Lecture Notes in Computer Science 3829

Commenced Publication in 1973
Founding and Former Series Editors:
Gerhard Goos, Juris Hartmanis, and Jan van Leeuwen

Paul Pettersson   Wang Yi (Eds.)

Formal Modeling and Analysis of Timed Systems

Third International Conference, FORMATS 2005
Uppsala, Sweden, September 26-28, 2005
Proceedings

 Springer

Volume Editors

Paul Pettersson
Wang Yi
Uppsala University
Department of Information Technology
P.O. Box 337, 751 05 Uppsala, Sweden
E-mail: {paupet,yi}@it.uu.se

Library of Congress Control Number: 2005937088

CR Subject Classification (1998): F.3, D.2, D.3, C.3, D.2.4

ISSN   0302-9743
ISBN-10   3-540-30946-2 Springer Berlin Heidelberg New York
ISBN-13   978-3-540-30946-8 Springer Berlin Heidelberg New York

Springer is a part of Springer Science+Business Media

springer.com

© Springer-Verlag Berlin Heidelberg 2005
Printed in Germany

Typesetting: Camera-ready by author, data conversion by Scientific Publishing Services, Chennai, India
Printed on acid-free paper   SPIN: 11603009   06/3142   5 4 3 2 1 0

Preface

This volume contains the proceedings of FORMATS 2005, the Third International Conference on Formal Modelling and Analysis of Timed Systems, held in Uppsala, Sweden, September 26–28, 2005, in conjunction with ARTIST2 summer school, September 29–October 2, 2005, on Component Modelling, Testing and Verification, and Static Analysis of Embedded Systems. FORMATS is an annual workshop series initiated in 2003. It is dedicated to the advancement of formal theories, techniques and software tools for modelling and analysis of timed systems. FORMATS 2003 was associated to CONCUR 2003 (International Conference on Concurrency Theory), held in Marseilles, France. FORMATS 2004 was organized in conjunction with FTRTFT (Formal Techniques in Real-Time and Fault Tolerant Systems), Grenoble, France.

This year, FORMATS received 43 submissions out of which 19 papers were selected for presentation by the Program Committee. Each of the submitted papers has been reviewed by at least three PC members and their sub-reviewers. The scientific program of FORMATS 2005 contained three invited talks: Lothar Thiele (Modular Performance Analysis of Distributed Embedded Systems), Karl-Erik Årzén (Timing Analysis and Simulation Tools for Real-Time Control) and Parosh Abdulla (Verification of Parameterised Timed Systems). The 19 selected contributions cover work on semantics and modelling of timed systems, formalisms for modelling and verification including timed automata, hybrid automata, and timed Petri nets, games for verification and synthesis, model-checking, case studies and issues related to implementation, security and performance analysis.

We would like to thank all the PC members for their efforts in the reviewing and selection process. We thank Ulrika Anderssson, Anders Hessel, Patrik Johansson, and Leonid Mokrushin for taking care of practical matters in the local organization.

The Program Committee of FORMATS 2005 comprised: Parosh Abdulla (Uppsala Univ., Sweden), Eugene Asarin (LIAFA, France), Patricia Bouyer (LSV, France), Ed Brinksma (Univ. of Twente, Netherlands), Flavio Corradini (Univ. of Camerino, Italy), Joost-Pieter Katoen (Aachen Univ., Germany), Marta Kwiatkowska (Univ. of Birmingham, UK), Yassine Lakhnech (Verimag, France), Kim G. Larsen (Aalborg Univ., Denmark), Insup Lee (Univ. of Pennsylvania, USA), Oded Maler (Verimag, France), Jens Palsberg (UCLA, USA), Paul Pettersson (Co-chair, Uppsala Univ., Sweden), Jean-Francois Raskin (ULB, Belgium), Marille Stoelinga (Univ. of Twente, Netherlands), P.S. Thiagarajan (National Univ. of Singapore), Stavros Tripakis (Verimag, France), Frits Vaandrager (Radboud Univ. Nijmegen, Netherlands), Walter Vogler (Univ. of Augsburg, Germany), and Wang Yi (Co-chair, Uppsala Univ., Sweden).

The Steering Committee of FORMATS consisted of Rajeev Alur (Univ. of Pennsylvania, USA), Flavio Corradini (Univ. of Camerino, Italy), Kim G. Larsen (Aalborg Univ., Denmark), Oded Maler (Verimag, France), Walter Vogler (Univ. Augsburg, Germany), and Wang Yi (Uppsala Univ., Sweden).

We would also like to thank the following sub-reviewers who assisted us in the evaluation of the submitted papers: Yasmina Abdeddaim, Dave Arney, Michael Balser, Elmar Bihler, Benedikt Bollig, Hanifa Boucheneb, Thomas Brihaye, Scott Cotton, Pedro D'Argenio Martin De Wulf, Laurent Doyen, Arvind Easwaran, Marco Faella, Sebastian Fischmeister, Wan Fokkink, Laurent Fribourg, Greg Goessler, Anders Hessel, David Jansen, Victor Khomenko, Jesung Kim, Tomas Krilavicius, Didier Lime, Birgitta Lindstrm, Dejan Nickovic, Thomas Noll, Laurent Mazare, George Pappas, Pierre-Alain Reynier, Olivier H. Roux, Usa Sammapun, Mark Schäfer, Insik Shin, Natalia Sidorova, Volker Stolz, Laurent Van Begin, and Tim Willemse.

September 2005   Paul Pettersson and Wang Yi

Table of Contents

Invited Talk

Hybrid Systems

Petri Nets

Semantics

Semantics and Modelling

Modular Performance Analysis of Distributed Embedded Systems

Lothar Thiele

Institute TIK, Switzerland
thiele@tik.ee.ethz.ch

Embedded computer systems are getting increasingly distributed. This can not only be seen on a small scale, e.g. in terms of multiprocessors on a chip, but also in terms of embedded systems that are connected via various communication networks. Whereas classical methods from the worst case timing analysis and real-time community focus on single resources, new models and methods need to be developed that enable the design and analysis of systems that guarantee end-to-end properties.

The talk covers a new class of methods based on real-time calculus. They can be considered as a deterministic variant of queuing theory and allow for (a) bursty input events and event streams, (b) heterogeneous composition of scheduling methods (EDF, FP, TDMA, WFQ, ...), (c) distributed computation and communication resources (d) detailed modeling of event stream correlations and resource behavior and (d) hard worst case bounds. In addition, the methods have been combined with formal assume/guarantee interfaces. Besides introducing the basic models and methods, some application studies are covered also.

It appears that this class of new methods provide a major step towards the analysis and design of predictable distributed systems.

P. Pettersson and W. Yi (Eds.): FORMATS 2005, LNCS 3829, p. 1, 2005.
© Springer-Verlag Berlin Heidelberg 2005

Real Time Temporal Logic: Past, Present, Future[*]

Oded Maler[1], Dejan Nickovic[1], and Amir Pnueli[2,3]

[1] Verimag, 2 Av. de Vignate, 38610 Gières, France
{Dejan.Nickovic, Oded.Maler}@imag.fr
[2] Weizmann Institute of Science, Rehovot 76100, Israel
[3] New York University, 251 Mercer St. New York, NY 10012, USA
Amir.Pnueli@cs.nyu.edu

Abstract. This paper attempts to improve our understanding of timed languages and their relation to timed automata. We start by giving a constructive proof of the folk theorem stating that timed languages specified by the past fragment of MITL, can be accepted by deterministic timed automata. On the other hand we provide a proof that certain languages expressed in the future fragment of MITL are not deterministic,[1] and analyze the reason for this asymmetry.

1 Introduction

In this paper we compare the past and future fragments of the real-time temporal logic MITL [AFH96] with respect to the recognizability of their models by *deterministic* timed automata. To put our work in context we first discuss past and future in untimed temporal logic, the question of online and offline monitoring as well as some related work on real-time logics and timed languages.

1.1 Past and Future in LTL

Propositional linear-time temporal logic (LTL) is a commonly-accepted formalism for specifying properties of finite-state discrete systems [MP95b]. The semantic models for LTL are typically sequences which are *infinite* toward the *future* and *finite* toward the *past*.[2] On this semantic domain there is a "typing" asymmetry between models of properties expressed in the *past* fragment of LTL, which are star-free[3] regular *languages*, and models for formulae written using the *future* fragment which are star-free regular *ω-languages*. To facilitate a closer comparison of the expressive power of the two

---

[*] This work was partially supported by the European Community project IST-2003-507219 PROSYD (Property-based System Design).

[1] As far as we know, no systematic techniques for proving such facts have been developed for timed automata since their introduction 15 years ago until recently.

[2] In other words the "carrier set" is isomorphic to $\mathbb{N}$, not $\mathbb{Z}$. Languages over bi-infinite sequences have been studied in [NP86].

[3] The word *star-free* comes from the characterization of these languages as those definable using a special class of regular expressions the do not use the Kleene star but allow intersection and complementation, see [MNP71].

P. Pettersson and W. Yi (Eds.): FORMATS 2005, LNCS 3829, pp. 2–16, 2005.

formalisms, one can unify their semantic domains by interpreting future LTL over finite sequences. This can be done, for example, by extending LTL semantics to include "truncated" (finite) paths as in [EFH$^+$03]. Getting rid of the ω-dimension we can focus on the differences between the two formalisms which are related to the *direction* of the temporal modalities.

When an automaton reads a sequence, the current state of the automaton represents (the equivalence class of) the prefix read so far. Past LTL fits naturally this point of view as satisfaction is determined *now* by what happened from time zero *until now*. Future LTL, on the other hand, states at time zero what it expects to see or not to see in the future. As time progresses, some of those "obligations" are fulfilled (or violated) and some new ones are generated. Satisfaction is established if all obligations are met at the end of the sequence. The translation from LTL formulae to automata that accept their models is one of the cornerstones of formal verification [VW86], and most of the work on the topic focused on future properties and ω-automata. From a future LTL formula one can construct naturally an alternating or a non-deterministic automaton that accepts the language. Such an automaton can be determinized either by the non-trivial construction of Safra for ω-automata [Saf88], or by the simpler subset construction if we take the finitary interpretation. The translation from past LTL to automata is more folklore, but it is not hard to see that it translates *naturally* to deterministic automata, a fact the also explains the simplicity of the online monitoring procedure in [HR02]. So the bottom line for LTL is that both the past and future fragments can be eventually translated into deterministic automata.[4]

1.2 Deterministic Automata and Online Monitors

Monitoring is the process of testing whether a given behavior ξ satisfies a property φ (or, equivalently, belongs to the corresponding language L). This process can be performed in two different fashions. Offline monitoring starts *after* the whole sequence is given. Online monitoring is interleaved with the process of reading the sequence and is similar to the way the sequence is read by an automaton. Online monitors can detect violation or satisfaction *as soon as they happen*, which can be after a small prefix of the sequence.[5] This is advantageous for two reasons: for monitoring *real* systems (rather than simulated ones) offline monitoring is a post-factum analysis and can be too late to be useful. Even for simulated systems, where monitoring is used as a lightweight alternative to formal verification, early detection may reduce simulation time significantly. In analog circuits, the application domain that triggered this work, simulations can be *very* long.

---

[4] We mention the results of [MP90] which show how to go from counter-free automata to past LTL formulae and from counter-free ω-automata to mixed past-future formulae which are Boolean combinations of formulae of the form $\Box \Diamond \varphi$ where φ is a past formula. An alternative proof of the fact that all LTL formulae can be brought to this normal form appears in [LPZ85].

[5] To be more precise, violation or satisfaction of a property based on a prefix can be declared when all possible continuations of the prefix are equivalent with respect to the formula. Such a prefix is called "definitive" in [EFH$^+$03]. If the corresponding automaton is minimal, this fact can be easily detected by entering a "sink"state, either rejecting (for violation of safety) or accepting (satisfaction of eventuality). For non-minimal automata the analysis is a bit more involved.

In [MN04] we have developed an offline monitoring procedure for the real-time logic MITL$_{[a,b]}$. This procedure, which was used to monitor properties of real-valued signals, scans the signal from the end backwards and propagates truth values from sub-formulae "upward" and from the present to the past. In order to have an online version of this procedure, we somehow need to produce an automaton-like mechanism that reads Boolean signals, and whose state during reading is sufficiently detailed to detect acceptance or rejection as they occur. To follow the same recipe as in the untimed case, one would like to transform a formula to a timed automaton to be used as a monitoring procedure. However, the natural translation of MITL yields non-deterministic or alternating timed automata which, in the general case, do not determinize [AD94]. There are several remedies for this problem:

1. Use the important observation of Tripakis [Tri02, KT04] that on-the-fly determinization with respect to a *given* non-Zeno signal is possible for any timed automaton. The reason for non-determinizability of certain automata is the need to memorize the times of *all* events that have occurred within a bounded time window, without any a-priori bound on their number. In monitoring, we observe a signal with a *fixed* number of events, which can generate only a finite number of non-deterministic choices and hence the restriction of the automaton to this signal is amenable to subset construction.
2. Develop a piecewise-backward version of the procedure in [MN04] which after every new event or sampling point, restarts the propagation of truth values backwards (in most cases the propagation need not go back too far).
3. Use specification formalisms that correspond to deterministic timed automata.

This work is the result of attempting to follow the third approach.

1.3   Related Work

The study of real-time specification formalisms started in the eighties and generated numerous logics, results and papers. The reader is advised to look at surveys and discussions of these logics [AH92a, Hen98, HR04], of timed automata [Alu99] and timed languages in general [Asa04]. Without purporting to be exhaustive, we mention some relevant results.

The real-time logic MITL was introduced in [AFH96] as a restriction of the more general logic MTL (metric temporal logic) of [Koy90]. The restriction of time modalities to positive-length intervals was intended to guarantee decidability but recent results [OW05, LW05] show that this restriction is not necessary for deciding MTL over finitary event-based semantics. The original version of MITL contained only future temporal operators and [AFH96] give a procedure for translating an MITL formula into a non-deterministic timed automaton with the satisfiability and model-checking problems being EXPSPACE-complete. The non-determinizable nature of MITL is hinted in the paper.

Event-recording automata, where only the time of the *last* occurrence of every input letter can be remembered by a clock, have been shown to be determinizable in [AFH99]. Event-clock automata, introduced in the same paper, constitute a generalization of the latter which allow also "event-predicting" clocks. Event-clock logic is another decidable real-time logic which is equally expressive as MITL [RSH98] and which can be naturally translated into determinizable event-clock automata. However those become non-deterministic when expressed as classical Alur-Dill automata.[6]

An investigation of past and future versions of MITL was carried out in [AH92b] where the "prediction" feature of event-clock automata was replaced by the ability of the automaton to change the direction of reading. The authors describe a strict hierarchy of timed languages based on the number of direction reversals needed to recognize them (which corresponds roughly to the nesting depth of past and future operators). The deterministic nature of the past fragment of MITL is mentioned as a corollary of that hierarchy but no explicit proof is given.

Real-time monitoring tools often rely on temporal logics as their property specification language, but typically under a *discrete-time* interpretation. For example, [KPA03] use LTL_t, standard LTL augmented with *freeze quantifiers*, while in [TR04] the monitoring procedure uses MITL. In [Gei02] the dense semantics is preserved but additional restrictions on MITL are imposed in order to guarantee determinizability. These include the restriction of timed modalities to intervals of the form $[0, d]$ and disallowing arbitrary nesting of temporal operators.

In [MP04] we started focusing on deterministic timed automata because of the belief that some fundamental concepts of automata theory are better studied in a deterministic framework. We have defined there a notion of *recognizability* and have shown that is coincides with acceptance by deterministic timed automata. The current paper is part of the quest for a matching specification formalism.

The rest of the paper is organized as follows. In Section 2 we describe signals along with the logic MITL. In Section 3 we define the variant of timed automata that we use as signal acceptors. The proof of determinizability of the past fragment of MITL is given in Section 4 followed, in Section 5, by the proof of non-determinizability of the future fragment and a discussion of the reasons. Further contemplations close the paper.

2   Signals and Their Temporal Logic

Two basic semantic domains can be used to describe timed behaviors. *Time-event sequences* consist of instantaneous events separated by time durations while discrete-valued *signals* are functions from time to some discrete domain. The reader may consult the introduction to [ACM02] or [Asa04] for more details on the algebraic characterization of these domains. In this work we use Boolean signals as the semantic domain, but the extension of the results to time-event sequences (which are equivalent to the timed traces used by Alur and Dill [AD94]) need not be a difficult exercise.

Let the time domain $\mathbb{T}$ be the set $\mathbb{R}_{\geq 0}$ of non-negative real numbers. A finite length Boolean signal ξ is a partial function $\xi : \mathbb{T} \to \mathbb{B}^n$ whose domain of definition is an interval $I = [0, r)$, $r \in \mathbb{N}$. We say that the length of the signal is r and denote this

---

[6] One may argue that deterministic event-clock automata preserve one essential feature of determinism, namely, a unique run for every input signal, but this comes at the expense of losing the *causality* of the runs due to the prediction feature which amounts to going back and forth in time.

fact by $|\xi| = r$. We use $\xi[t]$ for the value of the signal at time t and the notation $\sigma_1^{t_1} \cdot \sigma_2^{t_2} \cdots \sigma_k^{t_k}$ for a signal of length $t_1 + \cdots + t_k$ whose value is σ_1 at the interval $[0, t_1)$, σ_2 in the interval $[t_1, t_1 + t_2)$, etc. We use $t \oplus [a, b]$ to denote $[t+a, t+b] \cap [0, r)$ and $t \ominus [a, b]$ for $[t - b, t - a) \cap [0, r)$, that is, the Minkowski sum (difference) of $\{t\}$ and $[a, b]$ restricted to the domain of definition of the signal in question. We call these operations, respectively, forward and backward shifting.

We define the logic $\text{MITL}_{[a,b]}$ as a bounded version of the real-time temporal logic MITL [AFH96], such that all temporal modalities are restricted to intervals of the form $[a, b]$ with $0 \le a < b$ and $a, b \in \mathbb{N}$. The use of bounded temporal properties is one way to interpret temporal logic over finite-duration traces. The basic formulae of $\text{MITL}_{[a,b]}$ are defined by the grammar

$$\varphi := p \mid \neg\varphi \mid \varphi_1 \vee \varphi_2 \mid \varphi_1 \mathcal{S}_{[a,b]} \varphi_2 \mid \varphi_1 \mathcal{U}_{[a,b]} \varphi_2$$

where p belongs to a set $P = \{p_1, \ldots, p_n\}$ of propositions corresponding naturally to the coordinates of the n-dimensional Boolean signal considered. The future and past fragments of MITL use only the $\mathcal{U}$ and $\mathcal{S}$ modalities, respectively. The satisfaction relation $(\xi, t) \models \varphi$, indicating that signal ξ satisfies φ at position t, is defined inductively below. We use $p[t]$ to denote the projection of $\xi[t]$ on the dimension that corresponds to variable p.

$$\begin{aligned}
(\xi, t) &\models p & &\leftrightarrow t \in [0, r) \wedge p[t] = \top \\
(\xi, t) &\models \neg\varphi & &\leftrightarrow (\xi, t) \not\models \varphi \\
(\xi, t) &\models \varphi_1 \vee \varphi_2 & &\leftrightarrow (\xi, t) \models \varphi_1 \text{ or } (\xi, t) \models \varphi_2
\end{aligned}$$

$$(\xi, t) \models \varphi_1 \mathcal{S}_{[a,b]} \varphi_2 \leftrightarrow \exists t' \in t \ominus [a, b] \; (\xi, t') \models \varphi_2 \text{ and } \forall t'' \in [t', t], (\xi, t'') \models \varphi_1$$

$$(\xi, t) \models \varphi_1 \mathcal{U}_{[a,b]} \varphi_2 \leftrightarrow \exists t' \in t \oplus [a, b] \; (\xi, t') \models \varphi_2 \text{ and } \forall t'' \in [t, t'], (\xi, t'') \models \varphi_1$$

The satisfaction of a formula φ by the whole signal ξ is defined differently for the past and future fragments. For the past it is defined backwards as[7] $(\xi, |\xi|) \models \varphi$, and for the future as $(\xi, 0) \models \varphi$.

From basic $\text{MITL}_{[a,b]}$ operators one can derive other standard Boolean and temporal operators, in particular the time-constrained *sometime in the past*, *always in the past*, *eventually in the future* and *always in the future* operators whose semantics is defined as

$$\begin{aligned}
(\xi, t) &\models \Diamond\!\!\!\!-_{[a,b]} \varphi \leftrightarrow \exists t' \in t \ominus [a, b] \; (\xi, t') \models \varphi \\
(\xi, t) &\models \Box\!\!\!\!-_{[a,b]} \varphi \leftrightarrow \forall t' \in t \ominus [a, b] \; (\xi, t') \models \varphi \\
(\xi, t) &\models \Diamond_{[a,b]} \varphi \leftrightarrow \exists t' \in t \oplus [a, b] \; (\xi, t') \models \varphi \\
(\xi, t) &\models \Box_{[a,b]} \varphi \leftrightarrow \forall t' \in t \oplus [a, b] \; (\xi, t') \models \varphi
\end{aligned}$$

Note that our definition of the semantics of the time-bounded *since* and *until* operators differs slightly from their conventional definition in discrete time as it requires a time instant t' where *both* $(\xi, t') \models \varphi_2$ and $(\xi, t') \models \varphi_1$.

---

[7] To be more precise, it is the right limit of $(\xi, t) \models \varphi$ at $t \to r$.

3 Timed Automata

We use a variant of TA which differs from the classical definitions [AD94, HNSY94] by the following features:

1. It reads multi-dimensional *dense* Boolean signals, hence the alphabet letters are associated with *states* rather than with *transitions*.
2. Acceptance conditions are more refined and may include constraints on clock values.
3. Clock values may include the special symbol $\perp$ indicating that the clock is currently *inactive*.
4. Transitions can be labeled by the usual resets of the form $x := 0$ or $x := \perp$ as well as by *copy assignments* of the form $x_i := x_j$.

The last three features do not change the expressive power of timed automata, see [SV96], but allow us to treat clocks in a more "dynamic" fashion. Note that clock inactivity in a state can be encoded implicitly by the fact that in all paths emanating from the state, the clock is reset to zero before being tested [DY96]. The use of signals is motivated by our application domain and replicating our results to event-based semantics is left as an exercise.

The set of valuations of a set $C = \{x_1, \dots, x_n\}$ of clock variables, each denoted as $v = (v_1, \dots, v_n)$, defines the clock space $\mathcal{H} = (\mathbb{R}_{\geq 0} \cup \{\perp\})^n$. A *configuration* of a timed automaton is a pair of the form (q, v) with q being a discrete state. For a clock valuation $v = (v_1, \dots, v_n)$, $v + t$ is the valuation $(v'_1, \dots, v'_n)$ such that $v'_i = v_i$ if $v_i = \perp$ and $v'_i = v_i + t$ otherwise. A *clock constraint* is a Boolean combination of conditions of the forms $x \geq d$ or $x > d$ for some integer d.

Definition 1 (Timed Automaton). *A timed automaton over signals is a tuple $\mathcal{A} = (\Sigma, Q, C, \lambda, I, \Delta, q_0, F)$ where Σ is the input alphabet ($\mathbb{B}^n$ in this paper), Q is a finite set of discrete states and C is a set of clock variables. The labeling function $\lambda : Q \to \Sigma$ associates a letter of the alphabet to every state while the staying condition (invariant) I assigns to every state q a subset I_q of $\mathcal{H}$ defined by a conjunction of inequalities of the form $x \leq d$, for some clock x and integer d. The transition relation Δ consists of elements of the form (q, g, ρ, q') where q and q' are discrete states, the transition guard g is a subset of $\mathcal{H}$ defined by a clock constraint and ρ is the update function, a transformation of $\mathcal{H}$ defined by a set of copy assignments and resets on C. Finally q_0 is the initial state and F is the acceptance condition, a subset of $Q \times \mathcal{H}$ defined for each state by a clock constraint.*

The behavior of the automaton as it reads a signal ξ consists of an alternation between time progress periods where the automaton stays in a state q as long as $\xi[t] = \lambda(q)$ and I_q holds , and discrete instantaneous transitions guarded by clock conditions. Formally, a *step* of the automaton is one of the following:

- A time step: $(q, v) \xrightarrow{\sigma^t} (q, v + t)$, $t \in \mathbb{R}_+$ such that $\lambda(q) = \sigma$ and $v + t$ satisfies I_q (due to the structure of I_q this holds as well for every t', $0 \leq t' < t$).
- A discrete step: $(q, v) \xrightarrow{\delta} (q', v')$, for some transition $\delta = (q, g, \rho, q') \in \Delta$, such that v satisfies g and $v' = \rho(v)$.

A *run* of the automaton starting from a configuration (q_0, v_0) is a finite sequence of alternating time and discrete steps of the form

$$\xi: \quad (q_0, v_0) \xrightarrow{\sigma_1^{t_1}} (q_0, v_0 + t_1) \xrightarrow{\delta_1} (q_1, v_1) \xrightarrow{\sigma_2^{t_2}} (q_1, v_1 + t_2) \xrightarrow{\delta_2} \cdots \xrightarrow{\sigma_n^{t_n}} (q_f, v_f)$$

A run is accepting if the last configuration $(q_f, v_f) \in F$. The signal carried by the run is $\sigma_1^{t_1} \cdot \sigma_2^{t_2} \cdots \sigma_n^{t_n}$. The language of the automaton consists of all signals carried by accepting runs.

A timed automaton is *input-deterministic* if every input signal admits a unique run, a property guaranteed by the following two conditions:

1. Transition determinism: for every two transitions (q, g_1, ρ_1, q_1) and (q, g_2, ρ_2, q_2), $\lambda(q_1) = \lambda(q_2)$ implies $g_1 \cap g_2 = \emptyset$.
2. Time determinism: for every state q and transition (q, g, ρ, q'), if $\lambda(q) = \lambda(q')$ then the interior of $I_q \cap g$ is empty.

These two conditions imply that while reading a given signal, the automaton cannot be in two or more configurations simultaneously for any positive-length duration.

4   From Past MITL$_{[a,b]}$ to Deterministic Timed Automata

In this section we show how to build a deterministic timed automaton for any past MITL$_{[a,b]}$ formula. The construction follows the same lines as the compositional construction of [Pnu03] for untimed future temporal logic, where an automaton for a formula observes the states of the automata that correspond to its sub-formulae. This construction is particularly attractive for past temporal logic where the correspondence between states in the automaton and satisfaction of a sub formula is more direct.

We illustrate the idea underlying the proof on the formula $\diamondsuit_{[a,b]} \varphi$ for some past formula φ. Intuitively, an automaton that accepts such a language should monitor the truth value of φ and memorize, using clocks, the times when this value has changed. Memorizing all such changes may require an unbounded number of clocks, but as we shall see, only a finite number of those is sufficient since not all occurrence times of these changes need to be remembered.

Consider signal φ of Figure 1-(a), a clock x_i reset to zero at the ith time φ becomes true and a clock y_i reset when φ becomes false. For this example $\diamondsuit_{[a,b]} \varphi$ is true exactly when $(x_1 \geq a \wedge y_1 \leq b) \vee (x_2 \geq a \wedge y_2 \leq b)$. Due to the monotonicity of the clock dynamics, whenever y_1 goes beyond b, its value becomes irrelevant for the satisfaction of the acceptance condition, it can be discarded together with x_1. By itself, this fact does not guarantee finiteness of the number of clocks because we assume no a-priori bound on the variability of φ.

Consider now Figure 1-(b), where the second rise of φ is less than $b - a$ time after the preceding fall. In this case, condition $(x_1 \geq a \wedge y_1 \leq b) \vee (x_2 \geq a \wedge y_2 \leq b)$ becomes equivalent to $x_1 \geq a \wedge y_2 \leq b$. Since the values of y_1 and x_2 do not matter anymore we may disactivate them and forget this short episode of $\neg \varphi$. When φ falls again we may re-use clock y_1 to record the occurrence time and let the acceptance condition be $x_1 \geq a \wedge y_1 \leq b$. Hence the maximal number of events to be remembered before the

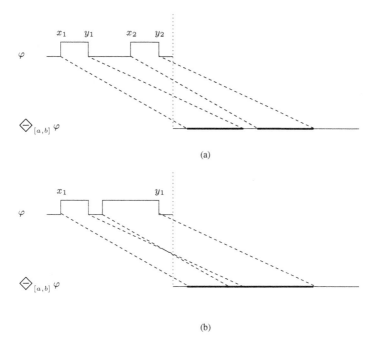

Fig. 1. Memorizing changes in the truth value of φ: (a) $x_2 - y_1 \geq b - a$; (b) $x_2 - y_1 < b - a$

oldest among them expires is $m = b/(b-a) - 1$ and at most $2m$ clocks are sufficient for monitoring such a formula. Note that for a "punctual" modality where $a = b$, m goes to infinity.

The automaton depicted in Figure 2, is a kind of an *"event recorder"* for accepting signals satisfying $\diamondsuit_{[a,b]} \varphi$. Its set of discrete states Q is partitioned into

$$Q_{\neg\varphi} = \{(01)^i 0\}_{i=0..m} \text{ and } Q_{\varphi} = \{(01)^i\}_{i=1..m},$$

with the intended meaning that the Boolean sequences that encode states correspond to the qualitative histories that they memorize, that is, the patterns of remembered rising and falling of φ that have occurred less than b time ago. The clocks of the automaton are $\{x_1, y_1, \ldots, x_m, y_m\}$, each measuring the time since its corresponding event. Naturally, clock x_i is active only at states $(01)^j$ and $(01)^j 0$ for $j \geq i$ and clock y_i at $(01)^j 0$ $(01)^{j+1}$ for $j \geq i$.

When φ first occurs the automaton moves from 0 to 01 and resets x_1. When φ becomes false it moves to 010 while resetting y_1. From there the following three continuations are possible:

Table 1. The effect of the clock shifting operation while taking a transition from $(01)^i$ to $(01)^{i-1}$

c	x_1	y_1	$\cdots$	x_{i-1}	y_{i-1}	x_i	y_i	$\cdots$	x_m	y_m
v	u_1	v_1	$\cdots$	u_{i-1}	v_{i-1}	u_i	$\perp$	$\cdots$	$\perp$	$\perp$
$s(v)$	u_2	v_2	$\cdots$	u_i	$\perp$	$\perp$	$\perp$	$\cdots$	$\perp$	$\perp$

1. If φ remains false for more than b time, the true episode of φ can be forgotten and the automaton moves to 0.
2. If φ becomes true within less than $b - a$ time, the false episode is forgotten and the automaton returns to 01.
3. If φ becomes true after more than $b - a$ time the automaton resets x_2 and moves to 0101.

Transitions of type 1 may happen in all states that record 2 changes or more. They occur when the first falling of φ is more than b time old and hence the values of clocks x_1 and y_1 can be forgotten. In order to keep the number of clocks bounded, this transition is accompanied by "shifting" the clocks values, that is, applying the operations $x_i := x_{i+1}$ and $y_i := y_{i+1}$ for all i as well as $x_m := y_m := \perp$. The effect of this shifting operation when a transition from $(01)^i$ to $(01)^{i-1}$ is taken is illustrated in Table 1.

Lemma 1. *The event recorder automaton, running in parallel with the automaton $\mathcal{A}_\varphi$, accepts the signals satisfying $\Diamond_{[a,b]} \varphi$ whenever x_1 is active and satisfies $x_1 \geq a$.*

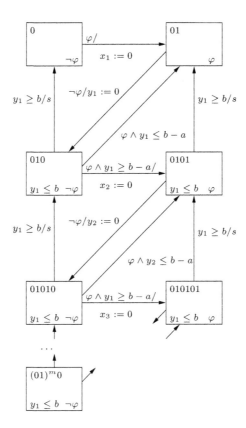

Fig. 2. An $[a, b]$ event recorder. The input labels and staying conditions are written on the bottom of each state. Transitions are decorated by the input labels of the target states and by clock resets. The clock shift operator is denoted by the symbol s.

Sketch of Proof: We need to show that in every state of the form $(01)^i 0$ there have been i risings and fallings of φ that have occurred less than b time ago such that each falling has lasted for more than $b - a$ time, and that the corresponding clocks represent the times elapsed since they have occurred. When this is the case and since $y_1 \leq b$ by construction, $x_1 \geq a$ at time t iff there was a time $t' \in t \ominus [a, b]$ in which φ was true. The proof is by induction on the length of the run. The claim is trivially true at the initial state. The inductive step starts with a configuration of the automaton satisfying the above, and proceeds by showing that it is preserved under time passage and transitions. The proof for states of the form $(01)^i$ is similar. ⌐

Lemma 2. *Given deterministic timed automata $\mathcal{A}_\varphi$ and $\mathcal{A}_\psi$ accepting $[\![\varphi]\!]$ and $[\![\psi]\!]$, respectively, one can construct a deterministic timed automaton accepting $\varphi \, \mathcal{S}_{[a,b]} \psi$.*

Proof: Observe first that $\varphi \, \mathcal{S} \psi$ can be seen as a restriction of $\diamondsuit \psi$ to periods where φ holds *continuously*. In other words, the automaton need not measure times of changes in ψ after which φ became false. Hence the $\mathcal{S}$-automaton (Figure 3) consists of an event recorder for ψ augmented with an additional initial state $\neg \varphi$. Whenever φ becomes true the automaton moves to the initial state of the event recorder and whenever φ becomes false it moves (from any state) back to $\neg \varphi$ while forgetting all the past history of ψ. ⌐

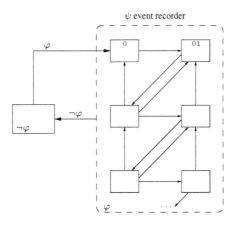

Fig. 3. The automaton for $\varphi \, \mathcal{S}_{[a,b]} \psi$

Theorem 1 (Past MITL is Deterministic). *Given a past MITL$_{[a,b]}$ formula φ, one can construct a deterministic timed automaton $\mathcal{A}$ accepting $[\![\varphi]\!]$.*

Proof: By induction on the structure of the formula. For a proposition p we build the deterministic two-state automaton $\mathcal{A}_p$ which moves to and from the accepting state according to the current value of p. For $\neg \varphi$ we take the automaton $\mathcal{A}_\varphi$ and complement its acceptance condition while for $\varphi \vee \psi$ we do a Cartesian product of $\mathcal{A}_\varphi$ and $\mathcal{A}_\psi$. Combining this with the previous lemma the result is established. ⌐

5 Future MITL is Non-deterministic

In this section we demonstrate the existence of a timed language L, definable in future MITL, which cannot be accepted by any deterministic automaton. Consider the formula

$$\Box_{[0,a]}(p \Rightarrow \Diamond_{[a,b]}q). \tag{1}$$

and the language L consisting of all signals of length $a+b$ that satisfy it. Models of this formula are two-dimensional Boolean signals that satisfy some relation between the times p is true in the interval $[0, a]$ and times when q holds in $[a, a + b]$ (see Figure 4). An automaton for L reads first the p part and memorizes what is required to memorize in order to determine whether the q part is accepted.

The syntactic (Nerode) right-congruence $\sim$ associated with a language L is defined as:

$$u \sim v \text{ iff } \forall w \; u \cdot w \in L \Leftrightarrow v \cdot w \in L.$$

For untimed languages acceptance by a finite (deterministic) automaton is equivalent to $\sim$ having a finite number of equivalence classes. In [MP04] we have shown that for timed languages, finiteness can be replaced by some special kind of *boundedness* which, among other things, implies:

Proposition 1 (MP04). *If a language is accepted by a deterministic timed automaton then there is some n such that all signals with n changes are Nerode equivalent to signals with less than n changes.*[8]

We now show that this is not the case for L, for which only signals which are identical are equivalent.

Claim. Let u and v be two p-signals of length a. Then, $u \neq v$ implies $u \not\sim v$ with respect to L.

Proof: Let t be the first time when u and v differ. Assume that p is true on $[t, t + \varepsilon]$ in u and false on that interval in v. We can then construct a distinguishing signal w such that $uw \notin L$ and $vw \in L$. Let w be the q-signal $1^t \cdot 0^{b-a+\varepsilon} \cdot 1^{a-t-\varepsilon}$, i.e. a signal which is true throughout $[a, a + b]$ except for the interval $[t + a, t + b + \varepsilon]$ (see Figure 5). Clearly uw will be rejected due to unfulfilled eventuality in the interval while vw will be accepted because v generates no obligations for this interval which are not fulfilled by the true values of w on both sides of the interval.   ∎

Hence, while reading the p-part the automaton should memorize the exact form of the signal, and since its variability is not bounded, an unbounded number of clocks is needed to memorize the times when p changes.

Corollary 1 (Future MITL is not Deterministic). *There are languages expressible in future MITL which cannot be recognized by any deterministic timed automaton.*

---

[8] Note that the converse is not true: consider, for instance, the language consisting of all signals where p holds continuously, and whose duration is a prime number. All signals with one or more changes in p value are rejected and hence equivalent, yet the language cannot be accepted by a deterministic (or non-deterministic) timed automaton.

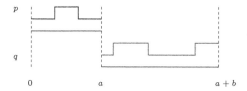

Fig. 4. A candidate signal for satisfying the formula; values of p and q are specified only in the relevant intervals, $[0, a]$ for p and $[a, a + b]$ for q

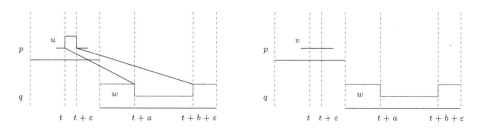

Fig. 5. Signal u, v and w such that $u \cdot w \notin L$ and $v \cdot w \in L$

This raises an intriguing question: why for specifications expressed in past MITL, the automaton *can* forget certain small changes in p that persist less than $b - a$ time? Below we give an answer to this question.

Consider first a "punctual" version of the future formula (1), where q should follow *exactly* b time after p:

$$\square_{[0,a]}(p \Rightarrow \lozenge_b q)$$

This formula admits a "dual" past formula

$$\boxminus_{[0,a]}(\neg q \Rightarrow \boxminus_b \neg p)$$

which is semantically equivalent on signals of length $a + b$. In other words, the first-order interpretations

$$\forall t \in [0, a]\ p[t] \Rightarrow q[t + b]$$

and

$$\forall t' \in [b, b + a]\ \neg q[t'] \Rightarrow \neg p[t' - b]$$

are equivalent (see Figure 6).

However, when we relax punctuality and use interval time modalities, the symmetry between past and future is broken and the automaton for the corresponding past formula

$$\boxminus_{[0,a]}(\neg q \Rightarrow \lozenge_{[a,b]} \neg p) \tag{2}$$

can ignore short episodes. The reason is due to the inter-relationship between the direction of the implication and the Minkowski sum. In a future interval modality, an event that happens at t may create an obligation for something to hold somewhere or throughout the future interval $t \oplus [a, b] = [t + a, t + b]$. In the past modality a future

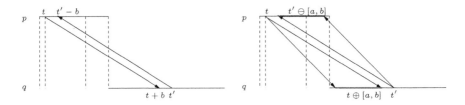

Fig. 6. Punctual modalities are past-future symmetric; interval modalities are not

event at time t' is implied by something that could/should have happened at the interval $t' \ominus [a, b] = [t' - b, t' - a]$. Anything that lasts less then $b - a$ does not generate its own specific obligations (obligations that are not already generated by neighboring segments of the signal). Logically speaking, (2) translates into the the first-order formula

$$\forall t' \in [b, a + b] \, (\neg q[t'] \Rightarrow \exists t \in t' \ominus [a, b] \, \neg p[t])$$

or equivalently

$$\forall t' \in [b, a + b] \, ((\forall t \in t' \ominus [a, b] \, p[t]) \Rightarrow q[t']).$$

Consider now two p-signals $p_1 = \xi \cdot 0^{t_1} 1^{t_2} 0^{t_3}$ and $p_2 = \xi \cdot 0^{t_1 + t_2 + t_3}$ that differ only by the true episode of length $t_2 < b - a$ in p_1. It is not hard to see that for any $t' \in [b, a + b]$

$$\forall t \in t' \ominus [a, b] \, p_1[t] \iff \forall t \in t' \ominus [a, b] \, p_2[t]$$

because any $t' \ominus [a, b]$ that intersects the true segment 1^{t_2} in p_2 also intersects at least one of its neighboring false segments. Hence the same obligations for t' are generated by p_1 and p_2 and they are Nerode equivalent.

So in conclusion, the difference between past and future in real-time temporal logic turns out to be due to a syntactic artifact that generates some bounded variability "filtering" for past interval modalities, but not for the future ones.

6   Discussion

It seems that the current paper does not conclude the search for a specification formalism which is natural, powerful and yet determinizable. Past MITL lacks the first property and future MITL is not deterministic. As another candidate we have explored a star-free version of the timed regular expressions presented in [ACM02]. The concatenation operator is more symmetric then the *since* and *until* operators and it could be interesting to see how it behaves. However it turns out that variations on both the future (1) and past (2) formulae can be defined by expressions such as

$$\neg(U \cdot (p \cdot U \wedge \neg(\langle U \cdot q \rangle_{[a,b]} \cdot U)))$$

and

$$\neg(U \cdot (U \cdot p \wedge \neg(U \cdot \langle q \cdot U \rangle_{[a,b]})) \cdot U),$$

respectively, where U is a special symbol denoting the universal timed language. This shows the star-free expressions are not deterministic either.

It looks as if determinizability can be obtained by enforcing some minimal duration for sub-formulae that imply something toward the future, for example p in (1). In past MITL this is automatically guaranteed by the structure of the formulae. We are currently contemplating sufficient syntactic conditions that will guarantee a similar property for the future fragment. In this context it is worth mentioning the *inertial bi-bounded delay* operator used for expressing delays in abstract models of digital circuits, which was formalized using timed automata in [MP95a]. This operator allows one to relate two signals by an inclusion of the form

$$\xi' \in D^c_{[a,b]}(\xi)$$

where $c \leq a$, meaning that every change in ξ that *persists for at least c time*, is propagated to ξ' within $t \in [a, b]$ time. Observe that this type of persistence constraint can be expressed within MITL. For example, the future formula (1) can be transformed into

$$\Box_{[0,a]}(\Box_{[0,b-a]}p \Rightarrow \Diamond_{[a,b]}q)$$

which is determinizable. Further investigations of these issues belong to the future.

Acknowledgments. This work benefited from discussions with E. Asarin, S. Tripakis and Y. Lakhnech and from comments made by D. Fisman, T. Henzinger and anonymous referees.

References

[Alu99]   R. Alur, Timed Automata, *Proc. CAV'99*, LNCS 1633, 8-22, Springer, 1999.

[AD94]   R. Alur and D.L. Dill, A Theory of Timed Automata, *Theoretical Computer Science* 126, 183–235, 1994.

[AFH96]   R. Alur, T. Feder, and T.A. Henzinger. The Benefits of Relaxing Punctuality. *Journal of the ACM*, 43(1):116–146, 1996.

[AFH99]   R. Alur, L. Fix, and T.A. Henzinger, Event-Clock Automata: A Determinizable Class of Timed Automata, *Theoretical Computer Science* 211, 253-273, 1999.

[AH92a]   R. Alur and T.A. Henzinger. Logics and Models of Real-Time: A Survey. *Proc. REX Workshop, Real-time: Theory in Practice*, pages 74–106. LNCS 600, Springer, 1992.

[AH92b]   R. Alur and T.A. Henzinger, Back to the Future: Towards a Theory of Timed Regular Languages, *Proc. FOCS'92*, 177-186, 1992.

[Asa04]   E. Asarin, Challenges in Timed Languages, *Bulletin of EATCS* 83, 2004.

[ACM02]   E. Asarin, P. Caspi and O. Maler, Timed Regular Expressions *The Journal of the ACM* 49, 172-206, 2002.

[DY96]   C. Daws and S. Yovine, Reducing the Number of Clock Variables of Timed Automata, *Proc. RTSS'96*, 73-81, IEEE, 1996.

[EFH+03]   C. Eisner, D. Fisman, J. Havlicek, Y. Lustig, A. McIsaac, and D. Van Campenhout, Reasoning with Temporal Logic on Truncated Paths, *Proc. CAV'03*, 27-39. LNCS 2725, Springer, 2003.

[Gei02]   M.C.W. Geilen. *Formal Techniques for Verification of Complex Real-time Systems*. PhD thesis, Eindhoven University of Technology, 2002.

[Hen98]   T.A. Henzinger. It's about Time: Real-time Logics Reviewed. In *Proc. CONCUR'98*, pages 439–454. LNCS 1466, Springer, 1998.

[HR02]   K. Havelund and G. Rosu. Synthesizing Monitors for Safety Properties. In *Proc. TACAS'02*, pages 342–356. LNCS 2280, Springer, 2002.

[HNSY94]   T. Henzinger, X. Nicollin, J. Sifakis, and S. Yovine, Symbolic Model-checking for Real-time Systems, *Information and Computation* 111, 193–244, 1994.

[HR04]   Y. Hirshfeld and A. Rabinovich Logics for Real Time: Decidability and Complexity, *Fundamenta Informaticae* 62, 1-28, 2004.

[Koy90]   R. Koymans, Specifying Real-time Properties with with Metric Temporal Logic, *Real-time Systems*, pages 255-299. 1990.

[KPA03]   K.J. Kristoffersen, C. Pedersen, and H.R. Andersen. Runtime Verification of Timed LTL using Disjunctive Normalized Equation Systems. In *Proc. RV'03*. ENTCS 89(2), 2003.

[KT04]   M. Krichen and S. Tripakis. Black-box Conformance Testing for Real-time Systems. In *Proc. SPIN'04*, pages 109–126. LNCS 2989, Springer, 2004.

[LPZ85]   O. Lichtenstein, A. Pnueli and L.D. Zuck, The Glory of the Past, *Proc. Conf. on Logic of Programs*, 196-218, LNCS, 1985.

[LW05]   S. Lasota and L. Walukiewicz, Alternating Timed Automata, In *Proc. FOSSACS'05*, pages 250–265. LNCS 3441, Springer.

[MN04]   O. Maler and D. Nickovic, Monitoring Temporal Properties of Continuous Signals, *proc. FORMATS/FTRTFT'04*, LNCS 3253, 2004.

[MP90]   O. Maler and A. Pnueli, Tight Bounds on the Complexity of Cascaded Decomposition of Automata. *proc. FOCS'90*, 672-682, 1990.

[MP95a]   O. Maler and A. Pnueli, Timing Analysis of Asynchronous Circuits using Timed Automata, in *Proc. CHARME'95*, LNCS 987, 189-205, Springer, 1995.

[MP04]   O. Maler and A. Pnueli. On Recognizable Timed Languages. In *Proc. FOSSACS'04*, pages 348–362. LNCS 2987, Springer, 2004.

[MP95b]   Z. Manna and A. Pnueli. *Temporal Verification of Reactive Systems: Safety*. Springer, 1995.

[MNP71]   R. McNaughton and S. Papert, *Counter Free Automata*, MIT Press, Cambridge, MA, 1971.

[NP86]   M. Nivat and D. Perrin, Ensembles Reconnaissables de Mots Bi-infinis, *Canadian J. of Mathematics* 38, 513-537, 1986.

[OW05]   J. Ouaknine and J. Worrell, On the Decidability of Metric Temporal Logic, In *Proc. LICS'05*, (to appear), 2005.

[Pnu03]   A. Pnueli. Verification of Reactive Systems. Lecture Notes, NYU, 2003. http://cs.nyu.edu/courses/fall03/G22.3033-007/lecture4.pdf.

[RSH98]   J.-F. Raskin, P.Y. Schobbens and T.A. Henzinger, Axioms for Real-Time Logics, *Proc. Concur'98*, 219-236, 1998.

[Saf88]   S. Safra, On the Complexity of ω-automata, *Proc. FOCS'88*, 319-327, 1998.

[SV96]   J.G. Springintveld and F.W. Vaandrager, Minimizable Timed Automata, *Proc. FTRTFT'96*, 130-147, LNCS 1135, Springer, 1996.

[TR04]   P. Thati and G. Rosu. Monitoring Algorithms for Metric Temporal Logic Specifications. In *Proc. of RV'04*, 2004.

[Tri02]   S. Tripakis. Fault Diagnosis for Timed Automata. In *Proc. FTRTFT'02*, pages 205–224. LNCS 2469, Springer, 2002.

[VW86]   M.Y. Vardi and P. Wolper. An Automata-theoretic Approach to Automatic Program Verification. In *Proc. LICS'86*, pages 322–331. IEEE, 1986.

Translating Timed I/O Automata Specifications for Theorem Proving in PVS*

Hongping Lim, Dilsun Kaynar, Nancy Lynch, and Sayan Mitra

Massachusetts Institute of Technology,
Computer Science and Artificial Intelligence Laboratory,
32 Vassar Street, Cambridge MA 02139, USA
{hongping, dilsun, lynch, mitras}@csail.mit.edu

Abstract. Timed Input/Output Automaton (TIOA) is a mathematical framework for specification and analysis of systems that involve discrete and continuous evolution. In order to employ an interactive theorem prover in deducing properties of a TIOA, its state-transition based description has to be translated to the language of the theorem prover. In this paper, we describe a tool for translating TIOA to the language of the Prototype Verification System (PVS)—a specification system with an integrated interactive theorem prover. We describe the translation scheme, discuss the design decisions, and briefly present three case studies to illustrate the application of the translator in the verification process.

1 Introduction

Timed Input/Output Automata [1, 2] is a mathematical framework for compositional modeling and analysis of systems that involve discrete and continuous evolution. The state of a timed I/O automaton changes discretely through *actions*, and continuously over time intervals through *trajectories*. A formal language called TIOA [3, 4] has been designed for specifying timed I/O automata. Like in its predecessor IOA [5], in the TIOA language, discrete transitions are specified in the precondition-effect style. In addition, TIOA introduces new constructs for specifying trajectories. Based on the TIOA language, a set of software tools is being developed [3]; these tools include a front-end type checker, a simulator, and an interface to the Prototype Verification System (PVS) theorem prover [6] (see Figure 1). This paper describes the new features of the TIOA language and a tool for translating specifications written in TIOA to the language of PVS; this tool is a part of the third component of the TIOA toolkit.

Motivation. Verification of timed I/O automata properties typically involves proving invariants or simulation relations between pairs of automata. The timed I/O automata framework provides a means for constructing very stylized proofs, which take the form of induction over the length of the executions of an automaton or a pair of automata, and a systematic case analysis of the actions and the

---

* This research has been supported by Air Force Contract FA9550-04-C-0084.

P. Pettersson and W. Yi (Eds.): FORMATS 2005, LNCS 3829, pp. 17–31, 2005.

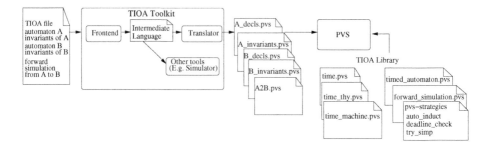

Fig. 1. Theorem proving on TIOA specifications

trajectories. Therefore, it is possible to partially automate such proofs by using an interactive theorem prover, as shown in [7]. Apart of partial automation, theorem prover support is useful for (a) managing large proofs, (b) re-checking proofs after minor changes in the specification, and (c) generating human readable proofs from proof scripts. We have chosen to use the PVS theorem prover because it provides an expressive specification language and an interactive theorem prover with powerful decision procedures. PVS also provides a way of developing special strategies or tactics for partially automating proofs, and it has been used in many real life verification projects [8].

To use a theorem prover like PVS for verification, one has to write the description of the timed I/O automaton model of the system in the language of PVS, which is based on classical, typed higher-order logic. One could write this automaton specification directly in PVS, but using the TIOA language has the following advantages. (a) TIOA preserves the state-transition structure of a timed I/O automaton, (b) allows the user to write programs to describe the transitions using operational semantics, whereas in PVS, transition definitions have to be functions or relations, (c) provides a natural way for describing trajectories using differential equations, and also (d) allows one to use other tools in the TIOA toolkit. Therefore, it is desirable to be able write the description of a timed I/O automaton in the TIOA language, and then use an automated tool to translate this description to the language of PVS.

Related Work and Contributions. Various tools have been developed to translate IOA specifications to different theorem provers, for example, Larch [9, 10], PVS [11], and Isabelle [12, 13]. Our implementation of the TIOA to PVS translator builds upon [9]. However, unlike IOA, TIOA allows the state of a timed I/O automaton to evolve continuously over time through *trajectories*. The main contribution of this paper is the design of a translation scheme from TIOA to PVS that can handle trajectories, and the implementation of the translator.

The Timed Automata Modeling Environment (TAME) [7] provides a PVS theory template for describing MMT automata [14]— a special type of I/O automaton that adds time bounds for enabled actions. This theory template has to be manually instantiated with the states, actions, and transitions of an automaton. A similar template is instantiated automatically by our translator to specify timed I/O automata in PVS. This entails translating the operational descriptions of transitions in TIOA to their corresponding functional descriptions in PVS. Moreover, unlike a timed I/O automaton which uses trajectories, an MMT automaton uses a *time passage action* to model continuous behavior. In TAME, this time passage action is written as another action of the automaton, with the properties of the pre- and post-state expressed in the enabling condition of the action. This approach, however, if applied directly to translate a trajectory, does not allow assertion of properties that must hold throughout the duration of the trajectory. Our translation scheme solves this problem by embedding the trajectory as a functional parameter of the time passage action.

We illustrate the application of the translator in three case studies: Fischer's mutual exclusion algorithm, a two-task race system, and a simple failure detector [15, 2]. The TIOA specifications of the system and its properties are given as input to the translator and the output is a set of PVS theories. The PVS theorem prover is then used to verify the properties using inductive invariant proofs. In two of these case studies, we describe time bounds on the actions of interest using an abstract automaton, and then prove the timing properties by a simulation relation from the system to this abstraction. The simulation relations typically involve inequalities between variables of the system and its abstraction. Our experience with the tool suggests that the process of writing system descriptions in TIOA and then proving system properties using PVS on the translator output can be helpful in verifying more complicated systems.

In the next section we give a brief overview of the timed I/O automata framework and the TIOA language. In Section 3, we describe the translation scheme; in Section 4, we illustrate the application of the translator with brief overviews of three case studies. Finally, we conclude in Section 5.

2   TIOA Mathematical Model and Language

Here we briefly describe the timed I/O automaton model and refer the reader to [1] for a complete description of the mathematical framework.

2.1   TIOA Mathematical Model

Let V be the set of variables of a timed I/O automaton. Each variable $v \in V$ is associated with a *static type*, $type(v)$, which is the set of values v can assume. A *valuation* for V is a function that associates each variable $v \in V$ to a value in $type(v)$. $val(V)$ denotes the set of all valuations of V. Each variable $v \in V$ is also associated with a *dynamic type*, which is the set of trajectories v may follow.

The time domain T is a subgroup of $(R, +)$. A time interval J is a nonempty, left-closed sub-interval of R. J is said to be *closed* if it is also right-closed. A trajectory τ of V is a mapping $\tau : J \to val(V)$, where J is a time interval starting with 0. The domain of τ, $\tau.dom$, is the interval J. A *point trajectory* is one with the trivial domain $\{0\}$. The first time of τ, $\tau.ftime$, is the infimum of $\tau.dom$. If $\tau.dom$ is closed then τ is *closed* and its limit time, $\tau.ltime$, is the supremum of $\tau.dom$. For any variable $v \in V$, $\tau \downarrow v(t)$ denotes the restriction of τ to the set $val(v)$. Let τ and τ' be trajectories for V, with τ closed. The *concatenation* of τ and τ' is the union of τ and the function obtained by shifting $\tau'.dom$ until $\tau.ltime = \tau'.ftime$. The *suffix* of a trajectory τ is obtained by restricting $\tau.dom$ to $[t, \infty)$, and then shifting the resulting domain by $-t$.

A *timed automaton* $\mathcal{A}$ is a tuple of $(X, Q, \Theta, E, H, D, \mathcal{T})$ where:

1. X is a set of *variables*.
2. $Q \subseteq val(X)$ is a set of *states*.
3. $\Theta \subseteq Q$ is a nonempty set of *start states*.
4. A is a set of actions, partitioned into *external* E and *internal actions* H.
5. $\mathcal{D} \subseteq Q \times A \times Q$ is a set of *discrete transitions*. We write a transition $(\mathbf{x}, a, \mathbf{x}') \in \mathcal{D}$ in short as $\mathbf{x} \xrightarrow{a} \mathbf{x}'$. We say that a is *enabled* in $\mathbf{x}$ if $\mathbf{x} \xrightarrow{a} \mathbf{x}'$ for some $\mathbf{x}'$.
6. $\mathcal{T}$ is a set of trajectories for X such that $\tau(t) \in Q$ for every $\tau \in \mathcal{T}$ and every $t \in \tau.dom$, and $\mathcal{T}$ is closed under prefix, suffix and concatenation.

A *timed I/O automaton* is a timed automaton with the set of external actions E partitioned into input and output actions. This distinction is necessary for composing timed I/O automata. In this paper, we consider only individual timed I/O automata and so we do not differentiate input and output actions. We use the terms timed I/O automaton and timed automaton synonymously.

An *execution fragment* of a timed I/O automaton $\mathcal{A}$ is an alternating sequence of actions and trajectories $\alpha = \tau_0 a_1 \tau_1 a_2 \ldots$, where $\tau_i \in \mathcal{T}, a_i \in A$, and if τ_i is not the last trajectory in α then τ_i is finite and $\tau_i.lstate \xrightarrow{a_{i+1}} \tau_{i+1}.fstate$. An execution fragment is *closed* if it is a finite sequence and the domain of the final trajectory is a finite closed interval. An *execution* is an execution fragment whose first state is a start state of $\mathcal{A}$. A state of $\mathcal{A}$ is *reachable* if it is the last state of some execution. An *invariant* property is one which is true in all reachable states of $\mathcal{A}$. A *trace* of an execution fragment α is obtained from α by removing internal actions and modifying the trajectories to contain only information about the amount of elapsed time. $traces_{\mathcal{A}}$ denotes the set of all traces of $\mathcal{A}$. We say that automaton $\mathcal{A}$ *implements* automaton $\mathcal{B}$ if $traces_{\mathcal{A}} \subseteq traces_{\mathcal{B}}$. A *forward simulation relation* [1] from $\mathcal{A}$ to $\mathcal{B}$ is a sufficient condition for showing that $\mathcal{A}$ implements $\mathcal{B}$. A *forward simulation* from automaton $\mathcal{A}$ to $\mathcal{B}$ is a relation $R \subseteq Q_{\mathcal{A}} \times Q_{\mathcal{B}}$ satisfying the following conditions for all states $\mathbf{x}_{\mathcal{A}} \in Q_{\mathcal{A}}$ and $\mathbf{x}_{\mathcal{B}} \in Q_{\mathcal{B}}$:

1. If $\mathbf{x}_{\mathcal{A}} \in \Theta_{\mathcal{A}}$ then there exists a state $\mathbf{x}_{\mathcal{B}} \in \Theta_{\mathcal{B}}$ such that $\mathbf{x}_{\mathcal{A}} R \mathbf{x}_{\mathcal{B}}$.
2. If $\mathbf{x}_{\mathcal{A}} R \mathbf{x}_{\mathcal{B}}$ and α is a transition $\mathbf{x} \xrightarrow{a}_{\mathcal{A}} \mathbf{x}'$, then $\mathcal{B}$ has a closed execution fragment β with $\beta.fstate = \mathbf{x}_{\mathcal{B}}$, $trace(\beta) = trace(\alpha)$, and $\alpha.lstate R \beta.lstate$.
3. If $\mathbf{x}_{\mathcal{A}} R \mathbf{x}_{\mathcal{B}}$ and α is an execution fragment of $\mathcal{A}$ consisting of a single closed trajectory, with $\alpha.fstate = \mathbf{x}_{\mathcal{A}}$, then $\mathcal{B}$ has a closed execution fragment β with $\beta.fstate = \mathbf{x}_{\mathcal{B}}$, $trace(\beta) = trace(\alpha)$, and $\alpha.lstate R \beta.lstate$.

2.2   TIOA Language

The TIOA language [3] is a formal language for specifying the components and properties of timed I/O automata. The states, actions and transitions of a timed

I/O automaton are specified in TIOA in the same way as in the IOA language [5]. New features of the TIOA language include trajectories and a new `AugmentedReal` data type. The trajectories are defined using differential and algebraic equations, invariants and stopping conditions. This approach is derived from [16], in which the authors had used differential equations and English informally to describe trajectories. Figure 2 shows an example of a TIOA specification. The `AugmentedReal` type extends reals with a constructor for infinity. Each variable has an explicitly defined static type, and an implicitly defined dynamic type. The dynamic type of a `Real` variable is the set of piecewise-continuous functions; the dynamic type of a variable of any other simple type or of the type **discrete** `Real` is the set of piecewise constant functions.

```
   automaton TwoTaskRace(a1,a2,b1,b2 : Real)
 2 where (a1 > 0) ∧ (a2 > 0) ∧ (b1 ≥ 0) ∧ (b2 > 0) ∧ (a2 ≥ a1) ∧ (b2 ≥ b1)

 4 signature
     internal increment, decrement, set
 6   output report

 8 states
     count: Int := 0, flag: Bool := false,
10   reported: Bool := false, now: Real := 0,
     first_main: Real := a1, last_main: AugmentedReal := a2,
12   first_set: Real := b1, last_set: AugmentedReal := b2

14 transitions
     internal increment                    internal decrement
16   pre                                    pre
       ¬flag ∧ now ≥ first_main               flag ∧ count > 0 ∧ now ≥ first_main
18   eff                                    eff
       count := count + 1;                    count := count - 1;
20     first_main:= (now + a1);               first_main := (now + a1);
       if (now+a2) ≥ 0 then                   if (now+a2) ≥ 0 then
22       last_main := now+a2                    last_main := (now+a2)
       fi                                     fi
24
     internal set                          output report
26   pre                                    pre
       ¬flag ∧ now ≥ first_set                flag ∧ count = 0 ∧ ¬reported
28   eff                                      ∧ now ≥ first_main
       flag := true;                        eff
30     first_set := 0;                        reported := true;
       last_set := infty                      first_main := 0;
32                                            last_main := infty

     trajectories
34     trajdef traj1
         invariant now ≥ 0
36       stop when now = last_main ∨ now = last_set
         evolve d(now) = 1
```

Fig. 2. TIOA description of *TwoTaskRace*

The set of trajectories of a timed I/O automaton is defined systematically by a set of trajectory definitions. A *trajectory definition* w is defined by an invariant $inv(w)$, a stopping condition $stop(w)$, and a set of differential and algebraic equations $daes(w)$ (see definition of `traj1` in Figure 2, lines 34–37). $W_{\mathcal{A}}$ denotes the set of trajectory definitions of $\mathcal{A}$. Each $w \in W_{\mathcal{A}}$ defines a set of trajectories, denoted by $traj(w)$. A trajectory τ belongs to $traj(w)$ if the following conditions hold: for each $t \in \tau.dom$: (a) $\tau(t) \in inv(w)$. (b) If $\tau(t) \in stop(w)$, then $t = \tau.ltime$. (c) τ satisfies the set of differential and algebraic equations in $daes(w)$. (d) For each non-real variable v, $(\tau \downarrow v)(t) = (\tau \downarrow v)(0)$; that is, the value of v

is constant throughout the trajectory. The set of trajectories $\mathcal{T}_{\mathcal{A}}$ of automaton $\mathcal{A}$ is the concatenation closure of the functions in $\bigcup_{w \in W_{\mathcal{A}}} traj(w)$.

3 Translation Scheme

For generating PVS theories that specify input TIOA descriptions, our translator implements the approach prescribed in TAME [7]. The translator instantiates a predefined PVS theory *template* that defines the components of a generic automaton. The translator automatically instantiates the template with the states, actions, and transitions of the input TIOA specification. This instantiated theory, together with several supporting library theories, completely specifies the automaton, its transitions, and its reachable states in the language of PVS (see Figure 1). Figure 3 shows the translator output in PVS for the TIOA description in Figure 2. In the following sections, we describe in more detail the translation of the various components of a TIOA description.

```
TwoTaskRace_decls: THEORY
2  BEGIN
     IMPORTING common_decls
4  states: TYPE =
        [#count: int, flag: bool,
6         reported: bool, now: real,
          first_main: real, last_main: time,
8         first_set: real, last_set: time#]

10 start(s: states): bool =
        (count(s) = 0 ∧ flag(s) = FALSE ∧
12      reported(s) = FALSE ∧ now(s) = 0 ∧
        first_main(s) = a₁ ∧ last_main(s) = fintime(a₂) ∧
14      first_set(s) = b₁ ∧ last_set(s) = fintime(b₂))

16 interval(i, j: (fintime?)): TYPE =
        {s: (fintime?) | i ≤ s ∧ s ≤ j ∧ i ≤ j}
18 f_type(i, j: (fintime?)): TYPE =
        [interval(i, j) → states]

20
     actions: DATATYPE
22    BEGIN
        nu_traj1(delta_t: {t: (fintime?) | dur(t) ≥ 0},
24            F: f_type(zero, delta_t) nu_traj1?
        increment: increment?
26      decrement: decrement?
        set: set?
28      report: report?
     END actions

30
     visible(a: actions): bool =
32    CASES a OF
        nu_traj1(delta_t, F): TRUE, increment: FALSE,
34      decrement: FALSE, set: FALSE, report: TRUE
     ENDCASES

36
     timepassageactions(a: actions): bool =
38    CASES a OF
        nu_traj1(delta_t, F): TRUE, increment: FALSE,
40      decrement: FALSE, set: FALSE, report: FALSE
     ENDCASES
```

```
42  enabled(a: actions, s: states): bool =
       CASES a OF
44     nu_traj1(delta_t, F):
          ∀ (t: interval(zero, delta_t)):
46        ((now(F(t)) ≥ 0) ∧
           (fintime(now(F(t))) = last_main(F(t)) ∨
48         fintime(now(F(t))) = last_set(F(t)))
50        ⇒ t = delta_t) ∧
           F(t) = s WITH [now := now(s) + 1 × dur(t)],
       increment: ((¬ flag(s)) ∧ (now(s) ≥ first_main(s))),
52     decrement:
           ((flag(s) ∧ (count(s) > 0)) ∧
54         (now(s) ≥ first_main(s))),
       set: ((¬ flag(s)) ∧ (now(s) ≥ first_set(s))),
56     report:
           (((flag(s) ∧ (count(s) = 0)) ∧
58         (¬ reported(s))) ∧ (now(s) ≥ first_main(s)))
       ENDCASES

60
     trans(a: actions, s: states): states =
62    CASES a OF
        nu_traj1(delta_t, F): F(delta_t),
64      increment: s WITH
           [first_main := (now(s) + a₁),
66         last_main := (IF ((now(s) + a₂) ≥ 0)
                           THEN fintime(now(s) + a₂)
68                         ELSE last_main(s) ENDIF),
           count := (count(s) + 1)],
70      decrement: s WITH
           [first_main := (now(s) + a₁),
72         last_main := (IF ((now(s) + a₂) ≥ 0)
                           THEN fintime(now(s) + a₂)
74                         ELSE last_main(s) ENDIF),
           count := (count(s) − 1)],
76      set: s WITH
           [last_set := infinity, first_set := 0, flag := TRUE],
78      report: s WITH
           [first_main:=0, reported:=TRUE, last_main:=infinity]
80     ENDCASES

82  END TwoTaskRace_decls
```

Fig. 3. PVS description of *TwoTaskRace*

3.1   Data Types, Automaton Parameters, and States

Simple static types of the TIOA language Bool, Char, Int, Nat, Real and String have their equivalents in PVS. PVS also supports declaration of TIOA types enumeration, tuple, union, and array in its own syntax. The type AugmentedReal is translated to the type time introduced in the time theory of TAME. time is defined as a DATATYPE consisting of two subtypes: fintime and infinity. The subtype fintime consists of only non-negative reals; infinity is a constant constructor.

The TIOA language allows the user to introduce new types and operators by declaring the types and the signature of the operators within the TIOA description. The semantics of these types and operators are written in PVS library theories, which are imported by the translator output.

The TIOA language provides the construct **states** for declaring the variables of an automaton (see Figure 2, lines 8–12). Each variable can be assigned an initial value at the start state. An optional **initially** predicate can be used to specify the start states. An automaton can have parameters which can be used in expressions within the description of the automaton (see Figure 2, lines 1–2).

In PVS, the state of an automaton is defined as a record with fields corresponding to the variables of the automaton. A boolean predicate start returns true when a given state satisfies the conditions of a start state (see Figure 3, lines 3–15). Assignments of initial values to variables in the TIOA description are translated as equalities in the start predicate in PVS, while the **initially** predicate is inserted as an additional conjunction into the start predicate. Automaton parameters are declared as constants in a separate PVS theory common_decls (see Figure 3, line 2) with axioms stating the relationship between them.

3.2   Actions and Transitions

In TIOA, actions are declared as **internal** or external (**input** or **output**). In PVS, these are declared as subtypes of an action DATATYPE. A visible predicate returns true for the external and time passage actions.

In TIOA, discrete transitions are specified in precondition-effect style using the keyword **pre** followed by a predicate (precondition), and the keyword **eff** followed by a program (effect). We define a predicate enabled in PVS parameterized on an action a and a state s to represent the preconditions. enabled returns true when the corresponding TIOA precondition for a is satisfied at s.

The program of the effect clause specifies the relation between the post-state and the pre-state of the transition. The program consists of sequential statements, which may be assignments, **if-then-else** conditionals or **for** loops (see Figure 2, lines 14–32). A non-deterministic assignment is handled by adding extra parameters to the action declaration and constraining the values of these parameters in the enabled predicate of the action.

In TIOA, the effect of a transition is typically written in an imperative style using a sequence of statements. We translate each type of statement to its corresponding functional relation between states, as shown in Table 1. The term P is a program, while $trans_P(s)$ is a function that returns the state obtained by

Table 1. Translation of program statements. v is a state variable; t is an expression; *pred* is a predicate; A is a finite set; choose picks an element from the given set A. WITH makes a copy of the record s, assigning the field v with a new value t.

program P	$trans_P(s)$
v := t	s WITH $[v := t]$
if pred then P_1 fi	IF pred THEN $trans_{P_1}(s)$ ELSE s ENDIF
if pred then P_1 else P_2 fi	IF pred THEN $trans_{P_1}(s)$ ELSE $trans_{P_2}(s)$ ENDIF
for v in A do P_1 od	forloop(A, s): RECURSIVE states = IF empty?(A) THEN s
	ELSE LET v=choose(A), s'=forloop(remove(v, A), s) IN
	$trans_{P_1}(s')$ ENDIF MEASURE card(A)

```
signature
    internal foo(i: int), bar
transitions
    internal foo(i: Int)            internal bar
        eff x := x + i;                 eff t := x;
            y := x * x;                     if x ≠ y then
            x := x - 1;                         x := y;
            y := y + 1                          y := t
                                            fi
```

Fig. 4. Actions and transitions in TIOA

performing program P on state s. In PVS, we define a function trans parameterized on an action a and a state s, which returns the post-state of performing the corresponding TIOA effect of a on s. Sequential statements like $P_1; P_2$ are translated to a composition of the corresponding functions $trans_{P_2}(trans_{P_1}(s))$. Our translator can perform this composition in following two ways:

Substitution method: We first compute $trans_{P_1}$, then substitute each variable in $trans_{P_2}$ with its intermediate value obtained from $trans_{P_1}$. This approach explicitly specifies the resulting value of each variable in the post-state in terms of the variables in the pre-state [9]. Figure 4 shows a simple example to illustrate this approach. foo performs some arithmetic, while bar swaps x and y if they are not equal. The translation is shown in the left column of Figure 5. In the transition of bar, x and y are assigned new values only when their values are not equal in the pre-state. Otherwise, they are assigned their previous values.

```
trans(a: actions, s: states): states =          trans(a: actions, s: states): states = CASES a OF
    CASES a OF                                       foo(i):
        foo(i): s WITH                                   (LET s: states = s WITH [x := x(s) + i] IN
            [x := (x(s) + i) - 1,                        (LET s: states = s WITH [y := x(s) × x(s)] IN
             y := (x(s) + i) × (x(s) + i) + 1],          (LET s: states = s WITH [x := x(s) - 1] IN
        bar: s WITH                                      (LET s: states = s WITH [y := y(s) + 1] IN s)))),
            [y := (IF (x(s) ≠ y(s)) THEN x(s)        bar:
                ELSE y(s) ENDIF),                        (LET s: states = s WITH [t := x(s)] IN
             x := (IF (x(s) ≠ y(s)) THEN y(s)            (LET s: states =
                ELSE x(s) ENDIF),                            IF (x(s) ≠ y(s)) THEN
             t := x(s)]                                         (LET s: states = s WITH [x := y(s)] IN
    ENDCASES                                                    (LET s: states = s WITH [y := t(s)] IN s))
                                                             ELSE s ENDIF
                                                             IN s))
                                                     ENDCASES
```

Fig. 5. Translation of transitions using substitution (left) and LET (right)

LET method: Instead of performing the substitution explicitly, we make use of the PVS LET keyword to obtain intermediate states on which to apply subsequent programs. The program P_1; P_2 can be written as LET $s = trans_{P_1}(s)$ IN $trans_{P_2}(s)$. The right column in Figure 5 shows the translation of the effects of foo and bar using LET statements.

In the substitution method, the translator does the work of expressing the final value of a variable in terms of the values of the variables in the pre-state. In the LET method, the prover has to perform these substitutions to obtain an expression for the post-state in an interactive proof. Therefore, the substitution method is more efficient for theorem proving, whereas the LET method preserves the sequential structure of the program, which is lost with the substitution method. Since the style of translation in some cases may be a matter of preference, we currently support both approaches as an option for the user.

3.3 Trajectories

The set of trajectories of an automaton is the concatenation closure of the set of trajectories defined by the trajectory definitions of the automaton. A trajectory definition w is specified by the **trajdef** keyword in a TIOA description followed by an **invariant** predicate for $inv(w)$, a **stop when** predicate for $stop(w)$, and an **evolve** clause for specifying $daes(w)$ (see traj1 in Figure 2, lines 34–37).

```
actions: DATATYPE                          enabled(a: actions, s: states): bool =
  BEGIN                                      CASES a OF
    nu_progress(delta_t: {t: (fintime?) | dur(t) ≥ 0},   nu_progress(delta_t, F, x_r):
      F: f_type(zero, delta_t), x_r: real) : nu_progress?   x_r ≥ 0 ∧ x_r ≤ 2 ∧
  END actions                                 (∀ (t: interval(zero, delta_t)):
                                                 (x(F(t)) ≥ 0) ∧
  trans(a: actions, s: states): states =        (((x(F(t)) ≤ 10)) ⇒ t = delta_t) ∧
    CASES a OF nu_progress(delta_t, F, x_r):     F(t) = s WITH
      F(delta_t)                                   [x := x(s) + x_r × dur(t)])
  ENDCASES                                   ENDCASES
```

Fig. 6. Using an additional parameter to specify rate of evolution

Each trajectory definition in TIOA is translated as a time passage action in PVS containing the trajectory map as one of its parameters. The precondition of this time passage action contains the conjunction of the predicates corresponding to the invariant, the stopping condition, and the evolve clause of the trajectory definition. In general, translating an arbitrary set of differential and algebraic equations (DAES) in the evolve clause to the corresponding precondition may be hard, but our translation scheme is designed to handle a large class of DAES, including the most common classes like constant and linear differential equations, and ordinary differential equations. The translator currently handles algebraic equations, constant differential equations and inclusions; it is being extended to handle linear differential equations.

Like other actions, a time passage action is declared as a subtype of the action DATATYPE, and specified using enabled-trans predicates. A time passage action has two required parameters: the length of the time interval of the trajectory, delta_t, and a trajectory map F mapping a time interval to a state of the automaton.

The transition function of the time passage action returns the last state of the trajectory, obtained by applying the trajectory map F on delta_t (see Figure 3, line 63). The precondition of a time passage action has conjunctions stating (1) the trajectory invariant, (2) the stopping condition, and (3) the evolution of variables (see nu_traj1 in Figure 3, lines 44-50, corresponding to traj1 in Figure 2).

If the **evolve** clause contains a constant differential inclusion of the form $d(x) \leq k$, we introduce an additional parameter x_r in the time passage action for specifying the rate of evolution. We then add a fourth conjunction into the precondition to assert the restriction x_r $\leq k$. The following example uses a constant differential inclusion that allows the rate of change of x to be between 0 and 2. The PVS output in Figure 6 contains an additional parameter x_r as the rate of change of x. The value of x_r is constrained in the precondition.

trajdef progress invariant x $\geq$ 0 stop when x = 10
    evolve d(x) $\geq$ 0; d(x) $\leq$ 2

3.4   Correctness of Translation

Consider a timed I/O automaton $\mathcal{A}$, and its PVS translation $\mathcal{B}$. A closed execution of $\mathcal{B}$ is an alternating finite sequence of states and actions (including time passage actions): $\beta = s_0, b_1, s_1, b_2, \ldots, b_r, s_r$, where s_0 is a start state, and for all i, $0 \leq i \leq r$, s_i is a state of $\mathcal{B}$, and b_i is an action of $\mathcal{B}$. We define the following two mappings:

Let $\beta = s_0, b_1, s_1, b_2, \ldots, b_r, s_r$ be a closed execution of $\mathcal{B}$. We define the mapping $\mathcal{F}(\beta)$ as a sequence $\tau_0, a_1, \tau_1, \ldots$ obtained from β by performing the following: (1) Each state s_i is replaced with a point trajectory τ_j such that $\tau_j.fstate = \tau_j.lstate = s_i$. (2) Each time passage action b_i is replaced by $T(b_i)$, where $T(b_i)$ is the parameter F of b_i, which is the same as the corresponding trajectory in $\mathcal{A}$. (3) Consecutive sequences of trajectories are concatenated into single trajectories.

Let $\alpha = \tau_0, a_1, \tau_1, \ldots$ be a closed execution of $\mathcal{A}$. We define the mapping $\mathcal{G}(\alpha)$ as a sequence $s_0, b_1, s_1, b_2, \ldots, b_r, s_r$ obtained from α by performing the following. Let τ_i be a concatenation of $\tau_{(i,1)}, \tau_{(i,2)}, \ldots$, such that $\tau_{(i,j)} \in traj(w_j)$ for some trajectory definition w_j of $\mathcal{A}$. Replace $\tau_{(i,1)}, \tau_{(i,2)}, \ldots$ with $\tau_{(i,1)}.fstate$, $\nu(\tau_{(i,1)})$, $\tau_{(i,1)}.lstate$, $\nu(\tau_{(i,2)})$, $\tau_{(i,2)}.lstate$, $\ldots$, where $\nu(\tau)$ denotes the corresponding time passage action in $\mathcal{B}$ for τ.

Using these mappings, we state the correctness of our translation scheme as a theorem, in the sense that any closed execution (or trace) of a given timed I/O automaton $\mathcal{A}$ has a corresponding closed execution (resp. trace) of the automaton $\mathcal{B}$, and vice versa, where $\mathcal{B}$ is described by the PVS theories generated by the translator. Owing to limited space, we state the theorem and omit the proof, which will be available in a complete version of the paper.

Theorem 1. *(a) For any closed execution β of $\mathcal{B}$, $\mathcal{F}(\beta)$ is a closed execution of $\mathcal{A}$. (b) For any closed execution α of $\mathcal{A}$, $\mathcal{G}(\alpha)$ is a closed execution of $\mathcal{B}$.*

3.5   Implementation

Written in Java, the translator is a part of the TIOA toolkit (see Figure 1). The implementation of the tool builds upon the existing IOA to Larch translator [9, 17]. Given an input TIOA description, the translator first uses the front-end type checker to parse the input, reporting any errors if necessary. The front-end produces an intermediate language which is also used by other tools in the TIOA toolkit. The translator parses the intermediate language to obtain Java objects representing the TIOA description. Finally, the translator performs the translation as described in this paper, and generates a set of files containing PVS theories specifying the automata and their properties. The translator accepts command line arguments for selecting the translation style for transitions, as well as for specifying additional theories that the output should import for any user defined data types. The current version of the translator can be found at: http://web.mit.edu/hongping/www/tioa/tioa2pvs-translator.

4   Proving Properties in PVS

In this section, we briefly discuss our experiences in verifying systems using the PVS theorem prover on the theories generated by our translator. To evaluate the translator we have so far studied the following three systems. We have specifically selected distributed systems with timing requirements so as to test the scalability and generality of our proof techniques. Although these distributed systems are typically specified component-wise, we use a single automaton, obtained by composing the components, as input to the translator for each system.

(1) *Fischer's mutual exclusion algorithm* [15]: In this algorithm, each process proceeds through different phases like try, test, etc. in order to get to the critical phase where it gains access to the shared resource. The *safety property* we want to prove is that no two processes are simultaneously in the critical phase, as shown in Figure 7. Each process is indexed by a positive integer; pc is an array recording the region each process is in. Notice that we are able to state the invariant using universal quantifiers without having to bound the number of processes.

(2) The *two-task race system* [15, 4] (see Figure 2) increments a variable count repeatedly, within a1 and a2 time, a1 < a2, until it is interrupted by a set action. This set action can occur within b1 and b2 time from the start, where b1 ≤ b2. After set, the value of count is decremented (every [a1, a2] time) and a report action is triggered when count reaches 0. We want to show that the time

```
invariant of fischer_me:
   ∀ i: Int ∀ j: Int
   ((i > 0 ∧ j > 0 ∧ i ≠ j) ⇒
    ((pc[i] ≠ pc_crit) ∨
     (pc[j] ≠ pc_crit)))
```

$Inv(s: states): bool =$
  $\forall (i: int): (\forall (j: int):$
   $(((((i > 0) \land (j > 0)) \land (i \neq j)) \Rightarrow$
    $((pc(s)(i) \neq pc\_crit) \lor (pc(s)(j) \neq pc\_crit)))))$
  $lemma:$ LEMMA $(\forall (s: states): reachable(s) \Rightarrow Inv(s));$

Fig. 7. TIOA and PVS descriptions of the mutual exclusion property

bounds on the occurrence of the `report` action are: *lower bound*: if a2 < b1 then
`min(b1,a1)` $+ \frac{(b1-a2)*a1}{a2}$ else a1, and *upper bound*: b2 + a2 + $\frac{b2*a2}{a1}$. To prove
this, we create an abstract automaton `TwoTaskRaceSpec` which performs a `report`
action within these bounds, and show a forward simulation from `TwoTaskRace` to
`TwoTaskRaceSpec`.

(3) A simple *failure detector system* [2] consisting of a sender, a delay prone
channel, and a receiver. The sender sends messages to the receiver, within u1 time
after the previous message. A `timed_queue` delays the delivery of each message by
at most b. A failure can occur at any time, after which the sender stops sending.
The receiver timeouts after not receiving a message for at least u2 time. We are
interested in proving two properties for this system: (a) *safety*: a timeout occurs
only after a failure has occurred, and (b) *timeliness*: a timeout occurs within
u2 + b time after a failure. As in the two-task race example, to show the time
bound, we first create an abstract automaton that timeouts within u2 + b time
of occurrence of a failure, and then we prove a forward simulation.

We specify the systems and state their properties in the TIOA language. The
translator generates separate PVS theory files for the automaton specifications,
invariants, and simulation relations (see Figure 1). We invoke the PVS-prover
on these theories to interactively prove the translated lemmas and theorems.

One advantage of using a theorem prover like PVS is the ability to develop
and use special strategies to partially automate proofs. PVS strategies are written to apply specific proof techniques to recurring patterns found in proofs.
In proving the system properties, we use special PVS strategies developed for
TAME and TIOA [7, 18]. As many of the properties involve inequalities over
real numbers, we also use the strategies in the Manip [19] and the Field [20]
packages.

PVS generates Type Correctness Conditions (TCCs), which are proof obligations to show that certain expressions have the right type. As we have defined
the `enabled` predicate and `trans` function separately, it is sometimes necessary to
add conditional statements into the `eff` program of the TIOA description, so as
to ensure type correctness in PVS.

Prior to proving the properties using the translator output, we had proved the
same properties using hand-translated versions of the system specifications [4].
These hand-translations were done assuming that all the differential equations
are constant, and that the all invariants and stopping conditions are convex. In
the proof of invariants, we are able to use a strategy to handle the induction
step involving the parameterized trajectory, thus the length of the proofs in the
hand translated version were comparable to those with the translators output.
However, such a strategy is still not available for use in simulation proofs, and
therefore additional proof steps were necessary when proving simulation relations
with the translator output, making the proofs longer by 105% in the worst
case[1]. Nonetheless, the advantage of our translation scheme is that it is general
enough to work for a large class of systems and that it can be implemented in
software.

---

[1] We did not attempt to make the proofs compact.

4.1   Invariant Proofs for Translated Specifications

To prove that a property holds in all reachable states, we use induction to prove that (a) the property holds in the start states, and (b) given that the property holds in any reachable pre-state, the property also holds in the post-state obtained by performing any action that is enabled in the pre-state.

We use the `auto_induct` strategy to inductively prove invariants. This strategy breaks down the proofs into a base case, and one subgoal for each action type. Trivial subgoals are discharged automatically, while other simple branches are proved by using TIOA strategies like `apply_specific_precond` and `try_simp` with decision procedures of PVS. Harder subgoals require more careful user interaction in the form of using simpler invariants and instantiating formulas.

In branches involving time passage actions, to obtain the post-state, we instantiate the universal quantifier over the domain of the trajectory in the time passage action with the limit time of the trajectory. A commonly occurring type of invariant asserts that a continuously evolving variable, say v, does not cross a deadline, say d. Within the trajectory branch of the proof of such an invariant, we instantiate the universal quantifier over the domain of the trajectory with the time required for v to reach the value of d. In particular, if v grows at a constant rate k, we instantiate with $(d - v)/k$. We have also written a PVS strategy `deadline_check` which performs this instantiation.

The strategies provided by Field and Manip deals only with real values, while our inequalities may involve time values. For example, in the two-task race system, we want to show that last_set $\geq$ fintime(now). Here, last_set is a time value, that is, a positive real or infinity, while now is a real value. If last_set is infinite, the inequality follows from the definitions of $\geq$ and infinity in the time theory of TAME. For the finite case, we extract the real value from last_set, and then prove the version of the same inequality involving only reals.

4.2   Simulation Proofs for Translated Specifications

In our examples, we prove a forward simulation relation from the system to the abstract automaton to show that the system satisfies the timing properties. The proof of the simulation relation involves using induction, performing splits on the actions, and verifying the inequalities in the relation. The induction hypothesis assumes that a pre-state $\mathbf{x}_{\mathcal{A}}$ of the system automaton $\mathcal{A}$ is related to a pre-state $\mathbf{x}_{\mathcal{B}}$ of the abstract automaton $\mathcal{B}$. If the action $a_{\mathcal{A}}$ is an external action or a time passage action, we show the existence of a corresponding action $a_{\mathcal{B}}$ in $\mathcal{B}$ such that the $a_{\mathcal{B}}$ is enabled in $\mathbf{x}_{\mathcal{B}}$ and that the post-states obtained by performing $a_{\mathcal{A}}$ on $\mathbf{x}_{\mathcal{A}}$ and $a_{\mathcal{B}}$ on $\mathbf{x}_{\mathcal{B}}$ are related. If the action $a_{\mathcal{A}}$ is internal, we show that the post-state of $a_{\mathcal{A}}$ is related to $\mathbf{x}_{\mathcal{B}}$. To show that two states are related, we prove that the relation holds between the two states using invariants of each automaton, as well as techniques for manipulating inequalities and the time type. We have not used automaton-specific strategies in our current proofs for simulation relations. Such strategies have been developed in [21]. Once tailored to our translation scheme, they will make the proofs shorter.

A time passage action contains the trajectory map as a parameter. When we show the existence of a corresponding action in the abstract automaton, we need to instantiate the time passage action with an appropriate trajectory map. For example, in the proof of the simulation relation in the two-task race system, the time passage action nu_traj1 of TwoTaskRace is simulated by the following time passage action of TwoTaskRaceSpec:

$$\text{nu\_post\_report}(\text{delta\_t}(\text{a\_A}), \text{ LAMBDA}(t: \text{TTRSpec\_decls.interval}(\text{zero}, \text{delta\_t}(\text{a\_A}))):$$
$$\text{s\_B WITH } [\text{now} := \text{now}(\text{s\_B}) + \text{dur}(t)])$$

The time passage action nu_post_report of TwoTaskRaceSpec (abbreviated as TTR-Spec) has two parameters. The first parameter has value equal to the length of a_A, the corresponding time passage action in the automaton TwoTaskRace. The second parameter is a function that maps a given time interval of length t to a state of the abstract automaton. This state is same as the pre-state s_B of TwoTaskRaceSpec, except that the variable now is incremented by t.

5   Conclusion and Future Work

In this paper we have introduced the TIOA language and presented a tool for translating TIOA descriptions to the language of the PVS theorem prover. Although the TIOA language provides convenient and natural constructs for describing a timed I/O automaton, it cannot be used directly in a theorem prover such as PVS. Our tool performs the translation from TIOA to PVS, translating programs in the transition effects of TIOA descriptions into functional relations in PVS, and trajectories into parameterized time passage actions. We have described briefly three case studies in which we have successfully written the systems in TIOA, and proved properties of the systems in PVS using the output of the translator. Our experience suggests that the process of writing system descriptions in TIOA and then proving system properties using PVS on the translator output is useful for analyzing more complicated systems.

Some features remain to be implemented in the translator tool, like `for` loops, and composition of automata. In future, we want to develop PVS strategies to exploit the structure of the translator output for shorter and more readable proofs. We will continue to work on other case studies to evaluate the translator as a theorem proving interface for the TIOA language. These examples include clock synchronization algorithms and implementation of atomic registers.

References

1. Kaynar, D., Lynch, N., Segala, R., Vaandrager, F.: Timed I/O automata: A mathematical framework for modeling and analyzing real-time systems. In: RTSS 2003: The 24th IEEE International Real-Time Systems Symposium, Cancun, Mexico (2003)
2. Kaynar, D., Lynch, N., Segala, R., Vaandrager, F.: The theory of timed I/O automata. Technical Report MIT/LCS/TR-917, MIT Laboratory for Computer Science (2003) Available at `http://theory.lcs.mit.edu/tds/reflist.html`.

3. Kaynar, D., Lynch, N., Mitra, S., Garland, S.: TIOA Language. MIT Computer Science and Artificial Intelligence Laboratory, Cambridge, MA. (2005)
4. Kaynar, D., Lynch, N., Mitra, S.: Specifying and proving timing properties with tioa tools. In: Work in progress session of the 25th IEEE International Real-Time Systems Symposium (RTSS 2004), Lisbon, Portugal (2004)
5. Garland, S., Lynch, N., Tauber, J., Vaziri, M.: IOA User Guide and Reference Manual. MIT Computer Science and Artificial Intelligence Laboratory, Cambridge, MA. (2003) Available at http://theory.lcs.mit.edu/tds/ioa.html.
6. Owre, S., Rajan, S., Rushby, J., Shankar, N., Srivas, M.: PVS: Combining specification, proof checking, and model checking. In Alur, R., Henzinger, T.A., eds.: Computer-Aided Verification, CAV '96. Number 1102 in Lecture Notes in Computer Science, New Brunswick, NJ, Springer-Verlag (1996) 411–414
7. Archer, M.: TAME: PVS Strategies for special purpose theorem proving. Annals of Mathematics and Artificial Intelligence **29** (2001)
8. Owre, S., Rushby, J., Shankar, N., Stringer-Calvert, D.: PVS: an experience report. In Hutter, D., Stephan, W., Traverso, P., Ullman, M., eds.: Applied Formal Methods—FM-Trends 98. Volume 1641 of Lecture Notes in Computer Science., Boppard, Germany, Springer-Verlag (1998) 338–345
9. Bogdanov, A., Garland, S., Lynch, N.: Mechanical translation of I/O automaton specifications into first-order logic. In: Formal Techniques for Networked and Distributed Sytems - FORTE 2002 : 22nd IFIP WG 6.1 International Conference, Texas, Houston, USA (2002) 364–368
10. Garland, S.J., Guttag, J.V.: A guide to LP, the Larch prover. Technical report, DEC Systems Research Center (1991) Available at http://nms.lcs.mit.edu/Larch/LP.
11. Devillers, M.: Translating IOA automata to PVS. Technical Report CSI-R9903, Computing Science Institute, University of Nijmegen (1999) Available at http://www.cs.ru.nl/research/reports/info/CSI-R9903.html.
12. Ne Win, T.: Theorem-proving distributed algorithms with dynamic analysis. Master's thesis, Massachusetts Institute of Technology, Cambridge, MA (2003)
13. Paulson, L.C.: The Isabelle reference manual. Technical Report 283, University of Cambridge (1993)
14. Merritt, Modugno, Tuttle: Time-constrained automata. In: CONCUR: 2nd International Conference on Concurrency Theory, LNCS, Springer-Verlag (1991)
15. Lynch, N.A.: Distributed Algorithms. Morgan Kaufmann Publishers Inc. (1996)
16. Lynch, N., Segala, R., Vaandrager, F.: Hybrid I/O automata. Information and Computation **185** (2003) 105–157
17. Bogdanov, A.: Formal verification of simulations between I/O automata. Master's thesis, Massachusetts Institute of Technology, Cambridge, MA (2000) Available at http://theory.lcs.mit.edu/tds/ioa.html.
18. Mitra, S., Archer, M.: Reusable PVS proof strategies for proving abstraction properties of I/O automata. In: STRATEGIES 2004, IJCAR Workshop on strategies in automated deduction, Cork, Ireland (2004)
19. Muñoz, C., Mayero, M.: Real automation in the field. Technical Report NASA/CR-2001-211271 Interim ICASE Report No. 39, ICASE-NASA Langley, ICASE Mail Stop 132C, NASA Langley Research Center, Hampton VA 23681-2199, USA (2001)
20. Vito, B.: A PVS prover strategy package for common manipulations (2003) Available at http://shemesh.larc.nasa.gov/people/bld/manip.html.
21. Mitra, S., Archer, M.: PVS strategies for proving abstraction properties of automata. Electronic Notes in Theoretical Computer Science **125** (2005) 45–65

Specification and Refinement of Soft Real-Time Requirements Using Sequence Diagrams

Atle Refsdal[1], Knut Eilif Husa[1,2], and Ketil Stølen[1,3]

[1] Department of Informatics, University of Oslo, Norway
[2] Ericsson, Norway
[3] SINTEF ICT, Norway

Abstract. Soft real-time requirements are often related to communication in distributed systems. Therefore it is interesting to understand how UML sequence diagrams can be used to specify such requirements. We propose a way of integrating soft real-time requirements in sequence diagram specifications by adding probabilities to timed sequence diagrams. Our approach builds on timed STAIRS, which is an approach to the compositional and incremental development of sequence diagrams supporting specification of mandatory as well as potential behavior.

1 Introduction

A soft real-time requirement is a time requirement that needs to be met only by a certain percentage of the relevant behavior. A hard real-time requirement can be seen as a special case of a soft real-time requirement; it is a soft real-time requirement that needs to be met in 100% of the cases. When a delay depends on factors that are hard to measure, highly complex or outside our control, a soft real-time requirement is often more appropriate than a hard constraint.

Time constraints are often related to some kind of communication scenario. Therefore it is important to be able to express soft real-time constraints in sequence diagrams. Sequence diagrams show how a task is performed by sending messages between lifelines.

In this paper we enable specification of soft real-time constraints with sequence diagrams by extending STAIRS presented in [HS03], [HHRS05a] and [HHRS05b] with the possibility of assigning probabilities. The probabilities are added independently from the time constraints, so our approach supports probabilistic specifications in general.

The rest of this paper is organized as follows: Section 2 introduces a specification to illustrate aspects of probabilistic STAIRS throughout the paper. Section 3 defines events, traces and some basic operators. Timed STAIRS is introduced in section 4, while section 5 discusses the relation between mandatory choice and probabilities. Probabilistic STAIRS is introduced in section 6, and section 7 shows how this enables the addition of a soft real-time requirement to the example specification. In section 8 the refinement relation is defined. Section 9 demonstrates refinement of the example specification. We discuss some related work in section 10 before concluding in section 11.

P. Pettersson and W. Yi (Eds.): FORMATS 2005, LNCS 3829, pp. 32–48, 2005.

2   The Automatic Teller Machine Example

We use as example a scenario where a customer withdraws money from an automatic teller machine (atm). This section gives a brief and informal explanation of the example. Figure 1 shows the first version of the specification. It serves two purposes. Firstly, it introduces the basic UML sequence diagram notation. Secondly, it allows us to characterize the need for more expressiveness. We come back to this example in later sections to illustrate our approach. Since our main concern is demonstration of real-time specifications we have omitted some details that would belong in a real-life scenario, such as the entering of a PIN code. The scenario describes the case where the transaction succeeds.

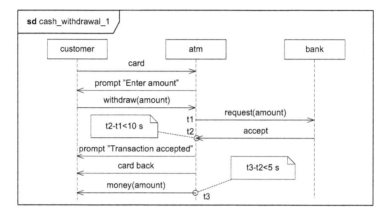

Fig. 1. A cash withdrawal scenario

It is an interaction between three *lifelines*: the customer, the atm and the bank. Lifelines represent the entities taking part in the interaction. The intuition behind the specification is the following: First the customer inserts her/his card, and the atm displays the text "Enter amount". The customer then enters the desired amount, and the atm sends a request to the bank asking whether the transaction is acceptable. A hard real-time requirement has been placed on the reply from the bank, stating that it should take no more than 10 seconds from the atm sends its request to the reply is received.[1] After the atm receives a positive reply from the bank, it displays the text "Transaction accepted", returns the card, and finally delivers the desired amount of money. A second hard real-time requirement has been put on the delivery of money stating that the delay from the atm receives a positive reply from the bank to the money is delivered should be less than five seconds.

UML sequence diagrams describe *traces* representing execution histories, and categorize traces as positive (valid) or negative (invalid). Positive traces represent

---

[1] We have chosen to use a different notation for real-time requirements than in UML 2.0, since we find our notation more suitable when the requirement crosses an operator boundary, as will happen in later specifications. Graphical (concrete) syntax is not a main issue in this paper.

acceptable executions, while negative traces represent unacceptable executions. All other traces are inconclusive, meaning that the specification does not say whether they are acceptable [OMG04–p. 526]. According to the specification in Figure 1, the positive traces are those where 1) messages are sent in the order shown in the diagram and 2) both real-time requirements are fulfilled. The negative traces are those that fulfill 1) but not 2).

The delay from the request is sent from the atm to a reply is received may depend on several complex factors, so we might want to replace the hard real-time requirement with a soft real-time requirement. Timed STAIRS gives a formal semantics to (a subset of) UML sequence diagrams with hard real-time requirements. Specifying soft real-time constraints, however, is not possible. Enabling the specification of soft real-time requirements within the framework of timed STAIRS is the aim of this paper.

3   Events, Traces and Basic Operators

In this section we define the notions of events and traces. We also introduce a number of helpful operators. Most of the definitions and explanations in this section are taken from [HHRS05a].

For any set A, A^ω denotes the set of finite as well as infinite sequences of elements of A. $\mathbb{N}$ denotes the set of natural numbers, while $\mathbb{N}_0$ denotes the set of natural numbers including 0. We define the functions

$$\#\_ \in A^\omega \to \mathbb{N}_0 \cup \{\infty\}, \quad \_[\_] \in A^\omega \times \mathbb{N} \to A, \qquad \_ \frown \_ \in A^\omega \times A^\omega \to A^\omega,$$
$$\_|\_ \in A^\omega \times \mathbb{N}_0 \to A^\omega, \qquad \_\circledS\_ \in \mathbb{P}(A) \times A^\omega \to A^\omega$$

to yield the length of a sequence, the nth element of a sequence, the concatenation of two sequences, truncation of a sequence and the filtering of a sequence. Hence, $\#a$ yields the number of elements in a, and $a[n]$ yields a's nth element if $n \leq \#a$. To concatenate two sequences means to glue them together. Therefore, $a_1 \frown a_2$ denotes a sequence of length $\#a_1 + \#a_2$ that equals a_1 if a_1 is infinite, and is prefixed by a_1 and suffixed by a_2 otherwise. For any $0 \leq i \leq \#a$, $a|_i$ denotes the prefix of a of length i. By $B \circledS a$ we denote the sequence obtained from the sequence a by removing all elements in a that are not in the set B.

We also need filtering of pairs of sequences. The filtering function

$$\_\textcircled{T}\_ \in \mathbb{P}(A \times B) \times (A^\omega \times B^\omega) \to A^\omega \times B^\omega$$

can be understood as a generalization of $\circledS$. For any set of pairs of elements P and pairs of sequences t, $P \textcircled{T} t$ denotes the pair of sequences obtained from t by

- truncating the longest sequence in t at the length of the shortest sequence in t if the two sequences are not of equal length;
- for each $j \in [1...k]$, where k is the length of the shortest sequence in t, selecting or deleting the two elements at index j in the two sequences, depending on whether the pair of these elements is in the set P.

For example, we have that

$$\{(1,f),(1,g)\} \circledT (\langle 1,1,2,1,2\rangle, \langle f,f,f,g,g\rangle) = (\langle 1,1,1\rangle, \langle f,f,g\rangle)$$

For a formal definition of $\circledT$, see [BS01].

π_i is a projection operator returning element number i of a tuple.

3.1   Events

A message is a triple (s, re, tr) of a signal s, a receiver re and a transmitter tr. $\mathcal{M}$ denotes the set of all messages. The receiver and transmitter are lifelines. $\mathcal{L}$ denotes the set of all lifelines.

An event may be of two kinds; a transmission event tagged by "!" or a reception event tagged by "?".[2] Every event occurring in a sequence diagram has a timestamp tag. $\mathcal{T}$ denotes the set of timestamp tags. We use logical formulas with timestamp tags as free variables to impose constraints on the timing of events. By $\mathbb{F}(v)$ we denote the set of logical formulas whose free variables are contained in the set of timestamp tags v.

An event is a triple $(k, m, t) \in \{!, ?\} \times \mathcal{M} \times \mathcal{T}$ of a kind, a message and a timestamp tag. $\mathcal{E}$ denotes the set of all events. We define the functions

$$k._- \in \mathcal{E} \to \{?, !\}, \quad m._- \in \mathcal{E} \to \mathcal{M}, \quad t._- \in \mathcal{E} \to \mathcal{T}, \quad tr._- \in \mathcal{E} \to \mathcal{L}, \quad re._- \in \mathcal{E} \to \mathcal{L}$$

to yield the kind, message, timestamp tag, transmitter and receiver of an event, respectively. Since we are primarily interested in communication scenarios, we do not give a semantic interpretation to events, except that the timestamp tag is assigned a timestamp in form of a real number. $\mathbb{R}$ denotes the set of timestamps. The set $[\![\,\mathcal{E}\,]\!]$ of event interpretations is therefore defined by

$$[\![\,\mathcal{E}\,]\!] \stackrel{\text{def}}{=} \{(k, m, t \mapsto r) \mid (k, m, t) \in \mathcal{E} \wedge r \in \mathbb{R}\} \tag{1}$$

$t \mapsto r$ means that timestamp r is assigned to timestamp tag t. We also define the function

$$r._- \in [\![\,\mathcal{E}\,]\!] \to \mathbb{R}$$

to yield the timestamp of an event interpretation. In the following, we use "event" and "event interpretation" interchangeably.

3.2   Traces

A trace $h \in [\![\,\mathcal{E}\,]\!]^\omega$ is a finite or infinite sequence of events. Traces represent executions of the system under specification, and must satisfy a number of well-formedness conditions. Firstly, we require the events of h to be ordered by time:

$$\forall\, i, j \in [1..\#h] : i < j \Rightarrow r.h[i] \leq r.h[j] \tag{2}$$

---

[2] Note that in timed STAIRS [HHRS05a] "?" represents consumption. We have chosen to use "?" for reception since we do not concider consumption events in this paper.

Note that two events may occur at the same time.

Secondly, we allow the same event to occur only once in the same trace:

$$\forall\, i,j \in [1..\#h] : i \neq j \Rightarrow h[i] \neq h[j] \tag{3}$$

Thirdly, time will eventually progress beyond any finite point in time. The following constraint states that for each lifeline l represented by infinitely many events in the trace h, and for any possible timestamp t there must exist an l-event in h whose timestamp is greater than t:

$$\forall\, l \in \mathcal{L} : (\#e.l \circledS h = \infty \Rightarrow \forall\, t \in \mathbb{R} : \exists\, i \in \mathbb{N} : r.(e.l \circledS h)[i] > t) \tag{4}$$

where $e.l$ denotes the set of events that may take place on the lifeline l. Formally:

$$e.l \overset{\text{def}}{=} \{e \in [\![\, \mathcal{E}\,]\!] \mid (k.e =!\, \wedge tr.e = l) \vee (k.e =?\, \wedge re.e = l)\} \tag{5}$$

We also require that for any single message, transmission happens before reception. But we need to take into account that the transmitter or receiver of a certain message might not be included in the sequence diagram. Thus we get the following well-formedness requirement on traces, stating that if at any point in the trace we have a transmission event, up to that point we must have had at least as many transmissions as receptions of that particular message:

$$\forall\, i \in [1..\#h] : k.h[i] =! \Rightarrow \tag{6}$$

$$\#(\{!\} \times \{m.h[i]\} \times U) \circledS h|_i > \#(\{?\} \times \{m.h[i]\} \times U) \circledS h|_i$$

where $U \overset{\text{def}}{=} \{t \mapsto r \mid t \in \mathcal{T} \wedge r \in \mathbb{R}\}$.

$\mathcal{H}$ denotes the set of well-formed traces. Traces are written as a sequence of events enclosed by $\langle\rangle$, for example $\langle e_1, e_2, e_3\rangle$.

4 Syntax and Semantics for Timed STAIRS

In the following we explain how a timed sequence diagram can be represented by a *specification pair* (p, n) where p is a set of positive traces and n is a set of negative traces. (This is a simplification of timed STAIRS, where a sequence diagram is represented by a set of specification pairs.) $\mathcal{O}$ denotes the set of specification pairs. A specification pair (p, n) is contradictory if $p \cap n \neq \varnothing$. $[\![\, d\,]\!]$ denotes the specification pair representing sequence diagram d.

4.1 Textual Syntax for Timed Sequence Diagrams

The set of syntactically correct sequence diagrams, $\mathcal{D}$, is defined inductively as the least set such that: [3]

---

[3] Timed STAIRS [HHRS05a] also include the operators loop, assert and xalt. We have omitted these operators to save space. There is also a formal requirement stating that if we have a message in the diagram and both the transmitter and the receiver lifelines of that message are present in the diagram, then both the transmit and the receive event of that message must be present in the diagram as well. This requirement is also omitted here to save space.

- $\mathcal{E} \subset \mathcal{D}$
- $d \in \mathcal{D} \Rightarrow \mathsf{neg}\ d \in \mathcal{D}$
- $d_1, d_2 \in \mathcal{D} \Rightarrow d_1\ \mathsf{par}\ d_2 \in \mathcal{D} \wedge d_1\ \mathsf{seq}\ d_2 \in \mathcal{D} \wedge d_1\ \mathsf{alt}\ d_2 \in \mathcal{D}$
- $d \in \mathcal{D} \wedge C \in \mathbb{F}(tt.d) \Rightarrow d\ \mathsf{tc}\ C \in \mathcal{D}$

where $tt.d$ yields the set of timestamp tags occurring in d. The base case implies that any event is a sequence diagram. Any other sequence diagram is constructed from the basic ones through the application of operations for negation, potential choice (alternative), weak sequencing, parallel execution and time constraint.

4.2 Denotational Semantics for Timed STAIRS

Event. The semantics of an event is the specification pair whose positive set consists of infinitely many unary positive traces – one for each possible assignment of a timestamp to its timestamp tag. The negative set is empty.

$$[\![\ (k, m, t)\ ]\!] \overset{\text{def}}{=} (\{\langle(k, m, t \mapsto r)\rangle \mid r \in \mathbb{R}\}, \varnothing) \quad \text{if } (k, m, t) \in \mathcal{E} \tag{7}$$

Negation. Undesired behavior is defined by the use of the neg construct. To negate a specification means to move every positive trace to the negative set. Negative traces remain negative. The empty trace is defined as positive to enable positive traces in a composition. Negation of a specification is defined by

$$[\![\ \mathsf{neg}\ d\ ]\!] \overset{\text{def}}{=} \neg [\![\ d\ ]\!] \tag{8}$$

where

$$\neg\ (p, n) \overset{\text{def}}{=} (\{\langle\rangle\}, n \cup p) \tag{9}$$

Parallel Execution. The operator for parallel execution is represented semantically by $\|$. Ignoring for the time being the sets of negative traces, a parallel execution defines the set of traces we get by merging one trace from one (positive) set with one trace from the other (positive) set. Informally, for sets of traces s_1 and s_2, $s_1 \| s_2$ is the set of all traces such that:

- all events from one trace in s_1 and one trace in s_2 are included (and no other events),
- the ordering of events from each of the traces is preserved.

Formally:

$$s_1 \| s_2 \overset{\text{def}}{=} \{h \in \mathcal{H} \mid \exists\, or \in \{1, 2\}^{\infty} : \tag{10}$$

$$\pi_2((\{1\} \times [\![\ \mathcal{E}\ ]\!]) \textcircled{T} (or, h)) \in s_1 \wedge$$

$$\pi_2((\{2\} \times [\![\ \mathcal{E}\ ]\!]) \textcircled{T} (or, h)) \in s_2\}$$

In this definition we make use of an oracle, the infinite sequence or, to resolve the non-determinism in the interleaving. It determines the order in which events from traces in s_1 and s_2 are sequenced.

The semantics of parallel execution may then be defined as

$$\llbracket d_1 \text{ par } d_2 \rrbracket \stackrel{\text{def}}{=} \llbracket d_1 \rrbracket \parallel \llbracket d_2 \rrbracket \qquad (11)$$

where

$$(p_1, n_1) \parallel (p_2, n_2) \stackrel{\text{def}}{=} (p_1 \parallel p_2, (n_1 \parallel (p_2 \cup n_2)) \cup (p_1 \parallel n_2)) \qquad (12)$$

Note that the merging of a negative trace with another (positive or negative) trace always results in a negative trace.

Weak Sequencing. Weak sequencing is the implicit composition mechanism combining constructs of a sequence diagram. The operator for weak sequencing is represented semantically by $\succeq$. We again temporarily ignore the sets of negative traces, and let s_1 and s_2 be trace sets. Since lifelines are independent, the constraint for the ordering of events applies to each lifeline; events that occur on different lifelines are interleaved. For $s_1 \succeq s_2$ we therefore have the constraint that events on one lifeline from one trace in s_1 should come before events from one trace in s_2 on the same lifeline:

$$s_1 \succeq s_2 \stackrel{\text{def}}{=} \{h \in \mathcal{H} \mid \exists h_1 \in s_1, h_2 \in s_2 : \qquad (13)$$

$$\forall l \in L : e.l \circledS h = e.l \circledS h_1 \frown e.l \circledS h_2\}$$

The semantics of weak sequencing may then be defined as

$$\llbracket d_1 \text{ seq } d_2 \rrbracket \stackrel{\text{def}}{=} \llbracket d_1 \rrbracket \succeq \llbracket d_2 \rrbracket \qquad (14)$$

where

$$(p_1, n_1) \succeq (p_2, n_2) \stackrel{\text{def}}{=} (p_1 \succeq p_2, (n_1 \succeq (p_2 \cup n_2)) \cup (p_1 \succeq n_2)) \qquad (15)$$

Weak sequencing involving at least one negative trace results in a negative trace.

Time Constraint. Time requirements are imposed by the use of a time constraint, denoted by $\wr C$, where C is a predicate over timestamp tags. When a time constraint is applied to a trace set all traces not fulfilling the constraint are removed. Formally, time constraint for a trace set s is defined as

$$s \wr C \stackrel{\text{def}}{=} \{h \in s \mid h \models C\} \qquad (16)$$

where $h \models C$ holds if for all possible assignments of timestamps to timestamp tags done by h, there is an assignment of timestamps to the remaining timestamp tags in C (possibly none) such that C evaluates to true. For example, if

$$h = \langle (k_1, m_1, t_1 \mapsto r_1), (k_2, m_2, t_2 \mapsto r_2), (k_3, m_3, t_3 \mapsto r_3) \rangle \text{ and } C = t_3 < t_1 + 5$$

then $h \models C$ if $r_3 < r_1 + 5$.

To apply a time requirement to a specification means to define failure to meet the requirement as negative behavior. The positive traces of the operand that do not fulfill the requirement become negative. The semantics of a time constraint is defined as

$$\llbracket d \text{ tc } C \rrbracket \stackrel{\text{def}}{=} \llbracket d \rrbracket \wr C \qquad (17)$$

where

$$(p, n) \wr C \stackrel{\text{def}}{=} (p \wr C, n \cup (p \wr \neg C)) \tag{18}$$

Potential Choice. The alt construct is used to express underspecification by grouping together traces that from the specifier's point of view serve the same purpose. This means that they are seen as equally desirable (for positive traces) or undesirable (for negative traces). For two trace sets where both are positive or both are negative, this can be represented semantically simply by taking the union of the sets. Hence, potential choice corresponds to the pairwise union of the positive sets and the negative sets. Formally, the semantics of the alt is defined by

$$[\![d_1 \text{ alt } d_2]\!] \stackrel{\text{def}}{=} [\![d_1]\!] \uplus [\![d_2]\!] \tag{19}$$

where

$$(p_1, n_1) \uplus (p_2, n_2) \stackrel{\text{def}}{=} (p_1 \cup p_2, n_1 \cup n_2) \tag{20}$$

5   Mandatory Choice and Probabilities

In STAIRS the alt operator as formally defined above enables underspecification, what we also refer to as potential choice. Underspecification means to leave some freedom of choice to the developers that will eventually implement (or further refine) the specification. This is for example useful when different design alternatives fulfill a function equally well from the specifier's point of view.

STAIRS supports also the specification of mandatory choice. For this purpose the STAIRS specific xalt operator is used. Mandatory choice means that all alternatives must be possible. It is often needed within security, for example in relation to information flow [Ros95]. When specifying a password generator, for instance, it is vital that all alternatives remain possible in the final implementation – otherwise in the extreme case we might end up with an implementation that always generates the same password.

Mandatory choice is also useful for other purposes. Sometimes non-determinism is employed to model the behavior of the environment of the system under specification. The mandatory choice operator is then used to represent alternative inputs from the environment that the designer has considered. If some of these alternatives are removed from the final specification, the implementation will not be able to handle the relevant input as intended.

Sometimes an application is non-deterministic by nature, for example in games. If we want to specify a dice, we obviously need to ensure that all alternatives, one through six, are possible outcomes in the implementation.

In probabilistic STAIRS we generalize the xalt operator into an operator for the specification of probabilities called palt. We may then also specify with what probability the different alternatives should occur. In the dice example, the probability of every outcome should be exactly $\frac{1}{6}$. Of course, if an alternative has an exact probability greater than zero, then this alternative must be a possible outcome of a valid implementation. For this reason, probabilistic choice can be viewed as a special case of mandatory choice. This view is consistent with the one presented in [MM99].

If an alternative is assigned a *set* of acceptable probabilities, then this set represents underspecification. Such underspecification is usually present in soft real-time requirements. A specification might say that the probability of a certain delay being less than 10 seconds should be 0.8 or more. This amounts to saying that the set of acceptable probabilities is $[0.8, .., 1.0]$. According to this specification, an implementation that gives a probability of 0.9 is certainly valid; the developer only needs to achieve one of the acceptable probabilities.

6   Syntax and Semantics for Probabilistic STAIRS

In the following we explain how a probabilistic sequence diagram can be represented by a multiset of *probability obligations* (also called *p-obligations*). A p-obligation $((p, n), Q)$ consists of a specification pair (p, n) and a set of probabilities Q, with the following interpretation: The traces implementing (p, n) should occur with a probability greater than or equal to a probability in Q. Only traces in $\mathcal{H} \setminus n$ are allowed to implement (p, n). The probability for these traces may be greater than the values in Q only if some or all of the traces are also positive or inconclusive according to some other p-obligation. We use a multiset instead of just a set because multiple occurrences of the same p-obligation (which may result from the composition operators) means that the specification pair should occur with a probability greater than or equal to the sum of probabilities from each instance of the p-obligation. For example, if the p-obligation $((p, n), [0.3, ..., 0.4])$ occurs twice in a specification, then this means that the traces implementing (p, n) should occur with a probability greater than or equal to a value in $[0.6, ..., 0.8]$. $\mathcal{P}$ denotes the set of p-obligations. In probabilistic STAIRS we may have underspecification with respect to traces and with respect to probabilities. Underspecification with respect to traces is captured by the fact that we may choose among the non-negative traces within a specification pair. Underspecification with respect to probabilities is modeled by the possibility of selecting among the probabilities within a p-obligation.

6.1   Textual Syntax for Probabilistic Sequence Diagrams

The set of syntactically correct sequence diagrams $\mathcal{D}$ is defined simply by adding the following case to the inductive definition in 4.1:

- $d_1, d_2 \in \mathcal{D} \wedge Q_1, Q_2 \subseteq [0...1] \Rightarrow d_1; Q_1 \text{ palt } d_2; Q_2 \in \mathcal{D}$

6.2   Denotational Semantics for Probabilistic STAIRS

Event. Probabilities can be assigned only by the use of the palt. The traces specified by a sequence diagram without occurrences of palt must occur with probability 1 in their relevant context. Therefore the set of probabilities associated with an event is $\{1\}$.

$$[\![\, (k, m, t) \,]\!] \stackrel{\text{def}}{=} \{((\{\langle (k, m, t \mapsto r) \rangle \mid r \in \mathbb{R}\}, \varnothing), \{1\})\} \quad \text{if } (k, m, t) \in \mathcal{E} \quad (21)$$

Negation and Time Constraint. Negation and time constraint are not affected by probabilities. They are defined by

$$[\![\, \text{neg } d \,]\!] \stackrel{\text{def}}{=} \{(\neg \, o, Q) \mid (o, Q) \in [\![\, d \,]\!]\} \tag{22}$$

$$[\![\, d \text{ tc } C \,]\!] \stackrel{\text{def}}{=} \{(o \wr C, Q) \mid (o, Q) \in [\![\, d \,]\!]\} \tag{23}$$

Parallel Execution and Weak Sequencing. When executing two specifications in parallel or sequentially, we get the mulitset of p-obligations obtained from choosing one p-obligation from the first and one p-obligation from the second and composing them in parallel or sequentially. Choosing the two p-obligations to be composed is seen as two independent probabilistic choices; therefore the sets of probabilities are multiplied. Formally, parallel execution and weak sequencing is defined by

$$[\![\, d_1 \text{ par } d_2 \,]\!] \stackrel{\text{def}}{=} \{(o_1 \parallel o_2, Q_1 * Q_2) \mid (o_1, Q_1) \in [\![\, d_1 \,]\!] \wedge (o_2, Q_2) \in [\![\, d_2 \,]\!]\} \tag{24}$$

$$[\![\, d_1 \text{ seq } d_2 \,]\!] \stackrel{\text{def}}{=} \{(o_1 \succsim o_2, Q_1 * Q_2) \mid (o_1, Q_1) \in [\![\, d_1 \,]\!] \wedge (o_2, Q_2) \in [\![\, d_2 \,]\!]\} \tag{25}$$

where multiplication of probability sets is defined by

$$Q_1 * Q_2 \stackrel{\text{def}}{=} \{q_1 * q_2 \mid q_1 \in Q_1 \wedge q_2 \in Q_2\} \tag{26}$$

Potential Choice. The alt construct captures underspecification with respect to traces (and not with respect to probabilities). When combining two p-obligations the probabilities that are not in both probability sets are removed. Otherwise, we might realize the composed specification with traces from only the first operand with a probability allowed only by the second operand.

$$[\![\, d_1 \text{ alt } d_2 \,]\!] \stackrel{\text{def}}{=} \{(o_1 \uplus o_2, Q_1 \cap Q_2) \mid (o_1, Q_1) \in [\![\, d_1 \,]\!] \wedge (o_2, Q_2) \in [\![\, d_2 \,]\!]\} \tag{27}$$

Probabilistic Choice. The palt construct expresses probabilistic choice (and therefore mandatory choice). Before defining the semantics of the palt we introduce the notion of probability decoration. Probability decoration is used to assign the probabilities associated with the operands of a palt. It is defined by

$$[\![\, d; Q' \,]\!] \stackrel{\text{def}}{=} \{(o, Q * Q') \mid (o, Q) \in [\![\, d \,]\!]\} \tag{28}$$

The palt operator is meant to describe the probabilistic choice between two alternative operands whose joint probability should add up to one. Formally, the palt is defined by

$$[\![\, d_1 \text{ palt } d_2 \,]\!] \stackrel{\text{def}}{=} [\![\, d_1 \,]\!] \cup [\![\, d_2 \,]\!] \cup \{(\oplus([\![\, d_1 \,]\!] \cup [\![\, d_2 \,]\!]), \{1\})\} \tag{29}$$

Note that the syntactic restrictions ensure that d_1 and d_2 are of the form $d; Q$ (see section 6.1). The p-obligation in the multiset to the right in 29 requires the probabilities of the two operands to add up to one. $\oplus$ characterizes the traces allowed by the two operands together: A trace t is positive if it is positive according to at least one p-obligation and not inconclusive according to any; t is negative only if it is negative according to all p-obligations; traces that are inconclusive according to at least one p-obligation remain inconclusive. Formally, the operator $\oplus$ for combining the specification pairs of a multiset S of p-obligations into a single specification pair is therefore defined by

$$\oplus S \stackrel{\text{def}}{=} ((\bigcup_{((p,n),Q)\in S} p) \cap (\bigcap_{((p,n),Q)\in S} p \cup n), \bigcap_{((p,n),Q)\in S} n) \tag{30}$$

7 Adding a Soft Real-Time Requirement to the Atm

We now replace the first hard real-time requirement in the atm example with a soft real-time requirement. Consider the sequence diagram in Figure 2.

This specification is modeled semantically by three p-obligations, we call these po_1, po_2 and po_3. The result of choosing the first palt operand is modeled semantically by po_1. The positive traces of po_1 are only those in which it takes less than 10 seconds before the reply arrives from the bank and it takes less than five seconds from the reply arrives to the money is delivered. Traces where one or both of these constraints are not met are negative in po_1. The acceptable range of probability for this p-obligation is $[0.8, ..., 1]$.

The result of choosing the second palt operand is modeled semantically by po_2. The positive traces of po_2 are all traces where it takes 10 seconds or more before the reply arrives from the bank and it takes less than five seconds from

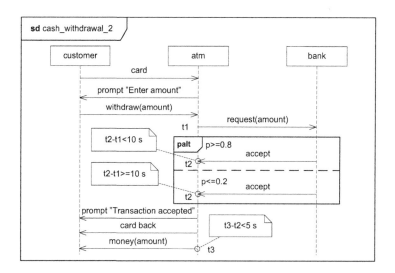

Fig. 2. Cash withdrawal with soft real-time constraint.

the reply arrives to the money is delivered. Traces where one or both of these constraints are not met are negative in po_2. The acceptable range of probability for this p-obligation is $[0, ..., 0.2]$.

The last p-obligation, po_3, models the combination of the two operands, which means that $po_3 = (\oplus\{po_1, po_2\}, \{1\})$. This means that the positive traces of po_3 are all traces where it takes less than five seconds to get money after the reply is received from the bank, regardless of how long it takes to get the reply. The negative traces are only those where it takes five seconds or more to get the money.

Traces where messages are not exchanged between the customer, the atm and the bank as described by Figure 2 (but ignoring the time requirements) are inconclusive according to po_1, po_2 and po_3.

8   Refinement

Refinement of a specification means to reduce underspecification by adding information so that the specification becomes closer to an implementation. Semantically, in our setting this can be done at the level of p-obligations or at the level of multisets of p-obligations. We first define refinement semantically for p-obligations. Then we lift this definition to specifications that are represented semantically by multisets of p-obligations.

8.1   Refinement of P-obligations

As in [HHRS05b], a specification pair is refined by moving positive traces to the set of negative traces or by moving traces from the set of inconclusive traces to either the positive or the negative set. STAIRS [HHRS05b] refers to the first option as narrowing and the second option as supplementing. As argued in [HHRS05b], narrowing reduces the set of positive traces to capture new design decisions or to match the problem more accurately. Supplementing categorizes (to this point) inconclusive behavior as either positive or negative recognizing that early descriptions normally lack completeness.

A p-obligation is refined by either refining its specification pair or reducing its set of probabilities. Formally, a p-obligation $((p', n'), Q')$ is a refinement of a p-obligation $((p, n), Q)$, written $((p, n), Q) \rightsquigarrow ((p', n'), Q')$, iff

$$n \subseteq n' \wedge p \subseteq p' \cup n' \wedge Q' \subseteq Q \qquad (31)$$

8.2   Refinement of Specifications

All p-obligations at the given (more abstract) level represent a mandatory alternative. Therefore each p-obligation needs to be represented by a p-obligation also at the refined (more concrete) level. However, there are three additional considerations to take into account when defining the refinement relation.

Firstly, if a p-obligation has 0 as an acceptable probability, this means that it does not need to be implemented. Therefore p-obligations with 0 in the probability set need not be represented at the refined level.

Secondly, we need to ensure that any combination of p-obligations at the abstract level is refined at the concrete level. For example, if a p-obligation po occurs several times at the abstract level it is not enough just to ensure that there is a single p-obligation po' at the concrete level such that $po \rightsquigarrow po'$.

Thirdly, it should be possible to refine a p-obligation at the abstract level by the combination of a submultiset of p-obligations at the concrete level, as long as the combination of these p-obligations is a refinement of the abstract p-obligation. Suppose now that we have two specifications d_1 and d_2 such that $((\{t_1, t_2\}, \{t_3\}), [0.4, ..., 0.6]) \in [\![d_1]\!]$ and such that there is no p-obligation $((p, n), Q)$ in $[\![d_2]\!]$ such that $Q \subseteq [0.4, ..., 0.6]$. Then it should still be possible for d_2 to be a refinement of d_1, as long as there is a submultiset S of $[\![d_2]\!]$ such that the combination of all p-obligations in S is a refinement of $((\{t_1, t_2\}, \{t_3\}), [0.4, ..., 0.6])$. This is the case for example if $[\![d_2]\!]$ contains the p-obligations $((\{t_1\}, \{t_2, t_3\}), \{0.3\})$ and $((\{t_2\}, \{t_1, t_3\}), \{0.2\})$. Taken together, these two p-obligations are certainly a valid refinement of $((\{t_1, t_2\}, \{t_3\}), [0.4, ..., 0.6])$.

Each p-obligation represents a probabilistic choice. The probability for a combination of choices is the sum of probabilities for each choice. Let $\{Q_1, ..., Q_n\}$ be a multiset of probability sets. We then define

$$\sum_{i=1}^{n} Q_i \stackrel{\text{def}}{=} \{\min(1, \sum_{i=1}^{n} q_i) \mid q_i \in Q_i\} \tag{32}$$

Note that the upper limit of probabilities is 1.

We are now ready to define refinement of specifications. Formally, a specification d' is a refinement of a specification d, written $d \rightsquigarrow d'$, iff

$$\forall S \subseteq [\![d]\!] : 0 \notin \pi_2.\bar{\oplus}S \Rightarrow \exists S' \subseteq [\![d']\!] : \bar{\oplus}S \rightsquigarrow \bar{\oplus}S' \tag{33}$$

where the operator $\bar{\oplus}$ characterizes the combination of all p-obligations in a multiset S into a single pair $((p, n), Q)$. Formally, $\bar{\oplus}$ is defined by

$$\bar{\oplus}S \stackrel{\text{def}}{=} (\oplus S, \sum_{po \in S} \pi_2.po) \tag{34}$$

9   Refining the Atm Specification

Figure 3 shows a refinement of the specification in Figure 2.

The change that has been made to "cash_withdrawal_2" is to impose an upper limit to the acceptable response time from the bank also in the second operand, stating that the reply should be received within 20 seconds. In addition we have narrowed the acceptable range of probability for both operands. It is now required that the reply from the bank should be received within 10 seconds in at least 90% of the cases, instead of just 80%.

The specification "cash_withdrawal_3" is modeled semantically by three p-obligations, we call these po_1', po_2' and po_3'. The p-obligation po_1' represents

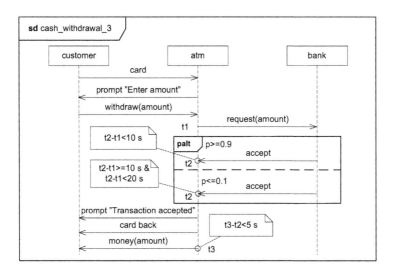

Fig. 3. A refinement of Figure 2

the result of choosing the first operand of the palt. The positive and negative traces of po_1' are the same as for po_1, while the set of acceptable probabilities for po_1' is $[0.9, ..., 1]$, which is a subset of the probability set of po_1. This means that $po_1 \rightsquigarrow po_1'$.

The result of choosing the second palt operand is modeled semantically by po_2'. The positive and negative traces of po_2' are the same as for po_2, except that traces where it takes more than 20 seconds to get a reply from the bank are positive in po_2 and negative in po_2'. Since the probability set of po_2', $[0, ..., 0.1]$, is a subset of the probability set of po_2, we get $po_2 \rightsquigarrow po_2'$.

The last p-obligation, po_3', models the combination of the two operands, which means that $po_3' = (\oplus\{po_1', po_2'\}, \{1\})$. According to po_3' the positive traces are all traces where it takes less than 20 seconds to get an answer from the bank and less than five seconds to get money after the reply is received from the bank. The negative traces are those where it takes 20 seconds or more to get a reply or five seconds or more to get the money. Since the probability sets of po_3 and po_3' are both $\{1\}$ and the only difference with respect to traces is that the traces where it takes 20 seconds or more to get a reply from the bank are positive in po_3 and negative in po_3', we get $po_3 \rightsquigarrow po_3'$.

The above shows that condition 33 is fulfilled for every singleton set that is a submultiset of the semantics of "cash_withdrawal_2". It is easy to verify that $\bar{\oplus}\{po_1, po_2\} \rightsquigarrow \bar{\oplus}\{po_1', po_2'\}$, $\bar{\oplus}\{po_2, po_3\} \rightsquigarrow \bar{\oplus}\{po_2', po_3'\}$, $\bar{\oplus}\{po_1, po_3\} \rightsquigarrow \bar{\oplus}\{po_1', po_3'\}$ and $\bar{\oplus}\{po_1, po_2, po_3\} \rightsquigarrow \bar{\oplus}\{po_1', po_2', po_3'\}$. This means that condition 33 is fulfilled, so the specification "cash_withdrawal_3" is a refinement of "cash_withdrawal_2".

We also have that the original specification "cash_withdrawal_1" with its hard real-time constraint is a refinement of "cash_withdrawal_2". To see this, note that the specification "cash_withdrawal_1" is represented semantically by $\{(\pi_1.po_1, \{1\})\}$, and that $(\pi_1.po_1, \{1\})$ is a valid refinement of both po_1 and po_3. Since $0 \in \pi_2.po_2$, this shows that condition 33 is fulfilled for every singleton set that is a submultiset of the semantics of "cash_withdrawal_2". In addition, we see that $(\pi_1.po_1, \{1\})$ is a valid refinement of $\overline{\oplus}\{po_1, po_2\}$, $\overline{\oplus}\{po_2, po_3\}$ and $\overline{\oplus}\{po_1, po_2, po_3\}$. Condition 33 is therefore fulfilled. A similar argument shows that "cash_withdrawal_1" is also a refinement of "cash_withdrawal_3".

10   Related Work

[Seg95] uses probabilistic automata to address the problem of verification of randomized distributed algorithms. The analysis includes timed systems, so that real-time properties can be investigated in a probabilistic setting. [Jan03] introduces a stochastic extension to statecharts called StoCharts to allow the quantification of the time between events according to a stochastic distribution, and defines a formal semantics that can be analyzed by tools. [JL91] presents a formalism for specifying probabilistic transition systems where transitions have sets of allowed probabilities, and defines two refinement relations on such systems. These formalisms address many of the same issues as we do, but rely on complete specifications of the communicating entities since the models are automata and statecharts.

Various dialects of sequence diagrams have been used informally for several decades. The latest versions of the most known variants are UML 2.0 [OMG04] and MSC-2000 [ITU99].

Live Sequence Charts [DH01], [HM03] is an extension of MSC where (a part of) a chart may be designated as universal (mandatory) or existential (optional). Explicit criteria in the form of pre-charts are given for when a chart applies: Whenever the system exhibits the communication behavior of its pre-chart its own behavior must conform to that prescribed by the chart. Timing constraints are included and alternatives may be assigned exact probabilities.

The UML Profile for Schedulability, Performance and Time [OMG05] extends UML by adding stereotypes and annotations for defining values for performance measures such as response time and CPU demand time. The profile is envisaged to be used with a suitable modeling tool based on for example schedulability analysis, Petri Nets or stochastic process algebra. The profile enables specification of a wide range of time-related requirements, including soft real-time requirements. However, no formal semantics is defined for the language.

Most closely related to the work presented in this paper is of course timed STAIRS as presented in [HHRS05a]. Here the notions of positive and negative behavior, mandatory choice and refinement are formalized in relation to sequence diagrams. Timed STAIRS has a more fine-grained analysis of refinement than presented here. This is partly due to a richer semantical model for events and traces. Events in timed STAIRS can be of three different types: transmit, receive and consume. This enables the distinction between two forms of refinement: glass-box refinement, which take the full semantics into account, and black box refinement, which only considers externally visible changes. The approach presented in this paper can easily be generalized to take this into account. Timed STAIRS does not address probabilities.

11 Conclusion

We have extended the work presented in [HHRS05a]. Our contribution is to generalize the approach to handle probabilities. This enables specification of soft real-time constraints as well as probabilistic specifications in general. The resulting approach, which we call probabilistic STAIRS, offers a powerful language for specifying a wide range of communicating systems, underpinned by a formal semantics that allows analysis of functional and non-functional properties, as well as formal definition of incremental development. The full report [RHS05] on which this paper is based contains additional composition operators (loop, assert, palt with n operands), a discussion on how probability spaces relate to probabilistic STAIRS specifications and proofs of various properties such as transitivity of refinement. In the future we intend to explore the relationship between probabilistic STAIRS and state machines with time and probabilities.

Acknowledgments

The research on which this paper reports has been carried out within the context of the IKT-2010 project SARDAS (15295/431) and the IKT SOS project ENFORCE (164382/V30), both funded by the Research Council of Norway. We thank Rolv Bræk, Øystein Haugen, Birger Møller Pedersen, Mass Soldal Lund, Judith Rossebø, Ragnhild Kobro Runde, Manfred Broy, Ina Schieferdecker, Thomas Weigert and the anonymous reviewers for helpful feedback.

References

[BS01]   M. Broy and K. Stølen. *Specification and Development of Interactive Systems: Focus on Streams, Interfaces, and Refinement.* Springer, 2001.

[DH01]   W. Damm and D. Harel. LSCs: Breathing life into message sequence charts. *Formal Methods in System Design*, 19(1):45–80, 2001.

[HHRS05a] Ø. Haugen, K. E. Husa, R. K. Runde, and K. Stølen. Why timed sequence diagrams require three-event semantics. Technical Report 309, Department of Informatics, University of Oslo, 2005.

[HHRS05b] Ø. Haugen, K.E. Husa, R.K. Runde, and K. Stølen. STAIRS towards formal design with sequence diagrams. *Software and System Modeling*, 00:1–13, 2005.

[HM03]   D. Harel and R. Marelly. *Come, Let's Play: Scenario-Based Programming Using LSC's and the Play-Engine.* Springer, 2003.

[HS03]   Ø. Haugen and K. Stølen. STAIRS — Steps to analyze interactions with refinement semantics. In *Sixth International Conference on UML*, number 2863 in Lecture Notes in Computer Science, pages 388–402. Springer, 2003.

[ITU99]   International Telecommunication Union. *Recommendation Z.120 — Message Sequence Chart (MSC)*, 1999.

[Jan03]   D. N. Jansen. *Extensions of Statecharts with Probability, Time, and Stochastic Timing*. PhD thesis, University of Twente, 2003.

[JL91]   B. Jonsson and K. G. Larsen. Specification and refinement of probabilistic processes. In *Proceedings of the Sixth Annual IEEE Symposium on Logic in Computer Science*, pages 266–277, Amsterdam, The Netherlands, 1991.

[MM99]   C Morgan and A McIver. pGCL: Formal reasoning for random algorithms. *South African Computer Journal*, 22:14–27, 1999.

[OMG04]   Object Management Group. *UML 2.0 Superstructure Specification*, ptc/04-10-02 edition, 2004.

[OMG05]   Object Management Group. *UML Profile for Schedulability, Performance and Time Specification*, version 1.1 formal/05-01-02 edition, jan 2005.

[RHS05]   A. Refsdal, K. E. Husa, and K. Stølen. Specification and refinement of soft real-time requirements using sequence diagrams. Technical Report 323, Department of Informatics, University of Oslo, 2005.

[Ros95]   A. W. Roscoe. CSP and determinism in security modelling. In *Proceedings of the 1995 IEEE Symposium on Security and Privacy*, pages 114–127, Washington, DC, USA, 1995. IEEE Computer Society.

[Seg95]   R. Segala. *Modeling and Verification of Randomized Distributed Real-Time Systems*. PhD thesis, Massachusetts Institute of Technology, 1995.

On Optimal Timed Strategies

Thomas Brihaye[1], Véronique Bruyère[1], and Jean-François Raskin[2]

[1] Faculté des Sciences, Université de Mons-Hainaut,
Avenue du Champ de Mars 6, B-7000 Mons, Belgium
[2] Département d'Informatique, Université Libre de Bruxelles,
Boulevard du Triomphe CP 212, B-1050-Bruxelles, Belgium

Abstract. In this paper, we study timed games played on weighted timed automata. In this context, the reachability problem asks if, given a set T of locations and a cost C, Player 1 has a strategy to force the game into T with a cost less than C no matter how Player 2 behaves. Recently, this problem has been studied independently by Alur et al and by Bouyer et al. In those two works, a semi-algorithm is proposed to solve the reachability problem, which is proved to terminate under a condition imposing the non-zenoness of cost. In this paper, we show that in the general case the existence of a strategy for Player 1 to win the game with a bounded cost is undecidable. Our undecidability result holds for weighted timed game automata with five clocks. On the positive side, we show that if we restrict the number of clocks to one and we limit the form of the cost on locations, then the semi-algorithm proposed by Bouyer et al always terminates.

1 Introduction

Weighted timed automata are an extension of timed automata with costs : each discrete transition has an associated non-negative integer cost to be paid when the transition is taken, and each location has an associated cost rate that has to be paid with respect to the time spent in the location. If the most important problem for timed automata is *reachability*, the natural extension for weighted timed automata is *optimal cost reachability*, that is, given an initial state, what is the minimum cost to be paid to reach a given location. This problem has been solved independently in [6] and [8]. The complexity of this problem is similar to the complexity of classical reachability in timed automata [3]. The more general problem of model-checking on weighted timed automata is investigated in [10].

Timed automata and weighted timed automata are models for closed systems, where every transition is controlled. If we want to distinguish between actions of a *controller* and actions of an *environment* we have to consider *timed games* on those formalisms. In one round of the timed game played on a timed automaton, Player 1 (the controller) chooses an action a and a time $t \geq 0$, Player 2 (the environment) updates the state of the automaton either by playing an uncontrollable action at time $t' \leq t$ or by playing the action a at time t as proposed by Player 1. We say that Player 1 has a winning *strategy* to reach a set T of

P. Pettersson and W. Yi (Eds.): FORMATS 2005, LNCS 3829, pp. 49–64, 2005.

target locations if it can force Player 2 to update the automaton in a way that the control of the automaton eventually reaches a location of T. When the timed game is played on a weighted timed automaton, we can ask if Player 1 can force Player 2 to update the control of the automaton in a way to reach T with a cost bounded by a given value. We can also ask to compute the optimal cost for Player 1 winning such a game.

While games on timed automata are already well studied, see for example [11], [1] and [2], and are known to be decidable, only preliminary results about games on weighted timed automata are known. First results on reachability with an optimal cost appear in [7], where the cost is equal the time spent to reach a target location in a timed automaton. Optimal reachabitility is aslo studied in [13] with any costs and weighted automata that are acyclic. In [4], Alur et al study the k-bounded optimal game reachability problem, i.e. given an initial state s of a weighted timed automaton $\mathcal{A}$, a cost bound C and a set T of locations, determine if Player 1 has a strategy to enforce the game started in state s into a location of T within k rounds, while ensuring that the cost is bounded by C. Their algorithmic solution has an exponential-time worst case complexity. In [9], the authors study winning strategies to reach a set of target locations with an optimal cost in a weighted timed automaton $\mathcal{A}$. To compute the optimal cost and to synthetize an optimal winning strategy, they provide a semi-algorithm for which they can guarantee the termination under a condition called *strict non-zenoness of cost*. This condition imposes that every cycle in the region automaton of $\mathcal{A}$ has a cost bounded away from zero. The general case where this condition is not imposed, is left open in both papers [4] and [9].

In this paper, we consider timed games played on a weighted timed automaton as they are introduced in [4], and following the lines of [9] we study the two problems of the existence of a winning strategy with a bounded cost, and of the existence of a winning strategy with an optimal cost (Section 2). We prove the unexpected negative result that for weighted timed automata, the existence of a winning strategy with a cost bounded by a given value is undecidable (Section 3, Theorem 1). The proof is based on a reduction of the halting problem for two-counter machines. The weighted timed automaton simulating the two-counter machine has five clocks and a cost rate equal to 0 or 1 on the locations. On the positive side, we show that if we restrict the number of clocks to one and we limit the cost rate to 0 or d where d is a fixed integer, then the two problems mentioned above are decidable (Section 4, Corollary 3). The proof follows the approach of [9] but we can prove the termination of their semi-algorithm without the non-zenoness of cost hypothesis.

2   Timed Games

In this section, we recall the notion of timed game on a weighted timed automaton as it is defined in [4]. In this context we introduce the concept of winning strategy and the related cost problems as mentioned in [9]. We begin with the definition of weighted timed automaton.

2.1   Weighted Timed Automata

Let X be a finite set of clocks. Let $\mathbb{R}_+$ be the set of all non-negative reals and let $\mathbb{N}$ be the set of all non-negative integers. A clock valuation is a map $\nu : X \to \mathbb{R}_+$. The set of constraints over X, denoted $G(X)$, is the set of boolean combinations of constraints of the form $x \sim \alpha$ or $x - y \sim \alpha$ where $x, y \in X$, $\alpha \in \mathbb{N}$, and $\sim \in \{<, \leq, =, \geq, >\}$. The way a clock valuation ν over X satisfies a constraint g over X is defined naturally; it is denoted by $\nu \models g$.

Definition 1. *A weighted timed automata, WTA for short, is a tuple $\mathcal{A} = (L, L_F, X, \Sigma, \delta, Inv, W_L, W_\delta)$ where L is a finite set of locations, $L_F \subseteq L$ is a set of target locations, Σ is a finite set of actions that contains the special symbol u, $\delta \subseteq L \times \Sigma \times G(X) \times 2^X \times L$ is a transition relation, $Inv : L \to G(X)$ is an invariant function, $W_L : L \to \mathbb{N}$ gives the cost for each location, and $W_\delta : \delta \to \mathbb{N}$ gives the cost for each transition.*

For a transition $e = (l, a, g, Y, l') \in \delta$, the label of e is a, and it is denoted by $\mathsf{Action}(e)$. Transitions labeled with u model *uncontrolled* transitions. The other ones are the *controlled* transitions.

A *state* of $\mathcal{A}$ is a pair $q = (l, \nu)$ where $l \in L$ is a location and ν is a valuation over X. Let Q denote the set of all states. For a clock valuation ν and a value $t \in \mathbb{R}_+$, $\nu + t$ denotes the clock valuation ν' where $\nu'(x) = \nu(x) + t$, for each $x \in X$. For any clock valuation ν, and any subset of clocks $Y \subseteq X$, $\nu[Y := 0]$ denotes the clock valuation ν' such that $\nu'(x) = \nu(x)$ for any $x \in X \setminus Y$ and $\nu'(x) = 0$ for any $x \in Y$.

A *timed transition* in $\mathcal{A}$ is of the form $(l, \nu) \to^t (l, \nu + t)$, where $(l, \nu), (l, \nu + t) \in Q$, $t \in \mathbb{R}_+$, and $\nu + t' \models Inv(l)$ for every t', $0 \leq t' \leq t$. A *discrete transition* in $\mathcal{A}$ is of the form $(l, \nu) \to^e (l', \nu')$ where e is a transition $(l, a, g, Y, l') \in \delta$ such that $\nu \models Inv(l)$, $\nu \models g$, $\nu' = \nu[Y := 0]$ and $\nu' \models Inv(l')$.

In this paper, without loss of generality, we make the assumption that a WTA $\mathcal{A}$ is *c-deterministic*, i.e. if $q \to^e q'$ and $q \to^{e'} q''$ with e, e' two controlled transitions such that $\mathsf{Action}(e) = \mathsf{Action}(e')$, then $q' = q''$.

Hypothesis 1. A WTA $\mathcal{A}$ is supposed to be c-deterministic.

A *run* ρ of a WTA $\mathcal{A}$ is a finite or infinite sequence of alternating timed and discrete transitions

$$\rho = q_1 \to^{t_1} q_1' \to^{e_1} q_2 \to^{t_2} q_2' \to^{e_2} \cdots \to^{t_k} q_k' \to^{e_k} q_{k+1} \cdots .$$

The run ρ is also denoted as $q_1 \to^{t_1 \cdot e_1} q_2 \to^{t_2 \cdot e_2} \cdots \to^{t_k \cdot e_k} q_{k+1} \cdots$. When ρ is the finite run $q_1 \to^{t_1 \cdot e_1} \cdots \to^{t_k \cdot e_k} q_{k+1}$, with $q_i = (l_i, \nu_i)$ for each i, we define the *cost* $W(\rho)$ of ρ as

$$W(\rho) = \sum_{i=1}^{k} W_L(l_i) \cdot t_i + \sum_{i=1}^{k} W_\delta(e_i).$$

2.2   Timed Games and Related Cost Problems

We now present the notion of timed game on a WTA and some related problems.

The *timed game* on a WTA $\mathcal{A} = (L, L_F, X, \Sigma, \delta, Inv, W_L, W_\delta)$ is played by two players, *Player 1* (the *controller*) and *Player 2* (the *environment*). Let $\Sigma_u = \Sigma \setminus \{u\}$. At any state q, Player 1 picks a time t and an action $a \in \Sigma_u$ such that there is a transition $q \rightarrow^{t \cdot e} q'$ with $\mathsf{Action}(e) = a$. Player 2 has two choices:

- either it can wait for time t', $0 \leq t' \leq t$, and execute a transition $q \rightarrow^{t' \cdot e'} q''$ with $\mathsf{Action}(e') = u$,
- or it can decide to wait for time t and execute the[1] transition $q \rightarrow^{t \cdot e} q'$ proposed by Player 1.

The game then evolves to a new state (according to the choice of Player 2) and the two players proceed to play as before.

Comments 1. In the definition of a timed game, it is implicitly supposed that Player 1 can always formulate a choice (t, a) in any reachable state q of the game.

We present the concept of strategy. A *(Player 1) strategy* is a function $\lambda : Q \mapsto \mathbb{R}_+ \times \Sigma_u$. A finite or infinite run $\rho = q_1 \rightarrow^{t_1 \cdot e_1} q_2 \rightarrow^{t_2 \cdot e_2} \cdots \rightarrow^{t_k \cdot e_k} q_{k+1} \cdots$ is said to be played[2] *according to* λ if for every i, if $\lambda(q_i) = (t'_i, a_i)$, then either $t_i \leq t'_i$ and $\mathsf{Action}(e_i) = u$, or $t_i = t'_i$ and $\mathsf{Action}(e_i) = a_i$. The run ρ is *winning* if for some i, $q_i = (l_i, \nu_i)$ with $l_i \in L_F$ being a target location. Suppose that q_i is the first state of ρ such that $l_i \in L_F$, and let ρ' be the prefix run of ρ equal to $q_1 \rightarrow^{t_1 \cdot e_1} \cdots \rightarrow^{t_{i-1} \cdot e_{i-1}} q_i$. Then we say that $W(\rho')$ is *the cost of ρ to reach L_F* and we abusively denote it by $W(\rho)$. Given a state q and a strategy λ, we define $\mathsf{Outcome}(q, \lambda)$ as the set of runs starting from q and played according to λ. The strategy λ is *winning* from state q if all runs of $\mathsf{Outcome}(q, \lambda)$ are winning.

Finally, we define two notions of cost as proposed in [9], and we state the problems studied in this paper. The *cost* $\mathsf{Cost}(q, \lambda)$ associated with a winning strategy λ and a state q is defined by

$$\mathsf{Cost}(q, \lambda) = \sup\{W(\rho) \mid \rho \in \mathsf{Outcome}(q, \lambda)\}.$$

Intuitively, the presence of the supremum is explained by the fact that Player 2 tries to make choices that lead to cost $W(\rho)$ as large as possible. The *optimal cost* $\mathsf{OptCost}(q)$ is then equal to

$$\mathsf{OptCost}(q) = \inf\{\mathsf{Cost}(q, \lambda) \mid \lambda \text{ is a winning strategy}\}.$$

A winning strategy λ from q is called *optimal* whenever $\mathsf{Cost}(q, \lambda) = \mathsf{OptCost}(q)$.

Problem 1. Given a WTA $\mathcal{A}$, a state q of $\mathcal{A}$ and a constant $c \in \mathbb{N}$, decide if there exists a winning strategy λ from q such that $\mathsf{Cost}(q, \lambda) \leq c$.

---

[1] Recall that $\mathcal{A}$ is assumed to be c-deterministic.

[2] This definition is from [4]. A third condition appears in the definition given in [9],[11].

Problem 2. Given a WTA $\mathcal{A}$ and a state q of $\mathcal{A}$, determine the optimal cost $\mathsf{OptCost}(q)$ and decide whether there exists an optimal winning strategy.

Comments 2. Concerning Problem 2, there is an optimal winning strategy from state q iff the infimum can be replaced by a minimum in the definition of $\mathsf{OptCost}(q)$. Notice that Problem 1 is decidable if Problem 2 can be solved. Indeed, there exists a winning strategy λ from q such that $\mathsf{Cost}(q, \lambda) \leq c$ iff either $\mathsf{OptCost}(q) < c$, or $\mathsf{OptCost}(q) = c$ and there is an optimal strategy from q.

3   Undecidability Results

This section is devoted to the main result of this article, that is, Problems 1 is undecidable. By Comments 2, it follows Problem 2 cannot be solved.

Theorem 1. *Problem 1 is undecidable.*

Proof. The idea of the proof is the following one. Given a two-counter machine M, we will construct a WTA $\mathcal{A}$ and propose a timed game on $\mathcal{A}$. In this game, Player 1 will simulate the execution of M, and Player 2 will observe the possible simulation errors done by Player 1. We will prove that for a well-chosen state q, there exists a winning strategy λ from q with $\mathsf{Cost}(q, \lambda) \leq 1$ iff the machine M halts. It will follow that Problem 1 is undecidable.

We here consider the classical model of two-counter machine [12]. The two counters are denoted by c_1 and c_2, and the different types of labeled instructions are given in Table 1.[3] A *configuration* of the machine M is given by a triple

Table 1. The possible instructions of a two-counter machine

zero test	k : if $c_i = 0$ then goto k' else goto k''
increment	k : $c_i := c_i + 1$
decrement	k : $c_i := c_i - 1$
stop	k : STOP

(k, c_1, c_2) which represents the (label of the) current instruction of M and two counter values. The first instruction of M is supposed to be labeled by k_0 and the stop instruction for which M halts, is supposed to be labeled by k_s. The initial configuration of M is thus $(k_0, 0, 0)$.

   We first define how the counter values are encoded in the states of $\mathcal{A}$. We encode the value of counter c_1 using three clocks x_1, y_1, z_1 and the value of counter c_2 using three clocks x_2, y_2, z_2[4]. The clock values are always between 0 and 1. To keep the notation simple, we use the same notation to denote the clock

---

[3] We assume that there is a zero test before each decrementation instruction such that the counter value is not modified each time it is equal to zero.

[4] An encoding using five clocks is possible, but the exposition would be more technical.

or its value. When clear from the context, we often drop the subscript, that is, counter c is described by clocks x, y and z. Counter c_i, $i = 1, 2$, has value $n \in \mathbb{N}$,

$$c_i = n \qquad (1)$$

iff one of the following three conditions is satisfied :

- $0 \leq x_i \leq y_i \leq z_i \leq 1$, $y_i - x_i = \frac{1}{2^{n+1}}$, and $x_i + (1 - z_i) = \frac{1}{2^{n+1}}$,
- $0 \leq z_i \leq x_i \leq y_i \leq 1$, $y_i - x_i = \frac{1}{2^{n+1}}$, and $x_i - z_i = \frac{1}{2^{n+1}}$,
- $0 \leq y_i \leq z_i \leq x_i \leq 1$, $(1 - x_i) + y_i = \frac{1}{2^{n+1}}$, and $x_i - z_i = \frac{1}{2^{n+1}}$.

The first condition is given in Figure 1.[5] We say that the encoding is in *normal form* if $x_i = 0$ (see Figure 2).

Fig. 1. One among the three encodings of $c_1 = n$, with $\alpha + \beta = \frac{1}{2^{n+1}}$

Fig. 2. The encoding of $c_1 = n$ in normal form

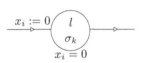

Fig. 3. Location labeled by σ_k

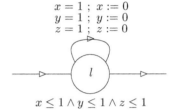

Fig. 4. Widget to let the value of a counter unchanged

The automaton $\mathcal{A} = (L, L_F, X, \Sigma, \delta, Inv, W_L, W_\delta)$ has thus a set X of six clocks (x_i, y_i and z_i, $i = 1, 2$). The costs given by function W_L to the locations are either 0 or 1. The function W_δ assigns a null cost to each transition.[6] The set L contains a location for each label k of the machine M, which is labeled by σ_k in a way to remember the label k. For each such k, the related location l is as depicted in Figure 3 where i is equal to 1 or 2. We notice that the control spends no time in location l, and that one of the two counters, c_i, is encoded in normal form. This is the way configurations (k, c_1, c_2) of the machine M are encoded by states (l, ν) of the automaton $\mathcal{A}$ with locations l like in Figure 3. In particular, the stop instruction of M which is labeled by k_s is encoded by a location l like in Figure 3, such that σ_{k_s} replaces σ_k and $l \in L_F$ is a target location.

In the sequel, we present *widgets* used by Player 1 to simulate the instructions of the machine M. These widgets are fragments of the automaton $\mathcal{A}$; they

---

[5] The two other conditions are cyclic– or mod 1, representations of the first condition.
[6] In the following figures, the cost if not indicated is supposed to be equal to zero.

are depicted in Figures 4–11. In these figures, target locations $l \in L_F$ are surrounded by a double circle, uncontrolled transitions are labeled by the action u, and controlled transitions are those that are not labeled. It is supposed that controlled transitions leaving a given location are labeled by distinct actions of Σ_u, in a way to have a c-deterministic WTA $\mathcal{A}$ (see Hypothesis 1). Notice that the constructed automaton $\mathcal{A}$ will satisfy the assumptions of Comments 1.

With the construction of these widgets and a particular state q of $\mathcal{A}$, we will see that the machine M halts iff Player 1 has a winning strategy λ from q with $\mathsf{Cost}(q, \lambda) \leq 1$. Let us describe this idea, the complete proof will be given later:

– If M halts, then the strategy of Player 1 is to faithfully simulate the instructions of M. If Player 2 lets Player 1 playing, then the cost of simulating M equals 0, otherwise the cost equals 1. In both cases the game always reaches a target location. This shows that λ is a winning strategy with $\mathsf{Cost}(q, \lambda) \leq 1$.
– Suppose that M does not halt. Either the timed game simulates the instructions of M and thus never finishes. Or it does not simulate the instructions of M and Player 2 is able to force the game to reach a target location with a cost strictly greater than 1. Therefore in both cases, Player 1 has no winning strategy λ with $\mathsf{Cost}(q, \lambda) \leq 1$.

Widget W_1 to let a counter value unchanged - The first widget allows, when time elapses in a location l, to keep the value of counter c unchanged. Such a widget is useful when, for instance, the value of one counter is incremented while the value of the other counter is not modified. See Figure 4. If the control enters location l at time t with clock values x, y, z encoding the value n of counter c, and leave location l at time $t'' \geq t$, then for all t', $t \leq t' \leq t''$, the current clock values x', y', z' still encode the value n. Indeed the clock values cyclically rotate among the three possible conditions for encoding n (see (1)).

The widget W_1 is often useful in combination with other widgets. To keep the figures of those widgets readable, we often omit widget W_1 inside them.

Widget W_2 for normal form - Figure 5 presents a widget to put a counter encoding in normal form. When the control enters location l with clocks values x, y, z encoding the value n of counter c, the control reaches location l' with x, y, z encoding n and $x = 0$. The control instantaneoulsy leaves location l' due to the invariant $x = 0$.

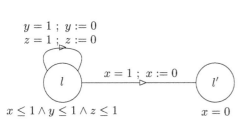

Fig. 5. Widget to put a counter encoding in normal form

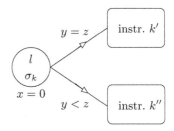

Fig. 6. Widget for zero test

Widget W_3 *for zero test* - We here indicate how to simulate a zero test instruction, i.e. an instruction k : if $c = 0$ then goto k' else goto k''. The widget for zero test is given in Figure 6. We assume that the control reaches location l with the value n of counter c encoded by x, y, z in normal form[7], that is, $x = 0$, $y = \frac{1}{2^{n+1}}$ and $z = 1 - \frac{1}{2^{n+1}}$. We notice that location l is like locations described in Figure 3. No time can elapse in l. Clearly to test that $n = 0$ is equivalent to test that $y = z$ as done in this widget.

Widget W_4 *for increment* - In this paragraph, we indicate how to simulate an increment instruction $k : c := c + 1$. While the previous widgets have controlled transitions only, and null costs on every location, the widget for incrementing counter c uses two uncontrolled transitions, and have cost equal to 1 for certain locations. This widget is composed of several parts.

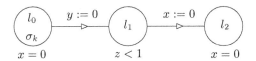

Fig. 7. First part of the widget for increment

(1) First part of widget W_4
Consider Figure 7. We can suppose that the control reaches location l_0 with the value n of counter c encoded by x, y, z in normal form, such that $x = 0$, $y = \frac{1}{2^{n+1}}$ and $z = 1 - \frac{1}{2^{n+1}}$. The transition from l_0 to l_1 has to be taken immediately. As the transition from l_1 to l_2 is controlled, Player 1 has to choose the amount of time t that it waits in l_1 before taking the transition to l_2. Because of the invariant labeling l_1, we know that $t < \frac{1}{2^{n+1}}$. When entering location l_2, the clock values are as follows: $x = 0$, $y = t$ and $z = 1 - \frac{1}{2^{n+1}} + t$. Note that to faithfully simulate the increment of counter c, Player 1 should choose $t = \frac{1}{2^{n+2}}$. It is easy to verify that in location l_2,

$$t = \frac{1}{2^{n+2}} \Leftrightarrow y + z = 1. \tag{2}$$

So, we are in the following situation: to verify that Player 1 has faithfully chosen t to simulate the increment of counter c, we simply have to check that in l_2, $y + z = 1$. Hereafter, we show how Player 2 observes in location l_2 the possible simulation errors of Player 1. Notice that in l_2, the clock values x, y, z satisfy $0 = x < y < z \le 1$.

(2) Part of widget W_4 to check if $y + z \ne 1$
For clarity, we distinguish the case where (i) $y + z > 1$ from the case where (ii) $y + z < 1$. We begin with Case (i). The widget $W^>$ is given in Figure 8. Notice that the first location of this widget is equal to the last one of the widget

---

[7] This is always possible by using widget W_2.

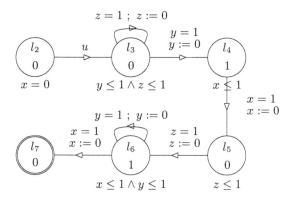

Fig. 8. Widget $W^>$

of Figure 7, and that the first transition is uncontrolled. Location l_7 is a target location, i.e. $l_7 \in L_F$. The idea is as follows: we use the cost $W(\rho)$ of the run ρ from l_2 to l_7 to compute the value $y + z$. The cost of each location is null except for locations l_4 and l_6 where $W_L(l_4) = 1$ and $W_L(l_6) = 1$. Let ρ be a run from l_2 to l_7 such that y and z are clock values in l_2. Recall that in location l_2, the clock values x, y, z satisfy $0 = x < y < z \leq 1$. We can verify that the cost of ρ is equal to $y + z$ (a cost y in location l_4 and a cost z in location l_6). Hence we have

$$y + z > 1 \Leftrightarrow W(\rho) > 1. \tag{3}$$

We now consider Case (ii). The widget $W^<$ is given in Figure 9. As for widget $W^>$ the first location of this widget is equal to location l_2 of Figure 7, and the first transition is uncontrolled. Location l'_6 is a target location. The idea is similar to Case (i) : along the run ρ' from l_2 to l'_6, the value n of counter c is left unchanged, and the cost of ρ' is equal to $(1 - y) + (1 - z)$ (a cost $1 - y$ in l'_3 and a cost $1 - z$ in l'_5). As $y + z < 1$ is equivalent to $(1 - y) + (1 - z) > 1$, then

$$y + z < 1 \Leftrightarrow W(\rho') > 1. \tag{4}$$

(3) Complete widget for increment
The complete widget for increment is composed of the widgets given in Figures 7, 8 and Figure 9, as it is schematically given in Figure 10. The counter that we want to increment has value n. First the control enters the first part of the widget for incrementation with $x = 0$, $y = \frac{1}{2^{n+1}}$, $z = 1 - \frac{1}{2^{n+1}}$. As we have seen before, Player 1 has to choose the amount of time t that it waits in l_1 before taking the transition to l_2. The only way to reach l_2 with $y + z = 1$ is to simulate faithfully the increment of the counter (see (2)). Then in location l_2, Player 1 proposes to Player 2 to move the control to the widget that encodes the next instruction of the machine M. Player has three choices: either accept the move of Player 1, or move the control to the widget $W^>$, or move the control to the widget $W^<$.

So, looking at Figure 10, the situation is as follows. Suppose that Player 1 faithfully simulates the increment instruction, i.e. $y + z = 1$ (see (2)). Either

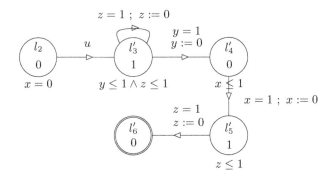

Fig. 9. Widget $W^<$

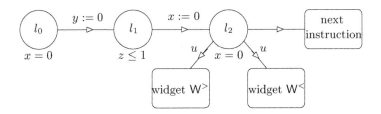

Fig. 10. Widget W_4 for increment

Player 2 lets the game evolving to the next instruction of M, and the cost remains null. Or it decides to use one of the two widgets $W^>$, $W^<$, and the game reaches a target location with a cost equal to 1 (see (3) and (4)). So whatever the Player 2's decision, the cost is bounded by 1. Suppose now that Player 1 does not simulate the increment instruction, i.e. $y + z \neq 1$, then Player 2 can take a decision such that the game reaches a target location with a cost strictly greater than 1. Indeed, if $y + z > 1$, it decides to use the widget $W^>$ (see (3)), otherwise it uses the widget $W^<$ (see (4)).

Widget W_5 for decrement - As for the increment, the widget for decrement is in several parts. We only present the first part in details, where Player 1 has to faithfully simulate the decrement. The other parts where Player 2 observes the possible errors of Player 1 are identical to Cases (i), (ii) of the increment widget.

Let us assume that we enter location l_0 of the widget of Figure 11 with $x = 0$, $y = \frac{1}{2^{n+1}}$ and $z = 1 - \frac{1}{2^{n+1}}$. We also assume that $n > 1$ (see footnote 3).

When the control leaves location l_1, the clock values are respectively equal to $x = 0$, $z = 1$, and $y = \frac{1}{2^{n+1}} + \frac{1}{2^{n+1}}$. Then Player 1 has to choose the amount of time t that it waits in location l_2 before taking the transition to l_3. To faithfully simulate the decrement, Player 1 should choose $t = \frac{1}{2^n}$. In location l_4, we are now in the same situation as in location l_2 of the increment widget (see Figure 10): $t = \frac{1}{2^n} \Leftrightarrow y + z = 1$. So, we just have to plug in l_4 the two widgets $W^>$, $W^<$ and a transition to the next instruction of the machine M. The situation is the same as for the increment. Indeed if Player 1 faithfully simulates the decrement instruction, then the cost is bounded by 1 whatever the Player 2's decision. If Player 1 does not simulate it, then Player 2 can take a decision such that the game reaches a target location with a cost strictly greater than 1.

It should now be clear why we can reduce the halting of a two-counter machine to the existence of a winning strategy for Player 1 to reach a target location with a cost bounded by 1. Let M be a two-counter machine and $\mathcal{A}$ the WTA constructed from the widgets as above. The target locations of $\mathcal{A}$ are either the location associated with the stop instruction of M, or the target locations of the widgets of Figures 8 and 9. Let $q = (l, \nu)$ be the state of $\mathcal{A}$ encoding the initial configuration $(k_0, 0, 0)$ of M, that is, l is the location labeled by σ_{k_0}, and ν is the clock valuation such that $x_1 = x_2 = 0$ and $y_1 = z_1 = y_2 = z_2 = \frac{1}{2}$. Let us prove that M halts iff there exists a winning strategy λ from q with $\mathsf{Cost}(q, \lambda) \leq 1$.

Suppose that M halts, then the strategy λ of Player 1 is to faithfully simulate the instructions of M. Let ρ be a run of $\mathsf{Outcome}(q, \lambda)$. If along ρ, Player 2 lets Player 1 simulating M, then ρ reaches the target location of $\mathcal{A}$ associated with the stop instruction of M with a cost $W(\rho) = 0$. If Player 2 decides to use one of the two widgets $\mathsf{W}^>$, $\mathsf{W}^<$, then ρ reaches the target location of this widget with $W(\rho) = 1$. Therefore, λ has a winning strategy from q satisfying $\mathsf{Cost}(q, \lambda) \leq 1$.

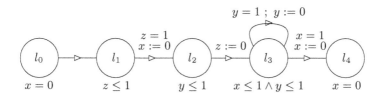

Fig. 11. First part of the widget for decrement

Suppose that there is a winning strategy λ from q with $\mathsf{Cost}(q, \lambda) \leq 1$. Assume that M does not halt, the contradiction is obtained as follows. If λ consists in simulating the instructions of M, then Player 2 decides to let Player 1 simulating M. The corresponding run $\rho \in \mathsf{Outcome}(q, \lambda)$ will never reach a target location since M does not halt. This is impossible since λ is winning. Thus suppose that λ does not simulate the instructions of M, and let $\rho \in \mathsf{Outcome}(q, \lambda)$. As soon as Player 2 observes a simulation error along ρ, it decides to use one of the widgets $\mathsf{W}^>$, $\mathsf{W}^<$ such that ρ reaches the target location of this widget with $W(\rho) > 1$. This is impossible since λ is winning with a cost $\mathsf{Cost}(q, \lambda) \leq 1$. □

4   Symbolic Analysis of Timed Games

4.1   The Pre Operator

In order to symbolically analyse timed games, we present a controllable predecessor operator. The main result is Proposition 1 relating the iteration of this operator with the existence of a winning strategy with a bounded cost. The content of this section is close to [9], but with a different and simpler presentation.[8]

Let $\mathcal{A} = (L, L_F, X, \Sigma, \delta, Inv, W_L, W_\delta)$ be a WTA. An *extended state* of $\mathcal{A}$ is a tuple (l, ν, w) where $l \in L$ is a location, ν is a clock valuation over X, and $w \in \mathbb{R}_+$ is called the *credit*. Intuitively, the credit models a sufficient amount of resource that allows Player 1, when in state (l, ν), to reach a target location of L_F whatever Player 2 decides to do, with a cost less than or equal to w. The set of extended states is denoted by Q_E.

We now define the following Pre operator.

Definition 2. *Let $\mathcal{A}$ be a WTA and $R \subseteq Q_E$. Then $(l, \nu, w) \in \mathsf{Pre}(R)$ iff there exist $t \in \mathbb{R}_+$ and a controlled transition $e \in \delta$ such that*

- *there exists an extended state $(l', \nu', w') \in R$, with $(l, \nu) \rightarrow^{t \cdot e} (l', \nu')$, and $w \geq w' + W_L(l) \cdot t + W_\delta(e)$,*
- *and for every t', $0 \leq t' \leq t$, every uncontrolled transition $e' \in \delta$, and every state (l', ν') such that $(l, \nu) \rightarrow^{t' \cdot e'} (l', \nu')$, there exists an extended state $(l', \nu', w') \in R$ with $w \geq w' + W_L(l) \cdot t' + W_\delta(e')$.*

The Pre operator satisfies the following nice properties. Given a WTA $\mathcal{A}$, we define the set $\mathsf{Goal} = \{(l, \nu, w) \mid l \in L_F \text{ and } w \geq 0\}$, and the set

$$\mathsf{Pre}^*(\mathsf{Goal}) = \bigcup_{k \geq 0} \mathsf{Pre}^k(\mathsf{Goal}).^9$$

A set $R \subseteq Q_E$ of extended states is said *upward closed* if whenever $(l, \nu, w) \in R$, then $(l, \nu, w') \in R$ for all $w' \geq w$.

Lemma 1.   *1. For all $R \subseteq Q_E$, the set $\mathsf{Pre}(R)$ is upward closed.*
2. The set Goal and $\mathsf{Pre}^*(\mathsf{Goal})$ are upward closed.

Proposition 1. *Let $\mathcal{A}$ be a WTA. Then $(l, \nu, w) \in \mathsf{Pre}^*(\mathsf{Goal})$ iff there exists a winning strategy λ from state $q = (l, \nu)$ such that $\mathsf{Cost}(q, \lambda) \leq w$.*

Proposition 1 leads to several comments in the case a symbolic representation[10] for $\mathsf{Pre}^*(\mathsf{Goal})$ can be computed. In such a case, we say that $\mathsf{Pre}^*(\mathsf{Goal})$ has an *effective representation*.

Comments 3. By Proposition 1, Problem 1 is decidable if (i) $\mathsf{Pre}^*(\mathsf{Goal})$ has an effective representation, and (ii) the belonging of an extended state (l, ν, w) to $\mathsf{Pre}^*(\mathsf{Goal})$ can be effectively checked. We now know from Theorem 1 that one of the conditions (i), (ii) cannot be fulfilled in general.

---

[8] In [9], timed games on WTA's are reduced to games on linear hybrid automata where the cost is one of the variables.
[9] For $k = 0$, $\mathsf{Pre}^k(\mathsf{Goal}) = \mathsf{Goal}$, and for $k > 0$, $\mathsf{Pre}^k(\mathsf{Goal}) = \mathsf{Pre}\left(\mathsf{Pre}^{k-1}(\mathsf{Goal})\right)$.
[10] For instance this representation could be given in a decidable logical formalism like the first-order theory of the reals with order and addition.

Comments 4. Let $\mathcal{A}$ be a WTA and $q = (l, \nu)$ be a state of $\mathcal{A}$. Problem 2 asks to determine the optimal cost $\mathsf{OptCost}(q)$. This is possible under the following hypotheses: (i) $\mathsf{Pre}^*(\mathsf{Goal})$ has an effective representation, (ii) the value $\inf\{w \mid (l, \nu, w) \in \mathsf{Pre}^*(\mathsf{Goal})\}$ can be effectively computed. This value is exactly $\mathsf{OptCost}(q)$.

Moreover the existence of an optimal winning strategy from q is decidable if one can determine the value $c = \mathsf{OptCost}(q)$, and the belonging of (l, ν, c) to $\mathsf{Pre}^*(\mathsf{Goal})$ can be effectively checked. Indeed, an optimal strategy exists iff c is the minimum value of the set $\{w \mid (l, \nu, w) \in \mathsf{Pre}^*(\mathsf{Goal})\}$ (see Comments 2).

In [9], Problem 2 has been solved for the class of WTA's $\mathcal{A}$ such that the cost function of is strictly non-zeno, i.e. every cycle in the region automaton associated with $\mathcal{A}$ has a cost which is bounded away from zero. The authors of this paper translate Problem 2 into some linear hybrid automata where the cost is one of the variables. For this class of hybrid automata, the conditions mentioned above in these comments are fulfilled. Of course the automaton we have contructed in the proof of Theorem 1 does not fall into this class of automata.

4.2   One Clock

In Section 3, Problem 1 was shown undecidable by a reduction of the halting problem of a two-counter machine. The WTA in the proof uses five clocks, has no cost on the transitions and cost 0 or 1 on the locations. We here study WTA's with one clock and such that for any location l, $W_L(l) \in \{0, d\}$ with $d \in \mathbb{N}$ a given constant. For this particular class of automata, we solve Problem 2 by following the lines of Comments 4. By Comments 2, Problem 1 is thus also solved. The proof is only detailed for $d = 1$.

To facilitate the computation of the Pre operator, we first introduce another operator denoted by π, that is largely inspired from the one of [9]. We need to generalize some notation to extended states: a timed transition $(l, \nu) \to^t (l', \nu')$ is extended to $(l, \nu, w) \to^t (l', \nu', w - W_L(l) \cdot t)$, similarly with $(l, \nu) \to^e (l', \nu')$ extended to $(l, \nu, w) \to^e (l', \nu', w - W_\delta(e))$. Given $R \subseteq Q_E$ and $a \in \Sigma$ we define

$$\mathsf{Pre}^a(R) = \{r \in Q_E \mid \exists r' \in R \text{ such that } r \to^e r' \text{ with } \mathsf{Action}(e) = a\},$$

as well as $\mathsf{cPre}(R) = \cup_{a \in \Sigma_u} \mathsf{Pre}^a(R)$, and $\mathsf{uPre}(R) = \mathsf{Pre}^u(R)$. We also define the following set $\mathsf{tPre(R,S)}$, with $R, S \subseteq Q_E$. Intuitively, an extended state r is in $\mathsf{tPre}(R, S)$ if from r we can reach r' by time elapsing and along the timed transition from r to r' we avoid S. This set is defined by

$$\mathsf{tPre}(R, S) = \{r \in Q_E \mid \exists t \in \mathbb{R}_+ \text{ with } r \to^t r', r' \in R, \text{ and } \mathsf{Post}_{[0,t]}(s) \subseteq \overline{S}\}$$

where $\mathsf{Post}_{[0,t]}(s) = \{r' \in Q_E \mid \exists t', 0 \leq t' \leq t, \text{ such that } r \to^{t'} r'\}$. The new operator π is then defined by :

$$\pi(R) = \mathsf{tPre}\big(\mathsf{cPre}(R), \mathsf{uPre}(\overline{R})\big). \tag{5}$$

The next lemmas indicate useful properties of the various operators.

Lemma 2. *1.* $\mathsf{cPre}(R_1 \cup R_2) = \mathsf{cPre}(R_1) \cup \mathsf{cPre}(R_2),$
2. $\mathsf{uPre}(R_1 \cup R_2) = \mathsf{uPre}(R_1) \cup \mathsf{uPre}(R_2),$
3. $\mathsf{tPre}(R_1 \cup R_2, S) = \mathsf{tPre}(R_1, S) \cup \mathsf{Pre}_t(R_2, S),$
4. $\mathsf{tPre}(R, S_1 \cup S_2) = \mathsf{tPre}(R, S_1) \cap \mathsf{Pre}_t(R, S_2).$

Lemma 3. *1. If $R \subseteq Q_E$ is upward closed, then $\pi(R) = \mathsf{Pre}(R)$.*
2. $\mathsf{Pre}^*(\mathsf{Goal}) = \pi^*(\mathsf{Goal}).$

We now study WTA's $\mathcal{A}$ with one clock x, such that $W_L(l) \in \{0, 1\}$ for every location l. Let C be the largest constant used in the guards of $\mathcal{A}$. As done in [5] for timed automata, we define an equivalence relation on Q_E in order to obtain a partition of this set.

Definition 3. *Let $(\nu, w), (\nu', w') \in \mathbb{R}_+^2$. Then $(\nu, w) \sim (\nu', w')$ if the following conditions hold.*

1. Either $\lfloor \nu \rfloor = \lfloor \nu' \rfloor$, or $\nu, \nu' > C$; $\lfloor w \rfloor = \lfloor w' \rfloor$;
2. For $\nu, \nu' \leq C$, $fract(\nu) = 0$ iff $fract(\nu') = 0$; $fract(w) = 0$ iff $fract(w') = 0$;
3. For $\nu, \nu' \leq C$, $fract(\nu) + fract(w) \sim 1$ iff $fract(\nu') + fract(w') \sim 1$, with $\sim \in \{<, =, >\}$.

An example of equivalence relation $\sim$ is given in Figure 12. We extend the relation $\sim$ to Q_E by defining $(l, \nu, w) \sim (l', \nu', w')$ iff $l = l'$ and $(\nu, w) \sim (\nu', w')$. Let $\mathcal{P}$ be the partition of Q_E obtained with this relation.

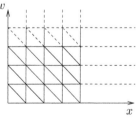

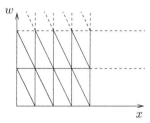

Fig. 12. The relation $\sim$ with $C = 4$ **Fig. 13.** The partition $\mathcal{P}_2$

The partition $\mathcal{P}$ is *stable* under π, that is, given $R \in \mathcal{P}$, $\pi(R)$ is a union of equivalence classes of $\mathcal{P}$. The reader could convince himself as follows. Let $R \in \mathcal{P}$. Clearly, the sets $\mathsf{cPre}(R)$ and $\mathsf{uPre}(R)$ are union of equivalences classes of $\mathcal{P}$. Now due to Lemma 2, it remains to check that given $R, S \in \mathcal{P}$, the set $\mathsf{tPre}(R, S)$ is a union of equivalence classes taking into account that $W_L(l) \in \{0, 1\}$. We summarize this result in the next lemma.

Lemma 4. *$\mathcal{P}$ is stable under π.*

By this lemma, the next corollary is straightforward since Goal is a union of equivalence classes of $\mathcal{P}$ and by Lemmas 1 and 3.

Corollary 1. *The set* Pre*(Goal) *is a union of equivalence classes of* $\mathcal{P}$. *Given a state* q *of* $\mathcal{A}$, *the optimum cost* OptCost(q) *is a non-negative integer*[11].

Even if the proposed partition $\mathcal{P}$ is infinite, we are able to prove that the computation of Pre*(Goal) terminates. We first define the *set* Up($\mathcal{P}$) *of upward closed sets w.r.t.* $\mathcal{P}$: Up($\mathcal{P}$) = $\{R \mid R = \cup R_i, R_i \in \mathcal{P}$ and R is upward closed$\}$.

Lemma 5. *The partially ordered set* $\langle$Up($\mathcal{P}$), $\supseteq\rangle$ *is Artinian*[12].

Corollary 2. Pre*(Goal) *can be effectively computed.*

Looking at Comments 4, we get the next corollary.

Corollary 3. *Let* $\mathcal{A}$ *be a WTA with one clock and such that* $W_L(l) \in \{0, 1\}$ *for all locations* l. *Then Problems 1 and 2 can be solved.*

Comments 5. The arguments given in this section are easily extended to a cost function $W_L(l) \in \{0, d\}$ for any location l, where $d \geq 1$ is a fixed integer. The same approach holds but with a partition $\mathcal{P}_d$ different from $\mathcal{P}$. This partition is similar to $\mathcal{P}$, except that we only need horizontal lines of the form $w = d \cdot n$ (with $n \in \mathbb{N}$) and each anti-diagonal of the form $x + w = c$ is removed and replaced by the lines of equations $d \cdot x + w = d \cdot n$ (with $n \in \mathbb{N}$). See Figure 13.

References

1. L. de Alfaro and T.A. Henzinger and R. Majumdar. Symbolic algorithms for infinite-state games. In *Proceedings of CONCUR'01, Lect. Notes Comput. Sci.* **2154**, 536–550, Springer, 2001.
2. L. de Alfaro and M. Faella and T.A. Henzinger and R. Majumdar and M. Stoelinga". The element of surprise in timed games". In *Proceedings of CON-CUR'03, Lect. Notes Comput. Sci.* **2761**, 144–158, Springer, 2003.
3. R. Alur and P. Madhusudan. Decision problems for timed automata: A survey. In *Proceedings of SFM'04, Lect. Notes Comput. Sci.* **3185**, 1–24, Springer, 2004.
4. R. Alur, M. Bernadsky, and P. Madhusudan. Optimal reachability for weighted timed games. In *Proceedings of ICALP'04, Lect. Notes Comput. Sci.* **3142**, 122–133, Springer, 2004.
5. R. Alur and D.L. Dill. A theory of timed automata. *Theoret. Comput. Sci.* **126**, 183–235, 1994.
6. R. Alur, S. La Torre, and G.J. Pappas. Optimal paths in weighted timed automata. In *Proceedings of HSCC'01, Lect. Notes Comput. Sci.* **2034**, 49–62, Springer, 2001.
7. E. Asarin and O. Maler. As soon as possible: Time optimal control for timed automata. In *Proceedings of HSCC'99, Lect. Notes Comput. Sci.* **1569**, 19–30, Springer, 1999.
8. G. Behrmann, A. Fehnker, T. Hune, K. Larsen, P. Pettersson, J. Romijn, and F. Vaandrager. Minimum-cost reachability for priced timed automata. In *Proceedings of HSCC'01, Lect. Notes Comput. Sci.* **2034**, 147–161. Springer-Verlag, 2001.

---

[11] It is possible to find an example of WTA with two clocks and an optimum cost which is rational.

[12] Every decreasing chain is finite.

9. P. Bouyer, F. Cassez, E. Fleury, and K.G. Larsen. Optimal strategies in priced timed game automata. In *Proceedings of FSTTCS'04*, **3328** *Lect. Notes Comput. Sci.* **3328**, 148–160, Springer, 2004.

10. T. Brihaye, V. Bruyère, and J.-F. Raskin. Model-Checking for Weighted Timed Automata. In *Proceedings of FORMATS-FTRTFT'04*, *Lect. Notes Comput. Sci.* **3253** , 277–292, Springer, 2004.

11. O. Maler, A. Pnueli, and J. Sifakis. On the synthesis of discrete controllers for timed systems. In *Proceedings of STACS'95*, *Lect. Notes Comput. Sci.* **900**, 229–242, Springer, 1995.

12. M. Minsky. *Computation: Finite and Infinite Machines*. Prentice Hall, 1967.

13. S. La Torre, S. Mukhopadhyay, and A. Murano. Optimal-reachability and control for acyclic weighted timed automata. In *Proceedings of IFIP TCS'02*, *IFIP Conference Proceedings* **223**, 485–497, Kluwer, 2002.

Average Reward Timed Games*

Bo Thomas Adler[1], Luca de Alfaro[1], and Marco Faella[1,2]

[1] School of Engineering, University of California, Santa Cruz, USA
[2] Dipartimento di Scienze Fisiche, Università di Napoli "Federico II", Italy

Abstract. We consider real-time games where the goal consists, for each player, in maximizing the average reward he or she receives per time unit. We consider zero-sum rewards, so that a reward of $+r$ to one player corresponds to a reward of $-r$ to the other player. The games are played on discrete-time game structures which can be specified using a two-player version of timed automata whose locations are labeled by reward rates. Even though the rewards themselves are zero-sum, the games are not, due to the requirement that time must progress along a play of the game.

Since we focus on control applications, we define the value of the game to a player to be the maximal average reward per time unit that the player can ensure. We show that, in general, the values to players 1 and 2 do not sum to zero. We provide algorithms for computing the value of the game for either player; the algorithms are based on the relationship between the original, infinite-round game, and a derived game that is played for only finitely many rounds. As memoryless optimal strategies exist for both players in both games, we show that the problem of computing the value of the game is in NP∩coNP.

1 Introduction

Games provide a setting for the study of control problems. It is natural to view a system and its controller as two players in a game; the problem of synthesizing a controller given a control goal can be phrased as the problem of finding a controller strategy that enforces the goal, regardless of how the system behaves [Chu63, RW89, PR89]. In the control of real-time systems, the games must not only model the interaction steps between the system and the controller, but also the amount of time that elapses between these steps. This leads to *timed games,* a model that was first applied to the synthesis of controllers for safety, reachability, and other ω-regular goals [MPS95, AH97, AMAS98, HHM99, dAFH+03]. More recently, the problem of designing controllers for *efficiency* goals has been addressed, via the consideration of *priced* versions of timed games [BCFL04, ABM04]. In priced timed games, price rates (or, symmetrically, reward rates) are associated with the states of the game, and prices (or rewards) with its transitions. The problem that has so far been addressed is the synthesis of minimum-cost controllers for reachability goals [BCFL04, ABM04]. In this paper, we focus instead on the problem of synthesizing controllers that maximize the average reward[1] per time unit accrued along an infinite play of the game. This is an expressive

---

* This research was supported in part by the NSF CAREER award CCR-0132780, by the ONR grant N00014-02-1-0671, and by the ARP award TO.030.MM.D.
[1] With a sign change, this is obviously equivalent to minimizing the average cost.

P. Pettersson and W. Yi (Eds.): FORMATS 2005, LNCS 3829, pp. 65–80, 2005.

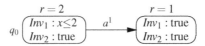

Fig. 1. A game automaton where player 1 can freeze time to achieve a higher average reward

and widely applicable efficiency goal, since many real-time systems are modeled as non-terminating systems which exhibit infinite behaviors.

We consider timed games played between two players over discrete-time game structures with finite state space. At each round, both players independently choose a move. We distinguish between *immediate moves*, which correspond to control actions or system transitions and take 0 time, and *timed moves*. There are two timed moves: the move Δ_0, which signifies the intention to wait for 0 time, and the move Δ_1, which signifies the intention of waiting for 1 time unit. The two moves chosen by the players jointly determine the successor state: roughly, immediate moves take the precedence over timed ones, and unit-length time steps occur only when both players play Δ_1. Each state is associated with a reward rate, which specifies the reward obtained when staying at the state for one time unit. We consider zero-sum rewards, so that a reward of $+r$ to one player corresponds to a reward of $-r$ to the other player. These game structures can be specified using a notation similar to that of timed automata. Each location is labeled by a reward rate, and by two invariants (rather than one), which specify how long the two players can stay at the location; the actions labeling the edges correspond to the immediate moves of the players.

The goal of each player is to maximize the long-run average reward it receives per time unit; however, this goal is subordinate to the requirement that players should not block the progress of time by playing forever zero-delay moves (immediate moves, or Δ_0). As an example, consider the game of Figure 1. The strategy that maximizes the reward per time unit calls for player 1 staying forever at q_0: this yields an average reward per time unit of 4. However, such a strategy would block time, since the clock x would not be able to increase beyond the value 2, due to the player-1 invariant $x \leq 2$ at q_0. If player 1 plays move a^1, time can progress, but the average reward per time unit is 1. To prevent players from blocking time in their pursuit of higher average reward, we define the value of a play of the game in a way that enforces time progress. If time diverges along the play, the value of the play is the average reward per time unit obtained along it. If time does not diverge along the play, there are two cases. If a player contributes to blocking the progress of time, then the value of the play to the player is $-\infty$; if the progress of time is blocked entirely by the other player, then the value of the play to the player is $+\infty$. These definitions are based on the treatment of time divergence in timed games of [dAFH+03, dAHS02]. According to these definitions, even though the reward rate is zero-sum, and time-divergent plays have zero-sum values, the games are not zero-sum, due to the treatment of time divergence. Since we are interested in the problem of controller design, we define the value of a game to a player to be the maximal play value that the player is able to secure, regardless of how the adversary plays. The resulting games are not determined: that the values that the two players can secure do not sum to zero. We show that there is no symmetrical formulation that can at the same time enforce time progress, and lead to a determined setting.

We provide algorithms for computing the value of the game for either player. The algorithms are based on the relationship between the original, infinite-round, game, and a derived game that is played on the same discrete-time game structure, but for only finitely many rounds. As in [EM79], the derived game terminates whenever one of the two players closes a loop; our construction, however, differs from [EM79] in how it assigns a value to the loops, due to our different notion of value of a play. We show that a player can achieve the same value in the finite game, as in the original infinite-round game. Our proof is inspired by the argument in [EM79], and it closes some small gaps in the proof of [EM79].

The equivalence between finite and infinite games provides a PSPACE algorithm for computing the value of average reward discrete-time games. We improve this result by showing that both finite and infinite games admit memoryless optimal strategies for each player. Once we fix a memoryless strategy for a player, the game is reduced to a graph. We provide a polynomial-time algorithm that enables the computaton of the value of the graph for the other player. The algorithm is based on polynomial-time graph transformations, followed by the application of Karp's algorithm for computing the minimum/maximal average cost of a cycle [Kar78]. The existence of memoryless strategies, together with this algorithm, provide us with a polynomial witness and with a polynomial-time algorithm for checking the witness. Since this analysis can be done both for the winning strategies of a player, and for the "spoiling" strategies of the opponent, we conclude that the problem of computing the value of an average-reward timed game, for either player, is in NP ∩ coNP. This matches the best known bounds for several other classes of games, among which are turn-based deterministic parity games [EJ91] and turn-based stochastic reachability games [Con92]. Since the maximum average reward accumulated in the first n time units cannot be computed by iterating n times a dynamic-programming operator, the weakly-polynomial algorithm of [ZP96] cannot be adapted to our games; the existence of polynomial algorithms is an open problem.

The goal of minimizing the long-run average cost incurred during the life of a real-time system has been considered previously in [BBL04]. There, the underlying model is a timed automaton, and the paper solves the verification problem ("what is the minimum long-run average cost achievable?"), or equivalently, the control problem for a fully deterministic system. In contrast, the underlying computational model in this paper is a timed game, and the problem solved is the control of a nondeterministic real-time system.

Compared to other work on priced timed games [BCFL04, ABM04], our models for timed games are simplified in two ways. First, rewards can only be accrued by staying at a state, and not by taking transitions. Second, we study the problem in discrete time. On the other hand, our models are more general in that, unlike [BCFL04, ABM04], we do not impose structural constraints on the game structures that ensure the progress of time. There is a tradeoff between imposing structural constraints and allowing rewards for transitions: had we introduced constraints that ensure time progress, we could have easily accommodated for rewards on the transitions. The restriction to discrete-time limits somewhat the expressiveness of the models. Nevertheless, control problems where the control actions can be issued only at discrete points in time are very common: most real controllers are driven by a periodic clock; hence, the discrete-time restriction is not unduly limiting as far as the controller actions are concerned. We note that there are also many cases where the system actions can be considered to occur in discrete-time: this is the case, for instance, whenever the state of the system is sampled regularly in time.

2 Discrete-Time Game Structures

We define *discrete-time game structures* as a discrete-time version of the timed game structures of [dAFH+03]. A discrete-time game structure represents a game between two players, which we denote by 1, 2; we indicate by $\sim i$ the opponent of $i \in \{1,2\}$ (that is, player $3 - i$). A *discrete-time game structure* is a tuple $\mathcal{G} = (S, Acts_1, Acts_2, \Gamma_1, \Gamma_2, \delta, r)$, where:

- S is a finite set of states.
- $Acts_1$ and $Acts_2$ are two disjoint sets of actions for player 1 and player 2, respectively. We assume that $\Delta_0, \Delta_1 \notin Acts_i$ and write $M_i = Acts_i \cup \{\Delta_0, \Delta_1\}$ for the sets of moves of player $i \in \{1,2\}$.
- For $i \in \{1,2\}$, the function $\Gamma_i : S \mapsto 2^{M_i} \setminus \emptyset$ is an enabling condition, which assigns to each state s a set $\Gamma_i(s)$ of moves available to player i in that state.
- $\delta : S \times (M_1 \cup M_2) \mapsto S$ is a destination function that, given a state and a move of either player, determines the next state in the game.
- $r : S \mapsto \mathbb{Z}$ is a function that associates with each state $s \in S$ the *reward rate* of s: this is the reward that player 1 earns for staying for one time unit at s.

The move Δ_0 represents an always-enabled stuttering move that takes 0 time: we require that for $s \in S$ and $i \in \{1,2\}$, we have $\Delta_0 \in \Gamma_i(s)$ and $\delta(s, \Delta_0) = s$. The moves in $\{\Delta_0\} \cup Acts_1 \cup Acts_2$ are known as the *zero-time* moves. The move Δ_1 represents the decision of waiting for 1 time unit. We do not require that Δ_1 be always enabled: if we have $\Delta_1 \notin \Gamma_i(s)$ for player $i \in \{1,2\}$ at a state $s \in S$, then player i cannot wait, but must immediately play a zero-time move. We define the *size* of a discrete-time game structure by $|\mathcal{G}| = \sum_{s \in S} (|\Gamma_1(s)| + |\Gamma_2(s)|)$.

2.1 Move Outcomes, Runs, and Strategies

A timed game proceeds as follows. At each state $s \in S$, player 1 chooses a move $a^1 \in \Gamma_1(s)$, and simultaneously and independently, player 2 chooses a move $a^2 \in \Gamma_2(s)$. The set of successor states $\widetilde{\delta}(s, a^1, a^2) \subseteq S$ is then determined according to the following rules.

- *Actions take precedence over stutter steps and time steps.* If $a^1 \in Acts_1$ or $a^2 \in Acts_2$, then the game takes an action a selected nondeterministically from $A = \{a^1, a^2\} \cap (Acts_1 \cup Acts_2)$, and $\widetilde{\delta}(s, a^1, a^2) = \{\delta(s, a) \mid a \in A\}$.
- *Stutter steps take precedence over time steps.* If $a^1, a^2 \in \{\Delta_0, \Delta_1\}$, there are two cases.
  - If $a^1 = \Delta_0$ or $a^2 = \Delta_0$, the game performs a stutter step, and $\widetilde{\delta}(s, a^1, a^2) = \{s\}$.
  - If $a^1 = a^2 = \Delta_1$, then the game performs a time step of duration 1, and the game proceeds to $\widetilde{\delta}(s, a^1, a^2) = \{\delta(s, \Delta_1)\}$.

An *infinite run* (or simply *run*) of the discrete-time game structure $\mathscr{G}$ is a sequence $s_0, \langle a_1^1, a_1^2 \rangle, s_1, \langle a_2^1, a_2^2 \rangle, s_2, \dots$ such that $s_k \in S$, $a_{k+1}^1 \in \Gamma_1(s_k)$, $a_{k+1}^2 \in \Gamma_2(s_k)$, and $s_{k+1} \in \widetilde{\delta}(s_k, a_{k+1}^1, a_{k+1}^2)$ for all $k \geq 0$. A *finite run* σ is a finite prefix of a run that terminates at a state s, we then set $last(\sigma) = s$. We denote by *FRuns* the set of all finite runs of the game structure, and by *Runs* the set of its infinite runs. For a finite or infinite run σ, and a number $k < |\sigma|$, we denote by $\sigma_{\leq k}$ the prefix of σ up to and including state σ_k. A state s' is *reachable* from another state s if there exists a finite run $s_0, \langle a_1^1, a_1^2 \rangle, s_1, \dots, s_n$ such that $s_0 = s$ and $s_n = s'$.

A *strategy* π_i for player $i \in \{1, 2\}$ is a mapping $\pi_i : FRuns \mapsto M_i$ that associates with each finite run $s_0, \langle a_1^1, a_1^2 \rangle, s_1, \dots, s_n$ the move $\pi_i(s_0, \langle a_1^1, a_1^2 \rangle, s_1, \dots, s_n)$ to be played at s_n. We require that the strategy only selects enabled moves, that is, $\pi_i(\sigma) \in \Gamma_i(last(\sigma))$ for all $\sigma \in FRuns$. For $i \in \{1, 2\}$, let Π_i denote the set of all player i strategies. A strategy π_i for player $i \in \{1, 2\}$ is *memoryless* if for all $\sigma, \sigma' \in FRuns$ we have that $last(\sigma) = last(\sigma')$ implies $\pi_i(\sigma) = \pi_i(\sigma')$. For strategies $\pi_1 \in \Pi_1$ and $\pi_2 \in \Pi_2$, we say that a run $s_0, \langle a_1^1, a_1^2 \rangle, s_1, \dots$ is *consistent* with π_1 and π_2 if, for all $n \geq 0$ and $i = 1, 2$, we have $\pi_i(s_0, \langle a_1^1, a_1^2 \rangle, s_1, \dots, s_n) = a_{n+1}^i$. We denote by $Outcomes(s, \pi_1, \pi_2)$ the set of all runs that start in s and are consistent with π_1, π_2. Note that in our timed games, two strategies and a start state yield a *set* of outcomes, because if the players both propose actions, a nondeterministic choice between the two moves is made. According to this definition, strategies can base their choices on the entire history of the game, consisting of both past states and moves.

2.2 Discrete-Time Game Automata

We specify discrete-time game structures via *discrete-time game automata,* which are a discrete-time version of the *timed automaton games* of [dAFH⁺03]; both models are two-player versions of timed automata [AD94]. A *clock condition* over a set C of clocks is a boolean combination of formulas of the form $x \preceq c$ or $x - y \preceq c$, where c is an integer, $x, y \in C$, and $\preceq$ is either $<$ or $\leq$. We denote the set of all clock conditions over C by $ClkConds(C)$. A *clock valuation* is a function $\kappa : C \mapsto \mathbb{R}_{\geq 0}$, and we denote by $K(C)$ the set of all clock valuations for C.

A *discrete-time game automaton* is a tuple $\mathscr{A} = (Q, C, Acts_1, Acts_2, E, \theta, \rho, Inv_1, Inv_2, Rew)$, where:

- Q is a finite set of locations.
- C is a finite set of clocks.
- $Acts_1$ and $Acts_2$ are two disjoint, finite sets of actions for player 1 and player 2, respectively.
- $E \subseteq Q \times (Acts_1 \cup Acts_2) \times Q$ is an edge relation.
- $\theta : E \mapsto ClkConds(C)$ is a mapping that associates with each edge a clock condition that specifies when the edge can be traversed. We require that for all $(q, a, q_1), (q, a, q_2) \in E$ with $q_1 \neq q_2$, the conjunction $\theta(q, a, q_1) \wedge \theta(q, a, q_2)$ is unsatisfiable. In other words, the game move and clock values determine uniquely the successor location.
- $\rho : E \mapsto 2^C$ is a mapping that associates with each edge the set of clocks to be reset when the edge is traversed.

- $Inv_1, Inv_2 : Q \mapsto ClkConds(C)$ are two functions that associate with each location an invariant for player 1 and 2, respectively.
- $Rew : Q \mapsto \mathbb{Z}$ is a function that assignes a reward $Rew(q) \in \mathbb{Z}$ with each $q \in Q$.

Given a clock valuation $\kappa : C \mapsto \mathbb{R}_{\geq 0}$, we denote by $\kappa + 1$ the valuation defined by $(\kappa + 1)(x) = \kappa(x) + 1$ for all clocks $x \in C$. The clock valuation $\kappa : C \mapsto \mathbb{R}_{\geq 0}$ *satisfies* the clock constraint $\alpha \in ClkConds(C)$, written $\kappa \models \alpha$, if α holds when the clocks have the values specified by κ. For a subset $C' \subseteq C$ of clocks, $\kappa[C' := 0]$ denotes the valuation defined by $\kappa[C' := 0](x) = 0$ if $x \in C'$, and by $\kappa[C' := 0](x) = \kappa(x)$ otherwise.

The discrete-time game automaton $\mathscr{A}$ induces a discrete-time game structure $[\![\mathscr{A}]\!]$, whose states consist of a location of $\mathscr{A}$ and a clock valuation over C. The idea is the following. The move Δ_0 is always enabled at all states $\langle q, \kappa \rangle$, and leads again to $\langle q, \kappa \rangle$. The move Δ_1 is enabled for player $i \in \{1, 2\}$ at state $\langle q, \kappa \rangle$ if $\kappa + 1 \models Inv_i(q)$; the move leads to state $\langle q, \kappa + 1 \rangle$. For player $i \in \{1, 2\}$ and $a \in Acts_i$, the move a is enabled at a state $\langle q, \kappa \rangle$ if there is a transition (q, a, q') in E which is enabled at $\langle q, \kappa \rangle$, and if the invariant $Inv_i(q')$ holds for the destination state $\langle q', \kappa[\rho(q, a, q') := 0] \rangle$. If the values of the clocks can grow unboundedly, this translation would yield an infinite-state discrete-time game structure. However, we can define *clock regions* similarly to timed automata [AD94], and we can include in the discrete-time game structure only one state per clock region; as usual, this leads to a finite state space.

3   The Average Reward Condition

In this section, we consider a discrete-time game structure $\mathscr{G} = (S, Acts_1, Acts_2, \Gamma_1, \Gamma_2, \delta, r)$, unless otherwise noted.

3.1   The Value of a Game

We consider games where the goal for player 1 consists in maximizing the average reward per time unit obtained along a game outcome. The goal for player 2 is symmetrical, and it consists in minimizing the average reward per time unit obtained along a game outcome. To make these goals precise, consider a finite run $\sigma = \sigma_0, \langle \sigma_1^1, \sigma_1^2 \rangle, \sigma_1, \ldots, \sigma_n$. For $k \geq 1$, the time D_k elapsed at step k of the run is defined by $D_k(\sigma) = 1$ if $\sigma_k^1 = \sigma_k^2 = \Delta_1$, and $D_k(\sigma) = 0$ otherwise; the reward R_k accrued at step k of the run is given by $R_k(\sigma) = r(\sigma_{k-1}) \cdot D_k(\sigma)$. The time elapsed during σ and the reward achieved during σ are defined in the obvious way, by $D(\sigma) = \sum_{k=1}^{n} D_k(\sigma)$ and $R(\sigma) = \sum_{k=1}^{n} R_k(\sigma)$. Finally, we define the long-run average reward of an infinite run σ' by:

$$\bar{r}(\sigma') = \liminf_{n \to \infty} \frac{R(\sigma'_{\leq n})}{D(\sigma'_{\leq n})}.$$

A first attempt to define the goal of the game consists in asking for the maximum value of this long-run average reward that player 1 can secure. According to this approach, the value for player 1 of the game at a state s would be defined by

$$\tilde{v}(\mathscr{G}, s) = \sup_{\pi_1 \in \Pi_1} \inf_{\pi_2 \in \Pi_2} \inf\{\bar{r}(\sigma) \mid \sigma \in Outcomes(s, \pi_1, \pi_2)\}.$$

However, this approach fails to take into account the fact that, in timed games, players must not only play in order to achieve the goal, but must also play realistic strategies that guarantee the advancement of time. As an example, consider the game of Figure 1. We have $\tilde{v}(\langle q_0, [x := 0]\rangle) = 4$, and the optimal strategy of player 1 consists in staying at q_0 forever, never playing the move a^1. Due to the invariant $x \leq 2$, such a strategy blocks the progress of time: once $x = 2$, the only move player 1 can play is Δ_0. It is easy to see that the only strategies of player 1 that do not block time eventually play move a^1, and have value 1. Note that the game does not contain any blocked states, i.e., from every reachable state there is a run that is time-divergent: the lack of time progress of the above-mentioned strategy is due to the fact that player 1 values more obtaining high average reward, than letting time progress.

To ensure that winning strategies do not block the progress of time, we modify the definition of value of a run, so that ensuring time divergence has higher priority than maximizing the average reward. Following [dAFH$^+$03], we introduce the following predicates:

- For $i \in \{1,2\}$, we denote by $blameless^i(\sigma)$ ("$blameless\ i$") the predicate defined by $\exists n \geq 0. \forall k > n. \sigma_k^i = \Delta_1$. Intuitively, $blameless^i(\sigma)$ holds if, along σ, player i beyond a certain point cannot be blamed for blocking time.
- We denote by $td(\sigma)$ ("time-divergence") the predicate defined by $\forall n \geq 0. \exists k > n. [(\sigma_k^1 = \Delta_1) \wedge (\sigma_k^2 = \Delta_1)]$.

We define the value of a run $\sigma \in Runs$ for player $i \in \{1,2\}$ by:

$$w_i(\sigma) = \begin{cases} +\infty & \text{if } blameless^i(\sigma) \wedge \neg td(\sigma); \\ (-1)^{(i+1)} \bar{r}(\sigma) & \text{if } td(\sigma); \\ -\infty & \text{if } \neg blameless^i(\sigma) \wedge \neg td(\sigma). \end{cases} \quad (1)$$

It is easy to check that, for each run, exactly one of the three cases of the above definition applies. Notice that if $td(\sigma)$ holds, then $w_1(\sigma) = -w_2(\sigma)$, so that the value of time-divergent runs is defined in a zero-sum fashion. We define the value of the game for player i at $s \in S$ as follows:

$$v_i(\mathcal{G}, s) = \sup_{\pi_i \in \Pi_i} \inf_{\pi_{\sim i} \in \Pi_{\sim i}} \inf\{w_i(\sigma) \mid \sigma \in Outcomes(s, \pi_1, \pi_2)\}. \quad (2)$$

We omit the argument $\mathcal{G}$ from $v_i(\mathcal{G}, s)$ when clear from the context.

We say that a state $s \in S$ is *well-formed* if, for all $i \in \{1,2\}$, we have $v_i(s) > -\infty$. From (1) and (2), a state is well-formed if both players can ensure that time progresses from that state, unless blocked by the other player: this is the same notion of well-formedness introduced in [dAHS02, dAFH$^+$03]. Since we desire games where time progresses, we consider only games consisting of well-formed states.

3.2 Determinacy

A game is *determined* if, for all $s \in S$, we have $v_1(s) + v_2(s) = 0$: this means that if player $i \in \{1,2\}$ cannot enforce a reward $c \in \mathbb{R}$, then player $\sim i$ can enforce at least reward $-c$. The following theorem provides a strong non-determinacy result for average-reward discrete-time games.

Theorem 1. *(non-determinacy) For all $c > 0$, there exists a game structure $\mathcal{G} = (S, Acts_1, Acts_2, \Gamma_1, \Gamma_2, \delta, r)$ with a state $s \in S$, and two "spoiling" strategies $\pi_1^* \in \Pi_1$, $\pi_2^* \in \Pi_2$, such that the following holds:*

$$\sup_{\pi_1 \in \Pi_1} \sup\{w_1(\sigma) \mid \sigma \in Outcomes(s, \pi_1, \pi_2^*)\} \leq -c$$

$$\sup_{\pi_2 \in \Pi_2} \sup\{w_2(\sigma) \mid \sigma \in Outcomes(s, \pi_1^*, \pi_2)\} \leq -c.$$

As a consequence, $v_1(s) \leq -c$ and $v_2(s) \leq -c$.

Note that in the theorem we take sup, rather than inf as in (2), over the set of outcomes arising from the strategies. Hence, the theorem states that even if the choice among actions is resolved in favor of the player trying to achieve the value, there is a game with a state s where $v_1(s) + v_2(s) \leq -2c < 0$. Moreover, in the theorem, the adversary strategies are fixed, again providing an advantage to the player trying to achieve the value.

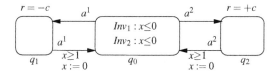

Fig. 2. A game automaton. Unspecified guards and invariants are "true".

Proof. Consider the game of Figure 2. We take for $\pi_1^* \in \Pi_1$ and $\pi_2^* \in \Pi_2$ the strategies that play always Δ_0 in q_0, and Δ_1 elsewhere. Let $s_0 = \langle q_0, [x := 0] \rangle$, and consider the value

$$\widehat{v}_1(s_0) = \sup_{\pi_1 \in \Pi_1} \sup\{w_1(\sigma) \mid \sigma \in Outcomes(s_0, \pi_1, \pi_2^*)\}.$$

There are two cases. If eventually player 1 plays forever Δ_0 in s_0, player 1 obtains the value $-\infty$, as time does not progress, and player 1 is not blameless. If player 1, whenever at s_0, eventually plays a^1, then the value of the game to player 1 is $-c$. Hence, we have $\widehat{v}_1(s_0) = -c$. The analysis for player 2 is symmetrical. ∎

The example of Figure 2, together with the above analysis, indicates that we cannot define the value of an average reward discrete-time game in a way that is symmetrical, leads to determinacy, and enforces time progress. In fact, consider again the case in which player 2 plays always Δ_0 at s_0. If, beyond some point, player 1 plays forever Δ_0 in s_0, time does not progress, and the situation is symmetrical wrt. players 1 and 2: they both play forever Δ_0. Hence, we must rule out this combination of strategies (either by assigning value $-\infty$ to the outcome, as we do, or by some other device). Once this is ruled out, the other possibility is that player 1, whenever in s_0, eventually plays a^1. In this case, time diverges, and the average value to player 1 is $-c$. As the analysis is symmetrical, the value to both players is $-c$, contradicting determinacy.

4 Solution of Average Reward Timed Games

In this section, we solve the problem of computing the value of an average reward timed game with respect to both players. First, we define a turn-based version of the timed game. Such version is equivalent to the first game when one is concerned with the value achieved by a specific player. Then, following [EM79], we define a finite game and we prove that it has the same value as the turn-based infinite game. This will lead to a PSPACE algorithm for computing the value of the game. We then show that the finite and, consequently, the infinite game admit memoryless optimal strategies for both players; as mentioned in the introduction, this will enable us to show that the problem of computing the value of the game is in NP∩coNP.

In the remainder of this section, we consider a fixed discrete-time game structure $\mathscr{G} = (S, Acts_1, Acts_2, \Gamma_1, \Gamma_2, \delta, r)$, and we assume that all states are well-formed. We focus on the problem of computing $v_1(s)$, as the problem of computing $v_2(s)$ is symmetrical. For a finite run σ and a finite or infinite run σ' such that $last(\sigma) = first(\sigma')$, we denote by $\sigma \cdot \sigma'$ their concatenation, where the common state is included only once.

4.1 Turn-Based Timed Game

We describe a turn-based version of the timed game, where at each round player 1 chooses his move before player 2. Player 2 can thus use her knowledge of player 1's move to choose her own. Moreover, when both players choose an action, the action chosen by player 2 is carried out. This accounts for the fact that in the definition of $v_1(s)$, nondeterminism is resolved in favor of player 2 (see (2)). Notice that if player 2 prefers to carry out the action chosen by player 1, she can reply with the stuttering move Δ_0. Definitions pertaining this game have a "t∞" superscript that stands for "turn-based infinite". We define the *turn-based joint destination function* $\widetilde{\delta}^{\mathrm{t}} : S \times M_1 \times M_2 \mapsto S$ by

$$\widetilde{\delta}^{\mathrm{t}}(s, a^1, a^2) = \begin{cases} \delta(s, \Delta_1) & \text{if } a^1 = a^2 = \Delta_1 \\ \delta(s, \Delta_0) & \text{if } \{a^1, a^2\} \subseteq \{\Delta_0, \Delta_1\} \text{ and } a^1 = \Delta_0 \text{ or } a^2 = \Delta_0 \\ \delta(s, a^1) & \text{if } a^1 \in Acts_1 \text{ and } a^2 \in \{\Delta_0, \Delta_1\} \\ \delta(s, a^2) & \text{if } a^2 \in Acts_2 \end{cases}$$

As before, a run is an infinite sequence $s_0, \langle a_1^1, a_1^2 \rangle, s_1, \langle a_2^1, a_2^2 \rangle, s_2, \ldots$ such that $s_k \in S$, $a_{k+1}^1 \in \Gamma_1(s_k)$, $a_{k+1}^2 \in \Gamma_2(s_k)$, and $s_{k+1} \in \widetilde{\delta}^{\mathrm{t}}(s_k, a_{k+1}^1, a_{k+1}^2)$ for all $k \geq 0$. A 1-*run* is a finite prefix of a run ending in a state s_k, while a 2-*run* is a finite prefix of run ending in a move $a \in M_1$. For a 2-run $\sigma = s_0, \langle a_1^1, a_1^2 \rangle, s_1, \ldots, s_n, \langle a_{n+1}^1 \rangle$, we set $last(s_0, \langle a_1^1, a_1^2 \rangle, s_1, \ldots, s_n, \langle a_{n+1}^1 \rangle) = s_n$ and $lasta(s_0, \langle a_1^1, a_1^2 \rangle, s_1, \ldots, s_n, \langle a_{n+1}^1 \rangle) = a_{n+1}^1$. For $i \in \{1, 2\}$, we denote by $FRuns_i$ the set of all i-runs. Intuitively, i-runs are runs where it is player i's turn to move. In the turn-based game, a *strategy* π_i for player $i \in \{1, 2\}$ is a mapping $\pi_i : FRuns_i \mapsto M_i$ such that $\pi_i(\sigma) \in \Gamma_i(last(\sigma))$ for all $\sigma \in FRuns_i$. For $i \in \{1, 2\}$, let Π_i^{t} denote the set of all player i strategies; notice that $\Pi_1^{\mathrm{t}} = \Pi_1$. Player-1 memoryless strategies are defined as usual. We say that a player-2 strategy $\pi \in \Pi_2^{\mathrm{t}}$ is *memoryless* iff, for all $\sigma, \sigma' \in FRuns_2$, $last(\sigma) = last(\sigma')$ and $lasta(\sigma) = lasta(\sigma')$ imply $\pi(\sigma) = \pi(\sigma')$.

For strategies $\pi_1 \in \Pi_1^{\mathrm{t}}$ and $\pi_2 \in \Pi_2^{\mathrm{t}}$, we say that a run $s_0, \langle a_1^1, a_1^2 \rangle, s_1, \ldots$ is *consistent* with π_1 and π_2 if, for all $n \geq 0$ and $i = 1, 2$, we have $\pi_1(s_0, \langle a_1^1, a_1^2 \rangle, s_1, \ldots, s_n) = a_{n+1}^1$

and $\pi_2(s_0, \langle a_1^1, a_1^2 \rangle, s_1, \ldots, s_n, \langle a_{n+1}^1 \rangle) = a_{n+1}^2$. Since $\widetilde{\delta}^t$ is deterministic, for all $s \in S$, there is a unique run that starts in s and is consistent with π_1 and π_2. We denote this run by $outcomes^{t\infty}(s, \pi_1, \pi_2)$. The value assigned to a run, to a strategy and to the whole game are defined as follows. We set $w_1^{t\infty}(\sigma) = w_1(\sigma)$, and

$$v_1^{t\infty}(s, \pi_1) = \inf_{\pi_2 \in \Pi_2^t} w_1^{t\infty}(outcomes^{t\infty}(s, \pi_1, \pi_2)); \qquad v_1^{t\infty}(s) = \sup_{\pi_1 \in \Pi_1^t} v_1^{t\infty}(s, \pi_1).$$

The following theorem follows from the definition of turn-based game and from (2).

Theorem 2. *For all $s \in S$, it holds $v_1(s) = v_1^{t\infty}(s)$.*

4.2   Turn-Based Finite Game

We now define a finite turn-based game that can be played on a discrete-time game structure. Definitions pertaining this game have a "tf" superscript that stands for "turn-based finite". The finite game ends as soon as a loop is closed. A *maximal run* in the finite game is a 1-run $\sigma = s_0, \langle a_1^1, a_1^2 \rangle, s_1, \ldots, s_n$ such that s_n is the first state that is repeated in σ. Formally, n is the least number such that $s_n = s_j$, for some $j < n$. We set $loop(\sigma)$ to be the suffix of σ: $s_j, \langle a_{j+1}^1, a_{j+1}^2 \rangle, \ldots, s_n$. For $\pi_1 \in \Pi_1^t$, $\pi_2 \in \Pi_2^t$, and $s \in S$, we denote by $outcomes^{tf}(s, \pi_1, \pi_2)$ the unique maximal run that starts in s and is consistent with π_1 and π_2.

In the finite game, a maximal run σ ending with the loop λ is assigned the value of the infinite run obtained by repeating λ forever. Formally, $w_1^{tf}(\sigma) = w_1(\sigma \cdot \lambda^\omega)$, where λ^ω denotes the concatenation of numerably many copies of λ. The value assigned to a strategy $\pi_1 \in \Pi_1^t$ and the value assigned to the whole game are defined as follows.

$$v_1^{tf}(s, \pi_1) = \inf_{\pi_2 \in \Pi_2^t} w_1^{tf}(outcomes^{tf}(s, \pi_1, \pi_2)); \qquad v_1^{tf}(s) = \sup_{\pi_1 \in \Pi_1^t} v_1^{tf}(s, \pi_1).$$

Notice that since this game is finite and turn-based, for all $s \in S$, it holds:

$$\sup_{\pi_1 \in \Pi_1} \inf_{\pi_2 \in \Pi_2} w_1^{tf}(outcomes^{tf}(s, \pi_1, \pi_2)) = \inf_{\pi_2 \in \Pi_2} \sup_{\pi_1 \in \Pi_1} w_1^{tf}(outcomes^{tf}(s, \pi_1, \pi_2)). \qquad (3)$$

4.3   Mapping Strategies

We introduce definitions that allow us to relate the finite game to the infinite one. For a 1-run $\sigma = s_0, \langle a_1^1, a_1^2 \rangle, s_1, \ldots, s_n$, let *firstloop*$(\sigma)$ be the operator that returns the first simple loop (if any) occurring in σ. Similarly, let *loopcut*(σ) be the operator that removes the first simple loop (if any) from σ. Formally, if σ is a simple run (i.e. it contains no loops) we set *firstloop*$(\sigma) = \varepsilon$ (the empty sequence), and *loopcut*$(\sigma) = \sigma$. Otherwise, let $k \geq 0$ be the smallest number such that $\sigma_j = \sigma_k$, for some $j < k$; we set

$$\textit{firstloop}(\sigma) = \sigma_j, \langle a_{j+1}^1, a_{j+1}^2 \rangle, \ldots, \langle a_k^1, a_k^2 \rangle, \sigma_k;$$

$$\textit{loopcut}(\sigma) = \sigma_0, \langle a_1^1, a_1^2 \rangle, \ldots, \sigma_j, \langle a_{k+1}^1, a_{k+1}^2 \rangle, \ldots, \sigma_n.$$

We now define the *quasi-segmentation* $QSeg(\sigma)$ to be the sequence of simple loops obtained by applying *firstloop* repeatedly to σ.

$$QSeg(\sigma) = \begin{cases} \varepsilon & \text{if } firstloop(\sigma) = \varepsilon \\ firstloop(\sigma) \cdot QSeg(loopcut(\sigma)) & \text{otherwise} \end{cases}$$

For an infinite run σ, we set $QSeg(\sigma) = \lim_{n \to \infty} QSeg(\sigma_{\leq n})$. Given a finite run σ, *loopcut* can only be applied a finite number of times before it converges to a fixpoint. We call this fixpoint $resid(\sigma)$. Notice that for all runs σ, $resid(\sigma)$ is a simple path and therefore its length is bounded by $|S|$.

For simplicity, we developed the above definitions for 1-runs. The corresponding definitions of $resid(\sigma)$ and $QSeg(\sigma)$ for 2-runs σ are similar.

For all $i \in \{1,2\}$ and all strategies $\pi \in \Pi_i^t$, we define the strategy $\tilde{\pi}$ as $\tilde{\pi}(\sigma) = \pi(resid(\sigma))$ for all $\sigma \in FRuns_i$. Intuitively, $\tilde{\pi}$ behaves like π until a loop is formed. At that point, $\tilde{\pi}$ *forgets* the loop, behaving as if the whole loop had not occurred. We now give some technical lemmas.

Lemma 1. *Let $\pi_1 \in \Pi_1^t$, $\pi_2 \in \Pi_2^t$, and $\sigma = outcomes^{t\infty}(s, \tilde{\pi}_1, \pi_2)$. For all $k > 0$, $resid(\sigma_{\leq k})$ is a prefix of a finite run consistent with π_1. Formally, there is $\pi_2' \in \Pi_2^t$ and $\sigma' = outcomes^{tf}(s, \pi_1, \pi_2')$ such that $\sigma' = resid(\sigma_{\leq k}) \cdot \rho$.*

Similarly, let $\sigma = outcomes^{t\infty}(s, \pi_1, \tilde{\pi}_2)$. For all $k > 0$, there is $\pi_1' \in \Pi_1^t$ and $\sigma' = outcomes^{tf}(s, \pi_1', \pi_2)$ such that $\sigma' = resid(\sigma_{\leq k}) \cdot \rho$.

Proof. We prove the first statement, as the second one is analogous. We proceed by induction on the length of $QSeg(\sigma_{\leq k})$. If $QSeg(\sigma_{\leq k})$ is the empty sequence (i.e. $\sigma_{\leq k}$ contains no loops), the result is easily obtained, as $\tilde{\pi}_1$ coincides with π_1 until a loop is formed. So, we can take $\pi_2' = \pi_2$ and obtain the conclusion.

On the other hand, suppose $QSeg(\sigma_{\leq k}) = \lambda_1, \ldots, \lambda_n$. For simplicity, suppose $\lambda_1 \neq \lambda_2$. As illustrated in Figure 3, let σ_j be the first state after λ_1 that does not belong to λ_1. Then, σ_{j-1} belongs to λ_1 and there is another index $i < j-1$ such that $\sigma_i = \sigma_{j-1}$. So, the game went twice through σ_{j-1} and two different successors were taken. However, player 1 must have chosen the same move in σ_i and σ_{j-1}, as by construction $\tilde{\pi}_1(\sigma_{\leq i}) = \tilde{\pi}_1(\sigma_{\leq j-1})$. Therefore, the change must be due to a different choice of π_2. It is easy to devise π_2' that coincides with π_2, except that λ_1 may be skipped, and at σ_i, the successor σ_j is chosen. We can then obtain a run $\rho = outcomes^{t\infty}(s, \tilde{\pi}_1, \pi_2')$ and an integer $k' \geq 0$ such that $QSeg(\rho_{\leq k'}) = \lambda_2, \ldots, \lambda_n$ and $resid(\rho_{\leq k'}) = resid(\rho)$. The thesis is obtained by applying the inductive hypothesis to ρ and k'. ∎

Using this lemma, we can show that for all $\pi_1 \in \Pi_1$, each loop occurring in the infinite game under $\tilde{\pi}_1$ can also occur in the finite game under π_1.

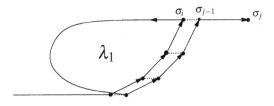

Fig. 3. Nodes linked by dashed lines represent the same state of the game

Lemma 2. *Let $\pi_1 \in \Pi_1^t$, $\pi_2 \in \Pi_2^t$, and $\sigma = outcomes^{t\infty}(s, \tilde{\pi}_1, \pi_2)$. For all $\lambda \in QSeg(\sigma)$, λ can occur as the final loop in a maximal run of the finite game. Formally, there is $\pi_2' \in \Pi_2^t$ and $\sigma' = outcomes^{tf}(s, \pi_1, \pi_2')$ such that $\lambda = loop(\sigma')$.*

Similarly, let $\sigma = outcomes^{t\infty}(s, \pi_1, \tilde{\pi}_2)$. For all $\lambda \in QSeg(\sigma)$, there is $\pi_1' \in \Pi_1^t$ and $\sigma' = outcomes^{tf}(s, \pi_1', \pi_2)$ such that $\lambda = loop(\sigma')$.

The next lemma states that if the strategy π_1 of player 1 achieves value v in the finite turn-based game, the strategy $\tilde{\pi}_1$ achieves at least as much in the infinite turn-based game.

Lemma 3. *For all $s \in S$ and $\pi_1 \in \Pi_1^t$, it holds $v_1^{t\infty}(s, \tilde{\pi}_1) \geq v_1^{tf}(s, \pi_1)$.*

Proof. Let $v = v_1^{tf}(s, \pi_1)$. We show that $\tilde{\pi}_1$ can ensure reward v in the infinite game. The result is trivially true if $v = -\infty$. So, in the following we assume that $v > -\infty$.

Fix a player 2 strategy $\pi_2 \in \Pi_2^t$, and let $\sigma = outcomes^{t\infty}(s, \tilde{\pi}_1, \pi_2)$. Let $QSeg(\sigma) = \lambda_1, \lambda_2 \ldots$. We distinguish two cases, according to whether time diverges or not in σ. If time diverges, all loops λ_j that contain no tick give no contribution to the value of σ and can therefore be ignored.

For all λ_j containing (at least) a time step, by Lemma 2, λ_j is a possible terminating loop for the finite game under π_1. Thus, $R(\lambda_j) \geq v \cdot D(\lambda_j)$. Now, the value of σ can be split as the value due to loops containing time steps, plus the value due to the residual. For all $n \geq 0$, let m_n be the number of loops in $QSeg(\sigma_{\leq n})$. We obtain:

$$w_1^{t\infty}(\sigma) =$$

$$\liminf_{n \to \infty} \frac{R(\sigma_{\leq n})}{D(\sigma_{\leq n})} = \liminf_{n \to \infty} \frac{R(resid(\sigma_{\leq n})) + \sum_{j=1}^{m_n} R(\lambda_j)}{D(resid(\sigma_{\leq n})) + \sum_{j=1}^{m_n} D(\lambda_j)} = \liminf_{n \to \infty} \frac{\sum_{j=1}^{m_n} R(\lambda_j)}{\sum_{j=1}^{m_n} D(\lambda_j)} \geq v.$$

Consider now the case when σ contains only finitely many time steps. Let $k \geq 0$ be such that no time steps occur in σ after σ_k. Consider a loop λ_j entirely occurring after σ_k. Obviously λ_j contains no time steps. Moreover, by Lemma 2, λ_j is a terminating loop for a maximal run ρ in the finite game under π_1. Since $v_1^{tf}(s, \pi_1) > -\infty$, it must be $w_1^{tf}(\rho) = +\infty$. Consequently, it holds $blameless^1(\rho)$ and in particular player 1 is blameless in all edges in λ_j.

Now, let $k' \geq 0$ be such that each state (and edge) after $\sigma_{k'}$ will eventually be part of a loop of $QSeg(\sigma)$. Let $k'' = \max\{k, k'\}$. Then, all edges that occur after k'' will eventually be part of a loop where player 1 is blameless. Consequently, k'' is a witness to the fact that $blameless^1(\sigma)$, and therefore $w_1^{t\infty}(\sigma) = +\infty \geq v$. ∎

Lemma 4. *For all $s \in S$ and $\pi_2 \in \Pi_2^t$, it holds $v_1^{t\infty}(s, \tilde{\pi}_2) \leq v_1^{tf}(s, \pi_2)$.*

Proof. Let $v = v_1^{tf}(s, \pi_2)$. Similarly to Lemma 3, we can rule out the case $v = +\infty$ as trivial. Fix a player 1 strategy π_1, and let $\sigma = outcomes^{t\infty}(s, \pi_1, \tilde{\pi}_2)$. We show that $w_1^{t\infty}(\sigma) \leq v$. If time diverges on σ, the proof is similar to the analogous case in Lemma 3. Otherwise, let $k \geq 0$ be such that no time steps occur in σ after σ_k. Consider a loop $\lambda \in QSeg(\sigma)$, entirely occurring after σ_k. Obviously λ contains no time steps. Moreover, by Lemma 2, λ is a terminating loop for a maximal run ρ in the finite game under π_1. Since $v_1^{tf}(s, \pi_1) < +\infty$, it must be $w_1^{tf}(\rho) = -\infty$. Consequently, it holds $\neg blameless^1(\rho)$ and in particular player 1 is blamed in some edge of λ. This shows that $\neg blameless^1(\sigma)$, and consequently $w_1^{t\infty}(\sigma) = -\infty \leq v$. ∎

Lemmas 3 and 4 show that the infinite game is no harder than the finite one, for both players. Considering also (3), we obtain the following result.

Theorem 3. *For all $s \in S$, $v_1^{t\infty}(s) = v_1^{tf}(s)$.*

Theorems 2 and 3 allow us to use the finite game to compute the value of the original timed game. The length of the finite game is bounded by $|S|$. It is well-known that a recursive, backtracking algorithm can compute the value of such game in PSPACE.

Theorem 4. *For all $s \in S$, $v_1(s)$ can be computed in PSPACE.*

4.4 Memory

By following the "forgetful game" construction and proofs used by [EM79], we can derive a similar result on the existence of memoryless strategies for both players. The proof depends on the fact that the value of forgetful game is the same as the turn-based finite game (and hence, the same as the infinite game, from Theorem 3), and follows the same inductive steps as provided in [EM79].

Theorem 5. *For all $i \in \{1,2\}$, and $t \in S$, there exists a memoryless optimal strategy for player i. Formally, there exists $\pi_i \in \Pi_i$ such that $v_1(t, \pi_i) = v_1(t)$.*

4.5 Improved Algorithms

We show that, given $s \in S$, $v \in \mathbb{Q}$ and $i \in \{1,2\}$, the problem of checking whether $v_i^{tf}(s) \geq v$ is in NP$\cap$coNP. The decision problem $v_1^{tf}(s) \geq v$ is in NP because a memoryless strategy for player 1 acts as a polynomial-time witness: once such a strategy π_1 is fixed, we can compute in polynomial time the value $v_1^{tf}(s, \pi_1)$. The problem is also in coNP because, once a memoryless strategy of player 2 is fixed, we can compute in polynomial time the value $v_1^{tf}(s, \pi_2)$.

Once we fix a memoryless strategy for player $i \in \{1,2\}$, the finite game is reduced to a multigraph where all the choices belong to player $\sim i$. It is convenient to define the set of vertices of the multigraph as $U = \{\{s\} \mid s \in S\}$, rather than simply as S. Let E be the set of edges of the multigraph. Each edge $e \in E$ is labeled with the pair of moves $\langle a^1, a^2 \rangle \in M_1 \times M_2$ played by the players along e. We label e with *tick* whenever $a^1 = a^2 = \Delta_1$, and with bl_i whenever $a^i \in Acts_i \cup \{\Delta_0\}$; every edge e from $\{s\}$ to $\{t\}$ is also associated with reward $r(s)$ if it has label *tick*, and reward 0 otherwise. We indicate paths in this graph by $u_0, e_1, u_1, e_2, \ldots, u_n$, where e_i is an edge from u_{i-1} to u_i, for $1 \leq i \leq n$. Given a strongly connected component (SCC) (V, F), where $V \subseteq U$ and $F \subseteq E$, we *collapse* (V, F) as follows: (i) we replace in U the vertices in V by the single vertex $\bigcup V$; (ii) we remove all edges in F; (iii) we replace every edge from $v \in V$ to $u \in U \setminus V$ (resp. from $u \in U \setminus V$ to $v \in V$) with an edge of the same label from $\bigcup V$ to u (resp. from u to $\bigcup V$); (iv) we replace every edge $e \notin F$ from $v \in V$ to $v' \in V$ with a self-loop of the same label from $\bigcup V$ to $\bigcup V$.

To determine the value of this multigraph to player 1, we first transform the multigraph so that all edges are labeled with *tick*, and we then apply Karp's algorithm for computing the loop with minimum or maximum average reward [Kar78]. We proceed depending on whether player 1, or player 2, fixes a memoryless strategy. When player 1 fixes a memoryless strategy:

1. Find a maximal SCC (V, F), where $V \subseteq U$ and $F \subseteq E$, such that all edges in F are labeled with $\neg tick$ and $\neg bl_1$. Player 2 will want to avoid following this SCC forever; thus, we collapse it. Repeat until no more SCCs can be collapsed.

2. If a vertex $u \in U$ has no outgoing edges, it means that player 2 could not avoid entering and following one of the SCCs collapsed above. Hence, for each $u \in U$ without outgoing edges, remove u from the graph along with all incoming edges, and assign value $+\infty$ to all $s \in u$. Repeat until no more vertices can be removed.

3. Find all the loops whose edges are all labeled with $\neg tick$. Due to the collapsing in the above steps, each of these loops contains at least one edge labeled bl_1, so its value when followed forever is $-\infty$. Remove all such vertices from the graph, and assign value $-\infty$ to the corresponding states.

4. From the resulting multigraph G, construct a multigraph G' with the same vertices as G. For each simple path in G of the form $u_0, e_1, u_1, \ldots, u_n, e_{n+1}, u_{n+1}$ where the edges $e_1, \ldots, e_n$ are labeled by $\neg tick$, and the edge e_{n+1} is labeled by $tick$, we insert in G' an edge from u_0 to u_{n+1} labeled by the same reward as e_{n+1}.

5. Use the algorithm of [Kar78] to find the loop with minimal average reward in G' (the algorithm of [Kar78] is phrased for graphs, but it can be trivially adapted to multigraphs). If r is the average reward of the loop thus found, all the vertices of the loop, and all the vertices that can reach the loop, have value r. Remove them from G', and assign value r to the corresponding states. Repeat this step until all vertices have been removed.

Similarly (but not symmetrically), if player 2 fixes a memoryless strategy, we can compute the value for player 1 as follows:

1. Find all the loops where all the edges are labeled with $\neg tick$ and $\neg bl_1$. These loops, and all the vertices that can reach them, have value $+\infty$. Remove them from the graph, and assign value $+\infty$ to the corresponding states.

2. Find a maximal SCC (V, F), where $V \subseteq U$ and $F \subseteq E$, such that all edges in F are labeled with $\neg tick$. Due to the previous step, every loop in (V, F) contains at least one edge labeled bl_1, and player 1 will want to avoid following forever such an SCC: thus, we collapse (V, F).

3. For each $u \in U$ without outgoing edges, remove u from the graph along with all incoming edges, and assign value $-\infty$ to all $s \in u$. Repeat until no more vertices can be removed.

4. From the resulting multigraph G, construct a multigraph G' as in step 4 of the previous case.

5. This step is the same as step 5 of the previous case, except that in each iteration we find the loop with *maximal* average reward.

Since the algorithm of [Kar78], as well as the above graph manipulations, can all be done in polynomial time, we have the following result.

Theorem 6. *The problem of computing the value to player $i \in \{1, 2\}$ of a discrete-time average reward game is in NP∩coNP.*

We note that the maximal reward that a player can accrue in the first n time units cannot be computed by iterating n times a dynamic-programming operator, as is the case for untimed games. In fact, each player can play an unbounded number of zero-time moves in the first n time units, so that even the finite time-horizon version of our games requires the consideration of time divergence. Hence, it does not seem possible to adapt the approach of [ZP96] to obtain a weakly-polynomial algorithm. Whether polynomial-time algorithms can be achieved by other means is an open problem.

References

[ABM04]   R. Alur, M. Bernadsky, and P. Madhusudan. Optimal reachability for weighted timed games. In *Proc. 31st Int. Colloq. Aut. Lang. Prog.*, volume 3142 of *Lect. Notes in Comp. Sci.* Springer-Verlag, 2004.

[AD94]   R. Alur and D.L. Dill. A theory of timed automata. *Theor. Comp. Sci.*, 126:183–235, 1994.

[AH97]   R. Alur and T.A. Henzinger. Modularity for timed and hybrid systems. In *CONCUR 97: Concurrency Theory. 8th Int. Conf.*, volume 1243 of *Lect. Notes in Comp. Sci.*, pages 74–88. Springer-Verlag, 1997.

[AMAS98]   E. Asarin, O. Maler, A.Pnueli, and J. Sifakis. Controller synthesis for timed automata. In *Proc. IFAC Symposium on System Structure and Control*, pages 469–474. Elsevier, 1998.

[BBL04]   P. Bouyer, E. Brinksma, and K.G. Larsen. Staying alive as cheaply as possible. In *Proc. of 7th Intl. Workshop on Hybrid Systems: Computation and Control (HSCC)*, volume 2993 of *Lect. Notes in Comp. Sci.*, pages 203–218. Springer-Verlag, 2004.

[BCFL04]   P. Bouyer, F. Cassez, E. Fleury, and K.G. Larsen. Optimal strategies in priced timed game automata. In *Found. of Software Technology and Theoretical Comp. Sci.*, volume 3328 of *Lect. Notes in Comp. Sci.*, pages 148–160. Springer-Verlag, 2004.

[Chu63]   A. Church. Logic, arithmetics, and automata. In *Proc. International Congress of Mathematicians, 1962*, pages 23–35. Institut Mittag-Leffler, 1963.

[Con92]   A. Condon. The complexity of stochastic games. *Information and Computation*, 96:203–224, 1992.

[dAFH+03]   L. de Alfaro, M. Faella, T.A. Henzinger, R. Majumdar, and M. Stoelinga. The element of surprise in timed games. In *CONCUR 03: Concurrency Theory. 14th Int. Conf.*, volume 2761 of *Lect. Notes in Comp. Sci.*, pages 144–158. Springer-Verlag, 2003.

[dAHS02]   L. de Alfaro, T.A. Henzinger, and M. Stoelinga. Timed interfaces. In *Proceedings of the Second International Workshop on Embedded Software (EMSOFT 2002)*, volume 2491 of *Lect. Notes in Comp. Sci.*, pages 108–122. Springer-Verlag, 2002.

[EJ91]   E.A. Emerson and C.S. Jutla. Tree automata, mu-calculus and determinacy (extended abstract). In *Proc. 32nd IEEE Symp. Found. of Comp. Sci.*, pages 368–377. IEEE Computer Society Press, 1991.

[EM79]   A. Ehrenfeucht and J. Mycielski. Positional strategies for mean payoff games. *Int. Journal of Game Theory*, 8(2):109–113, 1979.

[HHM99]   T.A. Henzinger, B. Horowitz, and R. Majumdar. Rectangular hybrid games. In *CONCUR'99: Concurrency Theory. 10th Int. Conf.*, volume 1664 of *Lect. Notes in Comp. Sci.*, pages 320–335. Springer-Verlag, 1999.

[Kar78]   R.M. Karp. A characterization of the minimum cycle mean in a digraph. *Discrete Mathematics*, 23:309–311, 1978.

[MPS95]   O. Maler, A. Pnueli, and J. Sifakis. On the synthesis of discrete controllers for timed systems. In *Proc. of 12th Annual Symp. on Theor. Asp. of Comp. Sci.*, volume 900 of *Lect. Notes in Comp. Sci.*, pages 229–242. Springer-Verlag, 1995.

[PR89]   A. Pnueli and R. Rosner. On the synthesis of a reactive module. In *Proceedings of the 16th Annual Symposium on Principles of Programming Languages*, pages 179–190. ACM Press, 1989.

[RW89]   P.J.G. Ramadge and W.M. Wonham. The control of discrete event systems. *IEEE Transactions on Control Theory*, 77:81–98, 1989.

[ZP96]   U. Zwick and M. Paterson. The complexity of mean payoff games on graphs. *Theor. Comp. Sci.*, 158:343–359, 1996.

Beyond Liveness: Efficient Parameter Synthesis for Time Bounded Liveness

Gerd Behrmann, Kim G. Larsen, and Jacob Illum Rasmussen

Department of Computer Science, Aalborg University, Denmark
{behrmann, kgl, illum}@cs.aau.dk

Abstract. In this paper, we deal with the problem of parameter synthesis for a subset of parameterised TCTL over timed automata. The problem was proved decidable by V. Bruyere et al. in [10] for general parameterised TCTL using a translation to Presburger arithmetic and also considered by F. Wang in [13] using a parametric region construction. In contrast, we provide two efficient zone based algorithms for a useful subset of parameterised TCTL. The subset has obvious applications to worst case execution time (WCET) analysis. In [11] WCET is performed via model checking, but their approach uses a binary search strategy over several invocations of the model checker. In contrast, both our algorithms synthesise the bound directly. We provide experimental results based on a prototype implementation in UPPAAL for two case studies: The first concerns response time analysis of a well known train gate scenario. The second is an execution time analysis of task graph problems where tasks have uncertain execution times.

1 Introduction

For most real-time systems it is essential that liveness properties come equipped with acceptable upper time-bound guarantees in order to be of use. Merely knowing that a particular service will be provided "eventually" once requested or that the execution of a given set of tasks will "eventually" terminate is of limited use. What we need in addition are hard real-time guarantees.

The temporal logic TCTL [1] provides a convenient formalism for expressing bounded as well as unbounded liveness properties for timed systems, and tools like KRONOS [9] and (partially) UPPAAL [5] offer support for automatically checking whether real time systems modelled as timed automata [2] satisfy given TCTL properties.

As an example, consider a task graph [12] scheduling instance with a number of interdependent tasks to be executed on a limited number of processors. The interdependencies state that no task can execute until all tasks preceding it in the graph are terminated. Now assume given lower and upper bounds on the execution time for each task and a given (dynamic) policy for assigning processors to tasks a natural problem is to provide guarantees as to the maximum execution time for the entire task graph instance. Now assuming that $\mathsf{Task}_i.\mathsf{End}$

P. Pettersson and W. Yi (Eds.): FORMATS 2005, LNCS 3829, pp. 81–94, 2005.

is a proposition indicating termination of task i, the following TCTL property guarantees that the overall execution time does not exceed p:

$$A\Diamond_{\leq p} \bigwedge_{i=1...n} \mathsf{Task}_i.\mathsf{End} \qquad (1)$$

Bounded response or leads-to properties is another class of typical bounded liveness properties. As an example consider the well-known train-gate scenario distributed with UPPAAL. The scenario models a railway control system which controls the access to a bridge for several trains. The bridge is a critical shared resource that should only be crossed by at most one train at a time. To ensure this, the controller applies a policy for holding trains back in critical situations. However, it is also important that the applied policy guarantees that each individual train will make it to the bridge within a guaranteed time bound. Now assume $\mathsf{Train}_i.\mathsf{Appr}$ and $\mathsf{Train}_i.\mathsf{Cross}$ are propositions indicating that train i is approaching respectively crossing the bridge. The following TCTL property guarantees that whenever train i approaches it will be granted access to the bridge within p time-units:

$$A\Box\,(\,\mathsf{Train}_i.\mathsf{Appr} \implies A\Diamond_{\leq p}\mathsf{Train}_i.\mathsf{Cross}\,) \qquad (2)$$

Though (1) and (2) nicely express useful bounded liveness properties it remains to find valid values for the time bound p in a systematic way. In fact we might already have established that the particular real-time systems satisfy the corresponding unbounded liveness properties, thus knowing that the bounded liveness properties hold for some bounds.[1] At the same time all our attempts of identifying concrete values for p for which (1) (or (2)) holds might have failed. What we really want is a method for automatically *synthesising* the smallest value of p for which (1) (or ((2)) holds.

The above synthesis problem was shown decidable by V. Bruyere et al [10] for general parameterised TCTL using a translation to Presburger arithmetic and considered by F. Wang in [13] using a parametric region graph construction. The contribution of this paper is to provide *efficient* zone-based algorithms for parameter synthesis for TCTL properties of the forms $A\Diamond_{\leq p}\phi$ and $A\Box(\psi \implies A\Diamond_{\leq p}\phi)$ where ϕ and ψ are restricted to be propositions (state properties). Thus we cover the two prototypical examples of (1) and (2). The paper offers two approaches for parameter synthesis:

Our first approach assumes that the (unbounded) liveness property (e.g. $A\Diamond\phi$) is already known to hold. This enables the parameter synthesis to be reduced to a simple reachability analysis on an extended timed automaton model with an additional clock for measuring time. This is in contrast to the method in [11] for worst case execution time (WCET) analysis, where a binary search strategy is used under the assumption that a bound exists (and is known).

In our second approach the algorithm for model checking the unbounded liveness property $A\Diamond\phi$ [7] is extended to directly synthesise the smallest p such that $A\Diamond_{\leq p}\phi$ holds (or conclude that such a p does not exist).

---

[1] A simple argument based on the region-based model checking algorithm for TCTL.

The structure of the remainder of the paper is as follows. Section 2 provides the notational conventions of the paper, Sections 3 and 4 present the two approaches and Section 5 offers an extensive experimental investigation of the two approaches on instances of the train gate scenario and task graph scheduling.

2   Notation

In this section we briefly define timed automata and the notation used throughout the rest of the paper. Timed automata are finite state automata extended with variables over the non-negative reals, called clocks. Edges of a timed automaton are guarded by an expression over the clocks in addition a set of clocks to be reset when executing the edge. Locations have an invariant expression, that must be satisfied when the automaton is in that location. Timed automata can be composed into networks of communicating timed automata, but for simplicity and without loss of generality we operate on a single timed automaton. More formally, we define timed automata as follows.

Definition 1 (Timed Automaton). *If X is a set of clocks, then $\mathcal{B}(X)$ is the set of conjunctions over expressions on the form $x \bowtie n$ for $x \in X$, $n \in \mathbb{N}$ and $\bowtie \in \{<, \leq, \geq, >\}$. A timed automaton over X is a tuple (L, l_0, E, G, U, I), where L is a set of locations, $l_0 \in L$ is the initial location, $E \subseteq L \times L$ if a set of edges, $G : E \to \mathcal{B}(X)$ assigns guards to edges, $U : E \to \mathcal{P}(X)$ assigns a set of clocks to edges, and $I : L \to \mathcal{B}(X)$ assigns invariants to locations.*

A state of a timed automaton over a set of clocks X is a pair (l, u), where l is a location and u a valuation over the clocks in X. Clock valuations are functions $X \to \mathbb{R}_{\geq 0}$ that assign non-negative real values to clocks. The set of all clock valuations is $\mathbb{R}_{\geq 0}^X$. Given a set of clocks $Y \subseteq X$ and clock valuation u over X, $\pi_Y(u) \in \mathbb{R}_{\geq 0}^Y$ is the projection of u onto Y. Two useful operations on clock valuations are increment all clocks by some amount, $(u + d)(x) = u(x) + d$, and reset a set of clocks r, $u[r \mapsto 0](x) = 0$ if $x \in r$, $u(x)$ otherwise. The satisfaction relation $u \models g$ for $g \in \mathcal{B}(X)$ is defined in the obvious way.

We skip the concrete semantics of a timed automaton, but notice that the state space is infinite. As usual, the solution to this problem is to define the simulation graph of a timed automaton.

Definition 2 (Simulation Graph). *The simulation graph of a timed automaton (L, l_0, E, G, U, I) over a set of clocks X has a vertex set $\{(l, W) \in L \times \mathcal{P}(\mathbb{R}_{\geq 0}^X) \mid \forall u \in W : u \models I(l)\}$, and an edge set, $\Rightarrow$, as defined below. We distinguish between discrete (a.k.a. action) transitions and delay transitions:*

$$(l, W) \overset{e}{\Rightarrow} (l', W') \Leftrightarrow e \in E \wedge e = (l, l') \wedge W' = (W \wedge G(e))[U(e) \mapsto 0] \wedge I(l')$$

$$(l, W) \overset{\delta}{\Rightarrow} (l', W') \Leftrightarrow$$
$$l = l' \wedge W' = \{u + d \mid u \in W \wedge d \in \mathbb{R}_{\geq 0} \wedge \forall 0 \leq d' \leq d : u + d' \models I(l)\}$$

The vertices of the simulation graph are called symbolic states and describe a possibly infinite set of concrete states. We define $\max_x((l, W)) = \max_x(W) = \sup\{u(x) \mid u \in W\}$ to be the supremum of the clock x in any valuation of the symbolic state.

A zone is a set of clock valuations characterizable by a conjunction of expressions $x \bowtie n$ and $x - y \bowtie n$, where x and y are clocks, n is an integer and $\bowtie \in \{<, \leq, \geq, >\}$. It is easy to see that the initial state $S_0 = (l_0, \{u_0\})$, where $\forall x \in X : u_0(x) = 0$, is a zone. An important property of timed automata is that the successor of a zone is itself a zone, thus making zones a good choice for representing symbolic states. Using zones, we obtain a countable state space. In order to get a finite state space, exact abstractions over symbolic states are used. An abstraction function is a partial function $\mathfrak{a} : \mathcal{P}(\mathbb{R}_{\geq 0}^X) \hookrightarrow \mathcal{P}(\mathbb{R}_{\geq 0}^X)$, such that $W \subseteq \mathfrak{a}(W)$. If the set of zones is closed under a given abstraction, then the abstraction is an extrapolation. For thee definitions of finite, sound and complete abstractions we refer the interested reader to [8, 4, 3]. Several such abstractions exist, all based on the maximum constant $M(x)$ to which a clock x is compared in a guard or in an invariant [8].[2]

A state formula, φ, is a predicate over expressions of the form $x \bowtie n$, $x - y \bowtie n$, and l, where x and y are clocks in X, n is an integer, and $\bowtie \in \{<, \leq\}$ and l is a location. The satisfaction relation is defined in the natural way and we write $(l, u) \models \varphi$ when (l, u) satisfies φ. A symbolic state satisfies a state formula if any of the concrete states in the symbolic state satisfies the formula, i.e., $(l, W) \models \varphi \Leftrightarrow \exists u \in W : (l, u) \models \varphi$.

3   Reduction to Reachability Analysis

In this section we present an algorithm for synthesising the smallest p such that $A\lozenge_{\leq p}\varphi$ holds under the assumption that $A\lozenge\varphi$ is known to hold. The problem is reduced to building the state space of an annotated model. Our approach is similar to that of [11], although their model uses discrete time and deadlocks as soon as the goal condition φ is satisfied. They extend the model with an extra counter c, which is zero in the initial state and incremented at every time tick. Properties of the form $E\lozenge(\varphi \wedge c \geq p)$ for different values of p are model checked, and a binary search strategy to find the maximum p for which the property holds is used. In contrast, we use continuous time and extend the timed automaton model with an additional clock, c, which is zero in the initial state and is neither reset nor tested in the model. Instead of performing a binary search on different values of p, we generate all states up to a depth where φ holds and record the maximum value of c, see Fig. 1. This value is the smallest p s.t. $A\lozenge_{\leq p}\varphi$ holds, assuming that $A\lozenge\varphi$ holds.

It is important that the algorithm never computes any successors of states satisfying φ – otherwise the resulting value for p would not be tight. Therefore we introduce the following delay operation:

---

[2] Variations include using two maximum constants per clock [4] or using location specific maximum constants [3].

proc $Reachable(S_0, \varphi) \equiv$
    $pre(S_0 \models A\Diamond\varphi)$
    $Wait := \{delay(S_0[c \mapsto 0], \neg\varphi)\}$
    $Passed := \emptyset$
    $p := 0$ Initial estimate of p is zero
    while $Wait \neq \emptyset$ **do**
        let $S \in Wait$
        $Wait = Wait \setminus \{S\}$
        $p := \max(p, \max_c(S))$ The estimate is enlarged as needed
        $S := S \wedge \neg\varphi$ Here S might become empty
        foreach $S' : S \overset{a}{\Rightarrow} S'$ **do**   For all action successors
            $S' := delay(S', \neg\varphi)$ Delay under $\neg\varphi$, see Def. 3
            $(S' := extrapolate(S')^{\ddagger})$ See text on extrapolation and pruning
            if $\forall S'' \in Passed : S' \not\subseteq S''$ Unvisited state?
                then $Passed := Passed \cup \{T\}$
                    $Wait := Wait \cup \{T\}$
        fi
        od
    od
    exit(p)
end

Fig. 1. An algorithm for finding the smallest p s.t. $s_0 \models A\Diamond_{\leq p}\varphi$. The algorithm uses two sets of symbolic states: $Wait$ is the set of reached but not yet explored states; $Passed$ is the set of explored states. The algorithm takes a symbolic state, S, from $Wait$, updates the estimate for p and restricts S to the states not satisfying φ. For each action successor S', the delay under $\neg\varphi$ is computed. Finally, if the successor was not previously explored, it is added to the $Passed$ and $Wait$ sets.

Definition 3 (Restricted Delay). *We define a function* delay $: (L \times \mathbb{R}^X_{\geq 0}) \times \Phi \to \mathcal{P}(\mathbb{R}^X_{\geq 0})$ *mapping a state and a state formula to the set of clock valuations that can be reached by delaying from the state without violating the state formula.*

$$delay((l, v), \varphi) = \{ u \mid u \models I(l)$$
$$\wedge \exists d \geq 0 : u = v + d \wedge \forall 0 \leq d' < d : (l, v + d') \models \varphi \wedge I(l)\}$$

The operation can easily be extended to operate on symbolic states.

If the symbolic state is a zone, then restricted delay is implementable using DBMs, although the result will be non-convex and thus must be represented as a list of zones. If the state formula does not constrain any clocks, then the operation is trivial to implement using the unrestricted delay operation.

    As mentioned in Section 2, timed automata have an infinite state space and model checking is typically based on the simulation graph of the timed automaton. The use of exact abstractions is crucial in obtaining a finite simulation graph. In our case we must ensure that the timing information recorded in the extra clock, c, is not destroyed by this abstraction while still guaranteeing termination. First we argue that even without the use of an abstraction function, a zone based implementation of the algorithm outlined before, will terminate. Second, we argue that the efficiency of the algorithm can be improved by using any of the standard abstractions and setting the maximum constant for c to infinity. Third, we argue that the efficiency can be further improved by using a special operator to prune parts of the search.

Termination. Termination follows from the fact that $A\Diamond\varphi$ holds. Since φ will eventually hold and the algorithm in Fig. 1 does not explore the successors of states in which φ holds, this guarantees termination of the algorithm.

Extrapolation. In timed automata model checking there are two reasons for performing the analysis using an abstraction: The first is to ensure finiteness and hence to guarantee termination; the second is for efficiency, as a coarser abstraction results in a smaller simulation graph. In our case, termination is guaranteed even when no abstraction function is used. Hence, we are mainly interested in the second aspect. In [4] all extrapolation operators are defined over a set of maximum constants derived from the model - one for each clock. We have the following result:

Lemma 1. *Let $\mathfrak{a}$ be any of the extrapolation operators defined in [4]. For any clock x for which the maximum constant is infinity, we have:*

$$(l_0, \{v_0\}) \Rightarrow^*_{\mathfrak{a}} (l, Z) \text{ implies } \forall v \in Z : \exists v' \in Z : v(x) = v'(x) \wedge (l_0, v_0) \to^* (l, v')$$

In other words, if the maximum constant of a clock is infinity, then the value of the clock is preserved in the abstraction. Thus the bound, p, produced by the algorithm in Fig. 1 using any of the mentioned extrapolation operators, with the maximum constant of the extra clock, c, being infinity, is valid (i.e, $A\Diamond_{\leq p}\varphi$ holds) and tight (i.e. $A\Diamond_{\leq q}\varphi$ is false for any $q < p$). Validity follows from completeness of the abstractions and tightness follows from lemma 1.

Pruning. Let X be the set of clocks in the model, and let $c \notin X$ be an additional unrestricted clock. Given two concrete states (l, v) and (l, v'), such that $\pi_X(v) = \pi_X(v')$ and $v(c) < v'(c)$, there is no point in exploring (l, v) when (l, v') has already been explored, as the later can simulate the former with a bigger value of c. We now describe how this observation can be used to prune the search. Let us first introduce a new operation on zones.

Definition 4. *Let c be a clock that is neither reset nor tested in the model. Let X be the set of all clocks, excluding the additional c clock. The $\ddagger$ operator is overloaded on both symbolic states and zones, and is defined as:*

$$(l, Z)^\ddagger = (l, Z^\ddagger)$$
$$Z^\ddagger = \{v \mid \exists v' \in Z : 0 \leq v(c) \leq v'(c) \wedge \pi_X(v) = \pi_X(v')\}$$

The $\ddagger$ operation enlarges a zone by including those valuations that are identical to the valuations already in the zone except that c has a smaller value, see Fig. 2. We have the following result:

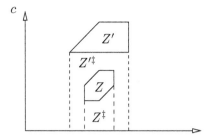

Fig. 2. The ‡ operator performs a downwards closure on the extra clock c. Thus symbolic states that are "cheaper" and smaller are included in "expensive" and bigger states.

Lemma 2. *The ‡-operation respects symbolic transitions in the sense that* (l, Z) $\Rightarrow (l, Z')$ *iff* $(l, Z)^{\ddagger} \Rightarrow (l, Z'')$ *for* $Z'^{\ddagger} = Z''^{\ddagger}$.

It follows that applying the ‡ operation to all successors computed in the algorithm of Fig. 1 does not change the return value of the algorithm. It is useful to note that using the LU extrapolation of [4] with a maximum lower bound of ∞ and a maximum upper bound of $-\infty$ has the same effect as using ∞ for both bounds and applying the ‡ operation on the result, i.e., $\mathfrak{a}_{\prec_{LU}}(Z) = \mathfrak{a}_{\prec_{LU}}(Z)^{\ddagger}$ if $U(c) = -\infty$.

4   Parameterised Liveness Checking

In the previous section we assumed that φ would eventually be satisfied. One way of checking that this is in fact the case, is to use the model checker to verify that $A\Diamond\varphi$ holds in the initial state. In this section we present an alternative algorithm to first checking that φ will eventually hold followed by finding the bound using the algorithm described in the previous section: The algorithm either establishes that $A\Diamond\varphi$ does not hold; or if it does hold provides the smallest p s.t. that $A\Diamond_{\leq p}\varphi$ holds. As an easy extension, we provide an algorithm for finding the smallest p s.t. $A\Box(\psi \implies A\Diamond_{\leq p}\varphi)$ holds, i.e. the smallest p such that whenever ψ holds, φ is guaranteed to hold before p time units – we call this time bounded leads-to synthesis. The usefulness of time bounded leads-to synthesis is demonstrated in Section 5.

Searching for Counter Examples. Before presenting the new algorithm, we review the algorithm currently used in UPPAAL for checking $A\Diamond\varphi$. This algorithm is strongly inspired by [7], and finds counter examples disproving $A\Diamond\varphi$, i.e., any maximal path where $\neg\varphi$ holds in all states. A path is maximal if either it ends in a state with no outgoing transitions, ends in a state from which an unbounded delay is possible, or is infinite. The algorithm for this is shown in Fig. 3. It takes an initial symbolic state, S_0, and a state formula, φ. The algorithm is essentially a depth first search restricted to states not satisfying φ, with detection

proc $Eventually(S_0, \varphi) \equiv$
  $ST := \emptyset$
  $Passed := \emptyset$
  $Search(delay(S_0, \neg\varphi))$
  exit($true$)
end
proc $Search(S) \equiv$
  if $loop(S, ST)$ **then exit**($false$) **fi**   Maximal path found
  $push(ST, S)$ Add to stack
  $S := S \wedge \neg\varphi$ Only explore states where $\neg\varphi$
  if $unbounded(S) \vee deadlocked(S)$ **then exit**($false$) **fi**   Maximal path found
  if $\forall S' \in Passed : S \not\sqsubseteq S'$ If unvisited state
    then foreach $S' : S \overset{a}{\Rightarrow} S'$ **do**   For all successors
      $Search(delay(S', \neg\varphi))$ Recursive call
     od
  fi
  $Passed := Passed \cup \{pop(ST)\}$ Move from stack to $Passed$
end

Fig. 3. Recursive algorithm for checking $S_0 \models A\Diamond\varphi$. The algorithm maintains a set, $Passed$, of previously explored states and a call stack, ST, for easy loop detection. The recursive sub-procedure operates by first restricting the symbolic state S to the subset not satisfying φ (i.e. it never explores states satisfying φ). If the result is unbounded or contains deadlock states, then a counter example, i.e. a maximal path satisfying $\neg\varphi$, has been found. Otherwise, if the state has not been explored before (it is not in $Passed$), then the algorithm is called recursively for all successors. Notice that **exit** terminates the algorithm.

of maximal paths. As an optimisation the $Passed$ set is used to remember states known eventually to satisfy φ. States are added to this set during backtracking.[3]

Finding the bound. An algorithm for finding the smallest p such that $A\Diamond_{\leq p}\varphi$ holds is shown in Fig. 4. The main difference to the algorithm in Fig. 3 is the addition of an extra clock, c, that is not used in the actual model and which is reset to zero in the initial state. The algorithm maintains an estimate for p while searching for maximal paths satisfying $\neg\varphi$. Initially, the estimate is zero. Whenever a state satisfying φ is found to have a value for c larger than our current estimate, the estimate is enlarged accordingly.

Pruning. As before, the ‡ operation can safely be used to enlarge all zones without affecting the maximum value of c in any zone encountered.

Correctness. Figure 5 illustrates how unexplored states are picked up, stored on the stack and pushed to the $Passed$ set when backtracking. We observe that the

---

[3] A loop in the simulation graph does not necessarily imply that all concrete state in a symbolic state of the loop are part of a concrete infinite trace. This is only the case if the symbolic loop is pre- and post-stable [7]. Fortunately, any loop in the simulation graph is known to contain such a pre- and post-stable loop, and since we are only interested in the existence of such a loop, we do not need to compute it.

proc $Eventually'(S_0, \varphi) \equiv$
   $p := 0$
   $ST := \emptyset$
   $Passed := \emptyset$
   $Search'(delay(S_0[c \mapsto 0], \neg\varphi))$ c is zero in the initial state
   exit(p)
end
proc $Search'(S) \equiv$
   if $loop(\pi_X(S), \pi_X(ST))$ **then** **exit**$(false)$ **fi**   Notice project on X
   $p := \max(p, \max_c(S))$ Enlarge estimate
   $push(ST, S^{\ddagger})$ Notice use of $\ddagger$
   $S := S \wedge \neg\varphi$
   if $unbounded(S) \vee deadlocked(S)$ **then** **exit**$(false)$ **fi**
   if $\forall S' \in Passed : S \not\subseteq S'$
      then **foreach** $S' : S \overset{a}{\Rightarrow} S'$ **do**
            $Search'(delay(S', \neg\varphi))$
      od
   fi
   $Passed := Passed \cup \{pop(ST)\}$
end

Fig. 4. The algorithm returns the smallest p such that $S_0 \models A\lozenge_{\leq p}\varphi$ or *false* if no such p exists

following invariants hold for $Search'$ in Fig. 4.

$$\forall s \in Passed : \pi_X(s) \models A\lozenge_{\leq p - s(c)}\varphi \tag{3}$$

$$\forall 0 \leq p' < p : \exists s \in Passed : s(c) > p' \tag{4}$$

$\forall s \in Passed \cup WP \cup ST : \exists s_0 \in S_0 :$

$$\text{there is a path from } s_0 \text{ to } s \text{ with delay } s(c) \quad (5)$$

Invariant (3) states that from all states s in *Passed*, φ will hold within $p - s(c)$ time units. In particular, once S_0 is in *Passed* we have $S_0 \models A\lozenge_{\leq p}\varphi$ since c is zero in the initial state. Invariant (4) states that for all values smaller than p, there is a state in *Passed* in which c is larger. Finally, invariant (5) states that c accurately measures the time along some path originating at an initial state. Validity follows from (3) whereas tightness follows from (4) and (5).

Termination. We first observe that the *Passed* set is not necessary for guaranteeing termination. Also notice that the projection of the extended simulation graph (extended in the sense that we added an extra clock c that is not abstracted by the extrapolation operation) onto X is finite. Assume that the algorithm does not terminate. Then there must be an infinite path in the extended simulation graph such that φ never holds. The projection of this path onto X must necessarily contain a loop since the projected simulation graph is finite. But such

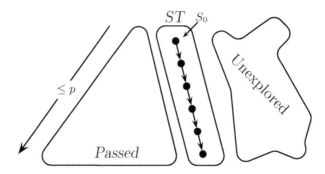

Fig. 5. The algorithm in Fig. 4 uses a stack, ST, to hold the trace to the currently explored state. During backtracking, states are moved to the *Passed* set. It is an invariant of the algorithm that the distance (in time units) between the initial state and any state in *Passed* is not larger than p.

a loop would be detected by the *loop* function contradicting that the algorithm does not terminate.

Time Bounded Leads-to Synthesis. In UPPAAL, the reachability checker and the liveness checker can be combined to check leads-to properties, i.e., properties on the form $A\square(\psi \implies A\Diamond\varphi)$, also written $\psi \rightsquigarrow \varphi$. This is done by using the reachability checker to generate all reachable symbolic states, S, satisfying ψ and then using the liveness checker (Fig. 3) to check $S \models A\Diamond\varphi$ for each of them. As an optimisation, the *Passed* set can be reused between invocations of the liveness checker, as we only add states from which φ will eventually hold. The same approach can be used to find the smallest p such that $A\square(\psi \implies A\Diamond_{\leq p}\varphi)$, i.e., time bounded leads-to synthesis: Once again the model is extended with an additional clock, c. The reachability checker is used to find all reachable states, S, satisfying ψ. We then invoke $Search'(delay(S[c \mapsto 0], \neg\varphi))$ on each of them, maintaining *Passed* and p between calls. If *Search'* returns *false* we conclude that $\psi \rightsquigarrow \varphi$ does not hold; otherwise p is a valid and tight bound. It is important though, that c is reset as soon as ψ starts to hold, i.e., when computing successors, the reachability checker must first compute the action successors, then perform a restricted delay under $\neg\psi$ (i.e., $delay(S, \neg\psi)$), then reset c and invoke the liveness checker on the subset actually satisfying ψ, and then continue with an unrestricted delay operation as usual. With this approach, c accurately captures the time between ψ holding and φ holding.

5   Experiments

We have implemented a prototype of the above algorithms in the most recent development build of UPPAAL. The prototype is limited to state formula over locations and integer variables, thus simplifying the implementation of the restricted delay operation. In the following, we describe experimental results for

| | Liveness | | | Reachability | | | |
Instance	$A\lozenge_{\le p}$	$A\lozenge$	$E\lozenge$	Total	Binary	DF	w/o Extrap.
rand0000	23,1s	2.0s	0.5s	2.5s	3.5s	10.7	1.8s
rand0010	31.0s	2.8s	0.7s	3.5s	5.1s	14.0s	3.2s
rand0020	31.5s	2.4s	0.5s	2.9s	4.1s	14.9s	0.9s
rand0030	19.6s	1.4s	0.4s	1.8s	2.6s	9.1s	0.9s
rand0040	22.6s	2.0s	0.6s	2.6s	4.3s	10.4s	2.9s
rand0050	24.6s	1.5s	0.3s	1.8s	2.4s	11.4s	0.7s
rand0060	24.2s	1.6s	1.8s	3.4s	14.2s	11.3s	1.9s
rand0070	2.8	0.5s	0.6s	1.1s	4.4s	1.3s	1.3s
rand0080	29.6s	1.9s	0.4s	2.3s	3.2s	14.0s	1.0s
rand0090	20.6s	1.7s	0.4s	2.1s	2.9s	9.4s	1.2s
rand0100	17.1s	1.3s	0.3s	1.6s	2.6s	7.7s	1.3s

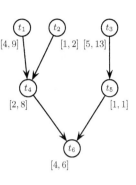

Fig. 6. 11 instances of task graphs with 100 task running on 2 machines using fixed priority scheduling. The experiments were conducted on a 1.3GHz Pentium M with 512MB memory.

both the bounded liveness property, $A\lozenge_{\le p}\varphi$, and the bounded response or leads-to property, $A\square(\psi \implies A\lozenge_{\le p}\varphi)$, also denoted $\psi \leadsto_{\le p} \varphi$.

We test the bounded liveness property on the task graph problem and the bounded response property on the train gate problem. A task graph is a directed acyclic graph where the nodes represent tasks and the arcs represent dependencies among the tasks in the sense that a task is released when all parents have finished executing. The right side of Fig. 6 depicts a task graph with 6 tasks. Now, the task graph scheduling problem is, given a number of processor and an execution time for each task, find a non-preemptive schedule that minimises the total execution time while respecting all precedence constraints. In order to perform WCET analysis on task graphs, we choose a fixed scheduling strategy, in this case fixed priorities, and assign to each task an execution time interval giving best and worst case execution times. This means that the system keeps a priority queue with available tasks and whenever the last dependency of a task finishes execution, that task is added to the queue. We can then synthesise p for the property $A\lozenge_{\le p}$ "all tasks finished" on the system. In other words, using the scheduling strategy, what is the latest time when all tasks are finished.

In the first five columns of Figure 6 we compare the two approaches presented in this paper to the approach of [11]. The experiments have been conducted on 11 task graph instances with 100 tasks from the standard task graph set, [12]. Column 1 displays the results for the parameterized liveness algorithm of Figure 4 and columns 2 and 3 provide the execution time of checking the liveness property and running the parameterized reachability algorithm of Figure 1 and summed in column 4. Column 5 gives the results for the binary search approach presented in [11] and were performed by searching between the upper bound of assuming no parallelism and the lower bound of full parallelism.

The results in Fig. 6 clearly indicate that the reachability-based algorithm, even when the verification time of the $A\lozenge$ property is added, outperforms the parameterized liveness algorithm. For most of the instances, the difference is approximately an order of magnitude.

Furthermore, the parameterized reachability approach also outperforms the binary search method of [11]. Actually, the execution time of the parameterized reachability algorithm is comparable to the execution time of a single model checking problem of the binary search approach, thus making it a clear improvement for using model checkers to synthesize parameters for bounded liveness problems.

The major difference between the parameterized liveness algorithm and the parameterized reachability algorithm is that the former is based on depth-first search while the latter on breadth-first. In order investigate whether this difference can explain the difference in performance of the two algorithms, column 6 of Figure 6 displays the performance of the parameterized reachability algorithm using depth-first search instead of breadth-first. The results show that there is, roughly, a factor two difference between the depth-first reachability algorithm and the parameterized liveness algorithm indicating that the depth-first strategy of the parameterized liveness algorithm is responsible for the worse performance.

Finally, column 7 of Figure 6 gives the execution times for the problems without implementing the extrapolation introduced in Definition 4. By comparing these results with those of column 3 it is clear that performing the extrapolation operation significantly improves performance of the parameterized reachability algorithm up to a factor of four.

For verifying the bounded leads-to property $\leadsto_{\leq p}$ we use the train gate controller example as introduced in Section 1. The right of Fig. 7 depicts a timed automata of a train for the train gate controller system. A train initially starts in the Safe location. At any point in time, the train can move to the Appr location, indicating that the train is approaching the gate. If nothing happens within ten time units, the train can move to the Cross location, indicating that the train is passing the gate. However, if the train receives a message to stop it proceeds to the Stop location. Here, the train waits until it receives a notification that it is allowed to proceed, it then moves to the Start location and further to the Cross location within a given time interval. As stated in Section 1, an important

Trains	$\leadsto_{\leq p}$	$\leadsto$
4	0.2s	0.06s
5	0.4s	0.2s
6	3.8s	1.3s
7	25.7s	9.3s
8	268.1s	88.7s

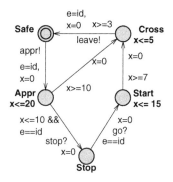

Fig. 7. 5 instances of the train gate controller. The experiments were conducted on a 2.6GHz Pentium4 with 2GB memory.

property to verify is that whenever a train approaches it is eventually granted permission to cross, i.e Train.Appr⤳Train.Cross. However, knowing that a train will eventually pass might, in practice, be unimportant if we do not know the longest waiting time a train can experience.

The table in Fig. 7 shows experimental results for instances of the train gate controller with five to eight trains. The experiments compare the running time of verifying the leads-to property ($\leadsto$) versus the bounded leads-to property ($\leadsto_{\leq p}$). The results show that the penalty for verifying $\leadsto_{\leq p}$ and synthesising the parameter p is approximately a factor four as opposed to verifying $\leadsto$.

6   Conclusions

In this paper we have contributed results on efficient zone-based parameter synthesis for time bounded liveness in timed automata. We have presented two different approaches to the synthesis, one based on reduction to reachability analysis and one based on a modified and extended version of the algorithm for unbounded liveness checking. We have demonstrated the usefulness of the analysis via two case studies. The experimental results showed (not quite unexpected) that the reachability based approach is much faster than the approach based on liveness checking and also faster than the binary search approach presented in [11]. It is slightly more surprising that running an unbounded liveness analysis *and* the reachability-based synthesis is more efficient than using the modified liveness algorithm for synthesizing the parameter directly. The experiments indicate that the reason for the difference in performance is the fact that the parameterized liveness algorithm uses a depth-first search, whereas the reachability-based approach uses a breadth-first strategy, since changing the reachability-based algorithm to use depth-first search provides similar results to the liveness-based approach. Thus, the parameterized liveness algorithm could benefit from a breadth-first type implementation as opposed to depth-first. Furthermore, we have provided an extrapolation operation for the algorithm and shown its efficiency through experiments.

There is still room for improvement in the algorithms. Analogous to our work in [6], it is possible to prune the search if an upper bound on the remaining time for reaching the goal condition can be provided (either by the user or derived from the model). Also, any guiding towards the most expensive goal state can be used to quickly obtain good estimates of p, thus making it possible to prune more states.

As our experimental investigation showed the reachability based approach to be significantly faster, it might be a good idea to also use it for time bounded leads-to synthesis. This is possible when $\psi \leadsto \varphi$ is known to hold for a given model; the approach is similar to the one described in Section 4, except that instead of invoking the liveness-based algorithm for every state satisfying ψ we invoke the reachability-based algorithm.

Finally, we leave it for further work to extend the time bounded liveness synthesis for timed automata to cost bounded liveness synthesis for priced timed automata.

References

1. Rajeev Alur, Costas Courcoubetis, and David Dill. Model-checking for real-time systems. In *Proc. 5th IEEE Symposium on Logic in Computer Science (LICS'90)*, pages 414–425. IEEE Computer Society Press, 1990.
2. Rajeev Alur and David Dill. A theory of timed automata. *Theoretical Computer Science (TCS)*, 126(2):183–235, 1994.
3. Gerd Behrmann, Patricia Bouyer, Emmanuel Fleury, and Kim G. Larsen. Static guard analysis in timed automata verification. In *Proc. 9th International Conference on Tools and Algorithms for the Construction and Analysis of Systems (TACAS'2003)*, volume 2619 of *Lecture Notes in Computer Science*, pages 254–277. Springer, 2003.
4. Gerd Behrmann, Patricia Bouyer, Kim G. Larsen, and Radek Pelanek. Lower and upper bounds in zone based abstractions of timed automata. In *TACAS 2004*, volume 2988 of *Lecture Notes in Computer Science*, pages 312–326, 2004.
5. Gerd Behrmann, Alexandre David, and Kim G. Larsen. A tutorial on UPPAAL. In Marco Bernardo and Flavio Corradini, editors, *Formal Methods for the Design of Real-Time Systems*, volume 3185 of *Lecture Notes in Computer Science*. Springer, 2004.
6. Gerd Behrmann, Ansgar Fehnker, Thomas Hune, Kim G. Larsen, Paul Pettersson, Judi Romijn, and Frits Vaandrager. Efficient guiding towards cost-optimality in UPPAAL. In *Proc. 7th International Conference on Tools and Algorithms for the Construction and Analysis of Systems (TACAS'01)*, volume 2031 of *Lecture Notes in Computer Science*, pages 174–188. Springer, 2001.
7. Ahmed Bouajjani, Stavros Tripakis, and Sergio Yovine. On-the-fly symbolic model-checking for real-time systems. In *Proc. 18th IEEE Real-Time Systems Symposium (RTSS'97)*, pages 25–35. IEEE Computer Society Press, 1997.
8. Patricia Bouyer. Untameable timed automata! In *Proc. 20th Annual Symposium on Theoretical Aspects of Computer Science (STACS'03)*, volume 2607 of *Lecture Notes in Computer Science*, pages 620–631. Springer, 2003.
9. Marius Bozga, Conrado Daws, Oded Maler, Alfredo Olivero, Stavros Tripakis, and Sergio Yovine. KRONOS: a model-checking tool for real-time systems. In *Proc. 10th International Conference on Computer Aided Verification (CAV'98)*, volume 1427 of *Lecture Notes in Computer Science*, pages 546–550. Springer, 1998.
10. Véronique Bruyère, Emmanuel Dall'Olio, and Jean-François Raskin. Durations, parametric model-checking in timed automata with presburger arithmetic. In *STACS'03*, volume 2607 of *Lecture Notes in Computer Science*, pages 687–698, 2003.
11. Alexander Metzner. Why model checking can improve wcet analysis. In *CAV 2004*, volume 3114 of *Lecture Notes in Computer Science*, pages 334–347, 2004.
12. T. Tobita, M. Kouda, and H. Kasahara. Performance evaluation of minimum execution time multiprocessor scheduling algorithms using standard task graph set. *Proc. of PDPTA'00*, pages 745–751, 2000.
13. F. Wang. Parametric analysis of computer systems. *Journal of Formal Methods in Systems Design*, 17:39–60, 2000.

Verification of Parameterized Timed Systems

Parosh Aziz Abdulla

Uppsala University, Sweden
parosh@it.uu.se

One of the prominent methods for program verification is that of *model checking* [CES86, QS82]. In the last decade there has been an extensive research effort in order to extend the applicability of model checking to systems with infinite state spaces. There are at least two reasons why a system may be infinite-state:

- A system may operate on data structures with unbounded domains. Examples include real-valued clocks in timed automata [AD94], stacks in push-down automata [BEM97], queues in communicating processes [AJ96], counters in counter machines, etc.
- A system can also be infinite-state because it is *parameterized*. This means that the description of the system is parameterized by the number of components inside the system. In such a case, we would like to verify correctness of the system regardless of the number of processes.

We consider systems which contain both sources of infiniteness; namely parameterized systems of processes each of which behaves as a timed automaton.

Parameterized verification has recently received a lot of attention. One of the earliest works for model checking of parameterized systems was reported by German and Sistla [GS92]. The paper considers systems consisting of an unbounded number of *finite-state processes*, and reduces the problem to a corresponding one for *Vector Addition Systems with States*, a model which is computationally equivalent to Petri nets.

Another important line of research in this area is that of *Regular Model Checking*. Regular model checking was advocated by the paper [KMM+01] as a uniform framework for the analysis of parameterized systems. The idea of regular model checking is to perform symbolic reachability analysis, using regular sets as a symbolic representation of the state space of the parameterized system. Examples of parameterized systems which can be analyzed in this manner are systems consisting of homogeneous finite-state processes connected in linear, ring-formed, or tree-like topologies [AJNS04, ALdR05, BT02, BLW03].

We consider verifying safety properties for *Timed Networks (TNs)* [AJ03]: systems consisting of an arbitrary set of timed automata. Such systems embody both of the two reasons for being infinite-state: they use an infinite data structure (namely clocks which can assume values from the set of real numbers), and they are parameterized in allowing an arbitrary set of processes. TNs cannot be analyzed within earlier frameworks for parameterized verification, since the individual components are no longer finite-state processes.

There are several examples of protocols which can be modelled as TNs. For instance, Fischer's protocol [SBM92] achieves mutual exclusion among an arbitrary set of timed processes. This protocol, together with other protocols, such as the Lynch-Shavit protocol [LS92] and the Phillips audio control protocol [BGK+96], are designed to operate

P. Pettersson and W. Yi (Eds.): FORMATS 2005, LNCS 3829, pp. 95–97, 2005.

correctly regardless of the number of participants. Therefore, parameterized verification is relevant in order to prove correctness of the entire family in one step.

We will consider a hierarchy of TNs defined by the number of clocks allowed inside each timed automaton. First, we consider *single-clock TNs* in which each process is restricted to operate on one clock. Despite this restriction, a single-clock TN operates on an unbounded number of clocks, and hence its behaviour cannot be captured by that of a timed automaton [AD94]. Therefore, it cannot be analyzed through existing tools for timed automata such as KRONOS and UPPAAL. We present a symbolic algorithm for verifying safety properties for *single clock TNs*. The symbolic representation we use is a variant of that of *zones* widely used in tools for model checking timed automata. The difference is that, in our case, all variables of the zone are existentially quantified. As an example, we use our algorithm to verify parameterized versions of Fischer's protocol and the Lynch-Shavit protocol (i.e., we show their correctness regardless of the number of participating processes).

On the other hand, there are many protocols in the literature which can be modelled as TNs where each of the timed automata has more than one clock. For instance, the Phillips audio protocol has two clocks per process. Also, the system described in [MT01] consists of an arbitrary number of nodes, each of which is connected to a set of LANs. Each node maintains timers to keep track of sending and receiving of messages from other nodes connected to the same set of LANs. In a similar way to Fischer's protocol, it is clearly relevant to ask whether we can verify correctness of the protocol in [BGK+96] regardless of the number of senders, or the protocol in [MT01] regardless of the number of nodes. The question is then whether the decidability result can be extended form single-clock systems to multi-clock systems. We answer this question negatively [ADM04a]. In fact, we show that *two-clock TNs* are Turing-powerful, implying undecidability of all non-trivial verification problems.

Finally, we consider TNs which operate on the discrete time domain. In this case, we show that safety properties can be checked regardless on the number of clocks inside each component.

Considering the undecidability result for the dense-time case, we also study restricted classes of TNs [ADM04b]:

– *Open TNs* in which only strict inequalities are allowed on clock values. We show that undecidability is maintained in this case.
– *Closed TNs* in which only non-strict inequalities are allowed on clock values. In a similar manner to discrete TNs, we show that the problem becomes decidable regardless of the number of clocks inside each process
– *Robust TNs*. Using the *robust semantics*, a computation is accepted only if all neighbouring computations are also accepted. We show that undecidability is maintained in the case of robust TNs.

References

[AD94]   R. Alur and D. Dill. A theory of timed automata. *Theoretical Computer Science*, 126:183–235, 1994.
[ADM04a]   P. A. Abdulla, J. Deneux, and P. Mahata. Multi-clock timed networks. In *Proc. LICS' 04 20th IEEE Int. Symp. on Logic in Computer Science*, pages 345–354, 2004.

[ADM04b] P. A. Abdulla, J. Deneux, and P. Mahata. Open, closed and robust timed networks. In *Proc. INFINITY '04, 6th International Workshop on Verification of Infinite-State Systems*, 2004.

[AJ96] P. A. Abdulla and B. Jonsson. Verifying programs with unreliable channels. *Information and Computation*, 127(2):91–101, 1996.

[AJ03] P. A. Abdulla and B. Jonsson. Model checking of systems with many identical timed processes. *Theoretical Computer Science*, 290(1):241–264, 2003.

[AJNS04] P.A. Abdulla, B. Jonsson, M. Nilsson, and M. Saksena. A survey of regular model checking. In *Proc. CONCUR 2004, 15th Int. Conf. on Concurrency Theory*, pages 348–360, 2004.

[ALdR05] P. A. Abdulla, A. Legay, J. d'Orso, and A. Rezine. Simulation-based iteration of tree transducers. In *Proc. TACAS '05, 11th Int. Conf. on Tools and Algorithms for the Construction and Analysis of Systems*, volume 3440 of *Lecture Notes in Computer Science*, pages 30–44, 2005.

[BEM97] A. Bouajjani, J. Esparza, and O. Maler. Reachability Analysis of Pushdown Automata: Application to Model Checking. In *Proc. Intern. Conf. on Concurrency Theory (CONCUR'97)*. LNCS 1243, 1997.

[BGK+96] J. Bengtsson, W. O. D. Griffioen, K.J. Kristoffersen, K.G. Larsen, F. Larsson, P. Pettersson, and W. Yi. Verification of an audio protocol with bus collision using UP-PAAL. In *Proc. 8th Int. Conf. on Computer Aided Verification*, volume 1102 of *Lecture Notes in Computer Science*, pages 244–256, 1996.

[BLW03] Bernard Boigelot, Axel Legay, and Pierre Wolper. Iterating transducers in the large. In *Proc. 15th Int. Conf. on Computer Aided Verification*, volume 2725 of *Lecture Notes in Computer Science*, pages 223–235, 2003.

[BT02] Ahmed Bouajjani and Tayssir Touili. Extrapolating Tree Transformations. In *Proc. 14th Int. Conf. on Computer Aided Verification*, volume 2404 of *Lecture Notes in Computer Science*, 2002.

[CES86] E.M. Clarke, E.A. Emerson, and A.P. Sistla. Automatic verification of finite-state concurrent systems using temporal logic specification. *ACM Trans. on Programming Languages and Systems*, 8(2):244–263, April 1986.

[GS92] S. M. German and A. P. Sistla. Reasoning about systems with many processes. *Journal of the ACM*, 39(3):675–735, 1992.

[KMM+01] Y. Kesten, O. Maler, M. Marcus, A. Pnueli, and E. Shahar. Symbolic model checking with rich assertional languages. *Theoretical Computer Science*, 256:93–112, 2001.

[LS92] N. A. Lynch and N. Shavit. Timing-based mutual exclusion. In *IEEE Real-Time Systems Symposium*, pages 2–11, 1992.

[MT01] I. A. Mason and C. L. Talcott. Simple network protocol simulation within maude. In Kokichi Futatsugi, editor, *Electronic Notes in Theoretical Computer Science*, volume 36. Elsevier, 2001.

[QS82] J.P. Queille and J. Sifakis. Specification and verification of concurrent systems in cesar. In *5th International Symposium on Programming, Turin*, volume 137 of *Lecture Notes in Computer Science*, pages 337–352. Springer Verlag, 1982.

[SBM92] F. B. Schneider, B. Bloom, and K. Marzullo. Putting time into proof outlines. In de Bakker, Huizing, de Roever, and Rozenberg, editors, *Real-Time: Theory in Practice*, volume 600 of *Lecture Notes in Computer Science*, 1992.

Model Checking the Time to Reach Agreement*

Martijn Hendriks

Institute for Computing and Information Sciences,
Radboud University Nijmegen,
Toernooiveld 1, 6525 ED Nijmegen, The Netherlands
M.Hendriks@cs.ru.nl

Abstract. The timed automaton framework of Alur and Dill is a natural choice for the specification of partially synchronous distributed systems (systems which have only partial information about timing, e.g., only an upper bound on the message delay). The past has shown that verification of these systems by model checking usually is very difficult. The present paper demonstrates that an agreement algorithm of Attiya et al, which falls into a – for model checkers – particularly problematic subclass of partially synchronous distributed systems, can easily be modeled with the UPPAAL model checker, and that it is possible to analyze some interesting and non-trivial instances with reasonable computational resources. Although existing techniques are used, this is an interesting case study in its own right that adds to the existing body of experience. Furthermore, the agreement algorithm has not been formally verified before to the author's knowledge.

1   Introduction

Distributed systems are in general hard to understand and to reason about due to their complexity and inherent non-determinism. That is why formal models play an important role in the design of these systems: one can specify the system and its properties in an unambiguous and precise way, and it enables a formal correctness proof. The I/O-automata of Lynch and Tuttle provide a general formal modeling framework for distributed systems [1, 2, 3]. Although the models and proofs in this framework can be very general (e.g., parameterized by the number of processes or the network topology), the proofs require – as usual – a lot of human effort.

Model checking provides a more automated, albeit less general way of proving the correctness of systems [4]. The approach requires the construction of a model of the system and the specification of its correctness properties. A model checker then automatically computes whether the model satisfies the properties or not. The power of model checkers is that they are relatively easy to use compared to manual verification techniques or theorem provers, but they also have some clear drawbacks. In general only *instances* of the system can be verified (i.e., the

---

* Supported by the European Community Project IST-2001-35304 AMETIST (Advanced Methods for Timed Systems), http://ametist.cs.utwente.nl/.

P. Pettersson and W. Yi (Eds.): FORMATS 2005, LNCS 3829, pp. 98–111, 2005.

algorithm can be verified for 3 processes, but not for n processes). Furthermore, model checking suffers from the state space explosion problem: the number of states grows exponentially in the number of system components. This often renders the verification of realistic systems impossible.

A class of distributed systems for which model checking has yielded no apparent successes is the subclass of *partially synchronous systems* in which (i) message delay is bounded by some constant, and (ii) many messages can be in transit simultaneously. In the partially synchronous model, system components have some information about timing, although the information might not be exact. It lies between the extremes of the synchronous model (the processes take steps simultaneously) on one end and the asynchronous model (the processes take steps in an arbitrary order and at arbitrary relative speeds) on the other end [3]. The timed automata framework of Alur and Dill [5] is a natural choice for the specification of partially synchronous systems (as is the Timed I/O-automaton framework [6], which, however, does not support model checking). Verification of the above mentioned subclass of "difficult" partially synchronous systems by model checking, however, is often very difficult since every message needs its own clock to model the bounds on message delivery time. This is disastrous since the state space of a timed automaton grows exponentially in the number of clocks. Moreover, if messages may get lost or message delivery is unordered, then on top of that also the discrete part of the model explodes rapidly.

Many realistic algorithms and protocols fall into the class of "difficult" partially synchronous systems. Examples include the sliding window protocol for the reliable transmission of data over unreliable channels [7, 8], a protocol to monitor the presence of network nodes [9, 10, 11], and the ZeroConf protocol whose purpose is to dynamically configure IPv4 link-local addresses [12, 13]. Furthermore, the agreement algorithm described in [14] (see also Chapter 25 of [3]) also is a partially synchronous system that is difficult from the perspective of model checking. The analysis of this algorithm with the UPPAAL model checker is the subject of the present paper. The main contribution consists of the formal verification of some non-trivial instances of the algorithm, which has not been done before to the author's knowledge. Although standard modeling and verification techniques are used, the case study is interesting in its own right, and increases the existing body of case-study experience. Independently of the present work, Leslie Lamport has also analyzed a distributed algorithm that falls into the class of difficult partially synchronous systems as defined above [15].

The remainder of this paper is structured as follows. The timed automaton framework and the UPPAAL model checker are very briefly introduced in Section 2. Section 3 then presents an informal description of the distributed algorithm of [14], which consists of two parts: a timeout task and a main task. Section 4 describes the UPPAAL model that is used to verify the timeout task. A model for the parallel composition of the timeout task and the main task is proposed in Section 5. Two properties of the timeout task that have been verified in Section 4 are used to reduce the complexity of this latter model. Finally, Section 6 discusses the present work. The UPPAAL models from this paper are available at http://www.cs.ru.nl/ita/publications/papers/martijnh/. Note that the UPPAAL development version 3.5.7 has been used.

2 Timed Automata

This section provides a very brief overview of timed automata and their semantics, and of the UPPAAL tool, which is a model checker for timed automata. The reader is referred to [16] and [17] for more details.

Timed automata are finite automata that are extended with real valued clock variables [5]. Let X be a set of clock variables, then the set $\Phi(X)$ of clock constraints ϕ is defined by the grammar $\phi := x \sim c \mid \phi_1 \wedge \phi_2$, where $x \in X$, $c \in \mathbb{N}$, and $\sim \in \{<, \leq, =, \geq, >\}$. A clock interpretation ν for a set X is a mapping from X to $\mathbb{R}^+$, where $\mathbb{R}^+$ denotes the set of positive real numbers including zero. A clock interpretation ν for X satisfies a clock constraint ϕ over X, denoted by $\nu \models \phi$, if and only if ϕ evaluates to *true* with the values for the clocks given by ν. For $\delta \in \mathbb{R}^+$, $\nu + \delta$ denotes the clock interpretation which maps every clock x to the value $\nu(x) + \delta$. For a set $Y \subseteq X$, $\nu[Y := 0]$ denotes the clock interpretation for X which assigns 0 to each $x \in Y$ and agrees with ν over the rest of the clocks. We let $\Gamma(X)$ denote the set of all clock interpretations for X.

A timed automaton then is a tuple $(L, l^0, \Sigma, X, I, E)$, where L is a finite set of locations, $l^0 \in L$ is the initial location, Σ is a finite set of labels, X is a finite set of clocks, I is a mapping that labels each location $l \in L$ with some clock constraint in $\Phi(X)$ (the *location invariant*) and $E \subseteq L \times \Sigma \times \Phi(X) \times 2^X \times L$ is a set of edges. An edge $(l, a, \phi, \lambda, l')$ represents a transition from location l to location l' on the symbol a. The clock constraint ϕ specifies when the edge is enabled and the set $\lambda \subseteq X$ gives the clocks to be reset with this edge. The semantics of a timed automaton $(L, l^0, \Sigma, X, I, E)$ is defined by associating a transition system with it. A state is a pair (l, ν), where $l \in L$, and $\nu \in \Gamma(X)$ such that $\nu \models I(l)$. The initial state is (l^0, ν^0), where $\nu^0(x) = 0$ for all $x \in X$. There are two types of transitions (let $\delta \in \mathbb{R}^+$ and let $a \in \Sigma$). First, $((l, \nu), (l, \nu + \delta))$ is a δ-*delay transition* iff $\nu + \delta' \models I(l)$ for all $0 \leq \delta' \leq \delta$. Second, $((l, \nu), (l', \nu'))$ is an a-*action transition* iff an edge $(l, a, \phi, \lambda, l')$ exists such that $\nu \models \phi$, $\nu' = \nu[\lambda := 0]$ and $\nu' \models I(l')$. Note that location invariants can be used to specify progress, and that they can cause time deadlocks.

The transition system of a timed automaton is infinite due to the real valued clocks. The region and zone constructions, however, are finite abstractions that preserve Timed Computation Tree Logic (TCTL) formulas and a subset of TCTL formulas (most notably reachability) respectively [18, 19]. This enables the application of finite state model checking techniques as implemented, for instance, by the UPPAAL tool.

The UPPAAL modeling language extends the basic timed automata as defined above with bounded integer variables and binary blocking (CCS style) synchronization. Systems are modeled as a set of communicating timed automata. The UPPAAL tool supports simulation of the model and the verification of reachability and invariant properties. The question whether a state satisfying ϕ is reachable can be formalized as $\mathbf{EF}(\phi)$. The question whether ϕ holds for all reachable states is formalized as $\mathbf{AG}(\phi)$. If a reachability property holds or an invariant property does not hold, then UPPAAL can provide a run that proves this. This run can be replayed in the simulator, which is very useful for debugging purposes.

3   Description of the Algorithm

This section presents an informal description of an algorithm that solves the problem of *fault-tolerant distributed agreement* in a partially synchronous setting [14] (see also Chapter 25 of [3]). A system of n processes, denoted by $p_1, ..., p_n$, is considered, where each process is given an input value and at most f processes may fail. Each process that does not fail must eventually (termination) choose a decision value such that no two processes decide differently (agreement), and if any process decides for v, then this has been the input value of some process (validity)[1]. The process's computation steps are atomic and take no time, and two consecutive computation steps of a non-faulty process are separated c_1 to c_2 time units. The processes can communicate by sending messages to each other. The message delay is bounded by d time units, and message delivery is unordered. Furthermore, messages can get neither lost nor duplicated. The constant D is defined as $d+c_2$. As mentioned above, f out of the n processes may fail. A failure may occur at any time, and if a process fails at some point, then an arbitrary subset of the messages that would have been sent in the next computation step, is sent. No further messages are sent by a failed process. It is convenient to regard the algorithm, which is run by every process, as the merge of a *timeout task* and a *main task*, such that a process's computation step consists of a step of the timeout task followed by a step of the main task.

3.1   Description of the Timeout Task

The goal of the timeout task is to maintain the running state of all other processes. To this end, every process p_j broadcasts an $(alive, j)$ message in every computation step. If process p_i has run for sufficiently many computation steps without receiving an $(alive, j)$ message, then it assumes that p_j halted either by decision or by failure[2]. Figure 1 contains the description of a computation step of the timeout task of process p_i in precondition-effect style.

The boolean variable *blocked* is used by the main task to stop the timeout task. Initially, this boolean is *false*. It is set to *true* if the process decides. The other state components are a set $halted \subseteq \{1, ..., n\}$, initially $\emptyset$, and for every

---

[1] This is required to avoid trivial solutions in which every process always decides for some predetermined constant value.

[2] The message complexity of this algorithm is quite high. Recently, an alternative with an adjustable "probing load" for each node has been proposed in [9], further analyzed in [10], and improved in [11].

Precondition:
  ¬ *blocked*
Effect:
  broadcast($(alive,i)$)
  for $j := 1$ **to** n **do**
    $counter(j) := counter(j) + 1$
    if $(alive,j) \in buff$ **then**
      remove $(alive,j)$ from *buff*
      $counter(j) := 0$
    else if $counter(j) \geq \lfloor \frac{D}{c_1} \rfloor + 1$ **then**
      add j to *halted*
  od

Fig. 1. The timeout task for process p_i

$j \in \{1, ..., n\}$ a counter $counter(j)$, initially set to -1. Additionally, every process has a message buffer *buff* (a set), initially $\emptyset$. Two properties of the timeout task have been proven in [14].

A_1 If any p_i adds j to *halted* at time t, then p_j halts, and every message sent from p_j to p_i is delivered strictly before time t.

A_2 If p_j halts at time t, then every p_i either halts or adds j to *halted* by time $t + T$, where $T = D + c_2 \cdot (\lfloor \frac{D}{c_1} \rfloor + 1)$.

These two properties are used in [14] for the correctness proof of the complete algorithm. In this paper, these two properties are first mechanically verified for a number of instances of the algorithm. Consequently, they are used to make an abstract model of the complete algorithm in Section 5.

3.2 Description of the Main Task

Figure 2 contains the description of a computation step of the main task of process p_i in precondition-effect style. Apart from the input value v_i and the state components used by the timeout task, there is one additional state component, namely the round counter r, initially zero. The input values are assumed to be either zero or one for simplicity[3].

Each process tries to decide in each round. Note that a process may decide for 0 only in even rounds, and for 1 only in odd rounds. Furthermore, if a process fails to decide in round r, then it broadcasts r before going to round $r + 1$. On the other hand, if a process decides in round r, it broadcasts $r+1$ before halting. In order for a process to decide in a round $r \geq 1$, it ensures that it has received the message $r - 1$ from all non-halted processes, and no message r from any process. Three main results that are obtained in [14] are the following.

---

[3] An extension to an arbitrary input domain is discussed in [14].

Precondition:
  $r = 0 \wedge v_i = 1$
Effect:
  broadcast$((0,i))$
  $r := 1$

Precondition:
  $r \geq 1 \wedge \exists_j \ (r,j) \in buff$
Effect:
  broadcast$((r,i))$
  $r := r + 1$

Precondition:
  $r = 0 \wedge v_i = 0$
Effect:
  broadcast$((1,i))$
  decide(0)

Precondition:
  $r \geq 1 \wedge \forall_{j \notin halted} \ (r-1,j) \in buff \ \wedge$
  $\neg \exists_j \ (r,j) \in buff$
Effect:
  broadcast$((r+1,i))$
  decide$(r \bmod 2)$

Fig. 2. The main task for process p_i

M_1 (Agreement, Lemma 5.9 of [14]). No two processes decide on different values.

M_2 (Validity, Lemma 5.10 of [14]). If process p_i decides on n, then $n = v_j$ for some process j.

M_3 (Termination, Theorem 5.1 of [14]). The upper bound on the time to reach agreement equals $(2f - 1)D + max\ \{T, 3D\}$.

These results are mechanically verified in Section 5 for a number of non-trivial instances of the algorithm.

4   Verification of the Timeout Task

4.1   Modeling the Timeout Task

Note that every process runs the same algorithm, and that the timeout parts of different processes do not interfere with each other. Therefore, only two processes are considered, say p_i and p_j. By the same argument, only one direction of the timeout task is considered: p_i (*Observer*) keeps track of the running state of p_j (*Process*).

Figure 3 shows the UPPAAL automaton of the merge of the timeout task and abstract main task of *Process* (the only functionality of the main task is to halt). It has one local clock x to keep track of the time between two consecutive computation steps. The *Process* automaton must spend exactly c_2 time units in the initial location *init* before it takes the transition to location *comp* (the reason for this is explained below). It then immediately either fails or does a computation step. Failure of *Process* is modeled by the pair of edges to *halted*, which models the non-deterministic choice of the subset of messages to send. The computation step is modeled by the self-loop and by the upper transition

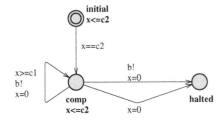

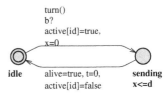

Fig. 3. The *Process* automaton   **Fig. 4.** The broadcast template

to *halted* (a decision transition that blocks the timeout task)[4]. Note that x is reset on every edge to *halted* for verification purposes.

As required by the algorithm, *Process* broadcasts an *alive* message at each computation step. This action is modeled by a b-synchronization, which activates an instance of the broadcast template, shown in Figure 4. This template is parameterized with a constant *id* in order to give each instance a unique identifier. Clearly, the UPPAAL model must ensure *output enabledness* of *Process*: it must be able to broadcast the alive message when it wants to. Since the maximal number of simultaneous broadcasts equals $\lfloor \frac{d}{c_1} \rfloor + 2$, this many instances of the broadcast template must be present in the model. The guard *turn()* and the assignments to *active[id]* implement a trick to reduce the reachable state space by partially exploiting the symmetry among the broadcast instances[5]. After a b-synchronization, a broadcast automaton may spend at most d time units in location *sending*, which is modeled using the local clock x. The actual message delivery is modeled by the assignment *alive=true* on the transition back to *idle*. The reset of the global clock t is used for the verification of property A_1.

Figure 5 shows the automaton for the *Observer*, which is the composition of an abstract main task (whose only purpose again is to halt) and the "receiving part" of the timeout task. It has a local integer variable *cnt*, initialized to -1, and a local clock x. Furthermore, the boolean *has_halted* models whether $Process \in halted_{Observer}$. The *Observer* automaton must first spend c_2 time units in the initial location before taking the edge to location *comp*. Then, it must immediately either do a computation step or fail. The computation step is modeled by the self-loop and by the upper transition to *halted*. The procedure *update()* updates the variables *cnt*, *has_halted* and *alive* as specified in Figure 6. Failure is modeled by the lower edge to *halted*.

Both the *Observer* automaton and the *Process* automaton must first spend c_2 time units in their initial location. This is a modeling trick to fulfill the requirement from [14] that "every process has a computation or failure event

---

[4] A straightforward model contains a third edge to *halted* with the guard $x \geq c_1$, the synchronization $b!$, and the reset $x = 0$. Such an edge is, however, "covered" by the present upper edge to *halted* and can therefore be left out.

[5] A next release of UPPAAL will hopefully support symmetry reduction, which can automatically exploit the symmetry among broadcast automata [20].

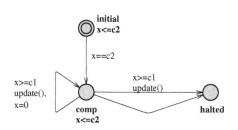

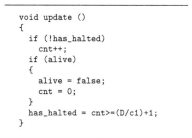

Fig. 5. The *Observer* automaton   **Fig. 6.** The *update()* function

at time 0". I.e., our model starts at time $-c_2$. (If UPPAAL would allow the initialization of a clock to any natural number, then both initial locations can be removed.)

4.2 Verifying the Timeout Task

Property A_1 is translated to the following invariant property of the UPPAAL model (a broadcast automaton with identifier i is denoted by b_i):

$$\mathbf{AG} \left(\begin{array}{c} has\_halted \longrightarrow \\ (Process.halted \wedge \forall_i \ b_i.idle \wedge t > 0) \end{array} \right) \tag{1}$$

The state property $\forall_i \ b_i.idle \wedge t > 0$ ensures that all messages from *Process* to *Observer* are delivered strictly before the conclusion of *Observer* that *Process* halted. Property A_2 is translated as follows:

$$\mathbf{AG} \left(\begin{array}{c} (Process.halted \wedge Process.x > T) \\ \longrightarrow \\ (Observer.halted \vee has\_halted) \end{array} \right) \tag{2}$$

The branching time nature of A_2 is specified by this invariance property due to the structure of our model: *Process.x* measures the time that has been elapsed since *Process* arrived in the location *halted*.

Properties (1) and (2) have been verified for the following parameter values[6]:

- $c_1 = 1$, $c_2 = 1$ and $d \in \{0 - 5\}$,
- $c_1 = 1$, $c_2 = 2$ and $d \in \{0 - 5\}$, and
- $c_1 = 9$, $c_2 = 10$ and $d \in \{5, 9 - 11, 15, 20, 50\}$.

Each of the above instances could be verified within 5 minutes using at most 25 MB of memory.

---

[6] A 3.4 GHz Pentium 4 machine with 2 GB of main memory running Fedora Core 4 has been used for all measurements. The tool *memtime* (available via the UPPAAL website http://www.uppaal.com/) has been used to measure the time and memory consumption.

5   Verification of the Algorithm

The UPPAAL model of the parallel composition of the main task and the timeout task, which is used to verify properties M_1–M_3, is presented in this section. It is assumed that every process receives an input by time zero (synchronous start), since otherwise the state space becomes too large to handle interesting instances. If the timeout task is modeled explicitly, then many *alive* messages must be sent every computation step, which results in an overly complex model. Using properties A_1 and A_2, however, the explicit sending of *alive* messages can be abstracted away.

5.1   Modeling the Algorithm

Figure 7 shows the UPPAAL template of the behavior of the algorithm. This template is parameterized with two constants, namely its unique identifier *id*, and a boolean *mayFail* which indicates whether this process may fail[7].

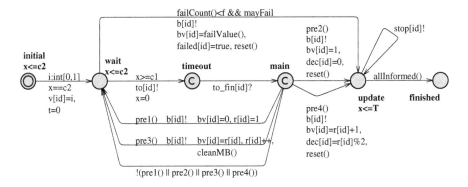

Fig. 7. The process template

Similar to the model of the timeout task, a process first waits c_2 time units in its initial location. Then, it non-deterministically chooses an input value in $\{0,1\}$ on the edge to *wait*. The global clock t is used to measure the running time of the algorithm, and is only reset on this edge. Then it either starts a computation step or fails. A computation step first activates the timeout automaton of the process, which is described below, on the edge to *timeout*. When the timeout automaton finishes (it may have updated the *halted* set), the edge to *main* is taken. Then there are five possibilities: one of the four preconditions of the main task transitions is satisfied (note that they are all mutually exclusive), or none of them is satisfied. In the first case, the specified actions are taken, and in the second case nothing is done. The committed locations (those with a "C"

---

[7] Again, this is a trick that exploits the symmetry of processes to reduce the reachable state space.

inside) specify that a computation step is atomic and that it takes no time (if a committed location is active, then no delay is allowed and the next action transition must involve a committed component). Note that broadcasting the message (m, i) is achieved by assigning m to $bv[id]$ on an edge with a $b[id]$-synchronization. Figure 8 shows the functions that implement the preconditions of the four transitions of the main task (see also Figure 2).

```
bool pre1 ()                          bool pre2 ()
{                                     {
  return r[id]==0 && v[id]==1;          return r[id]==0 && v[id]==0;
}                                     }

bool pre3 ()                          bool pre4 ()
{                                     {
  if (r[id]<=0)                         if (r[id]<=0 || pre3())
    return false;                         return false;
  for (j:pid_t)                         for (j:pid_t)
    if (buff[id][r[id]][j])              if (!halted[id][j] &&
      return true;                          !buff[id][r[id]-1][j])
  return false;                            return false;
}                                       return true;
                                      }
```

Fig. 8. The preconditions for the four transitions of the main task

A failure is modeled by the edge from *wait* to *update*. This edge is only enabled if fewer than f failures already have occurred. The *failValue()* function computes the value that would have been broadcast during the next computation step.

In location *update* the process has halted either by decision or by failure. It can stay there for a maximum of T time units and it provides a *stop[id]*-synchronization. This is used for the abstraction of the timeout task, which is explained below. When all other processes have been informed that this process has halted (*allInformed()* returns *true*), then the transition to location *finished* is enabled.

Similar to the model of the timeout task, the broadcasts are modeled by instances of the broadcast template which is shown in Figure 9.

The template is parameterized with two constants, namely *id*, the identifier of the process automaton this broadcast automaton belongs to, and *bid*, an identifier that is unique among the other broadcast automata of process au-

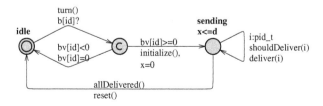

Fig. 9. The broadcast template

tomaton *id*. The broadcast automaton is started – if it is its turn[8] – with a
b[id]-synchronization. If the value of *bv[id]* is smaller than zero, then nothing
is done (this is convenient for modeling in the process template). In location
sending it starts delivering the message that has been passed to it in *bv[id]*. The
shouldDeliver() and *allDelivered()* functions ensure that it delivers all messages
on time, but only if necessary. I.e., it is not useful to deliver a message to a process that already has halted, since that message is never used; it only increases
the reachable state space.

Each process automaton has a separate timeout automaton that has two
functions. First, it is activated at the beginning of each computation step of the
process it belongs to in order to update the *halted* set of the process. Second,
it serves as a test automaton to ensure that the process it belongs to is output
enabled[9]. The timeout template is shown in Figure 10. It has one parameter,
namely the constant *id*, which refers to the process it belongs to.

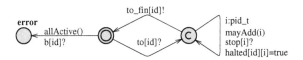

Fig. 10. The timeout template

When a timeout process is activated, it non-deterministically picks a subset of
processes that have halted and adds them to the *halted* set. Here properties A_1
and A_2 of the timeout task come in. The function *mayAdd()* checks for a given
process *j* whether all messages from *j* to this process have been delivered. If not,
then it may not add *j* to *halted* (property A_1). Furthermore, the synchronization
over the channel *stop[j]* must be enabled. In Figure 7 can be seen that this is
only the case for the *T* time units after *j* has halted (property A_2). But if this
process has not added *j* to halted by that time, then *j* cannot proceed to location
finished (in that case *allInformed()* returns *false*), with a time deadlock as result.
This is exactly the case when $T - p_i.x < c_1 - p_j.x$ for processes *i* and *j*. We
believe that this abstraction of the timeout task is safe, i.e., every admissible
computation path in the original model of [14] can be mapped to an equivalent
path in the UPPAAL model.

The second function of the timeout template is implemented by the edge to
the *error* location. This location is reachable if the process wants to broadcast
and all its broadcast automata are active already. In a correct model, the *error*
location therefore is not reachable.

---

[8] Similarly as in the model of the timeout task in the previous section, the guard
turn() partially exploits the symmetry between the broadcast automata of a single
process to reduce the reachable state space.
[9] In this model, the number of necessary broadcast automata is no longer easily to
determine. Therefore, an explicit check is useful.

5.2   Verifying the Algorithm

Properties M_1–M_3 are translated as follows (where U is the upper bound on the running time of the protocol as specified before).

$$Agreement: \ \mathbf{AG}\left(\forall_{i,j} \ dec_i \geq 0 \wedge dec_j \geq 0 \longrightarrow dec_i = dec_j\right) \qquad (3)$$

$$Validity: \ \mathbf{AG}\left(\forall_i \ dec_i \geq 0 \longrightarrow \exists_j \ dec_i = v_j\right) \qquad (4)$$

$$Termination: \ \mathbf{AG}\left((\exists_i \ p_i.wait) \longrightarrow t \leq U\right) \qquad (5)$$

The following properties are health checks to ensure that (i) the processes are output enabled, and (ii) the only deadlocks in the model are those that are expected.

$$\mathbf{AG}\left(\neg\exists_i \ T_i.error\right) \qquad (6)$$

$$\mathbf{AG}\left(deadlock \longrightarrow (\forall_i \ p_i.finished \ \vee \ \exists_{i,j} \ p_j.x - p_i.x > T - c_1)\right) \qquad (7)$$

The properties (3)–(6) have been verified (using the convex-hull approximation of UPPAAL with a breadth-first search order) for the following parameter values[6]:

- $n = 3$, $f \in \{0, 1\}$, $c_1 = 1$, $c_2 = 1$, and $d \in \{0, 1, 2, 3, 5, 10\}$,
- $n = 3$, $f \in \{0, 1\}$, $c_1 = 1$, $c_2 = 2$, and $d \in \{0, 1, 2, 3, 5, 10\}$, and
- $n = 3$, $f \in \{0, 1\}$, $c_1 = 9$, $c_2 = 10$, and $d \in \{5, 9 - 11, 15, 20, 50, 100\}$.

Each of the above instances could be verified within 11 minutes using at most 1014 MB of memory. Property (7) has been verified for a subset of the above parameter values, namely for the models with the three smallest values for d in each item. This property is more difficult to model check since the convex-hull approximation is not useful and it involves the *deadlock* state property, which disables UPPAAL's LU-abstraction algorithm [21] (a less efficient one is used instead), and which is computationally quite complex due to the symbolic representation of states.

6   Conclusions

Despite the fact that model checkers are in general quite easy to use (in the sense that their learning curve is not so steep as for instance the one of theorem provers), making a good model still is difficult. The algorithm that has been analyzed in this paper can easily be modeled "literally". The message complexity then, however, is huge due to the many broadcasts of *alive* messages, with the result that model checking interesting instances becomes impossible. This has been solved by a non-trivial abstraction of the timeout task. Ideally of course, model checkers can even handle such "naive" models. Fortunately, much research still is aimed at improving these tools. For instance, the UPPAAL model checker is getting more and more mature, both w.r.t. usability as efficiency. An example of the former is the recent addition of a C-like language. This makes the modeling of the agreement protocol much easier, and makes the model more efficient. A loop over an array, as for instance used in the *pre3()* and *pre4()* functions shown in Figure 8, can now be encoded with a C-like function instead of using a cycle of committed locations and/or an auxiliary variable. This saves the allocation and deallocation of intermediate states and possibly a state variable. Other examples of efficiency improvements of UPPAAL are enhancements like symmetry reduction [20] and the sweep line method [22], which are planned to be added to UPPAAL soon. Especially symmetry reduction would greatly benefit distributed systems, which often exhibit full symmetry. Furthermore, recent research also focuses on distributing UPPAAL, which may even give a super-linear speed-up [23, 24].

It seems that the class of partially synchronous systems, which is notoriously difficult from the perspective of model checking, now slowly comes within reach of present model checking tools. Therefore, these tools have the potential to play a valuable role in the design of these systems. They may provide valuable early feedback on subtle design errors and hint at system invariants that can subsequently be used in the general correctness proof.

Acknowledgements. The author thanks Frits Vaandrager and Jozef Hooman for valuable discussions and comments on earlier versions of the present paper.

References

1. Lynch, N.A., Tuttle, M.R.: An introduction to Input/Output automata. CWI-Quarterly **2** (1989) 219–246
2. Lynch, N.A., Tuttle, M.R.: Hierarchical correctness proofs for distributed algorithms. In: PODC'87. (1987) 137–151 A full version is available as MIT Technical Report MIT/LCS/TR-387.
3. Lynch, N.A.: Distributed Algorithms. Morgan Kaufmann Publishers (1996)
4. Clarke, E.M., Grumberg, O., Peled, D.A.: Model Checking. The MIT Press (2000)
5. Alur, R., Dill, D.L.: A theory of timed automata. Theoretical Computer Science **126** (1994) 183–235
6. Kaynar, D.K., Lynch, N.A., Segala, R., Vaandrager, F.W.: A framework for modelling timed systems with restricted hybrid automata. In: RTSS'03, IEEE Computer Society Press (2003) 166–177 A full version is available as MIT Technical Report MIT/LCS/TR-917.
7. Tanenbaum, A.S.: Computer Networks. Prentice–Hall (1996)
8. Chkliaev, D., Hooman, J., de Vink, E.: Verification and improvement of the sliding window protocol. In: TACAS'03. Number 2619 in LNCS, Springer–Verlag (2003) 113–127
9. Bodlaender, M., Guidi, J., Heerink, L.: Enhancing discovery with liveness. In: CCNC'04, IEEE Computer Society Press (2004)
10. Katoen, J.P., Bohnenkamp, H., Klaren, R., Hermanns, H.: Embedded software analysis with MOTOR. In: SFM'04. Number 3185 in LNCS, Springer–Verlag (2004) 268–293
11. Bohnenkamp, H., Gorter, J., Guidi, J., Katoen, J.P.: Are you still there? A lightweigth algorithm to monitor node absence in self-configuring networks. In: Proceedings of DSN 2005. (2005)

12. Cheshire, S., Aboba, B., Guttman, E.:   Dynamic configuration of IPv4 link-local addresses (2004) *http://www.ietf.org/internet-drafts/draft-ietf-zeroconf-ipv4-linklocal-17.txt.*
13. Zhang, M., Vaandrager, F.: Analysis of a protocol for dynamic configuration of IPv4 link local addresses using Uppaal. Technical report, NIII, Radboud University Nijmegen (2005) To appear.
14. Attiya, H., Dwork, C., Lynch, N.A., Stockmeyer, L.: Bounds on the time to reach agreement in the presence of timing uncertainty. Journal of the ACM **41** (1994) 122–152
15. Lamport, L.: Real-time model checking is really simple. In Borrione, D., Paul, W., eds.: CHARME 2005. LNCS, Springer (2005) To appear.
16. Behrmann, G., David, A., Larsen, K.G.: A tutorial on Uppaal. In: SFM'04. Volume 3185 of LNCS., Springer (2004) 200–236
17. Bengtsson, J., Yi, W.: Timed automata: Semantics, algorithms and tools. In Desel, J., Reisig, W., Rozenberg, G., eds.: Lectures on Concurrency and Petri Nets: Advances in Petri Nets. Number 3098 in LNCS, Springer–Verlag (2004) 87–124
18. Alur, R., Courcoubetis, C., Dill, D.L.: Model checking in dense real time. Information and Computation **104** (1993) 2–34
19. Dill, D.L.: Timing assumptions and verification of finite-state concurrent systems. In: Automatic Verification Methods for Finite State Systems. Number 407 in LNCS, Springer–Verlag (1989) 197–212
20. Hendriks, M., Behrmann, G., Larsen, K.G., Niebert, P., Vaandrager, F.W.: Adding symmetry reduction to Uppaal. In: FORMATS'03. Number 2791 in LNCS, Springer–Verlag (2004) 46–59
21. Behrmann, G., Bouyer, P., Larsen, K.G., Pelánek, R.: Lower and upper bounds in zone based abstractions of timed automata. In: TACAS'04. Number 2988 in LNCS, Springer–Verlag (2004) 312–326
22. Christensen, A., Kristensen, L.M., Mailund, T.: A sweep-line method for state space exploration. In: TACAS'01. Number 2031 in LNCS, Springer–Verlag (2001) 450–464
23. Behrmann, G., Hune, T., Vaandrager, F.W.: Distributed timed model checking – how the search order matters. In: CAV'00. Number 1855 in LNCS, Springer–Verlag (2000) 216–231
24. Behrmann, G.: Distributed reachability analysis in timed automata. Software Tools for Technology Transfer **7** (2005) 19–30

Diagonal Constraints in Timed Automata: Forward Analysis of Timed Systems

Patricia Bouyer, François Laroussinie, and Pierre-Alain Reynier

LSV – CNRS & ENS Cachan – France
{bouyer, fl, reynier}@lsv.ens-cachan.fr

Abstract. Timed automata (TA) are a widely used model for real-time systems. Several tools are dedicated to this model, and they mostly implement a forward analysis for checking reachability properties. Though diagonal constraints do not add expressive power to classical TA, the standard forward analysis algorithm is not correct for this model. In this paper we survey several approaches to handle diagonal constraints and propose a refinement-based method for patching the usual algorithm: erroneous traces found by the classical algorithm are analyzed, and used for refining the model.

1 Introduction

Model checking. The development of reactive, critical or embedded systems requires the use of formal verification methods. Model checking consists in verifying automatically that a model fulfills its specification and has been widely and successfully applied to industrial systems. It is often necessary to consider quantitative informations on time elapsing in both the model description and the property to be verified. Timed automata (TA) have been proposed by Alur and Dill [AD94] to model such real-time systems. Since then, many theoretical results have been obtained: decidability of reachability properties [AD94], model checking for timed temporal logics [ACD93, HNSY94], *etc*.

Reachability in timed automata. Decidability of reachability properties in timed automata is based on the construction of the so-called region automaton, which finitely abstracts behaviours of timed automata [AD94]. However in practice this construction is not implemented, and symbolic on-the-fly algorithms have been proposed to overcome the complexity blow-up induced by timing constraints. These procedures are often based on *zones* and *DBMs* to represent the sets of clock valuations. In particular, an on-the-fly forward reachability algorithm using zones has been developed and implemented in tools like UPPAAL [LPY97] or KRONOS [DOTY96]. Even if timed automata form a decidable class, the exact forward computation may not terminate. To overcome this problem, an *abstraction* operator over zones needs to be used [DT98].

Guards in timed automata. Classical timed automata [AD94] consider only simple constraints $x \sim c$ and *diagonal constraints* $x - y \sim c$. Surprisingly the standard forward reachability algorithm based on zones has been recently shown to be correct only for TA with simple constraints, but not always correct for TA using diagonal constraints [Bou03, BY03]: locations of TA with diagonal constraints may be found reachable by

P. Pettersson and W. Yi (Eds.): FORMATS 2005, LNCS 3829, pp. 112–126, 2005.

the algorithm while they are not! This problem comes from the use of the abstraction operator over zones.

From [AD94, BDGP98] we know that diagonal constraints can be removed from TA. This gives a procedure for verifying TA with diagonal constraints: construct a TA without diagonal constraints and then apply the standard forward analysis algorithm. However, removing diagonal constraints induces a blowup in the size of the model (it is exponential in the number of diagonal constraints). This is clearly too expensive to be used on real-life systems. Moreover diagonal constraints do not always raise wrong diagnosis (only few examples can be found in the literature) and a systematic removal of all diagonal constraints may therefore not be pertinent.

Our contribution. In this paper we propose a refinement-based method which does not systematically remove all diagonal constraints. The core of our method is an algorithm which analyzes an erroneous trace provided by the classical algorithm and selects a set G of diagonal constraints which causes the error. We then remove diagonal constraints of G from the model and re-run the classical algorithm on the refined model.

Outline of the paper. In Section 2 we introduce basic notions of timed automata, forward reachability analysis, zones and abstractions. In Section 3 we survey several approaches to handle diagonal constraints and propose a refinement-based method for patching the usual algorithm. In section 4 we describe our algorithm for selecting pertinent diagonal constraints. For this, we introduce an extension of the DBM data structure which allows us to store information on the dependence of computed zones w.r.t. diagonal constraints. We prove correctness and progress of our refinement-based method.

Proofs are omitted due to lack of space, and can be found in [BLR05].

2   Forward Analysis of Timed Automata

Basic definitions, timed automata. We consider as time domain $\mathbb{T}$ the set $\mathbb{Q}^+$ of non-negative rationals or the set $\mathbb{R}^+$ of non-negative reals. We consider a finite set X of variables, called *clocks*. A *clock valuation* over X is a mapping $v : X \to \mathbb{T}$ that assigns to each clock a time value. The set of all clock valuations over X is denoted $\mathbb{T}^X$. Let $t \in \mathbb{T}$, the valuation $v + t$ is defined by $(v + t)(x) = v(x) + t, \forall x \in X$. For a subset r of X, we denote by $[r \leftarrow 0]v$ the valuation such that for each $x \in r$, $([r \leftarrow 0]v)(x) = 0$ and for each $x \in X \setminus r$, $([r \leftarrow 0]v)(x) = v(x)$.

Given a set of clocks X, we introduce two sets of clock constraints over X. The most general one, denoted by $\mathcal{C}(X)$, is defined by the grammar "$g ::= x \sim c \mid x - y \sim c \mid g \wedge g \mid \mathtt{tt}$" where $x, y \in X$, $c \in \mathbb{Z}$, $\sim \in \{\leq, =, \geq\}$ and $\mathtt{tt}$ stands for true. We also use the proper subset $\mathcal{C}_{df}(X)$ of *diagonal-free* constraints where the constraints of the form $x - y \sim c$ (called *diagonal constraints*) are not allowed. To simplify, we do not consider strict inequalities, but everything presented in this paper extends easily to strict inequalities. We write $v \models g$ when the clock valuation v satisfies the clock constraint g. A clock constraint is said k-*bounded* whenever it only uses constraints with constants between $-k$ and $+k$.

A *timed automaton* (TA for short) over $\mathbb{T}$ is a tuple $\mathcal{A} = (\Sigma, X, L, \ell_0, T)$, where Σ is a finite alphabet of actions, X is a finite set of clocks, L is a finite set of locations,

$\ell_0 \in L$ is the initial location, and $T \subseteq L \times [\mathcal{C}(X) \times \Sigma \times 2^X] \times L$ is a finite set of edges (or transitions). If only diagonal-free constraints are used on transitions, the timed automaton is said to be *diagonal-free*. A *state* of $\mathcal{A}$ is a pair $\langle \ell, v \rangle$ where $\ell \in L$ is the current location and $v \in \mathbb{T}^X$ represents the current values of clocks. The initial state is $\langle \ell_0, v_0 \rangle$ where v_0 is the valuation mapping all clocks in X to 0. The semantics of $\mathcal{A}$ can be described as an infinite transition system whose states are states of $\mathcal{A}$ and whose transitions correspond to time elapsing followed by an enabled edge in $\mathcal{A}$. More precisely, from a state $\langle \ell, v \rangle$, it is possible to reach a state $\langle \ell', v' \rangle$ if there exist $\delta \in \mathbb{T}$ and $(\ell, g, a, r, \ell') \in T$ such that $v + \delta \models g$ and $v' = [r \leftarrow 0](v + \delta)$. Now we can define a *run* of $\mathcal{A}$ as a finite sequence of such steps, it is denoted:

$$\langle \ell_0, v_0 \rangle \xrightarrow[t_1]{g_1, a_1, r_1} \langle \ell_1, v_1 \rangle \xrightarrow[t_2]{g_2, a_2, r_2} \cdots \xrightarrow[t_p]{g_p, a_p, r_p} \langle \ell_p, v_p \rangle$$

where t_i is the amount of time elapsed since state $\langle \ell_0, v_0 \rangle$—the duration of time elapsing in the i-th location is then $\delta_i = t_{i+1} - t_i$. In the following we abstract away names of actions because we will only consider reachability properties.

Reachability in timed automata. Reachability is a fundamental problem in verification. For timed automata, it is stated as follows: given a timed automaton $\mathcal{A}$ and a set of locations L_f, does there exist a run leading to some state $\langle \ell, v \rangle$, with $l \in L_f$? This problem has been proved decidable (and PSPACE-complete) by Alur and Dill [AD94]. The proof is based on the well-known *region* construction: the (infinite) set of states of $\mathcal{A}$ is partitioned into a finite set of regions such that two states which belong to the same region satisfy the same reachability properties.

Algorithms for reachability. In practice the region construction is not used to check reachability properties because the number of regions is too high: it is not abstracted enough to be applied successfully over non-trivial systems. For this purpose, symbolic and on-the-fly algorithms have been proposed and implemented [LPY97]. They use the constraints of $\mathcal{C}(X)$ as symbolic representations for the sets of valuations. In this framework such a constraint is called a *zone* and is usually implemented with DBMs (Difference Bound Matrices [BM83, Dil90]). Backward analysis raises no real problem but forward analysis is more convenient for verifying timed automata with useful features like integer variables. Given a zone Z and an edge $e = (\ell, g, a, r, \ell')$, $\mathsf{Post}(Z, e)$ denotes the zone corresponding to the set $\{[r \leftarrow 0](v+t) \in \mathbb{T}^X \mid v \in Z, t \geq 0, \text{and } v+t \models g\}$. Symbolic transitions can then be defined over *symbolic states* (ℓ, Z) using the $\mathsf{Post}(\cdot)$ operator. The symbolic graph may however be infinite, because constants used in zones may grow for ever. The forward computation does not terminate in general. To avoid this phenomenon, an abstraction operator, called the k-*extrapolation* (k is a constant supposed to be greater than the maximal constant occurring in $\mathcal{A}$), is used at each iteration: $\mathsf{Extra}_k(Z)$ denotes the smallest zone containing Z and defined by a k-bounded clock constraint. Together with inclusion checking (line 9. of the algorithm), this clearly entails the termination of the classical procedure described as Algorithm **FRA** (see Algorithm 1). If a location of L_f is found as reachable, Algorithm **FRA** returns a witness trace (*i.e.* a sequence of consecutive edges).

Completeness and correctness. Obviously, as the k-extrapolation of zones is an overapproximation, this algorithm is complete: any reachable location is found as reachable

---

Algorithm 1. Forward Reachability Analysis – FRA

---

1. Algorithm FRA ($\mathcal{A}$: timed automaton; L_f: set of final locations) {
2.   Define k as the maximal constant appearing in $\mathcal{A}$;
3.   Visited := $\emptyset$;   (⋆ Visited stores the visited states ⋆)
4.   Waiting := $\{(\ell_0,\mathsf{Extra}_k(Z_0))\}$;   (⋆ $Z_0 = \{v_0\}$ ⋆)
5.   Repeat
6.   Get and Remove (ℓ,Z) from Waiting;
7.   If $\ell \in L_f$ (⋆ ℓ is a final location ⋆)
8.   then {Return "Yes" and a witness trace;}
9.   else {If there is no $(\ell,Z') \in$ Visited s.t. $Z \subseteq Z'$ (⋆ inclusion checking ⋆)
10.   then {Visited := Visited $\cup \{(\ell,Z)\}$;
11.   Succ := $\{(\ell',\mathsf{Extra}_k(\mathsf{Post}(Z,e)))\mid e$ edge from ℓ to $\ell'\}$;
12.   Waiting := Waiting $\cup$ Succ;}}
13.   Until (Waiting = $\emptyset$);
14.   Return "No"; }

---

by the algorithm. The correctness ("only reachable locations are found as reachable by the algorithm") is more difficult to state. In [Bou03, BY03], Algorithm FRA has been proved correct for diagonal-free timed automata and it has been shown to be **not correct** for timed automata using also diagonal constraints. Figure 1 illustrates this correctness problem: Algorithm FRA sees location "Error" of $\mathcal{A}$ as reachable whereas it is not (see [BLR05] for details). This problem is not due to the choice of constant k or to the definition of $\mathsf{Extra}_k(\cdot)$: if we replace the operator $\mathsf{Extra}_k(\cdot)$ by any operator $\mathsf{Extra}_K(\cdot)$ for some K or even by any abstraction operator Abs such that for every zone Z, $\mathsf{Abs}(Z)$ is a zone containing Z, and $\{\mathsf{Abs}(Z) \mid Z$ zone$\}$ is finite (to ensure termination of the forward analysis algorithm), then the algorithm will not be correct and will announce state "Error" as reachable in $\mathcal{A}$ (see [Bou04]).

Extrapolation and zones. As explained above, zones are a suitable symbolic representation for clock valuations but contrary to what is sometimes assumed, zones are

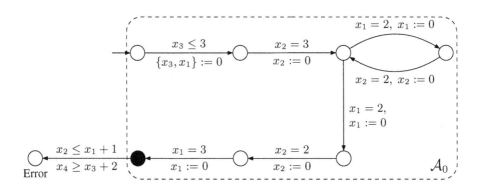

Fig. 1. Automaton $\mathcal{A}$

not a symbolic way of handling regions: there is indeed no simple correspondence between zones and (sets of) regions, which explains the correctness problem encountered in Algorithm FRA. For example, in the diagonal-free case, there exist k-bounded zones which are strictly included in a region. Concerning models with diagonal constraints, one can compute (using Algorithm FRA) a zone Z such that there is a region R with $Z \cap R = \emptyset$ while $\mathsf{Extra}_k(Z) \cap R \neq \emptyset$. Such a phenomenon appears for example in the automaton of Figure 1. This emphasizes the fact that we have always to be careful when handling regions and zones, and to separately consider methods based on regions and methods based on zones. This seems related to abstraction problems encountered in the verification of infinite-state systems, and we will use classical refinement techniques [CGJ+00] to solve our problem.

3   Methods for Handling Diagonal Constraints

Our aim is to propose an efficient forward algorithm based on zones for checking reachability properties in timed automata with diagonal constraints. We can distinguish two main approaches. First there are the ones based on a systematic removal of diagonal constraints: the original TA is replaced by a diagonal-free TA and a standard algorithm is then applied. Secondly there are methods in which diagonal constraints are treated only when they induce spurious traces: if the constraints generate no problem, then these methods provide no extra-cost compared with the standard reachability algorithm. This last criterion is very important because there are only few problematic cases.

3.1   Systematic Removal of Diagonal Constraints

It is well known that given a TA $\mathcal{A}$ with diagonal constraints, it is possible to build a diagonal-free TA $\mathcal{A}'$ s.t. $\mathcal{A}$ and $\mathcal{A}'$ verify the same reachability properties [BDGP98]. This construction combined with the classical reachability algorithm for diagonal-free TA provides a correct forward algorithm for TA, and such a method avoids the expensive region automaton construction. Nevertheless removing diagonal constraints entails a complexity blow-up: if n is the number of diagonal constraints in $\mathcal{A}$, the size of $\mathcal{A}'$ is in $\mathcal{O}(|\mathcal{A}| \cdot 2^n)$. This approach is clearly too expensive, especially if we assume that diagonal constraints mostly raise no error.

Intuitively, if we want to avoid problems with diagonal constraints, it seems sufficient to ensure the following property: $\forall Z$ computed, $\forall g$ diagonal, $Z \subseteq g \lor Z \subseteq \neg g$ ($*$). The method proposed by Bengtsson and Yi in [BY04] relies on this criterion: after each application of the extrapolation operator, the zone which is obtained is split so that Property ($*$) holds. Like the construction of [BDGP98], this solution suffers from an exponential blow-up of the number of zones visited during the computation. Indeed, the complexity of Algorithm FRA crucially depends on the number of zones which need to be handled, and with both two previous methods, the number of zones is multiplied by 2^n, where n is the number of diagonal constraints of the initial automaton.

Finally we could also restrict the removal of the two previous methods to the *active* diagonal constraints in the current control location, following the idea proposed for clocks by Daws and Yovine in [DY96], and generalized in [BBFL03].

Note that all these methods induce a complexity blow-up even if there is no false-positive execution. Indeed, timed automata with diagonal constraints are exponentially more succinct than diagonal-free timed automata [BC05].

3.2 Target Methods for Spurious Traces

In this case, the aim is to develop special heuristics when a false-positive is found. This would permit to have algorithms as efficient as the standard one when there is no problem with diagonal constraints.

First note that given a symbolic execution, it is easy to check whether it is consistent (*i.e.* whether a corresponding run actually exists in $\mathcal{A}$) or if it is a *false positive*. This can be done by using a forward computation with no extrapolation (the finiteness of the execution ensures termination).

Therefore a natural (but wrong!) method could be: (1) use the standard reachability algorithm, (2) if a location is found reachable through a symbolic execution ρ, check whether ρ is a false positive, (3) if ρ is a false positive, run further the algorithm. But this procedure is not complete: some reachable locations may be missed by this algorithm. For example, assume that a false positive contains a symbolic state (ℓ, Z), and assume that later in the algorithm, a symbolic state (ℓ, Z') is computed with $Z' \subseteq Z$. Because of the inclusion checking, Algorithm FRA will stop the computation, whereas it is possible that a valid run goes through symbolic state (ℓ, Z'): inclusion between extrapolated zones does not imply inclusion between exact zones (see [BLR05] for an example). On the other hand, removing states of the false positive trace from the list of visited states could prevent termination of the computation.

We now consider two methods that extend this idea in order to have a complete and correct algorithm.

Combining forward and backward computation. Since diagonal constraints are correctly handled with the backward computation, a possible approach consists in combining forward and backward computations. This algorithm works in two steps. First one performs a forward analysis: If a location is found reachable with a correct execution, the algorithm stops; If a false-positive execution is found, it is stored in the visited states list and the algorithm continues. At the end of the first step, either a correct execution has been found (and the answer is YES), or no spurious execution has been found (and the answer is NO), otherwise the second step begins. It consists in a backward computation from the target states of the spurious executions. This backward computation is restricted to the set of visited states computed in the first step. Such a method would work, but it has an important drawback: the backward computation does not handle additional data: in UPPAAL for ex., it is possible to add integer variables and operations over these data, they can be treated in forward computations but not in backward. This restricts a lot the applicability of the method.

A refinement-based and pure forward method. We now propose to use a refinement-based method (illustrated on Figure 2): (a) use the standard algorithm over a model M, (b) when a false positive ρ is found, refine the model in such a way that ρ will be correctly treated in the refined model M', and (c) restart the procedure over M'. Such a methodology has been proposed in [CGJ$^+$00] and has been applied to many kinds of infinite-state systems (constraint-based programs [HJMS02], hybrid systems [ADI03], *etc*). In our case, a refinement step will consist in removing some diagonal constraints of the initial automaton. Termination is clearly ensured if at least one diagonal constraint is selected at each iteration. As removing diagonal constraints is expensive, the key idea is to refine w.r.t. diagonal constraints only if it is necessary: when a false positive ρ is found, we want to find as few diagonal constraints as possible such that if we remove these diagonal constraints in the model, then the same false positive will not be found again by Algorithm FRA. Selecting pertinent diagonal constraints is the core of our algorithm and will be presented in the next section. We now briefly present the refinement step of our algorithm.

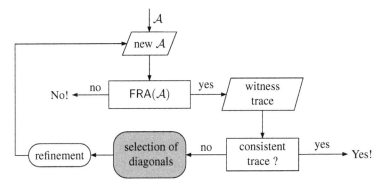

Fig. 2. Refinement-based method

Refinement w.r.t. a constraint g. Given a TA $\mathcal{A} = (\Sigma, X, L, \ell_0, T)$ and a diagonal constraint $g = (x - y \sim c)$, we consider the method proposed in [BDGP98] to remove g from $\mathcal{A}$: the truth value of g is encoded into locations of the refined automaton $\mathcal{A}_g$. This boolean value is not changed by time elapsing, it can only be modified by a reset of x or y. Locations of $\mathcal{A}_g$ are pairs (ℓ, ϵ) with $\ell \in L$ and $\epsilon \in \{\top, \bot\}$, and edges are directly derived from those of $\mathcal{A}$: they either relate locations with the same or opposite truth value depending on the reset of the corresponding edge in $\mathcal{A}$, and the occurrences of the guard $x - y \sim c$ are just replaced by their truth value in the current location. This construction can be directly extended to a set of diagonal constraints. If G is a finite set of diagonal constraints and $\mathcal{A}$ a TA, we note $\mathsf{Split}(\mathcal{A}, G)$ the TA which is obtained after refinement w.r.t. the constraints in G.

4   Diagonal Constraint Analysis

We assume a timed automaton $\mathcal{A} = (\Sigma, X, L, \ell_0, T)$ is given, and we set n the cardinal of set X. Let k be an integer greater than the maximal constant occurring in $\mathcal{A}$. Let $\mathsf{Diag}(\mathcal{A})$ be the set of diagonal constraints occurring in the guards of $\mathcal{A}$. In this section, we propose an algorithm which, given an erroneous trace ρ, selects a set of diagonal guards $G \subseteq \mathsf{Diag}(\mathcal{A})$ which satisfies the two following conditions: (i) $G \neq \emptyset$, and (ii) in $\mathsf{Split}(\mathcal{A}, G)$, the erroneous trace ρ doesn't exist anymore. Condition (i) ensures termination of the refinement method (as $\mathsf{Diag}(\mathcal{A})$ is a finite set), and condition (ii) is a *progress* condition: a given erroneous path will never be found twice.

Of course, the set of all diagonal guards appearing along the erroneous trace satisfies both conditions. But our aim is to select as few guards as possible. Our algorithm builds a possibly much smaller set of guards, and it does not increase the complexity: it is linear in the length of the run, like the consistency checking.

4.1 Erroneous Traces

Algorithm **FRA** returns a witness trace whenever a final state is found as reachable (a *trace* ρ is a sequence of consecutive edges of $\mathcal{A}$). Such a trace is *erroneous* whenever no real run follows the same edges as the trace. To formalize this notion, we associate with a trace ρ two zones: the zone Z_ρ^e which corresponds to all valuations which are reachable following trace ρ, and Z_ρ^a which corresponds to all valuations which are found as reachable when applying the abstract symbolic computation [1] along ρ. We can define these two families of zones inductively as follows. For the empty trace (denoted ϵ), $Z_\epsilon^e = Z_\epsilon^a = \{v_0\}$, and if ρ is a trace and α an edge such that $\rho.\alpha$ is also a trace, we have $Z_{\rho.\alpha}^e = \mathsf{Post}(Z_\rho^e, \alpha)$, and $Z_{\rho.\alpha}^a = \mathsf{Extra}_k(\mathsf{Post}(Z_\rho^a, \alpha))$. Note that the zones defined here only depend on ρ and not on automaton $\mathcal{A}$. A trace ρ is said *erroneous* (we also say that it is a *false positive*) for $\mathcal{A}$ when $Z_\rho^e = \emptyset$ whereas $Z_\rho^a \neq \emptyset$.

Algorithm **FRA** is correct for diagonal-free timed automata. Thus, if ρ is an erroneous trace, there must exist some diagonal guard along ρ which is the cause of the error. One hope could be that when the exact and the abstract computations disagree, the last guard encountered is diagonal (as it is the case for the automaton in Figure 1), and that it is sufficient to refine $\mathcal{A}$ w.r.t. this guard to get rid of the erroneous trace. This is however not the case: this guard can be a simple non diagonal constraint. Automaton in Figure 3 illustrates this point ($\mathcal{A}_0$ refers to the automaton depicted on Figure 1): the last transition, whose guard is non-diagonal, leads to an empty exact computation while the abstract one is not empty. Understanding the role of diagonal constraints along an erroneous trace thus requires a precise analysis of the whole execution.

Fig. 3. The problem occurs on the simple constraint $x_2 \leq 1$

4.2 Propagation of Constraints, the EDBM Data Structure

For analyzing an erroneous trace ρ which is output by Algorithm **FRA**, we will use a forward computation. We want to understand precisely the effect of each diagonal constraint and therefore we will study the differences between the zones Z_-^e and Z_-^a. We won't directly reason on these zones but on their representations with DBMs. A

---

[1] e stands for exact and a for abstract.

DBM $M = (m_{i,j})_{0 \leq i,j \leq n}$ is a square matrix of size $n + 1$ (where n is the number of clocks) whose entries belong to $\mathbb{Z} \cup \{\infty\}$. Its semantics is the zone $[\![M]\!] = \{v \in \mathbb{T}^X \mid \forall i, j \quad x_i - x_j \leq m_{i,j}\}$ (we use a clock x_0 assumed to be equal to 0 in order to represent constraints $x_i \sim c$ as a difference constraint $x_i - x_0 \sim c$). To have a non-ambiguous representation of zones by DBMs, we need to compute *normal forms*: it consists in applying Floyd's Algorithm for shortest paths over the implicit weighted oriented graph described by such a matrix (see [Dil90, Bou04] for classical results over DBMs).

As we use a shortest paths algorithm, the values of the entries depend not only on the last guard we intersect but also on other entries. Just as it is done in Floyd's Algorithm in order to compute all shortest paths, we will store the "dependence" of each entry.

For example, if the current zone is $x_2 \leq 5$, and if the next transition of the trace is $\xrightarrow{g,\{x_2\}}$ where g is $x_1 - x_2 \leq 3$, the next zone which is computed is $x_1 \leq 8 \wedge x_2 = 0 \wedge x_1 - x_2 \leq 8$, and we will store that the constraints $x_1 \leq 8$ and $x_1 - x_2 \leq 8$ depend on g (because they are inherited from the intersection of g with $x_2 \leq 5$). On the contrary, the constraint $x_2 = 0$ does not depend on g (it is solely due to the reset of clock x_2). For storing such a dependence information, we need to enrich the DBMs, we thus define the EDBM data structure:

Definition 1 (Extended DBM — EDBM). *An* extended DBM *is a pair* $(M, \mathcal{S})$ *of square matrices of size* $n + 1$ *where* M *is a classical DBM and* $\mathcal{S}$ *is a matrix whose entries are non-empty sets of subsets of* $\mathsf{Diag}(\mathcal{A})$.

Let $(M, \mathcal{S})$ be an EDBM with $M = (m_{i,j})_{i,j=0...n}$ and $\mathcal{S} = (\mathcal{S}_{i,j})_{i,j=0...n}$. This EDBM represents the same zone as M, and the set $\mathcal{S}_{i,j}$ informally contains all diagonal guards on which entry $m_{i,j}$ may depend. In a weighted graph, it may exist several shortest paths between two vertices. The same holds for dependence sets: the set $\mathcal{S}_{i,j}$ may contain several subsets of $\mathsf{Diag}(\mathcal{A})$, each one contains sufficient information on the dependence of $m_{i,j}$ w.r.t. diagonal guards. Each set $G \in \mathcal{S}_{i,j}$ will be a candidate set for the refinement step whenever entry $m_{i,j}$ is detected as non correct. We store every possible set so as to choose the minimal (*i.e.* smallest) one at the end.

Operations on EDBMs. Given a constraint g, we use $Set(g)$ to denote $\{\{g\}\}$ if g is diagonal and $\{\emptyset\}$ otherwise. We first define the two following basic operations on non-empty sets of sets:

(i) $\mathcal{S}_1 \vee \mathcal{S}_2 = \{G \mid G \in \mathcal{S}_1 \cup \mathcal{S}_2\}$
(ii) $\mathcal{S}_1 \wedge \mathcal{S}_2 = \{G_1 \cup G_2 \mid G_1 \in \mathcal{S}_1 \text{ and } G_2 \in \mathcal{S}_2\}$

We can now extend classical operations on DBMs (needed by Algorithm FRA) to EDBMs. We consider two EDBMs $(M, \mathcal{S})$ and $(M', \mathcal{S}')$ with $M = (m_{i,j})_{i,j=0...n}$, $\mathcal{S} = (\mathcal{S}_{i,j})_{i,j=0...n}$, $M' = (m'_{i,j})_{i,j=0...n}$, and $\mathcal{S}' = (\mathcal{S}'_{i,j})_{i,j=0...n}$. We assume in addition that the DBM M is in normal form.

Future. $(M', \mathcal{S}') = \overrightarrow{(M, \mathcal{S})}$ whenever:

$$(m'_{i,j}, \mathcal{S}'_{i,j}) = \begin{cases} (\infty, \{\emptyset\}) & \text{if } j = 0 \\ (m_{i,j}, \mathcal{S}_{i,j}) & \text{otherwise} \end{cases}$$

Reset of clock x_k. $(M', \mathcal{S}') = [x_k \leftarrow 0](M, \mathcal{S})$ whenever

$$(m'_{i,j}, \mathcal{S}'_{i,j}) = \begin{cases} (0, \{\emptyset\}) & \text{if } i, j \in \{0, k\} \\ (m_{i,0}, \mathcal{S}_{i,0}) & \text{if } j = k, \\ (m_{0,j}, \mathcal{S}_{0,j}) & \text{if } i = k, \\ (m_{i,j}, \mathcal{S}_{i,j}) & \text{otherwise} \end{cases}$$

Intersection with $g = (x_k - x_l \leq c)$. $(M', \mathcal{S}') = \mathsf{Inter}((M, \mathcal{S}), g)$ whenever:

$$(m'_{i,j}, \mathcal{S}'_{i,j}) = \begin{cases} (m_{i,j}, \mathcal{S}_{i,j}) & \text{if } m_{i,j} < m \\ (m_{i,j}, \mathcal{S}_{i,j} \lor \overline{\mathcal{S}}) & \text{if } m_{i,j} = m \\ (m, \overline{\mathcal{S}}) & \text{if } m_{i,j} > m \end{cases}$$

where $m = m_{i,k} + c + m_{l,j}$ and $\overline{\mathcal{S}} = \mathcal{S}_{i,k} \wedge \mathsf{Set}(g) \wedge \mathcal{S}_{l,j}$

Note that the intersection operation contains a normalization step in order to tighten every entry w.r.t. the new constraint g. In fact, the resulting DBM M' is in normal form after each of these three operations. Following UPPAAL implementation of forward analysis [BBLP05], these operations are sufficient for computing the exact reachable zones along a trace. Computing successors w.r.t. an edge $\xrightarrow{g,r}$ is done by computing the future, then computing successively the intersection with all atomic guards forming g^2, and finally computing resets of all clocks in r:

$$\ell \xrightarrow{\wedge_{j=1}^{p} g_j, r} \ell' \quad \text{is transformed into} \quad \ell \xrightarrow{Fut.} \xrightarrow{\cap g_1} \cdots \xrightarrow{\cap g_p} \xrightarrow{r \leftarrow 0} \ell'$$

From now on, we decompose in this way every transition and then the whole trace ρ into elementary steps $(\alpha_i)_{i=1\ldots p}$ (even if it is an abuse of notation, we write $\rho = \alpha_1 \ldots \alpha_p$) such that each step is either an intersection with an atomic guard, a reset of clock, or a future operation. This decomposition allows us to consider each atomic guard successively and then to detect the atomic guard causing the error (emptiness is of course due to an intersection). Computing the symbolic execution along ρ then corresponds to applying successively each operation α_i (for $i = 1 \ldots p$). We keep previous notations Z_ρ^e and Z_ρ^a, and we denote $(M_\rho, \mathcal{S}_\rho)$ the EDBM obtained after having applied successively operations α_i to the EDBM $(M_\epsilon, \mathcal{S}_\epsilon)$ where each entry of M_ϵ is 0, whereas each entry of $\mathcal{S}_\epsilon$ is $\{\emptyset\}$. Obviously, for every trace ρ, $[\![M_\rho]\!] = Z_\rho^e$. To ease the reading, we write $M_\rho(i, j)$ (resp. $\mathcal{S}_\rho(i, j)$) the entry (i, j) of the matrix M_ρ (resp. $\mathcal{S}_\rho$). We are now ready for presenting our algorithm which selects diagonal guards for the refinement step.

4.3   Correctness and Progress of the Algorithm

Presentation of the algorithm. Our algorithm for selecting diagonal guards along an erroneous trace is presented as Algorithm 2 and is called Select_guards. At the i-th step of the iteration, the EDBM stored in $(M', \mathcal{S}')$ is the EDBM $(M_{\rho_i}, \mathcal{S}_{\rho_i})$ with $\rho_i = \alpha_1 \ldots \alpha_{i-1}$. As ρ is an erroneous trace, there exists some $1 \leq i \leq p$ such that $[\![M_{\rho_i}]\!] \neq$

---

[2] An atomic guard is a guard of the form $x \sim c$ or $x - y \sim c$ with $\sim \in \{\leq, \geq\}$.
[3] k or l is possibly 0.

Algorithm 2. Selection of diagonal guards – Select_guards

---
1. Algorithm Select_guards ($\rho = \alpha_1 \ldots \alpha_p$ an erroneous trace in $\mathcal{A}$) {
2.   Initialize EDBMs (M, S) and (M', S') to (M_ϵ, S_ϵ);
3. $i := 0$;
4.   Repeat
5. $i := i + 1$;
6. $(M, S) := (M', S')$;
7.   If α_i is the future operation, $(M', S') := \overrightarrow{(M, S)}$;
8.   If α_i is the intersection with g_i, $(M', S') := \mathsf{Inter}((M, S), g_i)$;
9.   If α_i is the reset of clock x, $(M', S') := [x \leftarrow 0](M, S)$;
10.   Until $[\![M']\!] = \emptyset$
11.   Return $\mathcal{S}_{l,k} \wedge Set(g_i)$; }   (⋆ the last α_i is a guard g_i of the form $x_k - x_l \leq c$ ⋆)[3]

$\emptyset$ whereas $[\![M_{\rho_i . \alpha_i}]\!] = \emptyset$. The elementary step α_i is an intersection with some guard $g_i = (x_k - x_l \leq c)$ and we get that $M_{\rho_i}(l, k) + c < 0$ (otherwise $[\![M_{\rho_i . \alpha_i}]\!]$ would not be empty). Note that this inequality does not hold for the abstract computation because $Z^a_{\rho_i . \alpha_i} \neq \emptyset$. As a consequence, we get that the entry (l, k) is not correct in the abstract computation (i.e. in $Z^a_{\rho_i}$). That's why Algorithm Select_guards outputs the dependence set $\mathcal{S}_{\rho_i}(l, k)$, and adds the guard g_i whenever it is a diagonal guard. The refinement step will split the original automaton along all diagonals in some $G \in \mathcal{S}_{\rho'}(l, k) \wedge Set(g_i)$. Note that adding g_i is necessary: consider the automaton in Figure 3 in which the two last transitions are switched; there is no diagonal guard before the last transition. We will now prove correctness of this selection algorithm.

Correctness of the algorithm. If ρ is a trace, and G a subset of $\mathsf{Diag}(\mathcal{A})$, we denote $\rho[G \leftarrow \mathsf{tt}]$ the trace where the transitions labelled by some $g \in G$ are replaced by a transition labelled by the constraint tt. Roughly, the first lemma states that diagonal guards which are not selected by our algorithm are not involved in the computation of the corresponding entry.

Lemma 1. *Let $\mathcal{A}$ be a timed automaton, and ρ a trace in $\mathcal{A}$. Consider a pair (i, j) and a set of diagonal guards G.*

$$\text{If } \left(\exists G_0 \in \mathcal{S}_\rho(i, j) \text{ s.t. } G_0 \cap G = \emptyset \right) \text{ then } M_{\rho[G \leftarrow \mathsf{tt}]}(i, j) = M_\rho(i, j).$$

Proof (Sketch). The proof can be done by induction on the length of the trace ρ. It relies on the fact that all guards which may have been used for computing the current entry have been selected. Therefore, other guards can be removed safely.   □

Our algorithm outputs a set of sets G of diagonal guards, each set G contains candidates for splitting the original automaton during the refinement step. The following proposition states that if there is an erroneous trace in a timed automaton, then each set G which is part of the output of our algorithm is non-empty. This proves correctness of the refinement step: each time we need to refine, we will be able to do so.

Proposition 1. *Let $\mathcal{A}$ be a timed automaton, and ρ an erroneous trace in $\mathcal{A}$. Then* Select_guards(ρ) *does not contain the empty set.*

Proof. The proof is done by contradiction. Suppose this set contains the empty set. Using the previous lemma, we can remove all diagonal constraints appearing along this path and obtain an erroneous path which does not contain any diagonal constraint. This contradicts the correctness of the algorithm in the non-diagonal case.   □

The following proposition states that any set G selected by our algorithm is pertinent w.r.t. ρ. In the refined automaton $\mathsf{Split}(\mathcal{A}, G)$, the guards of G have been removed, and every location of $\mathcal{A}$ is split into $2^{|G|}$ locations so as to encode the truth value of guards in G. The trace ρ in $\mathcal{A}$ corresponds to a set of traces – denoted $\pi_{\mathcal{A},G}(\rho)$ – in $\mathsf{Split}(\mathcal{A}, G)$. The next proposition states that Algorithm **FRA** will not output as a witness trace any $\rho' \in \pi_{\mathcal{A},G}(\rho)$. This is formally expressed as follows:

Proposition 2. *Let $\mathcal{A}$ be a TA, and ρ an erroneous trace in $\mathcal{A}$. Let $G \in \mathsf{Select\_guards}(\rho)$ and $\mathcal{A}' = \mathsf{Split}(\mathcal{A}, G)$. For all $\rho' \in \pi_{\mathcal{A},G}(\rho)$, the abstract computation in $\mathcal{A}'$ for ρ' leads to an empty state, i.e. $Z_{\rho'}^a = \emptyset$.*

Proof. $\rho = \rho_1.\alpha$ is an erroneous trace such that $Z_{\rho_1}^e \neq \emptyset$, $Z_\rho^e = \emptyset$ while $Z_\rho^a \neq \emptyset$. Assume that the entry which is not correct in Z_ρ^a is (l, k). Algorithm $\mathsf{Select\_guards}$ returns $\mathcal{S}_{\rho_1}(l, k) \wedge \mathcal{S}et(g)$ where g is the guard labelling α.

Now consider $\overline{G} = \mathsf{Diag}(\mathcal{A}) \backslash G$. Lemma 1 ensures that the trace $\rho_1[\overline{G} \leftarrow \mathtt{tt}]$ leads in $\mathcal{A}$ to a zone with the same entry (l, k) via an exact forward computation: $M_{\rho_1[\overline{G} \leftarrow \mathtt{tt}]}(l, k) = M_{\rho_1}(l, k)$. Emptiness of Z_ρ^e then implies emptiness of $Z_{\rho[\overline{G} \leftarrow \mathtt{tt}]}^e$.

Let $\mathcal{A}_1$ be the timed automaton obtained from $\mathcal{A}$ by replacing any guard in $\overline{G}$ by $\mathtt{tt}$. The trace $\rho[\overline{G} \leftarrow \mathtt{tt}]$ is a trace of $\mathcal{A}_1$ and it leads also to an empty zone, as for the computation in $\mathcal{A}$, because this depends only on the trace and not on the automaton.

Now let $\mathcal{A}_2$ be $\mathsf{Split}(\mathcal{A}_1, G)$. Any trace ρ_2 in $\pi_{\mathcal{A}_1,G}(\rho[\overline{G} \leftarrow \mathtt{tt}])$ leads, as $\mathcal{A}_1$ along $\rho[\overline{G} \leftarrow \mathtt{tt}]$, to an empty zone: $Z_{\rho_2}^e = Z_{\rho[\overline{G} \leftarrow \mathtt{tt}]}^e = \emptyset$. There is no more diagonal constraint in $\mathcal{A}_2$. Thus, the abstract forward computation along trace ρ_2 leads also to an empty zone: $Z_{\rho_2}^a = \emptyset$.

Clearly $\mathcal{A}_2$ accepts more runs than $\mathcal{A}' = \mathsf{Split}(\mathcal{A}, G)$ because some guards have been replaced by $\mathtt{tt}$. This holds for the exact and the abstract computation. Any trace ρ' in $\pi_{\mathcal{A},G}(\rho)$ thus leads to an empty zone in the abstract computation: $Z_{\rho'}^a = \emptyset$.   □

The two propositions show the correctness of our algorithm for selecting diagonal constraints.

4.4   Comments on the Method

When ρ is an erroneous trace, $\mathsf{Select\_guards}(\rho)$ may output several non-empty sets of diagonal guards. For the refinement step, we can choose any such set. In particular, we can choose the smallest one, so that the refinement is not too expensive.

The key point of the method we propose is the $\mathsf{Select\_guards}$ algorithm because it may avoid the removal of all diagonal constraints. Note that our method is not formally optimal in the sense that it is possible that refining w.r.t. a proper subset of the selected set is sufficient to treat correctly the current trace. However, we may find such a subset with an incremental test: add successively each selected guard until the erroneous trace is eliminated (this procedure is linear in $|\rho|$). It is clearly more efficient than any method consisting in splitting every constraint in $\mathrm{Diag}(\mathcal{A})$, especially because most of the diagonal constraints do not raise wrong diagnosis. For example, as explained in [BY04], they are very useful for modeling scheduling problems (see for example [FPY02]). Such systems contain a lot of diagonal constraints[4] but, as the clocks of these systems are bounded, our algorithm will never find erroneous traces, and no refinement is needed (for this class of models the classical forward algorithm FRA will be correct). Then a systematic splitting is expensive and useless. In [BLR05], we give several examples of computations of Algorithm Select_guards.

The splitting step could be implemented in several ways and we could avoid building explicitly $\mathrm{Split}(\mathcal{A}, G)$. First we could consider on-the-fly techniques where the truth of guards in G are stored using a vector of booleans. Another possibility could be to modify the computation of Post operator in order to integrate the splitting of diagonal constraints.

4.5   Related Work

Several refinement-based methods have already been proposed in the past for timed systems [AIKY95, MRS02, Sor04] and more generally for hybrid systems [ADI03]. In these works the verification process starts assuming there is no timing information in the system, and then, when a spurious trace is found, the system is refined using relevant constraints (or predicates) of this spurious trace. For timed systems, predicates which are used for refining the model are predicates which separate regions, which ensures that the refinement process stops. In those works, abstraction and refinement are used either to avoid computing the regions or to compute the coarsest time-abstract bisimulation [TY01] before verifying the system.

In our work, the aim and the techniques are different. We do not want to propose a verification algorithm fully based on abstraction and refinement, but we want to use the refinement paradigm for patching the classical forward analysis algorithm with no over-cost when no spurious trace is detected. Indeed, this algorithm, which is for example implemented in UPPAAL, has already proven its efficiency in many case studies. Moreover, as this algorithm is correct for TA without diagonal constraints, we select predicates only among the diagonal constraints of the TA we verify.

5   Conclusion

In this paper we have studied the role of diagonal constraints in a forward analysis computation. We have described several approaches to handle diagonal constraints and proposed a refinement-based purely forward method for verifying reachability properties of timed automata with diagonal constraints. As diagonal constraints do not always raise wrong diagnosis, a systematic removal of all diagonal constraints appears as too expensive, and a refinement-based learning from erroneous traces of the classical algorithm seems more appropriate to patch the usual algorithm, as there will be no over-cost if no spurious trace is found. We think that, in practice, the cost of this approach is lower

---

[4] There are n^2 diagonal constraints where n is the number of tasks to be scheduled.

than the cost of the systematic removal of all diagonal constraints. As further developments, we would like to combine techniques we have proposed in this paper with more efficient refinement-based methods, as the lazy abstraction approach of [HJMS02]. We also plan to implement this method and to compare it with other approaches.

References

[ACD93]   Rajeev Alur, Costas Courcoubetis, and David Dill. Model-checking in dense real-time. *Information and Computation*, 104(1):2–34, 1993.

[AD94]   Rajeev Alur and David Dill. A theory of timed automata. *Theoretical Computer Science*, 126(2):183–235, 1994.

[ADI03]   Rajeev Alur, Thao Dang, and Franjo Ivančić. Counter-example guided predicate abstraction of hybrid systems. In *9th International Conference on Tools and Algorithms for the Construction and Analysis of Systems*, volume 2619 of *Lecture Notes in Computer Science*, pages 208–223. Springer, 2003.

[AIKY95]   Rajeev Alur, Alon Itai, Robert P. Kurshan, and Mihalis Yannakakis. Timing verification by successive approximation. *Information and Computation*, 118(1):142–157, 1995.

[BBFL03]   Gerd Behrmann, Patricia Bouyer, Emmanuel Fleury, and Kim G. Larsen. Static guard analysis in timed automata verification. In *Proc. 9th International Conference on Tools and Algorithms for the Construction and Analysis of Systems (TACAS'03)*, volume 2619 of *Lecture Notes in Computer Science*, pages 254–277. Springer, 2003.

[BBLP05]   Gerd Behrmann, Patricia Bouyer, Kim G. Larsen, and Radek Pelànek. Zone based abstractions for timed automata exploiting lower and upper bounds. *Software Tools for Technology Transfer*, 2005. To appear.

[BC05]   Patricia Bouyer and Fabrice Chevalier. On conciseness of extensions of timed automata. *Journal of Automata, Languages and Combinatorics*, 2005. To appear.

[BDGP98]   Béatrice Bérard, Volker Diekert, Paul Gastin, and Antoine Petit. Characterization of the expressive power of silent transitions in timed automata. *Fundamenta Informaticae*, 36(2–3):145–182, 1998.

[BLR05]   Patricia Bouyer, François Laroussinie, and Pierre-Alain Reynier. Diagonal constraints in timed automata — Forward analysis of timed systems. Research Report LSV-05-14, Laboratoire Spécification & Vérification, ENS de Cachan, France, 2005.

[BM83]   Bernard Berthomieu and Miguel Menasche. An enumerative approach for analyzing time Petri nets. In *Proc. IFIP 9th World Computer Congress*, volume 83 of *Information Processing*, pages 41–46. North-Holland/ IFIP, 1983.

[Bou03]   Patricia Bouyer. Untameable timed automata! In *Proc. 20th Annual Symposium on Theoretical Aspects of Computer Science (STACS'03)*, volume 2607 of *Lecture Notes in Computer Science*, pages 620–631. Springer, 2003.

[Bou04]   Patricia Bouyer. Forward analysis of updatable timed automata. *Formal Methods in System Design*, 24(3):281–320, 2004.

[BY03]   Johan Bengtsson and Wang Yi. On clock difference constraints and termination in reachability analysis of timed automata. In *Proc. 5th International Conference on Formal Engineering Methods (ICFEM 2003)*, volume 2885 of *Lecture Notes in Computer Science*, pages 491–503. Springer, 2003.

[BY04]   Johan Bengtsson and Wang Yi. Timed automata: Semantics, algorithms and tools. In *Proc. 4th Advanced Course on Petri Nets (ACPN'03)*, volume 3098 of *Lecture Notes in Computer Science*, pages 87–124. Springer, 2004.

[CGJ⁺00]   Edmund M. Clarke, Orna Grumberg, Somesh Jha, Yuan Lu, and Helmut Veith. Counterexample-guided abstraction refinement. In *Proc. 12th International Conference on Computer Aided Verification (CAV'00)*, volume 1855 of *Lecture Notes in Computer Science*, pages 154–169. Springer, 2000.

[Dil90]   David Dill. Timing assumptions and verification of finite-state concurrent systems. In *Proc. of the Workshop on Automatic Verification Methods for Finite State Systems (1989)*, volume 407 of *Lecture Notes in Computer Science*, pages 197–212. Springer, 1990.

[DOTY96]   Conrado Daws, Alfredo Olivero, Stavros Tripakis, and Sergio Yovine. The tool KRONOS. In *Proc. Hybrid Systems III: Verification and Control (1995)*, volume 1066 of *Lecture Notes in Computer Science*, pages 208–219. Springer, 1996.

[DT98]   Conrado Daws and Stavros Tripakis. Model-checking of real-time reachability properties using abstractions. In *Proc. 4th International Conference on Tools and Algorithms for the Construction and Analysis of Systems (TACAS'98)*, volume 1384 of *Lecture Notes in Computer Science*, pages 313–329. Springer, 1998.

[DY96]   Conrado Daws and Sergio Yovine. Reducing the number of clock variables of timed automata. In *Proc. 17th IEEE Real-Time Systems Symposium (RTSS'96)*, pages 73–81. IEEE Computer Society Press, 1996.

[FPY02]   Elena Fersman, Paul Petterson, and Wang Yi. Timed automata with asynchrounous processes: Schedulability and decidability. In *Proc. 8th International Conference on Tools and Algorithms for the Construction and Analysis of Systems (TACAS'02)*, volume 2280 of *Lecture Notes in Computer Science*, pages 67–82. Springer, 2002.

[HJMS02]   Thomas A. Henzinger, Ranjit Jhala, Rupak Majumdar, and Grégoire Sutre. Lazy abstraction. In *Proc. 29th ACM Symposium on Principles of Programming Languages (POPL'02)*, pages 58–70. ACM Press, 2002.

[HNSY94]   Thomas A. Henzinger, Xavier Nicollin, Joseph Sifakis, and Sergio Yovine. Symbolic model-checking for real-time systems. *Information and Computation*, 111(2):193–244, 1994.

[LPY97]   Kim G. Larsen, Paul Pettersson, and Wang Yi. UPPAAL in a nutshell. *Journal of Software Tools for Technology Transfer (STTT)*, 1(1–2):134–152, 1997.

[MRS02]   M. Oliver Möller, Harald Rueß, and Maria Sorea. Predicate abstraction for dense real-time systems. In *Proc. Theory and Practice of Timed Systems (TPTS'02)*, volume 65(6) of *Electronic Notes in Theoretical Computer Science*, pages 1–20. Elsevier, 2002.

[Sor04]   Maria Sorea. Lazy approximation for dense real-time systems. In *Proc. Joint Conference on Formal Modelling and Analysis of Timed Systems and Formal Techniques in Real-Time and Fault Tolerant System (FORMATS+FTRTFT'04)*, volume 3253 of *Lecture Notes in Computer Science*, pages 363–378. Springer, 2004.

[TY01]   Stavros Tripakis and Sergio Yovine. Analysis of timed systems using time-abstracting bisimulations. *Formal Methods in System Design*, 18(1):25–68, 2001.

A New Verification Procedure for Partially Clairvoyant Scheduling

K. Subramani* and D. Desovski

LDCSEE,
West Virginia University,
Morgantown, WV
{ksmani, desovski}@csee.wvu.edu

Abstract. In this paper, we describe a new algorithm for the problem of checking whether a real-time system has a Partially Clairvoyant schedule (PCS). Existing algorithms for the PCS problem are predicated on sequential quantifier elimination, i.e., the innermost quantifier is eliminated first, followed by the next one and so on. Our technique is radically different in that the quantifiers in the schedulability specification are eliminated in *arbitrary fashion*. We demonstrate the usefulness of this technique by achieving significant performance improvement over a wide range of inputs. Additionally, the analysis developed for the new procedure may find applications in domains such as finite model theory and classical logic.

1 Introduction

The design of Real-time systems mandates the appreciation of uncertainty in problem parameters. A significant concern in the scheduling of jobs in real-time systems is the non-constancy in their execution times. Consider a set of n, *ordered* jobs, $\mathcal{J} = \{J_1, J_2, \ldots, J_n\}$, with start times $\{s_1, s_2, \ldots, s_n\}$ and execution times $\{e_1, e_2, \ldots, e_n\}$. The execution time e_i of job J_i is an interval-valued constant $[l_i, e_i]$, i.e., during a run of the job set, e_i can assume any value in the range $[l_i, u_i]$ and *is not known before the job has finished executing*. The job set executes repeatedly in the same order, in scheduling windows of length L. There exists a set of relative timing constraints between pairs of jobs; the constraint set is expressed through the system

$$\mathbf{A} \cdot [\vec{\mathbf{s}} \; \vec{\mathbf{e}}]^{\mathbf{T}} \leq \vec{\mathbf{b}} \tag{1}$$

where $\mathbf{A}$ is an $m \times 2 \cdot n$ integral matrix, $\vec{\mathbf{b}}$ is an integral m-vector, $\vec{\mathbf{s}} = [s_1, s_2, \ldots, s_n]^T$ is the start time vector of the jobs and $\vec{\mathbf{e}} = [e_1, e_2, \ldots, e_n]^T$ is the execution time vector of the jobs. We only permit strict difference constraints between

---

* The research of this author was conducted in part at the Discrete Algorithms and Mathematics Department of Sandia National Laboratories. Sandia is a multiprogram laboratory operated by Sandia Corporation, a Lockheed-Martin Company, for the U.S. DOE under contract number DE-AC-94AL85000.

P. Pettersson and W. Yi (Eds.): FORMATS 2005, LNCS 3829, pp. 127–141, 2005.

job pairs. These constraints express the "relative distance" relationship between pairs of jobs and are hence known as relative timing constraints. For instance, the following types of constraints are permitted: (a) Job J_3 starts within 3 units of job J_1 finishing: $s_3 \leq s_1 + e_1 + 3$, (b) Job J_5 needs to wait at least 7 units after the conclusion of job J_2, to commence: $s_5 \geq s_2 + e_2 + 7$. Likewise, the requirement that the sum of the start times of the jobs not exceed 10 units of time is not a relative timing constraint. The job set is ordered, i.e., job J_1 starts and finishes before job J_2, which in turn starts and finishes before job J_3 and so on; the ordering constraints, $s_i + e_i \leq s_{i+1}$, $\forall i = 1, 2, \ldots, n - 1$, are part of the constraint system.

In Partially Clairvoyant scheduling, the goal is to check whether a set of jobs, subject to the constraints described by System (1), can be scheduled on the time line, *if* the start time of a job may depend upon the execution times of previously scheduled jobs. Accordingly, the schedulability predicate is:

$$\exists s_1 \forall e_1 \in [l_1, u_1] \ \exists s_2 \forall e_2 \in [l_2, u_2] \ldots \exists s_n \forall e_n \in [l_n, u_n]$$
$$\mathbf{A} \cdot [\vec{\mathbf{s}} \ \vec{\mathbf{e}}]^{\mathbf{T}} \leq \vec{\mathbf{b}} \tag{2}$$

The Partially Clairvoyant Schedulability problem (PCS) is then concerned with verifying the satisfiability of Predicate (2).

On rewriting the constraint system $\mathbf{A} \cdot [\vec{\mathbf{s}} \ \vec{\mathbf{e}}]^{\mathbf{T}} \leq \vec{\mathbf{b}}$ as $\mathbf{G} \cdot \vec{\mathbf{s}} + \mathbf{H} \cdot \vec{\mathbf{e}} \leq \vec{\mathbf{b}}$, we observe that every row in $\mathbf{G}$ has precisely one +1 and one −1; the same is true for $\mathbf{H}$ as well. Additionally, an entry in $\mathbf{H}$ is either equal to the corresponding entry in $\mathbf{G}$, or it is zero. In some ways, $\mathbf{H}$ is a "subset" of $\mathbf{G}$. We call this structure, the "standard" structure. Note that in the standard structure, each universally quantified variable e_i is associated with an existentially quantified variable s_i. We say that e_i corresponds to s_i.

2 Motivation and Related Work

Partially Clairvoyant scheduling (also called *Parametric Scheduling*) was introduced in [GPS95], wherein the first polynomial time algorithm for the PCS problem was proposed. This algorithm, which we shall refer to as the primal approach is based on quantifier elimination over a system of temporal constraints and has a worst case time complexity of $\Theta(n^3)$ and requires $\Theta(n^3)$ space. A dual-based approach (i.e., dual to the approach in [GPS95]), exploiting the network structure of difference constraints was proposed in [Sub03]. The key idea used in the design of the dual algorithm is the fact that a system of strict difference constraints specified for a job set has a Partially Clairvoyant schedule, if and only if the corresponding constraint network does not have a negative Partially Clairvoyant cost cycle. The dual algorithm has the same worst case time complexity as the approach in [GPS95]; however it is more space efficient in that it can be implemented in $\Theta(n^2)$ space. We point out that there has been no attempt in the literature to formally study the empirical performance of algorithms for Partially Clairvoyant Scheduling. The study in this paper is the first of its kind and plays an important role in the identification of practical issues involved in algorithm implementation of quantifier elimination procedures. The Arbitrary Dual algorithm has the same time and space complexity as the dual-based approach, but it permits a lot of flexibility, insofar as eliminating variables is concerned.

Given a quantifier string in which all the quantifiers are existential or all the quantifiers are universal, the order of quantifier elimination is irrelevant. However, in the presence of quantifier alternation, it is well known that the order of quantifier elimination matters; indeed elimination procedures eliminate the innermost variable first, followed by the variable preceding it and so on [Wei97]. It is to be noted that the logic demanding this order requires that the variables be discrete; to the best of our knowledge, the literature has not considered whether quantifier elimination must be sequential, if the variables are continuous. The work in this paper establishes that there exist non-trivial cases, in which quantifier elimination can indeed be conducted in a non-sequential fashion.

3   PCS Algorithms in the Literature

The primal algorithm has been describe and analyzed in detail in [GPS95] and we refer the reader to that article, for the sake of saving space.

3.1   The Dual Algorithm

The dual approach proceeds, by constructing the constraint network $G =< V, R >$ corresponding to a set of n jobs, with standard constraints imposed on their execution, where V is the set of vertices and R is the set of edges. G is constructed as per the following rules:

(a) $V =< s_1, s_2, \ldots, s_n >$, i.e., one node for the start time of each job,
(b) For every constraint of the form: $s_i + k \leq s_j$, construct a Type I arc $r_{ij}^{(1)}$: $s_i \rightsquigarrow s_j$, with weight $w_{ij}^{(1)} = -k$,
(c) For every constraint of the form: $s_i + e_i \leq s_j + k$, construct a Type II arc $r_{ij}^{(2)} : s_i \rightsquigarrow s_j$, with weight $w_{ij}^{(2)} = k - e_i$,
(d) For every constraint of the form: $s_i \leq s_j + e_j + k$, construct a Type III arc $r_{ij}^{(3)} : s_i \rightsquigarrow s_j$, with weight $w_{ij}^{(3)} = e_j + k$,
(e) For every constraint of the form: $s_i + e_i \leq s_j + e_j + k$, construct a Type IV arc $r_{ij}^{(4)} : s_i \rightsquigarrow s_j$, with weight $w_{ij}^{(4)} = e_j - e_i + k$.

The constraint network that is thus constructed, is provided as input to Algorithm (3.1). Algorithm (3.1) proceeds by eliminating one job after another from the constraint set, till either a negative Partially Clairvoyant cost cycle is discovered or all the jobs have been eliminated. In the former case it declares the constraint set to be infeasible from the perspective of obtaining a

Partially Clairvoyant schedule and in the latter case the constraint set is declared feasible. Note that eliminating a job J_i from the constraint set corresponds to eliminating the pair (s_i, e_i) from the constraint network. The correctness of Algorithm (3.1) follows from 2 simple observations: (a) A Partially Clairvoyant system of difference constraints is infeasible if and only if the corresponding constraint network has a cycle of negative Partially Clairvoyant cost, and (b) Algorithm (3.1) detects or preserves negative Partially Clairvoyant cost cycles. Algorithm (3.3) computes the Partially Clairvoyant cost of a cycle.

Function PARTIALLY-CLAIRVOYANT-STANDARD $(G =< V, R >)$
1: **for** $(i = n$ **down to** 1) **do**
2:    $G =$ELIMINATE-JOB (J_i, G).
3: **end for**
4: **return**(A Partially Clairvoyant schedule exists.)

Algorithm 3.1. The dual-based algorithm for Partially Clairvoyant Scheduling

4   The Arbitrary Dual Algorithm

In Algorithm (3.1), job J_i is eliminated before job J_{i-1}, $\forall i = n, n - 1, \ldots, 2$; indeed the ordered elimination was crucial in correctness proof in [Sub03]. On the other hand, Algorithm (4.1) eliminates jobs from the constraint network in arbitrary fashion.

As mentioned before, and as proved in [Sub03], a constraint system has a Partially Clairvoyant schedule, if and only if the corresponding constraint network does not have a Negative Partially Clairvoyant cost (NPCC) cycle. Accordingly, our strategy to prove the correctness of Algorithm (4.1) consists of two parts: Theorem (1) will focus on showing that Step (3) of the algorithm *either preserves or detects NPCC cycles*, while Theorem (2) shows that Step (3) does not create NPCC cycles, if none exist.

Theorem 1. *Step (3) of Algorithm (4.1) preserves or detects NPCC cycles in the constraint network G, i.e., if there exists a NPCC cycle, before the execution of Step (3), then at the execution of Step (3) in Algorithm (4.1), either Step (12) in Algorithm (4.2) is executed, or there exists a NPCC cost cycle, in the constraint network that results.*

Before providing a formal proof of Theorem (1), we briefly sketch the mechanics of the Arbitrary dual algorithm. Algorithm (4.1) chooses an arbitrary sequence of jobs to be eliminated from the constraint network. We stress that eliminating job J_i from the constraint network, involves the elimination of both its start time s_i and execution time e_i. Consequently, the elimination of J_i from G preserves the relative timing constraint structure ("standard" structure) of the constraint network, in that every edge between a pair of vertices in the new network continues to represent a standard constraint between the corresponding jobs. In other words, Algorithm (4.1) is incremental in nature.

Function ELIMINATE-JOB $(J_i, G =< V, R >)$
1: Let S_{in} denote the set of edges that are directed into vertex s_i.
2: Let S_{out} denote the set of edges that are directed from vertex s_i.
3: {Note that edges of different types, between the same pair of vertices are treated as distinct edges; in order to simplify the notation we do not explicitly mention the types of edges.}
4: **for** (each edge $r_{ki} \in S_{in}$) **do**
5:    Adjust w_{ki} to reflect the substitution $e_i = l_i$
6:    **for** (each edge $r_{ij} \in S_{out}$) **do**
7:       Adjust w_{ij} to reflect the substitution $e_i = u_i$
8:       Create a new edge r'_{kj} with cost $w'_{kj} = w_{ki} + w_{ij}$
9:       **if** $(k = j)$ **then**
10:          {A cycle has been detected}
11:          **if** $(w'_{kj} < 0)$ **then**
12:             **return**(A Partially Clairvoyant schedule does not exist).
13:          **else**
14:             Discard r_{kj}. {Self-loops are deleted from the constraint network.}
15:             **continue**
16:          **end if**
17:       **end if**
18:       **if** (there exists an edge r_{kj} in G of the same type as r'_{kj}, having smaller weight) **then**
19:          Discard r'_{kj}
20:       **else**
21:          {Either no edge r_{kj} of the same type as r'_{kj} existed, in which case, we assume that there exists an edge with weight $w_{kj} = \infty$, or the weight of the existing edge was greater than w'_{kj}. In either case, r'_{kj} replaces the existing edge.}
22:          Set $r_{kj} = r'_{kj}$ with weight $w_{kj} = w'_{kj}$.
23:       **end if**
24:    **end for**
25: **end for**
26: Let G' denote the new network after all the above changes have been carried out.
27: **return**(G')

Algorithm 3.2. Eliminating job J_i from the constraint network

At the heart of the ELIM-ARBITRARY-JOB() procedure, and therefore at that of Algorithm (4.1), is the DETERMINE-FEASIBILITY() procedure. This procedure takes as input a constraint network, having precisely 2 vertices and 2 edges and checks whether there is a NPCC cycle in this network. It is important to note that the function DETERMINE-FEASIBILITY() eliminates jobs in the correct order, i.e., the higher numbered job before the lower numbered job. Thus, the predicate

$$\exists s_i \forall e_i \in [l_i, u_i] \exists s_k \forall e_k \in [l_k, u_k] \ G$$

is checked in case $(i < k)$; otherwise, we check the predicate

$$\exists s_k \forall e_k \in [l_k, u_k] \exists s_i \forall e_i \in [l_i, u_i] \ G$$

Function COMPUTE-PARTIALLY-CLAIRVOYANT-COST $(C, \{i_1, i_2, \ldots, i_k\})$

1: $\{C$ is a cycle on the vertices $\{i_1, i_2, \ldots, i_k\}$ The list $< i_1, i_2, \ldots, i_k >$ is a list of vertex indices, with each $i_j \in \{1, 2, \ldots, n\}$, $j = 1, 2, \ldots, k$. Without loss of generality, we assume that $i_1 < i_2 < \ldots < i_k.\}$
2: **if** $(k = 2)$ **then**
3:    $\{$Since C is a simple cycle, there are precisely 2 vertices and 2 edges in C; further, there is precisely one edge into vertex s_{i_2} and one edge into s_{i_1}. Adjust weight $w_{i_2 i_1}$ to reflect the substitution $e_{i_2} = u_{i_2}$ and weight $w_{i_1 i_2}$ to reflect the substitution $e_{i_2} = l_{i_2}.\}$
4:    Let $cost = w_{i_1 i_2} + w_{i_2 i_1}$.
5:    Adjust $cost$ to reflect the substitution $e_{i_1} = u_{i_1}$ if $cost$ is a decreasing function of e_{i_1} and $e_{i_1} = l_{i_1}$ otherwise. $\{$It is important to note that if e_{i_1} appears in $cost$, it is either as e_{i_1} or as $-e_{i_1}.\}$
6:    **return**($cost$)
7: **else**
8:    $\{$We eliminate s_{i_k} from the cycle.$\}$
9:    Let s_{i_p} and s_{i_q} denote the vertices in C to which s_{i_k} is connected; further, we assume that the edges of C are $s_{i_p} \leadsto s_{i_k}$ and $s_{i_k} \leadsto s_{i_q}$.
10:    Adjust $w_{i_p i_k}$ to reflect the substitution $e_{i_k} = l_{i_k}$ and $w_{i_k i_q}$ to reflect the substitution $e_{i_k} = u_{i_k}$.
11:    Create a new edge $s_{i_p} \leadsto s_{i_q}$ having weight $w_{i_p i_q} = w_{i_p i_k} + w_{i_k i_q}$.
12:    $\{$Since C is a cycle, there did not exist an edge from s_{i_p} to s_{i_q} prior to the above step.$\}$
13:    Let C' denote the new cycle, thus created.
14:    **return**(COMPUTE-PARTIALLY-CLAIRVOYANT-COST $(C, \{i_1, i_2, \ldots, i_{k-1}\})$.)
15: **end if**

Algorithm 3.3. Computing the Partially Clairvoyant cost of a simple, directed cycle

---

Function ARBITRARY-DUAL $(G =< V, R >)$

1: Consider an arbitrary permutation π of the set $\{1, 2, \ldots, n\}$.
2: **for** $(i = 1$ **down to** $n)$ **do**
3:    $G =$ELIMINATE-ARBITRARY-JOB $(J_{\pi(i)}, G)$.
4: **end for**
5: **return** (A Partially Clairvoyant schedule exists.)

Algorithm 4.1. The Arbitrary Dual algorithm for Partially Clairvoyant Scheduling

In other words, for constraint networks having precisely 2 vertices and 2 edges, we call PARTIALLY-CLAIRVOYANT-STANDARD() to eliminate jobs in the correct order; it follows from [Sub03], that DETERMINE-FEASIBILITY() returns (**true**) if and only if the $2-$vertex, $2-$edge input constraint network G *does not* contain a NPCC cycle. Note that the constraint network G that is input to DETERMINE-FEASIBILITY() is an ordered, directed cycle of length 2.

Function ELIMINATE-ARBITRARY-JOB $(J_i,\ G =<V, R>)$

1: Let S_{in} denote the set of edges that are directed into vertex s_i.
2: Let S_{out} denote the set of edges that are directed out of vertex s_i.
3: **for** (each edge $r_{ki} \in S_{in}$) **do**
4:    **for** (each edge $r_{ij} \in S_{out}$) **do**
5:      **if** ($k = j$) **then**
6:        $\{s_k \rightsquigarrow s_i \rightsquigarrow s_k$ is a cycle$\}$
7:        Construct a 2-vertex network G^2 with vertices labeled s_i and s_k and edges r_{ki} and r_{ik}.
8:        **if** (DETERMINE-FEASIBILITY(G^2, i, k) **then**
9:          $\{$This constraint pair does not create infeasibility$\}$
10:           **continue**
11:        **else**
12:           **return**(A Partially Clairvoyant schedule does not exist).
13:        **end if**
14:      **end if**
15:      $\{$The following portion is executed only if $k \neq j$.$\}$
16:      **if** $((k > i)$ and $(j > i))$ **then**
17:        Create a new edge r'_{kj} with weight $w'_{kj} = w_{ki} + w_{ij}$.
18:        Adjust w'_{kj} to reflect the substitution $e_i = u_i$, if w'_{kj} is a decreasing function of e_i and $e_i = l_i$ otherwise. $\{$Note that due to the nature of the constraint system, e_i will appear in w_{kj} either as e_i or as $-e_i$. Further, w'_{kj} is a standard weight in that it is a function of the execution times e_k and e_j only and not e_i.$\}$
19:        GRAPH-INSERT(G, r'_{kj})
20:        **continue**
21:      **end if**
22:      $\{$The following portion is executed, only if $j \neq k$ and at least one of j and k is less than i.$\}$
23:      Adjust w_{ki} to reflect the substitution $e_i = l_i$; Adjust w_{ij} to reflect the substitution $e_i = u_i$.
24:      Create a new edge r'_{kj} with cost $w'_{kj} = w_{ki} + w_{ij}$. $\{r'_{kj}$ now represents a strict difference constraint between the jobs J_j and J_k.$\}$
25:      GRAPH-INSERT(G, r'_{kj})
26:      $\{$This completes the process of adjusting the constraint network to account for the new constraints which are created as a result of the elimination.$\}$
27:    **end for**
28: **end for**
29: Let G' be the network that results after the above changes have been carried out.
30: $\{$Observe that the standard constraint structure is preserved in that G' also represents an instance of a Partially Clairvoyant Scheduling problem, albeit with fewer jobs$\}$
31: **return**(G')

Algorithm 4.2. Eliminating job J_i from the constraint network in the Arbitrary approach

---

Function GRAPH-INSERT (G, r'_{kj})
1: {We are inserting the standard constraint represented by r'_{kj} into the constraint
    network G.}
2: **if** (there exists an edge r_{kj} in G of the same type as r'_{kj}, having smaller weight)
    then
3:    Discard r'_{kj}.
4: **else**
5:    {Either no edge r_{kj} of the same type as r'_{kj} existed, in which case, we assume
      that there exists an edge with weight $w_{kj} = \infty$, or the weight of the existing
      edge was greater than w'_{kj}. In either case, r'_{kj} replaces the existing edge.}
6:    Set $r_{kj} = r'_{kj}$ with weight $w_{kj} = w'_{kj}$.
7: **end if**

Algorithm 4.3. Inserting edge r'_{kj} into the constraint network

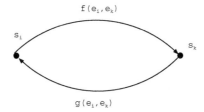

Fig. 1. Arbitrary dual on a 2-vertex network

Now consider the sequence of events when an arbitrary job, J_i, is eliminated from the constraint network by the ELIMINATE-ARBITRARY-JOB() procedure. Steps (5) through (14) of this algorithm focus on identifying NPCC cycles of length 2, by feeding constraint networks having precisely 2 vertices and 2 edges (i.e., ordered, directed cycles) to DETERMINE-FEASIBILITY(). If none of these constraint networks *is* a NPCC cycle, we know that there are no NPCC cycles of length 2, involving J_i in the current constraint network.

Pick any NPCC cycle (say C) of length greater than 2, involving J_i. Let s_a denote the vertex with the edge directed into s_i and let s_b denote the vertex with the edge directed out of s_i. Observe that if both $a > i$ and $b > i$, then when evaluating the Partially Clairvoyant cost of C, it is necessary for the variable e_i to remain unsubstituted till s_i is contracted; in all other cases, e_i needs to be substituted before the contraction of s_i. This is precisely what is achieved by Steps (16) through (24) of Algorithm (4.2).

We now provide a formal proof of the correctness of Algorithm (4.1).

Proof (of Theorem (1)): We use induction on the number of jobs, n, i.e., the number of vertices in the constraint network G. Note that the base case of the induction is $n = 2$, since there can be no constraints in the case of a job set with a single job. Recall that we permit relative timing constraints only and hence every constraint involves a pair of jobs.

Consider the constraint network corresponding to a set of 2 jobs. As per the construction procedure outlined in Section §3.1, the corresponding constraint network contains 2 vertices s_1 and s_2. We need to consider the following 2 cases:

(a) Job J_2, i.e, vertex s_2 is chosen first for contraction - In this case, we note that Algorithm (4.1) is identical to Algorithm (3.1) and its correctness follows from the correctness of Algorithm (3.1).

(b) Job J_1, i.e., vertex s_1 is chosen first for contraction - In this case, Steps (5) through (14) of Algorithm (4.2) create constraint networks corresponding to each cycle in G, and these networks are input to DETERMINE-FEASIBILITY(), which as discussed before, correctly handles networks representing simple, directed cycles of length 2.

Function DETERMINE-FEASIBILITY (G, i, k)
1: **if** $(i < k)$ **then**
2:   Call PARTIALLY-CLAIRVOYANT-STANDARD() on G, so that J_k is eliminated and then J_i.
3:   **if** (PARTIALLY-CLAIRVOYANT-STANDARD() detects infeasibility in G) **then**
4:     **return(false)**
5:   **else**
6:     **return(true)**
7:   **end if**
8: **else**
9:   DETERMINE-FEASIBILITY (G, k, i).
10: **end if**

Algorithm 4.4. Determining the feasibility of a constraint network, having precisely 2 vertices and 2 edges

We have thus proved the base case of the induction.

Assume that Theorem (1) is true for all job sets of size at most $k > 1$. Now consider a job set of size $k + 1$. Let J_i be the first job that is picked to be eliminated by the random permutation π in Algorithm (4.1). The following cases arise:

(a) $i = k + 1$, i.e., job J_{k+1} is chosen - In this case, we need to eliminate (s_{k+1}, e_{k+1}) from the constraint network. However, this step is identical to executing a single step of Algorithm (3.1) and the correctness of Algorithm (3.1) immediately implies that NPCC cycles are detected or preserved.

(b) $i \neq k + 1$, i.e., a job other than the last one is chosen - Let C be a simple directed cycle in G, having negative Partially Clairvoyant cost. If C has length 2, it is detected by the DETERMINE-FEASIBILITY() procedure, in Steps (5) through (14) of Algorithm (4.2). If C has length greater than 2, the splicing process indicated in Figure (2) is carried out.

The crucial observation is that if s_i is the smallest index in C, then, e_i is not eliminated till s_i is crushed; otherwise, e_i is substituted first, because that

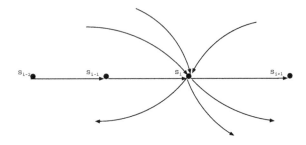

Fig. 2. Arbitrary job elimination

is exactly how the algorithm in [Sub03] evaluates the Partially Clairvoyant cost of C. Thus, eliminating s_i has not resulted in C being eliminated. However, it is possible that an edge created by contracting s_i is eliminated by the GRAPH-INSERT() procedure. Notice though, that the only way this can happen, is if there is a cycle having Partially Clairvoyant cost, even lower than C; in other words, NPCC cycles are preserved in the resultant constraint network.

Thus, the validity of Theorem (1) follows by mathematical induction.   □

Theorem 2. *Step (3) of Algorithm (4.1) does not introduce negative Partially Clairvoyant cost cycles into G, i.e., if there did not exist a negative Partially Clairvoyant cost cycle in G, before the execution of Step (3) of Algorithm (4.1), then there does not exist one, after its execution.*

Proof: The argument is somewhat similar to the one used in Theorem (1). The key observation, is that deleting edges does not create NPCC cycles. The only point at which NPCC cycles can be introduced is during the GRAPH-INSERT() procedure. It is not hard to see though, that if a NPCC cycle is created in this step, then it must have been the case that the cycle existed in the network, prior to the contraction of s_i. In other words, if there did not exist a NPCC cycle, before the execution of Step (3), then there does not exist one after the execution of Step (3).   □

From Theorem (1) and Theorem (2), we know that Algorithm (4.1) declares that a constraint specification does not have a Partially Clairvoyant schedule if and only if the corresponding constraint network has a NPCC cycle, as required by [Sub03]. It therefore follows that Algorithm (4.1) correctly decides whether or not a system of standard constraints has a Partially Clairvoyant schedule.

The correctness of the Algorithm (4.1) is reinforced by our empirical analysis. In every single instance of a constraint structure, the primal, the dual and the Arbitrary dual, produced the same answer to the schedulability query.

Theorem 1 allows us to conclude that:

Corollary 1. *Let*

$$\exists x_1 \, \forall y_1 \in [l_1, u_1] \, \exists x_2 \, \forall y_2 \in [l_2, u_2] \, \ldots \exists x_n \, \forall y_n \in [l_n, u_n] \quad \mathbf{G} \cdot \vec{\mathbf{x}} + \mathbf{H} \cdot \vec{\mathbf{y}} \leq \vec{\mathbf{b}}, (3)$$

be a Quantified Linear Program where $(\mathbf{G}, \ \mathbf{H})$ has the standard structure, described before. Then there exists a polynomial time quantifier elimination proce-

dure for determining the truth of the proposition, which eliminates existentially quantified variables (and the corresponding universally quantified variables) in arbitrary fashion.

5   Implementation

In the full paper, we shall provide a detailed description of the implementation issues. Here, we confine ourselves to discussing our observations. The parameter for discriminating inputs was the length of the NPCC cycles. Our implementational profile mirrors the study of negative cost cycle algorithms in [CGR96].

Observe that as per the proof of the Arbitrary Dual algorithm we could specify any arbitrary elimination order, e.g., sorting vertices based on degree product and the algorithm would still function correctly. Accordingly, we consider three versions of the Arbitrary Dual algorithm, viz., Min-Dual (mdual), Heap-Dual (hdual) and Randomized Dual (rdual). Both Min-Dual and Heap-Dual are predicated on the principle that it is advantageous to eliminate the job with the least number of dependencies. For a vertex s_i, in the dual constraint network, we define the degree product as $d_{in}(s_i) \cdot d_{out}(s_i)$. In the case of Min-Dual, the degree-products of the vertices are stored in a simple array. In this case, accessing the vertex with least degree-product takes $O(n)$ time and adjusting the degree-products of vertices, in the post-elimination phase, takes an additional $O(n)$ time. In the Heap-Dual case, vertices are organized as a heap; in this case, selecting the vertex with the least degree-product takes $O(\log n)$ time, whereas adjusting the degree-products of vertices, in the post-elimination phase takes $O(n \cdot \log n)$. In either case, the time spent on the additional data structuring can be absorbed by the $O(n^2)$ time it takes to eliminate a vertex from the network. In the Randomized Dual algorithm, the job to be eliminated is chosen uniformly, and at random from the jobs which have not yet been eliminated.

5.1   Results

For the empirical analysis of the algorithms, we characterize a constraint network by the length of its NPCC cycles. Accordingly, we get the following classes of constraint networks:

(Na) Constraint networks with no NPCC cycles, (Nb) Constraint networks with few NPCC cycles of large length, (Nc) Constraint networks with many NPCC cycles of small length, and (Nd) Cruel Adversary constraint networks.

The Cruel Adversary type of constraint network represents instances of the PCS problem in which some of the jobs are heavily constrained, while the rest have very few constraints associated with them. Since these networks are globally sparse, i.e., the total number of constraints is $O(n)$, it is fair to expect that algorithms for the PCS problem terminate quickly on these instances. However, insofar as existing algorithms are concerned, the position of the "cruel" vertices, i.e., the jobs which are heavily constrained in the sequence play an important role in the time taken to terminate.

Consider the constraint network in Figure (3); this constraint system is taken from [LSW03] and describes the constraints associated with an embedded controlled for a coffee machine. Each of the jobs $\{J_1...J_{n-1}\}$ has just 3 constraints associated with it, whereas job J_n has $\Omega(n)$ constraints associated with it. The constraint network is clearly sparse since it has $O(n)$ edges. If we first eliminate J_n from the constraint network, as demanded by the Primal and the Dual algorithms, a *complete* constraint network, having $\Omega(n^2)$ edges will result. The complete network is the worst case input for all of the algorithms. However eliminating the other jobs before job J_n is eliminated avoids this problem, and for this case and similar cases the Heap-Dual, Min-Dual and even the Randomized Dual algorithms perform better than existing algorithms.

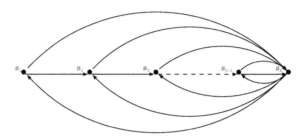

Fig. 3. A Cruel Adversary type of constraint network

A second example of a Cruel Adversary constraint network is described in [MSC+97], where the real-time system is an embedded controlled used by NASA. In this case, the $\frac{n}{2}^{th}$ job in the sequence is the heavily constrained job, while all other jobs are lightly constrained.

Each of the constraint networks (Na), (Nb) and (Nc) can have two subtypes, viz., sparse, and dense. The Cruel Adversary constraint networks are necessarily sparse. For the purposes of our analysis, we use the following definitions:

(i) Sparse networks have at most $10n$ edges, (ii) Dense networks have at least $\frac{n^2}{8}$ edges.

Our experiments were categorized as follows: (a) For networks with few NPCC cycles of large length, we performed the tests on networks having one negative cycle with length $\frac{8}{10}n$, (b) For networks with many NPCC cycles of small length, we have performed the tests on cycles with length 5, with the total number of cycles equal to $\frac{8}{5\cdot10}n$, (e) Since the worst case execution time of all algorithms occurs when there is no NPCC cycle, i.e., a Partially Clairvoyant schedule exists, we have tested Cruel Adversary networks only for the case when a schedule exists. For the Cruel Adversary case, we considered extensions of both examples described above, i.e., the case in which the cruel vertex was s_n and the case in which the cruel vertex was $s_{\frac{n}{2}}$.

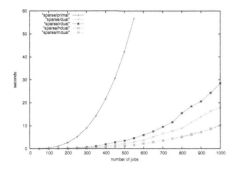

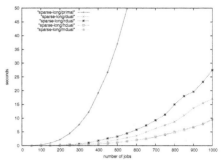

Fig. 4. Implementation execution times on sparse constraint networks with no negative clairvoyant cycles

Fig. 5. Implementation execution times on sparse constraint networks with a long negative clairvoyant cycle

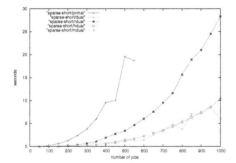

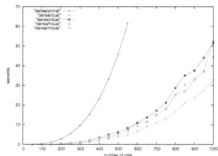

Fig. 6. Implementation execution times on sparse constraint networks with many short negative clairvoyant cycles

Fig. 7. Implementation execution times on dense constraint networks with no negative clairvoyant cycles

Observations on sparse constraint networks. The results of running the implementations on sparse constraint networks with no NPCC cycles are presented in Figure (5), while the results on sparse constraint networks with a single, long, NPCC cycle are described in Figure (6). Figure (7) details our observations on sparse constraint networks with many short NPCC cycles. The primal implementation could not finish the instances with more than 850 jobs, on account of memory constraints. From the figures, it is clear that implementations of the Arbitrary Dual algorithm are indeed superior to existing algorithms for this case.

Observations on dense constraint networks. Figures (8), (9) and (10) characterize our observations on dense constraint networks, with no NPCC cycles, a single, long NPCC cycle and many short NPCC cycles respectively. Once again the figures demonstrate the superiority of the Arbitrary Dual algorithm.

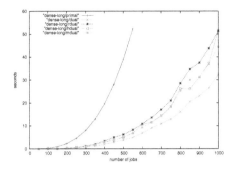

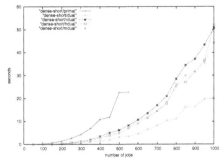

Fig. 8. Implementation execution times on dense constraint networks with long negative clairvoyant cycle

Fig. 9. Implementation execution times on dense constraint networks with many short negative clairvoyant cycles

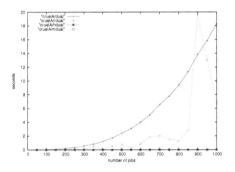

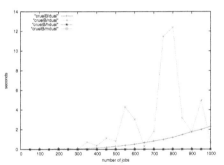

Fig. 10. Implementation execution times on the Cruel Adversary network with cruel vertex s_n

Fig. 11. Implementation execution times on the Cruel Adversary network with cruel vertex $s_{n/2}$

Observations on Cruel Adversary type of constraint networks. It is precisely in case of such constraint networks that the Arbitrary dual algorithm plays such a pivotal role in performance improvement.

If it is apriori known that the scheduling instance has the unbalanced structure of a Cruel Adversary, then it would be best to use the Min-Dual or Heap-Dual versions of the Arbitrary dual algorithm. Indeed, as the figures show, even the Randomized Dual algorithm fares better than the primal and dual-based approaches, for these instances.

References

[CGR96]   Boris V. Cherkassky, Andrew V. Goldberg, and T. Radzik. Shortest paths algorithms: Theory and experimental evaluation. *Mathematical Programming*, 73:129–174, 1996.

[GPS95]   R. Gerber, W. Pugh, and M. Saksena. Parametric Dispatching of Hard Real-Time Tasks. *IEEE Transactions on Computers*, 1995.

[LSW03]   Kim G. Larsen, B. Steffen, and C. Weise. Continuous modelling of real time and hybrid systems. Technical report, Aalborg Universitet, 2003. BRICS Technical Report.

[MSC+97]   N. Muscettola, B. Smith, S. Chien, C. Fry, G. Rabideau, K. Rajan, and D. Yan. In-board planning for autonomous spacecraft. In *The Fourth International Symposium on Artificial Intelligence, Robotics, and Automation for Space (i-SAIRAS)*, July 1997.

[Sub03]   K. Subramani. An analysis of partially clairvoyant scheduling. *Journal of Mathematical Modelling and Algorithms*, 2(2):97–119, 2003.

[Wei97]   Volker Weispfenning. Simulation and optimization by quantifier elimination. *Journal of Symbolic Computation*, 24(2):189–208, August 1997. Applications of quantifier elimination (Albuquerque, NM, 1995).

Timing Analysis and Simulation Tools for Real-Time Control

Karl-Erik Årzén

Lund University, Sweden

The temporal non-determinism introduced by computing and communication in the form of delay and jitter can lead to significant performance degradation. To achieve good performance in systems with limited computer resources, e.g. embedded systems, the resource constraints of the implementation platform must be taken into account at design time. To facilitate this, software tools are needed to analyze and simulate how the timing affects the control performance. Recently two new such tools, JITTERBUG and TRUETIME have been developed at the Department of Automatic Control, Lund University.

JITTERBUG is a MATLAB-based toolbox that makes it possible to compute a quadratic performance criterion for a linear control system under various timing conditions. The tool can also compute the spectral density of the signals in the system. Using the toolbox, one can easily and quickly assert how sensitive a control system is to delay, jitter, lost samples, etc., without resorting to simulation. The tool is quite general and can also be used to investigate jitter-compensating controllers, aperiodic controllers, and multi-rate controllers. The main contribution of the toolbox, which is built on well-known theory (LQG theory and jump linear systems), is to make it easy to apply this type of stochastic analysis to a wide range of problems.

The use of JITTERBUG assumes knowledge of sampling period and latency distributions. This information can be difficult to obtain without access to measurements from the true target system under implementation. Also, the analysis cannot capture all the details and nonlinearities (especially in the real-time scheduling) of the computer system. A natural approach is to use simulation instead. However, today's simulation tools make it difficult to simulate the true temporal behaviour of control loops. What is normally done is to introduce time delays in the control loop representing average-case or worst-case delays. Taking a different approach, the MATLAB/Simulink-based tool TRUETIME facilitates simulation of the temporal behaviour of a multitasking real-time kernel executing controller tasks. The tasks are controlling processes that are modelled as ordinary Simulink blocks. TRUETIME also makes it possible to simulate simple models of wired and wireless communication networks and their influence on networked control loops. Different scheduling policies may be used (e.g., priority-based preemptive scheduling and earliest-deadline-first (EDF) scheduling).

TRUETIME can also be used as an experimental platform for research on dynamic real-time control systems. For instance, it is possible to study compensation schemes that adjust the control algorithm based on measurements of actual timing variations (i.e., to treat the temporal uncertainty as a disturbance and manage it with feed-forward or gain-scheduling). It is also easy to experiment with more flexible approaches to real-time scheduling of controllers, such as feedback scheduling [1]. There the available

P. Pettersson and W. Yi (Eds.): FORMATS 2005, LNCS 3829, pp. 142–143, 2005.

CPU or network resources are dynamically distributed according the current situation (CPU load, the performance of the different loops, etc.) in the system.

More information about JITTERBUG and TRUETIME can be found in [2]. The toolboxes can be downloaded from http://www.control.lth.se/user/dan/truetime/ and http://www.control.lth.se/user/lincoln/jitterbug/

References

1. A. Cervin, J. Eker, B. Bernhardsson, and K.E. Årzén. Feedback-feedforward scheduling of control tasks. *Real-Time Systems*, 23(3), 2002.
2. A. Cervin, D. Henriksson, B. Lincoln, and K.-E. Årzén. How does control timing affect performance? *IEEE Control Systems Magazine*, 23(1):16–30, 2003.

Automatic Rectangular Refinement of Affine Hybrid Systems

Laurent Doyen[1],[*], Thomas A. Henzinger[2],[3],[**], and Jean-François Raskin[1]

[1] Université Libre de Bruxelles (ULB) Brussels, Belgium
[2] École Polytechnique Fédérale de Lausanne (EPFL) Lausanne,
Switzerland
[3] University of California (UC) Berkeley, U.S.A.

Abstract. We show how to automatically construct and refine rectangular abstractions of systems of linear differential equations. From a hybrid automaton whose dynamics are given by a system of linear differential equations, our method computes automatically a sequence of rectangular hybrid automata that are increasingly precise overapproximations of the original hybrid automaton. We prove an optimality criterion for successive refinements. We also show that this method can take into account a safety property to be verified, refining only relevant parts of the state space. The practicability of the method is illustrated on a benchmark case study.

1 Introduction

Hybrid systems are digital real-time systems embedded in analog environments. A paradigmatic example of a hybrid system is a digital embedded control program for an analog plant environment, like a furnace or an airplane: the controller state moves discretely between control modes, and in each control mode, the plant state evolves continuously according to physical laws. Those systems combine discrete and continuous dynamics. Those aspects have been studied in computer science and in control theory. Computer scientists have introduced *hybrid automata* [8], a formal model that combines discrete control graphs, usually called *finite state automata*, with continuously evolving variables.

When the evolution of continuous variables are subject to rectangular flow constraints, that is, constraints of the form $\dot{x} \in [a, b]$, hybrid automata are called *rectangular*. For that subclass of hybrid automata, there exists a reasonably efficient algorithm to compute the flow successor [1]. Based on this algorithm, there exists an iterative method that computes the exact set of reachable states when it terminates. This semi-algorithm can be used to establish or refute *safety properties*. On the other hand, if the evolution of continuous variables are subject to more complicated flow constraints, for example affine dynamics like $\dot{x} = 3x - y$, computing the flow successor is more difficult and only approximate methods are known.

---

[*] Research fellow supported by the Belgian National Science Foundation (FNRS).
[**] Supported in part by the AFOSR MURI grant F49620-00-1-0327 and the NSF grants CCR-0208875 and CCR-0225610.

Rectangular hybrid automata have the additional property that they can over-approximate, at any level of precision, the set of behaviors of more complex hybrid automata. A general methodology to analyze complex hybrid automata using rectangular approximations has been proposed in [10]. This methodology can be summarized as follows: to establish a safety property on a complex hybrid automata A, construct a rectangular approximation B of A and check the safety property on B. If the property is established on B, then it also holds on A. If the property is not established on B, then use a more precise rectangular approximation B'.

So far, the construction of the abstraction B and its refinement B' was supposed to be obtained manually. In this paper, we show how to efficiently automate this methodology for the class of affine hybrid automata, that is, hybrid automata whose continuous dynamics are defined by systems of linear differential equations. More precisely, we show (i) how to compute automatically rectangular approximations for affine hybrid automata, (ii) how to refine automatically and in an optimal way rectangular approximations that fail to establish a given safety property, (iii) how to target refinement only to relevant parts of the state space.

Refinements are obtained by splitting location invariants. A split is optimal if it minimizes some measure of the imprecision of the resulting rectangular approximation. Intuitively, the imprecision corresponds to the size of the interval defining the rectangular flow, because the smaller the imprecision, the closer the rectangular dynamics is to the exact dynamics. In this paper, we minimize the maximal imprecision of the dynamics in the split location of the refined automaton.

We have implemented our methodology and applied it to the navigation benchmark proposed in [5], for which we have implemented a prototype. The first results that we have obtained are encouraging. We therefore expect further improvements to the theory of refinement, as well as to the design and implementation of algorithms, to be fruitful, and we plan to continue investigating this field.

Structure of the Paper. In Section 2 we recall the classical definitions of hybrid automata, giving their semantics as timed transition systems. We show how rectangular overapproximations of affine hybrid automata can be constructed. The methodology to obtain successive refinements of such rectangular approximations is detailed in Section 3 in the form of an optimization problem whose solution is intended to give an optimal way of refining. We give an algorithm to solve the problem in 2 dimensions (when the hybrid systems has 2 variables), and we give an approximation technique for higher dimensions in the form of a more abstract optimization problem that can be solved in general. Finally, the refinement-based verification algorithm is explained in Section 4 and a case study is presented in Section 5. Complete proofs of the theorems can be found at the following web page: `http://www.ulb.ac.be/di/ssd/cfv/publications.html`.

2   Hybrid Automata and Abstraction

Intervals. An *interval* is a nonempty convex subset of the set $\mathbb{R}$ of real numbers. For a bounded interval I, we denote the left (resp. right) end-point of I by l_I

(resp. r_I). For an interval I, we define $\mathsf{size}(I) = r_I - l_I$ if I is bounded, and $\mathsf{size}(I) = +\infty$ otherwise. A bounded interval I is *closed* if $l_I \in I$ and $r_I \in I$. Given two closed intervals I_1 and I_2, their *convex hull* is the closed interval $I_3 = I_1 \sqcup I_2$ such that $l_{I_3} = \min(l_{I_1}, l_{I_2})$ and $r_{I_3} = \max(r_{I_1}, r_{I_2})$.

Predicates. Let $X = \{x_1, \ldots, x_n\}$ be a finite set of variables. A *valuation* over X is a function $v : X \to \mathbb{R}$. Alternatively, it can be seen as a tuple $(v_1, \ldots, v_n) = (v(x_1), \ldots, v(x_n))$ in $\mathbb{R}^n$. Given $v : X \to \mathbb{R}$ and $Y \subseteq X$, define $v_{|Y} : Y \to \mathbb{R}$ by $v_{|Y}(x) = v(x) \; \forall x \in Y$. A *linear term* over X is an expression of the form $y \equiv a_0 + \sum_{x_i \in X} a_i x_i$ where $a_i \in \mathbb{Q}$ $(0 \leq i \leq n)$ are rational constants. Given a valuation v over X, we write $[\![y]\!]_v$ for the real number $a_0 + \sum_{x_i \in X} a_i v(x_i)$. We denote by $\mathsf{LTerm}(X)$ the set of all linear terms over X. A *rectangular predicate* over X is a formula of the form $\bigwedge_{x \in X} x \in I_x$ where I_x $(x \in X)$ are closed intervals. We denote by $\mathsf{Rect}(X)$ the set of all rectangular predicates over X. Given two rectangular predicates $p = \bigwedge_{x \in X} x \in I_x$ and $q = \bigwedge_{x \in X} x \in J_x$, we define the *size* of p by $|p| = \max_{x \in X}\{\mathsf{size}(I_x)\}$ and the *rectangular hull* of p and q by $p \sqcup q = \bigwedge_{x \in X} x \in I_x \sqcup J_x$. A *linear constraint* over X is a formula of the form $y \bowtie 0$ where $y \in \mathsf{LTerm}(X)$ is a linear term over X and $\bowtie \in \{<, \leq, =, >, \geq\}$. A *linear predicate* over X is a finite conjunction of linear constraints over X. We denote by $\mathsf{Lin}(X)$ the set of all linear constraints over X. For a (rectangular or linear) predicate p over X, we write $[\![p]\!]$ for the set of all valuations $v \in [X \to \mathbb{R}]$ satisfying p. A *polytope* is a closed bounded set $[\![p]\!]$ defined by a linear predicate p. An *affine dynamics predicate* over X is a formula of the form $\bigwedge_{x \in X} \dot{x} = t_x$ where $t_x \in \mathsf{LTerm}(X)$ $(x \in X)$ are linear terms over X and $\dot{x}$ represents the first derivative of x. Let $\dot{X} = \{\dot{x} \mid x \in X\}$. We denote by $\mathsf{Affine}(X, \dot{X})$ the set of all affine dynamics predicates over X. For an affine dynamics predicate p, we write $[\![p]\!]$ for the set of all valuations $v \in [X \cup \dot{X} \to \mathbb{R}]$ satisfying p.

Lines and Hyperplanes. A function $f : \mathbb{R}^n \to \mathbb{R}$ is called *affine* if it is of the form $f(x) = a_0 + \sum_i a_i x_i$ with $a_i \in \mathbb{Q}$ $(0 \leq i \leq n)$. We say that two affine functions f_1 and f_2 are *parallel* if for some $\lambda \in \mathbb{R}$ the function $f(x) = f_1(x) + \lambda f_2(x)$ is independent of x (that is, ∇f is identically 0). Given a function $f : A \to B$ and $b \in B$, define the *level set* of f corresponding to b by $f^{-1}(b) = \{a \in A \mid f(a) = b\}$. For $C \subseteq B$, define $f^{-1}(C) = \{a \in A \mid f(a) \in C\}$. A *hyperplane* is a level set of an affine function. Given an affine function $f : \mathbb{R}^n \to \mathbb{R}$, we write $\pi \equiv f(x) = 0$ to denote the hyperplane $\pi = f^{-1}(0)$. In $\mathbb{R}^2$ a hyperplane is a *line*. Given two points $a, b \in \mathbb{R}^2$, let $line(a, b)$ denote the line passing by a and b. We write $[a, b]$ for the *line segment* connecting a and b, i.e. the set of convex combinations $\{\lambda a + (1 - \lambda)b \mid 0 \leq \lambda \leq 1\}$.

Transition Systems. A TTS (*timed transition system*) $\mathcal{T}$ is a tuple $\langle S, S_0, S_f, \Sigma, \to \rangle$ where S is a (possibly infinite) set of states, $S_0 \subseteq S$ is the set of initial state, $S_f \subseteq S$ is the set of final states, Σ is a finite set of labels including the *silent* label τ, and $\to \subseteq S \times (\Sigma \cup \mathbb{R}^{\geq 0}) \times S$ is the transition relation. If $(q, \sigma, q') \in \to$ we write $q \xrightarrow{\sigma} q'$. Define the *successors* of a set $A \subseteq S$ in $\mathcal{T}$ to be the set $\mathsf{Post}_\mathcal{T}(A) = \{s' \in S \mid \exists s \in A, \exists \sigma \in \Sigma \cup \mathbb{R}^{\geq 0} : s \xrightarrow{\sigma} s'\}$. Similarly, the *predecessors* of A in $\mathcal{T}$ are given by $\mathsf{Pre}_\mathcal{T}(A) = \{s \in S \mid \exists s' \in A, \exists \sigma \in \Sigma \cup \mathbb{R}^{\geq 0} : s \xrightarrow{\sigma} s'\}$.

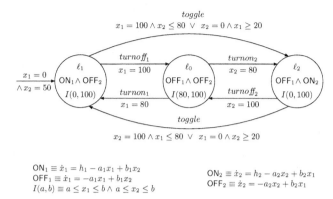

ON$_1 \equiv \dot{x}_1 = h_1 - a_1 x_1 + b_1 x_2$
OFF$_1 \equiv \dot{x}_1 = -a_1 x_1 + b_1 x_2$
$I(a, b) \equiv a \le x_1 \le b \wedge a \le x_2 \le b$

ON$_2 \equiv \dot{x}_2 = h_2 - a_2 x_2 + b_2 x_1$
OFF$_2 \equiv \dot{x}_2 = -a_2 x_2 + b_2 x_1$

Fig. 1. A shared gas-burner

The *reachable states* of $\mathcal{T}$ is the set $\mathsf{Reach}(\mathcal{T}) = \bigcup_{i \in \mathbb{N}} \mathsf{Post}^i_{\mathcal{T}}(S_0)$ where $\mathsf{Post}^0_{\mathcal{T}}(A) = A$ and recursively $\mathsf{Post}^i_{\mathcal{T}}(A) = \mathsf{Post}_{\mathcal{T}}(\mathsf{Post}^{i-1}_{\mathcal{T}}(A))$. Let $\mathsf{Reach}^{-1}(\mathcal{T}) = \bigcup_{i \in \mathbb{N}} \mathsf{Pre}^i_{\mathcal{T}}(S_f)$ where $\mathsf{Pre}^0_{\mathcal{T}}(A) = A$ and recursively $\mathsf{Pre}^i_{\mathcal{T}}(A) = \mathsf{Pre}_{\mathcal{T}}(\mathsf{Pre}^{i-1}_{\mathcal{T}}(A))$. Finally, let $\mathsf{Unsafe}(\mathcal{T}) = \mathsf{Reach}(\mathcal{T}) \cap \mathsf{Reach}^{-1}(\mathcal{T})$ be the set of reachable states that can reach the final states. The complement of $\mathsf{Unsafe}(\mathcal{T})$ is the set of safe states.

Given the TTS $\mathcal{T} = \langle S, S_0, S_f, \Sigma, \rightarrow \rangle$, we define the *stutter-closed relation* $\twoheadrightarrow \subseteq S \times (\Sigma \backslash \{\tau\} \cup \mathbb{R}^{\ge 0}) \times S$ as follows: if $\sigma \in \Sigma \backslash \{\tau\}$, then $s \overset{\sigma}{\twoheadrightarrow} s'$ iff there exists a finite sequence $s_0, \dots, s_k \in S$ of states such that $s = s_0$ and $s_0 \overset{\tau}{\rightarrow} s_1 \overset{\tau}{\rightarrow} \dots \overset{\tau}{\rightarrow} s_k \overset{\sigma}{\rightarrow} s'$; if $t \in \mathbb{R}^{\ge 0}$, then $s \overset{t}{\twoheadrightarrow} s'$ iff there exists a finite sequence $s_0, \dots, s_{2k} \in S$ of states and a finite sequence $t_0, \dots, t_k \in \mathbb{R}^{\ge 0}$ of constants such that $s = s_0$ and $s_0 \overset{t_0}{\rightarrow} s_1 \overset{\tau}{\rightarrow} s_2 \overset{t_1}{\rightarrow} \dots \overset{\tau}{\rightarrow} s_{2k} \overset{t_k}{\rightarrow} s'$ and $t = t_0 + \dots + t_k$.

Hybrid Automata. We define two types of hybrid automata, with either affine or rectangular dynamics [1, 11].

Definition 1 [Hybrid Automaton]. An *hybrid automaton* H is a tuple $\langle$ Loc, Lab, Edg, X, Init, Inv, Flow, Jump, Final$\rangle$ where: (*i*) Loc $= \{\ell_1, \dots, \ell_m\}$ is a finite set of *locations*. (*ii*) Lab is a finite set of *labels* containing the silent label τ. (*iii*) Edg $\subseteq$ Loc$\times$Lab$\times$Loc is a finite set of *edges*. (*iv*) $X = \{x_1, \dots, x_n\}$ is a finite set of *variables*. (*v*) Init : Loc $\rightarrow$ Lin(X) gives the *initial condition* Init(ℓ) of location ℓ. The automaton can start in ℓ with an initial valuation v lying in $[\![$Init(ℓ)$]\!]$. (*vi*) Inv : Loc $\rightarrow$ Lin(X) gives the *invariant condition* Inv(ℓ) of location ℓ. We require that $[\![$Inv(ℓ)$]\!]$ is bounded for every $\ell \in$ Loc. The automaton can stay in ℓ as long as the values of its variables lie in $[\![$Inv(ℓ)$]\!]$ (*vii*) Flow governs the evolution of the variables in each location:

- either Flow : Loc $\rightarrow$ Affine($X, \dot{X}$) and H is called an *affine dynamics* hybrid automaton,
- or Flow : Loc $\rightarrow$ Rect($\dot{X}$) and H is called a *rectangular dynamics* hybrid automaton;

(*viii*) Jump : Edg $\rightarrow$ Lin($X \cup X'$) with $X' = \{x'_1, \ldots, x'_n\}$ gives the *jump condition* Jump(e) of edge e. The variables in X' refer to the updated values of the variables after the edge has been traversed. (*ix*) Final : Loc $\rightarrow$ Lin(X) gives the *final condition* Final(ℓ) of location ℓ. In general, final conditions specify the unsafe states of the system.

Example. Fig. 1 represents an affine dynamics hybrid automaton modeling a single gas-burner that is, shared for heating alternatively two water tanks. It has three locations ℓ_0, ℓ_1, ℓ_2 and two variables x_1 and x_2, the temperature in the two tanks. The gas-burner can be either switched off (in ℓ_0) or turned on heating one of the two tanks (in ℓ_1 or ℓ_2). The dynamics in each location is given by a combination of the predicates ON_i and OFF_i ($i = 1, 2$) where the constants a_i model the heat exchange rate of the tank i with the room in which the tanks are located, b_i model the heat exchange rate between the two tanks and h_i depends on the power of the gas-burner. On every edge of the automaton, we have omitted the condition $x'_1 = x_1 \wedge x'_2 = x_2$ also written as $stable(x_1, x_2)$ that asserts that the values of the variables have to be maintained when the edge is traversed. In the sequel, we fix the constants $h_1 = h_2 = 2$, $a_1 = a_2 = 0.01$ and $b_1 = b_2 = 0.005$.

Definition 2 [Semantics of hybrid automata]. The *semantics* of an hybrid automaton $H = \langle \text{Loc}, \text{Edg}, X, \text{Init}, \text{Inv}, \text{Flow}, \text{Jump}, \text{Final} \rangle$ is the TTS $[\![H]\!] = \langle S, S_0, S_f, \Sigma, \rightarrow \rangle$ where $S = \text{Loc} \times \mathbb{R}^n$ is the *state space*, $S_0 = \{(\ell, v) \in S \mid v \in [\![\text{Init}(\ell)]\!]\}$ is the *initial space*, $S_f = \{(\ell, v) \in S \mid v \in [\![\text{Final}(\ell)]\!]\}$ is the *final space*, $\Sigma = \text{Lab}$ and $\rightarrow$ contains all the tuples $((\ell, v), \sigma, (\ell', v'))$ such that:

- either there exists $e = (\ell, \sigma, \ell') \in \text{Edg}$ such that $(v, v') \in [\![\text{Jump}(e)]\!]$,
- or $\ell = \ell'$ and $\sigma = \delta \in \mathbb{R}^{\geq 0}$ and there exists a continuously differentiable function $f : [0, \delta] \rightarrow [\![\text{Inv}(l)]\!]$ such that $f(0) = v$, $f(\delta) = v'$ and for all $t \in [0, \delta]$:
  - either H has affine dynamics and $(f(t), \dot{f}(t)) \in [\![\text{Flow}(\ell)]\!]$,
  - or H has rectangular dynamics and $\dot{f}(t) \in [\![\text{Flow}(\ell)]\!]$.

Such a function f is called a *witness* for the transition $((\ell, v), \delta, (\ell', v'))$.

An hybrid automaton H is said *empty* if no final state of H is reachable, that is, if $\text{Reach}([\![H]\!]) \cap \bigcup_{\ell \in \text{Loc}} [\![\text{Final}(\ell)]\!] = \varnothing$. The question to determine if a given hybrid automaton is empty is known as the *emptiness problem*.

To attack this problem, many of the existing tools (*a.o.* HYTECH [9], d/dt [2], PHAVER [7]) use a symbolic analysis of the hybrid automaton with a forward and/or backward approach: starting from the initial (resp. unsafe) states, iterate the operator $\text{Post}_{[\![H]\!]}$ (resp. $\text{Pre}_{[\![H]\!]}$) until a fix point is reached and then check emptiness of the intersection with the unsafe (resp. initial) states. Those procedures are not guaranteed to terminate since the emptiness problem is undecidable for both affine and rectangular dynamics hybrid automata [11].

Remark. The more efficient tool PHAVER does not implement the backward analysis. Nevertheless, for a rectangular dynamics automaton H it is possible to define the *reverse automaton* $-H$ such that $\text{Pre}_{[\![H]\!]} = \text{Post}_{[\![-H]\!]}$, and so such that $\mathsf{Reach}^{-1}_{[\![H]\!]} = \mathsf{Reach}_{[\![-H]\!]}$. Roughly, the construction consists in reversing the flow dynamics (an interval $[a, b]$ is replaced by the interval $[-b, -a]$) and the jump conditions (by permuting primed and unprimed variables). The other components are kept unchanged except the initial and unsafe sets which are swapped [11].

Overapproximations. The formal link between an automaton and its approximation will be drawn with the notion of *weak simulation*[12].

Definition 3 [Weak simulation]. Given two TTS $T_1 = \langle S^1, S_0^1, S_f^1, \Sigma, \rightarrow^1 \rangle$ and $T_2 = \langle S^2, S_0^2, S_f^2, \Sigma, \rightarrow^2 \rangle$ with the same set of labels, we write $T_1 \succeq T_2$ and say that T_1 *weakly simulates* T_2 if there exists a relation $R \subseteq S^1 \times S^2$ such that:

1. for all $(s_1, s_2) \in R$, for each $\sigma \in \Sigma\backslash\{\tau\} \cup \mathbb{R}^{\geq 0}$, if $s_2 \overset{\sigma}{\longrightarrow} s_2'$, then there exists $s_1' \in S^1$ such that $s_1 \overset{\sigma}{\longrightarrow} s_1'$ and $(s_1', s_2') \in R$,
2. for all $s_2 \in S_0^2$, there exists $s_1 \in S_0^1$ such that $(s_1, s_2) \in R$,
3. and for all $s_2 \in S_f^2$, for all $s_1 \in S^1$, if $(s_1, s_2) \in R$, then $s_1 \in S_f^1$.

Such a relation R is called a *simulation relation* for $T_1 \succeq T_2$.

For a relation $S \subseteq S^1 \times S^2$, let the inverse of S be the relation $S^{-1} = \{(s_2, s_1) \mid (s_1, s_2) \in S\}$.

Definition 4 [Weak bisimulation]. Two TTS T_1 and T_2 are *weakly bisimilar* (noted $T_1 \approx T_2$) if there exists a simulation relation R for $T_1 \succeq T_2$ and a simulation relation S for $T_2 \succeq T_1$ such that $R = S^{-1}$.

In the sequel, we also use a slightly different notion of simulation where only the unsafe states are to be simulated, because of the following observation: a state that has been proven to be safe in T_1 is necessarily safe in T_2 if $T_1 \succeq T_2$ and therefore the emptiness problem for an hybrid automaton H has the same answer as the emptiness problem on H with some of its safe states forbidden. So, it is sufficient to refine the automaton in its unsafe states. More details are given in Section 4.

Definition 5 [Weak simulation for unsafe behaviours]. Given two TTS $T_1 = \langle S^1, S_0^1, S_f^1, \Sigma, \rightarrow^1 \rangle$ and $T_2 = \langle S^2, S_0^2, S_f^2, \Sigma, \rightarrow^2 \rangle$ with the same set of labels, we write $T_1 \succeq_{unsafe} T_2$ and say that T_1 *weakly simulates the unsafe behaviours of* T_2 if there exists a relation $R \subseteq S^1 \times \mathsf{Unsafe}(T_2)$ such that:

1. for all $(s_1, s_2) \in R$, for each $\sigma \in \Sigma\backslash\{\tau\} \cup \mathbb{R}^{\geq 0}$, if $s_2 \overset{\sigma}{\longrightarrow} s_2'$ and $s_2' \in \mathsf{Unsafe}(T_2)$, then there exists $s_1' \in S^1$ such that $s_1 \overset{\sigma}{\longrightarrow} s_1'$ and $(s_1', s_2') \in R$,
2. for all $s_2 \in S_0^2$, there exists $s_1 \in S_0^1$ such that $(s_1, s_2) \in R$,
3. and for all $s_2 \in S_f^2$, for all $s_1 \in S^1$, if $(s_1, s_2) \in R$, then $s_1 \in S_f^1$.

Such a relation R is called a *simulation relation* for $T_1 \succeq_{unsafe} T_2$.

Definition 6 [Weak bisimulation for unsafe behaviours]. Two TTS $\mathcal{T}_1$ and $\mathcal{T}_2$ are *weakly bisimilar for unsafe behaviours* (noted $\mathcal{T}_1 \approx_{unsafe} \mathcal{T}_2$) if there exists a simulation relation R for $\mathcal{T}_1 \succeq_{unsafe} \mathcal{T}_2$ and a simulation relation S for $\mathcal{T}_2 \succeq_{unsafe} \mathcal{T}_1$ such that $R = S^{-1}$.

Lemma 7. *Let $\mathcal{T}_1$ and $\mathcal{T}_2$ be two TTS. If $\mathcal{T}_1 \succeq \mathcal{T}_2$, then $\mathcal{T}_1 \succeq_{unsafe} \mathcal{T}_2$.*

Theorem 8. *Let H and H' be two hybrid automata such that $[\![H']\!] \succeq_{unsafe} [\![H]\!]$. If H' is empty, then so is H.*

Definition 9 [Rectangular phase-portrait approximation]. We say that a hybrid automaton H' is a *rectangular phase-portrait approximation* of an hybrid automaton H if $[\![H']\!] \succeq [\![H]\!]$ and H' has rectangular dynamics.

A natural way for constructing a rectangular phase-portrait approximation $H' = \mathsf{rect}(H)$ of an affine dynamics hybrid automaton H is to replace in each location ℓ of H the affine flow condition $\mathsf{Flow}_H(\ell) = \bigwedge_{x \in X} \dot{x} = t_x$ by the rectangular predicate $\mathsf{Flow}_{H'}(\ell) = \bigwedge_{x \in X} \dot{x} \in I_x$ where I_x is the tightest interval containing the set $\{[\![t_x]\!]_v \mid v \in [\![\mathsf{Inv}(l)]\!]\}$. The bounds of I_x can be determined by a linear program since t_x is a linear term and $\mathsf{Inv}(l)$ is a linear predicate. The proof that $[\![H']\!] \succeq [\![H]\!]$ is obvious since for any $v \in [\![\mathsf{Flow}_H(\ell)]\!]$ we have $v_{|\dot{X}} \in [\![\mathsf{Flow}_{H'}(\ell)]\!]$.

Example. Fig. 2(a) depicts the result of this construction when applied to the location ℓ_1 of the shared gas-burner automaton.

For an hybrid automaton H with set of locations Loc_H, let $\mathsf{SafeLoc}(H) = \{\ell \in \mathsf{Loc}_H \mid \nexists(\ell, v) \in \mathsf{Unsafe}([\![H]\!])\}$.

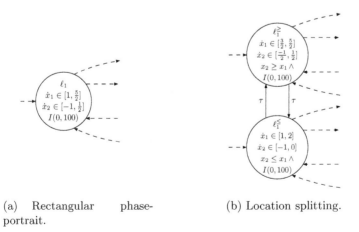

(a) Rectangular phase-portrait.

(b) Location splitting.

Fig. 2. Location ℓ_1 of the shared gas-burner

Lemma 10. *For every affine dynamics hybrid automaton H, we have* $\mathsf{SafeLoc}(\mathsf{rect}(H)) \subseteq \mathsf{SafeLoc}(H)$.

3 Abstraction Refinement for Hybrid Automata

Definition 11 [Refined approximation]. Given H' and H'' two rectangular phase-portrait approximations of an hybrid automaton H, we say that H'' *refines* H' if $[\![H']\!] \succeq [\![H'']\!]$.

A natural way of refining an approximation of an affine dynamics hybrid automaton is to *split* its locations by partitioning or covering their invariant.

Definition 12 [Cut]. Given a polytope $P \subseteq \mathbb{R}^n$ and a hyperplane $\pi \equiv f(x) = 0$, we define the *cut* $P/\pi = \langle P^+, P^- \rangle$ where $P^+ = P \cap f^{-1}(\mathbb{R}^{\geq 0})$ and $P^- = P \cap f^{-1}(\mathbb{R}^{\leq 0})$. The cut P/π is said *non-trivial* if $P^+ \neq \varnothing$ and $P^- \neq \varnothing$.

Thus a non-trivial cut P/π of a polytope P is a *cover* of P but not a partition since the two pieces are closed sets and they share the points in $P \cap \pi$.

Definition 13 [Location splitting]. Given an hybrid automaton $H = \langle \mathsf{Loc}, \mathsf{Lab}, \mathsf{Edg}, X, \mathsf{Init}, \mathsf{Inv}, \mathsf{Flow}, \mathsf{Jump}, \mathsf{Final} \rangle$, one of its locations $\ell^\star \in \mathsf{Loc}$ and a hyperplane $\pi \equiv f_\pi(x) = 0$ in $\mathbb{R}^{|X|}$, the *splitting* of H by the hyperplane π in location $\ell^\star$ is the hybrid automaton $\mathsf{split}(H, \ell^\star, \pi) = \langle \mathsf{Loc}', \mathsf{Lab}', \mathsf{Edg}', X', \mathsf{Init}', \mathsf{Inv}', \mathsf{Flow}', \mathsf{Jump}', \mathsf{Final}' \rangle$ where: (i) $\mathsf{Loc}' = \mathsf{Loc}\backslash\{\ell^\star\} \cup \{(\ell^\star, P), (\ell^\star, Q)\}$ where $P = \mathsf{Inv}(\ell^\star) \wedge f_\pi(x) \leq 0$ and $Q = \mathsf{Inv}(\ell^\star) \wedge f_\pi(x) \geq 0$. For $\ell' \in \mathsf{Loc}'$, let $loc(\ell') = \ell'$ if $\ell' \in \mathsf{Loc}$ and $loc(\ell') = \ell^\star$ otherwise. (ii) $\mathsf{Lab}' = \mathsf{Lab}$. (iii) $\mathsf{Edg}' = E_1 \cup E_2$ where $E_1 = \{(\ell, \sigma, \ell') \mid \ell, \ell' \in \mathsf{Loc}' \wedge (loc(\ell), \sigma, loc(\ell')) \in \mathsf{Edg}\}$ is the set of edges inherited from H and $E_2 = \{(\ell, \tau, \ell') \mid \ell, \ell' \in \mathsf{Loc}' \wedge loc(\ell) = loc(\ell') = \ell^\star\}$ are silent edges between the two copies of the location $\ell^\star$. (iv) $X' = X$. (v) $\mathsf{Init}'(\ell') = \mathsf{Init}(loc(\ell'))$ for each $\ell' \in \mathsf{Loc}'$. (vi) $\mathsf{Inv}'(\ell') = \mathsf{Inv}(\ell')$ for each $\ell' \in \mathsf{Loc}\backslash\{\ell^\star\}$, $\mathsf{Inv}'(\ell^\star, P) = P$ and $\mathsf{Inv}'(\ell^\star, Q) = Q$. (vii) $\mathsf{Flow}'(\ell') = \mathsf{Flow}(loc(\ell'))$ for each $\ell' \in \mathsf{Loc}'$. $(viii)$ for every $e = (\ell, \sigma, \ell') \in E_1$ we have $\mathsf{Jump}'(e) = \mathsf{Jump}(loc(\ell), \sigma, loc(\ell))$, and for every $e \in E_2$ we have $\mathsf{Jump}'(e) = stable(X)$. (ix) $\mathsf{Final}'(\ell') = \mathsf{Final}(loc(\ell'))$ for each $\ell' \in \mathsf{Loc}'$.

Example. Fig. 2(b) shows the rectangular phase-portrait approximation of the splitting of the location ℓ_1 of the shared gas-burner by the line $x_1 = x_2$. The resulting automaton is a refinement since the ranges of the rectangular dynamics have decreased in each of the two splitted locations.

This technique is very general and has been applied to hybrid automata with nonlinear dynamics [10]. However, in that last reference, the proof of correctness (that the refined automaton $\mathsf{split}(H, \ell^\star, \pi)$ weakly simulates the original automaton H) relies crucially on the fact that the split of an invariant is derived from a finite *open cover*, that is, a location $\ell^\star$ is replaced by $(\ell^\star, P)$ and $(\ell^\star, Q)$ where P, Q are open sets such that $\mathsf{Inv}(\ell^\star) \subseteq P \cup Q$. Unfortunately, the proof cannot be extended to closed covers: for example, the continuously differentiable function $f : \mathbb{R}^{\geq 0} \to \mathbb{R}$ defined by $f(0) = 0$ and $f(t) = t^2 \sin(1/t)$ for $t > 0$, oscillates infinitely in every interval $[0, \epsilon]$ ($\epsilon > 0$). So that if $f_{|[0,\delta]}$ was the witness of a transition $((\ell, v), \delta, (\ell, v'))$ of an automaton H with variable $X_H = \{y\}$, it would be impossible for the automaton $\mathsf{split}(H, \ell, y = 0)$ to mimic that transition since time cannot progress by any amount while maintaining either $y \geq 0$ or $y \leq 0$. However, this kind of pathological behaviour can not appear as a solution of a system of affine dynamics flow conditions (even though spiral trajectories are still possible) because such solutions are *analytic* and zeroes of analytic functions are isolated.

Theorem 14. *For every hybrid automaton H, for every of its location ℓ, and every hyperplane π, we have $[\![\mathsf{split}(H, \ell, \pi)]\!] \approx [\![H]\!]$, that is, $[\![\mathsf{split}(H, \ell, \pi)]\!]$ and $[\![H]\!]$ are weakly bisimilar.*

With the remark above, the proof of Theorem 14 is straightforward.

In this section, we are interested in finding *automatically* an optimal cut for refining the state space. We consider the general problem to split a location in an optimal way, that is, to minimize the imprecision of the resulting rectangular phase-portrait approximation. The definition of the imprecision could have several forms. We decide to minimize the maximal size of the rectangular predicates that appear as flow conditions in the rectangular approximation of the splitted automaton (and particularly in the splitted location). It may be necessary to scale the variables in order to give sense to the comparison of their dynamics range. We now discuss our choice. On the one hand, this criterion is natural since the precision of the approximation is directly connected to the size of the rectangular predicates. Further, minimizing the maximal size ensures that the approximation becomes more precise. On the other hand, other criteria we have tried (minimizing the sum of the squares of the sizes, minimizing the size of the reachable set, etc.) gave rise to computational difficulties due to their non-linear form. Our criterion can be handled with linear programming techniques, and showed practical applicability with promising results (see Section 5).

3.1   Optimization Criteria

We ask to split the invariant of a location into two convex pieces, minimizing the maximal size of the flow intervals obtained in the approximation. We define two versions of this problem, one called *concrete* when the given dynamics is affine on the invariant, and one called *abstract* when the invariant is already covered by a number of pieces each with its rectangular dynamics. The second formulation is introduced because we have no simple algorithm in nD for $n \geq 3$ for solving the concrete problem, while we have a general algorithm for the abstract one. Therefore, it may be of interest to discretize the original affine system in order to get an approximation of the best split. We show that the result can be made arbitrarily close to the exact solution.

In Definition 15, we associate to each subset $Q \subseteq P$ of the invariant P of a location the tightest rectangular dynamics that contains the exact dynamics in the set Q (which is defined by an affine predicate of the form $\bigwedge_{x_i \in X} \dot{x}_i = f_i(x_1, \ldots, x_n)$). Then, the *imprecision* of a cut of P into two pieces is defined to be the maximal size of the rectangular predicates associated to each piece.

Definition 15 [Concrete imprecision]. Let $X = \{x_1, \ldots, x_n\}$ be a finite set of variables. Let $P \subset \mathbb{R}^n$ be a polytope and $F = \{f_1, \ldots, f_n\}$ a set of n affine functions $f_i : \mathbb{R}^n \to \mathbb{R}$ ($1 \le i \le n$). For a polytope $Q \subseteq P$, we define the rectangular predicate $\mathsf{range}^F(Q) = \bigwedge_{x \in X} x \in I_x$ where for each $x_i \in X$, we have $I_{x_i} = f_i(Q)$. We define the *concrete imprecision* of a cut $P/\pi = \langle P^+, P^- \rangle$ by $\mathsf{sizeRange}^F(P/\pi) = \max\{|\mathsf{range}^F(P^+)|, |\mathsf{range}^F(P^-)|\}$.

Definition 16 [Concrete optimal-cut problem]. An *instance of the concrete optimal-cut problem* is a tuple $\langle P, X, F \rangle$ where: $P \subset \mathbb{R}^n$ is a polytope, $X = \{x_1, \ldots, x_n\}$ is a set of n variables, and F is a set of n affine functions $f_i : \mathbb{R}^n \to \mathbb{R}$ ($1 \le i \le n$).

The *concrete optimal-cut problem* is to determine a hyperplane $\pi^\star \subset \mathbb{R}^n$ such that for every hyperplane $\pi \subset \mathbb{R}^n$, $\mathsf{sizeRange}^F(P/\pi^\star) \le \mathsf{sizeRange}^F(P/\pi)$.

We define an abstract version of the optimal-cut problem where the invariants of the locations are originally given as a union of polytopes $\mathcal{P}$, and the flow condition in each piece is rectangular. This form of the problem is obtained when we discretize the concrete problem according to $\mathcal{P}$. The abstract problem asks to split the location into only *two* pieces such that the maximal flow interval in the two pieces is minimized.

Definition 17 [Abstract imprecision]. Let $X = \{x_1, \ldots, x_n\}$ be a finite set of variables. Let $P \subset \mathbb{R}^n$ be a polytope covered by a finite set of polytopes $\mathcal{P} = \{P_1, \ldots, P_m\}$, that is, such that $P = P_1 \cup \cdots \cup P_m$. Let $\mathsf{Flow} : \mathcal{P} \to \mathsf{Rect}(\dot{X})$ be a function that associates to each piece of $\mathcal{P}$ a rectangular dynamics. For a polytope $Q \subseteq P$, we define the rectangular predicate $\mathsf{range}^{\mathsf{Flow}}(Q) = \bigsqcup_{P_j \in \mathcal{P}, P_j \cap Q \ne \varnothing} \mathsf{Flow}(P_j)$. We define the *abstract imprecision* of a cut $P/\pi = \langle P^+, P^- \rangle$ by $\mathsf{sizeRange}^{\mathsf{Flow}}(P/\pi) = \max\{|\mathsf{range}^{\mathsf{Flow}}(P^+)|, |\mathsf{range}^{\mathsf{Flow}}(P^-)|\}$.

Definition 18 [Abstract optimal-cut problem]. An *instance of the abstract optimal-cut problem* is a tuple $\langle P, \mathcal{P}, X, \mathsf{Flow} \rangle$ where: $P \subset \mathbb{R}^n$ is a polytope, $\mathcal{P} = \{P_1, \ldots, P_m\}$ is finite set of polytopes such that $P = P_1 \cup \cdots \cup P_m$, $X = \{x_1, \ldots, x_n\}$ is a set of n variables, and $\mathsf{Flow} : \mathcal{P} \to \mathsf{Rect}(\dot{X})$.

The *abstract optimal-cut problem* asks to determine a hyperplane $\pi^\star \subset \mathbb{R}^n$ such that for every hyperplane $\pi \subset \mathbb{R}^n$, $\mathsf{sizeRange}^{\mathsf{Flow}}(P/\pi^\star) \le \mathsf{sizeRange}^{\mathsf{Flow}}(P/\pi)$.

3.2   Solution of the Abstract Optimal-Cut Problem

We give an algorithm for solving the abstract problem and show how it can be used to approximate the solution of the concrete problem.

Definition 19 [Separability]. Two sets $A, B \subseteq \mathbb{R}^n$ are *separable* if there exists an affine function $f : \mathbb{R}^n \to \mathbb{R}$ such that $\forall x \in A : f(x) \leq 0$ and $\forall x \in B : f(x) \geq 0$.

This definition extends to sets of sets: we say that $\mathcal{A} \subseteq 2^{\mathbb{R}^n}$ and $\mathcal{B} \subseteq 2^{\mathbb{R}^n}$ are separable if $\bigcup \mathcal{A}$ and $\bigcup \mathcal{B}$ are separable. Separability can be tested using the *convex hull* of a set, denoted $\mathcal{C}Hull(\cdot)$.

Lemma 20. *Two sets $A, B \subseteq \mathbb{R}^n$ are separable iff there exists a hyperplane $\pi \subset \mathbb{R}^n$ such that $\mathcal{C}Hull(A) \cap \mathcal{C}Hull(B) \subseteq \pi$.*

An optimal cut for the abstract problem $\langle P, \mathcal{P}, X, \mathsf{Flow} \rangle$ is solved by Algorithm 1. It uses two external functions *value* and *separable* taking as input two sets $\mathcal{A}$ and $\mathcal{B}$ of polytopes. The function *value* returns the number $\mathsf{sizeRange}^{\mathsf{Flow}}(\langle \bigcup \mathcal{A}, \bigcup \mathcal{B} \rangle)$ and the boolean function *separable* returns true iff $\mathcal{A}$ and $\mathcal{B}$ are separable. Lemma 20 suggests a natural implementation of *separable*.

This algorithm constructs two sets of pieces $G^+ \subseteq \mathcal{P}$ and $G^- \subseteq \mathcal{P}$ to be separated from each other, and maintains a set $G_0 = \mathcal{P} \backslash (G^+ \cup G^-)$ of untreated pieces. Initially, we have $G^+ = G^- = \varnothing$ and $G_0 = \mathcal{P}$. The call $split(\varnothing, \varnothing, \mathcal{P})$ returns two sets G^+ and G^- that are separable and such that any separating hyperplane of G^- and G^+ is an optimal cut for $\langle P, \mathcal{P}, X, \mathsf{Flow} \rangle$. Intuitively, the function *split* iteratively selects two pieces $P_i, P_j \in \mathcal{P}$ that are forced to be separated because their flow interval $\mathsf{range}^{\mathsf{Flow}}(P_i \cup P_j)$ is maximal. The separation constraint can be represented as an edge between P_i and P_j in a graph whose vertices is the set $\mathcal{P}$. We can add new such constraints while the graph is 2-colorable with the additional requirement that the two sets of pieces induced by the 2-coloring is physically separable by a hyperplane. In the case the new edge is already connected to the rest of the graph, the color of the common vertex imposes the color of the other. Otherwise, the algorithm has to explore two choices (corresponding to put P_i in G^- and P_j in G^+ or vice versa). An obvious argument shows that this can occur only n times (where $n = |X|$ is the number of variables) so that the the algorithm is in $O(m.2^n)$, assuming constant execution time of external functions. We do not know if this bound is tight for the problem.

Theorem 21. *Algorithm 1 is correct and always terminates.*

The Algorithm 1 can be used to solve the concrete optimal-cut problem up to a precision $\epsilon \in \mathbb{Q}^{>0}$, as stated by Theorem 23. It suffices to discretize the polytope with a grid of size ϵ: given a set $F = \{f_1, \ldots, f_n\}$ of n affine functions in $\mathbb{R}^n$, let $\mathsf{Grid}^F_\epsilon = \{ \bigcap_{1 \leq i \leq n} f_i^{-1}([k_i \, \epsilon, (k_i + 1) \, \epsilon]) \mid (k_1, \ldots, k_n) \in \mathbb{Z}^n \}$. In practice, the complexity blows up since the number of elements in the grid is exponential in $1/\epsilon$.

Definition 22 [ϵ-discretization of a concrete optimal-cut problem]. Let $Q = \langle P, X, F \rangle$ be an instance of the concrete optimal-cut problem in $\mathbb{R}^n$, and let $\epsilon \in \mathbb{Q}^{>0}$. The ϵ-*discretization* of Q is the instance $Q_\epsilon = \langle P, \mathcal{P}, X, \mathsf{Flow} \rangle$ of the abstract optimal-cut problem such that:

Algorithm 1. Algorithm for the abstract optimal-cut problem

Input : An instance $\langle P, \mathcal{P}, X, \mathsf{Flow} \rangle$ of the abstract optimal-cut problem.
Result: Two separable sets G^- and G^+ such that any separating hyperplane of G^- and G^+
         is an optimal cut for $\langle P, \mathcal{P}, X, \mathsf{Flow} \rangle$.
begin
   | **return** $split(\varnothing, \varnothing, \mathcal{P})$;
end

external function $value(\mathcal{A}, \mathcal{B}$: set of polytopes$)$: $\mathbb{R}^{\geq 0}$

external function $separable(\mathcal{A}, \mathcal{B}$: set of polytopes$)$: $\{\mathsf{true}, \mathsf{false}\}$

function $split(G^-, G^+, G_0$: set of polytopes$)$: $2^{\mathcal{P}} \times 2^{\mathcal{P}} \times \mathbb{R}^{\geq 0}$ **begin**

  1   Let $P_i, P_j \in \mathcal{P}$ maximizing $\mathsf{range}^{\mathsf{Flow}}(P_i \cup P_j)$ subject to $P_i \in G_0 \lor P_j \in G_0$;
  2   **if** no such P_i, P_j exists **then return** $\langle G^-, G^+, value(G^- \cup G_0, G^+ \cup G_0) \rangle$;
  3   **if** $P_i \in G_0 \land P_j \in G_0$ **then**
  4 $v_A \leftarrow \infty$;
  5 $v_B \leftarrow \infty$;
  6   **if** $separable(G^- \cup \{P_i\}, G^+ \cup \{P_j\})$ **then**
  7 | $\langle A_1, A_2, v_A \rangle \leftarrow split(G^- \cup \{P_i\}, G^+ \cup \{P_j\}, G_0 \backslash \{P_i, P_j\})$;
  8   **if** $separable(G^- \cup \{P_j\}, G^+ \cup \{P_i\})$ **then**
  9 | $\langle B_1, B_2, v_B \rangle \leftarrow split(G^- \cup \{P_j\}, G^+ \cup \{P_i\}, G_0 \backslash \{P_i, P_j\})$;
 10   **if** $v_A = v_B = \infty$ **then return** $\langle G^-, G^+, value(G^- \cup G_0, G^+ \cup G_0) \rangle$;
 11   **if** $v_A \leq v_B$ **then**
 12 | **return** $\langle A_1, A_2, v_A \rangle$;
             else
 13 | **return** $\langle B_1, B_2, v_B \rangle$;
      else
 14   Assume w.l.o.g. that $P_i \in G^-$;
 15   **if** $separable(G^-, G^+ \cup \{P_j\})$ **then**
 16 | **return** $split(G^-, G^+ \cup \{P_j\}, G_0 \backslash \{P_j\})$;
           else
 17 | **return** $\langle G^-, G^+, value(G^- \cup G_0, G^+ \cup G_0) \rangle$;

end

- $\mathcal{P} = \{P \cap box \mid box \in \mathsf{Grid}_\epsilon^F \land P \cap box \neq \varnothing\}$. Notice that $\mathcal{P}$ is finite since P is bounded;
- for each $P_j \in \mathcal{P}$, we have $\mathsf{Flow}(P_j) = \mathsf{range}^F(P_j)$ which is a rectangular predicate of size at most ϵ.

Theorem 23. *Let $Q = \langle P, X, F \rangle$ be an instance of the concrete optimal-cut problem and let $Q_\epsilon = \langle P, \mathcal{P}, X, \mathsf{Flow} \rangle$ be its ϵ-discretization for some $\epsilon \in \mathbb{Q}^{>0}$. If $\pi^\star$ is a solution for Q and $\pi_\epsilon^\star)$ is a solution for Q_ϵ, then $\mathsf{sizeRange}^F(P/\pi_\epsilon^\star) - \mathsf{sizeRange}^F(P/\pi^\star) < \epsilon$.*

3.3   Solution of the Concrete Optimal-Cut Problem in $\mathbb{R}^2$

We propose an algorithm to solve the concrete optimal-cut problem $\langle P, X, F \rangle$ in two dimensions ($P \subset \mathbb{R}^2$) when $F = \{f_1, f_2\}$ contains two functions. It is shown as Algorithm 2. This algorithm is inspired by the abstract Algorithm 1 applied to an ϵ-discretization of the concrete problem with $\epsilon \to 0$. The main trick is to translate the condition of separability expressed with convex hulls into a more

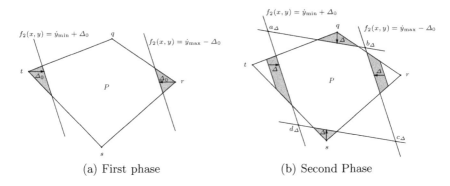

(a) First phase   (b) Second Phase

Fig. 3. Algorithm 2

continuous condition. We show that this condition can be expressed as a linear program.

Let us execute Algorithm 2 and explain informally why it is correct. The input is an instance $\langle P, X, \{f_1, f_2\}\rangle$ of the concrete optimal-cut problem. We represent P on Fig. 3(a).

At lines 2,2 we compute the interval image of P by f_1 and f_2, and the size of the those intervals (r_x and r_y). The assumption of line 2 implies that the points r and t on Fig. 3(a) are such that $\mathsf{sizeRange}^F(\{r, t\}) = \mathsf{sizeRange}^F(P)$. Therefore, any cut that separates those points is better than any other cut. This remains true for the shaded regions defined by Δ_0 on Fig. 3(a) until:

- either Δ_0 becomes equal to $r_y - r_x$,
- or Δ_0 reaches the value $\frac{r_y}{2}$, and the optimal-cut is given by the line $\ell \equiv f_2(x, y) = \dot{y}_{\min} + \frac{r_y}{2}$.

This alternative is tested at line 2: the condition $r_y \geq 2\, r_x$ is equivalent to $\frac{r_y}{2} \leq r_y - r_x$. If $r_y < 2\, r_x$, the algorithm continues as depicted on Fig. 3(b), separating all pairs of points that give the largest range for function f_1 and f_2. The four regions P_q, P_r, P_s and P_t (containing respectively q, r, s and t) are growing altogether at the same "rate". The algorithm will stop whenever it becomes impossible to separate both P_q from P_s and P_r from P_t. As in the abstract algorithm, there are two branches to explore, corresponding to separate either $\{P_q, P_r\}$ from $\{P_s, P_t\}$ or $\{P_q, P_t\}$ from $\{P_r, P_s\}$. On Fig. 3(b), is represented the intersection of the level sets of f_1 and f_2 as $a_\Delta, b_\Delta, c_\Delta$ and d_Δ. The subscript emphasizes the fact that those points are moving when Δ varies.

Intuitively, $\{P_q, P_r\}$ and $\{P_s, P_t\}$ are separable iff a_Δ and c_Δ are outside P, a possible separating line being the line connecting a_Δ and c_Δ. Similarly, $\{P_q, P_t\}$ and $\{P_r, P_s\}$ are separable iff b_Δ and d_Δ are outside P. Assume that, as Δ increases, one of the points b_Δ and d_Δ first enters P. Then, it becomes impossible to separate $\{P_q, P_t\}$ from $\{P_r, P_s\}$. But since $\{P_q, P_r\}$ and $\{P_s, P_t\}$ are still separable, the algorithm can continue. When either a_Δ or c_Δ enters P, the algorithm stops (with say $\Delta = \Delta^\star$). An optimal line cut is given by the line passing by $a_{\Delta^\star}$ and $c_{\Delta^\star}$.

Algorithm 2. Algorithm for computing the concrete optimal-cut in 2D

Input : An instance $S = \langle P, X, F \rangle$ of the concrete optimal-cut problem with $P \subset \mathbb{R}^2$,
$X = \{x, y\}$, and $F = \{f_1, f_2\}$.

Result: A line that solves the concrete optimal-cut problem for S.

begin

1    $[\dot{x}_{\min}, \dot{x}_{\max}] \leftarrow f_1(P)$; $[\dot{y}_{\min}, \dot{y}_{\max}] \leftarrow f_2(P)$;

2    $r_x \leftarrow \dot{x}_{\max} - \dot{x}_{\min}$; $r_y \leftarrow \dot{y}_{\max} - \dot{y}_{\min}$;

3   Assume w.l.o.g. that $r_y \geq r_x$;

4   **if** $r_y \geq 2\,r_x$ **then return** $\ell \equiv f_2(x, y) = \dot{y}_{\min} + \frac{r_y}{2}$;

5    $\Delta_0 \leftarrow r_y - r_x$;

6   Let Δ be a symbolic parameter ;

7    $a_\Delta \leftarrow f_2^{-1}(\dot{y}_{\min} + \Delta_0 + \Delta) \cap f_1^{-1}(\dot{x}_{\min} + \Delta)$;

8    $b_\Delta \leftarrow f_1^{-1}(\dot{x}_{\min} + \Delta) \cap f_2^{-1}(\dot{y}_{\max} - \Delta_0 - \Delta)$;

9    $c_\Delta \leftarrow f_2^{-1}(\dot{y}_{\max} - \Delta_0 - \Delta) \cap f_1^{-1}(\dot{x}_{\max} - \Delta)$;

10    $d_\Delta \leftarrow f_1^{-1}(\dot{x}_{\max} - \Delta) \cap f_2^{-1}(\dot{y}_{\min} + \Delta_0 + \Delta)$;

11   **for** $z = a$ **to** d **do** $\Delta_z \leftarrow \min\{\Delta \mid z_\Delta \in P\}$;

12    $\Delta_1 \leftarrow \min(\Delta_a, \Delta_c)$; $\Delta_2 \leftarrow \min(\Delta_b, \Delta_d)$;

13   **if** $\Delta_1 \geq \frac{r_y}{2} - \Delta_0 \vee \Delta_2 \geq \frac{r_y}{2} - \Delta_0$ **then return** $\ell \equiv f_2(x, y) = \dot{y}_{\min} + \frac{r_y}{2}$;

14    $Q_{\min} \leftarrow P \cap f_1^{-1}(\dot{x}_{\min})$; $Q_{\max} \leftarrow P \cap f_1^{-1}(\dot{x}_{\max})$;

15   **if** $f_2(Q_{\min}) \cap [\dot{y}_{\min}, \dot{y}_{\min} + \Delta_0] \neq \varnothing \wedge f_2(Q_{\min}) \cap [\dot{y}_{\max} - \Delta_0, \dot{y}_{\max}] \neq \varnothing$ **then**

16   **return** $\ell \equiv f_2(x, y) = \dot{y}_{\min} + \frac{r_y}{2}$;

17   **else if** $f_2(Q_{\min}) \cap [\dot{y}_{\min}, \dot{y}_{\min} + \Delta_0] \neq \varnothing \neq \varnothing$ **then**

18   **if** $f_2(Q_{\max}) \cap [\dot{y}_{\min}, \dot{y}_{\min} + \Delta_0] \neq \varnothing$ **then**

19   **return** $\ell \equiv f_2(x, y) = \dot{y}_{\min} + \frac{r_y}{2}$;

     else

20   **return** $line(b_{\Delta_2}, d_{\Delta_2})$;

21   **else if** $f_2(Q_{\min}) \cap [\dot{y}_{\max} - \Delta_0, \dot{y}_{\max}] \neq \varnothing$ **then**

22   **if** $f_2(Q_{\max}) \cap [\dot{y}_{\max} - \Delta_0, \dot{y}_{\max}] \neq \varnothing$ **then**

23   **return** $\ell \equiv f_2(x, y) = \dot{y}_{\min} + \frac{r_y}{2}$;

     else

24   **return** $line(a_{\Delta_1}, c_{\Delta_1})$;

25   **else if** $f_2(Q_{\max}) \cap [\dot{y}_{\max} - \Delta_0, \dot{y}_{\max}] \neq \varnothing \wedge f_2(Q_{\max}) \cap [\dot{y}_{\min}, \dot{y}_{\min} + \Delta_0] \neq \varnothing$ **then**

26   **return** $\ell \equiv f_2(x, y) = \dot{y}_{\min} + \frac{r_y}{2}$;

27   **else if** $f_2(Q_{\max}) \cap [\dot{y}_{\max} - \Delta_0, \dot{y}_{\max}] \neq \varnothing$ **then**

28   **return** $line(b_{\Delta_2}, d_{\Delta_2})$;

29   **else if** $f_2(Q_{\max}) \cap [\dot{y}_{\min}, \dot{y}_{\min} + \Delta_0] \neq \varnothing$ **then**

30   **return** $line(a_{\Delta_1}, c_{\Delta_1})$;

31   **else if** $\Delta_1 > \Delta_2$ **then**

32   **return** $line(a_{\Delta_1}, c_{\Delta_1})$;

   else

33   **return** $line(b_{\Delta_2}, d_{\Delta_2})$;

end

As it can be shown, for $z = a \ldots d$ the point z_Δ enters P for $\Delta_z = \min\{\Delta \mid z_\Delta \in P\}$. Then $\Delta^\star = \max(\min(\Delta_a, \Delta_c), \min(\Delta_b, \Delta_d))$. Finally, notice that there are several other special configurations that require a particular treatment by Algorithm 2 (lines 2–2).

Remark. The macro-instructions of Algorithm 2 (lines 2, 2, 2) can be seen as linear programs. In particular, the coordinates of a_Δ, b_Δ, c_Δ and d_Δ are linear in the parameter Δ so that the minimization of line 2 is a linear program.

Theorem 24. *Algorithm 2 is correct and always terminates.*

Algorithm 2 applies to the optimal-cut problem in 2D. A straightforward extension to higher dimension is not trivially feasible. Indeed, already in 3D, we have examples showing that the separability is not guaranteed even when the level sets (which are planes) are intersecting entirely outside the given polytope.

Example. On Fig. 4 is shown the invariant of location ℓ_1 of the shared gas-burner, with the position of the level sets of $f_1(x_1, x_2) = h_1 - a_1 x_1 + b_1 x_2$ and $f_2(x_1, x_2) = -a_2 x_2 + b_2 x_1$ at the end of Algorithm 2. The four arrows indicates the moving direction of the lines corresponding to increase the parameter Δ in the algorithm. The shaded regions corresponds to the pieces that are to be separated. The optimal cut is the dashed line $x_1 = x_2$.

4   Refinement-Based Safety Verification Algorithm

In this section, we explain the methodology to obtain automatically successive refinements of an affine hybrid automaton H for which to check emptiness.

A first rectangular phase-portrait approximation $H_0 = \mathsf{rect}(H)$ is computed from the original automaton H. Then the automaton H_0 is symbolically analyzed, both forward and backward as described in Section 2. This gives the two sets $\mathsf{Reach}(\llbracket H_0 \rrbracket)$ and $\mathsf{Reach}^{-1}(\llbracket H_0 \rrbracket)$. If their intersection $\mathsf{Unsafe}(\llbracket H_0 \rrbracket)$ is empty, then so is the set $\mathsf{Unsafe}(\llbracket H \rrbracket)$ (by Lemma 7 and Theorem 8) and the emptiness of H is established. Otherwise, we refine the automaton H by splitting one of its unsafe locations and restart the procedure. In fact, from Theorem 25 below and Lemma 10, it appears that refining the rectangular approximation of an automaton H in a safe location is useless for checking emptiness, since the emptiness problem has the same answer for H and its refinement in that case. In other words, the relevant part of the state-space to be refined is $\mathsf{Unsafe}(\llbracket H \rrbracket)$. This is stated by Corollary 26, using the notion of *pruning*.

For an hybrid automaton $H = \langle \mathsf{Loc}, \mathsf{Lab}, \mathsf{Edg}, X, \mathsf{Init}, \mathsf{Inv}, \mathsf{Flow}, \mathsf{Jump}, \mathsf{Final} \rangle$ and a subset $L \subseteq \mathsf{Loc}$ of its locations, let $\mathsf{prune}(H, L)$ be the hybrid automaton $\langle \mathsf{Loc}', \mathsf{Lab}, \mathsf{Edg}', X, \mathsf{Init}, \mathsf{Inv}, \mathsf{Flow}, \mathsf{Jump}, \mathsf{Final} \rangle$ where $\mathsf{Loc}' = \mathsf{Loc} \backslash L$, $\mathsf{Edg}' = \{(\ell, \sigma, \ell') \in \mathsf{Edg} \mid \ell, \ell' \in \mathsf{Loc}'\}$ and the other components are left unchanged.

Theorem 25. *For every hybrid automaton H, for every subset $L \subseteq \mathsf{SafeLoc}(H)$ of its safe locations, we have $\llbracket \mathsf{prune}(H, L) \rrbracket \approx_{unsafe} \llbracket H \rrbracket$, that is, $\llbracket \mathsf{prune}(H, L) \rrbracket$ and $\llbracket H \rrbracket$ are weakly bisimilar for the unsafe behaviours.*

Corollary 26. *For every hybrid automaton H, for every location $\ell \in \mathsf{SafeLoc}(\mathsf{rect}(H))$, and every hyperplane π, $\mathsf{rect}(H)$ is empty iff $\mathsf{rect}(\mathsf{split}(H, \ell, \pi))$ is empty.*

The core of the refinement based verification procedure is given below. Although the refinement loop is not guaranteed to terminate, we could stop when the size of the invariants run below a certain threshold with the conclusion that the system is not robustly correct for that threshold. In a variation of this procedure, the splitting can be iterated a fixed number of times in each loop, between successive analysis of the rectangularized system.

while Unsafe($[\![\text{rect}(H)]\!]$) $\neq \emptyset$ **do**
$\quad L \leftarrow \mathsf{SafeLoc}(\mathsf{rect}(H))$;
$\quad H' \leftarrow \mathsf{prune}(H, L)$;
$\quad$ Let ℓ be a location of H' and π be a hyperplane ;
$\quad H \leftarrow \mathsf{split}(H', \ell, \pi)$;

The splitting is done in the location ℓ having the greatest imprecision (the largest value of sizeRange on its invariant) and the hyperplane π is determined using one of the algorithm presented in Section 3. This is a natural choice for ℓ since our goal is to finally reduce the overall imprecision of the rectangular approximation. This way, the approximation can be made arbitrarily close to the original system (for an infinite-norm metric [10]) and so if the system is robust (in the sense that it is still correct under some small perturbation [6]), our procedure eventually establishes its correctness, provided the reachability analysis of the rectangular automata terminate. This contrasts with the counter-example based refinement abstraction method (CEGAR) developed by Clarke et al. [4] where the approximations are finite-state, but the refinement procedure is driven by the elimination of spurious counter-examples (executions of the approximation which have no concrete counterpart) and therefore not guaranteed to terminate.

5   Case Study

In practice, we use PPL (the Parma Polyhedra Library [3]) to overapproximate the differential equations by rectangular inclusions. PPL is a C++ library to manipulate polyhedrons with large rational coefficients and exact arithmetic. We analyze the rectangular system with PHAVer [7], a recent tool for the verification of hybrid systems. This tool is designed to verify affine dynamics hybrid automata, based on forward reachability analysis and user-defined rectangular approximations. In our case, since the successive rectangular approximations are obtained automatically, we have disabled the refinement features of PHAVer. Also, we use the reverse automaton construction of Section 2 to implement backward analysis.

We applied our methodology to the Navigation benchmark [5]. We present it briefly. An object is moving on a $m \times n$ grid divided in $m \cdot n$ cells. A map M associates to each cell either an integer i in $\{0, \dots, 7\}$ or a special symbol in $\{\mathsf{A}, \mathsf{B}\}$. The integer determines the *desired velocity* $\mathbf{v}_d(i) = (sin(i\pi/4), cos(i\pi/4))$ in the cell. Then the behaviour of the object (described by its position $\mathbf{x}$ and velocity $\mathbf{v}$) in such a cell is governed by the differential equations $\dot{\mathbf{x}} = \mathbf{v}$ and $\dot{\mathbf{v}} = A \cdot (\mathbf{v} - \mathbf{v}_d(i))$ where A is a 2×2 matrix such that the solution velocity $\mathbf{v}$ always converge to the desired velocity $\mathbf{v}_d(i)$. A cell mapped to B should be avoided and a cell mapped to A should be reached. We only verify the avoidance property and we assume that the object cannot leave the grid. An instance of the benchmark is characterized by the size of the grid, the map M, the matrix A and the initial positions and velocities.

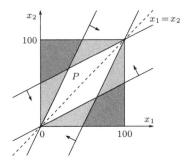

Fig. 4. The optimal cut of the invariant of location ℓ_1 of the shared gas-burner

Instance	Grid	Time	(PT)
NAV01	3×3	5s	(35s)
NAV02	3×3	10s	(62s)
NAV03	3×3	10s	(62s)
NAV04	3×3	75s	$(225s^i)$
NAV07	4×4	11mn	

^{i} obtained with a heuristic

Fig. 5. Execution times on a Xeon 3GHz with 4GB RAM (compared with PT = PHAVER times [7])

This navigation benchmark has 4 variables x_1, x_2, v_1, v_2 but only two of them (v_1 and v_2) appear in the right-hand side of the differential equations. So, the quality of the splitting is not influenced by the position variables x_1, x_2. Thus it is sufficient to consider line cuts in the plane $v_1 v_2$ of the velocities. In order to apply the procedure OptimalCut, we still have to choose two functions among the four defining the system of differential equations: v_1, v_2, $A_{1*} \cdot (\mathbf{v} - \mathbf{v}_d)$ or $A_{2*} \cdot (\mathbf{v} - \mathbf{v}_d(i))$ where A_{1*} (resp. A_{2*}) is the first (resp. second) row of A. In practice, the first two functions give better results, essentially due to a lower need in computational resources (mainly memory).

The results reported in Fig. 5 are encouraging since we were able to verify more efficiently than PHAVER itself the instances NAV01-04, while we used that tool as a black box for analysis of rectangular automata (thus with all heuristics disabled). Also notice that the instance NAV04 was solved by PHAVER after applying heuristic convex hull and bounding box approximations at particular moments of the analysis [7]. Our results are fragile, since another choice of affine functions has lead to computational difficulties, as mentioned above.

References

1. R. Alur, C. Courcoubetis, N. Halbwachs, T.A. Henzinger, P.-H. Ho, X. Nicollin, A. Olivero, J. Sifakis, and S. Yovine. The algorithmic analysis of hybrid systems. *Theoretical Computer Science*, 138:3–34, 1995.
2. Eugene Asarin, Thao Dang, Oded Maler, and Olivier Bournez. Approximate reachability analysis of piecewise-linear dynamical systems. In *Proceedings of HSCC 2000: Hybrid Systems, Computation and Control*, LNCS 1790, pages 20–31. Springer, 2000.
3. R. Bagnara, E. Ricci, E. Zaffanella, and P. M. Hill. Possibly not closed convex polyhedra and the Parma Polyhedra Library. In *Static Analysis: Proceedings of the 9th International Symposium*, LNCS 2477, pages 213–229, Springer, 2002.
4. Edmund M. Clarke, Orna Grumberg, Somesh Jha, Yuan Lu, and Helmut Veith. Counterexample-guided abstraction refinement. In *Proceedings of CAV 2000: Computer Aided Verification*, LNCS 1855, pages 154–169. Springer, 2000.

5. Ansgar Fehnker and Franjo Ivancic. Benchmarks for hybrid systems verification. In *HSCC 04: Hybrid Systems, Computation and Control*, LNCS 2993, pages 326–341. Springer, 2004.

6. Martin Fränzle. Analysis of hybrid systems: An ounce of realism can save an infinity of states. In *Proceedings of CSL 1999: Computer Science Logic*, LNCS 1683, pages 126–140. Springer, 1999.

7. Goran Frehse. Phaver: Algorithmic verification of hybrid systems past HyTech. In *HSCC 05: Hybrid Systems, Computation and Control*, LNCS 3414, pages 258–273. Springer, 2005.

8. T.A. Henzinger. The theory of hybrid automata. In *Proceedings of the 11th Annual Symposium on Logic in Computer Science*, pages 278–292. IEEE Computer Society Press, 1996.

9. T.A. Henzinger, P.-H. Ho, and H. Wong-Toi. A user guide to HyTech. In *TACAS 95: Tools and Algorithms for the Construction and Analysis of Systems*, LNCS 1019, pages 41–71. Springer, 1995.

10. T.A. Henzinger, P.-H. Ho, and H. Wong-Toi. Algorithmic analysis of nonlinear hybrid systems. *IEEE Transactions on Automatic Control*, 43:540–554, 1998.

11. T.A. Henzinger, P.W. Kopke, A. Puri, and P. Varaiya. What's decidable about hybrid automata? *Journal of Computer and System Sciences*, 57:94–124, 1998.

12. R. Milner. *A Calculus of Communicating Systems*. LNCS 92. Springer, 1980.

Reachability Problems on Extended O-Minimal Hybrid Automata

Raffaella Gentilini

Università di Udine (DIMI), Via Le Scienze 206, 33100 Udine - Italy
gentilin@dimi.uniud.it

Abstract. Within hybrid systems theory, o-minimal automata are often considered on the border between decidability and undecidability. In such classes of hybrid automata, the constraint of having only *constant reset* upon discrete jumps is a strong limitation for their applicability: hence, an important issue for both theoreticians and practitioners, is that of relaxing the above constraint, while not fall into undecidability.

In this paper we start considering the problem of *timed-bounded* reachability on o-minimal automata. This can be seen either as a reachability problem paired with time-constraints or as a classical reachability problem for a class of hybrid automata which properly extends the o-minimal one, with an extra variable representing time. Then, we directly face the problem of extending o-minimal automata by allowing some variables to retain their values upon a discrete jump, without crossing the undecidability border.

1 Introduction

Hybrid automata [10] allow formal modeling and reasoning on systems in which continuous and discrete dynamics mutually interact. A fundamental task, underlying automatic verification of hybrid systems, consists in solving a reachability problem i.e. in checking whether the hybrid systems trajectories can evolve to some (bad) region of the (infinite) state-space. The reachability problem is known to be undecidable for a great variety of hybrid automata families [10, 11, 2]. Indeed, the analysis of the border between decidability and undecidability stands as one of the major questions in hybrid systems theory. So far, the results in literature suggest that decidability can follow only from the imposition of strict constraints, either to the continuous flow or to the discrete transitions of systems [2, 11, 1, 9, 13]. To this purpose, the recently introduced family of o-minimal hybrid automata [13] is significant in that, on the one hand, it admits a great variety of possible continuous evolutions but, on the other hand, it imposes a very restrictive constraint on discrete transitions. Basically, upon each discrete jump of an o-minimal system, all continuous variables must be (non deterministically) reset to a constant. Stated in an other way, continuous and discrete dynamics are completely decoupled. In [13], the entire family of o-minimal systems was shown to admit finite bisimulation, and various classes of o-minimal automata were proved decidable, being the corresponding bisimulation algorithm computable.

P. Pettersson and W. Yi (Eds.): FORMATS 2005, LNCS 3829, pp. 162–176, 2005.

Because of the above positive results o-minimal systems are a family of hybrid automata having a great interest from a theoretical point of view; however, their application is rather limited since any continuous variable is never admitted to "remember" its value upon discrete transition.

Starting from the above considerations, in the first part of this paper we consider a variant of reachability problem for o-minimal systems: the *time-bounded reachability problem* (is a region reachable within a maximum time *t*?). Such a problem can be seen either as a reachability problem paired with time-constraints, or it can be reduced to a classical reachability problem for a class of hybrid automata which properly extends the o-minimal one, with an extra variable representing time. In order to show the decidability of our extended reachability problem, we use the first of the two above characterizations, and we introduce a proof technique that does not require the construction of a (finite) bisimulation abstraction. Basically, we build and solve an equivalent minimum-path problem on a suitable weighted-graph.

In the second part of the paper, we directly face the problem of adjoining o-minimal automata with variables that can maintain their value upon a discrete jump. To this purpose we introduce the class of *relaxed o-minimal automata* that we show to admit finite bisimulation. Finally, we rely on techniques introduced in the first part of the paper to study and prove decidability for a further extension of o-minimal automata, that we call *MasterSlaves o-minimal automata*. For space sake, we include complete proofs of the claims in this paper in [8].

2 Preliminaries

We introduce here the basic notions and the notation we will need in the sequel.

Definition 1 (Hybrid Automata [2]). *An Hybrid Automata is a tuple $H = (L, E, X, Init, Inv, F, G, R)$ with the following components:*

- *a finite set of* locations, *L;*
- *a finite set of* continuous variables, *$X = \{x_1, \ldots x_n\}$, that take value on $\mathbb{R}$;*
- *a finite set of* discrete transitions *(or* jumps*) $E \subseteq L \times L$;*
- *$F : L \times \mathbb{R}^n \mapsto \mathbb{R}^n$, assigning to each location $\ell \in L$ a vector field $F(\ell, \cdot)$ that defines the evolution of continuous variables within ℓ;*
- *an initial set of conditions: Init $\subseteq L \times \mathbb{R}^n$;*
- *Inv: $L \mapsto 2^{\mathbb{R}^n}$, the* Invariant *location labelling;*
- *$G : E \mapsto 2^{\mathbb{R}^n}$, the* Guard *edge labelling;*
- *$R : E \times \mathbb{R}^n \mapsto 2^{\mathbb{R}^n}$, the* Reset *edge labelling.*

We use the notation $\mathbf{v}$ to represent a valuation, $(v_1, \ldots, v_n) \in \mathbb{R}^n$, of the variables' vector $\mathbf{x} = (x_1, \ldots, x_n)$. $\|\mathbf{x}\|$ represents the usual euclidean vector norm, whereas $\dot{\mathbf{x}}$ denotes the first derivatives of the variables in $\mathbf{x}$. A *state* in H is a pair $s = (\ell, \mathbf{v})$, where $\ell \in L$ is called the *discrete component* of s and $\mathbf{v}$ is called the *continuous component* of s. An execution of $H = (L, E, X, Init, Inv, f, G, R)$, starts at any $(\ell, \mathbf{v}) \in Init$ and consists of continuous evolutions (within a location) and discrete transitions (between two locations). Formally, an execution of H is a path in the *timed transition system* of H (cfr. Definition 2, below), alternating discrete and continuous steps.

Definition 2. *The* timed transition system, T_H^t, *of the hybrid automata* $H = (L, E, X, Init, Inv, F, G, R)$ *is the labeled transition system* $T_H^t = (Q, Q_0, \Sigma, \rightarrow)$, *with* $Q \subseteq L \times \mathbb{R}^n, Q_0 \subseteq Q, \Sigma = \mathbb{R}^+ \cup E$, *where:*

  - $(\ell, \mathbf{v}) \in Q$ *if and only if* $\mathbf{v} \in Inv(\ell)$ *and* $(\ell, \mathbf{v}) \in Q_0$ *if and only if* $\mathbf{v} \in Init(\ell) \cap Inv(\ell)$;
  - *for each* $\delta \in \mathbb{R}^+$, *there is a continuous transition* $(\ell, \mathbf{v}) \rightarrow_\delta (\ell, \mathbf{v}')$, *if and only if there is a differentiable function* $f : [0, \delta] \rightarrow \mathbb{R}^n$, *with the first derivative* $\dot{f} : [0, \delta] \rightarrow \mathbb{R}^n$ *such that:*
    1. $f(0) = \mathbf{v}$ *and* $f(\delta) = \mathbf{v}'$;
    2. *for all* $\varepsilon \in (0, \delta)$, $f(\varepsilon) \in Inv(\ell)$, *and* $\dot{f}(\varepsilon) = F(\ell, f(\varepsilon))$.
  - *there is a discrete transition* $(\ell, \mathbf{v}) \rightarrow_e (\ell', \mathbf{v}')$ *if and only if* $e = (\ell, \ell') \in E$, $\mathbf{v} \in G(\ell)$ *and* $\mathbf{v}' \in R((\ell, \ell'), \mathbf{v})$

A run of H will be denoted by the sequence (of continuous and discrete steps) $r = (\ell_0, \mathbf{v_0}) \xrightarrow{t_0} (\ell_0, \mathbf{w_0}) \rightarrow (\ell_1, \mathbf{v_1}) \xrightarrow{t_1} (\ell_1, \mathbf{w_1}) \rightarrow \ldots (\ell_n, \mathbf{v_n}) \xrightarrow{t_n} (\ell_n, \mathbf{w_n})$, where $\sum_{i=0}^n t_i$ will be said the *duration* of r.

The *time abstract transition system* of H is the labeled transition system $T_H = (Q, Q_0, \Sigma \rightarrow)$, where $\Sigma = E \cup \{\tau\}$, that is obtain from T_H^t by replacing each label $\delta \in \mathbb{R}^+$ with the label τ.

A fundamental tool for resizing transition systems, while preserving crucial properties (such as reachability) is *bisimulation reduction*, that we introduce below. Consider a labeled transition system $T = (Q, Q_0, Q_F, \Sigma, \rightarrow)$, where Q_F denotes the set of final states, and let $\sim_\mathcal{B}$ to be an equivalence relation on Q.

Definition 3. $\sim_\mathcal{B}$ *is a* bisimulation *of* $T = (Q, Q_0, Q_F, \Sigma, \rightarrow)$ *if and only if:*

  - *both* Q_0 *and* Q_F *are* $\sim_\mathcal{B}$ *blocks (i.e. union of* $\sim_\mathcal{B}$ *classes);*
  - *for each* $\sim_\mathcal{B}$ *block,* B, *for each label* $a \in \Sigma$, *the region* $Pre_a(B) = \{q \in Q \mid \exists p \in B \quad \wedge \quad q \rightarrow_a p\}$ *is a* $\sim_\mathcal{B}$-*block.*

2.1   O-Minimal Theories and O-Minimal Hybrid Automata

In this paper we consider a class of hybrid automata called *o-minimal automata* [13, 14]. O-minimal theories, introduced below, play a central role in the definition of o-minimal automata. We refer to [19, 18, 20] for a more comprehensive introduction to o-minimal theories.

Definition 4. *A theory of the reals is* o-minimal *if and only if every definable subset of* $\mathbb{R}$ *is a finite union of points and intervals (possibly unbounded).*

The class of o-minimal theories over the reals is quite rich: the theories $\mathsf{Li}(\mathbb{R}) = (\mathbb{R}, <, +, -, 0, 1)$ and $\mathsf{OF}(\mathbb{R}) = (\mathbb{R}, <, +, -, *, 0, 1)$ are both o-minimal. The extension of the above theories obtained by admitting, in the underlying language, a symbol for the exponential function, $\mathsf{OF_{exp}}(\mathbb{R}) = (\mathbb{R}, <, +, -, *, exp, 0, 1)$, is also o-minimal. Another important extension is obtained by introducing, in the underline language, a symbol for each *restricted analytic functions* and more extensions are discussed in [13]. By Definition 6, below, such a variety of o-minimal theories (over the reals) ensures that o-minimal automata is a large and important family of hybrid automata, admitting powerful continuous evolutions. In the following definitions, we will use the notation adopted in [13].

Definition 5. *Let $F : \mathbb{R}^n \mapsto \mathbb{R}^n$ a smooth vector field on $\mathbb{R}^n$. For each $\mathbf{v} \in \mathbb{R}^n$, let $\gamma_{\mathbf{v}}(t)$ to denote the integral curve of F which passes through $\mathbf{v}$ at $t = 0$, that is $\dot{\gamma}_{\mathbf{v}}(t) = F(\gamma_{\mathbf{v}}(t))$ and $\gamma_{\mathbf{v}}(0) = \mathbf{v}$. We say that F is* complete *if, for each $\mathbf{v} \in \mathbb{R}^n$, $\gamma_{\mathbf{v}}(t)$ is defined for all times t. For such an F, the* flow *of F is the function $\phi : \mathbb{R}^n \times \mathbb{R} \mapsto \mathbb{R}^n$, given by $\phi(\mathbf{v}, t) = \gamma_{\mathbf{v}}(t)$.*

Definition 6 (O-Minimal Hybrid Automata [13]). *The hybrid automaton $H = (L, E, X, \mathrm{Init}, \mathrm{Inv}, F, G, R)$ is said an o-minimal automata if and only if:*

- *for each $\ell \in L$ the smooth vector field $F(\ell, \cdot)$ is complete;*
- *for each $(\ell, \ell') \in E$, the reset function $R : E \mapsto \mathbb{R}^n$ does not depend on continuous variables (*constant resettings*);*
- *for each $\ell \in L$ and $(\ell, \ell') \in E$, the sets $\mathrm{Inv}(\ell)$, $R(\ell, \ell')$, $G(\ell)$, $\mathrm{Init}(\ell)$, and the flow of $F(\ell, \cdot)$ are definable in the same o-minimal theory*

Given an o-minimal theory, $\mathcal{T}$, we denote by o-minimal($\mathcal{T}$) automata the class of o-minimal automata induced by $\mathcal{T}$.

3   Related Work

The *reachability problem* for an hybrid automaton H, consists in the problem of determinimg, given a location ℓ and $V \subseteq \mathbb{R}^n$, if there exists a run of H ending at $(\ell, \mathbf{v})$ with $\mathbf{v} \in V$. In general, the latter problem is not decidable [11, 10]. So far, according to the results in the litterature, it seems that its decidability can be obtained only by imposing strict constraints either on the discrete transitions, or on the continuous evolution of hybrid automata [2, 11].

In *timed automata* [1] and *multirate automata* [11, 12], for example, the flow of continuous variables must be of constant slope one and general constant slope, respectively. In both cases, the reachability problem is decidable because the corresponding time-abstract transition systems can be (algorithmically) reduced to finite by *bisimulation* reduction [11]. *Initialized rectangular automata* [12] allow to specify derivatives of the continuous variables flows by means of a conjunction of inequality of the form $\dot{x} \approx c$, where $\approx \in \{<, >, =\}$ and $c \in \mathbb{Q}$. Moreover they impose an *initialization constraint* on discrete transitions. Given a discrete transition (ℓ, ℓ'), all the variables that have a different flow in ℓ and ℓ' must be reset to an interval over $\mathbb{R}$; The reachability problem is decidable for initialized rectangular automata, since the corresponding time abstract transition systems can be (algorithmically) reduced to finite by *simulation* reduction [9, 11].

O-minimal hybrid systems [13] are considered on the border between decidability and undecidability for the reachability problem. If H is an o-minimal automata, then T_H admits finite bisimulation [13, 14, 7]. This result does not guarantee the decidability of the entire family [14], because the bisimulation reduction is not computable, in general, for o-minimal automata. In order to decide reachability relying on bisimulation reduction, it is necessary to effectively:

1. represent sets of states;
2. perform set intersection, set complement, and check set emptiness;
3. given a set of states, Y, compute the set of states that can reach an element in Y following a discrete/continuous step.

The computability of the above operations depends on the o-minimal theory in which the flow of the hybrid automata, the *Inv* sets, the *Guard* sets, the *Reset* sets, and the *Initial* conditions are defined. In [14] it is proved the decidability of o-minimal(OF($\mathbb{R}$)) automata. Decidability depends on the fact that the theory (OF($\mathbb{R}$)) *admits quantifier elimination* [17, 4] i.e. each formula in the theory is equivalent to a quantifier free one that can be algorithmically determined. Thus, for example, checking set emptiness corresponds to first performing quantifier elimination, and then checking if the resulting formula is equivalent to *false*. The results in [13, 14] show that o-minimal(OF($\mathbb{R}$)) automata constitute a class of decidable hybrid systems admitting powerful coupled continuous dynamics. For example, the flow of continuous variables whose first derivatives is given by $\dot{\mathbf{x}} = A\mathbf{x}$, with A nilpotent (that is $\exists n\ A^n = 0$), is OF($\mathbb{R}$) definable [13]. On the converse, o-minimal(OF($\mathbb{R}$)) automata define the class of decidable hybrid systems with the strongest constraints on discrete transition: each variable must be nondeterministically reset to a constant upon each location switch.

In the next section we show how the above constraints on discrete transitions leave open the following decidability question for o-minimal automata.

Is it possible to decide if a region is reachable within a time interval?

The answer of such a question is positive for the other families of decidable hybrid automata (timed, multirate and initialized rectangular automata). We enclose the circle giving a positive answer also for o-minimal(OF($\mathbb{R}$)) automata. The construction we will give is interesting in itself, because it allows establishing an alternative proof that reachability is decidable for o-minimal(OF($\mathbb{R}$)) automata. Such a proof does not make use of bisimulation or simulation reduction and, in our opinion, allows to better understand the link relating the constraints defining both discrete and continuous components, in o-minimal automata, and the decidability of the reachability problem. Moreover, our proof is constructive and gives, as a free byproduct, an *optimal* reachability run i.e. a run whose duration is minimal. The problem of determining optimal runs, assuming both time constraints and discrete switches costs has been previously considered for the class of timed automata in [16, 5, 3].

We conclude this section citing the works in [15, 6] where the issue of extending o-minimal automata relaxing the constant reset constraint is taken into consideration, and some extensions leading to undecidability are presented.

4   Time Bounded Reachability Problem and O-Minimal Hybrid Automata

We start by formally defining the *time bounded reachability problem* on hybrid automata.

Definition 7. *The* timed bounded reachability problem *for an hybrid automata H, consists in determining, given a location ℓ, $V \subseteq \mathbb{R}^n$, and a time value $t \in \mathbb{Q}$, if there exists a run of H having duration $t' \leq t$ and ending at $(\ell, \mathbf{v})$, with $\mathbf{v} \in V$.*

For most families of decidable hybrid automata (but not for classes of o-minimal systems), the above problem can be reduced to a classical reachability problem on an augmented automata of the same family. In fact, assume for example to work with a timed, a multirate, or an initialized rectangular automata, H, and suppose that you want to state if the region (ℓ, V) is reachable within time $t \in \mathbb{Q}$. You can obtain a new automata of the same family, H', by augmenting the set of continuous variables with a new (time) variable x_t, where $\dot{x}_t = 1$ in all locations and $R(v_t) = v_t$ for all discrete transitions. Trivially, (ℓ, V) is reachable within the time t in H if and only if $(\ell, V \times \{t' \,|\, t' \leq t\})$ is reachable in H'. The construction does not work for o-minimal($\mathsf{OF}(\mathbb{R})$) automata, since o-minimal automata do not allow a variable to always maintain the same value upon a discrete transition.

In order to prove that time bounded reachability is still decidable for o-minimal($\mathsf{OF}(\mathbb{R})$) automata, we shall define an equivalent weighted graph minimum-path problem. The graph manipulated will be a labelling of the control graph of H, instead of a simulation or a bisimulation abstraction of T_H. The following lemma establishes a general property of o-minimal systems and will be central in the correctness of the encoding.

Lemma 1. *For each run of H,*
$$r = (\ell_0, \mathbf{v_0}) \xrightarrow{t_0} (\ell_0, \mathbf{w_0}) \to (\ell_1, \mathbf{v_1}) \ldots \xrightarrow{t_{n-1}} (\ell_{n-1}, \mathbf{w_{n-1}}) \to (\ell_n, \mathbf{v_n}),$$
there is a run of H,
$$r^* = (\ell'_0, \mathbf{v'_0}) \xrightarrow{t_0} (\ell'_0, \mathbf{w'_0}) \to (\ell'_1, \mathbf{v'_1}) \ldots \xrightarrow{t_{m-1}} (\ell'_{m-1}, \mathbf{w'_{m-1}}) \to (\ell'_m, \mathbf{v'_m}), \text{ where:}$$

- $\ell_0 = \ell'_0$, $\mathbf{v_0} = \mathbf{v'_0}$, $\ell_n = \ell'_m$, and $\mathbf{v_n} = \mathbf{v'_m}$
- $\forall\, 0 \leq i, j < m$, it holds $(i \neq j) \to (\langle \ell'_i, \ell'_{i+1} \rangle) \neq (\langle \ell'_j, \ell'_{j+1} \rangle)$
- *the duration of r^* is less or equal to the duration of r.*

Lemma 1 can be used to build, given an o-minimal automata H, an o-minimal automata H' with the following property: (ℓ, V) is reachable in H if and only if V is reachable (in a suitable location of H') through a path that passes *at most once* on each H'-location. More precisely, we define the *guard-expansion* of an o-minimal automata H, as below:

Definition 8. *The* guard-expansion *of $H = (L, E, X, \mathrm{Init}, \mathrm{Inv}, \mathsf{f}, G, R)$ is the o-minimal automata $H' = (L', E', X', \mathrm{Init}', \mathrm{Inv}', \mathsf{f}', G', R')$ where:*

- $L' = \{\ell_i^j \mid (\ell_j, \ell_i) \in E\} \cup \{\ell_i^\sharp \mid \ell_i \in L \text{ has not incoming edges}\};$
- $(\ell_i^j, \ell_p^i) \in E$ if and only if $(\ell_i, \ell_p) \in E$;
- for all $\ell_i^j \in L'$ we have $\mathrm{Init}'(\ell_i^j)=\mathrm{Init}(\ell_i)$, $\mathrm{Inv}'(\ell_i^j)=\mathrm{Inv}(\ell_i)$, $G(\ell_i^j, \ell_p^i)=G(\ell_i, \ell_p)$, $f'(\ell_i^j, \mathbf{x})=f(\ell_i, \mathbf{x})$;
- for all $(\ell_i^j, \ell_p^i) \in E$, $R'(\ell_i^j, \ell_p^i) = R(\ell_i, \ell_p)$.

The result in Lemma 2 follows directly by Definition 8 and by Lemma 1.

Lemma 2. *If (ℓ_i, V) is reachable in the o-minimal automata H within time t, then there exists j such that (ℓ_i^j, V) is reachable in the guard-expansion of H, through a run of duration $t' \leq t$ that never pass twice in the same location.*

5 An Algorithm for Time Bounded Reachability on Classes of O-Minimal Hybrid Automata

We prove here the decidability of time bounded reachability for o-minimal($\mathsf{OF}(\mathbb{R})$) automata. As anticipated, we will make use of the results in Section 4 to map the problem onto a weighted graph minimum-path problem.

Given an o-minimal($\mathsf{OF}(\mathbb{R})$) automata, H, the first step in the construction consists in obtaining the guard-expansion of H (cfr. Definition 8), H'. By Lemma 2, checking if H admits a run to a region R, of duration at most t, is equivalent to checking if there is a suitable acyclic run of duration at most t in H'. We represent in Figure 1 an o-minimal($\mathsf{OF}(\mathbb{R})$) automata and its guard-expansion[1]. In the rest of this section we will use exactly the automata of Figure 1 to illustrate the overall procedure.

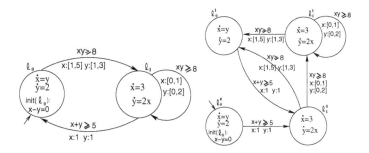

Fig. 1. An o-minimal($\mathsf{OF}(\mathbb{R})$) automaton and its guard-expansion

5.1 Phase 1: Labelling Scheme

Our next task is that of opportunely labeling the control graph of the guard-expansion automata H', obtaining a weighted graph $\mathcal{G}$. The set of nodes in $\mathcal{G}$ consists of the set of locations of H' plus an auxiliary final node F.

---

[1] Note that the continuous dynamics of the hybrid automata depicted in Figure 1 can be expressed within ($\mathsf{OF}(\mathbb{R})$) theory because the matrices involved in the underlying differential equations systems are *nilpotent* (see [14]).

If the target region, in our process, is in the location l_i of H, then F is linked to all the locations of H' into which l_i gets split. Hence, for example, if we would like to check time-bounded reachability of a region in the location ℓ_0, then $\mathcal{G}$ would have the structure depicted in Figure 2.

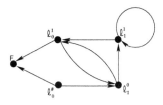

Fig. 2.

The weights in $\mathcal{G}$ are real numbers maintaining as much information as necessary to reduce our time bounded reachability problem to that of detecting a minimum weighted path in $\mathcal{G}$. Such weights are defined relying on the fact that $\mathsf{OF}(\mathbb{R})$ is a decidable theory that admits quantifier elimination. In fact, to label each edge of $\mathcal{G}$, we build a suitable $\mathsf{OF}(\mathbb{R})$ formula and we eliminate its quantifiers. As a byproduct, we obtain a real number that we use as a weight. More in detail, the labeling of $\mathcal{G}$ proceeds as follows:

- For each edge (l_i^j, l_p^i) in $\mathcal{G}$, we build the formula $\psi_{(l_i^j, l_p^i)}(t_0)$, that represents the *greatest lower bound* of the (o-minimal) set of times allowing to pass from a point in the reset region $R(l_j, l_i)$ of H, to a point in the guard region $G(l_i, l_p)$ of H. The formula $\psi_{(l_i^j, l_p^i)}(t_0)$ is given by:

$$\psi_{(l_i^j, l_p^i)}(t_0) = (Reach^{\Delta}_{(l_i^j, l_p^i)}(t_0) \vee Reach_{(l_i^j, l_p^i)}(t_0)) \wedge \\ \wedge \forall t(Reach_{(l_i^j, l_p^i)}(t) \to t \geq t_0)) \tag{1}$$

In $\psi_{(l_i^j, l_p^i)}(t_0)$, the subformula $Reach^{\Delta}_{(l_i^j, l_p^i)}(t_0)$ characterizes the time-point t_0 as the left extreme of an open interval, $\Delta = (t_0, t_0 + \epsilon)$, such that, for each $t_0 < t < t_0 + \epsilon$, the continuous components of H' can evolve from a value in $R(l_j, l_i)$ to a value in $G(l_i, l_p) \in H$, in time t. Similarly, the subformula $Reach_{(l_i^j, l_p^i)}(t)$ expresses the possibility to reach the guard-set $G(l_i, l_p) \in H$ from the reset-set $R(l_j, l_i) \in H$ in time t. If ϕ denotes the flow of the vector field $F(\ell_i, \cdot)$, then $Reach^{\Delta}_{(l_i^j, l_p^i)}(t_0)$ and $Reach_{(l_i^j, l_p^i)}(t)$ are the following $\mathsf{OF}(\mathbb{R})$ first-order formulas:

$$Reach^{\Delta}_{(l_i^j, l_p^i)}(t_0) = \exists \epsilon \forall t[(t_0 < t \wedge t < \epsilon) \to Reach_{(l_i^j, l_p^i)}(t)] \tag{2}$$

$$Reach_{(l_i^j, l_p^i)}(t) = \exists \mathbf{x}, \mathbf{y} \, [\mathbf{x} \in R(l_j, l_i) \wedge \mathbf{y} \in G(l_i, l_p) \wedge \phi(\mathbf{x}, t) = \mathbf{y} \wedge \\ \wedge \forall t'(0 \leq t' \leq t \to \phi(\mathbf{x}, t') \in Inv(l_i))] \tag{3}$$

If $\psi_{(l_i^j, l_p^i)}(t_0)$ is satisfiable, then there is a unique value that can be assigned to t_0 to have a true sentence. Hence, by using, for example, Collins cylindric algebraic decomposition algorithm [6] we can eliminate the quantifiers in $\psi_{(l_i^j, l_p^i)}(t_0)$ and obtain a real algebraic number witnessing (the unique) time-value satisfying $\psi_{(l_i^j, l_p^i)}(t_0)$. We use the computed greatest lower bound, say α, to label the edge (l_i^j, l_p^i) in $\mathcal{G}$. We also distinguish the case in which α is the left extreme of an *open* interval of times, from the case in which α is the left extreme of a *closed* interval of times (allowing to pass from $R(l_j, l_i)$ to $G(l_i, l_p))^2$. In the first case, we use a dotted edge to connect the vertex l_i^j to the vertex l_p^i in $\mathcal{G}$. Finally, if $\psi_{(l_i^j, l_p^i)}(t_0)$ is not satisfiable, the edge (l_i^j, l_p^i) is labeled with the value $+\infty$, meaning that it is never possible to reach location $l_p^i \in H'$ from $l_i^j \in H'$.

- For each edge $(l_i^{\#}, l_p^i)$ in $\mathcal{G}$, we derive the formula $\psi_{(l_i^{\#}, l_p^i)}(t_0)$, that represents the greatest lower bound on the time required to pass from a point in the initial region of $\ell_i \in H$ to a point in the guard region $G(l_i, l_p)$ of H. The process of construction of formula $\psi_{(l_i^{\#}, l_p^i)}(t_0)$ is equivalent to that of building formula $\psi_{(l_i^j, l_p^i)}(t_0)$, in Equation 1. The only difference is that we should use the initial-set $Init(l_i)$ in place of the reset-set $R(l_j, l_i)$, within the definition of the subformula in Equation 3. The edge $(l_i^{\#}, l_p^i)$ is finally labeled either with $+\infty$ or with the real number resulting from solving the expression derived from quantifier elimination applied to $\psi_{(l_i^{\#}, l_p^i)}(t_0)$.

- We follow an analogous approach to label each edge leading to the node F in $\mathcal{G}$. In this case, however, in place of guard-sets we use the final region V to define the formulae in Equations 1,2,3.

5.2 Phase 2: Time Bounded Acyclic Paths Detection

Since now we have never used the input information about the time bound. This information is necessary in the last phase of our procedure. In such a step we simply apply a classical algorithm for the (multiple sources) minimum-path problem[3] on $\mathcal{G}$, where F plays the role of target node, and the sources are the nodes associated with each initial location, $l_i^{\#}$, in H'. Then, we match the weight, w, of such a minimum path with the time bound, t_{max}. Finally we answer positively to our problem if and only if $w < t_{max}$ or $w = t_{max}$ and the corresponding minimum path does not contain any dotted edge.

Theorem 1. *Time-bounded reachability is decidable for o-minimal(OF($\mathbb{R}$)) hybrid automata.*

6   Generalizing Issues

The strategy discussed in previous sections to answer the time-bounded o-minimal reachability problem can be naturally translated into an approach to decide general reachability problem for o-minimal automata. Such an approach

---

[2] This can be done by simply checking if the sentence $\exists t_0 (Reach_{(l_i^j, l_p^i)}(t_0) \wedge \forall t (Reach_{(l_i^j, l_p^i)}(t) \rightarrow t \geq t_0))$ is equivalent to the free-quantifier sentence *true*.

[3] Note that it is possible to carry on the computation of the overall minimum path algorithm *symbolically*. This means that if α and α' are two edge labelling reals, represented by the two OF($\mathbb{R}$) quantifier free formulas $\phi(t)$ and $\phi'(t)$, then $\alpha + \alpha'$ can be obtained by eliminating the quantifiers in $\exists t_1, t_2 (\phi(t_1) \wedge \phi'(t_2) \wedge t_1 + t_2 = t_3)$.

is even simpler in the case of general reachability, in the sense that we only need to solve an equivalent connectivity problem on a directed (unlabeled) graph $\mathcal{G}$. Moreover, building the edges of $\mathcal{G}$ involves the definition and evaluation of $\mathsf{OF}(\mathbb{R})$ sentences simpler than the formulas in Equations 1, 2, 3. More in detail, consider again the o-minimal automata in Figure 1 and the problem of detecting the reachability of an $\mathsf{OF}(\mathbb{R})$ definable set of states within location ℓ_0. The directed unlabeled graph built to solve such problem has exactly the same set of nodes of the graph in Figure 2 (built for time-bounded reachability). The rule for defining the set of edges in $\mathcal{G}$, instead, changes: in particular, for each edge (l_i^j, l_p^i) in the guard expansion H', we build a corresponding edge $(l_i^j, l_p^i) \in \mathcal{G}$ if and only if the following sentence is equivalent to the quantifier free sentence *true*:

$$\exists \mathbf{x}, \mathbf{y}, t(\mathbf{x} \in R(l_j, l_i) \cap Inv(l_i) \wedge \mathbf{y} \in G(l_i, l_p) \cap Inv(l_i) \wedge$$

$$\wedge \phi(\mathbf{x}, t) = \mathbf{y} \wedge \forall t' \leq t(\phi(\mathbf{x}, t') \in Inv(l_i)) \tag{4}$$

The above sentence simply asserts the possibility of reaching a point in the guard region $G(l_i, l_p)$, from a point in the reset region $R(l_j, l_i)$. Note that, if it is not necessary to specify the invariant sets in our hybrid automata, then the sentence in Equation 4 uses *only* the existential fragment of the underlying theory.

With respect to traditional decision procedures in the litterature [13, 14], for deciding reachability in o-minimal automata, the above sketched strategy does not require to build the whole state-space of the bisimulation abstraction of T_H. Thus, it is valuable with respect to the, often fundamental in the verification field, space-efficiency parameter. Moreover, in our opinion, the outlined decision procedure for reachability *precisely localize* the decidability of o-minimal hybrid automata within the following two parameters:

- the constant resets imposed onto the discrete dynamics;
- the decidability of the (existential fragment) of the theory defining all relevant sets in the automata.

7   Relaxing O-Minimal Automata Constant Resets

7.1   Relaxed O-Minimal Automata

In this section, we directly face the problem of adjoining o-minimal automata with variables that can maintain their values upon a discrete jump. To this aim, Definition 9, below, introduces the class of *relaxed o-minimal automata*. In a relaxed o-minimal hybrid automata, say H, continuous variables can maintain their values along discrete transitions. However, for each cycle in the control graph of H, there must be at least one edge along which all variables are non deterministically reset to a constant. Let $\mathcal{T}$ to be an o-minimal theory:

Definition 9 (Relaxed O-Minimal($\mathcal{T}$) Automata). *A Relaxed o-minimal ($\mathcal{T}$) Automata is an hybrid automata $H = \langle L, E, X, Init, Inv, F, G, R \rangle$ in which:*

- $L, E, X, Init, Inv, F, G$ are defined as in o-minimal hybrid automata, inside the same o-minimal theory $\mathcal{T}$;
- the reset function $R = R_1 \times \ldots \times R_{n=|X|} : E \times \mathbb{R}^n \times 2^{\mathbb{R}^n}$ is defined as follows:
  1. for each edge $e \in E$, for each $1 \leq i \leq n$, $R_i(e, \cdot)$ is either equal to the identity function $id : \mathbb{R} \mapsto \mathbb{R}$, or it is a constant function mapping each value of the continuous variable x_i to an interval over $\mathbb{R}$;
  2. for each cycle $(\ell_1 \ldots \ell_k = \ell_1)$ in the control graph of H, $\mathcal{G} = (L, E)$, there exists an edge $e = (\ell_i, \ell_{i+1})$ upon which the reset function $R = R_1 \times \ldots \times R_n$ is composed only by constant functions.

Consider a (general) hybrid automata $H = \langle L, E, X, Init, Inv, F, G, R \rangle$ and let $T_H = \langle Q, Q_0, Q_F, \Sigma, \rightarrow \rangle$, were Q_F is a set of final states, to be the time-abstract transition system of H. We represent in Figure 3 a well known partition-refinement computational approach to determine the maximum bisimulation over T_H. The procedure in Figure 3 successively refines a partition onto Q coarser than the bisimulation quotient, iterating until a (finite) partition stable with respect to $\rightarrow = (\bigcup_{e \in E} \rightarrow_e) \cup \rightarrow_\tau$ is determined. It follows that $\text{BISIM}(H)$ computes the bisimilation quotient of T_H if and only if T_H admits a finite bisimulation. Theorem 2, at the end of this section, shows exactly that this is the case for the time abstract transition systems of relaxed o-minimal automata.

We start by observing that, in order to show bisimulation finiteness for o-minimal hybrid automata in [13], Pappas et al. used a partition refinement bisimulation algorithm simpler than the general one presented in Figure 3. Such an algorithm is depicted in Figure 4, and reduces to perform only the first for-loop of BISIM, splitting independently the state-space associated with each location $\ell \in L$. This, in turn, means that the discrete transitions are never considered within the splitting process. The correctness of the algorithm depends on the fact that o-minimal systems are constrained to *constant resets*. More precisely, if $G(e)$

$\text{BISIM}(H)$

(1)   Let $\mathcal{P}$ be the coarsest partition of $L \times \mathbb{R}^n$ compatible with respect to each block $\{\ell\} \times Z$, where $\ell \in L$, $Z \in \mathcal{A}_\ell$ and $\mathcal{A}_\ell = \{Inv(\ell), Init(\ell), Final(\ell)\}$
(2)   **Repeat**
(3) $old\mathcal{P} \leftarrow \mathcal{P}$
(4)   **for each** $(\ell \in L)$
(5)   **while** $(\exists B, B' \in \mathcal{P}$ such that $\emptyset \neq B \cap Pre_\tau(B') \neq B)$
(6) $B_1 \leftarrow B \cap Pre_\tau(B'); B_2 \leftarrow B \setminus Pre_\tau(B')$
(7) $\mathcal{P} \leftarrow (\mathcal{P} \setminus \{B\}) \cup \{B_1, B_2\}$
(8)   **for each** $(e = (\ell, \ell') \in E)$
(9)   **for each** $(\ell' \times V' = B' \in \mathcal{P}, \ell \times V = B \in \mathcal{P}$ such that $\emptyset \neq B \cap Pre_e(B') \neq B)$
(10) $B_1 \leftarrow B \cap Pre_e(B'); B_2 \leftarrow B \setminus Pre_e(B')$
(11) $\mathcal{P} \leftarrow (\mathcal{P} \setminus \{B\}) \cup \{B_1, B_2\}$
(13) **until** $(\mathcal{P} = old\mathcal{P})$

Fig. 3. The partition refinement bisimulation algorithm for general hybrid automata

---

BISIMLOC(H)

(1)   define $\mathcal{A}_\ell = \{Inv(\ell), Init(\ell), Final(\ell)\} \cup \{G(\ell, \ell'), R(\ell, \ell') \mid (\ell, \ell' \in E)\}$
(2)   Let $\mathcal{P}$ be the coarsest partition of $L \times \mathbb{R}^n$ compatible with respect
       to each block $\{\ell\} \times Z$, where $\ell \in L$, $Z \in \mathcal{A}_\ell$
(3)   for each $(\ell \in L)$
(4)   while $(\exists B, B' \in \mathcal{P}$ such that $\emptyset \neq B \cap Pre_\tau(B') \neq B)$
(5) $B_1 \leftarrow B \cap Pre_\tau(B'); B_2 \leftarrow B \setminus Pre_\tau(B')$
(6) $\mathcal{P} \leftarrow (\mathcal{P} \setminus \{B\}) \cup \{B_1, B_2\}$

Fig. 4. The partition refinement bisimulation algorithm for o-minimal automata in [13]

and $R(e)$ are classes in the initial partition $\mathcal{P}_0$, for each edge e, constant resets ensure that discrete transitions do not cause any partition refinement since:

$$Pre_e(B) = \begin{cases} \emptyset, & \text{if } B \cap R(e) = \emptyset; \\ G(e), & \text{otherwise.} \end{cases}$$

On the other hand, the *termination* of the refinement process within the bisimulation procedure used by [13] in Figure 4, only depends on the form of the following two components:

- the initial partition, which is a *finite* and composed by *classes definable in the o-minimal theory of H* ;
- the smooth and complete vector field that defines the relation of the transition system, whose flow is definable in the o-minimal theory of H.

The above facts will be used within the following Lemmas, preliminary to the main Theorem 2. Note that, since relaxed o-minimal automata allow identity resets, the procedure in Figure 4 [13] does not allow to define a bisimulation over the corresponding time-abstract transition systems. Consider a relaxed o-minimal automata, H, and let $\mathcal{P}_0$ to be the partition built in the initialization phase of BISIM(H).

Lemma 3. *Each execution of the first for-loop within* BISIM *terminates leading to a finite partition which refines* $\mathcal{P}_0$.

Theorem 2. *Relaxed o-minimal hybrid automata admit finite bisimulation.*

The corollary below, follows immediately from Theorem 2 and from the fact that the o-minimal theory $OF(\mathbb{R})$ admits quantifier elimination.

Corollary 1. *The reachability problem is decidable for Relaxed o-minimal(OF (ℝ)) automata.*

7.2   MasterSlaves O-Minimal Automata

In Section 5, we exploited Tarski quantifier elimination to obtain a real value that is a lower bound onto the time necessary to move among regions, within one o-minimal automaton location. Here we build up on this idea to define a further extension of o-minimal automata which does not cross the undecidability border, while relaxing the condition of having only constant reset on discrete jumps.

Briefly, this is achieved by endowing our automata with *two* classes of continuous variables. Precisely, *MasterSlaves* o-minimal hybrid automata will be endowed with a set of variables that we call *constant reset* variables (or *slaves variables*) plus a further variable that we call *free variable* (or *master variable*). We impose the continuous evolution of the master variable, say x^f, to be independent from slaves variables[4]: x^f is allowed to maintain its value upon a discrete transition if its flow does not change with the corresponding switch to a new location. Otherwise, the free variable must be reset to a constant. As far as slaves variables is concerned, we impose their discrete dynamics to be always constrained to constant reset.

Given a location ℓ, it is possible to define a $\mathcal{T}$ formula representing the set of times allowing to traverse[5] ℓ, using exactly the same techniques adopted in Section 5. We guarantee that such a set admits a *strictly positive* lower bound for MasterSlaves o-minimal automata. The above fact, together with *closed bounded invariant sets* (cfr. condition f) in Definition 10, below), is strongly related to the decidability results stated in Theorems 3 and 4, at the end of this section.

To equip the reader of some more intuition, before formally introducing MasterSlaves automata, we anticipate that conditions f), g) in Definition 10, and the form of continuous dynamics, allow to ensure the following properties:

1. $\forall \ell \in L$ there exists a *strictly positive* lower bound to the time required to traverse ℓ;
2. there exists a finite *upper bound* on the time that the free variable can spend evolving according to a given vector field, F^f, and subject to identity resetting, without violating invariants.

Definition 10 (MasterSlaves O-Minimal($\mathcal{T}$) Automata). *A* MasterSlaves o-minimal($\mathcal{T}$) Automata *is an Hybrid Automata* $H = (L, E, X, \mathrm{Init}, \mathrm{Inv}, F, G, R)$ *with:*

continuous dynamics

a) $X = X^c \cup \{x^f\}$, $x^f \notin X^c$. $X^c = \{x_1^c, \ldots, x_m^c\}$, $m \geq 1$, *is said the set of constant reset variables (or* slaves variables*), whereas* x^f *is said the* free variable *(or* master variable*);*

b) $\forall \ell \in L$, $F(\ell, \cdot) : \mathbb{R}^{m+1} \mapsto \mathbb{R}^{m+1}$ *is a complete smooth vector field whose flow is* $\mathcal{T}$*-definable.*

c) $\forall \ell \in L$, *the continuous evolution of the free variables does not depend on* X^c, *i.e. it can be represented as the solution of a complete smooth vector field,* $F^f(\ell) : \mathbb{R} \mapsto \mathbb{R}$. *Moreover, if* $v \in \mathrm{Inv}(\ell)\mid_{x^f}$, *then* $\|F^f(v)\| \neq 0$.

---

[4] In other words, for each location of a MasterSlaves automata, the flow of the free variable can be represented as the solution of a smooth vector field $F^f : \mathbb{R} \mapsto \mathbb{R}$.

[5] i.e. to reach a guard region in ℓ departing from any guard region associated to a discrete edge mapping to ℓ.

discrete dynamics

d) $\forall (\ell, \ell') \in E$, $R(\ell, \ell') = R^f \times R^c$, where $R^f(\ell, \ell')$ can be the identity function $id : \mathbb{R} \mapsto \mathbb{R}$ only if $F^f(\ell) = F^f(\ell')$ and $Inv(\ell)|_{x^f} = Inv(\ell')|_{x^f}$; otherwise $R^f(\ell, \ell')$ is a constant $\mathcal{T}$-definable function mapping to $2^{\mathbb{R}}$. $R^c(\ell, \ell') : \mathbb{R}^m \mapsto 2^{\mathbb{R}^m}$ is a constant $\mathcal{T}$-definable function;

relevant sets

e) $\forall (\ell, \ell') \in E, \ell \in L$, the guard-set $G(l, l')$, the invariant-set $Inv(\ell)$, and (if any) the initial set $Init(\ell)$ are definable within $\mathcal{T}$;

f) $\forall \ell \in L$, $Inv(\ell)$ is a closed and bounded set;

g) $\forall \ell \in L$, there exists a strict positive constant $d > 0$ such that:
   * for each $\mathbf{v} \in \bigcup_{\ell' | (\ell', \ell) \in E} R(\ell', \ell)(G(\ell', \ell)) \cup Init(\ell)$
   * for each $\mathbf{w} \in \bigcup_{\ell'' | (\ell, \ell'') \in E} G(\ell, \ell'')$
   the distance between $\mathbf{v}$ and $\mathbf{w}$ is at least d, i.e. $||\mathbf{v} - \mathbf{w}|| \geq d$.

Lemma 4 states that it is possible to solve a reachability problem on a given MasterSlave o-minimal automata, by checking only runs that traverse at most k edges, where k is a proper constant. The proof of Lemma 4 is based exactly on the two properties discussed before formalizing our automata.We rely on the same properties, and on the o-minimality of the theory underlying the definition of our systems, to prove Theorem 3, stating that MasterSlaves o-minimal automata admit finite bisimulation.

Lemma 4. *Let H be a partitioned o-minimal. There is a constant k such that for each state of H, $(\ell, \mathbf{w})$, $(\ell, \mathbf{w})$ is reachable in H if and only if H admits a run traversing at most k discrete edges and leading to $(\ell, \mathbf{w})$.*

Theorem 3. *MasterSlaves o-minimal automata admit finite bisimulation.*

The decidability of the reachability problem for MasterSlaves($\mathsf{OF}(\mathbb{R})$) automata follows directly from Theorem 3 (or, equivalently from Lemma 4) and from decidability of o-minimal $\mathsf{OF}(\mathbb{R})$ theory.

Theorem 4. *The reachability problem is decidable for MasterSlaves($\mathsf{OF}(\mathbb{R})$) o-minimal automata.*

8 Conclusions

In this paper we study a number of problems related both to the understanding and to the extension of the border between hybrid systems decidability and undecidability . Our starting point was the family of o-minimal automata, which is largely considered layering on such a border. In particular, we develop some not bisimulation-based proof techniques for showing decidability of (timed-bounded) reachability problems for classes of o-minimal systems. We finally analyze the possibility to explicitly introduce identity resetting variables in o-minimal automata, without crossing the undecidability border.

Acknowledgements. We thank prof. A. Policriti for many useful discussions.

References

1. R. Alur and D. L. Dill. A theory of timed automata. *Theoretical Computer Science*, 126(2):183–235, 1994.
2. R. Alur, T.A. Henzinger, G. Lafferriere, and G.J. Pappas. Discrete abstractions of hybrid systems. *Proceedings of the IEEE*, 88:971–984, 2000.
3. R. Alur, S. La Torre, and G. J. Pappas. Optimal paths in weighted timed automata. In *Proceedings of the 4th International Workshop on Hybrid Systems*, pages 49–62. Springer-Verlag, 2001.
4. D. S. Arnon, G. E. Collins, and S. McCallum. Cylindrical algebraic decomposition i: the basic algorithm. *SIAM J. Comput.*, 13(4):865–877, 1984.
5. G. Behrmann, A. Fehnker, T. Hune, K. G. Larsen, P. Pettersson, J. Romijn, and F. Vaandrager. Minimum-cost reachability for priced timed automata. In *Proceedings of the 4th International Workshop on Hybrid Systems*, pages 147–161. Springer-Verlag, 2001.
6. T. Brihaye, C. Michaux, C. Rivire, and C. Troestler. On o-minimal hybrid systems. In *Proceedings of the 7-th International Workshop on Hybrid Systems*, pages 219–233, 2004.
7. J.M. Davoren. Topologies, continuity and bisimulations. *Theoretical Informatics and Applications*, 33(4/5):357–381, 1999.
8. R. Gentilini. Reachability problems on extended o-minimal hybrid automata. RR 07-05, Dep. of Computer Science, University of Udine, Italy, 2005.
9. M. R. Henzinger, T. A. Henzinger, and P. W. Kopke. Computing simulations on finite and infinite graphs. In *Proceedings of the 36th Annual Symposium on Foundations of Computer Science*, page 453. IEEE, 1995.
10. T.A. Henzinger. The theory of hybrid automata. In M.K. Inan and R.P. Kurshan, editors, *Verification of Digital and Hybrid Systems*, NATO ASI Series F: Computer and Systems Sciences 170, pages 265–292. Springer-Verlag, 2000.
11. T.A. Henzinger, P.W. Kopke, A. Puri, and P. Varaiya. What's decidable about hybrid automata? In *Proceedings of the 27th Annual Symposium on Theory of Computing*, pages 373–382. ACM Press, 1995.
12. P.W. Kopke. *The Theory of Rectangular Hybrid Automata*. PhD thesis, Cornell University, 1996.
13. G. Lafferriere, G. Pappas, and S. Sastry. O-minimal hybrid systems. *Mathematics of Control, Signals, and Systems*, 13:1–21, 2000.
14. G. Lafferriere, J.G. Pappas, and S. Yovine. A new class of decidable hybrid systems. In *Proceedings of the Second International Workshop on Hybrid Systems*, pages 137–151. Springer-Verlag, 1999.
15. J.S. Miller. Decidability and complexity results for timed automata and semi-linear hybrid automata. In *Proceedings of the Third International Workshop on Hybrid Systems*, pages 296–309, 2000.
16. C. Courcoubetis R. Alur and T. A. Henzinger. Computing accumulated delays in real-time systems. *Formal Methods in System Design*, 11:137–156, 1997.
17. A. Tarski. A decision method for elementary algebra and geometry. 1951.
18. L. van den Dries. O-minimal structures. In W. Hodges, editor, *Logic: From Foundations to Applications*, pages 99–108. Clarendon Press, 1996.
19. L. van den Dries. *Tame topology and o-minimal structures*, volume 248 of *London Math. Soc. Lecture Note Ser.* Cambridge University Press, 1998.
20. A. J. Wilkie. Schanuel conjecture and the decidability of the real exponential field. *Algebraic Model Theory*, pages 223–230, 1997.

Counterexamples for Timed Probabilistic Reachability

Husain Aljazzar[1], Holger Hermanns[2], and Stefan Leue[1]

[1] Department of Computer and Information Science,
University of Konstanz, Germany
{Husain.Aljazzar, Stefan.Leue}@uni-konstanz.de
[2] Department of Computer Science,
Saarland University, Germany
hermanns@cs.uni-sb.de

Abstract. The inability to provide counterexamples for the violation of timed probabilistic reachability properties constrains the practical use of CSL model checking for continuous time Markov chains (CTMCs). Counterexamples are essential tools in determining the causes of property violations and are required during debugging. We propose the use of explicit state model checking to determine runs leading into property offending states. Since we are interested in finding paths that carry large amounts of probability mass we employ directed explicit state model checking technology to find such runs using a variety of heuristics guided search algorithms, such as Best First search and Z*. The estimates used in computing the heuristics rely on a uniformisation of the CTMC. We apply our approach to a probabilistic model of the SCSI-2 protocol.

1 Introduction

Overview. Stochastic models are widely used in system design to describe discrete phenomena that change randomly as time progresses. They are commonly employed to specify and reason about system performance and dependability characteristics. It is widely recognized that the availability of automated analysis tools is pivotal in the assurance of high quality system design, hence our interest in formal analysis of this type of properties. In this paper we are considering the use of explicit state Model Checking [1] (ESMC) in the formal analysis of stochastic system models. In particular, we use explicit state model checking to explain why probabilistic timed reachability properties are not satisfied by a stochastic model given in the form of a *Continuous-Time Markov Chain (CTMC)*.

A few model checking approaches for probabilistic models have been presented in the literature [2–9]. In [9], a branching time temporal logic named *Continuous Stochastic Logic (CSL)* for expressing real-time probabilistic properties on CTMCs has been proposed, based on [7]. Efficient approximative stochastic model checking algorithms to verify CSL formulae have been developed. We notice that in practice relevant CSL formulae are often non-nested and fall into the

P. Pettersson and W. Yi (Eds.): FORMATS 2005, LNCS 3829, pp. 177–195, 2005.

common fragment of (the timed stochastic variants of) CTL and LTL. In this paper we restrict ourselves to the consideration of an important class of safety properties that can be expressed in this restricted fragment of CSL, namely timed probabilistic reachability. A timed probabilistic reachability property is a property of the form:

> "The probability to reach a state s violating a state proposition ϑ, i.e satisfying $\varphi := \neg\vartheta$, within the time interval $[0,t]$ does not exceed a probability $p \in [0,1]$".

The CSL syntax of this property is $\mathcal{P}_{<p}(\Diamond^{\leq t}\varphi)$.

The practical applicability of CSL model checking is constrained by the inability of this approach to produce offending system execution traces, also called counterexamples in model checking parlance, that illustrate why a property was violated. In particular, the probabilistic nature of the CTMC model checking problem means that it cannot generally be assumed that a single state-transition sequence through the model proves the violation of a probabilistic timed reachability property, in case it is invalid. In ordinary model-checking, such state-transition sequences are the prime debugging information provided by the model checker, in case the property is refuted. In the context of CSL, the probability of the property is determined by the probability mass flowing along all those state-transition sequences which lead into a target state, and consequently, the model checking algorithm cannot return a single state-transition sequence explaining why such states were reachable with a certain probability. Instead, the model checker can only give the actual probability in response to the specified CSL property. This means that the stochastic model checking algorithm will not be able to determine which part of the model is responsible for the undesired event of exceeding a given probability bound. It is then left up to the user to inspect the model in order to manually determine the reason for the property violation.

Approach. We address this problem by reconciling ESMC with CSL model checking. ESMC checks state properties of a system model by systematically exploring the state space of the system, usually given as an implicit graph. ESMC commonly uses graph search algorithms such as *Depth-First Search (DFS)* and *Breadth-First Search (BFS)* in the state space exploration. For safety properties, if an error is found the model checker returns an offending system run in the form of a state-transition sequence explaining how the property violating state can be reached from the initial system state. Reachability analysis performed by ESMC over-approximates the verification of timed probabilistic reachability since it does not respect the time and probability bounds that the property imposes.

In order to reconcile both approaches, an important question is to define a meaningful notion of a *counterexample* in the probabilistic context. Assume we are facing a refuted timed probabilistic reachability property. This means that the probability to reach an undesired state before the given time bound is higher than the bound specified in the property. This is caused by an infinite set of time-stamped runs (forming a tree structure of infinite depth and – owed to varying real-timed time stamps – infinite branching), which has a probability measure higher than required. Now the question is: what portion of this infinite set is the one that is undesired? The set itself does not provide useful information to answer this question. Even more, there surely is no general answer since the question is context-dependent. However it appears intuitively very beneficial to understand the structure of this set by determining its largest portions, especially by identifying a selection of runs through the system along which most of the relevant probability mass flows toward the undesired state. In this paper we are thus interested in identifying system runs in the state graph which are meaningful in the sense that they carry a lot of probability mass, and interpret these as meaningful counterexamples to the timed probabilistic reachability properties that we analyze. To discriminate more meaningful runs leading to property offending states from less meaningful ones during the state space exploration we employ heuristics guided directed search algorithms.

We envisage our approach to be applied in combination with a numeric probability analyser, such as the one included in the CADP tool set [10, 11]. A typical usage scenario would proceed in two steps. First, the system is checked on the given timed probabilistic reachability property using the numeric analyser, i.e., the probabilistic model checker. Second, if the property is determined to be violated, then a counterexample is elicited by our directed state space exploration approach. Intermediate results of the numeric analysis can be applied in guiding the search process, as outlined in Section 3.2. While we assume that this is the most likely usage scenario, our approach does not depend on a preceding probabilistic model checking run. Even more, knowing that some state can be reached within some time with a relatively high probability can in itself constitute important information about the system, even if it is not a counterexample to a timed probabilistic reachability property in the above sense.

Structure of the Paper. In Section 2 we present some model foundations for performing reachability analysis on probabilistic models. In Section 3 we extend these concepts to include directed, heuristics guided model exploration. We introduce the modeling of the SCSI-2 protocol, which serves as case study in our paper, in Section 4. This section also gives the experimental results. We conclude in Section 5.

2   Explicit-State Analysis of Probabilistic Systems

2.1   Probabilistic Systems

In this section, we sketch the model for probabilistic systems that we use.

Definition 1. *A labelled discrete-time Markov chain (DTMC) is a triple (S, P, L), where*

- *S is a finite set of states, and*
- *$P : S \times S \longrightarrow [0, 1]$ is a probability matrix, satisfying that for each state, probabilities of outgoing probabilistic transitions cumulate to 1.*

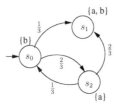

Fig. 1. A simple DTMC, or a CTMC with $E := \{(s_0, 3), (s_1, 0), (s_2, 5)\}$

- $L : S \longrightarrow 2^{AP}$ is labeling function, which assigns each state the subset of valid atomic propositions.

We often assume that there is a unique initial state s_{init} of the system. Figure 1 illustrates a simple DTMC consisting of 3 states and 4 transitions. s_0 is the initial state, $AP = \{a, b\}$ and L is given through the subsets of AP labeling the states.

Definition 2. *A labelled continuous-time Markov chain (CTMC) is a quadruple (S, P, E, L), where*

- (S, P, L), *is a DTMC, and*
- $E : S \longrightarrow \mathbb{R}_{>0}$ *is a rate vector, assigning exit rates to states.*

For example, the DTMC illustrated in Figure 1 can be extended to a CTMC with $E := \{(s_0, 3), (s_1, 0), (s_2, 5)\}$.

Paths, runs and probability measures. For a given DTMC (S, P, L), an infinite *run* is a sequence $s_0 \to s_1 \to s_2 \to \dots$ with, for $i \in \mathbb{N}$, $s_i \in S$ such that $P(s_i, s_{i+1}) > 0$ for all i. A finite run σ is a sequence $s_0 \to s_1 \to \dots s_{l-1} \to s_l$ such that s_l is absorbing[1], and $P(s_i, s_{i+1}) > 0$ for all $i < l$. A (finite or infinite) *path* through a CTMC (S, P, E, L) is a sequence $s_0 \xrightarrow{t_0} s_1 \xrightarrow{t_1} s_2 \xrightarrow{t_2} \dots$ such that $s_0 \to s_1 \to s_2 \to \dots$ is a run through (S, P, L) and $t_i \in \mathbb{R}_{>0}$ for all relevant i. For a given initial state s_0 in CTMC $\mathcal{C}$, a unique probability measure Pr on $Path(s_0)$ exists, where $Path(s_0)$ denotes the set of paths starting in s_0 [9]. The probability measure induces a probability measure on $Run(s_0)$, where $Run(s_0)$ denotes the set of runs starting in s_0. Because runs are time-abstract, the latter measure only depends on the embedded DTMC, and can be defined directly using $\Pr(s_0, s_0 \to s_1 \to s_2 \to \dots) = P(s_0, s_1) \cdot \Pr(s_1, s_1 \to s_2 \to \dots)$.

Transient probabilities. In a CTMC, the time-dependent state probability can be written as: $\pi(s', s, t) = \Pr\{\sigma \in Path(s) \mid \sigma @ t = s'\}$ where $\sigma @ t$ denotes the state occupied at time t on path σ. $\pi(s', s, t)$ determines the probability to be in state s' at time t, if starting in state s at time 0. Efficient techniques based on uniformisation exist to compute these probabilities. These thechniques use a specific *uniformised* DTMC to reduce the required computations to the discrete

---

[1] A state of a Markov chain is called absorbing if it has no outgoing transition leading to another state.

setting. In a DTMC the corresponding time dependency is given by the number of hops along runs, and the hop-dependent probability is $\pi(s', s, k) = \Pr\{\sigma \in Run(s) \mid \sigma(k) = s'\}$ where $\sigma(k)$ denotes the k-th state in run σ. Intuitively, $\pi(s', s, k)$ denotes the probability to be in state s' after k hops, if starting in state s (with 0 hops). The values of $\pi(\cdot, \cdot, k)$ are given by the entries of the matrix P^k as $\pi(s', s, k) = P^k(s, s')$.

Timed reachability probabilities. For a CTMC, the time-bounded reachability probability can be defined as $\rho(s', s, t) = \Pr\{\sigma \in Path(s) \mid \exists t' \in [0, t] : \sigma@t' = s'\}$. $\rho(s', s, t)$ determines the probability to hit state s' at the latest at time t, if starting in state s at time 0. The computation of $\rho(s', s, t)$ can be reduced to that of $\pi(s', s, t)$ by making s' absorbing (i.e., cutting all transitions) prior to the computation of $\pi(s', s, t)$ [9].

2.2 Reachability Analysis of Probabilistic Models

Consider a timed probabilistic reachability property of the previously discussed form $\phi := \mathcal{P}_{<p}(\Diamond^{\leq t}\varphi)$, to be checked on a given CTMC with initial state s_{init}. According to the semantics of CSL [7] (which we omit here), the validity of ϕ can be decided by comparing the probability bound p with the cumulated timed reachability probability $\sum_{s' \models \varphi} \rho(s', s_{init}, t)$. The computation of this quantity can be done in one transient analysis where all states satisfying φ are made absorbing [9].

This answers the question how timed probabilistic reachability properties are decided effectively. The goal of the present paper is more refined since we are aiming to provide debugging information in case the property is refuted. When that is the case, at least one offending state s' satisfying φ is reachable. For typical error state specifications, the number of such offending states is large, leading to a large number of counterexamples that all contribute to exceeding the probability bound p. We expect the user to be interested in a counterexample which carries a high probability and which is hence most informative. We aim specifically at identifying a finite run such that the contribution of this run to the timed reachability probability is large or even maximal.

To arrive there, we first have to introduce *timed run probabilities.* Recall that runs as such are time-abstract. Given a specific finite run $r = s_0 \rightarrow \ldots \rightarrow s_k$ of length k through the CTMC, the time-bounded run probability can be defined as

$$\gamma(r, t) = \Pr\{\sigma \in Path(s_0) \mid \exists t' \in [0, t] : \sigma@t' = s_k \wedge \sigma\!\downarrow_k = r\},$$

where $\sigma\!\downarrow$ is the projection of a path $s_0 \xrightarrow{t_0} s_1 \xrightarrow{t_1} s_2 \xrightarrow{t_2} \ldots$ on the run $s_0 \rightarrow s_1 \rightarrow s_2 \rightarrow \ldots$ obtained by removing the transition time stamps. The subscript $_k$ denotes the run truncated at depth k (thus ending in s_k which is contained in σ by construction). Intuitively, $\gamma(r, t)$ gives the probability that the CTMC moves along the run r and reaches $last(r)$ at the least at time t. For a finite run $r = s_0 \rightarrow s_1 \rightarrow s_2 \rightarrow \ldots \rightarrow s_n$ this timed run probability is given by

$$\gamma(r, t) = \int_0^t \left(p(s_1, s_0, t_1) \cdot \left(\ldots \left(\int_0^{t-t_{n-1}} p(s_n, s_{n-1}, t_n) \cdot dt_n \right) \ldots \right) \right) \cdot dt_1, \quad (1)$$

where $p(s', s, t) = P(s, s') \cdot (1 - e^{-E(s) \cdot t})$ is the probability to move from s to s' in the interval [0,t]. One can show that $\gamma(r, t)$ can be computed by $\rho(last(r), first(r), t)$ (with the obvious meaning of $first$ and $last$) on a CTMC where all states which are not touched along the run r are made absorbing.

3   Directed Reachability Analysis of CTMCs

3.1   Search Algorithms

In state space search, the most commonly used algorithms are depth-first search (DFS) and breadth-first search (BFS). Depth-first search (DFS) is memory efficient, but typically finds goal states only very deep in the search space which leads to very long counterexamples. Breadth-first search (BFS) is complete and can provide shortest counterexamples. However, BFS is in general too memory inefficient to be applied to models of realistic size [12]. For weighted graphs, Dijkstra's algorithm is known to deliver optimal solutions [13]. Originally, Dijkstra's algorithm uses the summation as a cost measure, i.e. the cost of path is the sum of the costs of the path's transitions. The cost (or merit) measure is a function used by the search algorithm to assign each explored state a number quantifying the costs of the path from the start state to a goal state over the current state, e.g., path length. The merit is often considered to be the negation of the costs. An optimal solution is a path whose merit is maximal (i.e., costs are minimal). Markov chains can easily be cast into weighted graphs. In the stochastic setting, however, the summation of costs that Dijkstra's algorithm requires makes little sense. We hence use Dijkstra's algorithm with a suitable but non-additive cost measure.

The algorithms DFS, BFS and Dijkstra are uninformed search algorithms. To the contrary, the exists a large class of informed algorithms that take advantage of knowledge about structural properties of the state graph or the goal state specification in order to improve the search. Belonging to this class, directed search algorithms use such knowledge to perform heuristics guided state space exploration. The guiding aims at finding optimal (e.g., shortest or cost-minimal) paths in the state space. Heuristics guided search algorithms exploit their knowledge during state expansion when deciding which node to expand next. The problem knowledge manifests itself in a heuristic evaluation function f which estimates the desirability of expanding a node. Amongst others, f relies on an estimate h of the optimal costs of the cheapest solution rooted in the current state. This algorithmic skeleton in its general form is called Best-first (BF) [14] search. If f is identical to h, the resulting greedy best first algorithm (GBestFS) will expand the successor node with the optimal value for h first. It often finds a solution fast but it is not optimal with respect to the cost of the path to a goal node since it can get stuck in sinks or local minima, as has been observed in work on directed explicit-state model checking (DESMC) which reconciles classical DFS based state space search with heuristics guided search [12].

In addition to GBestFS we also consider the Z*[2] search algorithm. According to Pearl [14], Z* is derived from BF by complying with the two following requirements:

- The use of a *recursively computed* evaluation function f, and by
- The use of a *delaying termination test* when deciding optimality of the expanded nodes.

The first requirement means that for each pair of states s and s', where s is the predecessor of s' in the traversal tree, $f(s')$ is computed by $f(s') := F[\psi(s), f(s), h(s')]$ for an arbitrary combination function F. $\psi(s)$ stands for a set of local parameters characterizing s. This requirement results in two efficiency improving features, namely computation sharing and selective updating [14]. The second requirement is needed to guarantee optimality of the search result that Z* delivers.

The optimality of Z* can only be guaranteed if the following two conditions are satisfied, in addition to the delaying termination test requirement:

1. The estimate h is *optimistic*, i.e. $h(s)$ is always an overestimate of the profit of expanding s.
2. The combining function F satisfies the *order-preservation* property illustrated in equation 2.

The property of h to be optimal has to be assured through its concrete definition in an application context. We then need to ascertain that F satisfies the order-preservation property:

$$
\begin{aligned}
F[\psi(s_1), f(s_1), h_1(s')] \geq F[\psi(s_2), f(s_2), h_1(s')] \Rightarrow \\
F[\psi(s_1), f(s_1), h_2(s')] \geq F[\psi(s_2), f(s_2), h_2(s')],
\end{aligned}
\tag{2}
$$

for all states s_1, s_2 and $s' \in succ(s_1) \cap succ(s_2)$ and all optimistic heuristics h_1 and h_2 (where $succ(s)$ enumerates the successor nodes of s). The order-preservation property states that if two paths σ_1 and σ_2 from s to s' are found, where σ_1 can be reached with less cost than σ_2, then the further search process will not reverse this order. In other words, by discarding the more expensive path we do not throw away the optimal path. This property is fundamental for the optimality of the algorithm.

3.2 Probabilistic Search Algorithms

In case a timed reachability property, say $\mathcal{P}_{<p}(\lozenge^{\leq t}\varphi)$, is refuted, we are aiming at identifying a run r through the CTMC leading to a state s with $s \vDash \varphi$ with a high, if not the highest, timed run probability. In a heuristics guided state-space search algorithm, the timed run probability $\gamma(r, t)$ will therefore serve as optimization

---

[2] The more prominent A* heuristics guided search algorithm is a variant of Z*, where an additive estimation function f is used. Since the costs in our context are probabilities that are multiplied along the path, we need a multiplicative estimation function. Therefore, A* is not applicable in this setting.

goal. However, the determination of the precise value of the integral in equation 1 is computationally very expensive and prone to numerical instability problems. Thus $\gamma(r, t)$ cannot be used as a merit measure in the search process. Therefore we propose in the following section an approximation of γ. The approximation relies on a uniformisation of the CTMC.

Approximative Cost Measure. We use a uniformisation method to turn the CTMC into a DTMC, which is then embedded in a Poisson process. Let $A = (S, P, E, L)$ be a CTMC. Using uniformisation we obtain an embedded DTMC $A' = (S, M, L)$, with M being defined as follows:

$$M = I + \frac{1}{\Gamma} \cdot E(s) \cdot (P - I), \qquad (3)$$

where Γ is not smaller than the maximum of E. The Poisson process in which A' is embedded looks as follows:

$$Prob\{N(t) = k\} := \frac{(\Gamma \cdot t)^k}{k!} \cdot e^{-\Gamma \cdot t}, \qquad k, t \geq 0. \qquad (4)$$

For fixed t, $N(t)$ is a random variable giving the (discrete) number of hops made in the uniformised model A' during the (continuous) time interval $[0, t]$ of A. For instance, the CTMC defined in Figure 1 can be uniformised using $\Gamma := max\{ E(s_0), E(s_1), E(s_2) \} = 5$. The uniformised model differs from the original model only in so far as the branching probabilities of the state s_0 are changed as follows: $s_0 \xrightarrow{\frac{1}{5}} s_1$, $s_0 \xrightarrow{\frac{2}{5}} s_2$ and additionally $s_0 \xrightarrow{\frac{2}{5}} s_0$.

The expected value of the Poisson process above is $N := \Gamma \cdot t$. Intuitively, N corresponds to the expected number of hops in the uniformised DTMC that may occur in t time units. The probability that N hops occur in time t is maximal. Now let t be the time bound given in the reachability property. Our search algorithm is performed on A' and selects a path leading to an error state which has at most N transitions and carries a maximal probability. Thus we limit the search process to states reachable within at most N transitions, i.e. states probably reachable in the time interval $[0, t]$.

In addition, $\gamma(r, t)$ is reduced to its discrete variant $\gamma'(r, N)$. While $\gamma(r, t)$ denotes the reachability probability in CTMC A along run r and bounded by time t, $\gamma'(r, N)$ denotes the reachability probability in DTMC A' along run r and bounded by hop count N. In the traversal tree spanned by the search algorithm there is always at most one run r between each pair of states, i.e., r is completely characterized by $first(r)$ and $last(r)$. Thus, instead of $\gamma'(r, N)$ we write $\gamma'(last(r), first(r), N)$, or even $\gamma'(last(r), N)$ if $first(r)$ is the start state. If $first(r)$ is different from the start state, $\gamma'(last(r), first(r), N)$ is computed as if $first(r)$ was the start state. We use π' to denote the restriction of π to the traversal tree. $\pi'(s, k)$ is just $\pi(s, s_{init}, k)$ (for start state s_{init}), but on the DTMC obtained from A' by redirecting all transitions which are not contained in the traversal tree – except for self-loops – to an absorbing state. For any state visited by the search algorithm, π' is computed as follows:

$$\pi'(s_{init}, k) = \begin{cases} 1, & k = 0 \\ M(s_{init}, s_{init}) \cdot \pi'(s_{init}, k - 1), & k > 0 \end{cases}$$

$$\pi'(s, k) = \begin{cases} 0, & k = 0 \\ M(pred(s), s) \cdot \pi'(pred(s), k - 1) + \\ \quad M(s, s) \cdot \pi'(s, k - 1), & k > 0 \end{cases} \tag{5}$$

where $pred(s)$ stands for the unique predecessor of s in the traversal tree. For some state s, $\gamma'(s, N)$ can be efficiently computed according the following expression:

$$\gamma'(s, N) = M(pred(s), s) \cdot \sum_{k=0}^{N-1} \pi'(pred(s), k), \tag{6}$$

where $pred(s)$ stands for the unique predecessor of s in the traversal tree. Using the approximation explained above we are now able to define an efficiently computable merit measure, namely $\gamma'(s, N)$.

In the following we demonstrate the computation of γ' by means of the uniformised variant of the the example illustrated in Figure 1. In the search process, at first s_0 is expanded generating s_1 and s_2. At this point $\gamma'(s_1, 2)$ is computed as follows:

$$\gamma'(s_1, 2) = \tfrac{1}{5} \cdot (\pi'(s_0, 0) + \pi'(s_0, 1)) = \tfrac{1}{5} \cdot (1 + \tfrac{2}{5} \cdot 1) = \tfrac{7}{25}.$$

Now we assume that the search algorithm expands the state s_2 generating the states s_0 and s_1. A new computation of $\gamma'(s_1, 2)$ is performed on the following way:

$$\begin{aligned} \gamma'(s_1, 2) &= \tfrac{2}{3} \cdot (\pi'(s_2, 0) + \pi'(s_2, 1)) \\ &= \tfrac{2}{3} \cdot (\pi'(s_2, 0) + \tfrac{2}{5} \cdot \pi'(s_0, 0) + 0 \cdot \pi'(s_2, 0)) = \tfrac{2}{3} \cdot (0 + \tfrac{2}{5} \cdot 1) = \tfrac{4}{15} \end{aligned}$$

Since $\tfrac{7}{25} > \tfrac{4}{15}$, the run $s_0 \to s_1$ is preferred over $s_0 \to s_2 \to s_1$ in order to reach s_1.

To give an impression of this approximation we consider an example CTMC that emphasizes a characteristic challenge in timed probabilistic search. We study the CTMC given on the left hand side of Figure 2, where E is defined as follows:

$$E(s) := \begin{cases} 2, & \text{if } s \in \{s_0, s_2\} \\ 20, & \text{otherwise} \end{cases}$$

Let s_0 be the start state, s_3 and s_{13} be goal states. We refer to the run from s_0 to s_{13} by r_1 and to s_3 by r_2. For small time bounds $t < 1.0$, $\gamma(r_1, t)$ is smaller than $\gamma(r_2, t)$, but for large time bounds $t \geq 1.0$, $\gamma(r_1, t)$ is higher than $\gamma(r_2, t)$. This observation implies that our search algorithm should select run r_1 for small time-bounds, and r_2 for larger bounds, in case it is a well-designed heuristics. The plot on the right side of figure 2 illustrates $\gamma(r_1, t)$ and $\gamma(r_2, t)$ and their approximations $\gamma'(r_1, N)$ and $\gamma'(r_2, N)$ depending on the time bound. We can

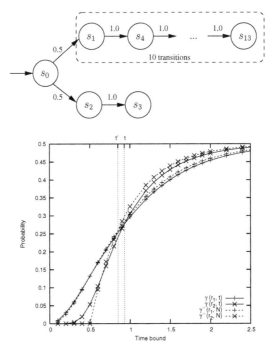

Fig. 2. An example of a CTMC

see that the approximated curves run rather closely by the accurate curves. The point of inflexion of the approximative curves where the higher probability mass changes from r_1 to r_2 is located quite close to the inflection point of the non-approximated curves. This illustrates that for a given time bound we are able to rather accurately determine the optimal path using our approximation.

As mentioned previously, the cost estimate function f used in Z^* takes a heuristic function h into account. In our setting h is an optimistic heuristics, i.e. for each state $h(s)$ is an overestimate of the maximal probability $h^*(s)$ to reach a goal state started from s within at most N transitions, more precisely:

$$h(s) \geq h^*(s) := max\{\gamma'(s', s, N) \mid s' \text{ is a goal state}\}. \tag{7}$$

f is defined formally in the following equation:

$$\begin{aligned} f(s') &:= F[\psi(s), f(s), h(s')] = F[\{\pi'(s, k) | 0 \leq k \leq N\}, M(s, s'), h(s')] \\ &= -\gamma'(s', N) \cdot h(s'). \end{aligned} \tag{8}$$

$\gamma'(s', N) \cdot h(s')$ is an estimate of the merit of the state s' and the costs are the negation of this value. If it is technically possible, information from the numerical analysis can be used in the computation of $\gamma'(s', N)$ and $h(s')$. This would increase the performance by computation sharing. The quality of h can also be improved. We remark that the property of f of being optimistic relies on the currently unproven conjecture that for each triple of states s_1, s_2 and s_3, where s_i is an ancestor of s_j in the traversal tree of the search algorithm for $i < j$, the following inequation holds:

$$\gamma'(s_2, s_1, N) \cdot \gamma'(s_3, s_2, N) \geq \gamma'(s_3, s_1, N). \tag{9}$$

This implies admissibility of f, and consequently the optimality of the algorithm. Our experiments confirm this conjecture since the search always finds optimal counterexamples and a reopening of nodes, which can have detrimental effects on the computational performance, was never observed. We point out, however, that optimality is not our essential goal. The experience in directed model checking has been that even inadmissible heuristics deliver good (sub-)optimal goals, if only the heuristic estimate is informative. We also remark that we have to store with each open state s, i.e. leaf state in the traversal tree, a vector of the size $N - depth(s)$ saving the probabilities to be in the state s after k transitions, for each $depth(s) \leq k \leq N$. However the effect of this additional space is imperceptible, hence the set of open states is very small relative to the whole state space.

To establish the optimality of Z^* we still have to establish order-preservation of f. This can be done by the following reasoning:

$$F[\psi(s_1), f(s_1), h_1(s')] \geq F[\psi(s_2), f(s_2), h_1(s')]$$
$$\Rightarrow -\gamma'(s_1, N) \cdot h_1(s') \geq -\gamma'(s_2, N) \cdot h_1(s')$$
$$\Rightarrow -\gamma'(s_1, N) \geq -\gamma'(s_2, N)$$
$$\Rightarrow -\gamma'(s_1, N) \cdot h_2(s') \geq -\gamma'(s_2, N) \cdot h_2(s')$$
$$\Rightarrow F[\psi(s_1), f(s_1), h_2(s')] \geq F[\psi(s_2), f(s_2), h_2(s')]$$

In the above proof we use the fact that h_1 and h_2 never take the value 0. Let $S' \subseteq S$ be the set containing all goal states. Note that $h_i(s) = 0$ for some state s implies that $h^*(s) = 0$ because $h_i(s) \geq h^*(s)$. That means, the probability to reach a goal state outgoing from s within N transitions is 0. In this case we are allowed to remove s and its in- and outgoing transitions from the state space.

3.3   Heuristic Functions

We now turn to the question how to efficiently compute informative heuristic estimates to be used in the search. Consider the property $\mathcal{P}_{<p}(\Diamond^{\leq t}\varphi)$. For every state s that we explore in the search we need an overestimating function for the maximal time-bounded run probability until a state satisfying φ is reached from s,

Table 1. A method to build heuristic functions for complex reachability properties

φ	h_φ	$\bar{h}_\varphi$
$\neg \varphi_1$	$\bar{h}_{\varphi_1}$	h_{φ_1}
$\varphi_1 \vee \varphi_2$	$max\{h_{\varphi_1}, h_{\varphi_2}\}$	$min\{\bar{h}_{\varphi_1}, \bar{h}_{\varphi_2}\}$
$\varphi_1 \wedge \varphi_2$	$min\{h_{\varphi_1}, h_{\varphi_2}\}$	$max\{\bar{h}_{\varphi_1}, \bar{h}_{\varphi_2}\}$

more precisely, $max\{\gamma'(s', s, N) \mid s' \vDash \varphi\}$ Let h_φ be an estimation for the maximal time-bounded run probability until a state *satisfying* φ is reached and $\bar{h}_\varphi$ an estimation for the maximal time-bounded run probability until a state *violating* φ is reached. If φ is an atomic proposition, the concrete heuristic estimation values are application dependent and we shall provide examples in the context of our case study in Section 4. However, the state formulae characterizing the state reachability conditions consist of boolean combinations of atomic state propositions, as for instance in the formula $\mathcal{P}_{<p}(\lozenge^{\leq t}(\varphi_1 \wedge \neg\varphi_2))$. Table 1 illustrates how heuristic estimates can be obtained from boolean combinations of atomic formulae. If the given heuristic functions of the atomic propositions are admissible, then the heuristic functions built according to Table1 are admissible. We can therefore assume that Z^* delivers paths leading into goal states with optimal costs.

4   Case Study: The SCSI-2 Protocol

SCSI-2 Protocol. To illustrate our approach we analyze a storage system of realistic size. This system consists of up to 8 devices, one disk controller and up to 7 hard disks. These devices are connected by a bus implementing the *Small Computer System Interface-2* (SCSI-2) standard [15]. Each device is assigned a unique SCSI number between 0 and 7. In [16], this system was analyzed regarding starvation problems for disks having SCSI numbers smaller than the SCSI number of the disk controller. Within the scope of that work the system was modelled in LOTOS [17] and transformed into an *interactive Markov chain (IMC)* by the CADP toolbox [10, 11]. We will use this model in our analysis.

In accordance with the SCSI-2 protocol definition, the controller can send a *command* (CMD) to the disk d. After processing this command, the disk sends a *reconnect* message (REC) to the controller. CMD and REC messages of every disk are stored in eight-place FIFO queues. CMD and REC messages circulate on the SCSI bus, which is shared by all devices. To avoid access conflicts on the bus, a bus arbitration policy is used.

Directed Reachability Analysis of the SCSI-2 Protocol. We analyse the storage system described above with respect to the probability of reaching an overload situation of the hard disks. The system consists of one controller and three disks. On one disk (the main disk) the operating system and all applications are installed. The two other disks are used to backup the data of the main disk (backup disks). In stress cases, the main disk is intensely loaded and has to serve many more access requests than the other disks. It is interesting to determine the probability to reach some state where the main disk is overloaded while the other disks are not busy. In this situation the command queue of the main disk is full and the queues of the backup disks are empty. Similarly we consider the system behavior during backup. In order to capture these situations we define the following atomic state propositions:

- For each disk d, the command queue of d is full: φ_d.
- For each disk d, the command queue of d is empty: ϑ_d.

Let 0 be the SCSI number of the main disk and 1 and 2 the numbers of the backup disks. We are interested in the following properties:

1. The main disk is overloaded and the backup disks are idle (MDOL):

$$\phi := \mathcal{P}_{<p}(\lozenge^{\leq t}\varphi_0 \wedge \vartheta_1 \wedge \vartheta_2) \tag{10}$$

2. One backup disk is overloaded and the two other disks are idle (BDOL):

$$\theta := \mathcal{P}_{<p}(\lozenge^{\leq t}\vartheta_0 \wedge (\varphi_0 \wedge \vartheta_1) \vee (\vartheta_0 \wedge \varphi_1)) \tag{11}$$

We first need heuristic estimation functions for the atomic propositions, as discussed in Section 3.3.[3] As we mentioned above, determining these estimates requires to exploit some domain specific insight.

Let D denote the set containing the SCSI numbers of the plugged disks. The map $cq : S \times D \longrightarrow \{0, 1, ..., 8\}$ gives for each disk the number of commands contained in its command queue in the current state.

1. The delay required to issue a new command to the disk d, for some $d \in D$, is modelled by a Markovian transition with rate λ_d.
2. The servicing time of the disk d is modelled by a Markovian transition with rate μ_d.

For the uniformisation of the model we have to determine a value which is not smaller than $E_{max} \geq max\{E(s) \mid s \in S\}$. It can easily be shown that $max\{E(s) \mid s \in S\} = \sum_{d \in D}(\lambda_d + \mu_d) =: E_{max}$. Thus in the uniformised model the branching probability of the transition $s \xrightarrow{rate} s'$ is $\frac{rate}{E_{max}}$. In each state s, transitions modeling sending a new command to disk d as well as processing a command by the disk d compete at least against the following Markovian delays (including the delay of the transition itself):

- λ_i for each disk i, where $cq(s, i) < 8$.
- μ_i for each disk i, where $cq(s, i) > 0$.

This leads to the following inequation, describing possible underestimations for the probabilities:

$$E(s) \geq \left(\sum_{\substack{i \in D \\ cq(s,i)<8}} \lambda_i + \sum_{\substack{i \in D \\ cq(s,i)>0}} \mu_i \right) =: E'(s). \tag{12}$$

In other words, the branching probability of leaving s, which we denote by $p_{out}(s)$, is not smaller than $\frac{E'(s)}{E_{max}}$. Thus, if s' is the other end state of such transition, then

$$\gamma'(s', s, N) \leq p \cdot \sum_{k=0}^{N-1}(1 - p_{out}(s))^k,$$

where p is the branching probability of the transition, i.e. $\frac{\lambda_i}{E_{max}}$ or $\frac{\mu_i}{E_{max}}$.

---

[3] Since negations of the atomic propositions do not occur in the property which we analyse we do not need to give heuristic functions for the negations $\bar{h}$.

In conclusion, relying on the the over-approximation above and the conjecture explained in Section 3.2, we can define the following optimistic heuristic functions:

$$h_{\varphi_d}(s) := (\frac{\lambda_d}{E_{max}} \cdot \sum_{k=0}^{N-1} (1 - p_{out}(s))^k))^{8-cq(s,d)} \tag{13}$$

$$h_{\vartheta_d}(s) := (\frac{\mu_d}{E_{max}} \cdot \sum_{k=0}^{N-1} (1 - p_{out}(s))^k))^{cq(s,d)} \tag{14}$$

More precisely, we conjecture the following relations:

$$h_{\varphi_d}(s) \geq h^*_{\varphi_d}(s) := max\{\gamma'(s, s', N) \mid cq(s', d) = 8\}$$
$$h_{\vartheta_d}(s) \geq h^*_{\vartheta_d}(s) := max\{\gamma'(s, s', N) \mid cq(s', d) = 0\}$$

The heuristic functions h_φ and h_ϑ are built according to Table 1[4].

Implementation and Experiments. As mentioned above we use GBestFS and Z^* as directed search algorithms and compare them to the undirected algorithms DFS, BFS and Dijkstra. The variant of Dijkstra's algorithm that we use interprets the $-\gamma'(s, N)$ values as a weight of the state s. We expect that BFS delivers the shortest solution while our variant of Dijkstra delivers the path with maximal time-bounded run probability.

We generate the models using the OPEN/ CÆSAR environment [18], also referred to as CADP, with which it is possible to generate a C graph module representing an implicit labeled transition system (LTS) corresponding to the given LOTOS model. We then transform the generated LTS into a CTMC[5]. We explore this CTMC on-the-fly by our search algorithms. If property violations are found, the search algorithm delivers a path leading from the initial state to a state violating the property. In order to preserve all probabilistic information of the model, the remainder of the model is replaced by a special absorbing state s_{out} to which we redirect all transitions which originate from some state on the path to the goal states, but which are not part of the path.

Table 2 shows an overview on the probabilities computed for the properties MDOL and BDOL. In order to assess the quality of some counterexample that we found we compare the reachability probability of the counterexamples with the precise reachability probability of the property in the original model, as determined by a transient analyser. For this purpose we generate the explicit state graph of the model in the BCG format of CADP and modify it by making all goal

---

[4] Note that heuristics built according to this table are monotone in case the heuristics for the atomic propositions are monotone. For the SCSI-2 example this is the case. The monotonicity manifests itself in the fact that we did not observe state re-openings in the experiments.

[5] In fact, in general the model resulting from this transformation is an interactive Markov chain (IMC), which in this particular case happens to correspond to a CTMC [16].

Table 2. Overview on the probabilities computed for the properties MDOL and BDOL for different time bounds, for main and backup disk load = 10

Prob.	Time bound		1	2	3	4	5	6	7	8	9	10
MDOL	Model		0.235	0.312	0.327	0.329	0.329	0.329	0.330	0.330	0.330	0.330
	DFS		-	-	-	-	-	-	0.000	-	-	0.000
	BFS		-	0.161	0.161	0.161	0.161	0.161	0.161	0.161	0.161	0.161
	Dijkstra	estimated	-	0.049	0.049	0.049	0.049	0.049	0.049	0.049	0.049	0.049
		precise	-	0.161	0.161	0.161	0.161	0.161	0.161	0.161	0.161	0.161
	GBestFS	estimated	-	0.005	0.005	0.005	0.005	0.005	0.005	0.005	0.005	0.005
		precise	-	0.012	0.012	0.012	0.012	0.012	0.012	0.012	0.012	0.012
	Z^*	estimated	-	0.049	0.049	0.049	0.049	0.049	0.049	0.049	0.049	0.049
		precise	-	0.161	0.161	0.161	0.161	0.161	0.161	0.161	0.161	0.161
BDOL	Model		0.008	0.008	0.008	0.008	0.008	0.008	0.008	0.008	0.008	0.008
	DFS		-	-	-	0.000	0.000	0.000	0.000	0.000	0.000	0.000
	BFS		-	0.002	0.002	0.002	0.002	0.002	0.002	0.002	0.002	0.002
	Dijkstra	estimated	-	0.001	0.001	0.001	0.001	0.001	0.001	0.001	0.001	0.001
		precise	-	0.002	0.002	0.002	0.002	0.002	0.002	0.002	0.002	0.002
	GBestFS	estimated	-	0.000	0.000	0.000	0.000	0.000	0.000	0.000	0.000	0.000
		precise	-	0.000	0.000	0.000	0.000	0.000	0.000	0.000	0.000	0.000
	Z^*	estimated	-	0.001	0.001	0.001	0.001	0.001	0.001	0.001	0.001	0.001
		precise	-	0.002	0.002	0.002	0.002	0.002	0.002	0.002	0.002	0.002

states absorbing. After that we analyze the modified model using the transient analyser of CADP. The resulting probabilities are given in the row labeled by "Model". For the probabilistic algorithms (Dijkstra, GBestFS, Z^*), two probability values are recorded in Table 2, namely the *estimated* and the *precise* ones, c.f. the table rows labeled "estimated" and "precise". The estimated value is $\gamma'(r, N)$ computed by the search algorithm. The precise probability of the counterexample is $\gamma(r, t)$ computed by the numeric transient analyser of CADP. To compute the precise value we run the transient analyser on the counterexample interpreted as a truncated CTMC (see Figure 5). When the search algorithm was unable to find a counterexample, then we denote this with an entry of the form '-'.

To interpret the results, we can first see that for both properties the probability of the run delivered by Z^* corresponds to the probability of the run using Dijkstra. This supports the optimality of Z^* and the optimality conjecture that we propose in Section 3.2. The probabilities of the counterexamples delivered by DFS are very close to zero which supports our claim that DFS is unsuitable in this setting. In many cases the DFS algorithm failed to find a counterexample at all. The reason is that we limited the search depth of DFS to N[6]. For time bound 1 no counterexample could be found since no goal state was reachable in the approximation within N state transitions. The optimal counterexample for both properties happens to be the shortest one. Only due to this BFS was able to select the optimal path in all experiments. The counterexamples found by GBestFS are inferior to the optimal ones.

Figures 3 and 4 compare the performance of the different algorithms with respect to CPU runtime, explored states and used memory space, respectively. Generally, we can observe that the guided algorithms (GBestFS and Z^*) have a

---

[6] C.f. also the incompleteness of depth bounded DFS discussed in [19].

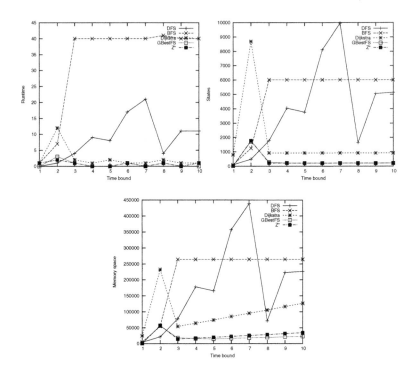

Fig. 3. Computational effort for MDOL depending on the time bound (main disk load = 5)

much better performance in terms of both runtime and memory space than the uninformed algorithms (DFS, BFS and Dijkstra). This suggests that the guided search algorithms will scale much better to larger problems than, in particular, Dijkstra's algorithm. In some situations GBestFS works more efficiently than Z^* but the difference is not very significant. The algorithms DFS and BFS perform badly in terms of both runtime and number of explored states. The number of explored states usually correlates with the memory space used by the algorithm. However the probabilistic algorithms (Dijkstra, GBestFS and Z^*) use additionally a vector of the size $\leq N$ for each open state s in order to save the values of $\pi(k)$, for $depth(s) \leq k \leq N$, c.f. section 3.2. Normally the effect of this additional space is imperceptible, hence the set of open states is very small relative to the whole state space. However, the effect can be noticed in Figure 4. Although BFS explores more states than Dijkstra, it requires less memory than BFS.

To assess the counterexamples found by our probabilistic algorithms qualitatively, we consider the following comparison. For the properties MDOL and BDOL, DFS finds an error state, if at all, over a very intricate run. These runs contribute almost nothing to the whole reachability probability of the property. In models in which short runs do not carry necessarily a large probability mass, we will detect the same effect for BFS. Certainly, such runs do not provide much insight in order to to locate the cause of the property violation. On the other

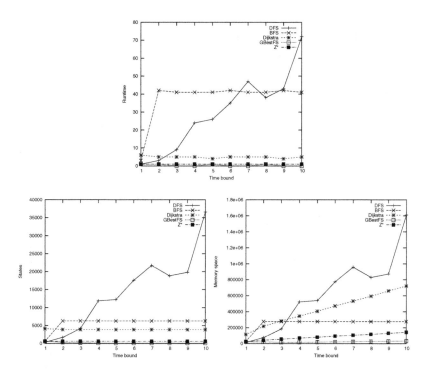

Fig. 4. Computational effort for BDOL depending on the time bound (backup disk load = 5)

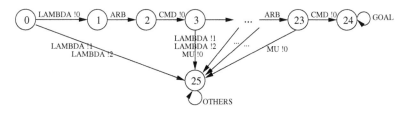

Fig. 5. A Counterexample for MDOL

hand, there are other runs that obviously carry larger probability mass. We illustrate one such run in Figure 5. It also corresponds to the counterexample that Z* finds for the MDOL property. This counterexample models the behavior of the system in the case that right from the start permanently new commands are sent to the main disk (disk 0) while the disk does not get the chance to service any of these commands. The counterexample largely consists of eight repetitions of the events **Lambda !0**, **ARB**, **CMD !0**. These correspond to a Markovian delay (**Lambda !0**), access to the data bus (**ARB**) and the sending of a command to disk 0 (**CMD !0**). This in fact corresponds to the most direct way to overload the main disk, a situation that is represented by the state labeled **GOAL**. All transitions which are not touched along this run are redirected to a sink state labeled OTH-ERS. By analysing this counterexample we can identify the following two factors contributing to the high probability of the property violation:

1. The Markov delay LAMBDA !0 modeling that the controller issues a new command for disk 0 is relative large, i.e. the disk is highly frequented.
2. Other Markov delays, especially MU !0 modeling the servicing delay of disk 0, are relative small, i.e. the disk can barely service the requests.

This leads to the following solution strategy. The main disk has to be replaced by a faster one which means increasing MU !0. At the same time the storage system load could be reduced, i.e. the value of LAMBDA !0 should be decreased.

In summary, the experiments show that our approach succeeds in efficiently finding counterexamples carrying large portion of the full probability and that are therefore meaningful in the debugging process. The estimated probabilities of the found counterexamples are relatively accurate, and comprise on average 50% for MDOL and 25% for BDOL of the total probability (c.f. line "Model" in the table).

5   Conclusion

We have described a method to determine counterexamples for timed probabilistic reachability properties of CTMCs. Our approach relies on heuristics directed explicit state search and employs uniformisation in order to efficiently compute heuristics. Using experimental data we illustrated that our approach succeeds in finding meaningful counterexamples in a way that is computationally superior to using other, non-directed search approaches.

Related work can largely be found in the area of model checking for stochastic systems, and in directed model checking, as cited earlier. We are not aware of other approaches to solving counterexample generation for stochastic model checking using heuristic search techniques. The method is also readily applicable to untimed probabilistic reachability counterexample generation.

Goals for future research include the use of appropriate search methods to approximate the timed probabilistic reachability problem from below, i.e., to determine a set of n runs in the model leading into goal states so that the combined probability of these runs exceeds the probability bound p. For appropriately structured models and small n this may be computationally advantageous compared to numerical stochastic model checking.

References

1. Clarke, E.M., Grumberg, O., Peled, D.A.: Model Checking. The MIT Press (1999 (third printing 2001))
2. Bianco, A., de Alfaro, L.: Model checking of probabalistic and nondeterministic systems. In: Proceedings of the 15th Conference on Foundations of Software Technology and Theoretical Computer Science, Springer-Verlag LNCS (1995) 499–513

3. A. Aziz, K. Sanwal, V. Singhal, R. K. Brayton: Verifying continuous-time Markov chains. In Rajeev Alur, Thomas A. Henzinger, eds.: Eighth International Conference on Computer Aided Verification CAV. Volume 1102., New Brunswick, NJ, USA, Springer Verlag LNCS (1996) 269–276

4. de Alfaro, L.: Formal Verification of Probabilistic Systems. Ph.d. dissertation, Stanford University (1997)

5. Baier, C.: On algorithmic verification methods for probabilistic systems. Habilitation Thesis. Habilitation thesis, University of Mannheim (1998)

6. Baier, C., Katoen, J.P., Hermanns, H.: Approximate symbolic model checking of continuous-time Markov chains. In: International Conference on Concurrency Theory, Springer Verlag LNCS (1999) 146–161

7. Aziz, A., Sanwal, K., Singhal, V., Brayton, R.: Model-checking Continuous-Time Markov Chains. ACM Transactions on Computational Logic **1** (2000) 162–170

8. Baier, C., Haverkort, B.R., Hermanns, H., Katoen, J.P.: Model checking continuous-time Markov chains by transient analysis. In: CAV '00: Proceedings of the 12th International Conference on Computer Aided Verification, Springer-Verlag LNCS (2000) 358–372

9. Baier, C., Haverkort, B., Hermanns, H., Katoen, J.P.: Model-checking algorithms for continuous-time Markov chains. IEEE Transions on Software Engineering **29** (2003)

10. H. Garavel, F. Lang, R.M.: An overview of CADP 2001. European Association for Software Science and Technology (EASST) Newsletter **4** (2002)

11. Hermanns, H., Joubert, C.: A set of performance and dependability analysis components for CADP. In Garavel, H., Hatcliff, J., eds.: Proceedings of the 9th International Conference on Tools and Algorithms for the Construction and Analysis of Systems TACAS'2003 (Warsaw, Poland). Volume 2619., Springer Verlag LNCS (2003) 425–430

12. Edelkamp, S., Lafuente, A.L., Leue, S.: Directed explicit-state model checking in the validation of communication protocols. Software Tools for Technology Transfer **5** (2004) 247–267

13. Dijkstra, E.W.: A note on two problems in connexion with graphs. Numerische Mathematik **1** (1959) 269–271

14. Pearl, J.: Heuristics – Intelligent Search Strategies for Computer Problem Solving. Addision–Wesley (1986)

15. (ANSI), A.N.S.I.: Small computer interface-2 – standard x3.131-1994 (1994)

16. Garavel, H., Hermanns, H.: On combining functional verification and performance evaluation using CADP. In: Proceedings of the International Symposium of Formal Methods Europe on Formal Methods - Getting IT Right, Springer-Verlag LNCS (2002) 410–429

17. ISO/IEC: LOTOS – a formal description technique based on temporal ordering of observational behaviour (1989)

18. Garavel, H.: OPEN/CÆSAR: An open software architecture for verification, simulation, and testing. In: TACAS '98: Proceedings of the 4th International Conference on Tools and Algorithms for Construction and Analysis of Systems, London, UK, Springer-Verlag LNCS (1998) 68–84

19. Holzmann, G.J.: The Spin Model Checker: Primer and Reference Manual. Addision–Wesley (2003)

Time Supervision of Concurrent Systems Using Symbolic Unfoldings of Time Petri Nets*

Thomas Chatain and Claude Jard

IRISA/ENS Cachan-Bretagne,
Campus de Beaulieu, F-35042 Rennes cedex, France
Thomas.Chatain@irisa.fr, Claude.Jard@bretagne.ens-cachan.fr

Abstract. Monitoring real-time concurrent systems is a challenging task. In this paper we formulate (model-based) supervision by means of hidden state history reconstruction, from event (e.g. alarm) observations. We follow a so-called true concurrency approach using time Petri nets: the model defines explicitly the causal and concurrency relations between the observable events, produced by the system under supervision on different points of observation, and constrained by time aspects. The problem is to compute on-the-fly the different partial order histories, which are the possible explanations of the observable events. We do not impose that time is observable: the aim of supervision is to infer the partial ordering of the events and their possible firing dates. This is achieved by considering a model of the system under supervision, given as a time Petri net, and the on-the-fly construction of an unfolding, guided by the observations. Using a symbolic representation, this paper presents a new definition of the unfolding of time Petri nets with dense time.

1   Introduction and Related Work

Monitoring real-time concurrent systems is a challenging task. In this paper we formulate model-based supervision by means of hidden state history reconstruction, from event (e.g. alarm) observations. We follow a so-called true concurrency approach using time Petri nets: the model defines explicitly the causal and concurrency relations between the observable events, produced by the system under supervision on different points of observation, and constrained by time aspects. The problem is to compute on-the-fly the different partial order histories, which are the possible explanations of the observable events. An important application is the supervision of telecommunications networks, which motivated this work.

Without considering time, a natural candidate to formalize the problem are safe Petri nets with branching processes and unfoldings. The previous work of our group used this framework to define the histories and a distributed algorithm to build them as a collection of consistent local views[2]. The approach defines

---

* This work was supported by the french RNRT projects Swan and Persiform, funded by the Ministère de la Recherche; partners of the Swan project are Inria, France Telecom R&D, Alcatel, QosMetrics, and University of Bordeaux; partners of the Persiform project are Inria, France Telecom R&D, INT, Orpheus, and University of Grenoble.

P. Pettersson and W. Yi (Eds.): FORMATS 2005, LNCS 3829, pp. 196–210, 2005.

the possible explanations as the underlying event structure of the unfolding of the product of the Petri net model and of an acyclic Petri net representing the partial order of the observed alarms.

In this paper we extend our method to time Petri nets, allowing the designer to model time constraints, restricting by this way the set of possible explanations, We do not impose that time is observable: the aim of supervision is to infer the partial ordering of the events and their possible firing dates. Using a symbolic representation, this paper presents a new definition of the unfolding of time Petri nets with dense time.

Model-based diagnosis using time Petri nets and partial orders has already been addressed in [12]. In this work, temporal reasoning is based on (linear) logic. The first reference to time Petri net unfolding seems to be in 1996, by A. Semenov, A. Yakovlev and A. Koelmans [13] in the context of hardware verification. They deal only with a quite restricted class of nets, called *time independent choice time Petri net*, in which any choice is resolved independently of time. In [1], T. Aura and J. Lilius give a partial order semantics to time Petri nets, based on the non-sequential processes semantics for untimed net systems. A time process of a time Petri net is defined as a traditionally constructed causal process that has a valid timing. An algorithm for checking validness of a given timing is presented. It is proved that the interleavings of the time processes are in bijection with the firing schedules. But unfortunately, they do not provide a way to represent all the valid processes using the notion of unfolding of time Petri net, as usual in the untimed case. A few years later (in 2002), H. Fleischhack and C. Stehno in [10] give the first notion of a finite prefix of the unfolding of a time Petri net. Their method relies on a translation towards an ordinary place/transition net. This requires to consider only discrete time and to enumerate all the situations. This also relies on the introduction of new transitions, which represent the clock ticks. Although relevant for model-checking, it is not clear that it allows us to recover causalities and concurrencies, as required in the diagnosis application. Furthermore, we are convinced that time constraints must be treated in a symbolic way, using the analog of state class constructions of B. Berthomieu [3, 4].

The rest of the paper is organized as follows. Section 2 defines the different ingredients of our model-based supervision, namely the diagnosis setup, the time Petri net model and its partial order semantics. Section 3 describes the symbolic unfolding technique used to compute the symbolic processes, which serve as explanations. Before entering the general case, we consider the simplest case of extended free-choice time Petri nets [5]. We conclude in Section 4. The proofs of the theorems are available in the research report [7].

2 Diagnosis, Time Petri Nets and Partial Order Semantics

2.1 Diagnosis: Problem

Let us consider a real distributed system, which produces on a given set of sensors some events (or alarms) during its life. We consider the following setup for

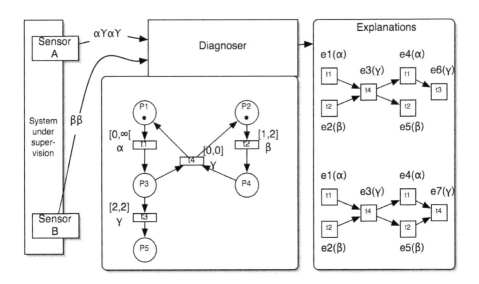

Fig. 1. Model-based diagnosis of distributed systems using time Petri nets

diagnosis, assuming that alarms are not lost. Each sensor records its local alarms in sequence, while respecting causality (i.e. the observed sequences cannot contradict the causal and temporal ordering defined in the model). The different sensors perform independently and asynchronously, and a single supervisor collects the records from the different sensors. Thus any interleaving of the records from different sensors is possible, and causalities and temporal ordering among alarms from different sensors are lost. This architecture is illustrated in Figure 1.

For the development of the example, we consider that the system under supervision produces the sequences $\alpha\gamma\alpha\gamma$ on sensor A, and $\beta\beta$ on sensor B. Given the time Petri net model of Figure 1 (left), the goal of the diagnoser is to compute all the possible explanations shown in Figure 1. Explanations are labelled partial orders. Each node is labeled by a transition of the Petri net model and a possible date given by a symbolic expression. Notice that the diagnoser infers the possible causalities between alarms, as well as the possible dates for each of them. The first alarms $\alpha\gamma\alpha$ and $\beta\beta$ imply that transitions t_1 and t_2 are fired twice and concurrently. The last γ can be explained by two different transitions in conflict (t_3 and t_4).

2.2 Time Petri Net: Definition

Notations. We denote f^{-1} the inverse of a bijection f. We denote $f_{|A}$ the restriction of a mapping f to a set A. The restriction has higher priority than the inverse: $f_{|A}^{-1} = (f_{|A})^{-1}$. We denote $\circ$ the usual composition of functions. Q denotes the set of nonnegative rational numbers.

Time Petri nets were introduced in [11].

A *time Petri net* (TPN) is a tuple $N = \langle P, T, pre, post, efd, lfd \rangle$ where P and T are finite sets of *places* and *transitions* respectively, *pre* and *post* map each transition $t \in T$ to its *preset* often denoted $^\bullet t \overset{\text{def}}{=} pre(t) \subseteq P$ ($^\bullet t \neq \emptyset$) and its *postset* often denoted $t^\bullet \overset{\text{def}}{=} post(t) \subseteq P$; $efd : T \longrightarrow Q$ and $lfd : T \longrightarrow Q \cup \{\infty\}$ associate the *earliest firing delay* $efd(t)$ and *latest firing delay* $lfd(t)$ with each transition t. A TPN is represented as a graph with two types of nodes: places (circles) and transitions (bars). The closed interval $[efd(t), lfd(t)]$ is written near each transition. For the purpose of supervision, we consider *labelled time Petri nets* $\langle N, \Lambda, \lambda \rangle$ where Λ is a set of event types (or alarms), and λ the typing of transitions (α, β, γ in Figure 1).

A *state* of a time Petri net is given by a triple $\langle M, dob, \theta \rangle$, where $M \subseteq P$ is a *marking* denoted with tokens (thick dots), $\theta \in Q$ is its date and $dob : M \longrightarrow Q$ associates a *date of birth* $dob(p) \leq \theta$ with each token (marked place) $p \in M$. A transition $t \in T$ is *enabled* in the state $\langle M, dob, \theta \rangle$ if all of its input places are marked: $^\bullet t \subseteq M$. Its *date of enabling* $doe(t)$ is the date of birth of the youngest token in its input places: $doe(t) \overset{\text{def}}{=} \max_{p \in ^\bullet t} dob(p)$. All the time Petri nets we consider in this article are *safe*, i.e. in each reachable state $\langle M, dob, \theta \rangle$, if a transition t is enabled in $\langle M, dob, \theta \rangle$, then $t^\bullet \cap (M \setminus {}^\bullet t) = \emptyset$.

A process of a TPN starts in an *initial state* $\langle M_0, dob_0, \theta_0 \rangle$, which is given by the *initial marking* M_0 and the initial date θ_0. Initially, all the tokens carry the date θ_0 as date of birth: $\forall p \in M_0 \quad dob_0(p) \overset{\text{def}}{=} \theta_0$.

The transition t can fire at date θ' from state $\langle M, dob, \theta \rangle$, if:

- t is enabled: $^\bullet t \subseteq M$;
- the minimum delay is reached: $\theta' \geq doe(t) + efd(t)$;
- time progresses: $\theta' \geq \theta$;
- the enabled transitions do not overtake the maximum delays:
  $\forall t' \in T \quad {}^\bullet t' \subseteq M \implies \theta' \leq doe(t') + lfd(t')$.

The firing of t at date θ' leads to the state $\langle (M \setminus {}^\bullet t) \cup t^\bullet, dob', \theta' \rangle$, where $dob'(p) \overset{\text{def}}{=} dob(p)$ if $p \in M \setminus {}^\bullet t$ and $dob'(p) \overset{\text{def}}{=} \theta'$ if $p \in t^\bullet$.

Finally we assume that time *diverges*: when infinitely many transitions fire, time necessarily diverges to infinity.

In the initial state of the net of Figure 1, p_1 and p_2 are marked and their date of birth is 0. t_1 and t_2 are enabled and their date of enabling is the initial date 0. t_2 can fire in the initial state at any time between 1 and 2. Choose time 1. After this firing p_1 and p_4 are marked, t_1 is the only enabled transition and it has already waited 1 time unit. t_1 can fire at any time θ, provided it is greater than 1. Consider t_1 fires at time 3. p_3 and p_4 are marked in the new state, and transitions t_3 and t_4 are enabled, and their date of enabling is 3 because they have just been enabled by the firing of t_1. To fire, t_3 would have to wait 2 time units. But transition t_4 cannot wait at all. So t_4 will necessarily fire (at time 3), and t_3 cannot fire.

Remark. The semantics of time Petri nets are often defined in a slightly different way: the state of the net is given as a pair $\langle M, I \rangle$, where M is the marking, and I maps each enabled transition t to the delay that has elapsed since it was enabled, that is $\theta - doe(t)$ with our notations. It is more convenient for us to attach time information on the tokens of the marking than on the enabled transitions. We have chosen the date of birth of the tokens rather than their age, because we want to make the impact of the firing of transitions as local as possible. And the age of each token in the marking must be updated each time a transition t fires, whereas the date of birth has to be set only for the tokens that are created by t. Furthermore, usual semantics often deal with the delay between the firing of two consecutive transitions. In this paper we use the absolute firing date of the transitions instead. This fits better to our approach in which we are not interested in the total ordering of the events.

2.3 Partial Order Semantics

Processes. We will define the set X of (finite) processes of a safe time Petri net starting at date θ_0 in the initial marking M_0. These processes are those described in [1]. We define them inductively and use a canonical coding like in [8]. The processes provide a partial order representation of the executions.

Each process will be a pair $x \stackrel{\text{def}}{=} \langle E, \Theta \rangle$, where E is a set of *events*, and $\Theta : E \longrightarrow Q$ maps each event to its firing date. Θ is sometimes represented as a set of pairs $(e, \Theta(e))$. Each event e is a pair $({}^{\bullet}e, \tau(e))$ that codes an occurrence of the transition $\tau(e)$ in the process. ${}^{\bullet}e$ is a set of pairs $b \stackrel{\text{def}}{=} ({}^{\bullet}b, place(b)) \in E \times P$. Such a pair is called a *condition* and refers to the token that has been created by the event ${}^{\bullet}b$ in the place $place(b)$. We say that the event $e \stackrel{\text{def}}{=} ({}^{\bullet}e, \tau(e))$ *consumes* the conditions in ${}^{\bullet}e$. Symmetrically the set $\{(e, p) \mid p \in \tau(e)^{\bullet}\}$ of conditions that are *created* by e is denoted $e^{\bullet}$.

For all set B of conditions, we denote $Place(B) \stackrel{\text{def}}{=} \{place(b) \mid b \in B\}$, and when the restriction of $place$ to B is injective, we denote $place_{|B}^{-1}$ its inverse, and for all $P \subseteq Place(B)$, $Place_{|B}^{-1}(P) \stackrel{\text{def}}{=} \{place_{|B}^{-1}(p) \mid b \in P\}$.

The set of conditions that remain at the end of the process $\langle E, \Theta \rangle$ (meaning that they are created by an event of E, and no event of E consumes them) is $\uparrow(E) \stackrel{\text{def}}{=} \bigcup_{e \in E} e^{\bullet} \setminus \bigcup_{e \in E} {}^{\bullet}e$ (it does not depend on Θ). The state that is reached after the process $\langle E, \Theta \rangle$ is $\langle Place(\uparrow(E)), dob, \max_{e \in E} \Theta(e) \rangle$, where for all $p \in Place(\uparrow(E))$, $dob(p) \stackrel{\text{def}}{=} \Theta({}^{\bullet}b)$, with $b \stackrel{\text{def}}{=} place_{|\uparrow(E)}^{-1}(p)$.

We define inductively the set X of (finite) processes of a time Petri net starting at date θ_0 in the initial marking M_0 as follows:

- $\langle \{\bot\}, \{(\bot, \theta_0)\} \rangle \in X$, where $\bot \stackrel{\text{def}}{=} (\emptyset, \epsilon)$ represents the initial event. Notice that the initial event does not actually represent the firing of a transition, which explains the use of the special value $\epsilon \notin T$. For the same reason, the set of conditions that are created by $\bot$ is defined in a special way: $\bot^{\bullet} \stackrel{\text{def}}{=} \{(\bot, p) \mid p \in M_0\}$.
- For all process $\langle E, \Theta \rangle \in X$ leading to state $\langle M, dob, \theta \rangle$, if a transition t can fire at date θ' from state $\langle M, dob, \theta \rangle$, then $\langle E \cup \{e\}, \Theta \cup \{(e, \theta')\} \rangle \in X$, where the event $e \stackrel{\text{def}}{=} (Place_{|\uparrow(E)}^{-1}({}^{\bullet}t), t)$ represents this firing of t.

We define the relation $\rightarrow$ on the events as: $e \rightarrow e'$ iff $e^\bullet \cap {}^\bullet e' \neq \emptyset$. The reflexive transitive closure $\rightarrow^*$ of $\rightarrow$ is called the *causality* relation. For all event e, we denote $\lceil e \rceil \overset{\text{def}}{=} \{ f \in E \mid f \rightarrow^* e \}$, and for all set E of events, $\lceil E \rceil \overset{\text{def}}{=} \bigcup_{e \in E} \lceil e \rceil$. We also define $cnds(E) \overset{\text{def}}{=} \bigcup_{e \in E} e^\bullet$ the set of *conditions* created by the events of E.

Two events of a process that are not causally related are said to be *concurrent*.

Symbolic Processes. We choose to group the processes that differ only by their firing dates to obtain what we call a *symbolic process*.

A symbolic process of a time Petri net is a pair $\langle E, pred \rangle$ with $pred : (E \longrightarrow Q) \longrightarrow \textbf{bool}$, such that for all mapping $\Theta : E \longrightarrow Q$, if $pred(\Theta)$, then $\langle E, \Theta \rangle \in X$.

In practice, $pred$ is described by linear inequalities. Examples of symbolic processes are given in Figure 1. The first explanation groups all the processes formally defined as $\langle E, \Theta \rangle$ where E contains the six following events, with the associated firing dates (the initial event $\bot$ is not represented):

$$
\begin{aligned}
1 &= (\{(\bot, P_1)\}, t_1) & \Theta(1) &\geq \Theta(\bot) \\
2 &= (\{(\bot, P_2)\}, t_2) & 1 &\leq \Theta(2) - \Theta(\bot) \leq 2 \\
3 &= (\{(1, P_3), (2, P_4)\}, t_4) & \Theta(3) &= \max\{\Theta(1), \Theta(2)\} \\
4 &= (\{(3, P_1)\}, t_1) & \Theta(4) &= \Theta(3) \\
5 &= (\{(3, P_2)\}, t_2) & \Theta(5) &= \Theta(3) + 2 \\
6 &= (\{(4, P_3)\}, t_3) & \Theta(6) &= \Theta(4) + 2
\end{aligned}
$$

2.4   Diagnosis: Formal Problem Setting

Consider a net N modeling a system and an observation O of this system, which associates a finite sequence of observed alarms $(\lambda_{s,1}, \ldots, \lambda_{s,n_s})$ with each sensor s. The set of sensors is denoted S. For each sensor s, Λ_s indicates which alarms the sensor observes.

To compute a diagnosis, we propose to build a net $\mathcal{D}(N, O)$ whose processes correspond to the processes of N which satisfy the observation O. The idea is to constrain the model by adding new places and transitions so that each transition of the model that sends an alarm to a sensor s is not allowed to fire until all the previous alarms sent to s have been observed.

To achieve this we create a place s_λ for each alarm λ that may be sent to the sensor s, plus one place $\bar{s}$. For each transition t that sends an alarm λ to the sensor s, we add s_λ to the postset of t. After the ith alarm is sent to s, a new transition $t_{s,i}$ which models the observation of this alarm by s, removes the token from s_λ and creates a token in the place $\bar{s}$, meaning that the alarm has been observed. $\bar{s}$ is added to the preset of each transition that sends an alarm to s, so that it cannot fire before the previous alarm has been observed. The transitions $t_{s,i}$ are connected through places $p_{s,i}$ so that they must fire one after another.

Formally, for a net $N \overset{\text{def}}{=} \langle P, T, pre, post, efd, lfd \rangle$ and an observation O from a set S of sensors, we define a net $\mathcal{D}(N, O) \overset{\text{def}}{=} \langle P', T', wpre', pre', post', efd', lfd' \rangle$. This net is almost a time Petri net: a *weak preset* $wpre'(t) \subseteq pre'(t)$, denoted ${}^\circ t$

has been added for each transition $t \in T'$; only the date of birth of the tokens in the weak preset participate in the definition of the *date of weak enabling* of t, which replaces the date of enabling in the semantics: $dowe(t) \stackrel{\text{def}}{=} \max_{p \in {}^\circ t} dob(p)$. In the processes, for each event e, we denote ${}^\circ e \stackrel{\text{def}}{=} Place_{|{}^\bullet e}^{-1}({}^\circ \tau(e))$.

$\mathcal{D}(N, O)$ is defined as follows (where $\uplus$ denotes the disjoint union):

- $P' \stackrel{\text{def}}{=} P \uplus \{\bar{s} \mid s \in S\} \uplus \{s_\lambda \mid s \in S \wedge \lambda \in \Lambda_s\} \uplus \{p_{s,i} \mid s \in S, \ i = 0, \ldots, n_s\};$
- $T' \stackrel{\text{def}}{=} T \uplus \{t_{s,i} \mid s \in S, \ i = 1, \ldots, n_s\};$
- for all $t \in T$, $\quad wpre'(t) \stackrel{\text{def}}{=} pre(t), \quad pre'(t) \stackrel{\text{def}}{=} wpre'(t) \uplus \{\bar{s} \mid \lambda(t) \in \Lambda_s\},$
  $post'(t) \stackrel{\text{def}}{=} post(t) \uplus \{s_{\lambda(t)} \mid \lambda(t) \in \Lambda_s\},$
  $efd'(t) \stackrel{\text{def}}{=} efd(t) \quad$ and $\quad lfd'(t) \stackrel{\text{def}}{=} lfd(t);$
- $wpre'(t_{s,i}) = pre'(t_{s,i}) \stackrel{\text{def}}{=} \{p_{s,i-1}, s_{\lambda_{s,i}}\}, \quad post'(t_{s,i}) \stackrel{\text{def}}{=} \{p_{s,i}, \bar{s}\} \quad$ and
  $efd'(t_{s,i}) = lfd'(t_{s,i}) \stackrel{\text{def}}{=} 0.$

Figure 2 shows the net of Figure 1 constrained by the observation $\alpha\gamma\alpha\gamma$ from sensor A and $\beta\beta$ from sensor B.

We call *diagnosis of observation O on net N* any set of symbolic processes of $\mathcal{D}(N, O)$, which contain all the processes $\langle E, \Theta \rangle$ of $\mathcal{D}(N, O)$ such that: $\{p_{s,n_s} \mid s \in S\} \uplus \{\bar{s}_\lambda \mid s \in S \wedge \lambda \in \Lambda_s\} \subseteq Place(\uparrow(E))$. Unless the model contains loops of non observable events, these processes can be described by a finite set of symbolic processes. These processes can be projected to keep only the conditions and events which correspond to places and transitions of the model. Then we obtain all the processes of N that are compatible with the observation O, as shown in Figure 1. The construction of the explanations is based on the unfolding of $\mathcal{D}(N, O)$. The notion of unfolding allows us to use a compact representation of the processes by sharing the common prefixes. The temporal framework leads naturally to consider the new notion of symbolic unfolding that we detail in the following section.

3   Symbolic Unfoldings of Time Petri Nets

Symbolic unfoldings have already been addressed in the context of high-level Petri nets [6]. In this section we define the symbolic unfolding of time Petri nets, i.e. a quite compact structure that contains all the possible processes and exhibits concurrency. Actually the time Petri nets are extended with weak presets, as required by our diagnosis approach (see Section 2.4). For symbolic unfoldings of classical time Petri nets (such that the underlying untimed Petri net is safe), consider that the weak preset ${}^\circ t$ of any transition $t \in T$ is equal to its preset ${}^\bullet t$.

3.1   Pre-processes

For the construction of symbolic unfoldings of time Petri nets, we need the notion of *pre-process*, that extends the notion of process.

For all process $\langle E, \Theta \rangle$, and for all nonempty, causally closed set of events $E' \subseteq E$ ($\bot \in E'$ and $\lceil E' \rceil = E'$), $\langle E', \Theta_{|E'} \rangle$ is called a *pre-process*. The definition

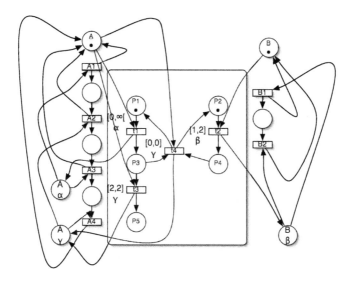

Fig. 2. Our example of TPN, constrained by the observation $\alpha\gamma\alpha\gamma$ from sensor A and $\beta\beta$ from sensor B

of the state that is reached after a process is also used for pre-processes. We define the *prefix* relation $\leq$ on pre-processes as follows:

$$\langle E, \Theta \rangle \leq \langle E', \Theta' \rangle \quad \text{iff} \quad E \subseteq E' \wedge \Theta = \Theta'_{|E}$$

3.2 Symbolic Unfoldings of Extended Free Choice Time Petri Nets

An *extended free choice* time Petri net is a time Petri net such that:

$$\forall t, t' \in T \quad {}^{\bullet}t \cap {}^{\bullet}t' \neq \emptyset \implies {}^{\bullet}t = {}^{\bullet}t'.$$

We define the *symbolic unfolding* U of an extended free choice time Petri net by collecting all the events that appear in its processes: $U \overset{\text{def}}{=} \bigcup_{\langle E, \Theta \rangle \in X} E$.

This unfolding has two important properties in the case of extended free choice time Petri nets:

Theorem 1. *Let $E \subseteq U$ be a nonempty finite set of events and $\Theta : E \longrightarrow Q$ associate a firing date with each event of E. $\langle E, \Theta \rangle$ is a pre-process iff:*

$$\begin{cases} \lceil E \rceil = E & \text{(E is causally closed)} \\ \nexists e, e' \in E \quad e \neq e' \wedge {}^{\bullet}e \cap {}^{\bullet}e' \neq \emptyset & \text{(E is conflict free)} \\ \forall e \in E \setminus \{\bot\} \quad lpred(e, \Theta) & \text{(all the events respect the firing delays)} \end{cases}$$

where

$$lpred(e, \Theta) \overset{\text{def}}{=} \begin{cases} \Theta(e) \geq \max_{b \in {}^{\bullet}e} \Theta({}^{\bullet}b) & \text{(t is strongly enabled when e fires)} \\ \Theta(e) \geq dowe(t) + efd(t) & \text{(the earliest firing delay is reached)} \\ \forall t' \in T \quad {}^{\bullet}t' = {}^{\bullet}t \implies \Theta(e) \leq dowe(t') + lfd(t') & \\ & \text{(the latest firing delays are respected)} \end{cases}$$

with $t \overset{\text{def}}{=} \tau(e)$ *and*

for all $t' \in T$ *such that* $\bullet t' = \bullet t$, $dowe(t') \overset{\text{def}}{=} \max_{b \in Place_{|\bullet_e}^{-1}(\circ t')} \Theta(\bullet b)$.

Theorem 2. *For all* $e \overset{\text{def}}{=} (B, t) \in cnds(U) \times T$,

$$
e \in U \text{ iff } \begin{cases} Place(B) = \bullet t \\ \nexists f, f' \in \lceil e \rceil \quad f \neq f' \ \wedge \ \bullet f \cap \bullet f' \neq \emptyset \\ \exists \Theta : \lceil e \rceil \longrightarrow Q \quad \forall f \in \lceil e \rceil \setminus \{\bot\} \quad lpred(f, \Theta) \end{cases}
$$

The first theorem gives a way to extract processes from the unfolding, while the second theorem gives a direct construction of the unfolding: adding a new event e just requires solving linear constraints on the $\Theta(f)$, $f \in \lceil e \rceil$. This also happens with symbolic unfoldings of high-level Petri nets introduced in [6].

3.3 Symbolic Unfoldings of Time Petri Nets: General Case

If we define the symbolic unfolding of a time Petri net in the general case as we have done for extended free choice time Petri nets, none of the two previous theorems hold: extracting a process from the unfolding becomes complex (see [1]); and especially we do not know any direct way to build the unfolding. It is also interesting to notice that the union of two pre-processes $\langle E, \Theta \rangle$ and $\langle E', \Theta' \rangle$ is not necessarily a pre-process, even if $\Theta_{|E \cap E'} = \Theta'_{|E \cap E'}$ and $E \cup E'$ is conflict free. In the example of Figure 1, we observe this if $\langle E, \Theta \rangle$ is the process which contains a firing of $t1$ at time 0 and a firing of $t2$ at time 1, and $\langle E', \Theta' \rangle$ is the pre-process that we obtain by removing the firing of $t2$ from the process made of $t1$ at time 0, $t2$ at time 2 and $t3$ at time 2. These difficulties come from the fact that the condition that allows us to extend a process $x \overset{\text{def}}{=} \langle E, \Theta \rangle$ with a new event e concerns all the state reached after the process x, and however the conditions in $\bullet e$ refer only to the tokens in the input places of $\tau(e)$.

From now on we assume that we know a partition of the set P of places of the net in sets $P_i \subseteq P$ of mutually exclusive places[1]; more precisely we demand that for all reachable marking M, $P_i \cap M$ is a singleton. For all place $p \in P_i$, we denote $\bar{p} \overset{\text{def}}{=} P_i \setminus \{p\}$. In the example of Figure 1, we will use the partition $\{p_1, p_3, p_5\}$, $\{p_2, p_4\}$.

Notion of partial state. A *partial state* of a time Petri net is a triple $\langle L, dob, \theta \rangle$ with $L \subseteq P$, $\theta \in Q$ is a date and $dob : L \longrightarrow Q$ associates a *date of birth* $dob(p) \leq \theta$ with each token (marked place) $p \in L$.

We define the relation $\sqsubseteq$ on partial states as follows:

$$
\langle L, dob, \theta \rangle \sqsubseteq \langle L', dob', \theta' \rangle \text{ iff } L \subseteq L' \ \wedge \ dob = dob'_{|L} \ \wedge \ \theta \leq \theta'
$$

---

[1] If we do not know any such partition, a solution is to extend the structure of the net with one complementary place for each place of the net and to add these new places in the preset (but not in the weak preset) and in the postset of the transitions such that in any reachable marking each place $p \in P$ is marked iff its complementary place is not. This operation does not change the behaviour of the time Petri net: since the weak presets do not change, the tokens in the complementary places do not participate in the definition of the date of enabling.

Firing a Transition from a Partial State. Although the semantics of time Petri nets requires to check time conditions for all the enabled transitions in the net, before firing a transition, there are cases when we know that a transition can fire at a given date θ', even if other transitions will fire before θ' in other parts of the net. As an example consider the net of Figure 1 starting at date 0 with the marking $\{p_1, p_2\}$. Although the semantics forbids to fire t_1 at date 10 before firing t_2, we feel that nothing can prevent t_1 from firing at date 10, because only t_1 can remove the token in place p_1. By contrast, the firing of t_3 highly depends on the firing date of t_2 because when t_4 is enabled it fires immediately and disables t_3. So if we want to fire t_3 we have to check whether p_2 or p_4 is marked.

A *partial state firing* is a triple (S, t, θ') where $S \stackrel{\text{def}}{=} \langle L, dob_L, \theta_L \rangle$ is a partial state, t is a transition such that $^\bullet t \subseteq L$, and $\theta' \geq \theta_L$ is a date.

The idea in partial state firings is that the partial state S gives enough information to be sure that t can fire at date θ'.

It will be crucial in the following to know how to select partial state firings. However several choices are possible. If we are given a predicate *PSF* on partial state firings, we can build extended processes by using only the extended processes that satisfy *PSF*. Then we will try to map these extended processes into pre-processes. If *PSF* is valid, then all the pre-processes we obtain are correct.

Extended Processes. Let *PSF* be a predicate on partial state firings. We will define a notion of *extended process* (parameterized by *PSF*), which is close to the notion of process, but the events are replaced by *extended events* which represent firings from partial states and keep track of all the conditions corresponding to the partial state, not only those that are consumed by the transition.

For all extended event $\dot{e} \stackrel{\text{def}}{=} \langle B, t \rangle$, we use the same notations as for events: $^\bullet \dot{e} \stackrel{\text{def}}{=} B$ and $\tau(\dot{e}) \stackrel{\text{def}}{=} t$, and we define $\dot{e}^\bullet \stackrel{\text{def}}{=} \{(\dot{e}, p) \mid p \in (Place(B) \setminus {}^\bullet t) \cup t^\bullet\}$. For all place $p \in Place(\dot{e}^\bullet)$, we define the extended event $origin(p, \dot{e})$ that actually created the token in the place p:

$$origin(p, \dot{e}) \stackrel{\text{def}}{=} \begin{cases} \dot{e} & \text{if } p \in t^\bullet \text{ or } \dot{e} = \bot \\ origin(p, {}^\bullet b) \text{ with } b \stackrel{\text{def}}{=} place_{|B}^{-1}(p) & \text{otherwise} \end{cases}$$

Like for processes, we define the set of conditions that remain at the end of the extended process $\langle \dot{E}, \Theta \rangle$ as $\uparrow(\dot{E}) \stackrel{\text{def}}{=} \bigcup_{\dot{e} \in \dot{E}} \dot{e}^\bullet \setminus \bigcup_{\dot{e} \in \dot{E}} {}^\bullet \dot{e}$. But for extended processes we define not only the global state that is reached after $\langle \dot{E}, \Theta \rangle$, but a partial state associated with each set of conditions $B \subseteq \uparrow(\dot{E})$. The partial state associated with B is $\langle L, dob_L, \theta_L \rangle$, where:

- $L \stackrel{\text{def}}{=} Place(B)$,
- $dob_L(p) \stackrel{\text{def}}{=} \Theta(origin(p, {}^\bullet b))$ with $b \stackrel{\text{def}}{=} place_{|B}^{-1}(p)$,
- $\theta_L \stackrel{\text{def}}{=} \max_{b \in B} \Theta({}^\bullet b)$.

We define the set $\dot{X}$ of *extended processes* of a time Petri net starting at date θ_0 in the initial marking M_0 as follows:

- Like for processes, $\langle \{\bot\}, \{(\bot, \theta_0)\} \rangle \in \dot{X}$, where $\bot \overset{\text{def}}{=} (\emptyset, \epsilon)$ represents the initial event. The set of conditions that are created by $\bot$ is defined as: $\bot^\bullet \overset{\text{def}}{=} \{(\bot, p) \mid p \in M_0\}$.
- For all extended process $\langle \dot{E}, \Theta \rangle \in \dot{X}$, for all $B \subseteq \uparrow(\dot{E})$ leading to the partial state S, for all t, θ', if $PSF(S, t, \theta')$, then $\langle \dot{E} \cup \{\dot{e}\}, \Theta \cup \{(\dot{e}, \theta')\} \rangle \in \dot{X}$, where the extended event $\dot{e} \overset{\text{def}}{=} (B, t)$ represents this firing of t.

Each extended event $\dot{e} \overset{\text{def}}{=} (B, t)$ can be mapped to the corresponding event $h(\dot{e}) \overset{\text{def}}{=} (B', t)$ with $B' \overset{\text{def}}{=} \left\{ \left(h(origin(p, \dot{f})), p\right) \mid (\dot{f}, p) \in Place_{|B}^{-1}(^\bullet t) \right\}$.

Corectness of PSF. We say that PSF is a *valid predicate on partial state firings* iff for all extended process $\langle \dot{E}, \Theta \rangle \in \dot{X}$, $\langle h(\dot{E}), \Theta \circ h_{|\dot{E}}^{-1} \rangle$ is a pre-process (notice that $h_{|\dot{E}}$ is injective). In other terms there exists a process $\langle E', \Theta' \rangle \in X$ such that $\langle h(\dot{E}), \Theta \circ h_{\dot{E}}^{-1} \rangle \leq \langle E', \Theta' \rangle$.

Symbolic Unfolding. As we did for extended free choice time Petri nets with events in Section 3.2, we define the *symbolic unfolding U* of a time Petri net by collecting all the extended events that appear in its extended processes: $U \overset{\text{def}}{=} \bigcup_{\langle \dot{E}, \Theta \rangle \in \dot{X}} \dot{E}$.

We have equivalents of the two theorems we had with symbolic unfoldings of extended free choice time Petri nets.

Theorem 3. *Let $\dot{E} \subseteq U$ be a nonempty finite set of extended events and $\Theta : \dot{E} \longrightarrow Q$ associate a firing date with each extended event of $\dot{E}$. $\langle \dot{E}, \Theta \rangle$ is an extended process iff:*

$$\begin{cases} \lceil \dot{E} \rceil = \dot{E} & \text{($\dot{E}$ is causally closed)} \\ \nexists \dot{e}, \dot{e}' \in \dot{E} \quad \dot{e} \neq \dot{e}' \; \wedge \; {}^\bullet\dot{e} \cap {}^\bullet\dot{e}' \neq \emptyset & \text{($\dot{E}$ is conflict free)} \\ \forall \dot{e} \in \dot{E} \setminus \{\bot\} \quad PSF(S, \tau(\dot{e}), \Theta(\dot{e})) & \text{(e corresponds to a partial state firing)} \\ \quad \text{where } S \text{ is the partial state associated with } {}^\bullet\dot{e}. \end{cases}$$

Theorem 4. *For all $\dot{e} \overset{\text{def}}{=} (B, t) \in cnds(U) \times T$,*

$$\dot{e} \in U \text{ iff } \begin{cases} \nexists \dot{f}, \dot{f}' \in \lceil \dot{e} \rceil \quad \dot{f} \neq \dot{f}' \; \wedge \; {}^\bullet\dot{f} \cap {}^\bullet\dot{f}' \neq \emptyset \\ \exists \Theta : \lceil \dot{e} \rceil \longrightarrow Q \quad \forall \dot{f} \in \lceil \dot{e} \rceil \setminus \{\bot\} \quad PSF(S, \tau(\dot{f}), \Theta(\dot{f})) \\ \quad \text{where } S \text{ is the partial state associated with } {}^\bullet\dot{f}. \end{cases}$$

Selecting Partial State Firings. The definition of extended processes is parameterized by a predicate PSF on partial state firings: each extended event must correspond to a partial firing that satisfies PSF, the others are forbidden. A good choice for PSF takes three notions into account: completeness, redundancy and preservation of concurrency.

Completeness. A predicate PSF on partial state firings is *complete* if for all process $\langle E, \Theta \rangle \in X$, there exists an extended process $\langle \dot{E}, \Theta' \rangle \in \dot{X}$ (with partial state firings in PSF) such that $\langle h(\dot{E}), \Theta' \circ h_{\dot{E}}^{-1} \rangle = \langle E, \Theta \rangle$.

Redundancy. Given a predicate *PSF* on partial state firings and a process $\langle E, \Theta \rangle \in X$, there may exist several extended processes $\langle \dot{E}, \Theta' \rangle \in \dot{X}$ (with partial state firings in *PSF*) such that $\langle h(\dot{E}), \Theta' \circ h_{\dot{E}}^{-1} \rangle = \langle E, \Theta \rangle$. This is called *redundancy*. In particular, if *PSF* contains two partial state firings $(\langle L, dob, \theta \rangle, t, \theta')$ and $(\langle L', dob', \theta \rangle, t, \theta')$ where $L' \subsetneq L$ and $dob' = dob_{|L'}$, then all the extended processes involving $(\langle L, dob, \theta \rangle, t, \theta')$ are redundant.

A trivial choice for PSF which does not preserve any concurrency. A trivial complete predicate *PSF* is the predicate that demands that the state S is a global state, and then check that t can fire at date θ' from S. In addition, this choice gives little redundancy. But the extended events of the extended processes that we obtain in this case are totally ordered by causality. In other words, these processes do not exhibit any concurrency at all. Actually we get what we call firing sequences in interleaving semantics.

A proposition for PSF. What we want is a complete predicate on partial state firings that generates as little redundancy as possible and that exhibits as much concurrency as possible.

We first define a predicate *PSF'* on partial state firings as follows:
$PSF'(\langle L, dob_L, \theta \rangle, t, \theta')$ iff

- t is enabled: $\bullet t \subseteq L$;
- the minimum delay is reached: $\theta' \geq doe(t) + efd(t)$;
- time progresses: $\theta' \geq \theta$;
- the transitions that may consume tokens of L are disabled or do not overtake the maximum delays:

$$\forall t' \in T \quad \bullet t' \cap L \neq \emptyset \implies \begin{cases} \exists p \in \bullet t' \quad \bar{p} \cap L \neq \emptyset \\ \vee \ \theta' \leq \max_{p \in \circ t' \cap L} dob(p) + lfd(t') \end{cases}$$

Now we define *PSF* by eliminating some redundancy in *PSF'*:
$PSF(\langle L, dob, \theta \rangle, t, \theta')$ iff $PSF'(\langle L, dob, \theta \rangle, t, \theta')$ and there exists no $L' \subsetneq L$ such that $PSF'(\langle L', dob_{|L'}, \theta \rangle, t, \theta')$.

It is important that the constraints solving (see Theorems 3 and 4) can be done automatically: with the definition of *PSF* we have proposed here, the quantifiers ($\forall$ and $\exists$) on places and transitions expand into disjunctions and conjunctions. The result is a disjunction of conjunctions of linear inequalities on the $\Theta(\dot{e})$. When a "max" appears in an inequality, this inequality can be rewritten into the desired form. These systems are shown near the events in Figure 3.

Theorem 5. *PSF is a valid, complete predicate on partial state firings.*

3.4   Example of Unfolding

We come back to our simple example of time Petri net given in Figure 1. Figure 3 shows a prefix of its symbolic unfolding. We have kept all the events concerned with the observations (this filtering is done by considering the time net $\mathcal{D}(N, O)$ defined in subsection 2.4). To keep the figure readable, we do not show in the unfolding the supplementary places and transitions induced by the observations).

In this unfolding we see three explanations as extended processes. In contrast, the explanations of Figure 1 are the symbolic processes that have been computed from the extended processes. The linear constraints that appear near the events of Figure 3 can be solved in order to find all the possible values for the dates of the events. The three maximal extended processes of Figure 3 share the prefix $\{e1, e2, e3, e4\}$. The first extended process contains also $e5$ and $e7$. It corresponds to the second explanation of Figure 1. The second extended process contains the prefix, plus $e5$ and $e8$ and the third contains the prefix, plus $e6$ and $e9$. These two extended processes correspond to the same explanation: the first of Figure 1.

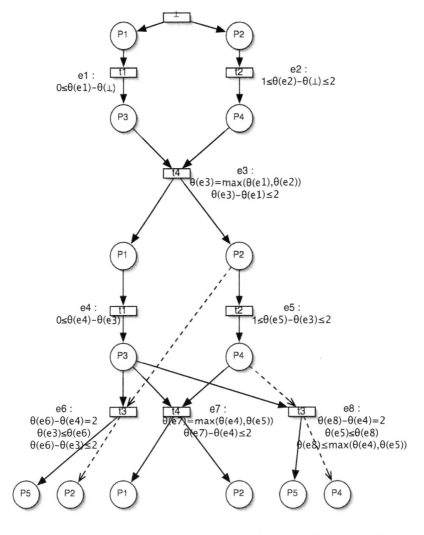

Fig. 3. A prefix of the symbolic unfolding of the time Petri net of Figure 1

This is what we have called redundancy. After solving the linear constraints we see that the second occurrence of t_1 must have occured immediately after $t4$ has fired and the second occurrence of t_2 must have fired 2 time units later. Actually the extended process with $e5$ and $e8$ and the one with $e6$ and $e9$ only differ by the fact that transition t_2 has fired *before* t_3 in the first one, whereas t_2 has fired *after* t_3 in the second one. Indeed, because of transition t_4, the firing of t_2 has a strong influence on the firing of t_3. This is the reason why there are too distinct cases in the unfolding.

4   Conclusion

We have presented a possible approach to the supervision/diagnosis of timed systems, using safe time Petri nets. In such nets, time constraints are given by interval of nonnegative rationals and are used to restrict the set of behaviours. The diagnosis problem is to recover the possible behaviours from a set of observations. We consider that the observations are given as a partial order (without any timing information) from the activity of several sensors. The goal of the supervisor is to select the possible timed behaviours of the model, which do not contradict the observations: i.e. presents the same set of events labelled by the alarms and orders the events in the same direction that the sensors do. This goal is achevied by considering a symbolic unfolding of time Petri nets, which is restricted by the observations. The result is a set of explanations, which explicit the causalities (both structural and temporal) between the observations. At the same time, our algorithm infers the possible delays before the firing of the transitions associated with them. Up to our knowledge, our symbolic unfolding for safe time Petri nets is original, and its application to compute symbolic explanations too.

A prototype implementation exists (a few thousands lines of Lisp code) and we plan to use it on real case studies. Another project is to define an algorithm to produce a complete finite prefix of the unfolding [9], which could be used for other applications than diagnosis (for which we do not need this notion since observations are finite sets).

At longer term, the notion of temporal diagnosis could be refined and revisited when considering timed distributed systems, in which alarms could bring a time information.

References

1. Tuomas Aura and Johan Lilius. Time processes for time Petri nets. In *ICATPN*, pages 136–155, 1997.
2. A. Benveniste, E. Fabre, C. Jard, and S. Haar. Diagnosis of asynchronous discrete event systems, a net unfolding approach. *IEEE Transactions on Automatic Control*, 48(5):714–727, May 2003.
3. Bernard Berthomieu and Michel Diaz. Modeling and verification of time dependent systems using time Petri nets. *IEEE Trans. Software Eng.*, 17(3):259–273, 1991.

4. Bernard Berthomieu and François Vernadat. State class constructions for branching analysis of time Petri nets. In *TACAS*, pages 442–457, 2003.

5. Eike Best. Structure theory of Petri nets: the free choice hiatus. In *Proceedings of an Advanced Course on Petri Nets: Central Models and Their Properties, Advances in Petri Nets 1986-Part I*, pages 168–205, London, UK, 1987. Springer-Verlag.

6. Thomas Chatain and Claude Jard. Symbolic diagnosis of partially observable concurrent systems. In *FORTE*, pages 326–342, 2004.

7. Thomas Chatain and Claude Jard. Time supervision of concurrent systems using symbolic unfoldings of time petri nets. Technical Report RR-5706, Institut National de Recherche en Informatique et en Automatique (INRIA), 2005.

8. Joost Engelfriet. Branching processes of Petri nets. *Acta Inf.*, 28(6):575–591, 1991.

9. Javier Esparza, Stefan Römer, and Walter Vogler. An improvement of McMillan's unfolding algorithm. In *TACAS*, pages 87–106, 1996.

10. Hans Fleischhack and Christian Stehno. Computing a finite prefix of a time Petri net. In *ICATPN*, pages 163–181, 2002.

11. P.M. Merlin and D.J. Farber. Recoverability of communication protocols – implications of a theorical study. *IEEE Transactions on Communications*, 24, 1976.

12. B. Pradin-Chézalviel, R. Valette, and L.A. Künzle. Scenario duration characterization of t-timed Petri nets using linear logic. In *IEEE PNPM*, pages 208–217, 1999.

13. Alexei Semenov and Alexandre Yakovlev. Verification of asynchronous circuits using time Petri net unfolding. In *DAC'96: Proceedings of the 33rd annual conference on Design automation*, pages 59–62, New York, NY, USA, 1996. ACM Press.

Comparison of the Expressiveness of Timed Automata and Time Petri Nets

Beatrice Bérard[1], Franck Cassez[2,*], Serge Haddad[1], Didier Lime[3],
and Olivier H. Roux[2,*]

[1] LAMSADE, Paris, France
{berard, haddad}@lamsade.dauphine.fr
[2] IRCCyN, Nantes, France
{Franck.Cassez, Olivier-h.Roux}@irccyn.ec-nantes.fr
[3] CISS, Aalborg, Denmark
didier@cs.aau.dk

Abstract. In this paper we consider the model of Time Petri Nets (TPN) where time is associated with transitions. We also consider Timed Automata (TA) as defined by Alur & Dill, and compare the expressiveness of the two models w.r.t. timed language acceptance and (weak) timed bisimilarity. We first prove that there exists a TA $\mathcal{A}$ s.t. there is no TPN (even unbounded) that is (weakly) timed bisimilar to $\mathcal{A}$. We then propose a structural translation from TA to (1-safe) TPNs preserving timed language acceptance. Further on, we prove that the previous (slightly extended) translation also preserves weak timed bisimilarity for a syntactical subclass $\mathcal{TA}_{syn}(\leq, \geq)$ of TA. For the theory of TPNs, the consequences are: 1) TA, bounded TPNs and 1-safe TPNs are equally expressive w.r.t. timed language acceptance; 2) TA are strictly more expressive than bounded TPNs w.r.t. timed bisimilarity; 3) The subclass $\mathcal{TA}_{syn}(\leq, \geq)$, bounded and 1-safe TPNs "à la Merlin" are equally expressive w.r.t. timed bisimilarity.

Keywords: Timed Language, Timed Bisimilarity, Time Petri Nets, Timed Automata, Expressiveness.

1 Introduction

In the last decade a number of extensions of Petri Nets with time have been proposed: among them are *Stochastic* Petri Nets, and different flavors of so-called *Time* or *Timed* Petri nets. Stochastic Petri Nets are now well known and a lot of literature is devoted to this model whereas the theoretical properties of the other timed extensions have not been investigated much.

Petri Nets with Time. Recent work [1, 11] considers Timed Arc Petri Nets where each token has a clock representing its "age" but a lazy (non-urgent) semantics of the net is assumed: this means that the firing of transitions may

---

* Work supported by the ACI CORTOS, a program of the French government.

P. Pettersson and W. Yi (Eds.): FORMATS 2005, LNCS 3829, pp. 211–225, 2005.

be delayed, even if this implies that some transitions are disabled because their input tokens become too old. Thus the semantics used for this class of Petri nets is such that they enjoy nice *monotonic* properties and fall into a class of systems for which many problems are decidable.

In comparison, the other timed extensions of Petri Nets (apart from Stochastic Petri Nets), *i.e.* Time Petri Nets (TPNs) [18] and Timed Petri Nets [20], do not have such nice monotonic features although the number of *clocks* to be considered is finite (one per transition). Also those models are very popular in the Discrete Event Systems and industrial communities as they allow to model real-time systems in a simple and elegant way and there are tools to check properties of Time Petri Nets [6, 14].

For TPNs a transition can fire within a time interval whereas for Timed Petri Nets it fires as soon as possible. Among Timed Petri Nets, time can be assigned to places or transitions [21, 19]. The two corresponding subclasses namely P-Timed Petri Nets and T-Timed Petri Nets are expressively equivalent [21, 19]. The same classes are defined for TPNs i.e. T-TPNs and P-TPNs, and both classes of Timed Petri Nets are included in both P-TPNs and T-TPNs [19]. P-TPNs and T-TPNs are proved to be incomparable in [16].

The class T-TPNs is the most commonly-used subclass of TPNs and in this paper we focus on this subclass that will be henceforth referred to as TPN.

Timed Automata. Timed Automata (TA) were introduced by Alur & Dill [3] and have since been extensively studied. This model is an extension of finite automata with (dense time) *clocks* and enables one to specify real-time systems. Theoretical properties of various classes of TA have been considered in the last decade. For instance, classes of determinizable TA such as *Event Clock Automata* are investigated in [4] and form a strict subclass of TA.

TA and TPNs. TPNs and TA are very similar and until now it is often assumed that TA have more features or are more expressive than TPNs because they seem to be a lower level formalism. Anyway the expressiveness of the two models have not been compared so far. This is an important direction to investigate as not much is known on the complexity or decidability of common problems on TPNs *e.g.* "is the universal language decidable on TPNs ?". Moreover it is also crucial for deciding which specification language one is going to use. If it turns out that TPNs are strictly less expressive (w.r.t. some criterion) than TA, it is important to know what the differences are.

Related Work. In a previous work [10] we have proved that TPN forms a subclass of TA in the sense that every TPN can be simulated by a TA (weak timed bisimilarity). A similar result can be found in [17] with a completely different approach. In another line of work in [15], the authors compare Timed State Machines and Time Petri Nets. They give a translation from one model to another that preserves timed languages. Nevertheless, they consider only the constraints with closed intervals and do not deal with general timed languages (*i.e.* Büchi timed languages). [9] also considers expressiveness problems but for a subclass of TPNs. Finally it is claimed in [9] that 1-safe TPNs with weak[1] constraints are strictly less expressive than TA with arbitrary types of constraints but a fair comparison should allow the same type of constraints in both models.

Our Contribution. In this article, we compare precisely the expressive power of TA vs. TPN using the notions of *Timed Language Acceptance* and *Timed Bisimilarity*. This extends the previous results above in the following directions: *i)* we consider general types of constraints (strict, weak); *ii)* we then show that there is a TA $\mathcal{A}_0$ s.t. no TPN is (even weakly) timed bisimilar to $\mathcal{A}_0$; *iii)* this leads us to consider weaker notions of equivalence and we focus on Timed Language Acceptance. We prove that TA (with general types of constraints) and TPN are equally expressive w.r.t. Timed Language Acceptance which is a new and somewhat surprising result; for instance it implies (using a result from [10]) that 1-safe TPNs and bounded TPNs are equally expressive w.r.t. Timed Language Acceptance; *iv)* to conclude we characterize a syntactical subclass of TA that is equally expressive to TPN without strict constraints w.r.t. Timed Bisimilarity. The results of the paper are summarized in Table 1: all the results are new except the one followed by [10]. We use the following notations: B-$\mathcal{TPN}_\varepsilon$ for the set of bounded TPNs with ε-transitions; 1-B-$\mathcal{TPN}_\varepsilon$ for the subset of B-$\mathcal{TPN}_\varepsilon$ with at most one token in each place (one safe TPN); B-$\mathcal{TPN}(\leq,\geq)$ for the subset of B-$\mathcal{TPN}_\varepsilon$ where only closed intervals are used; $\mathcal{TA}_\varepsilon$ for TA with ε-transitions; $\mathcal{TA}_{syn}(\leq,\geq)$ for the syntactical subclass of TA that is equivalent to B-$\mathcal{TPN}(\leq,\geq)$ (to be defined precisely in section 5). In the table $\preceq_\mathcal{L}$ or $\preceq_\mathcal{W}$ with $\preceq \in \{<,\leq\}$, respectively means "less expressive" w.r.t. Timed Language Acceptance and Weak Timed Bisimilarity; $=_\mathcal{L}$ means "equally expressive as" w.r.t. language acceptance and $\approx_\mathcal{W}$ "equally expressive as" w.r.t. weak timed bisimilarity.

Outline of the Paper. Section 2 introduces the semantics of TPNs and TA, Timed Languages and Timed Bisimilarity. In section 3 we prove our first result: there is a TA $\mathcal{A}_0$ s.t. there is no TPN that is (weakly) timed bisimilar to $\mathcal{A}_0$. In section 4 we focus on Timed Language Acceptance and we propose a structural translation from TA to 1-B-$\mathcal{TPN}_\varepsilon$ preserving timed language acceptance. We then prove that TA and bounded TPNs are equally expressive w.r.t. Timed Language Acceptance. This enables us to obtain new results for TPNs given by corollaries 3 and 4. Finally, in section 5, we characterize a syntactical subclass of TA ($\mathcal{TA}_{syn}(\leq,\geq)$) that is equivalent, w.r.t. Timed Bisimilarity, to the original version of TPNs (with closed intervals). This enables us to obtain new results for TPNs given by corollary 6.

2   Time Petri Nets and Timed Automata

Notations. Let Σ be a set (or alphabet). Σ^* (resp. Σ^ω) denotes the set of finite (resp. infinite) sequences of elements (or words) of Σ and $\Sigma^\infty = \Sigma^* \cup \Sigma^\omega$. By convention if $w \in \Sigma^\omega$ then the *length* of w denoted $|w|$ is ω; otherwise if

---

[1] Constraints using only $\leq$ and $\geq$.

Table 1. Summary of the Results

	Timed Language Acceptance	Timed Bisimilarity
	$\leq_{\mathcal{L}} \mathcal{TA}_\varepsilon$ [10]	$\leq_W \mathcal{TA}_\varepsilon$ [10]
B-$\mathcal{TPN}_\varepsilon$	$=_{\mathcal{L}}$ 1-B-$\mathcal{TPN}_\varepsilon =_{\mathcal{L}} \mathcal{TA}_\varepsilon$	$<_W \mathcal{TA}_\varepsilon$
		$\approx_W$ 1-B-$\mathcal{TPN}(\leq,\geq)$
B-$\mathcal{TPN}(\leq,\geq)$	$=_{\mathcal{L}} \mathcal{TA}_{syn}(\leq,\geq)$	$\approx_W \mathcal{TA}_{syn}(\leq,\geq)$

	Emptiness Problem	Universal Problem
B-$\mathcal{TPN}_\varepsilon$	Decidable [10]	Undecidable

$w = a_1 \cdots a_n$, $|w| = n$. We also use $\Sigma_\varepsilon = \Sigma \cup \{\varepsilon\}$ with $\varepsilon \notin \Sigma$, where ε is the empty word. B^A stands for the set of mappings from A to B. If A is finite and $|A| = n$, an element of B^A is also a vector in B^n. The usual operators $+, -, <$ and $=$ are used on vectors of A^n with $A = \mathbb{N}, \mathbb{Q}, \mathbb{R}$ and are the point-wise extensions of their counterparts in A. The set $\mathbb{B}$ denotes the boolean values $\{\mathsf{tt}, \mathsf{ff}\}$, $\mathbb{R}_{\geq 0}$ denotes the set of non-negative reals and $\mathbb{R}_{>0} = \mathbb{R}_{\geq 0} \setminus \{0\}$. A *valuation* ν over a set of variables X is an element of $\mathbb{R}_{\geq 0}^X$. For $\nu \in \mathbb{R}_{\geq 0}^X$ and $d \in \mathbb{R}_{\geq 0}$, $\nu + d$ denotes the valuation defined by $(\nu + d)(x) = \nu(x) + d$, and for $X' \subseteq X$, $\nu[X' \mapsto 0]$ denotes the valuation ν' with $\nu'(x) = 0$ for $x \in X'$ and $\nu'(x) = \nu(x)$ otherwise. $\mathbf{0}$ denotes the valuation s.t. $\forall x \in X, \nu(x) = 0$. An *atomic constraint* is a formula of the form $x \bowtie c$ for $x \in X$, $c \in \mathbb{Q}_{\geq 0}$ and $\bowtie \in \{<, \leq, \geq, >\}$. We denote $\mathcal{C}(X)$ the set of *constraints* over a set of variables X which consists of the conjunctions of atomic constraints. Given a constraint $\varphi \in \mathcal{C}(X)$ and a valuation $\nu \in \mathbb{R}_{\geq 0}^X$, we denote $\varphi(\nu) \in \mathbb{B}$ the truth value obtained by substituting each occurrence of x in φ by $\nu(x)$.

2.1   Timed Languages and Timed Transition Systems

Let Σ be a fixed finite alphabet s.t. $\varepsilon \notin \Sigma$. A is a finite set that can contain ε.

Definition 1 (Timed Words). *A* timed word w *over* Σ *is a finite or infinite sequence* $w = (a_0, d_0)(a_1, d_1) \cdots (a_n, d_n) \cdots$ *s.t. for each* $i \geq 0$, $a_i \in \Sigma$, $d_i \in \mathbb{R}_{\geq 0}$ *and* $d_{i+1} \geq d_i$.

A timed word $w = (a_0, d_0)(a_1, d_1) \cdots (a_n, d_n) \cdots$ over Σ can be viewed as a pair $(v, \tau) \in \Sigma^\infty \times \mathbb{R}_{\geq 0}^\infty$ s.t. $|v| = |\tau|$. The value d_k gives the absolute time (considering the initial instant is 0) of the action a_k.

We write $Untimed(w) = a_0 a_1 \cdots a_n \cdots$ for the untimed part of w, and $Duration(w) = \sup_{d_k \in \tau} d_k$ for the duration of the timed word w.

A *timed language* L over Σ is a set of timed words.

Definition 2 (Timed Transition System). *A* timed transition system (TTS) *over the set of actions* A *is a tuple* $S = (Q, Q_0, A, \longrightarrow, F, R)$ *where* Q *is a set of states,* $Q_0 \subseteq Q$ *is the set of initial states,* A *is a finite set of actions disjoint from* $\mathbb{R}_{\geq 0}$, $\longrightarrow \subseteq Q \times (A \cup \mathbb{R}_{\geq 0}) \times Q$ *is a set of edges. If* $(q, e, q') \in \longrightarrow$, *we also write* $q \xrightarrow{e} q'$. $F \subseteq Q$ *and* $R \subseteq Q$ *are respectively the set of* final *and* repeated *states.*

In the case of $q \xrightarrow{d} q'$ with $d \in \mathbb{R}_{\geq 0}$, d denotes a delay and not an absolute time. We assume that in any TTS there is a transition $q \xrightarrow{0} q'$ and in this case $q = q'$. A *run* ρ of length $n \geq 0$ is a finite ($n < \omega$) or infinite ($n = \omega$) sequence of alternating time and discrete transitions of the form

$$\rho = q_0 \xrightarrow{d_0} q_0' \xrightarrow{a_0} q_1 \xrightarrow{d_1} q_1' \xrightarrow{a_1} \cdots q_n \xrightarrow{d_n} q_n' \cdots$$

We write $first(\rho) = q_0$. We assume that a finite run ends with a time transition d_n. If ρ ends with d_n, we let $last(\rho) = q_n'$ and write $q_0 \xrightarrow{d_0 a_0 \cdots d_n} q_n'$. We write $q \xrightarrow{*} q'$ if there is run ρ s.t. $first(\rho) = q_0$ and $last(\rho) = q'$. The *trace* of an infinite run ρ is the timed word $trace(\rho) = (a_{i_0}, d_0 + \cdots + d_{i_0}) \cdots (a_{i_k}, d_0 + \cdots + d_{i_k}) \cdots$ that consists of the sequence of letters of $A \setminus \{\varepsilon\}$. If ρ is a finite run, we define the trace of ρ by $trace(\rho) = (a_{i_0}, d_0 + \cdots + d_{i_0}) \cdots (a_{i_k}, d_0 + \cdots + d_{i_k})$ where the a_{i_k} are in $A \setminus \{\varepsilon\}$.

We define $Untimed(\rho) = Untimed(trace(\rho))$ and $Duration(\rho) = \sum_{d_k \in \mathbb{R}_{\geq 0}} d_k$.

A run is *initial* if $first(\rho) \in Q_0$. A run ρ is *accepting* if *i)* either ρ is a finite initial run and $last(\rho) \in F$ or *ii)* ρ is infinite and there is a state $q \in R$ that appears infinitely often on ρ.

A timed word $w = (a_i, d_i)_{0 \leq i \leq n}$ is *accepted* by S if there is an accepting run of trace w. The *timed language* $\mathcal{L}(S)$ accepted by S is the set of timed words accepted by S.

Definition 3 (Strong Timed Similarity). *Let $S_1 = (Q_1, Q_0^1, A, \longrightarrow_1, F_1, R_1)$ and $S_2 = (Q_2, Q_0^2, A, \longrightarrow_2, F_2, R_2)$ be two TTS and $\preceq$ be a binary relation over $Q_1 \times Q_2$. We write $s \preceq s'$ for $(s, s') \in \preceq$. $\preceq$ is a* strong (timed) simulation *relation of S_1 by S_2 if: 1) if $s_1 \in F_1$ (resp. $s_1 \in R_1$) and $s_1 \preceq s_2$ then $s_2 \in F_2$ (resp. $s_2 \in R_2$); 2) if $s_1 \in Q_0^1$ there is some $s_2 \in Q_0^2$ s.t. $s_1 \preceq s_2$; 3) if $s_1 \xrightarrow{d}_1 s_1'$ with $d \in \mathbb{R}_{\geq 0}$ and $s_1 \preceq s_2$ then $s_2 \xrightarrow{d}_2 s_2'$ for some s_2', and $s_1' \preceq s_2'$; 4) if $s_1 \xrightarrow{a}_1 s_1'$ with $a \in A$ and $s_1 \preceq s_2$ then $s_2 \xrightarrow{a}_2 s_2'$ and $s_1' \preceq s_2'$.*

A TTS S_2 strongly simulates *S_1 if there is a strong (timed) simulation relation of S_1 by S_2. We write $S_1 \preceq_S S_2$ in this case.*

When there is a strong simulation relation $\preceq$ of S_1 by S_2 and $\preceq^{-1}$ is also a strong simulation relation[2] of S_2 by S_1, we say that $\preceq$ is a *strong (timed) bisimulation relation* between S_1 and S_2 and use $\approx$ instead of $\preceq$. Two TTS S_1 and S_2 are *strongly (timed) bisimilar* if there exists a strong (timed) bisimulation relation between S_1 and S_2. We write $S_1 \approx_S S_2$ in this case.

Let $S = (Q, Q_0, \Sigma_\varepsilon, \longrightarrow, F, R)$ be a TTS. We define the ε-abstract TTS $S^\varepsilon = (Q, Q_0^\varepsilon, \Sigma, \longrightarrow_\varepsilon, F, R)$ (with no ε-transitions) by:

- $q \xrightarrow{d}_\varepsilon q'$ with $d \in \mathbb{R}_{\geq 0}$ iff there is a run $\rho = q \xrightarrow{*} q'$ with $Untimed(\rho) = \varepsilon$ and $Duration(\rho) = d$,

---

[2] $s_2 \preceq^{-1} s_1 \iff s_1 \preceq s_2$.

- $q \xrightarrow{a}_\varepsilon q'$ with $a \in \Sigma$ iff there is a run $\rho = q \xrightarrow{*} q'$ with $Untimed(\rho) = a$ and $Duration(\rho) = 0$,
- $Q_0^\varepsilon = \{q \,|\, \exists q' \in Q_0 \,|\,\; q' \xrightarrow{*} q \text{ and } Duration(\rho) = 0 \wedge Untimed(\rho) = \varepsilon\}$.

Definition 4 (Weak Time Similarity). *Let $S_1 = (Q_1, Q_0^1, \Sigma_\varepsilon, \longrightarrow_1, F_1, R_1)$ and $S_2 = (Q_2, Q_0^2, \Sigma_\varepsilon, \longrightarrow_2, F_2, R_2)$ be two TTS and $\preceq$ be a binary relation over $Q_1 \times Q_2$. $\preceq$ is a* weak (timed) simulation relation *of S_1 by S_2 if it is a strong timed simulation relation of S_1^ε by S_2^ε. A TTS S_2* weakly simulates S_1 *if there is a weak (timed) simulation relation of S_1 by S_2. We write $S_1 \preceq_W S_2$ in this case.*

When there is a weak simulation relation $\preceq$ of S_1 by S_2 and $\preceq^{-1}$ is also a weak simulation relation of S_2 by S_1, we say that $\preceq$ is a *weak (timed) bisimulation relation* between S_1 and S_2 and use $\approx$ instead of $\preceq$. Two TTS S_1 and S_2 are *weakly (timed) bisimilar* if there exists a weak (timed) bisimulation relation between S_1 and S_2. We write $S_1 \approx_W S_2$ in this case. Note that if $S_1 \preceq_S S_2$ then $S_1 \preceq_W S_2$ and if $S_1 \preceq_W S_2$ then $\mathcal{L}(S_1) \subseteq \mathcal{L}(S_2)$.

2.2 Time Petri Nets

Time Petri Nets (TPN) were introduced in [18] and extend Petri Nets with timing constraints on the firings of transitions. In such a model, a clock is associated with each enabled transition, and gives the elapsed time since the more recent date at which it became enabled. An enabled transition can be fired if the value of its clock belongs to the interval associated with the transition. Furthermore, time can progress only if the enabling duration still belongs to the downward closure of the interval associated with any enabled transition. We consider here a generalized version[3] of TPN with accepting and repeated markings and prove our results for this general model.

Definition 5 (Labeled Time Petri Net). *A* Labeled Time Petri Net $\mathcal{N}$ *is a tuple $(P, T, \Sigma_\varepsilon, {}^\bullet(.), (.)^\bullet, M_0, \Lambda, I, F, R)$ where: P is a finite set of* places *and T is a finite set of* transitions *and $P \cap T = \emptyset$; Σ is a finite set of* actions *${}^\bullet(.) \in (\mathbb{N}^P)^T$ is the* backward *incidence mapping; $(.)^\bullet \in (\mathbb{N}^P)^T$ is the* forward *incidence mapping; $M_0 \in \mathbb{N}^P$ is the* initial *marking; $\Lambda : T \to \Sigma_\varepsilon$ is the* labeling function; *$I : T \to \mathcal{I}(\mathbb{Q}_{\geq 0})$ associates with each transition a* firing interval; *$R \subseteq \mathbb{N}^P$ is the set of* final *markings and $F \subseteq \mathbb{N}^P$ is the set of* repeated *markings.*

Semantics of Time Petri Nets. A *marking* M of a TPN is a mapping in $\mathbb{N}^P$ and $M(p_i)$ is the number of tokens in place p_i. A transition t is *enabled* in a marking M iff $M \geq {}^\bullet t$. We denote $En(M)$ the set of enabled transitions in M. To decide whether a transition t can be fired we need to know for how long it has been enabled: if this amount of time lies into the interval $I(t)$, t can actually be fired, otherwise it cannot. On the other hand, time can progress only if the enabling duration still belongs to the downward closure of the interval associated with any enabled transition. Let $\nu \in (\mathbb{R}_{\geq 0})^{En(M)}$ be a *valuation* such

---

[3] This is required to be able to define Büchi timed languages, which is not possible in the original version of TPN of [18].

that each value $\nu(t)$ is the time elapsed since transition t was last enabled. A *configuration* of the TPN $\mathcal{N}$ is a pair (M, ν). An *admissible configuration* of a TPN is a configuration (M, ν) s.t. $\forall t \in En(M), \nu(t) \in I(t)^{\downarrow}$. We let $ADM(\mathcal{N})$ be the set of admissible configurations.

In this paper, we consider the *intermediate semantics* for TPNs, based on [8, 5], which is the most common one. The key point in the semantics is to define when a transition is *newly enabled* and one has to reset its clock. Let $\uparrow enabled(t', M, t) \in \mathbb{B}$ be true if t' is *newly enabled* by the firing of transition t from marking M, and false otherwise. The firing of t leads to a new marking $M' = M - {}^{\bullet}t + t^{\bullet}$. The fact that a transition t' is newly enabled on the firing of a transition $t \neq t'$ is determined w.r.t. the intermediate marking $M - {}^{\bullet}t$. When a transition t is fired it is newly enabled whatever the intermediate marking is. Formally this gives:

$$\uparrow enabled(t', M, t) = \big(t' \in En(M - {}^{\bullet}t + t^{\bullet})\big) \wedge \big(t' \notin En(M - {}^{\bullet}t) \vee (t = t')\big) \quad (1)$$

Definition 6 (Semantics of TPN). *The semantics of a TPN $\mathcal{N} = (P, T, \Sigma_{\varepsilon},$ ${}^{\bullet}(.), (.)^{\bullet}, M_0, \Lambda, I, F, R)$ is a timed transition system $S_{\mathcal{N}} = (Q, \{q_0\}, T, \rightarrow, F', R')$ where: $Q = ADM(\mathcal{N})$, $q_0 = (M_0, \mathbf{0})$, $F' = \{(M, \nu) \mid M \in F\}$ and $R = \{(M, \nu) \mid M \in R\}$, and $\longrightarrow \in Q \times (T \cup \mathbb{R}_{\geq 0}) \times Q$ consists of the discrete and continuous transition relations: i) the discrete transition relation is defined $\forall t \in T$ by:*

$$(M, \nu) \xrightarrow{\Lambda(t)} (M', \nu') \ iff \ \begin{cases} t \in En(M) \wedge M' = M - {}^{\bullet}t + t^{\bullet} \\ \nu(t) \in I(t), \\ \forall t \in \mathbb{R}_{\geq 0}^{En(M')}, \nu'(t) = \begin{cases} 0 \ if \ \uparrow enabled(t', M, t), \\ \nu(t) \ otherwise. \end{cases} \end{cases}$$

and ii) the continuous transition relation is defined $\forall d \in \mathbb{R}_{\geq 0}$ by:

$$(M, \nu) \xrightarrow{d} (M, \nu') \ iff \ \begin{cases} \nu' = \nu + d \\ \forall t \in En(M), \nu'(t) \in I(t)^{\downarrow} \end{cases}$$

A run ρ of $\mathcal{N}$ is an initial run of $S_{\mathcal{N}}$. The timed language accepted by $\mathcal{N}$ is $\mathcal{L}(\mathcal{N}) = \mathcal{L}(S_{\mathcal{N}})$.

We simply write $(M, \nu) \xrightarrow{w}$ to emphasize that there is a sequence of transitions w that can be fired in $S_{\mathcal{N}}$ from (M, ν). If $Duration(w) = 0$ we say that w is an *instantaneous firing sequence*. The set of *reachable configurations* of $\mathcal{N}$ is $\mathsf{Reach}(\mathcal{N}) = \{M \in \mathbb{N}^P \mid \exists (M, \nu) \mid (M_0, \mathbf{0}) \xrightarrow{*} (M, \nu)\}$.

2.3 Timed Automata

Definition 7 (Timed Automaton). *A Timed Automaton $\mathcal{A}$ is a tuple $(L, l_0, X, \Sigma_{\varepsilon}, E, Inv, F, R)$ where: L is a finite set of locations; $l_0 \in L$ is the initial location; X is a finite set of positive real-valued clocks; $\Sigma_{\varepsilon} = \Sigma \cup \{\varepsilon\}$ is a finite* *set of* actions *and* ε *is the* silent *action;* $E \subseteq L \times \mathcal{C}(X) \times \Sigma_\varepsilon \times 2^X \times L$ *is a finite set of edges,* $e = \langle l, \gamma, a, R, l' \rangle \in E$ *represents an edge from the location* l *to the location* l' *with the guard* γ, *the label* a *and the reset set* $R \subseteq X$; $Inv \in \mathcal{C}(X)^L$ *assigns an invariant to any location. We restrict the invariants to conjuncts of terms of the form* $x \preceq r$ *for* $x \in X$ *and* $r \in \mathbb{N}$ *and* $\preceq \in \{<, \leq\}$. $F \subseteq L$ *is the set of* final locations *and* $R \subseteq L$ *is the set of* repeated locations.

Definition 8 (Semantics of a Timed Automaton). *The semantics of a timed automaton* $\mathcal{A} = (L, l_0, C, \Sigma_\varepsilon, E, Act, Inv, F, R)$ *is a timed transition system* $S_\mathcal{A} = (Q, q_0, \Sigma_\varepsilon, \rightarrow, F', R')$ *with* $Q = L \times (\mathbb{R}_{\leq 0})^X$, $q_0 = (l_0, \mathbf{0})$ *is the initial state,* $F' = \{(\ell, \nu) \mid \ell \in F\}$ *and* $R' = \{(\ell, \nu) \mid \ell \in R\}$, *and* $\rightarrow$ *is defined by: i) the discrete transitions relation* $(l, v) \xrightarrow{a} (l', v')$ *iff* $\exists (l, \gamma, a, R, l') \in E$ *s.t.* $\gamma(v) = \mathsf{tt}$, $v' = v[R \mapsto 0]$ *and* $Inv(l')(v') = \mathsf{tt}$; *ii) the continuous transition relation* $(l, v) \xrightarrow{t} (l', v')$ *iff* $l = l'$, $v' = v + t$ *and* $\forall 0 \leq t' \leq t$, $Inv(l)(v + t') = \mathsf{tt}$.

A run ρ *of* $\mathcal{A}$ *is an initial run of* $S_\mathcal{A}$. *The timed language accepted by* $\mathcal{A}$ *is* $\mathcal{L}(\mathcal{A}) = \mathcal{L}(S_\mathcal{A})$.

2.4   Expressiveness and Equivalence Problems

If B, B' are either TPN or TA, we write $B \approx_S B'$ (resp. $B \approx_W B'$) for $S_B \approx_S S_{B'}$ (resp. $S_B \approx_W S_{B'}$). Let $\mathcal{C}$ and $\mathcal{C}'$ be two classes of TPNs or TA.

Definition 9 (Expressiveness w.r.t. Timed Language Acceptance). *The class* $\mathcal{C}$ *is* more expressive *than* $\mathcal{C}'$ *w.r.t. timed language acceptance if for all* $B' \in \mathcal{C}'$ *there is a* $B \in \mathcal{C}$ *s.t.* $\mathcal{L}(B) = \mathcal{L}(B')$. *We write* $\mathcal{C}' \leq_\mathcal{L} \mathcal{C}$ *in this case. If moreover there is some* $B \in \mathcal{C}$ *s.t. there is no* $B' \in \mathcal{C}'$ *with* $\mathcal{L}(B) = \mathcal{L}(B')$, *then* $\mathcal{C}' <_\mathcal{L} \mathcal{C}$ *(read "strictly more expressive"). If both* $\mathcal{C}' \leq_\mathcal{L} \mathcal{C}$ *and* $\mathcal{C} \leq_\mathcal{L} \mathcal{C}'$ *then* $\mathcal{C}$ *and* $\mathcal{C}'$ *are equally expressive w.r.t. timed language acceptance, and we write* $\mathcal{C} =_\mathcal{L} \mathcal{C}'$.

Definition 10 (Expressiveness w.r.t. Timed Bisimilarity). *The class* $\mathcal{C}$ *is* more expressive *than* $\mathcal{C}'$ *w.r.t. strong (resp. weak) timed bisimilarity if for all* $B' \in \mathcal{C}'$ *there is a* $B \in \mathcal{C}$ *s.t.* $B \approx_S B'$ *(resp.* $B \approx_W B'$). *We write* $\mathcal{C}' \leq_S \mathcal{C}$ *(resp.* $\mathcal{C}' \leq_W \mathcal{C}$) *in this case. If moreover there is a* $B \in \mathcal{C}$ *s.t. there is no* $B' \in \mathcal{C}'$ *with* $B \approx_S B'$ *(resp.* $B \approx_W B'$), *then* $\mathcal{C}' <_S \mathcal{C}$ *(resp.* $\mathcal{C}' <_W \mathcal{C}$). *If both* $\mathcal{C}' <_S \mathcal{C}$ *and* $\mathcal{C} <_S \mathcal{C}'$ *(resp.* $<_W$) *then* $\mathcal{C}$ *and* $\mathcal{C}'$ *are equally expressive w.r.t. strong (resp. weak) timed bisimilarity, and we write* $\mathcal{C} \approx_S \mathcal{C}'$ *(resp.* $\mathcal{C} \approx_W \mathcal{C}'$).

In the sequel we will compare various classes of TPNs and TAs. We recall the following theorem adapted from [10]:

Theorem 1 ([10]). *For any* $\mathcal{N} \in B\text{-}\mathcal{TPN}_\varepsilon$ *there is a TA* $\mathcal{A}$ *s.t.* $\mathcal{N} \approx_W \mathcal{A}$, *hence* $B\text{-}\mathcal{TPN}_\varepsilon \leq_W \mathcal{TA}_\varepsilon$.

Moreover if $\mathcal{TA}(\leq, \geq)$ is the set of TA with only large constraints, we even have that $B\text{-}\mathcal{TPN}(\leq, \geq) \leq_W \mathcal{TA}(\leq, \geq)$.

3   Strict Ordering Results

In this section, we establish some results proving that TPNs are strictly less expressive w.r.t. weak timed bisimilarity than various classes of TA: $\mathcal{TA}(<)$ only including strict constraints and $\mathcal{TA}(\leq)$ only including large constraints.

Theorem 2. *There is no TPN weakly timed bisimilar to $\mathcal{A}_0 \in \mathcal{TA}(<)$ (Fig. 1).*

A similar theorem holds for a TA $\mathcal{A}_1$ with large constraints. Let $\mathcal{A}_1$ be the automaton $\mathcal{A}_0$ with the strict constraint $x < 1$ replaced by $x \leq 1$.

Theorem 3. *There is no TPN weakly timed bisimilar to $\mathcal{A}_1 \in \mathcal{TA}(\leq)$.*

The previous theorems entail B-$\mathcal{TPN}_\varepsilon <_W \mathcal{TA}(<)$ and B-$\mathcal{TPN}_\varepsilon <_W \mathcal{TA}(\leq)$ and as a consequence:

Corollary 1. *B-$\mathcal{TPN}_\varepsilon <_W \mathcal{TA}_\varepsilon$.*

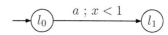

To be fair, one should notice that actually the class of bounded TPNs is strictly less expressive than $\mathcal{TA}(\leq)$ and $\mathcal{TA}(<)$ but also that, obviously unbounded TPNs are

Fig. 1. The Timed Automaton $\mathcal{A}_0$

more expressive than TA (because they are Turing powerful). Anyway the interesting question is the comparison between bounded TPNs and TA.

Following these negative results, we compare the expressiveness of TPNs and TA w.r.t. to Timed Language Acceptance and then characterize a subclass of TA that admits bisimilar TPNs without strict constraints.

4   Equivalence w.r.t. Timed Language Acceptance

In this section, we prove that TA and labeled TPNs are equally expressive w.r.t. timed language acceptance, and give an effective syntactical translation from TA to TPNs. Let $\mathcal{A} = (L, l_0, X, \Sigma_\varepsilon, E, Act, Inv, F, R)$ be a TA. As we are concerned in this section with the language accepted by $\mathcal{A}$ we assume the invariant function Inv is uniformly true. Let $\mathcal{C}_x$ be the set of atomic constraints on clock x that are used in $\mathcal{A}$. The Time Petri Net resulting from our translation is built from "elementary blocks" modeling the truth value of the constraints of $\mathcal{C}_x$. Then we link them with other blocks for resetting clocks.

Encoding Atomic Constraints. Let $\varphi \in \mathcal{C}_x$ be an atomic constraint on x. From φ, we define the TPN $\mathcal{N}_\varphi$, given by the widgets of Fig. 2 ((a) and (b)) and Fig. 3. In the figures, a transition is written $t(\sigma, I)$ where t is the name of the transition, $\sigma \in \Sigma_\varepsilon$ and $I \in \mathcal{I}(\mathbb{Q}_{\geq 0})$.

To avoid drawing too many arcs, we have adopted the following semantics: the grey box is seen as a macro place; an arc from this grey box means that there are as many copies of the transition as places in the grey box. For instance the TPN of Fig. 2.(b) has 2 copies of the target transition r: one with input places P_x and r_b and output places r_e and P_x and another fresh copy of r with input

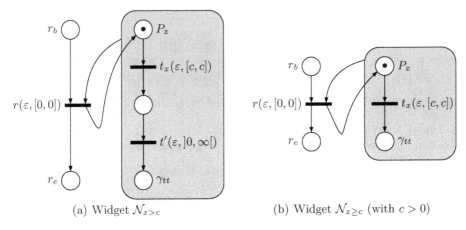

(a) Widget $\mathcal{N}_{x>c}$ (b) Widget $\mathcal{N}_{x\geq c}$ (with $c > 0$)

Fig. 2. Widgets for $\mathcal{N}_{x>c}$ and $\mathcal{N}_{x\geq c}$

places r_b and γ_{tt} and output places r_e and P_x. Note that in the widgets of Fig. 3 we put a token in γ_{tt} when firing r only on the copy of r with input place P_i (otherwise the number of tokens in place γ_{tt} could be unbounded).

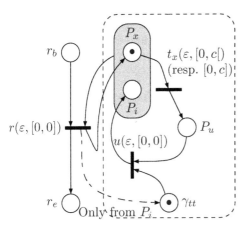

Fig. 3. Widget $\mathcal{N}_{x<c}$ (resp. $\mathcal{N}_{x\leq c}$)

Also we assume that the automaton $\mathcal{A}$ has no constraint $x \geq 0$ (as it evaluates to true they can be safely removed) and thus that the widget of Fig. 2.(b) only appears with $c > 0$. Each of these TPNs basically consists of a "constraint" subpart (in the grey boxes for Fig. 2 and in the dashed box for Fig. 3) that models the truth value of the atomic constraint, and another "reset" subpart that will be used to update the truth value of the constraint when the clock x is reset.

The "constraint" subpart features the place γ_{tt}: the intended meaning is that when a token is available in this place, the corresponding atomic constraint φ is true.

When a clock x is reset, all the grey blocks modeling an x-constraint must be set to their *initial* marking which has one token in P_x for Fig. 2 and one token in P_x and γ_{tt} for Fig. 3. Our strategy to reset a block modeling a constraint is to put a token in the r_b place (r_b stands for "reset begin"). Time cannot elapse from there on (strong semantics for TPNs), as there will be a token in one of the places of the grey block and thus transition r will be enabled.

Resetting Clocks. In order to reset all the blocks modeling constraints on a clock x, we chain all of them in some arbitrary order, the r_e place of the ith block

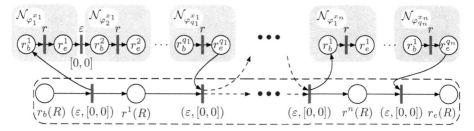

Fig. 4. Widget $\mathcal{N}_{Reset(R)}$ to reset the widgets of the constraints of clocks x_i, $1 \leq i \leq n$

is linked to the r_b place of the $i + 1^{th}$ block, via a 0 time unit transition ε. This is illustrated in Fig. 4 for clocks x_1 and x_n. Assume $R \subseteq X$ is a non empty set of clocks. Let $D(R)$ be the set of atomic constraints that are in the scope of R (the clock of the constraint is in R). We write $D(R) = \{\varphi_1^{x_1}, \varphi_2^{x_1}, \cdots, \varphi_{q_1}^{x_1}, \cdots, \varphi_{q_n}^{x_n}\}$ where $\varphi_i^{x_j}$ is the ith constraints of the clock x_j. To update all the widgets of $D(R)$, we connect the reset chains as described on Fig. 4. The picture inside the dashed box denotes the widget $\mathcal{N}_{Reset(R)}$. We denote by $r_b(R)$ the first place of this widget and $r_e(R)$ the last one. To update the (truth value of the) widgets of $D(R)$ it then suffices to put a token in $r_b(R)$. In null duration it will go to $r_e(R)$ and have the effect of updating each widget of $D(R)$ on its way.

The Complete Construction. First we create fresh places P_ℓ for each $\ell \in L$. Then we build the widgets $\mathcal{N}_\varphi$, for each atomic constraint φ that appears in $\mathcal{A}$. Finally for each $R \subseteq X$ s.t. there is an edge $e = (\ell, \gamma, a, R, \ell') \in E$ we build a reset widget $\mathcal{N}_{Reset(R)}$. Then for each edge $(\ell, \gamma, a, R, \ell') \in E$ with $\gamma = \wedge_{i=1,n}\varphi_i$ and $n \geq 0$ we proceed as follows:

1. assume $\gamma = \wedge_{i=1,n}\varphi_i$ and $n \geq 0$,
2. create a transition $f(a, [0, \infty[)$ and if $n \geq 1$ another one $r(\varepsilon, [0, 0])$,
3. connect them to the places of the widgets $\mathcal{N}_{\varphi_i}$ and $\mathcal{N}_{Reset(R)}$ as described on Fig. 5. In case $\gamma = \mathsf{tt}$ (or $n = 0$) there is only one input place to $f(a, [0, \infty[)$ which is P_ℓ. In case $R = \emptyset$ there is no transition $r(\varepsilon, [0, 0])$ and the output place of $f(a, [0, \infty[)$ is $P_{\ell'}$.

To complete the construction we just need to put a token in the place P_{ℓ_0} if ℓ_0 is the initial location of the automaton, and set each widget $\mathcal{N}_\varphi$ to its initial marking, for each atomic constraint φ that appears in $\mathcal{A}$, and this defines the initial marking M_0. The set of final markings is defined by the set of markings M s.t. $M(P_\ell) = 1$ for $\ell \in F$ and the set of repeated markings by the set of markings M s.t. $M(P_\ell) = 1$ for $\ell \in R$. We denote $\Delta(\mathcal{A})$ the TPN obtained as described previously. Notice that by construction 1) $\Delta(\mathcal{A})$ is 1-safe and moreover 2) in each reachable marking M of $\Delta(\mathcal{A})$ $(\sum_{\ell \in L} M(P_\ell)) \leq 1$. A widget related to an atomic constraint has a linear size w.r.t. its size, a clock resetting widget has a linear size w.r.t. the number of atomic constraints of the clock and a widget associated with an edge has a linear size w.r.t. its description size. Thus the size of $\Delta(\mathcal{A})$ is linear w.r.t. the size of $\mathcal{A}$ improving the quadratic complexity of the

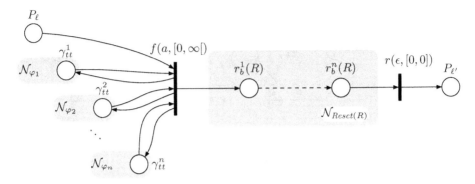

Fig. 5. Widget $\mathcal{N}_e$ of an edge $e = (\ell, \gamma, a, R, \ell')$

(restricted) translation in [15]. Finally, to prove $\mathcal{L}(\Delta(\mathcal{A})) = \mathcal{L}(\mathcal{A})$ we build two simulation relations $\preceq_1$ and $\preceq_2$ s.t. $\Delta(\mathcal{A}) \preceq_1 \mathcal{A}$ and $\mathcal{A} \preceq_2 \Delta(\mathcal{A})$. The complete proof is given in [7].

New Results for TPNs. The proofs of the following results can be found in [7].

Corollary 2. *The classes B-$\mathcal{TPN}_\varepsilon$ and $\mathcal{TA}_\varepsilon$ are equally expressive w.r.t. timed language acceptance, i.e. B-$\mathcal{TPN}_\varepsilon =_\mathcal{L} \mathcal{TA}_\varepsilon$.*

Corollary 3. *1-B-$\mathcal{TPN}_\varepsilon =_\mathcal{L}$ B-$\mathcal{TPN}_\varepsilon$.*

From the well-known result of Alur & Dill [3] and as our construction is effective, it follows that:

Corollary 4. *The universal language problem is undecidable for B-$\mathcal{TPN}_\varepsilon$ (and already for 1-B-$\mathcal{TPN}_\varepsilon$).*

5   Equivalence w.r.t. Timed Bisimilarity

In this section, we consider the class B-$\mathcal{TPN}(\leq, \geq)$ of TPNs without strict constraints, *i.e.* the original version of Merlin [18]. First recall that starting with a TPN $\mathcal{N} \in$ B-$\mathcal{TPN}(\leq, \geq)$, the translation from TPN to TA proposed in [10] gives a TA $\mathcal{A}$ with the following features:

- guards are of the form $x \geq c$ and invariants have the form $x \leq c$;
- between two resets of a clock x, the atomic constraints of the invariants over x are *increasing i.e.* the sequence of invariants encountered from any location is of the form $x \leq c_1$ and later on $x \leq c_2$ with $c_2 \geq c_1$ etc.

Let us now consider the syntactical subclass $\mathcal{TA}_{syn}(\leq, \geq)$ of TA defined by:

Definition 11. *The subclass $\mathcal{TA}_{syn}(\leq, \geq)$ of TA is defined by the set of TA of the form $(L, l_0, X, \Sigma_\varepsilon, E, Inv, F, R)$ where :*

- *guards are conjunctions of atomic constraints of the form $x \geq c$ and invariants are conjunction of atomic constraints $x \leq c$.*

- the invariants satisfy the following property; $\forall e = (\ell, \gamma, a, R, \ell') \in E$, if $x \notin R$ and $x \leq c$ is an atomic constraint in $Inv(\ell)$, then if $x \leq c'$ is $Inv(\ell')$ for some c' then $c' \geq c$.

We now adapt the construction of section 4 to define a translation from $\mathcal{TA}_{syn}(\leq, \geq)$ to B-$\mathcal{TPN}(\leq, \geq)$ preserving timed bisimulation. The widget $\mathcal{N}_{x \leq c}$ is modified as depicted in figure Fig. 6.(a). The widgets $\mathcal{N}_{x \geq c}$ and $\mathcal{N}_{reset}(R)$ are those of section 4 respectively in figures Fig. 2.(b) and Fig. 4.

The construction. As in section 4, we create a place P_ℓ for each location $\ell \in L$. Then we build the blocks $\mathcal{N}_\varphi$ for each atomic constraints $\varphi = x \geq c$ (Fig. 2.(b)) that appears in guards of $\mathcal{A}$ and we build the blocks $\mathcal{N}_\mathcal{I}$ for each atomic constraints $\mathcal{I} = x \leq c$ (Fig.6.(a)) that appears in an invariant of $\mathcal{A}$. Finally for each $R \subseteq X$ s.t. there is an edge $e = (\ell, \gamma, a, R, \ell') \in E$ we build a reset widget $\mathcal{N}_{Reset(R)}$ (Fig. 4). Then for each edge $(\ell, \gamma, a, R, \ell') \in E$ with $\gamma = \wedge_{i=1,n}\varphi_i$ and $n \geq 0$, we proceed exactly as in section 4 (Fig. 5). For each location $\ell \in L$ with $Inv(\ell) = \wedge_{k=1,n}\mathcal{I}_k$, we proceed as follows:

1. if $n \geq 1$, create a transition $I_k(\varepsilon, [0,0])$ for $1 \leq k \leq n$;
2. for $1 \leq k \leq n$ connect $I_k(\varepsilon, [0,0])$ to P_ℓ and to the place urg of block $\mathcal{N}_{\mathcal{I}_k}$, as depicted in figure Fig. 6.(b).

Let $\mathcal{A} = (L, \ell_0, X, \Sigma_\varepsilon, E, Inv, F, R)$ and assume that the set of atomic constraints of $\mathcal{A}$ is $\mathcal{C}_\mathcal{A} = \mathcal{C}_\mathcal{A}(\geq) \cup \mathcal{C}_\mathcal{A}(\leq)$ where $\mathcal{C}_\mathcal{A}(\bowtie)$ is the set of atomic constraints $x \bowtie c$, $\bowtie \in \{\leq, \geq\}$, of $\mathcal{A}$ and $X = \{x_1, \cdots, x_k\}$.

We denote $\Delta^+(\mathcal{A}) = (P, T, \Sigma_\varepsilon, {}^\bullet(.), (.)^\bullet, M_0, \Lambda, I, F_\Delta, R_\Delta)$ the TPN built as described previously. The place P_x and the transition t_x of a widget $\mathcal{N}_\varphi$ for $\varphi \in \mathcal{C}_\mathcal{A}$ are respectively written P_x^φ and t_x^φ in the sequel. Moreover, for a constraint $\varphi = x \geq c$, the place γ_{tt} of a widget $\mathcal{N}_\varphi$ is written γ_{tt}^φ and the place urg of a widget $\mathcal{N}_\varphi$ is written urg^φ. We can now build a bisimulation relation $\approx$ between $\mathcal{A}$ and $\Delta^+(\mathcal{A})$.

New Results for TPNs.

Corollary 5. *The classes B-$\mathcal{TPN}(\leq, \geq)$ and $\mathcal{TA}_{syn}(\leq, \geq)$ are equally expressive w.r.t. weak timed bisimulation, i.e. B-$\mathcal{TPN}(\leq, \geq) \approx_W \mathcal{TA}_{syn}(\leq, \geq)$.*

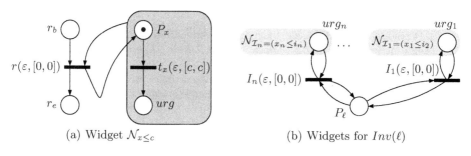

(a) Widget $\mathcal{N}_{x \leq c}$ (b) Widgets for $Inv(\ell)$

Fig. 6. Widget $\mathcal{N}_e$ of an edge $e = (\ell, \gamma, a, R, \ell')$

Corollary 6. *The classes* $1\text{-}B\text{-}\mathcal{TPN}(\leq,\geq)$ *and* $B\text{-}\mathcal{TPN}(\leq,\geq)$ *are equally expressive w.r.t. timed bisimulation i.e.* $1\text{-}B\text{-}\mathcal{TPN}(\leq,\geq) \approx_W B\text{-}\mathcal{TPN}(\leq,\geq)$.

6 Conclusion

In this paper, we have investigated different questions relative to the expressiveness of TPNs. First, we have shown that TA and bounded TPNs (strict constraints are permitted) are equivalent w.r.t. timed language equivalence. We have also provided an effective construction of a TPN equivalent to a TA. This enables us to prove that the universal language problem is undecidable for TPNs. Then we have addressed the expressiveness problem for weak time bisimilarity. We have proved that TA are strictly more expressive than bounded TPNs and given a subclass of TA expressively equivalent to TPN "à la Merlin".

Further work will consist in characterizing exactly the subclass of TA equivalent to TPN w.r.t. timed bisimilarity.

References

1. P.A. Abdulla and A. Nylén. Timed Petri nets and BQOs. In *ICATPN'01*, volume 2075 of *LNCS*, pages 53–72. Springer-Verlag, june 2001.
2. L. Aceto and F. Laroussinie. Is Your Model Checker on Time? On the Complexity of Model Checking for Timed Modal Logics. *Journal of Logic and Algebraic Programming*, volume 52-53, pages 7-51. Elsevier Science Publishers, august 2002.
3. R. Alur and D. Dill. A theory of timed automata. *Theoretical Computer Science B*, 126:183–235, 1994.
4. R. Alur and L. Fix and T.A. Henzinger. Event-Clock Automata: A Determinizable Class of Timed Automata. *Theoretical Computer Science*, 211:253–273, 1999.
5. T. Aura and J. Lilius. A causal semantics for time Petri nets. *Theoretical Computer Science*, 243(1–2):409–447, 2000.
6. B. Berthomieu, P.-O. Ribet and F. Vernadat. The tool TINA – Construction of Abstract State Spaces for Petri Nets and Time Petri Nets. *International Journal of Production Research*, 4(12), July 2004.
7. B. Bérard, F. Cassez, S. Haddad, D. Lime and O.H. Roux. Comparison of the Expressiveness of Timed Automata and Time Petri Nets. Research Report IRCCyN R2005-2 available at `http://www.lamsade.dauphine.fr/~haddad/publis.html` 2005.
8. B. Berthomieu and M. Diaz. Modeling and verification of time dependent systems using time Petri nets. *IEEE Transactions on Software Engineering*, 17(3):259–273, March 1991.
9. M. Boyer and M. Diaz. Non equivalence between time Petri nets and time stream Petri nets. In *Proceedings of 8th International Workshop on Petri Nets and Performance Modeling (PNPM'99)*, Zaragoza, Spain, pages 198–207.
10. F. Cassez and O.H. Roux. Structural Translation of Time Petri Nets into Timed Automata. In Michael Huth, editor, *Workshop on Automated Verification of Critical Systems (AVoCS'04)*, Electronic Notes in Computer Science. Elsevier, August 2004.

11. D. de Frutos Escrig, V. Valero Ruiz, and O. Marroquín Alonso. Decidability of properties of timed-arc Petri nets. In *ICATPN'00*, Aarhus, Denmark, volume 1825 of *LNCS*, pages 187–206, June 2000.

12. M. Diaz and P. Senac. Time stream Petri nets: a model for timed multimedia information. In *ATPN'94*, volume 815 of *LNCS*, pages 219–238, 1994.

13. D.L. Dill. Timing assumptions and verification of finite-state concurrent systems. In Proc. Workshop on Automatic Verification Methods for Finite State Systems, Grenoble, volume 407 of *LNCS*, 1989.

14. G. Gardey, D. Lime, M. Magin and O.H. Roux. ROMÉO: A Tool for Analyzing time Petri nets In *CAV '05*, Edinburgh, Scotland, UK, volume 3576 of *LNCS*, 2005, pages 418–423.

15. S. Haar, F. Simonot-Lion, L. Kaiser, and J. Toussaint. Equivalence of Timed State Machines and safe Time Petri Nets. In *Proceedings of WODES 2002*, Zaragoza, Spain, pages 119–126.

16. W. Khansa, J.P. Denat, and S. Collart-Dutilleul. P-Time Petri Nets for manufacturing systems. In *WODES'96*, Scotland, pages 94–102, 1996.

17. D. Lime and O.H. Roux. State class timed automaton of a time Petri net. In *PNPM'03*. IEEE Computer Society, September 2003.

18. P.M. Merlin. *A study of the recoverability of computing systems*. PhD thesis, University of California, Irvine, CA, 1974.

19. M. Pezzé and M. Young. Time Petri Nets: A Primer Introduction. Tutorial presented at the Multi-Workshop on Formal Methods in Performance Evaluation and Applications, Zaragoza, Spain, September 1999.

20. C. Ramchandani. *Analysis of asynchronous concurrent systems by timed Petri nets*. PhD thesis, Massachusetts Institute of Technology, Cambridge, MA, 1974.

21. J. Sifakis. Performance Evaluation of Systems using Nets. In *Net Theory and Applications, Advanced Course on General Net Theory of Processes and Systems, Hamburg*, volume 84 of *LNCS*, pages 307–319, 1980.

Quantifying Similarities Between Timed Systems*

Thomas A. Henzinger[1], Rupak Majumdar[2], and Vinayak S. Prabhu[3]

[1] Department of Computer and Communication Sciences, EPFL
tah@epfl.ch
[2] Department of Computer Science, UC Los Angeles
rupak@cs.ucla.edu
[3] Department of Electrical Engineering and Computer Sciences, UC Berkeley
vinayak@eecs.berkeley.edu

Abstract. We define quantitative similarity functions between timed
transition systems that measure the degree of closeness of two systems
as a real, in contrast to the traditional boolean yes/no approach to timed
simulation and language inclusion. Two systems are close if for each
timed trace of one system, there exists a corresponding timed trace in the
other system with the same sequence of events and closely corresponding
event timings. We show that timed CTL is robust with respect to our
quantitative version of bisimilarity, in particular, if a system satisfies a
formula, then every close system satisfies a close formula. We also define
a discounted version of CTL over timed systems, which assigns to every
CTL formula a real value that is obtained by discounting real time.
We prove the robustness of discounted CTL by establishing that close
states in the bisimilarity metric have close values for all discounted CTL
formulas.

1   Introduction

Timed systems model not only the sequence of system events but the timing
information as well. Unfortunately, most formal models for timed systems are
too precise: two states can be distinguished even if there is an arbitrarily small
mismatch between the timings of an event. For example, traditional timed language inclusion requires that each trace in one system be matched *exactly* by
a trace in the other system. Since formal models for timed systems are only
approximations of the real world, and subject to estimation errors, this presents
a serious shortcoming in the theory, and has been well noted in the literature
[15, 21, 23, 13, 18, 16, 3, 19, 17].

We develop a theory of refinement for timed systems that is *robust* with respect to small timing mismatches. The robustness is achieved by generalizing
timed refinement relations to metrics on timed systems that quantitatively estimate the closeness of two systems. That is, instead of looking at refinement

---

* This research was supported in part by the AFOSR MURI grant F49620-00-1-0327
and the NSF grants CCR-0208875, CCR-0225610, and CCR-0427202.

between systems as a boolean true/false relation, we assign a positive real number between zero and infinity to a pair of timed systems (T_r, T_s) which indicates how well T_r refines T_s. In the linear setting, we define the distance between two traces as ∞ if the untimed sequences differ, and as the supremum of the difference of corresponding time points otherwise. The distance between two systems is then taken to be the supremum of closest matching trace differences from the initial states. For example, the distance between the traces $a \xrightarrow{1} b$ and $a \xrightarrow{2} b$ is 1 unit, and occurs due to the second trace lagging the first by 1 unit at b. Similarly, the distance between the first trace and the trace $a \xrightarrow{100} b$ is 99. Intuitively, the first trace is "closer" to the second than the third; our metric makes this intuition precise.

Timed trace inclusion is undecidable on timed automata [2]. To compute a refinement distance between timed automata, we therefore take a branching view. We define quantitative notions of timed similarity and bisimilarity which generalize timed similarity and bisimilarity relations [6, 22] to metrics over timed systems. Given a positive real number ε, we define a state r to be ε-similar to another state s, if (1) the observations at the states match, and (2) if for every timed step from r there is a timed step from s such that the timing of events on the traces from r and s remain within ε. We provide algorithms to compute the similarity distance between two timed systems modeled as timed automata to within any given precision.

We show that bisimilarity metrics provide a robust refinement theory for timed systems by relating the metrics to timed computation tree logic (TCTL) specifications. We prove a *robustness theorem* that states close states in the metric satisfy TCTL specifications that have "close" timing requirements. For example, if the bisimilarity distance between states r and s is ε, and r satisfies the TCTL formula $\exists\Diamond_{\leq 5}a$ (i.e., r can get to a state where a holds within 5 time units), then s satisfies $\exists\Diamond_{\leq 5+2\varepsilon}a$. A similar robustness theorem for MITL was studied in [20]. However, they do not provide algorithms to compute distances between systems, relying on system execution to estimate the bound.

As an illustration, consider the two timed automata in Figure 1. Each automaton has four locations and two clocks x, y. Observations are the same as

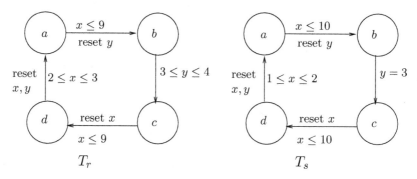

Fig. 1. Two similar timed automata

the locations. Let the initial states be $\langle a, x = 0, y = 0 \rangle$ in both automata. The two automata seem close on inspection, but traditional language refinement of T_s by T_r does not hold. The trace $\langle a, x = 0, y = 0 \rangle \xrightarrow{0} \langle b, 0, 0 \rangle \xrightarrow{4} \langle c, 4, 4 \rangle \ldots$ in T_r cannot be matched by a trace in T_s. The automaton T_s however, does have a similar trace, $\langle a, x = 0, y = 0 \rangle \xrightarrow{0} \langle b, 0, 0 \rangle \xrightarrow{3} \langle c, 3, 3 \rangle \ldots$ (the trace difference is 1 time unit). We want to be able to quantify this notion of similar traces. Our metric gives a directed distance of 1 between T_r and T_s: for every (timed) move of T_r from the starting state, there is a move for T_s such that the trace difference is never more than 1 unit. The two automata do have the same untimed languages, but are not timed similar. Thus, the traditional theory does not tell us if the timed languages are close, or widely different. Looking at TCTL specifications, we note T_s satisfies $\exists \Diamond (c \wedge \exists \Diamond_{\geq 7} d)$, while T_r only satisfies the more relaxed specification $\exists \Diamond (c \wedge \exists \Diamond_{\geq 5} d)$. Robustness guarantees a bound on the relaxation of timing requirements.

Once we generalize refinement to quantitative metrics, a natural progression is to look at logical formulae as functions on states, having real values in the interval $[0, 1]$. We use *discounting* [10, 12] for this quantification and define DCTL, a quantitative version of CTL for timed systems. Discounting gives more importance to near events than to those in the far future. For example, for the reachability query $\exists \Diamond a$, we would like to see a as soon as possible. If the shortest time to reach a from the state s is t_a, then we assign β^{t_a} to the value of $\exists \Diamond a$ at s, where β is a positive discount factor less than 1 in our multiplicative discounting. The subscript constraints in TCTL (e.g., ≤ 5 in $\exists \Diamond_{\leq 5} a$) may be viewed as another form of discounting, focusing only on events before 5 time units. Our discounting in DCTL takes a more uniform view; the discounting for a time interval depends only on the duration of the interval. We also show that the DCTL values are well behaved in the sense that close bisimilar states have close values for all DCTL specifications. For the discounted CTL formula $\exists \Diamond c$, the value in T_r is β^9 and β^{10} in T_s (shortest time to reach c on time diverging paths is 9 in T_r and 10 in T_s). They are again close (on the β scale).

The rest of the paper is organized as follows. In Section 2 we define quantitative notions of simulation and bisimilarity, and exhibit an algorithm to compute these functions to within any desired degree of accuracy for timed automata. In Section 3 we prove the robustness theorem for quantitative bisimilarity with respect to timed computation tree logic. In Section 4, we define DCTL, show its robustness, and give a model checking algorithm for a subset of DCTL over timed automata. Metrics have been studied before for discrete and probabilistic syetms in [14, 12, 17, 11], and for timed systems in [5, 17, 20]; this paper provides, to our knowledge, the first algorithms for computing refinement metrics on timed systems.

2   Quantitative Timed Simulation Functions

We define *quantitative* refinement functions on timed systems. These functions allow approximate matching of timed traces and generalize timed and untimed simulation relations.

2.1 Simulation Relations and Quantitative Extensions

A *timed transition system* (TTS) is a tuple $A = \langle Q, \Sigma, \rightarrow, \mu, Q_0 \rangle$ where

- Q is the set of states.
- Σ is a set of atomic propositions (the observations).
- $\rightarrow \subseteq Q \times \mathbb{R}^+ \times Q$ is the transition relation.
- $\mu : Q \mapsto 2^\Sigma$ is the observation map which assigns a truth value to atomic propositions true in a state.
- $Q_0 \subseteq Q$ is the set of initial states.

We write $q \xrightarrow{t} q'$ if $(q, t, q') \in \rightarrow$. A *state trajectory* is an infinite sequence $q_0 \xrightarrow{t_0} q_1 \xrightarrow{t_1} \ldots$, where for each $j \geq 0$, we have $q_j \xrightarrow{t_j} q_{j+1}$. The state trajectory is *initialized* if $q_0 \in Q_0$ is an initial state. A state trajectory $q_0 \xrightarrow{t_0} q_1 \ldots$ induces a *trace* given by the observation sequence $\mu(q_0) \xrightarrow{t_0} \mu(q_1) \xrightarrow{t_1} \ldots$. To emphasize the initial state, we say q_0-trace for a trace induced by a state trajectory starting from q_0. A trace is initialized if it is induced by an initialized state trajectory. A TTS A_i *refines* or *implements* a TTS A_s if every initialized trace of A_i is also an initialized trace of A_s. The general trace inclusion problem for timed systems is undecidable [2], simulation relations allow us to restrict our attention to a computable relation.

Let A be a TTS. A binary relation $\preceq \subseteq Q \times Q$ is a *timed simulation* if $q_1 \preceq q_2$ implies the following conditions:

1. $\mu(q_1) = \mu(q_2)$.
2. If $q_1 \xrightarrow{t} q_1'$, then there exists q_2' such that $q_2 \xrightarrow{t} q_2'$, and $q_1' \preceq q_2'$.

The state q is timed simulated by the state q' if there exists a timed simulation $\preceq$ such that $q \preceq q'$. A binary relation $\equiv$ is a *timed bisimulation* if it is a symmetric timed simulation. Two states q and q' are timed bisimilar if there exists a timed bisimulation $\equiv$ with $q \equiv q'$. Timed bisimulation is stronger than timed simulation which in turn is stronger than trace inclusion. If state q is timed simulated by state q', then every q-trace is also a q'-trace.

Untimed simulation and bisimulation relations are defined analogously by ignoring the duration of time steps. Formally, a binary relation $\preceq \subseteq Q \times Q$ is an (untimed) simulation if condition (2) above is replaced by

$(2)'$ If $q_1 \xrightarrow{t} q_1'$, then there exists q_2' and $t' \in \mathbb{R}^+$ such that $q_2 \xrightarrow{t'} q_2'$, and $q_1' \preceq q_2'$.

A symmetric untimed simulation relation is called an untimed bisimulation.

Timed simulation and bisimulation require that times be matched exactly. This is often too strict a requirement, especially since timed models are approximations of the real world. On the other hand, untimed simulation and bisimulation relations ignore the times on moves altogether. We now define *approximate* notions of refinement, simulation, and bisimulation that quantify if the behavior of an implementation TTS is "close enough" to a specification TTS. We begin by defining a metric on traces. Given two traces $\pi = r_0 \xrightarrow{t_0} r_1 \xrightarrow{t_1} r_2 \ldots$ and $\pi' = s_0 \xrightarrow{t_0'} s_1 \xrightarrow{t_1'} s_2 \ldots$, the distance $\mathcal{D}(\pi, \pi')$ is defined by

$$\mathcal{D}(\pi, \pi') = \begin{cases} \infty & : \quad \text{if } r_j \neq s_j \text{ for some } j \\ \sup_j \{ | \sum_{n=0}^{j} t_n - \sum_{n=0}^{j} t_n' | \} & : \quad \text{otherwise} \end{cases}$$

The trace metric $\mathcal{D}$ induces a *refinement distance* between two TTS. Given two timed transition systems A_r, A_s, with initial states Q_r, Q_s respectively, the *refinement distance* of A_r with respect to A_s is given by $\sup_{\pi_q} \inf_{\pi'_{q'}} \{\mathcal{D}(\pi_q, \pi'_{q'})\}$ where π_q (respectively, $\pi'_{q'}$) is a q-trace (respectively, q'-trace) for some $q \in Q_r$ (respectively, $q' \in Q_s$). Notice that the refinement distance is asymmetric: it is a *directed distance* [11].

We also generalize the simulation relation to a directed distance in the following way. For states r, s and $\delta \in \mathbb{R}$, the *simulation function* $\mathcal{S} : Q \times Q \times \mathbb{R} \to \mathbb{R}$ is the least fixpoint (in the absolute value sense) of the following equation:

$$\mathcal{S}(r,s,\delta) = \begin{cases} \infty & \text{if } \mu(r) \neq \mu(s) \\ \sup'_{t_r} \inf'_{t_s} \{\max'(\delta, \, \mathcal{S}(r',s',\delta + t_r - t_s)) \mid r \xrightarrow{t_r} r', s \xrightarrow{t_s} s'\} \text{ otherwise} \end{cases}$$

where $\sup'$, $\inf'$, $\max'$ consider only the modulus in the ordering, i.e., $x <' y$ iff $|x| < |y|$ in the standard real number ordering. We say r is ε-*simulated* by s if $|\mathcal{S}(r,s,0)| \leq \varepsilon$. Note the ε-simulation is *not* transitive in the traditional sense. If r is ε-simulated by s, and s is ε-simulated by w, then r is (2ε)-simulated by w.

Given two states r, s, it is useful to think of the value of $\mathcal{S}(r,s,\delta)$ as being the outcome of a game. Enviroment plays on r (and its successors), and chooses a move at each round. We play on s and choose moves on its successors. Each round adds another step to both traces (from r and s). The goal of the environment is to maximise the trace difference, our goal is to minimize. The value of $\mathcal{S}(r,s,\delta)$ is the maximum lead of the r trace with respect to the s trace when the simulation game starts with the r trace starting with a lead of δ. If from r, s the environment can force the game into a configuration in which we cannot match its observation, we assign a value of ∞ to $\mathcal{S}(r,s,\cdot)$. Otherwise, we recursively compute the maximum trace difference for each step from the successor states r', s'. For the successors r', s', the lead at the first step is $(\delta + t_r - t_s)$. The lead from the first step onwards is then $\mathcal{S}(r',s',\delta + t_r - t_s)$. The maximum trace difference is either the starting trace difference (δ), or some difference after the first step $(\mathcal{S}(r',s',\delta + t_r - t_s))$.

Note that different accumulated differences in the times in the two traces may lead to different strategies, we need to keep track of the accumulated delay or lead. For example, suppose the environment is generating a trace and is currently at state r, and our matching trace has ended up at state s. Suppose r can only take a step of length 1, and s can take two steps of lengths 0 and 100. If the two traces ending at r and s have an accumulated difference of 0 (the times at which r and s occur are exactly the same), then s should take the step of length 0. But if the r trace leads the s trace by say 70 time units, then s should take the step of length 100, the trace difference after the step will then be $|70 + 1 - 100| = 29$, if s took the 0 step, the trace difference would be $70 + 1 - 0 = 71$.

We also define the corresponding bisimulation function. For states $r, s \in Q$ and a real number δ, the *bisimulation function* $\mathcal{B} : Q \times Q \times \mathbb{R} \to \mathbb{R}$ is the least fixpoint (in the absolute value sense) of the equations $\mathcal{B}(r,s,\delta) = \infty$ if $\mu(r) \neq \mu(s)$, and

$$\mathcal{B}(r,s,\delta) = \max \begin{cases} \sup'_{t_r} \inf'_{t_s} \{\max'(\delta, \, \mathcal{B}(r',s',\delta + t_r - t_s)) \mid r \xrightarrow{t_r} r', s \xrightarrow{t_s} s'\}, \\ \sup'_{t_s} \inf'_{t_r} \{\max'(\delta, \, \mathcal{B}(r',s',\delta + t_r - t_s)) \mid r \xrightarrow{t_r} r', s \xrightarrow{t_s} s'\} \end{cases}$$

otherwise, where $\sup', \inf', \max'$ consider only the modulus in the ordering. The *bisimilarity distance* between two states r, s of a TTS is defined to be $\mathcal{B}(r, s, 0)$. States r, s are ε-bisimilar if $\mathcal{B}(r, s, 0) \leq \varepsilon$. Notice that $\mathcal{B}(r, s, 0) = 0$ iff r, s are timed bisimilar.

Proposition 1. *Let r and s be two states of a TTS. For every trace π_r from r, there is a trace π_s from s such that $\mathcal{D}(\pi_r, \pi_s) \leq |\mathcal{S}(r, s, 0)|$. The bisimilarity distance $\mathcal{B}(r, s, 0)$ is a pseudo-metric on the states of TTSs.*

Example 1. Consider the example in Fig. 2. The observations have been numbered for simplicity: $\mu(a_1) = a, \mu(b_i) = b, \mu(c_i) = c$. We want to compute $\mathcal{S}(a, a_1, 0)$. It can be checked that a is untimed similar to a_1 All paths have finite weights, so $\mathcal{S}(a, a_1, 0) < \infty$. Consider the first step, a takes a step of length 7 in A_r. A_s has two options, it can take a step to b_1 of length 5 or a step to b_2 of length 8, and to decide which one to take, it needs $\mathcal{S}(b, b_1, 2)$ and $\mathcal{S}(b, b_2, -1)$. $\mathcal{S}(b, b_2, -1)$ is $-1 + 10 - 4 = 5$. To compute $\mathcal{S}(b, b_1, 2)$, we look at b_1's options. In the next step, if we move to c_2, then the trace at the (c, c_2) configuration will be $2 + 10 - 9 = 3$. If we move to c_1, the trace difference will be $2 + 10 - 12 = 0$ (this is the better option). Thus $\mathcal{S}(b, b_1, 2) = 2$ (the 2 is due to the initial lead). Thus $\mathcal{S}(a, a_1, 0) = 2$. $\qquad\square$

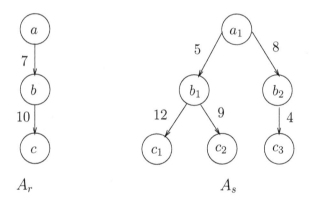

Fig. 2. A_r is 2-similar to A_s

2.2   Algorithms for Simulation Functions

Finite Weighted Graphs. We first look at computing ε-simulation on a special case of timed transition systems. A *finite timed graph* $T = (Q, \Sigma, E, \mu, W)$ consists of a finite set of locations Q, a set Σ of atomic propositions, an edge relation $E \subseteq Q \times Q$, an observation function $\mu : V \rightarrow 2^\Sigma$ on the locations, and an integer weight function $W : E \rightarrow \mathbb{N}^+$ on the edges. For vertices $s, s' \in Q$, we write $s \xrightarrow{t} s'$ iff there is an edge $(s, s') \in E$ with $W(s, s') = t$. The following theorem provides a bound on simulation functions on a finite timed graph.

Theorem 1. *Let A be a finite timed graph and let $n = |Q|$ be the number of nodes and $W_{max} = \max_{e \in E}\{W(e)\}$ the maximum weight of any edge. Let $f \in \{S, B\}$. (1) For every pair of vertices $r, s \in Q$, if $|f(r, s, 0)| < \infty$, then $|f(r, s, 0)| \leq 2n^2 \cdot W_{max}$. (2) The values $S(r, s, 0)$ and $B(r, s, 0)$ are computable over finite timed graphs in time polynomial in n and W_{max}.*

The proof of (1) is by contradiction, we give the argument for $S(r, s, 0)$. Since we are working on a finite graph, the sup-inf in the definiton of S can be replaced by a max-min. Consider the product graph $A \times A$ where if $r \xrightarrow{t_r} r'$ and $s \xrightarrow{t_s} s'$ in A, then $\langle r, s \rangle \xrightarrow{t_r - t_s} \langle r', s' \rangle$ in $A \times A$. The value of the max-min can be viewed as the outcome of a game, where the environment chooses a (maximising) move for the first vertex in the product graph, we choose a (minimising) move for the second vertex, and the game moves to the resulting vertex pair.

Suppose $n^2 W_{max} < |S(r, s, 0)| < \infty$. Since there are only n^2 locations in the pair graph, and since each composite move can cause at most W_{max} lead or lag, there must be a cycle of composite locations in the game, with non-zero accumulative weight. When the game starts, we would do our best to not to get into such a cycle. If we cannot *avoid* getting into such a cycle because of observation matching of the environment moves, $|S(v, s, 0)|$ will be ∞, because the enviroment will force us to loop around that cycle forever. If $|S(r, s, 0)| < \infty$, and we *choose* to go into such a cycle, it must be the case that there is an alternative path/cycle that we can take which has accumated delay of the opposite sign. For example, it may happen that at some point in the game we have an option of going into two loops, loop 1 has total gain 10, loop 2 has total gain -1000. We will take loop 1 the first 500 times, then loop 2 once, then repeat with loop 1. The leads and lags cancel out in part keeping $S(r, s, 0)$ bounded. A finite value value of $S(r, s, 0)$ is then due to 1) some initial hard observation matching contraint steps, with the number of steps being less than n^2 (no cycles), and 2) presence of different weight cycles (note we never need to go around the maximum weight cycle more than once). A cycle in the pair graph can have weight at most $n^2 W_{max}$. Hence the value of $|S(r, s, 0)|$ is bounded by $2n^2 W_{max}$.

Given the upper bound, the value of $S()$ can then be computed using dynamic programming (since all edges are integer valued, it suffices to restrict our attention to $S(\cdot, \cdot, \delta)$ for integer valued δ). Further, this bound is tight: there is a finite timed graph A and two states r, s of A with $S(r, s, 0)$ in $\Theta(n^2 W_{max})$.

Timed Automata. Timed automata provide a syntax for timed transition systems. A *timed automaton* A is a tuple $\langle L, \Sigma, C, \mu, \rightarrow, Q_0 \rangle$, where

- L is the set of locations.
- Σ is the set of atomic propositions.
- C is a finite set of clocks. A *clock valuation* $v : C \mapsto \mathbb{R}^+$ for a set of clocks C assigns a real value to each clock in C.
- $\mu : L \mapsto 2^\Sigma$ is the observation map (it does not depend on clock values).
- $\rightarrow \subseteq L \times L \times 2^C \times \Phi(C)$ gives the set of transitions, where $\Phi(C)$ is the set of clock contraints generated by $\psi := x \leq d \mid d \leq x \mid \neg\psi \mid \psi_1 \wedge \psi_2$.
- $Q_0 \subseteq L \times \mathbb{R}^{+|C|}$ is the set of initial states.

Each clock increases at rate 1 inside a location. A *state* is a location together with a clock valuation, the set of states is denoted $Q = L \times (\mathbb{R}^+)^{|C|}$. An edge $\langle l, l', \lambda, g \rangle$ represents a transition from location l to location l' when the clock values at l satisfy the constraint g. The set $\lambda \subseteq C$ gives the clocks to be reset with this transition. The semantics of timed automata are given as timed transition systems. This is standard [2], and omitted here.

For simplicity, we assume every clock of a timed automaton A stays within $M + 1$, where M is the largest constant in the system. A *region* R of a timed automaton A is a tuple $\langle l, h, \mathcal{P}(C) \rangle$ where

- l is a location of A.
- h is a function which specifies the integer values of clocks $h : C \to (\mathbb{N} \cap [0, M])$ (M is the largest constant in A).
- $\mathcal{P}(C)$ is a disjoint partition of the clocks $\{X_0, \ldots X_n \mid \uplus X_i = C, X_i \neq \emptyset$ for $i > 0\}$.

We say a state s with clock valuation v is in the region R when,

1. The location of s corresponds to the location of R
2. For all clocks x with $v(x) < M + 1$, $\lfloor v(x) \rfloor = h(x)$.
3. For $v(x) \geq M+1$, $h(x) = M$. (This is slightly more refined than the standard region partition, we have created more partitions in $[M, M+1)$, we map clock values which are greater than M into this interval. This is to simplify the proofs.)
4. Let frac(r) denote the fractional value of r. For any pair of clocks (x, y), frac$(v(x)) <$ frac$(v(y))$ iff $x \in X_i$ and $y \in X_j$ with $i < j$ (so, $x, y \in X_k$ implies frac$(v(x)) =$ frac$(v(y))$).
5. frac$(v(x)) = 0$ iff $x \in X_0$.

We say two states s, s' to be *region equivalent* if they belong to the same region.

We now show that given states r, s in a timed automaton A, the values of $\mathcal{S}(r, s, 0)$ and $\mathcal{B}(r, s, 0)$ can be computed to within any desired degree of accuracy. We use a *corner point abstraction* (similar to that in [4]) which can be viewed as a region graph augmented with additional timing information. We show that the corner points are at a close bisimilarity distance from the states inside the corresponding regions. Finally we use Theorem 1 to compute the approximation for $\mathcal{S}(\cdot)$ on the corner point graph.

A *corner point* is a tuple $\langle \alpha, R \rangle$, where $\alpha \in \mathbb{N}^{|C|}$ and R is a region. A region $R = \langle l, h, \{X_0, \ldots X_n\} \rangle$ has $n + 1$ corner points $\{\langle \alpha_i, R \rangle \mid 0 \leq i \leq n\}$:

$$\alpha_i(x) = \begin{cases} h(x) & : \quad x \in X_j \text{ with } j \leq i \\ h(x) + 1 & : \quad x \in X_j \text{ with } j > i \end{cases}$$

Intuitively, corner points denote the boundary points of the region.

Using the corner points, we construct a finite timed graph as follows. The structure is similar to the region graph, only we use corner points, and weights on some of the edges to model the passage of time. For a timed automaton A, the *corner point abstraction* CP(A) has corner points p of A as states. The observation of the state $\langle \alpha, \langle l, h, \mathcal{P}(C) \rangle \rangle$ is $\mu(l)$. The abstraction has the following weighted transitions :

Discrete. There is an edge $\langle \alpha, R \rangle \xrightarrow{0} \langle \alpha', R' \rangle$ if A has an edge $\langle l, l', \lambda, g \rangle$ $(l, l'$ are locations of R, R' respectively) such that (1) R satisfies the constraint g, and (2) $R' = R[\lambda \mapsto 0]$, $\alpha' = \alpha[\lambda \mapsto 0]$ (note that corner points are closed under resets).

Timed. For corner points $\langle \alpha, R \rangle, \langle \alpha', R \rangle$ such that $\forall x \in C$, $\alpha'(x) = \alpha(x) + 1$, we have an edge $\langle \alpha, R \rangle \xrightarrow{1} \langle \alpha', R \rangle$. These are the edges which model the flow of time. Note that for each such edge, there are concrete states in A which are arbitrarily close to the corner points, such that there is a time flow of length arbitralily close to 1 in between those two states.

Region flow. These transitions model the immediate flow transitions in between "adjacent" regions. Suppose $\langle \alpha, R \rangle, \langle \alpha, R' \rangle$ are such that R' is an immediate time successor of R, then we have an edge $\langle \alpha, R \rangle \xrightarrow{0} \langle \alpha, R' \rangle$. If $\langle \alpha + 1, R' \rangle$ is also a corner point of R', then we also add the transition $\langle \alpha, R \rangle \xrightarrow{1} \langle \alpha + 1, R' \rangle$.

Self loops. Each state also has a self loop transition of weight 0.

Transitive closure. We transitively close the timed, region flow, and the self loop transitions upto weight M (the subset of the full transitive closure where edges have weight less than or equal to M).

The number of states in the corner point abstraction of a timed automaton A is $O(|L| \cdot |C| \cdot (2M)^{|C|})$, where L is the set of locations in A, C the set of clocks, and M the largest constant in the system.

Lemma 1. *Let s be a state in a timed automaton A, and let p be a corner point of the region R corresponding to s in the corner point abstraction of A. Then s is ε-bisimilar to p for $\varepsilon = |C| + 1$, that is, $\mathcal{S}(s, \mathsf{p}, 0) \le |C| + 1$, where C is the set of clocks in A.*

Informally, each clock can be the cause of at most 1 unit of time difference, as the time taken to hit a constraint is always of the form $d - v(x)$ for some clock x and integer d. Once a clock is reset, it collapses onto a corner point, and the time taken from that point to reach a constraint controlled by x is the same as that for the corresponding corner point in $\mathrm{CP}(A)$.

Using Lemma 1 and Theorem 1, we can "blow" up the time unit for a timed automaton to compute ε-simulation and ε-bisimilarity to within any given degree of accuracy. This gives an EXPTIME algorithm in the size of the timed automaton and the desired accuracy.

Theorem 2. *Given two states r, s in a timed automaton A, and a natural number m, we can compute numbers $\gamma_1, \gamma_2 \in \mathbb{R}$ such that $\mathcal{S}(r, s, 0) \in [\gamma_1 - \frac{1}{m}, \gamma_1 + \frac{1}{m}]$ and $\mathcal{B}(r, s, 0) \in [\gamma_2 - \frac{1}{m}, \gamma_2 + \frac{1}{m}]$ in time polynomial in the number of states of the corner point abstraction and in $m^{|C|}$, where C is the set of clocks of A.*

3   Robustness of Timed Computation Tree Logic

TCTL. Timed computation tree logic (TCTL) [1] is a real time extension of CTL [7]. TCTL adds time contraints such as ≤ 5 to CTL formulae for specifying timing requirements. For example, while the CTL formula $\forall\Diamond a$ only requires a to eventually hold on all paths, the TCTL formula $\forall\Diamond_{\leq 5}a$ requires a to hold on all paths before 5 time units.

We will use $\sim$ to mean one of the binary relations $<, \leq, >, \geq$. The formulae of TCTL are given inductively as follows:

$$\varphi := a \mid \text{FALSE} \mid \neg\varphi \mid \varphi_1 \vee \varphi_2 \mid \varphi_1 \wedge \varphi_2 \mid \exists(\varphi_1\,\mathcal{U}_{\sim d}\varphi_2) \mid \forall(\varphi_1\,\mathcal{U}_{\sim d}\varphi_2)$$

where $a \in \Sigma$ and $d \in \mathbb{N}$.

The semantics of TCTL formulas is given over states of timed transition systems. For a state s in a TTS

$s \models a$ iff $a \in \mu(s)$; $s \not\models \text{FALSE}$; $s \models \neg\varphi$ iff $s \not\models \varphi$.

$s \models \varphi_1 \vee \varphi_2$ iff $s \models \varphi_1$ or $s \models \varphi_2$.

$s \models \varphi_1 \wedge \varphi_2$ iff $s \models \varphi_1$ and $s \models \varphi_2$.

$s \models \exists(\varphi_1\,\mathcal{U}_{\sim d}\varphi_2)$ iff for some run π_s starting from s, for some $t \sim d$, the state at time t, $\pi_s(t) \models \varphi_2$, and for all $0 \leq t' < t$, $\pi_s(t') \models \varphi_1$.

$s \models \forall(\varphi_1\,\mathcal{U}_{\sim d}\varphi_2)$ iff for all (infinite) paths π_s starting from s, for some $t \sim d$, the state at time t, $\pi_s(t) \models \varphi_2$, and for all $0 \leq t' < t$, $\pi_s(t') \models \varphi_1$.

We define the *waiting-for* operator as $\exists(\varphi_1\,\mathcal{W}_{\sim c}\varphi_2) = \neg\forall(\neg\varphi_2\,\mathcal{U}_{\sim c}\neg(\varphi_1 \vee \varphi_2))$, $\forall(\varphi_1\,\mathcal{W}_{\sim c}\varphi_2) = \neg\exists(\neg\varphi_2\,\mathcal{U}_{\sim c}\neg(\varphi_1\vee\varphi_2))$. The until operator in $\varphi_1\,\mathcal{U}_{\sim d}\varphi_2$ requires that φ_2 become true at some time, the waiting-for formula $\varphi_1\,\mathcal{W}_{\sim d}\varphi_2$ admits the possibility of φ_1 forever "waiting" for all times $t \sim d$ and φ_2 never being satisfied. Formally, $s \models \forall(\varphi\,\mathcal{W}_{\sim d}\theta)$ (respectively, $s \models \exists(\varphi\,\mathcal{W}_{\sim d}\theta)$) iff for all traces (respectively, for some trace) π_s from s, either 1) for all times $t \sim d$, $\pi_s(t) \models \varphi$, or 2) at some time t, $\pi_s(t) \models \theta$, and for all $(t' < t) \wedge (t' \sim d)$, $\pi_s(t') \models \varphi$. Using the waiting-for operator and the identities $\neg(\varphi\exists\mathcal{U}_{\sim d}\theta) = (\neg\varphi)\forall\mathcal{W}_{\sim d}(\neg\varphi \wedge \neg\theta)$ and $\neg(\varphi\forall\mathcal{U}_{\sim d}\theta) = (\neg\varphi)\exists\mathcal{W}_{\sim d}(\neg\varphi \wedge \neg\theta)$, we can write each TCTL formula φ in negation normal form by pushing the negation to the atomic propositions.

δ-weakened TCTL. For each TCTL forumla φ in negation normal form, and $\delta \in \mathbb{R}^+$, a δ-weakening $\zeta^\delta(\varphi)$ of φ with respect to δ is defined as follows:

$\zeta^\delta(a) := a,$ $\zeta^\delta(\neg a) := \neg a,$ $\zeta^\delta(\text{FALSE}) := \text{FALSE}$

$\zeta^\delta(\varphi_1 \vee \varphi_2) = \zeta^\delta(\varphi_1) \vee \zeta^\delta(\varphi_2),$ $\zeta^\delta(\varphi_1 \wedge \varphi_2) = \zeta^\delta(\varphi_1) \wedge \zeta^\delta(\varphi_2)$

$\zeta^\delta(\ddagger(\varphi_1\,\mathcal{U}_{\sim d}\varphi_2)) = \ddagger(\zeta^\delta(\varphi_1)\,\mathcal{U}_{\sim\delta(d,\sim)}\zeta^\delta(\varphi_2)),$

$\zeta^\delta(\ddagger(\varphi_1\,\mathcal{W}_{\sim d}\varphi_2)) = \ddagger(\zeta^\delta(\varphi_1)\,\mathcal{W}_{\sim\delta'(d,\sim)}\zeta^\delta(\varphi_2))$

where $\ddagger \in \{\exists, \forall\}$ and

$$\delta(d, \sim) = \begin{cases} d + \delta & \text{if } \sim\,\in \{<, \leq\} \\ d - \delta & \text{if } \sim\,\in \{>, \geq\} \end{cases} \qquad \delta'(d, \sim) = \begin{cases} d - \delta & \text{if } \sim\,\in \{<, \leq\} \\ d + \delta & \text{if } \sim\,\in \{>, \geq\} \end{cases}$$

The ζ^δ function relaxes the timing constraints by δ. The $\mathcal{U}$ and the $\mathcal{W}$ operators are weakened dually. Note that $\neg\zeta^\delta(\psi) \neq \zeta^\delta(\neg\psi)$. The discrepancy occurs because of the difference in how δ and δ' are defined.

Example 2. Let a and b be atomic propositions. We have $\zeta^2(\exists(a\,\mathcal{U}_{\leq 5}b))$ $= \exists(a\,\mathcal{U}_{\leq 7}b)$. Earlier, a state had to get to b within 5 time units, now it has 7 time units to satisfy the requirement. Similarly, $\zeta^2(\exists(a\,\mathcal{W}_{\leq 5}b)) = \exists(a\,\mathcal{W}_{\leq 3}b))$. The pre-weakened formula requires that either 1) for all $t \leq 5$ the proposition a must hold, or 2) at some time t, b must hold, and for all $(t' < t) \wedge (t' \leq 5)$ a must hold. The weakening operator relaxes the requirement on a holding for all times less than or equal to 5 to only being required to hold at times less than or equal to 3 (modulo the $(t' < t)$ clause in case 2). □

Proposition 2. *For all reals $\delta \geq 0$, TCTL formulae φ, and states s of a TTS, if $s \models \varphi$, then $s \models \zeta^\delta(\varphi)$.*

We now connect the bisimilarity metric with satisfaction of TCTL specifications. Of course, close states may not satisfy the *same* TCTL specifications. Take $\varphi = \forall\Diamond_{=5}a$, it requires a to occur at exactly 5 time units. One state may have traces that satisfy a at exactly 5 time units, another state at $5+\varepsilon$ for an arbitrarily small ε. The first state will satisfy φ, the second will not. However, two states close in the bisimilarity metric does satisfy "close" TCTL specifications. Theorem 3 makes this precise.

Theorem 3. *Let $\varepsilon > 0$. Let r, s be two ε-bisimilar states of a timed transition system, and let φ a TCTL formula in negation normal form. If $r \models \varphi$, then $s \models \zeta^{2\varepsilon}(\varphi)$.*

The proof proceeds by induction on formulae. The crucial point is to note that if r, s are ε-bisimilar, and if, starting from r, s the bisimilarity game arrives at the configuration r_1, s_1, then r_1, s_1 are 2ε-bisimilar. So if $r \overset{t_1}{\rightsquigarrow} r_1 \overset{t_2}{\rightsquigarrow} r_2$, and $s \overset{t'_1}{\rightsquigarrow} s_1 \overset{t'_2}{\rightsquigarrow} s_2$ (with r_i, s_i being the corresponding states), then $|t_2 - t'_2| \leq 2\varepsilon$. The states r_1 and s_1 are *not* ε-bisimilar in general, but the traces originating from the two states are close and remain within 2ε.

4   Discounted CTL for Timed Systems

Our next step is to develop a quantitative specification formalism that assigns real numbers in the interval $[0, 1]$ to CTL formulas. A value close to 0 is "bad," a value close to 1 "good." We use time and *discounting* for this quantification. Discounting gives more weight to the near future than to the far away future. The resulting logic is called DCTL.

Syntax, Semantics, and Robustness. We look at a subset of standard boolean CTL, with $\Diamond$ being the only temporal operator. The formulae of DCTL are inductively defined as follows:

$$\varphi := a \mid \text{FALSE} \mid \neg\varphi \mid \varphi_1 \vee \varphi_2 \mid \exists\Diamond\varphi \mid \forall\Diamond\varphi$$

where a ranges over atomic propositions. From this, we derive the formulas: $\exists\Box\varphi = \neg\forall\Diamond\neg\varphi$ and $\forall\Box\varphi = \neg\exists\Diamond\neg\varphi$.

The semantics of DCTL formulas are given as functions from states to the real interval $[0, 1]$. For a *discount parameter* $\beta \in [0, 1]$, and a timed transition system, the value of a formula φ at a state s is defined as follows:

$[\![a]\!](s) := 1$ if $s \models a$, 0 otherwise.

$[\![\text{FALSE}]\!](s) := 0; \qquad [\![\neg\varphi]\!](s) := 1 - [\![\varphi]\!](s)$

$[\![\varphi_1\{{}^\vee_\wedge\}\varphi_2]\!](s) := \{{}^{\max}_{\min}\}\{[\![\varphi_1]\!](s), [\![\varphi_2]\!](s)\}$

$[\![\{{}^\exists_\forall\}\Diamond\varphi]\!](s) := \{{}^{\sup}_{\inf}\}_{\pi_s} \sup_{t \in \mathbb{R}^+}\{\beta^t([\![\varphi]\!](\pi_s(t)))\}$

where π_s is an infinite time diverging path starting from state s, and $\pi_s(t)$ is the state on that path at time t. Intuitively, for the $\Diamond$ operator, the quicker we can get to a good state, the better, and the discounted value reflects this fact. The temporal operators can again be seen as playing a game. Environment chooses the path π_s, and we choose the best value on that path. In $\exists\Diamond$ the environment is cooperating and chooses the best path, in $\forall\Diamond$, it plays adversarially and takes the worst path. Note that $\beta = 1$ gives us the boolean case.

Example 3. Consider T_r in Figure 1. Assume we cannot stay at a location forever (location invariants can ensure this). The value of $\forall\Diamond b$ at the state $\langle a, x = 0, y = 0\rangle$ is β^6. The automaton must move from a to b within 6 time units, for otherwise it will get stuck at c and not be able to take the transition to d. Similarly, the value at the starting state in T_s is β^7.

Consider now the formula $\forall\Box(b \Rightarrow \forall\Diamond a) = \neg\exists\Diamond\neg(\neg b \vee \forall\Diamond a) = 1 - \exists\Diamond(\min(b, (1 - \forall\Diamond a)))$. What is its value at the starting state, $\langle a, 0, 0\rangle$, of T_r? The value of $\min(b, \cdot)$ is 0 at states not satisfying b, so we only need look at the b location in the outermost $\exists\Diamond$ clause. T_r needs to move out of b within 9 time units (else it will get stuck at c). Thus we need to look at states $\langle b, 0 \leq x \leq 9, 0 \leq y \leq 4\rangle$. On those states, we need the value of $\forall\Diamond a$. Suppose we enter b at time t. Then the b states encountered are $\{\langle b, t + z, z\rangle \mid z \leq 4, t + z \leq 9\}$. The value of $\forall\Diamond a$ at a state $\langle b, t + z, z\rangle$ is $\beta^{3+9-(t+z)}$ (we exit c at time $9 - (t + z)$, and can avoid a for 3 more time units). Thus the value of $\exists\Diamond(\min(b, (1 - \forall\Diamond a)))$ at the initial state is $\sup_{t,z}\{\beta^{t+z}(1 - \beta^{3+9-(t+z)}) \mid z \leq 4, t + z \leq 9\}$ (view $t + z$ as the elapsed time; the individual contributions of t and z in the sum depending on the choice of the path). The maximum value occurs when $t + z$ is 0. Thus the value of the sup is $1 - \beta^{12}$. So finally we have the value of $\forall\Box(b \Rightarrow \forall\Diamond a)$ at the starting state to be β^{12}. It turns out that the initial state in T_s has the same value for $\forall\Box(b \Rightarrow \forall\Diamond a)$. Both systems have the same "response" times for an a following a b. □

DCTL is robust with respect to ε-bisimilarity: close states in the bisimilarity metric have close DCTL values. Notice however that the closeness is not uniform and may depend on the nesting depth of temporal operators [10].

Theorem 4. *Let k be the number of nested temporal operators in a DCTL formula φ, and let β be a real discount factor in $[0, 1]$. For all states r, s in a TTS, if $|\mathcal{B}(r, s, 0)| \leq \varepsilon$, then $|[\![\varphi]\!](r) - [\![\varphi]\!](s)| \leq (k + 1)(1 - \beta^{2\varepsilon})$.*

Example 4. Consider $\forall\Diamond b$ at the starting states (which are 1-bisimilar) in T_r, T_s in Fig. 1. As shown in Ex. 3, the value in T_r is β^6, and β^7 in T_s. $\beta^6 - \beta^7 = \beta^6(1 - \beta) \leq 1 - \beta \leq 1 - \beta^2$. □

Model Checking dCTL over Timed Automata. We compute the value of $[\![\varphi]\!](s)$ as follows: for $\varphi = \exists \Diamond \theta$, first recursively obtain $[\![\theta]\!](v)$ for each state v in the TTS. The value of $[\![\varphi]\!](s)$ is then $\sup\{\beta^{t_v}([\![\theta]\!](v))\}$, where t_v is the shortest time to reach state v from state s. For $\varphi = \forall \Diamond \theta$, we need to be a bit more careful. We cannot simply take the longest time to reach states and then have an outermost inf (i.e., dual to the $\exists \Diamond$ case). The reason is that the $\exists \Diamond$ case had $\sup_{\pi_s} \sup_t$, and both the sups can be collapsed into one. The $\forall \Diamond$ case has $\inf_{\pi_s} \sup_t$, and the actual path taken to visit a state matters. For example, it may happen that on the longest path to visit a state v, we encounter a better value of θ before v say at u; and on some other path to v, we never get to see u, and hence get the true value of the inf. The value for a formula at a state in a finite timed graph can be computed using the algorithms in [10] (with trivial modifications). Timed automata involve real time and require a different approach. We show how to compute the values for a subset of DCTL on the states of a timed automaton.

Let $F_{\min}(s, Z)$ denote the set of times that must elapse in order for a timed automaton A to hit some configuration in the set of states Z starting from the state s. Then the minimum time to reach the set Z from state s (denoted by $t_{\min}(s, Z)$) is defined to be the inf of the set $F_{\min}(s, Z)$. The maximum time to reach a set of states Z from s for the first time ($t_{\max}(s, Z)$) can be defined dually.

Theorem 5 ([9]). *(1) For a timed automaton A, the minimum and maximum times required to reach a region R from a state s for the first time ($t_{\min}(s, R)$, $t_{\max}(s, R)$) are computable in time $O(|C| \cdot |G|)$ where C is the set of clocks in A, and G is the region automaton of A. (2) For regions R and R', either there is an integer constant d such that for every state $s \in R'$, we have $t_{\min}(s, R) = d$, or there is an integer constant d and a clock x such that for every state $s \in R'$, we have $t_{\min}(s, R) = d - \mathrm{frac}(t_x)$, where t_x is the value of clock x in s; and similarly for $t_{\max}(s, R)$.*

We note that for any state s, we have $[\![P]\!](s)$ is 0 or 1 for a boolean combination of propositions P, and this value is constant over a region. Thus the value of $[\![\exists \Diamond P]\!](s)$ is $\beta^{t_{\min}}$ where $t_{\min}$ is the shortest time to reach a region satisfying P from s. For computing $\forall \Diamond P$, we look at the inf-sup game where the environment chooses a path π_s, and we pick a state $\pi_s(t)$ on that path. The value of the game resulting from these choices is $\beta^t P(\pi_s(t))$. Enviroment is trying to minimise this value, and we are trying to maximise. Given a path, we will pick the earliest state on that path satisfying P. Thus the environment will pick paths which avoid P the longest. Hence, the value of $[\![\forall \Diamond P]\!](s)$ is $\beta^{t_{\max}}$ where $t_{\max}$ is the maximum time that can be spent avoiding regions satisfying P. The next theorem generalizes Theorem 5 to pairs of states. A state is integer (resp., rational) valued if its clock valuation maps each clock to an integer (resp., rational).

Theorem 6. *(1) Let r be an integer valued state in a timed automaton A. Then $t_{\min}(r, s)$, the minimum time to reach the state s from r is computable in time $O(|C| \cdot |G|)$ where C is the set of clocks in A, and G is the region automaton of A. (2) For a region R', either there is an integer constant d such that for every* state $s \in R'$, we have $t_{\min}(r, s) = d$; or there is an integer constant d and a clock x such that $t_{\min}(r, s) = d + \text{frac}(t_x)$, where t_x is the value of clock x in s.

Theorem 6 is based on the fact that if a timed automaton can take a transition from s to s', then 1) for every state w region equivalent to s, there is a transition $w \rightarrow w'$ where w' is region equivalent to s', and 2) for every state w' region equivalent to s', there is a transition $w \rightarrow w'$ where w is region equivalent to s. If π_r is a trajectory starting from r and ending at s with minimal delay, then for any other state s' region equivalent to s, there is a corresponding minimum delay trajectory π'_r from r which makes the same transitions as π_r, in the same order, going through the same regions of the region graph (only the timings may be different). Note that an integer valued state constitutes a seperate region by itself. Theorem 6 is easily generalised to rational valued initial states using the standard trick of multiplying automata guards with integers.

Theorem 7. *Let φ be a* DCTL *formula with no nested temporal operators. Then $[\![\exists \Diamond \varphi]\!](s)$ (and so $[\![\forall \Box \varphi]\!](s)$) can be computed for all rational-valued states s of a timed automaton.*

Let φ be a boolean combination of formulas of form $[\![\{{}^\exists_\forall\} \Diamond P]\!]$ (P a boolean combination of propositions). We have shown $[\![\varphi]\!](s')$ to be computable for all states (and moreover it to have a simple form over regions). The value of $[\![\exists \Diamond \varphi]\!](s)$ is then $\sup\{\beta^{t_{\min}(s,s')}[\![\varphi]\!](s')\}$. The sup as s' varies over a region is easily computable, as both $[\![\varphi]\!](s')$ and $t_{\min}(s, s')$ have uniform forms over regions. We can then take a max over the regions. Let $|G|$ be the size of the region graph, $|G(Q)|$ the number of regions. Then computation of φ over all regions takes time $O(|G(Q)| \cdot |C| \cdot |G|)$. The computation of the minimum time in Theorem 6 takes $O(|C| \cdot |G| \cdot m^{|C|})$, where m is the least common multiple of the denominators of the rational clock values. Thus, the value of the formula $\exists \Diamond \varphi$ can be computed in time $O(|C|^2 \cdot |G|^2 \cdot |G(Q)| \cdot m^{|C|})$, i.e., polynomial in the size of the region graph and in $m^{|C|}$.

We can also compute the maximum time that can elapse to go from a rational valued state to any (possibly irrational valued) state, but that does not help in the computation in the $\forall \Diamond \varphi$ case, as the actual path taken is important. We can do it for the first temporal operator since then φ is a boolean combination of propositions, and either 0 or 1 on regions. In the general case φ can have some real value in $[0, 1]$, and this boolean approach does not work. Incidentally, note that its not known whether the maximum time problem between two general states is decidable. The minimum time problem *is* decidable for general states via a complicated reduction to the additive theory of real numbers [8]. Whether these techniques may be used to get a model checking algorithm for DCTL is open.

5   Conclusion

Quantitative simulation and bisimulation functions precisely characterize the degree of closeness between timed systems, generalizing the (boolean) notions of timed simulation and bisimulation. For formal models of systems where the exact (infinite-precision) values of numerical quantities may not be known, such quantitative metrics provide a natural theory of refinement. Further, the metrics quantify the robust satisfaction of TCTL specifications: states close under the metric satisfy specifications with close timing requirements.

We also presented a quantitative theory for discounted CTL for timed systems. Discounted theories have been presented before for discrete systems [12, 10] which discount each individual transition by some discount factor. We discount *time* rather than individual *transitions*. Equal times are discounted by an equal amount irrespective of the number of transitions involved. We showed DCTL is robust: the values for a formula converge as the states converge in the bisimilarity metric. Finally, we showed a subset of DCTL to be computable over timed automata, and indicated why the continuous nature introduces difficulty over the discrete case. The general model checking problem for DCTL remains open.

References

1. R. Alur, C. Courcoubetis, and D.L. Dill. Model checking in dense real time. *Inf. and Comp.*, 104:2–34, 1993.
2. R. Alur and D.L. Dill. A theory of timed automata. *Theor. Comput. Sci.*, 126:183–235, 1994.
3. R. Alur, S. La Torre, and P. Madhusudan. Perturbed timed automata. In *HSCC 05*, LNCS 3414, pages 70–85. Springer, 2005.
4. P. Bouyer, E. Brinksma, and K.G. Larsen. Staying alive as cheaply as possible. In *HSCC 04*, LNCS 2993, pages 203–218. Springer, 2004.
5. P. Caspi and A. Benveniste. Toward an approximation theory for computerised control. In *EMSOFT 02*, LNCS 2491, pages 294–304. Springer, 2002.
6. K. Cerans. Decidability of bisimulation equivalences for parallel timer processes. In *CAV 92*, LNCS 663, pages 302–315. Springer, 1992.
7. E.M. Clarke, E.A. Emerson, and A.P. Sistla. Automatic verification of finite-state concurrent systems using temporal logic specifications. *ACM Trans. Program. Lang. Syst.*, 8:244–263, 1986.
8. H. Comon and Y. Jurski. Timed automata and the theory of real numbers. In *CONCUR 99*, LNCS 1664, pages 242–257. Springer, 1999.
9. C. Courcoubetis and M. Yannakakis. Minimum and maximum delay problems in real-time systems. *Formal Methods in System Design*, 1:385–415, 1992.
10. L. de Alfaro, M. Faella, T.A. Henzinger, R. Majumdar, and M. Stoelinga. Model checking discounted temporal properties. In *TACAS 04*, LNCS 2988, pages 77–92. Springer, 2004.
11. L. de Alfaro, M. Faella, and M. Stoelinga. Linear and branching metrics for quantitative transition systems. In *ICALP 04*, LNCS 3142, pages 97–109, 2004.
12. L. de Alfaro, T.A. Henzinger, and R. Majumdar. Discounting the future in systems theory. In *ICALP 03*, LNCS 2719, pages 1022–1037. Springer, 2003.
13. M. De Wulf, L. Doyen, N. Markey, and J.-F. Raskin. Robustness and implementability of timed automata. In *FORMATS 04*, LNCS 3253, pages 118–133. Springer, 2004.
14. J. Desharnais, V. Gupta, R. Jagadeesan, and P. Panangaden. Metrics for labeled Markov processes. *Theor. Comput. Sci.*, 318:323–354, 2004.

15. M. Fränzle. Analysis of hybrid systems: An ounce of realism can save an infinity of states. In *CSL 99*, LNCS 1683, pages 126–140. Springer, 1999.
16. V. Gupta, T.A. Henzinger, and R. Jagadeesan. Robust timed automata. In *HART 97*, LNCS 1201, pages 331–345. Springer, 1997.
17. V. Gupta, R. Jagadeesan, and P. Panangaden. Approximate reasoning for real-time probabilistic processes. In *QEST 04*, pages 304–313. IEEE, 2004.
18. T.A. Henzinger and J.-F. Raskin. Robust undecidability of timed and hybrid systems. In *HSCC 00*, LNCS 1790, pages 145–159. Springer, 2000.
19. J. Huang, J. Voeten, and M. Geilen. Real-time property preservation in approximations of timed systems. In *MEMOCODE 03*, pages 163–171. IEEE, 2003.
20. J. Huang, J. Voeten, and M. Geilen. Real-time property preservation in concurrent real-time systems. In *RTCSA 04*. Springer, 2004.
21. A. Puri. Dynamical properties of timed automata. In *FTRTFT 98*, LNCS 1486, pages 210–227. Springer, 1998.
22. S. Tasiran. *Compositional and Hierarchical Techniques for the Formal Verification of Real-Time Systems*. Dissertation, UC Berkeley, 1998.
23. M. De Wulf, L. Doyen, and J.-F. Raskin. Almost ASAP semantics: From timed models to timed implementations. In *HSCC 04*, LNCS 2993, pages 296–310. Springer, 2004.

Performance of Pipelined Asynchronous Systems

Flavio Corradini[1] and Walter Vogler[2]

[1] Dipartimento di Matematica e Informatica, Università di Camerino,
I–62032 Camerino (MC) - Italy
`flavio.corradini@unicam.it`
[2] Institut für Informatik, Universität Augsburg,
D–86135 Augsburg, Germany
`vogler@informatik.uni-augsburg.de`

Abstract. A testing-based faster-than relation has previously been developed that compares the worst-case efficiency of asynchronous systems. This approach reveals that pipelining does not improve efficiency in general; that it does so in practice depends on assumptions about the user behaviour. Accordingly, the approach was adapted to a setting where user behaviour is known to belong to a specific, but often occurring class of request-response behaviours; some quantitative results on the efficiency of the respective so-called response processes were given. In particular, it was shown that in the adapted setting a very simple case of pipelined process with two stages is faster than a comparable atomic processing. In this paper, we determine the performance of general pipelines, study whether the adapted faster-than relation is compatible with chaining (used to build pipelines) and two other operators, and give results on the performance of the resp. compositions, demonstrating also how rich the request-respond setting is.

1 Introduction

PAFAS (Process Algebra for Faster Asynchronous Systems) has been proposed as a useful tool for comparing the worst-case efficiency of asynchronous systems [3]. It is a CCS-like process description language [10] where a basic action is atomic and instantaneous but has an associated time bound specifying the maximal delay for its execution. (Time is discrete and, for simplicity, these bounds are always 1 or 0.) As discussed in [3], these upper time bounds give information on the efficiency of processes, but in contrast to most timed process algebras, time does not influence the functionality (i.e. which actions are performed); so like CCS, PAFAS treats the full functionality of asynchronous systems. Processes are compared via a variant of the testing approach [4] where processes are embedded into a test environment, which can be seen as a user of the process. A quantitative formulation of satisfying a test is given in [2]: the performance of a process is the function assigning to each test the maximal time it might take to satisfy the test or user; one process is faster than another, if it never has a larger performance value. These ideas were originally successfully studied in the Petri net formalism [12, 6]. We refer the reader to [3] for more details and results on PAFAS.

P. Pettersson and W. Yi (Eds.): FORMATS 2005, LNCS 3829, pp. 242–257, 2005.

Consider a task that can be performed in two stages. In a sequential architecture, the process performs both stages for such a task and only then starts with the next task. In PAFAS, we can model this process as 2-Seq $\equiv \mu x.\underline{in}.\tau.out.x$, where in is the input of data or some other request (the underbar indicating time bound 0), τ is an internal activity corresponding to the first stage, and the second stage is integrated into out, which outputs the result or gives a response to the request and takes time up to 1 as the first stage. Alternatively, one could use a pipelined architecture, where a second task can be accepted already when the first stage is over for the first task. This process is 2-Pipe $\equiv ((\mu x.\underline{in}.s.x)\|_{\{s\}}(\mu x.\underline{s}.out.x))/s$, where the first processing stage is integrated into the shift-action s in the first component.

Even though these are asynchronous systems, where the times needed by actions are not exactly known, one would expect that 2-Pipe is faster than 2-Seq since it allows more parallelism. But it turns out that 2-Pipe is not faster for the following reason: in the PAFAS-approach, if one system is faster than another, it also functionally refines this other system as in ordinary testing; in particular, it cannot perform new action sequences – but 2-Pipe can perform the sequence $in\ in$, which is not possible for 2-Seq.

Obviously, a theory for efficiency should be reconciled with the expectation that the general principle of pipelining improves efficiency in practice. The argument above reveals that the expectation of 2-Pipe being faster is based on some assumptions about the users, e.g. that their coordination will not be disturbed by the new action sequence $in\ in$. While a testing approach that considers all possible test environments usually leads to a precongruence, this cannot be expected in a test setting with a restricted class of users (or test environments), and it is not immediately clear what sort of results one can achieve.

In [2], we have adapted the timed testing scenario by considering only users U_n that want n tasks to be performed as fast as possible, i.e. possibly in parallel. While this is a severe restriction, the scenario is clearly of practical relevance: users that input a request and then just wait for a response are ubiquitous; one might think of queries to a database, messages being sent, or requiring access to a web page. That the requests are available in parallel corresponds to testing the respective system under heavy load. And from the theoretical perspective, the results and examples of [2] and of the present paper demonstrate that the scenario is still very rich, offering challenging problems. Given a process, its *response performance* (i.e. the adapted performance function) assigns to each U_n the time it takes in the worst case to satisfy U_n, i.e. it is essentially a function from natural numbers to natural numbers. For finite-state processes that are functionally correct in a sense to be defined (cf. Definition 9), we proved that the response performance is asymptotically linear, and showed how to determine its factor, which we called the *asymptotic performance*.

It then turned out that the asymptotic performance of 2-Pipe is indeed better than that of 2-Seq – justifying the expectation that pipelining increases efficiency. While we proved this explicitly, we just claimed that the response performance for 2-Pipe is $n + 1$, but refrained from giving the proof because already for this simple example the proof we had was pretty involved. In this paper, we determine the response performance for arbitrary pipelines, which might consist of an arbitrary number of stages and might have stages with arbitrary upper time bounds; in particular, 2-Pipe has two stages with each having upper bound 1, while 2-Seq consists of one stage with upper bound 2.

The proof is by induction on the number of stages; since the exact behaviour of the pipeline seems very difficult to describe due to asynchronicity, the essential idea is to approximate it. As an approximation from below, we give some behaviour that leads to the worst-case time of test-satisfaction. The difficult part is the approximation from above: we give a superset of the possible behaviour such that one can easily see the absence of behaviour with a worse time and such that the superset-property can be proven inductively.

Pipelines are built with the chaining operation, and our proof involves some compositional reasoning. In the present paper, chaining and two other composition operators are studied from the perspective of compositionality. The faster-than relations based on the response performance, the asymptotic performance resp., fail to be precongruences for these operators, which is not so surprising as already argued above. But we can show that the composition of correct processes is again a correct process, and we give estimates on its response performance.

Section 2 briefly recalls PAFAS and the timed testing scenario; see [3, 2] for more detailed explanations. The adapted testing scenario and the results from [2] are recalled in Sect. 3. Section 4 determines the response performance of general pipelines, and compatibility of our faster-than relations with the three composition operators is studied in Sect. 5. In Sect. 6, we give a conclusion and discuss related work. Due to lack of space, most proofs had to be omitted.

2   PAFAS

Largely repeating from [2], in this section we briefly introduce our CCS-like process description language PAFAS, its operational semantics and a testing-based preorder relating processes according to the worst-case efficiency. For an easier presentation, we will define the operational semantics of PAFAS using refusal sets. In [3], the operational semantics is defined in a way which is closer to intuition and independent of refusal sets, but more complicated.

$\mathbb{A}$ is an infinite set of actions $a, b, c, \ldots$ with the special action ω reserved for test processes to signal success; τ is an additional internal action. Actions in $\mathbb{A}_\tau = \mathbb{A} \cup \{\tau\}$ (ranged over by $\alpha, \beta, \ldots$) can let time 1 pass before their execution; i.e. 1 is their maximum delay after which they become *urgent* actions. $\underline{\mathbb{A}}_\tau = \{\underline{a} \mid a \in \mathbb{A}\} \cup \{\underline{\tau}\}$ denotes the set of urgent actions and is ranged over by $\underline{\alpha}, \underline{\beta}, \ldots$ (In most cases, longer delays can be specified by additional τ-prefixes.)

$\overline{X}$ is the set of process variables $x, y, z, \ldots$, used for recursive definitions. Take a function $\varPhi : \mathbb{A}_\tau \to \mathbb{A}_\tau$ such that the set $\{\alpha \in \mathbb{A}_\tau \mid \emptyset \neq \varPhi^{-1}(\alpha) \neq \{\alpha\}\}$ is finite, $\varPhi^{-1}(\omega) \subseteq \{\omega\}$ and $\varPhi(\tau) = \tau$; then $\varPhi$ is a *general relabelling function*. As shown in [3], general relabelling functions subsume the classically distinguished operations relabelling and hiding: P/A, where the actions in A are made internal, is the same as $P[\Phi_A]$, where the relabelling function Φ_A is defined by $\Phi_A(\alpha) = \tau$ if $\alpha \in A$ and $\Phi_A(\alpha) = \alpha$ if $\alpha \notin A$. A relabelling that maps $a_1, \ldots a_n$ to $b_1, \ldots, b_n$ and is the identity otherwise is written $b_1/a_1, \ldots, b_n/a_n$.

Definition 1. The set $\tilde{\mathbb{P}}$ of *(discretely timed) process terms* is the set of terms generated by the following grammar:

$$P ::= 0 \mid \alpha.P \mid \underline{\alpha}.P \mid P + P \mid P\|_A P \mid P[\Phi] \mid x \mid \mu x.P$$

where $x \in X$, $\alpha \in \mathbb{A}_\tau$, Φ a general relabelling function, $A \subseteq \mathbb{A}$ and recursion is time-guarded, i.e. variable x in $\mu x.P$ only appears within the scope of an $\alpha.()$-prefix with $\alpha \in \mathbb{A}_\tau$. $\mathbb{P}$ is the set of closed terms called *processes*. □

All operators are standard, e.g. P_1 and P_2 run in parallel in the parallel composition $P_1\|_A P_2$ having to synchronize on all actions from A, and $\alpha.P$ and $\underline{\alpha}.P$ is (action-)prefixing. Process $a.P$ performs a with a *maximal* delay of 1; hence, it can perform a immediately or it can idle for one time unit and become $\underline{a}.P$. As a stand-alone process, $\underline{a}.P$ must perform a immediately; but in a parallel context our processes are *patient*: as a component in $(\underline{a}.P)\|_{\{a\}}(a.Q)$, $\underline{a}.P$ has to wait for synchronization on a and this can take up to time 1, since component $a.Q$ may idle this long. That a process may perform a conditional time step, i.e. may take part in a time step in certain contexts, is the intuition behind refusal sets defined below. Now the purely functional behaviour of processes (i.e. which actions they can perform) is given by the following operational semantics.

Definition 2. The following SOS-rules define the transition relations $\xrightarrow{\alpha} \subseteq \tilde{\mathbb{P}} \times \tilde{\mathbb{P}}$ for $\alpha \in \mathbb{A}_\tau$, the *action transitions*. We write $P \xrightarrow{\alpha} P'$ if $(P,P') \in \xrightarrow{\alpha}$ and $P \xrightarrow{\alpha}$ if there exists a $P' \in \tilde{\mathbb{P}}$ such that $P \xrightarrow{\alpha} P'$, and similarly later on.

$$\text{Pref}_{a1} \quad \frac{}{\alpha.P \xrightarrow{\alpha} P} \qquad \text{Pref}_{a2} \quad \frac{}{\underline{\alpha}.P \xrightarrow{\alpha} P} \qquad \text{Rec}_a \quad \frac{P \xrightarrow{\alpha} P'}{\mu x.P \xrightarrow{\alpha} P'\{\mu x.P/x\}}$$

$$\text{Par}_{a1} \quad \frac{\alpha \notin A, \ P_1 \xrightarrow{\alpha} P_1'}{P_1\|_A P_2 \xrightarrow{\alpha} P_1'\|_A P_2} \qquad \text{Par}_{a2} \quad \frac{\alpha \in A, \ P_1 \xrightarrow{\alpha} P_1', \ P_2 \xrightarrow{\alpha} P_2'}{P_1\|_A P_2 \xrightarrow{\alpha} P_1'\|_A P_2'}$$

$$\text{Sum}_a \quad \frac{P_1 \xrightarrow{\alpha} P_1'}{P_1 + P_2 \xrightarrow{\alpha} P_1'} \qquad \text{Rel}_a \quad \frac{P \xrightarrow{\alpha} P'}{P[\Phi] \xrightarrow{\Phi(\alpha)} P'[\Phi]}$$

Additionally, there are symmetric rules for Par_{a1} and Sum_a for actions of P_2. An *activated action* of P is some $\alpha \in \mathbb{A}_\tau$ with $P \xrightarrow{\alpha}$. □

These rules are almost standard. Pref_{a1} and Pref_{a2} allow an activated action to occur (just as e.g. in CCS), and it makes *no* difference whether the action is urgent or not, i.e. Pref_{a1} allows to ignore the possible delay of α. Since passage of time will never deactivate actions or activate new ones, we capture all asynchronous behaviour that is possible in the standard CCS-like setting without time, and timing cannot be used to coordinate system behaviour.

We now give SOS-rules for so-called *refusal sets*. Performing such a set X is a conditional time step (of duration 1) and X consists of (some, but not necessarily all) actions which are *not* just waiting for synchronization; i.e. these actions are *not* urgent, the process does not have to perform them at this moment, and they can therefore be refused. If a process can perform a conditional time step, then it can take part in a 'real' time step in a suitable environment; the refusal set describes requirements for such an environment and the conditional time step also describes the effect on the process.

Definition 3. The following SOS-rules define $\xrightarrow{X}_r \subseteq \tilde{\mathbb{P}} \times \tilde{\mathbb{P}}$, where $X, X_i \subseteq \mathbb{A}$:

$$\text{Nil}_r \quad \frac{}{0 \xrightarrow{X}_r 0} \qquad \text{Pref}_{r1} \quad \frac{}{\alpha.P \xrightarrow{X}_r \underline{\alpha}.P} \qquad \text{Pref}_{r2} \quad \frac{\alpha \notin X \cup \{\tau\}}{\underline{\alpha}.P \xrightarrow{X}_r \underline{\alpha}.P}$$

$$\text{Par}_r \quad \frac{\forall_{i=1,2} \; P_i \xrightarrow{X_i}_r P_i', \; X \subseteq (A \cap \bigcup_{i=1,2} X_i) \cup ((\bigcap_{i=1,2} X_i) \setminus A)}{P_1 \|_A P_2 \xrightarrow{X}_r P_1' \|_A P_2'}$$

$$\text{Sum}_r \quad \frac{\forall_{i=1,2} \; P_i \xrightarrow{X}_r P_i'}{P_1 + P_2 \xrightarrow{X}_r P_1' + P_2'} \qquad \text{Rel}_r \quad \frac{P \xrightarrow{\Phi^{-1}(X \cup \{\tau\}) \setminus \{\tau\}}_r P'}{P[\Phi] \xrightarrow{X}_r P'[\Phi]}$$

$$\text{Rec}_r \quad \frac{P \xrightarrow{X}_r P'}{\mu x.P \xrightarrow{X}_r P'\{\mu x.P/x\}}$$

When $P \xrightarrow{X}_r P'$, we call this a (conditional) *time step* or, if $X = \mathbb{A}$, a *full time step*. In the latter case, we also write $P \xrightarrow{1} P'$. $\qquad \square$

For example, $\underline{a}.P$ ($a.Q$ resp.) can make a time step with refusal set $\mathbb{A} \setminus \{a\}$ (with refusal set $\mathbb{A}$ resp.) according to rule Pref_{r2} (Pref_{r1} resp.) and with rule Par_r we get $(\underline{a}.P) \|_{\{a\}} (a.Q) \xrightarrow{1} (\underline{a}.P) \|_{\{a\}} (\underline{a}.Q)$ as announced above.

The language of P is its behaviour as a stand-alone process; such a process never has to wait for a communication, hence all time steps in a run are full. As usual, we will abstract from internal behaviour; but note that internal actions gain some 'visibility' in timed behaviour, since their presence possibly allows more time to pass between the occurrence of visible actions.

Definition 4. For $P, P' \in \mathbb{P}$, we extend the transition relation $P \xrightarrow{\mu} P'$ for $\mu \in \mathbb{A}_\tau$ or $\mu = 1$ to sequences w as usual and write $P \xrightarrow{w} P'$; w is a *discrete τ-trace* of P.

For a sequence $w \in (\mathbb{A}_\tau \cup \mathfrak{P}(\mathbb{A}))^*$, let w/τ be the sequence w with all τ's removed and w/σ be the sequence w with all time steps removed. The *duration* $\zeta(w)$ of w is the number of time steps in w; note that $\zeta(w/\tau) = \zeta(w)$. We write $P \xrightarrow{v} P'$, if $P \xrightarrow{w} P'$ for some $w \in (\mathbb{A}_\tau \cup \{\mathbb{A}\})^*$ and $v = w/\tau$.

The *timed transition system* $\mathsf{TTS}(P)$ of P consists of all transitions $Q \xrightarrow{\mu} Q'$ with $\mu \in \mathbb{A}_\tau$ or $\mu = 1$ where Q is reachable from P via such transitions. The language of $\mathsf{TTS}(P)$ is $\mathsf{DL}(P) = \{w \mid P \xrightarrow{w}\}$, the *(discretely timed) language* of P, containing the *(discrete) traces* of P.

Similarly, $P \xrightarrow{\mu}_r P'$ if either $\mu = \alpha \in \mathbb{A}_\tau$ and $P \xrightarrow{\alpha} P'$, or $\mu = X \subseteq \mathbb{A}$ and $P \xrightarrow{X}_r P'$. For sequences w, we define $P \xrightarrow{w}_r P'$ (where w is a *refusal τ-trace*) and $P \xRightarrow{w}_r P'$ as above. $\mathsf{RT}(P) = \{w \mid P \xRightarrow{w}_r\}$ is the set of *refusal traces* of P.

The *refusal transition system* $\mathsf{RTS}(P)$ of P consists of all transitions $Q \xrightarrow{\mu}_r Q'$ with $\mu \in \mathbb{A}_\tau$ or $\mu \subseteq \mathbb{A}$ where Q is reachable from P via such transitions. If $\mathsf{RTS}(P)$ contains only finitely many processes, we call P *finite state*. □

Note that $\mathsf{RTS}(P \|_A Q)$ can be determined from $\mathsf{RTS}(P)$ and $\mathsf{RTS}(Q)$ according to the SOS-rules for parallel composition given above. $\mathsf{TTS}(P)$ can be obtained from $\mathsf{RTS}(P)$ by deleting time steps that are not full and processes that then are not reachable anymore. We now define the operation of chaining (called linking in [10]), which is central for this paper, and general pipelines.

Definition 5. Let P and Q be two process terms that have only the observable actions *in* and *out* in their language. Then the *chaining* of P and Q is $P \frown Q = (P[s/out] \|_{\{s\}} Q[s/in])/s$. For $l \geq 1$, we define an *in-out-sequence of length l* as $l\text{-}\mathsf{Seq} \equiv \mu x.\underline{in}.\tau^{l-1}.out.x$, where τ^{l-1} is a sequence of $l-1$ τ-prefixes. A *pipeline* is the chaining of a positive number of in-out-sequences. □

In $P \frown Q$, a request is first processed by P and then fed into Q for processing. For any sensible behaviour notion (and in particular for those treated in this paper), parallel composition with a fixed synchronization set is associative, and so is chaining; hence, pipelines do not need any bracketing. $l\text{-}\mathsf{Seq}$ generalizes $2\text{-}\mathsf{Seq}$ from the introduction, and $2\text{-}\mathsf{Pipe}$ is essentially the pipeline $1\text{-}\mathsf{Seq} \frown 1\text{-}\mathsf{Seq}$.

Proposition 6. *Let $P, Q \in \mathbb{P}$ be processes and $X, X' \subseteq \mathbb{A}$ with $P \xrightarrow{X}_r Q$. If $X' \subseteq X$, then $P \xrightarrow{X'}_r Q$. If X' does not contain an activated action of P, then $P \xrightarrow{X \cup X'}_r Q$.*

Let v be obtained from a sequence w of actions and time steps by deleting some time steps; then $P \xrightarrow{w}_r$ implies $P \xrightarrow{v}_r$.

Hence, the set of possible refusal sets for a process is downward closed w.r.t. set inclusion, and non-activated actions can always be refused. Thus, only the refusal of activated actions is relevant to determine the time steps of a process. behaviour including some time steps can just as well occur without these, corresponding to our idea of asynchronous behaviour with upper time bounds.

Definition 7. A process $P \in \mathbb{P}$ is *testable* if ω does not occur in P. Any process $O \in \mathbb{P}$ may serve as a *test process (observer)*. We write $\|$ for $\|_{\mathbb{A} \setminus \{\omega\}}$.

For O and a testable process $P \in \mathbb{P}$, we define the *performance function* p by

$$p(P, O) = \sup\{n \in \mathbb{N}_0 \mid \exists v \in \mathsf{DL}(P \| O) : \zeta(v) = n \text{ and } v \text{ does not contain } \omega\}.$$

If the set on the right-hand-side has no maximum, the supremum is ∞. The *performance function p_P of P* is defined by $p_P(O) = p(P, O)$.

For testable processes, P is a *faster implementation* of Q or *faster than Q*, $P \sqsupseteq Q$, if for all test processes O we have $p(P, O) \leq p(Q, O)$, i.e. $p_P \leq p_Q$. □

By definition, $P \sqsupseteq Q$ means that P is functionally a refinement of Q, since it is satisfactory for at least as many test processes as Q, and that additionally it is an improvement timewise. The following result states that timed tests can see refusal traces, which give quite a detailed account of the timed behaviour of processes; this is quite surprising, since we are in an asynchronous setting, where tests should have little temporal control over the tested systems.

Theorem 8. *For testable processes, $P \sqsupseteq Q$ if and only if $\mathsf{RT}(P) \subseteq \mathsf{RT}(Q)$.*

If P is not faster than Q, i.e. $P \not\sqsupseteq Q$, then there is a refusal trace of P that is not one of Q. If P and Q are finite-state, inclusion of refusal traces can be checked automatically; a corresponding tool, FastAsy, has been developed for a Petri net setting [1]; FastAsy has been redesigned recently, and adaptation to PAFAS is in progress.

3   Response Performance and Previous Results

3.1   Response Performance

Pipelining helps to improve efficiency only for restricted users; accordingly, the users considered in [2] issue requests with action *in* and expect responses via action *out*. In practice, these actions usually transfer data, but we abstract from these data; see [2]. We assume further that the only users of interest have a number of requests that they want to be answered as fast as possible, i.e. possibly in parallel; thus, we consider the users U_n defined by $U_1 \equiv \underline{in}.\underline{out}.\underline{\omega}.0$ and $U_{n+1} \equiv U_n \|_\omega \underline{in}.\underline{out}.\underline{\omega}.0$. Comparing processes w.r.t. these users means to compare their performance under heavy load.

The size of U_n is its number n of requests, and accordingly we define the *response performance* rp_P of a testable process P as the function from $\mathbb{N}$ to $\mathbb{N}_0 \cup \{\infty\}$ with $rp_P(n) = p_P(U_n)$. The aim of [2] was to evaluate the response performance of a process from its refusal transition system. This system is an arc-labelled graph, an arc (or directed edge) being a transition; as usual, a *path* is a sequence of transitions, each ending in a process from which the next transition starts, it is *closed* if the last and first process coincide. If apart from the latter coincidence all processes on a closed path are different, it is a *cycle*. Note that a finite transition system can only have finitely many different cycles.

3.2   Response Processes

The results on response performance only hold for processes that can reasonably serve the users U_n, and we define these processes in two stages.

Definition 9. For sequence w and action α, $\#(\alpha, w)$ denotes the number of occurrences of α in w, and similarly for a refusal set X in place of α. The *o-number* of a process Q is the number of pending *out* actions, i.e. it is $\sup\{\#(out, w) \mid Q \xrightarrow{w}_r$ and w does not contain *in*$\}$; due to Prop. 6, we can as well consider w without time steps only.

A testable process is a *response process* if it can only perform *in* and *out* as visible actions and is functionally correct in the following sense: if $P \xrightarrow{w}_r Q$, then $\#(in, w) - \#(out, w)$ is non-negative and the *o*-number of Q.   □

Thus, a response process P never performs too many *out* actions and is always able to perform the required number of these. Still, it might fail to do so in a bounded time; but then, the response performance would be ∞ for some n, meaning that some user will not be satisfied within any time bound, which is certainly an incorrect behaviour of the process.

Definition 10. A response process is *correct* if its response performance is finite for all n.   □

For a response process P, whenever a time step is performed in $\mathsf{RTS}(P)$ we can add to or remove from the refusal set arbitrary actions in $\mathbb{A} \setminus \{in, out\}$ by Prop. 6. Therefore, there are only four significant refusal sets, which for notational convenience we write as $\mathbb{A}$, $\{out\}$, $\{in\}$ and $\emptyset$. When we speak of $\mathsf{RTS}(P)$ in the following, we are referring to this slightly reduced version, which we will reduce even further below. Consequently, if P is *finite state*, $\mathsf{RTS}(P)$ also has finitely many transitions and is a *finite transition system*.

Theorem 11. *[2] Let $P \in \mathbb{P}$ be a testable process, Q reachable from P with o-number o and $Q \xrightarrow{\mu}_r Q'$.*

1. *Let P be a response process. Then o is finite. Furthermore, if μ is in, out resp., then the o-number of Q' is $o+1$, $o-1$ resp.; for all other cases of μ, it is o. The numbers of in's and of out's on a closed path in $\mathsf{RTS}(P)$ are equal.*
2. *If P is finite state, then it is decidable in time linear in the size of $\mathsf{RTS}(P)$ whether P is a response process.*

3.3   Results on the Response Performance

To find out about the response performance of a response process P, one considers specific paths in a reduced version of $\mathsf{RTS}(P)$.

Definition 12. The *reduced refusal transition system* $\mathsf{rRTS}(P)$ of a response process P is obtained from $\mathsf{RTS}(P)$ by deleting all time steps $Q \xrightarrow{X}_r Q'$ unless either the refusal set X is $\mathbb{A}$ or $\neg Q \xrightarrow{\mathbb{A}}_r Q'$, X is $\{out\}$ and the o-number of Q is positive; then, we delete all processes not reachable anymore.

We call a path in $\mathsf{rRTS}(P)$ *n-critical*, if it contains at most n in's and at most $n - 1$ out's and all time steps before the nth in are full.   □

Theorem 13. *[2] The response performance $rp_P(n)$ of a response process P is the supremum of the numbers of time steps taken over all n-critical paths.*

We call a function f from $\mathbb{N}$ to $\mathbb{N}_0$ *asymptotically linear*, if there are constants $a, c \in \mathbb{R}$ such that $an - c \leq f(n) \leq an + c$ for all $n \in \mathbb{N}$; we call a the *asymptotic factor* of such a function. Observe that the asymptotic factor of an asymptotically linear function can be determined whenever we know the function values for infinitely many parameter values. Other main results of [2] are that the response performance of a finite-state response process P is asymptotically linear, and that its asymptotic factor, which we call the *asymptotic performance* of P, can be determined efficiently.

Definition 14. A cycle in $\mathsf{rRTS}(P)$ for a response process P is *catastrophic*, if it contains a positive number of time steps but no *in*'s (and hence no *out*'s by 11.1). For P without catastrophic cycles, we consider cycles which can be reached from P by a path where all time steps are full and which themselves contain only time steps that are full; the *average performance* of such a cycle is the number of its full time steps divided by the number of its *in*'s, and the cycle is *bad*, if it has maximal average performance in $\mathsf{rRTS}(P)$. The *average performance* of a closed path with analogous properties is defined analogously.   □

Theorem 15. *[2] A finite-state response process P has a catastrophic cycle if and only if its response performance is ∞ for some n, i.e. if and only if it is not correct. If P is correct, the response performance is asymptotically linear, and the asymptotic performance of P is the average performance of a bad cycle.*

Our approach gives rise to two faster-than relations for correct response processes, the first being finer than the second.

Definition 16. For correct response processes P and Q, we say that P is *rp-faster than Q*, $P \sqsupseteq_{rp} Q$, if $rp(P) \leq rp(Q)$, and that P is *asp-faster than Q*, $P \sqsupseteq_{asp} Q$, if the asymptotic performance of P is at most that of Q.   □

4   Performance of Pipelines

First, we reformulate the definition of response performance; let $IN_n = \|_{\emptyset}^n \, \underline{in}$ be the parallel composition of n processes $\underline{in}.0$, and $OUT_n = \|_{\omega}^n \, \underline{out}.\underline{\omega}$ be the parallel composition (with synchronization over ω) of n processes $\underline{out}.\underline{\omega}.0$.

Proposition 17. *Let P and Q be correct response processes.*

1. $rp_P(n) = \sup\{m \in \mathbb{N}_0 \mid \exists v \in \mathsf{DL}((IN_n \, \|_{in} \, P) \, \|_{out} \, OUT_n) :$
     $\zeta(v) = m$ *and v does not contain ω*$\}$
2. $rp_P(n) = \sup\{m \in \mathbb{N}_0 \mid \exists v \in \mathsf{DL}((IN_n \, \|_{in} \, P)/in) :$
     $\zeta(v) = m$ *and v does contain at most $n - 1$ out*$\}$
3. $RT((IN_n \, \|_{in} \, (P \frown Q))/in) = RT((IN_n \, \|_{in} \, P)/in \frown Q)$

Interestingly, in Item 1 the user is separated into one part generating the requests and another part accepting the responses. This corresponds to an application, where P is a communication protocol. Compared to Thm. 13, Item 2 only considers very simple traces: the refusal traces of the process in Item 2 only have the action *out* and the refusal sets $\mathbb{A}$ (corresponding to $\{out\}$) and $\emptyset$. This simplicity will allow us to deal with the relevant behaviour of pipelines.

Item 3 will allow us to relate the behaviour of a pipeline to that of a shorter pipeline – essential for the inductive proof. We will show in Sect. 5, that the chaining of two correct response processes is again correct. This also implies that all pipelines are correct, since clearly all in-out-sequences are.

For the rest of this section, let $Pipe \equiv l_1\text{-Seq} ^\frown \ldots ^\frown l_k\text{-Seq}$ and $n \in \mathbb{N}$ be fixed; let $sum = \Sigma_{i=1}^k l_i$ and $mx = \max\{l_1, \ldots, l_k\}$. Our aim is to prove that $rp_{Pipe}(n) = sum + mx(n-1)$. For $k = 1$, this should be clear: $Pipe$ can always perform $l_1 = sum$ full time steps between an in and an out.

For the relevant case $k > 1$, we put $Pipe' \equiv l_1\text{-Seq} ^\frown \ldots ^\frown l_{k-1}\text{-Seq}$, and let sum' and mx' be defined analogously. Furthermore, we let $P \equiv (IN_n \|_{in} Pipe)/in$ and $P' \equiv (IN_n \|_{in} Pipe')/in$. Since out is the only visible action P and P' can ever perform, $\{out\}$ is equivalent to $\mathbb{A}$ in their refusal traces according to Prop. 6.

Lemma 18. $rp_{Pipe}(n) \geq sum + mx(n-1)$

Proof. In the proof, we repeatedly use

$$(a) \quad (\{out\}^* \; in \; \mathbb{A}^{l_k} \; \{in\}^* \; out)^n \; \{out\}^* \subseteq \mathsf{RT}(l_k\text{-Seq})$$

Observe that refusal sets can be deleted from such a refusal trace to give another refusal trace; in particular, we will sometimes delete some parts $\mathbb{A}^{l_k}$ below. Using Prop. 17.2, it suffices to show that

$$(b) \quad \{out\}^{sum} \; out \; (\{out\}^{mx} \; out)^{n-1}\{out\}^* \subseteq \mathsf{RT}(P)$$

This is the behaviour where only $Pipe$ delays the outputs; but if $Pipe$ is chained with an $l\text{-Seq}$ where $l > mx$, then the new component might block the output from $Pipe$; so for the inductive proof, we will also prove that

$$(c) \quad \{out\}^{sum} \; out \; (\emptyset^* \; out)^{n-1}\{out\}^* \subseteq \mathsf{RT}(P)$$

For the induction base $k = 1$, one can see from (a) that (b) and (c) hold: first, IN_n and $l_k\text{-Seq}$ communicate, and $\mathbb{A}^{l_k}$ from $l_k\text{-Seq}$ gives rise to $\{out\}^{sum}$ by $sum = l_k$, which is followed by out. Then either this is repeated and we obtain (b) by $mx = l_k$, or we obtain (c) by skipping $\mathbb{A}^{l_k}$ (see the remark above) since $\{in\}^*$ gives rise to $\emptyset^*$.

Now we assume, by induction, (b) and (c) to hold for P'. According to Prop. 17.3, we will show (b) and (c) with $\mathsf{RT}(P)$ replaced by $\mathsf{RT}(P' ^\frown l_k\text{-Seq})$. Observe that each refusal trace w in the latter set can be obtained from some $w' \in \mathsf{RT}(P')$ and $v \in \mathsf{RT}(l_k\text{-Seq})$ by merging an out in w' with an in in v into a τ (which we will write as τ_{io} although it really is not visible in w), by taking over each out in v, and by synchronizing refusal sets X and Y with $out \in X \vee in \in Y$ to give the set $\{out\}$ if $out \in Y$ or $\emptyset$ otherwise.

First consider $l_k \leq mx' = mx$. Combining refusal traces from (b) for P' and (a) according to the rules just described, we find that $\mathsf{RT}(P' ^\frown l_k\text{-Seq})$ contains

$$\{out\}^{sum'} \; \tau_{io} \; \{out\}^{l_k} \; out \; (\{out\}^{mx'-l_k} \; \tau_{io} \; \{out\}^{l_k} \; out)^{n-1}\{out\}^*.$$

Since $sum = sum' + l_k$ and $mx = mx' = mx' - l_k + l_k$, we have (b). Similarly, we get (c) from (c) for P' and (a), since (obtaining $\emptyset^*$ from $\emptyset^*$ and $\{in\}^*$ according to the remark made after (a)) $\mathsf{RT}(P' \frown l_k\text{-Seq})$ contains

$$\{out\}^{sum'}\ \tau_{io}\ \{out\}^{l_k}\ out\ (\tau_{io}\ \emptyset^*\ out)^{n-1}\{out\}^*.$$

Now consider the case $mx' \leq l_k = mx$. Combining refusal traces from (c) for P' and (a) according to the rules above, we find that $\mathsf{RT}(P' \frown l_k\text{-Seq})$ contains

$$\{out\}^{sum'}\ \tau_{io}\ \{out\}^{l_k}\ out\ (\tau_{io}\ \{out\}^{l_k}\ out)^{n-1}\{out\}^*.$$

Since $sum = sum' + l_k$ and $mx = l_k$, we have (b). Similarly, we get (c) from (c) for P' and (a) (recalling again the remark above), since $\mathsf{RT}(P' \frown l_k\text{-Seq})$ also in this case contains

$$\{out\}^{sum'}\ \tau_{io}\ \{out\}^{l_k}\ out\ (\tau_{io}\ \emptyset^*\ out)^{n-1}\{out\}^*. \qquad \square$$

Thus, we have shown as an approximation to $\mathsf{RT}(P)$ from below that there really is some behaviour where the user under consideration has to wait for $sum + mx(n-1)$ time steps. Now we have to prove an approximation from above in order to show that the waiting time cannot be worse. We will show by induction on k that each $w \in \mathsf{RT}(P)$ has the form

$$(*) \qquad \{out\}^{s_1}\ \emptyset^{t_1}\ out\ \ldots\ \{out\}^{s_n}\ \emptyset^{t_n}\ out\ \{out\}^{s}$$

(or can be obtained from such a sequence by replacing some sets $\{out\}$ by $\emptyset$ and taking prefixes) where $\forall\ j = 1, \ldots, n$ we have:

$$(\alpha)\ \ (\Sigma_{i=1}^{j-1}\ s_i + t_i) + s_j \leq sum + mx(j-1)$$

$$\text{or} \qquad (\beta)\ \ \exists\ j' > 1:\ j' \leq j\ \wedge\ (\Sigma_{i=j'}^{j-1}\ s_i + t_i) + s_j \leq mx(j - j' + 1)$$

Then we are done: if $w \in \mathsf{DL}(P) \subseteq \mathsf{RT}(P)$ has at most $n-1$ out, then it has the form $\{out\}^{s_1}\ out\ \ldots\ \{out\}^{s_{n-1}}\ out\ \{out\}^{s_n}$ or is a prefix of such a form, i.e. all the t_i according to $(*)$ are 0. By well-founded induction for $j = 1, \ldots, n$ we assume that for all $j' < j$ we already know that $\Sigma_{i=1}^{j'}\ s_i \leq sum + mx(j' - 1)$. If (α) applies for j, we also have this formula for j. Otherwise, (β) applies and for the respective j' we have $\Sigma_{i=1}^{j'-1}\ s_i \leq sum + mx(j' - 2)$ by induction as well as $\Sigma_{i=j'}^{j}\ s_i \leq mx(j - j' + 1)$; together these again show that $\Sigma_{i=1}^{j}\ s_i \leq sum + mx(j-1)$. Finally, we see that w takes at most $sum + mx(n-1)$ time.

For the induction base $k = 1$, a refusal trace w of P is a combination of a refusal trace from IN_n and some $v \in \mathsf{RT}(l_k\text{-Seq})$, which obviously has the form

$$(**) \qquad (\{out\}^*\ in\ \mathbb{A}^{\leq l_k}\ \{in\}^*\ out)^*$$

(or can be obtained from such a sequence by replacing some refusal sets by smaller sets and taking prefixes) where $\mathbb{A}^{\leq l_k}$ is a sequence of at most l_k $\mathbb{A}$. Since neither component can refuse in initially, we first have an internalized communication. Then, the at most l_k $\mathbb{A}$ from $l_k\text{-Seq}$ give rise to $s_1 \leq sum$ $\{out\}$ (thus (α) is satisfied for $j = 1$); t_1 $\{in\}$ from $l_k\text{-Seq}$ give rise to t_1 $\emptyset$. After out, this behaviour is repeated, where we get (β) for $j > 1$ choosing $j' = j$, since $s_j \leq l_k = mx$. Omitting the induction step, we concluded with Lemma 18:

Theorem 19. *For $Pipe \equiv l_1\text{-Seq} \frown \ldots \frown l_k\text{-Seq}$, $rp_{Pipe}(n) = sum + mx(n-1)$.*

In particular, this theorem reconfirms the claim from [2] that $rp_{2\text{-Pipe}}(n) = n + 1$, $rp_{2\text{-Seq}}(n) = 2n$ and hence 2-Pipe $\sqsubseteq_{rp}$ 2-Seq. Very generally, we have $rp_{l\text{-Seq}}(n) = ln$; breaking such a sequence up into a pipeline with more than one component and overall length l, gives always a faster response process, since it will have $sum = l$ and $mx < l$. Another aspect is that a chain k-Pipe of k components equal to 1-Seq (with time bound k for one request) has $rp_{k\text{-Pipe}}(n) = n + k - 1$, hence it is asymptotically faster than the in-out-sequence 2-Seq (with time bound just 2 for one request) even for large k, i.e. k-Pipe $\sqsubseteq_{asp}$ 2-Seq.

5   Compatibility with Parallel Composition

In our setting with very restricted test environments, we cannot expect to get a precongruence for parallel composition, but we will study in detail how our approach is compatible with parallel composition. Our parallel composition is indexed with a set of actions to be synchronized, and the only actions we are interested in are *in* and *out*. Synchronizing response processes on *in* only would give a process that answers each *in* by two *out*, which is not desirable here. Hence, the operations of interest are $\| = \|_A$ and $\|_\emptyset$, and we will also study $\frown$.

Theorem 20. *If P_1 and P_2 are correct response processes, then so is $P_1 \frown P_2$, and $\max(rp_{P_1}(n), rp_{P_2}(n)) \le rp_{P_1 \frown P_2}(n) \le rp_{P_1}(n) + rp_{P_2}(n)$ for all $n \in \mathbb{N}$.*

From the previous section, we know that e.g. $rp_{l\text{-Seq}}(n) = ln$, $rp_{k\text{-Seq}}(n) = kn$ and $rp_{l\text{-Seq} \frown k\text{-Seq}}(n) = \max(k,l)n + \min(k,l)$; here, at least the asymptotic performance of l-Seq $\frown$ k-Seq is the maximum of those of l-Seq and k-Seq.

On the other hand, consider $P_k \equiv \mu x.(in.out)^{k-1}.in.\tau^{k-1}.out.x$. Since every kth response requires time up to k, while the others do not require any time, we have $rp_{P_k}(n) = \lfloor \frac{n}{k} \rfloor k$, and hence $P_k \sqsupseteq_{rp}$ 1-Seq and $P_k \sqsupseteq_{asp}$ 1-Seq.

Now we compare the response performance of 1-Seq $\frown$ P_k and 1-Seq $\frown$ 1-Seq for multiples of k; we have $rp_{1\text{-Seq} \frown P_k}(kn) = (2k - 1)n + 1$: the first $k - 1$ responses may take time 1 each due to 1-Seq, the kth response may take time $k + 1$ due to both components; then this is repeated, except that after the kth response 1-Seq has already processed the next request, such that now every k responses may take time up to $2k - 1$. Thus, the asymptotic performance of 1-Seq $\frown$ P_k is $2 - \frac{1}{k}$; this is almost the sum of the asymptotic performances of its components. Furthermore, the asymptotic performance of 1-Seq $\frown$ 1-Seq is 1, hence neither 1-Seq $\frown$ P_k $\sqsupseteq_{asp}$ 1-Seq $\frown$ 1-Seq nor 1-Seq $\frown$ P_k $\sqsupseteq_{rp}$ 1-Seq $\frown$ 1-Seq. Almost the same results hold for $P_k \frown$ 1-Seq, hence both our preorders fail to be precongruences for $\frown$. On the positive side observe that, due to Thm. 19, they are precongruences if we only consider pipelines.

Theorem 21. *If P and Q are correct response processes, then so is $P \| Q$.*

E.g. for k-Seq and l-Seq, the response performance is simply the maximum of the component response performances, i.e. $rp_{k\text{-Seq} \| l\text{-Seq}}(n) = \max(k,l)n$.

In contrast to our results on chaining above and on $\|_\emptyset$ below, the proof for the above theorem does not allow to compute an upper bound on the asymptotic performance of $P\|Q$ from the asymptotic performances of P and Q. The following example demonstrates that it is in fact impossible to determine such a bound. For each $k > 1$, we will present two processes k-Bundle and P_k, which have asymptotic performance 1 (and even the same response performance) such that k-Bundle $\|$ 1-Seq has asymptotic performance k while $P_k \|$ 1-Seq has asymptotic performance < 2. (Thus $\sqsupseteq_{rp}$ and $\sqsupseteq_{asp}$ are not precongruences for $\|$.)

We define k-Bundle $\equiv (k\text{-sSeq} \|_s \ldots \|_s k\text{-sSeq})/s$ with k components k-sSeq which are in turn defined as $k\text{-sSeq} \equiv \mu x.\underline{in}.\tau^{k-1}.out.\underline{s}.x$. This process repeatedly gives a group of k responses within time k, so $rp_{k\text{-Bundle}}(n) = \lceil \frac{n}{k} \rceil k$. This is also the response performance of $P_k \equiv \mu x.\underline{in}.\tau^{k-1}.out.(\underline{in}.\underline{out})^{k-1}.x$.

For k-Bundle $\|$ 1-Seq the response performance of n is kn: because of 1-Seq, in and out have to alternate, because of k-Bundle each out takes up to time k. For $P_k \|$ 1-Seq the response performance of n is $n + \lceil \frac{n}{k} \rceil (k-1)$: because of 1-Seq, each out may take at least time 1, because of P_k the first and then each kth out may take up to time k, i.e. additional $k - 1$ time steps. The announced result follows, since $n + \lceil \frac{n}{k} \rceil(k-1) \le n + (\frac{n}{k} + 1)(k-1) = (2 - \frac{1}{k})n + k - 1$.

Intuitively, one might assume that $\|$ slows responses down (as in the above examples) because the components must synchronize on each response. So it might be quite surprising that the response performance of $P\|Q$ can be better than the response performances of both P and Q. To see this, consider for an arbitrary $k \ge 3$ the processes $P \equiv \mu x.\underline{in}.(in.\ \tau^{k-1}.out.\underline{out}.in.out.x + out.\underline{in}.out.x)$ and $Q \equiv \mu x.\underline{in}.out.\underline{in}.(in.\tau^{k-1}.out.\underline{out}.x + out.x)$.

To simplify the argument, we only deal with the asymptotic performance. We have $rp_P(3n) = rp_Q(3n) \ge (k+1)n$ since, using the first summand, dealing with 3 requests can take up to time $k + 1$. Thus, the asymptotic performance of P and Q is at least $\frac{k+1}{3} > 1$. In $P\|Q$, neither of the first summands can be used, so each request is answered within time 1, i.e. $rp_{P\|Q}(n) = n$ and the asymptotic performance is 1.

We close with results about the third reasonable composition operator $\|_\emptyset$.

Theorem 22. *If P and Q are correct response processes, then so is $P\|_\emptyset Q$. Furthermore, $rp_{P\|_\emptyset Q}(n) = \max\{rp_P(k), rp_Q(k) \mid k \le n\}$ for all n.*

As a first example, we will consider l-Seq and 1-Seq; one would assume intuitively that l-Seq $\|_\emptyset$ 1-Seq processes each group of $l + 1$ requests within time l – one request in l-Seq, the other l in 1-Seq –, and that therefore the response performance of n is $\lceil \frac{n}{l+1} \rceil l$. This would give e.g. for $l = 3$ and $n = 8$ time 6. That things are not so simple, and that this is actually false, can be seen from the following behaviour. The first four out are indeed produced within time 3; then, 1-Seq produces two more out within time 2. Within the same time, 3-Seq – being an asynchronous process – produces one out and then quickly "grabs" the last request, producing the last out at time 8.

The following example shows that $\sqsupseteq_{rp}$ is not a precongruence for $\|_\emptyset$. Let $R \equiv \mu x.\underline{in}.(out.\underline{s}.0\|_s\underline{in}.\tau.out.\underline{s}.x)/s$. R accepts two requests at a time and then produces an *out* after at most one time step and the second *out* after at most another time step; hence, $rp_R(n) = n$, i.e. the response performance is the same as that of 1-Seq.

Now define $P \equiv \text{1-Seq} \parallel_{\emptyset} R$ and $Q \equiv \text{1-Seq} \parallel_{\emptyset} \text{1-Seq}$. For Q, an asynchronous speed up of a response cannot produce a longer overall response time; hence, in the worst case, Q produces two *out* for each time step, showing $rp_Q(4n + 2) = 2n + 1$. To see that $rp_P(4n + 2) \geq 2n + 2$, consider a behaviour where every two time steps 1-Seq and R produce two *out* each, and where in the end R performs two *in* at time $2n$ and the last *out* at time $2n + 2$.

For the asymptotic performance, we have a positive result. For this result, let the *throughput* of a correct response process be the inverse of its asymptotic performance. Observe that the requirement "finite state" can be replaced by "finite state up to bisimilarity of the reduced refusal transition systems".

Theorem 23. *Let P and Q be correct and finite state with asymptotic performance a and b and throughput s and t. Then $P\parallel_{\emptyset}Q$ has throughput $s + t$, i.e. asymptotic performance $\frac{ab}{a+b}$. Hence, $\sqsupseteq_{asp}$ is a precongruence for such processes.*

As a small application, we consider again 3-Seq $\parallel_{\emptyset}$ 1-Seq; the asymptotic performance is by our theorem $\frac{3}{4}$, i.e. asymptotically 4 responses take time 3 corresponding to the intuition discussed above.

6   Conclusion

This paper follows a line of research about the efficiency of asynchronous systems, modelled as timed systems where activities have upper but no lower time bounds. In this line, the classical testing approach of [4] has been refined to timed testing – first in a Petri net setting [12, 6, 1] and later in process algebra [3] – and the resulting testing preorder is a suitable faster-than relation. Recently, a corresponding bisimulation based faster-than relation was studied in [7]. Upper time bounds have also been studied in the area of distributed algorithms; see e.g. [9]. A bisimulation based faster-than relation for asynchronous systems using lower time bounds has been suggested in [11]; this approach has been improved recently in [8]. We refer the reader to [3] for a further comparison of efficiency testing with the literature, in particular on other timed process algebras.

In order to prove pipelining to be efficient in the efficiency testing approach, this approach was adapted in [2] to a scenario where users only show a simple request-response behaviour corresponding to heavy load. A notion of correct response process was defined and shown to be decidable. The response performance, a suitable efficiency measure in the adapted scenario, was shown to be asymptotically linear for correct processes; cf. [5] and the discussion in [2] for the relation to results in $(max, +)$-algebras. Characterizations were given that help to determine the response performance and its constant factor, called the asymptotic performance. The response and the asymptotic performance give rise to two faster-than relations, the former being finer than the latter.

In the present paper, we have studied these notions further – based on the results of [2]. As one main result, we have shown what the response performance is for a pipeline consisting of any number of sequential stages. Then we have looked at three composition operators. While both faster-than relations fail to be precongruences for these operators, we were nevertheless able to show some compatibility results: the compositions of correct response processes are correct again and, in some cases, we have given bounds on the response or asymptotic performance of compositions. We have discussed examples to show the problems in obtaining or improving these bounds and to exhibit some pitfalls one might encounter in our approach.

We have settled what the response performance of the practically important class of pipelines is, which shows that in some cases the response performance of a chain of processes can be determined from its components and, consequently, that the two faster-than relations are precongruences for chaining on this class. It would be interesting to find similar results for other or more general classes. Synchronous behaviour can be seen as a strongly restricted sort of asynchronous behaviour in our approach; thus, it would be much simpler if we could obtain results on the basis of synchronous behaviour only, and therefore it would be very useful to find classes of correct response processes where such simplified considerations suffice.

The request-response users we considered correspond to a system working under heavy load. One could try to generalize this, but as already discussed in [2], this will not be easy. Another challenging task is to find typical user behaviour patterns other than just repetitions of *in–out* and to develop comparable, strong results for the resulting testing preorders. After several such case studies, one might consider *general strategies* to treat such assumptions on user behaviour.

References

1. E. Bihler and W. Vogler. Efficiency of token-passing MUTEX-solutions – some experiments. In J. Desel et al., editors, *Applications and Theory of Petri Nets 1998*, LNCS 1420, 185–204. Springer, 1998.
2. F. Corradini and W. Vogler. Measuring the performance of asynchronous systems with PAFAS. *Theoret. Comput. Sci.*, 335:187–213, 2005.
3. F. Corradini, W. Vogler, and L. Jenner. Comparing the worst-case efficiency of asynchronous systems with PAFAS. *Acta Informatica*, 38:735–792, 2002.
4. R. De Nicola and M.C.B. Hennessy. Testing equivalence for processes. *Theoret. Comput. Sci.*, 34:83–133, 1984.
5. S. Gaubert and Max Plus. Methods and applications of (max,+) linear algebra. In R. Reischuk et al., editors, *STACS 97*, LNCS 1200, 261–282. Springer, 1997.
6. L. Jenner and W. Vogler. Fast asynchronous systems in dense time. *Theoret. Comput. Sci.*, 254:379–422, 2001.
7. G. Lüttgen and W. Vogler. A faster-than relation for asynchronous processes. In K. Larsen, M. Nielsen, editors, *CONCUR 01*, LNCS 2154, 262–276. Springer, 2001.
8. G. Lüttgen and W. Vogler. Bisimulation on speed: Lower time bounds. In I. Walukiewicz, editor, *FOSSACS 2004*, LNCS 2987, 333–347. Springer, 2004.

9. N. Lynch. *Distributed Algorithms.* Morgan Kaufmann Publishers, 1996.
10. R. Milner. *Communication and Concurrency.* Prentice Hall, 1989.
11. F. Moller and C. Tofts. Relating processes with respect to speed. In J. Baeten and J. Groote, editors, *CONCUR '91*, LNCS 527, 424–438. Springer, 1991.
12. W. Vogler. Faster asynchronous systems. In I. Lee and S. Smolka, editors, *CONCUR 95*, LNCS 962, 299–312. Springer, 1995.

Is Timed Branching Bisimilarity
an Equivalence Indeed?

Wan Fokkink[1,3], Jun Pang[2], and Anton Wijs[3]

[1] Vrije Universiteit Amsterdam, Department of Theoretical Computer Science,
De Boelelaan 1081a, 1081 HV Amsterdam, The Netherlands
wanf@cs.vu.nl
[2] INRIA Futurs and LIX, École Polytechnique,
Rue de Saclay, 91128 Palaiseau Cedex, France
pangjun@lix.polytechnique.fr
[3] CWI, Department of Software Engineering,
PO Box 94079, 1090 GB Amsterdam, The Netherlands
wijs@cwi.nl

Abstract. We show that timed branching bisimilarity as defined by van der Zwaag [14] and Baeten & Middelburg [2] is not an equivalence relation, in case of a dense time domain. We propose an adaptation based on van der Zwaag's definition, and prove that the resulting timed branching bisimilarity is an equivalence indeed. Furthermore, we prove that in case of a discrete time domain, van der Zwaag's definition and our adaptation coincide.

1 Introduction

Branching bisimilarity [6, 7] is a widely used concurrency semantics for process algebras that include the silent step τ. Two processes are branching bisimilar if they can be related by some branching bisimulation relation. See [5] for a clear account on the strong points of branching bisimilarity.

Over the years, process algebras such as CCS, CSP and ACP have been extended with a notion of time. As a result, the concurrency semantics underlying these process algebras have been adapted to cope with the presence of time. Klusener [11–13] was the first to extend the notion of a branching bisimulation relation to a setting with time. The main complication is that while a process can let time pass without performing an action, such idling may mean that certain behavioural options in the future are being discarded. Klusener pioneered how this aspect of timed processes can be taken into account in a branching bisimulation context. Based on his work, van der Zwaag [14, 15] and Baeten & Middelburg [2] proposed new notions of a timed branching bisimulation relation.

A key property for a semantics is that it is an equivalence. In general, for concurrency semantics in the presence of τ, reflexivity and symmetry are easy to see, but transitivity is much more difficult. In particular, the transitivity proof for branching bisimilarity in [6] turned out to be flawed, because the transitive

P. Pettersson and W. Yi (Eds.): FORMATS 2005, LNCS 3829, pp. 258–272, 2005.
© Springer-Verlag Berlin Heidelberg 2005

closure of two branching bisimulation relations need not be a branching bisimulation relation. Basten [3] pointed out this flaw, and proposed a new transitivity proof for branching bisimilarity, based on the notion of a *semi*-branching bisimulation relation. Such relations are preserved under transitive closure, and the notions of branching bisimilarity and semi-branching bisimilarity coincide.

In a setting with time, proving equivalence of a concurrency semantics becomes even more complicated, compared to the untimed case. Still, equivalence properties for timed semantics are often claimed, but hardly ever proved. In [13, 14, 15, 2], equivalence properties are claimed without an explicit proof, although in all cases it is stated that such proofs do exist.

In the current paper, we study in how far for the notion of timed branching bisimilarity of van der Zwaag constitutes an equivalence relation. We give a counter-example to show that in case of a dense time domain, his notion is not transitive. We proceed to present a stronger version of van der Zwaag's definition (stronger in the sense that it relates fewer processes), and prove that this adapted notion does constitute an equivalence relation, even when the time domain is dense. Our proof follows the approach of Basten. Next, we show that in case of a discrete time domain, van der Zwaag's notion of timed branching bisimilarity and our new notion coincide. So in particular, in case of a discrete time domain, van der Zwaag's notion does constitute an equivalence relation.

In the appendix we show that our counter-example for transitivity also applies to the notion of timed branching bisimilarity by Baeten & Middelburg in case of a dense time domain; see [2–Section 6.4.1]. So that notion does not constitute an equivalence relation as well.

This paper is organized as follows. Section 2 contains the preliminaries. Section 3 features a counter-example to show that the notion of timed branching bisimilarity by van der Zwaag is not an equivalence relation in case of a dense time domain. A new definition of timed branching bisimulation is proposed in Section 4, and we prove that our notion of timed branching bisimilarity is an equivalence indeed. In Section 5 we prove that in case of a discrete time domain, our definition and van der Zwaag's definition of timed branching bisimilarity coincide. Section 6 gives suggestions for future work. In the appendix, we show that our counter-example for transitivity also applies to the notion of timed branching bisimilarity by Baeten & Middelburg [2].

2   Timed Labelled Transition Systems

Let Act be a nonempty set of visible actions, and τ a special action to represent internal events, with $\tau \notin Act$. We use Act_τ to denote $Act \cup \{\tau\}$.

The time domain *Time* is a totally ordered set with a least element 0. We say that *Time* is *discrete* if for each pair $u, v \in Time$ there are only finitely many $w \in Time$ such that $u < w < v$.

Definition 1 ([14]). *A timed labelled transition system (TLTS) [8] is a tuple* (S, T, U), *where:*

1. S is a set of states, including a special state $\sqrt{}$ to represent successful termination;
2. $T \subseteq S \times Act_\tau \times Time \times S$ is a set of transitions;
3. $U \subseteq S \times Time$ is a delay relation, which satisfies:
   - if $T(s, \ell, u, r)$, then $U(s, u)$;
   - if $u < v$ and $U(s, v)$, then $U(s, u)$.

Transitions (s, ℓ, u, s') express that state s evolves into state s' by the execution
of action ℓ at (absolute) time u. It is assumed that the execution of transitions
does not consume any time. A transition (s, ℓ, u, s') is denoted by $s \xrightarrow{\ell}_u s'$. If
$U(s, u)$, then state s can let time pass until time u; these predicates are used to
express time deadlocks.

3   Van der Zwaag's Timed Branching Bisimulation

Van Glabbeek and Weijland [7] introduced the notion of a *branching bisimulation*
relation for untimed LTSs. Intuitively, a τ-transition $s \xrightarrow{\tau} s'$ is invisible if it
does not lose possible behaviour (i.e., if s and s' can be related by a branching
bisimulation relation). See [5] for a lucid exposition on the motivations behind
the definition of a branching bisimulation relation.

The reflexive transitive closure of $\xrightarrow{\tau}$ is denoted by $\Rightarrow$.

Definition 2 ([7]). *Assume an untimed LTS. A symmetric binary relation $B \subseteq S \times S$ is a branching bisimulation if sBt implies:*

1. *if $s \xrightarrow{\ell} s'$, then*
   i either $\ell = \tau$ and $s'Bt$,
   ii or $t \Rightarrow \hat{t} \xrightarrow{\ell} t'$ with $sB\hat{t}$ and $s'Bt'$;
2. *if $s \downarrow$, then $t \Rightarrow t' \downarrow$ with sBt'.*

Two states s and t are branching bisimilar, denoted by $s \underline{\leftrightarrow}_b t$, if there is a branching bisimulation B with sBt.

Van der Zwaag [14] defined a timed version of branching bisimulation, which
takes into account time stamps of transitions and ultimate delays $U(s, u)$.

For $u \in Time$, the reflexive transitive closure of $\xrightarrow{\tau}_u$ is denoted by $\Rightarrow_u$.

Definition 3 ([14]). *Assume a TLTS (S, T, U). A collection B of symmetric binary relations $B_u \subseteq S \times S$ for $u \in Time$ is a timed branching bisimulation if $sB_u t$ implies:*

1. *if $s \xrightarrow{\ell}_u s'$, then*
   i either $\ell = \tau$ and $s'B_u t$,
   ii or $t \Rightarrow_u \hat{t} \xrightarrow{\ell}_u t'$ with $sB_u\hat{t}$ and $s'B_u t'$;
2. *if $s \downarrow$, then $t \Rightarrow_u t' \downarrow$ with $sB_u t'$;*

3. if $u < v$ and $U(s, v)$, then for some $n > 0$ there are $t_0, \ldots, t_n \in S$ with $t = t_0$ and $U(t_n, v)$, and $u_0 < \cdots < u_n \in Time$ with $u = u_0$ and $v = u_n$, such that for $i < n$, $t_i \Rightarrow_{u_i} t_{i+1}$, $sB_{u_i} t_{i+1}$ and $sB_{u_{i+1}} t_{i+1}$.

Two states s and t are timed branching bisimilar at u if there is a timed branching bisimulation B with $sB_u t$. States s and t are timed branching bisimilar, denoted by $s \underleftrightarrow{Z}_{tb} t$,[1] if they are timed branching bisimilar at all $u \in Time$.

Transitions can be executed at the same time consecutively. By the first clause in Definition 3, the behavior of a state at some point in time is treated like untimed behavior. The second clause deals with successful termination.[2] By the last clause, time passing in a state s is matched by a related state t with a "τ-path" where all intermediate states are related to s at times when a τ-transition is performed.

In the following examples, $\mathbb{Z}_{\geq 0} \subseteq Time$.

Example 1. Consider the following two TLTSs: $s_0 \xrightarrow{a}_2 s_1 \xrightarrow{b}_1 s_2$ and $t_0 \xrightarrow{a}_2 t_1$. We have $s_0 \underleftrightarrow{Z}_{tb} t_0$, since $s_0 B_w t_0$ for $w \geq 0$, $s_1 B_w t_1$ for $w > 1$, and $s_2 B_w t_1$ for $w \geq 0$ is a timed branching bisimulation.

Example 2. Consider the following two TLTSs: $s_0 \xrightarrow{a}_1 s_1 \xrightarrow{\tau}_2 s_2 \xrightarrow{b}_3 s_3$ and $t_0 \xrightarrow{a}_1 t_1 \xrightarrow{b}_3 t_2$. We have $s_0 \underleftrightarrow{Z}_{tb} t_0$, since $s_0 B_w t_0$ for $w \geq 0$, $s_1 B_w t_1$ for $w \leq 2$, $s_2 B_w t_1$ for $w \geq 0$, and $s_3 B_w t_2$ for $w \geq 0$ is a timed branching bisimulation.

Example 3. Consider the following two TLTSs: $s_0 \xrightarrow{a}_u s_1 \xrightarrow{\tau}_v s_2 \downarrow$ and $t_0 \xrightarrow{a}_u t_1 \downarrow$. If $u = v$, we have $s_0 \underleftrightarrow{Z}_{tb} t_0$, since $s_0 B_w t_0$ for $w \geq 0$, $s_1 B_u t_1$, and $s_2 B_w t_1$ for $w \geq 0$ is a timed branching bisimulation. If $u \neq v$, we have $s_0 \not\underleftrightarrow{Z}_{tb} t_0$, because s_1 and t_1 are not timed branching bisimilar at time u; namely, t_1 has a successful termination, and s_1 cannot simulate this at time u, as it cannot do a τ-transition at time u.

Example 4. Consider the following two TLTSs: $s_0 \xrightarrow{\tau}_u s_1 \xrightarrow{a}_v s_2 \downarrow$ and $t_0 \xrightarrow{a}_v t_1 \downarrow$. If $u = v$, we have $s_0 \underleftrightarrow{Z}_{tb} t_0$, since $s_0 B_w t_0$ for $w \geq 0$, $s_1 B_w t_0$ for $w \geq 0$, and $s_2 B_w t_1$ for $w \geq 0$ is a timed branching bisimulation. If $u \neq v$, we have $s_0 \not\underleftrightarrow{Z}_{tb} t_0$, because s_0 and t_0 are not timed branching bisimilar at time $\frac{u+v}{2}$.[3]

Van der Zwaag [14, 15] wrote about his definition: "It is straightforward to verify that branching bisimilarity is an equivalence relation." However, we found that in general this is not the case. A counter-example is presented below. Note that it uses a non-discrete time domain.

Example 5. Let p, q, and r defined as in Figures 1, 2 and 3, with $Time = \mathbb{Q}_{\geq 0}$. We depict $s \xrightarrow{a}_u s'$ as $s \xrightarrow{a(u)} s'$.

---

[1] The superscript Z refers to van der Zwaag, to distinguish it from the adaptation of his definition of timed branching bisimulation that we will define later.

[2] Van der Zwaag does not take into account successful termination, so the second clause is missing in his definition.

[3] $s_0 \underleftrightarrow{tb} t_0$ would hold for $u < v$ if in Definition 3 we would require that they are timed branching bisimilar at 0 (instead of at all $u \in Time$).

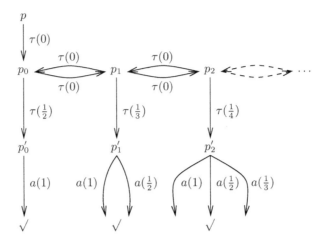

Fig. 1. A timed process p

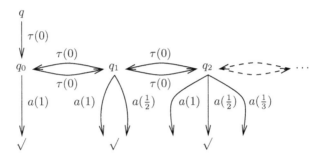

Fig. 2. A timed process q

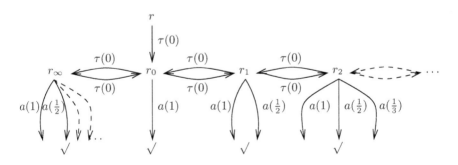

Fig. 3. A timed process r

$p \underset{tb}{\leftrightarrow}^{Z} q$, since pB_wq for $w \geq 0$, $p_iB_wq_i$ for $w \leq \frac{1}{i+2}$, and $p'_iB_wq_i$ for $w > 0$ (for $i \geq 0$) is a timed branching bisimulation.

Moreover, $q \underset{tb}{\leftrightarrow}^{Z} r$, since qB_wr for $w \geq 0$, $q_iB_wr_i$ for $w \geq 0$, $q_iB_0r_j$, and $q_iB_wr_\infty$ for $w = 0 \vee w > \frac{1}{i+2}$ (for $i, j \geq 0$) is a timed branching bisimulation.

(Note that q_i and r_∞ are *not* timed branching bisimilar in the time interval $\langle 0, \frac{1}{i+2}]$.)

However, $p \not\Leftrightarrow^Z_{tb} r$, due to the fact that none of the p_i can simulate r_∞. Namely, r_∞ can idle until time 1; p_i can only simulate this by executing a τ at time $\frac{1}{i+2}$, but the resulting process $\sum_{n=1}^{i+1} a(\frac{1}{n})$ is not timed branching bisimilar to r_∞ at time $\frac{1}{i+2}$, since only the latter can execute action a at time $\frac{1}{i+2}$.

4   A Strengthened Timed Branching Bisimulation

In this section, we propose a way to fix the definition of van der Zwaag (see Definition 3). Our adaptation requires the *stuttering property* [7] (see Definition 6) at all time intervals. That is, in the last clause of Definition 3, we require that $sB_w t_{i+1}$ for $u_i \leq w \leq u_{i+1}$. Hence, we achieve a stronger version of van der Zwaag's definition. We prove that this new notion of timed branching bisimilarity is an equivalence relation.

4.1   Timed Branching Bisimulaton

Definition 4. *Assume a TLTS (S, T, U). A collection B of binary relations $B_u \subseteq S \times S$ for $u \in$ Time is a timed branching bisimulation if $sB_u t$ implies:*

1. *if $s \xrightarrow{\ell}_u s'$, then*
   i *either $\ell = \tau$ and $s'B_u t$,*
   ii *or $t \Rightarrow_u \hat{t} \xrightarrow{\ell}_u t'$ with $sB_u \hat{t}$ and $s'B_u t'$;*
2. *if $t \xrightarrow{\ell}_u t'$, then*
   i *either $\ell = \tau$ and $sB_u t'$,*
   ii *or $s \Rightarrow_u \hat{s} \xrightarrow{\ell}_u s'$ with $\hat{s}B_u t$ and $s'B_u t'$;*
3. *if $s \downarrow$, then $t \Rightarrow_u t' \downarrow$ with $sB_u t'$;*
4. *if $t \downarrow$, then $s \Rightarrow_u s' \downarrow$ with $s'B_u t$;*
5. *if $u < v$ and $U(s, v)$, then for some $n > 0$ there are $t_0, \ldots, t_n \in S$ with $t = t_0$ and $U(t_n, v)$, and $u_0 < \cdots < u_n \in$ Time with $u = u_0$ and $v = u_n$, such that for $i < n$, $t_i \Rightarrow_{u_i} t_{i+1}$ and $sB_w t_{i+1}$ for $u_i \leq w \leq u_{i+1}$;*
6. *if $u < v$ and $U(t, v)$, then for some $n > 0$ there are $s_0, \ldots, s_n \in S$ with $s = s_0$ and $U(s_n, v)$, and $u_0 < \cdots < u_n \in$ Time with $u = u_0$ and $v = u_n$, such that for $i < n$, $s_i \Rightarrow_{u_i} s_{i+1}$ and $s_{i+1}B_w t$ for $u_i \leq w \leq u_{i+1}$.*

Two states s and t are timed branching bisimilar at u *if there is a timed branching bisimulation B with $sB_u t$. States s and t are* timed branching bisimilar, *denoted by $s \Leftrightarrow_{tb} t$, if they are timed branching bisimilar at all $u \in$ Time.*

It is not hard to see that the union of timed branching bisimulations is again a timed branching bisimulation.

Note that states q and r from Example 5 are not timed branching bisimilar according to Definition 4. Namely, none of the q_i can simulate r_∞ in the time interval $\langle 0, \frac{1}{i+2}]$, so that the stuttering property is violated.

Starting from this point, we focus on timed branching bisimulation as defined in Definition 4. We did not define this new notion of timed branching bisimulation as a symmetric relation (like in Definition 3), in view of the equivalence proof that we are going to present. Namely, in general the relation composition of two symmetric relations is not symmetric. Clearly any symmetric timed branching bisimulation is a timed branching bisimulation. Furthermore, it follows from Definition 4 that the inverse of a timed branching bisimulation is again a timed branching bisimulation, so the union of a timed branching bisimulation and its inverse is a symmetric timed branching bisimulation. Hence, Definition 4 and the definition of timed branching bisimulation as a symmetric relation give rise to the same notion.

4.2   Timed Semi-Branching Bisimulation

Basten [3] showed that the relation composition of two (untimed) branching bisimulations is not necessarily again a branching bisimulation. Figure 4 illustrates an example, showing that the relation composition of two timed branching bisimulations is not always a timed branching bisimulation. It is a slightly simplified version of an example from [3], here applied at time 0. Clearly, B and D are timed branching bisimulations. However, $B {\circ} D$ is not, and the problem arises at the transition $r_0 \xrightarrow{\tau}_0 r_1$. According to case 1 of Definition 3, since $r_0 \, (B {\circ} D) \, t_0$, either $r_1 \, (B {\circ} D) \, t_0$, or $r_0 \, (B {\circ} D) \, t_1$ and $r_1 \, (B {\circ} D) \, t_2$, must hold. But neither of these cases hold, so $B {\circ} D$ is not a timed branching bisimulation.

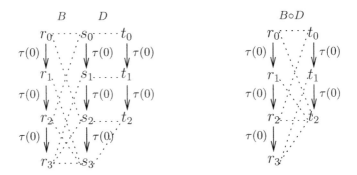

Fig. 4. Composition does not preserve timed branching bisimulation

Semi-branching bisimulation [7] relaxes case 1i of Definition 2: if $s \xrightarrow{\tau} s'$, then it is allowed that $t \Rightarrow t'$ with sBt' and $s'Bt'$. Basten proved that the relation composition of two semi-branching bisimulations is again a semi-branching bisimulation. It is easy to see that semi-branching bisimilarity is reflexive and symmetric. Hence, semi-branching bisimilarity is an equivalence relation. Then he proved that semi-branching bisimilarity and branching bisimilarity coincide, that means two states in an (untimed) LTS are related by a branching bisimulation relation if and only if they are related by a semi-branching bisimulation relation. We mimic the approach in [3] to prove that timed branching bisimilarity is an equivalence relation.

Definition 5. *Assume a TLTS (S, T, U). A collection B of binary relations $B_u \subseteq S \times Time \times S$ for $u \in Time$ is a* timed semi-branching bisimulation *if $s B_u t$ implies:*

1. *if $s \xrightarrow{\ell}_u s'$, then*
   i *either $\ell = \tau$ and $t \Rightarrow_u t'$ with $s B_u t'$ and $s' B_u t'$,*
   ii *or $t \Rightarrow_u \hat{t} \xrightarrow{\ell}_u t'$ with $s B_u \hat{t}$ and $s' B_u t'$;*
2. *if $t \xrightarrow{\ell}_u t'$, then*
   i *either $\ell = \tau$ and $s \Rightarrow_u s'$ with $s' B_u t$ and $s' B_u t'$,*
   ii *or $s \Rightarrow_u \hat{s} \xrightarrow{\ell}_u s'$ with $\hat{s} B_u t$ and $s' B_u t'$;*
3. *if $s \downarrow$, then $t \Rightarrow_u t' \downarrow$ with $s B_u t'$;*
4. *if $t \downarrow$, then $s \Rightarrow_u s' \downarrow$ with $s' B_u t$;*
5. *if $u < v$ and $U(s, v)$, then for some $n > 0$ there are $t_0, \ldots, t_n \in S$ with $t = t_0$ and $U(t_n, v)$, and $u_0 < \cdots < u_n \in Time$ with $u = u_0$ and $v = u_n$, such that for $i < n$, $t_i \Rightarrow_{u_i} t_{i+1}$ and $s B_w t_{i+1}$ for $u_i \le w \le u_{i+1}$;*
6. *if $u < v$ and $U(t, v)$, then for some $n > 0$ there are $s_0, \ldots, s_n \in S$ with $s = s_0$ and $U(s_n, v)$, and $u_0 < \cdots < u_n \in Time$ with $u = u_0$ and $v = u_n$, such that for $i < n$, $s_i \Rightarrow_{u_i} s_{i+1}$ and $s_{i+1} B_w t$ for $u_i \le w \le u_{i+1}$.*

Two states s and t are timed semi-branching bisimilar at u *if there is a timed semi-branching bisimulation B with $s B_u t$. States s and t are* timed semi-branching bisimilar, *denoted by $s \underline{\leftrightarrow}_{tsb} t$, if they are timed semi-branching bisimilar at all $u \in Time$.*

It is not hard to see that the union of timed semi-branching bisimulations is again a timed semi-branching bisimulation. Furthermore, any timed branching bisimulation is a timed semi-branching bisimulation.

Definition 6 ([7]). *A timed semi-branching bisimulation B is said to satisfy the* stuttering property *if:*

1. *$s B_u t$, $s' B_u t$ and $s \xrightarrow{\tau}_u s_1 \xrightarrow{\tau}_u \cdots \xrightarrow{\tau}_u s_n \xrightarrow{\tau}_u s'$ implies that $s_i B_u t$ for $1 \le i \le n$;*
2. *$s B_u t$, $s B_u t'$ and $t \xrightarrow{\tau}_u t_1 \xrightarrow{\tau}_u \cdots \xrightarrow{\tau}_u t_n \xrightarrow{\tau}_u t'$ implies that $s B_u t_i$ for $1 \le i \le n$.*

Lemma 1. *Any timed semi-branching bisimulation satisfying the stuttering property is a timed branching bisimulation.*

Proof. Let B be a timed semi-branching bisimulation that satisfies the stuttering property. We prove that B is a timed branching bisimulation.

Let $s B_u t$. We only consider case 1i of Definition 5, because cases 1ii, 2ii and 3-6 are the same for both timed semi-branching and branching bisimulation. Moreover, case 2i can be dealt with in a similar way as case 1i. So let $s \xrightarrow{\tau}_u s'$ and $t \Rightarrow_u t'$ with $s B_u t'$ and $s' B_u t'$. We distinguish two cases.

1. $t = t'$. Then $s' B_u t$, which agrees with case 1i of Definition 4.
2. $t \ne t'$. Then $t \Rightarrow_u t'' \xrightarrow{\tau}_u t'$. Since B satisfies the stuttering property, $s B_u t''$. This agrees with case 1ii of Definition 4.   □

4.3   Timed Branching Bisimilarity is an Equivalence

Our equivalence proof consists of the following main steps:

1. We first prove that the relation composition of two timed semi-branching bisimulation relations is again a semi-branching bisimulation relation (Proposition 1).
2. Then we prove that timed semi-branching bisimilarity is an equivalence relation (Theorem 1).
3. Finally, we prove that the largest timed semi-branching bisimulation satisfies the stuttering property (Proposition 2).

According to Lemma 1, any timed semi-branching bisimulation satisfying the stuttering property is a timed branching bisimulation. So by the 3rd point, two states are related by a timed branching bisimulation if and only if they are related by a timed semi-branching bisimulation.

Lemma 2. *Let B be a timed semi-branching bisimulation, and $sB_u t$.*

1. *$s \Rightarrow_u s' \implies (\exists t' \in S : t \Rightarrow_u t' \wedge s'B_u t')$;*
2. *$t \Rightarrow_u t' \implies (\exists s' \in S : s \Rightarrow_u s' \wedge t'B_u s')$.*

Proof. We prove the first part, by induction on the number of τ-transitions at u from s to s'.

1. *Base case:* The number of τ-transitions at u from s to s' is zero. Then $s = s'$. Take $t' = t$. Clearly $t \Rightarrow_u t'$ and $s'B_u t'$.
2. *Inductive case:* $s \Rightarrow_u s'$ consists of $n \geq 1$ τ-transitions at u. Then there exists an $s'' \in S$ such that $s \Rightarrow_u s''$ in $n - 1$ τ-transitions at u, and $s'' \xrightarrow{\tau}_u s'$. By the induction hypothesis, $t \Rightarrow_u t''$ with $s''B_u t''$. Since $s'' \xrightarrow{\tau}_u s'$ and B is a timed semi-branching bisimulation:
   - either $t'' \Rightarrow_u t'$ and $s''B_u t'$ and $s'B_u t'$;
   - or $t'' \Rightarrow_u \hat{t} \xrightarrow{\tau}_u t'$ with $s''B_u \hat{t}$ and $s'B_u t'$.
   In both cases $t \Rightarrow_u t'$ with $s'B_u t'$.

The proof of the second part is similar.   □

Proposition 1. *The relation composition of two timed semi-branching bisimulations is again a timed semi-branching bisimulation.*

Proof. Let B and D be timed semi-branching bisimulations. We prove that the composition of B and D (or better, the compositions of B_u and D_u for $u \in \text{Time}$) is a timed semi-branching bisimulation. Suppose that $rB_u sD_u t$ for $r, s, t \in S$. We check that the conditions of Definition 5 are satisfied with respect to the pair r, t. We distinguish four cases.

1. $r \xrightarrow{\tau}_u r'$ and $s \Rightarrow_u s'$ with $rB_u s'$ and $r'B_u s'$. Since $sD_u t$ and $s \Rightarrow_u s'$, Lemma 2 yields that $t \Rightarrow_u t'$ with $s'D_u t'$. Hence, $rB_u s'D_u t'$ and $r'B_u s'D_u t'$.

2. $r \xrightarrow{\ell}_u r'$ and $s \Rightarrow_u s'' \xrightarrow{\ell}_u s'$ with $r B_u s''$ and $r' B_u s'$. Since $s D_u t$ and $s \Rightarrow_u s''$, Lemma 2 yields that $t \Rightarrow_u t''$ with $s'' D_u t''$. Since $s'' \xrightarrow{\ell}_u s'$ and $s'' D_u t''$:
   - Either $\ell = \tau$ and $t'' \Rightarrow_u t'$ with $s'' D_u t'$ and $s' D_u t'$. Then $t \Rightarrow_u t'$ with $r B_u s'' D_u t'$ and $r' B_u s' D_u t'$.
   - Or $t'' \Rightarrow_u t''' \xrightarrow{\ell}_u t'$ with $s'' D_u t'''$ and $s' D_u t'$. Then $t \Rightarrow_u t''' \xrightarrow{\ell}_u t'$ with $r B_u s'' D_u t'''$ and $r' B_u s' D_u t'$.

3. $r \downarrow$. Since $r B_u s$, $s \Rightarrow_u s' \downarrow$ with $r B_u s'$. Since $s D_u t$ and $s \Rightarrow_u s'$, Lemma 2 yields that $t \Rightarrow_u t''$ with $s' D_u t''$. Since $s' \downarrow$ and $s' D_u t''$, $t'' \Rightarrow_u t' \downarrow$ with $s' D_u t'$. Hence, $t \Rightarrow_u t' \downarrow$ with $r B_u s' D_u t'$.

4. $u < v$ and $U(r, v)$. Since $r B_u s$, for some $n > 0$ there are $s_0, \dots, s_n \in S$ with $s = s_0$ and $U(s_n, v)$, and $u_0 < \cdots < u_n \in Time$ with $u = u_0$ and $v = u_n$, such that $s_i \Rightarrow_{u_i} s_{i+1}$ and $r B_w s_{i+1}$ for $u_i \le w \le u_{i+1}$ and $i < n$.
   For $i \le n$ we show that for some $m_i > 0$ there are $t_0^i, \dots, t_{m_i}^i \in S$ with $t = t_0^0$ and $U(t_{m_n}^n, v)$, and $v_0^i \le \cdots \le v_{m_i}^i \in Time$ with (A_i) $u_{i-1} = v_0^i$ (if $i > 0$) and (B_i) $u_i = v_{m_i}^i$, such that:

   (C_i) $t_j^i \Rightarrow_{v_j^i} t_{j+1}^i$ for $j < m_i$;
   (D_i) $t_{m_{i-1}}^{i-1} \Rightarrow_{u_{i-1}} t_0^i$ (if $i > 0$);
   (E_i) $s_i D_{u_{i-1}} t_0^i$ (if $i > 0$);
   (F_i) $s_i D_w t_{j+1}^i$ for $v_j^i \le w \le v_{j+1}^i$ and $j < m_i$.
   We apply induction with respect to i.

   - *Base case: $i = 0$.*
     Let $m_0 = 1$, $t_0^0 = t_1^0 = t$ and $v_0^0 = v_1^0 = u_0$. Note that B_0, C_0 and F_0 hold.
   - *Inductive case: $0 < i \le n$.*
     Suppose that $m_k, t_0^k, \dots, t_{m_k}^k, v_0^k, \dots, v_{m_k}^k$ have been defined for $0 \le k < i$. Moreover, suppose that B_k, C_k and F_k hold for $0 \le k < i$, and that A_k, D_k and E_k hold for $0 < k < i$.
     F_{i-1} for $j = m_{i-1} - 1$ together with B_{i-1} yields $s_{i-1} D_{u_{i-1}} t_{m_{i-1}}^{i-1}$. Since $s_{i-1} \Rightarrow_{u_{i-1}} s_i$, Lemma 2 implies that $t_{m_{i-1}}^{i-1} \Rightarrow_{u_{i-1}} t'$ with $s_i D_{u_{i-1}} t'$. We define $t_0^i = t'$ [then D_i and E_i hold] and $v_0^i = u_{i-1}$ [then A_i holds]. $s_i \Rightarrow_{u_i} \cdots \Rightarrow_{u_{n-1}} s_n$ with $U(s_n, v)$ implies that $U(s_i, u_i)$. Since $s_i D_{u_{i-1}} t_0^i$, according to case 5 of Definition 5, for some $m_i > 0$ there are $t_1^i, \dots, t_{m_i}^i \in S$ with $U(t_{m_i}^i, u_i)$, and $v_1^i < \cdots < v_{m_i}^i \in Time$ with $v_0^i < v_1^i$ and $u_i = v_{m_i}^i$ [then B_i holds], such that for $j < m_i$, $t_j^i \Rightarrow_{v_j^i} t_{j+1}^i$ [then C_i holds] and $s_i D_w t_{j+1}^i$ for $v_j^i \le w \le v_{j+1}^i$ [then F_i holds].

   Concluding, for $i < n$, $r B_{u_i} s_{i+1} D_{u_i} t_0^{i+1}$ and $r B_w s_{i+1} D_w t_{j+1}^{i+1}$ for $v_j^{i+1} \le w \le v_{j+1}^{i+1}$ and $j < m_i$. Since $v_j^i \le v_{j+1}^i$, $v_{m_i}^i = u_i = v_0^{i+1}$, $t = t_0^0$, $u = u_0 = v_0^0$, $t_j^i \Rightarrow_{v_j^i} t_{j+1}^i$, $t_{m_i}^i \Rightarrow_{u_i} t_0^{i+1}$, and $U(t_{m_n}^n, v)$, we are done.

So cases 1,3,5 of Definition 5 are satisfied. Similarly it can be checked that cases 2,4,6 are satisfied. So the composition of B and D is again a timed semi-branching bisimulation. $\qquad \square$

Theorem 1. *Timed semi-branching bisimilarity, $\underline{\leftrightarrow}_{tsb}$, is an equivalence relation.*

Proof. Reflexivity: Obviously, the identity relation on S is a timed semi-branching bisimulation.

Symmetry: Let B a timed semi-branching bisimulation. Obviously, B^{-1} is also a timed semi-branching bisimulation.

Transitivity: This follows from Proposition 1.   □

Proposition 2. *The largest timed semi-branching bisimulation satisfies the stuttering property.*

Proof. Let B be the largest timed semi-branching bisimulation on S. Let $s \xrightarrow{\tau}_u s_1 \xrightarrow{\tau}_u \cdots \xrightarrow{\tau}_u s_n \xrightarrow{\tau}_u s'$ with $sB_u t$ and $s'B_u t$. We prove that $B' = B \cup \{(s_i, t) \mid 1 \le i \le n\}$ is a timed semi-branching bisimulation.

We check that all cases of Definition 5 are satisfied for the relations $s_i B'_u t$, for $1 \le i \le n$. First we check that the transitions of s_i are matched by t. Since $s \Rightarrow_u s_i$ and $sB_u t$, by Lemma 2 $t \Rightarrow_u t'$ with $s_i B_u t'$.

- If $s_i \xrightarrow{\ell}_u s''$, then it follows from $s_i B_u t'$ that:
  - Either $\ell = \tau$ and $t' \Rightarrow_u t''$ with $s_i B_u t''$ and $s'' B_u t''$. Since $t \Rightarrow_u t' \Rightarrow_u t''$, this agrees with case 1i of Definition 5.
  - Or $t' \Rightarrow_u t''' \xrightarrow{\ell}_u t''$ with $s_i B_u t'''$ and $s'' B_u t''$. Since $t \Rightarrow_u t' \Rightarrow_u t'''$, this agrees with case 1ii of Definition 5.
- If $s_i \downarrow$, then it follows from $s_i B_u t'$ that $t' \Rightarrow_u t'' \downarrow$ with $s_i B_u t''$. Since $t \Rightarrow_u t' \Rightarrow_u t''$, this agrees with case 3 of Definition 5.
- If $u < v$ and $U(s_i, v)$, then it follows from $s_i B_u t'$ that for some $n > 0$ there are $t_0, \ldots, t_n \in S$ with $t' = t_0$ and $U(t_n, v)$, and $u_0 < \cdots < u_n \in Time$ with $u = u_0$ and $v = u_n$, such that for $i < n$, $t_i \Rightarrow_{u_i} t_{i+1}$ and $s_i B_w t_i$ for $u_i \le w \le u_{i+1}$. Since $t \Rightarrow_u t' \Rightarrow_u t_1$, this agrees with case 5 of Definition 5.

Next we check that the transitions of t are matched by s_i.

- If $t \xrightarrow{\ell}_u t'$, then it follows from $s'B_u t$ that:
  - Either $\ell = \tau$ and $s' \Rightarrow_u s''$ with $s'' B_u t$ and $s'' B_u t'$. Since $s_i \Rightarrow_u s' \Rightarrow_u s''$, this agrees with case 2i of Definition 5.
  - Or $s' \Rightarrow_u s''' \xrightarrow{\ell}_u s''$ with $s''' B_u t$ and $s'' B_u t'$. Since $s_i \Rightarrow_u s' \Rightarrow_u s'''$, this agrees with case 2ii of Definition 5.
- If $t \downarrow$, then it follows from $s'B_u t$ that $s' \Rightarrow_u s'' \downarrow$ with $s'' B_u t$. Since $s_i \Rightarrow_u s' \Rightarrow_u s''$, this agrees with case 4 of Definition 5.
- If $u < v$ and $U(t, v)$, then it follows from $s'B_u t$ that for some $n > 0$ there are $s'_0, \ldots, s'_n \in S$ with $s' = s'_0$ and $U(s_n, v)$, and $u_0 < \cdots < u_n \in Time$ with $u = u_0$ and $v = u_n$, such that for $i < n$, $s'_i \Rightarrow_{u_i} s'_{i+1}$ and $s'_{i+1} B_w t$ for $u_i \le w \le u_{i+1}$. Since $s_i \Rightarrow_u s' \Rightarrow_u s'_1$, this agrees with case 6 of Definition 5.

Hence B' is a timed semi-branching bisimulation. Since B is the largest, and $B \subseteq B'$, we find that $B = B'$. So B satisfies the first requirement of Definition 6.

Since B is the largest timed semi-branching bisimulation and $\underleftrightarrow{}_{tsb}$ is an equivalence, B is symmetric. Then B also satisfies the second requirement of Definition 6. Hence B satisfies the stuttering property.   □

As a consequence, the largest timed semi-branching bisimulation is a timed branching bisimulation (by Lemma 1 and Proposition 2). Since any timed branching bisimulation is a timed semi-branching bisimulation, we have the following two corollaries.

Corollary 1. *Two states are related by a timed branching bisimulation if and only if they are related by a timed semi-branching bisimulation.*

Corollary 2. *Timed branching bisimilarity, $\underleftrightarrow{}_{tb}$, is an equivalence relation.*

We note that for each $u \in \textit{Time}$, timed branching bisimilarity at time u is also an equivalence relation.

5   Discrete Time Domains

Theorem 2. *In case of a discrete time domain, $\underleftrightarrow{}_{tb}^{Z}$ and $\underleftrightarrow{}_{tb}$ coincide.*

Proof. Clearly $\underleftrightarrow{}_{tb} \subseteq \underleftrightarrow{}_{tb}^{Z}$. We prove that $\underleftrightarrow{}_{tb}^{Z} \subseteq \underleftrightarrow{}_{tb}$. Suppose B is a timed branching bisimulation relation according to Definition 3. We show that B is a timed branching bisimulation relation according to Definition 4. B satisfies cases 1-4 of Definition 4, since they coincide with cases 1-2 of Definition 3. We prove that case 5 of Definition 4 is satisfied.

Let $sB_u t$ and $U(s, v)$ with $u < v$. Let $u_0 < \cdots < u_n \in \textit{Time}$ with $u_0 = u$ and $u_n = v$, where $u_1, \ldots, u_{n-1}$ are all the elements from $\textit{Time}$ that are between u and v. (Here we use that $\textit{Time}$ is discrete.) We prove induction on n that there are $t_0, \ldots, t_n \in S$ with $t = t_0$ and $U(t_n, v)$, such that for $i < n$, $t_i \Rightarrow_{u_i} t_{i+1}$ and $sB_w t_{i+1}$ for $u_i \le w \le u_{i+1}$.

- *Base case: $n = 1$.* By case 3 of Definition 3 there is a $t_1 \in S$ with $U(t_1, v)$, such that $t \Rightarrow_u t_1$, $sB_u t_1$ and $sB_v t_1$. Hence, $sB_w t_1$ for $u \le w \le v$.
- *Inductive case: $n > 1$.* Since $U(s, v)$, clearly also $U(s, u_1)$. By case 3 of Definition 3 there is a $t_1 \in S$ such that $t \Rightarrow_u t_1$, $sB_u t_1$ and $sB_{u_1} t_1$. Hence, $sB_w t_1$ for $u \le w \le u_1$. By induction, $sB_{u_1} t_1$ together with $U(s, v)$ implies that there are $t_2, \ldots, t_n \in S$ with $U(t_n, v)$, such that for $1 \le i < n$, $t_i \Rightarrow_{u_i} t_{i+1}$, $sB_{u_i} t_{i+1}$ and $sB_{u_{i+1}} t_{i+1}$. Hence, $sB_w t_{i+1}$ for $u_i \le w \le u_{i+1}$.

We conclude that case 5 of Definition 4 holds. Similarly it can be proved that B satisfies case 6 of Definition 4. Hence B is a timed branching bisimulation relation according to Definition 4. So $\underleftrightarrow{}_{tb}^{Z} \subseteq \underleftrightarrow{}_{tb}$.   □

6   Future Work

We conclude the paper by pointing out some possible research directions for the future.

1. It is an interesting question whether a rooted version of timed branching bisimilarity is a congruence over a basic timed process algebra (such as

Baeten and Bergstra's $\text{BPA}^{ur}_{\rho\delta}$ [1], which is basic real time process algebra with time stamped urgent actions). Similar to equivalence, congruence properties for timed branching bisimilarity are often claimed, but hardly ever proved. We only know of one such congruence proof, in [13].

2. Van der Zwaag [14] extended the cones and foci verification method from Groote and Springintveld [9] to TLTSs. Fokkink and Pang [10] proposed an adapted version of this timed cones and foci method. Both papers take $\underline{\leftrightarrow}^Z_{tb}$ as a starting point. It should be investigated whether a timed cones and foci method can be formulated for $\underline{\leftrightarrow}_{tb}$ as defined in the current paper.

3. Van Glabbeek [4] presented a wide range of concurrency semantics for untimed processes with the silent step τ. It would be a challenge to try and formulate timed versions of these semantics, and prove equivalence and congruence properties for the resulting timed semantics.

References

1. J.C.M. Baeten and J.A. Bergstra. Real time process algebra. *Formal Aspects of Computing*, 3(2):142–188, 1991.

2. J.C.M. Baeten and C.A. Middelburg. *Process Algebra with Timing*. EATCS Monograph, Springer, 2002.

3. T. Basten. Branching bisimilarity is an equivalence indeed! *Information Processing Letters*, 58(3):141–147, 1996.

4. R.J. van Glabbeek. The linear time – branching time spectrum II: The semantics of sequential systems with silent moves. In (E. Best, ed.) *Proceedings of the 4th Conference on Concurrency Theory (CONCUR'93)*, Hildesheim, LNCS 715, pp. 66–81, 1993.

5. R.J. van Glabbeek. What is branching time and why to use it? In (M. Nielsen, ed.), *The Concurrency Column, Bulletin of the EATCS*, 53:190-198, 1994.

6. R.J. van Glabbeek and W.P. Weijland. Branching time and abstraction in bisimulation semantics. In (G. Ritter, ed.) *Proceedings of the IFIP 11th World Computer Congress (Information Processing '89)*, San Francisco, pp. 613–618, 1989.

7. R.J. van Glabbeek and W.P. Weijland. Branching time and abstraction in bisimulation semantics. *Journal of the ACM*, 43(3):555–600, 1996.

8. J.F. Groote, M.A. Reniers, J.J. van Wamel, and M.B. van der Zwaag. Completeness of timed μCRL. *Fundamenta Informaticae*, 50(3/4):361–402, 2002.

9. J.F. Groote and J.G. Springintveld. Focus points and convergent process operators. A proof strategy for protocol verification. *Journal of Logic and Algebraic Programming*, 49(1/2):31–60, 2001.

10. W.J. Fokkink and J. Pang. Formal verification of timed systems using cones and foci. In (I. Ulidowski, ed.) *Proceedings of the 6th Workshop on Real-Time Systems (ARTS'04)*, Stirling, ENTCS, 2005. To appear.

11. A.S. Klusener. Abstraction in real time process algebra. In (J.W. de Bakker, C. Huizing, W.P. de Roever, and G. Rozenberg, eds.) *Proceedings of the REX Workshop "Real-Time: Theory in Practice"*, Mook, LNCS 600, pp. 325–352, 1991.

12. A.S. Klusener. The silent step in time. In (R. Cleaveland, ed.) *Proceedings of the 3rd Conference on Concurrency Theory (CONCUR'92)*, LNCS 630, pp. 421–435, 1992.

13. A.S. Klusener. *Models and Axioms for a Fragment of Real Time Process Algebra*. PhD thesis, Eindhoven University of Technology, 1993.
14. M.B. van der Zwaag. The cones and foci proof technique for timed transition systems. *Information Processing Letters*, 80(1):33–40, 2001.
15. M.B. van der Zwaag. *Models and Logics for Process Algebra*. PhD thesis, University of Amsterdam, 2002.

A   Branching Tail Bisimulation

Baeten and Middelburg [2] defined the notion of *branching tail bisimulation*, which is closely related to van der Zwaag's definition of timed branching bisimulation. We show that in case of dense time, our counter-example (see Example 5) again shows that branching tail bisimilarity is not an equivalence relation.

In the absolute time setting of Baeten and Middelburg, states are of the form $<p, u>$ with p a process algebraic term and u a time stamp referring to the absolute time. They give operational semantics to their process algebras such that if $<p, u> \xrightarrow{v} <p, u+v>$ (where $\xrightarrow{v}$ for $v > 0$ denotes a time step of v time units), then $<p, u> \xrightarrow{w} <p, u+w>$ for $0 < w < v$; in our example this saturation with time steps will be mimicked. The relation $s \xmapsto{u} s'$ is defined by: either $s \Rightarrow \hat{s} \xmapsto{u} s'$, or $s \xmapsto{v} \hat{s} \xmapsto{w} s'$ with $v + w = u$.[4]

Branching tail bisimulation is defined as follows.[5]

Definition 7 ([2]). *Assume a TLTS in the style of Baeten and Middelburg. A symmetric binary relation $B \subseteq S \times S$ is a* branching tail bisimulation *if sBt implies:*

1. *if $s \xrightarrow{\ell} s'$, then*
   i *either $\ell = \tau$ and $t \Rightarrow t'$ with sBt' and $s'Bt'$;*
   ii *or $t \Rightarrow \hat{t} \xrightarrow{a} t'$ with $sB\hat{t}$ and $s'Bt'$;*
2. *if $s \xrightarrow{\ell} <\sqrt{}, u>$, then $t \Rightarrow t' \xrightarrow{\ell} <\sqrt{}, u>$ with sBt';*
3. *if $s \xmapsto{u} s'$, then*
   i *either $t \Rightarrow \hat{t} \xmapsto{v} \hat{t}' \xmapsto{w} t'$ with $v + w = u$, $sB\hat{t}$ and $s'Bt'$;*
   ii *or $t \Rightarrow \hat{t} \xmapsto{u} t'$ with $sB\hat{t}$ and $s'Bt'$.*

Two states s and t are branching tail bisimilar, *written $s \bisim_{tb}^{BM} t$, if there is a branching tail bisimulation B with sBt.*[6]

We proceed to transpose the TLTSs from Example 5 into the setting of Baeten and Middelburg. We now have the following transitions, for $i \geq 0$:$<p, 0> \xrightarrow{\tau}$

---

[4] Baeten and Middelburg also have a deadlock predicate ↑, which we do not take into account here, as it does not play a role in our counter-example.
[5] Baeten and Middelburg define this notion in the setting with relative time, and remark that the adaptation of this definition to absolute time is straightforward. Here we present this straightforward adaptation.
[6] The superscript *BM* refers to Baeten and Middelburg, to distinguish it from the notion of timed branching bisimulation as defined in this paper.

$<p_0, 0>$

$<p_i, 0> \xrightarrow{\tau} <p_{i+1}, 0>$

$<p_{i+1}, 0> \xrightarrow{\tau} <p_i, 0>$

$<p_i, u> \overset{v-u}{\longmapsto} <p_i, v>, \ 0 \le u < v \le \frac{1}{i+2}$

$<p_i, \frac{1}{i+2}> \xrightarrow{\tau} <p'_i, \frac{1}{i+2}>$

$<p'_i, u> \overset{v-u}{\longmapsto} <p'_i, v>, \ \frac{1}{i+2} \le u < v \le 1$

$<p'_i, \frac{1}{n}> \xrightarrow{a} <\surd, \frac{1}{n}>, \ n = 1, \ldots, i+1$

$<q, 0> \xrightarrow{\tau} <q_0, 0>$

$<q_i, 0> \xrightarrow{\tau} <q_{i+1}, 0>$

$<q_{i+1}, 0> \xrightarrow{\tau} <q_i, 0>$

$<q_i, u> \overset{v-u}{\longmapsto} <q_i, v>, \ 0 \le u < v \le 1$

$<q_i, \frac{1}{n}> \xrightarrow{a} <\surd, \frac{1}{n}>, \ n = 1, \ldots, i+1$

$<r, 0> \xrightarrow{\tau} <r_0, 0>$

$<r_i, 0> \xrightarrow{\tau} <r_{i+1}, 0>$

$<r_{i+1}, 0> \xrightarrow{\tau} <r_i, 0>$

$<r_i, u> \overset{v-u}{\longmapsto} <r_i, v>, \ \frac{1}{i+2} \le u < v \le 1$

$<r_i, \frac{1}{n}> \xrightarrow{a} <\surd, \frac{1}{n}>, \ n = 1, \ldots, i+1$

$<r_0, 0> \xrightarrow{\tau} <r_\infty, 0>$

$<r_\infty, 0> \xrightarrow{\tau} <r_0, 0>$

$<r_\infty, u> \overset{v-u}{\longmapsto} <r_\infty, v>, \ 0 \le u < v \le 1$

$<r_\infty, \frac{1}{n}> \xrightarrow{a} <\surd, \frac{1}{n}>, \ n \in \mathbb{N}$

$<p, 0> \underset{tb}{\overset{BM}{\leftrightarrow}} <q, 0>$, since $<p, w>B<q, w>$ for $w \ge 0$, $<p_i, w>B<q_i, w>$ for $w \le \frac{1}{i+2}$, and $<p'_i, w>B<q_i, w>$ for $w > 0$ (for $i \ge 0$) is a branching tail bisimulation.

Moreover, $<q, 0> \underset{tb}{\overset{BM}{\leftrightarrow}} <r, 0>$, since $<q, w>B<r, w>$ for $w \ge 0$, $<q_i, w>B<r_i, w>$ for $w \ge 0$, $<q_i, 0>B<r_j, 0>$, and $<q_i, w>B<r_\infty, w>$ for $w = 0 \vee w > \frac{1}{i+2}$ (for $i, j \ge 0$) is a branching tail bisimulation.

However, $<p, 0> \underset{tb}{\overset{BM}{\not\leftrightarrow}} <r, 0>$, since p cannot simulate r. This is due to the fact that none of the p_i can simulate r_∞. Namely, r_∞ can idle until time 1. p_i can only simulate this by executing a τ at time $\frac{1}{i+2}$, but the resulting process $<p'_i, \frac{1}{i+2}>$ is not timed branching bisimilar to $<r_\infty, \frac{1}{i+2}>$, since only the latter can execute action a at time $\frac{1}{i+2}$.

Implementation of Timed Automata:
An Issue of Semantics or Modeling?[*]

Karine Altisen and Stavros Tripakis

Verimag Centre Equation,
2, avenue de Vignate, 38610 Gières, France
{altisen, tripakis}@imag.fr

Abstract. We examine to what extent implementation of timed automata can be achieved using the standard semantics and appropriate
modeling, instead of introducing new semantics. We propose an implementation methodology which allows to transform a timed automaton
into a program and to check whether the execution of this program on
a given platform satisfies a desired property. This is done by modeling
the program and the execution platform, respectively, as an untimed
automaton and a collection of timed automata. We also study the problem of property preservation, in particular when moving to a "better"
execution platform. We show that some subtleties arise regarding the
definition of "better", in particular for digital clocks. The fundamental
issue is that faster clocks result in better "sampling" and therefore can
introduce more behaviors.

1   Introduction

Model-based design is being established as an important paradigm for the development of embedded systems today. This paradigm advocates using models all
the way from design to implementation. Using models, rather than, say, building
and testing prototypes, is important in order to cut development costs and time.
However, using models alone is not enough. Being abstractions of reality, models
often make "idealizing" assumptions, which break down during implementation.
Thus, it is necessary to bridge, somehow, the gap between high-level models and
low-level implementations.

In this context, this paper studies the problem of implementation of timed
automata. Timed automata [1] are a popular model for describing real-time
systems. Numerous model-checking techniques and tools exist for this model,
e.g. [7, 14], permitting to prove automatically, at least in principle, properties on
a given model. Synthesis techniques and tools also exist, permitting to compute
automatically controllers that are correct by construction for a given plant and
property, meaning that the closed-loop system (plant, controller) satisfies this
property. Such controllers can sometimes be represented as timed automata.

---

[*] Work partially supported by CNRS STIC project "CORTOS" and by IST Network
of Excellence "ARTIST2".

Regardless of whether a timed-automaton controller is synthesized automatically or "by hand", an important problem remains, namely, how to pass from the timed-automaton model to an implementation. This is a typical bridging-the-gap situation like the ones discussed above. Indeed, the semantics of timed automata are "ideal" in a number of ways ("continuous sampling" of guards using "perfect" clocks, zero execution and communication times, etc.).

A number of works exist on the timed automata implementation problem [4, 21, 13]. The main motivation for our work has been [21]. In summary, the results of [21] are as follows. Given a TA A, the authors define a new semantics of A, parameterized by a delay Δ, called *almost ASAP semantics* and denoted $[A]_\Delta$. They also define a *program semantics* for A, parameterized by two delays Δ_P (modeling the period of the digital clock of the execution platform where the program runs) and Δ_L (modeling the worst-case execution time of the loop-body of the program), denoted $[A]_{\Delta_P, \Delta_L}$.

The authors then prove three main results. First, an implementability result stating that if $\Delta > 4\Delta_P + 3\Delta_L$ then $[A]_{\Delta_P, \Delta_L}$ refines $[A]_\Delta$. Second, a "faster is better" result stating that if $\Delta' < \Delta$ then $[A]_{\Delta'}$ refines $[A]_\Delta$. Third, a modeling result which permits to transform A into a TA A_Δ such that $[A]_\Delta$ equals the standard semantics of A_Δ. The refinement relation used guarantees that if $\mathcal{S}$ correctly controls a given environment then any $\mathcal{S}'$ that refines $\mathcal{S}$ also controls correctly this environment. Thus, the three results above provide the cornerstones of a solution to the implementability problem: first Δ_P and Δ_L can be fixed according to the execution platform; then Δ can be chosen so that it satisfies the inequality above; finally, A_Δ can be verified against an appropriate environment model and a specification. If the specification is met, then there exists a program (implementing $[A]_{\Delta_P, \Delta_L}$) which is guaranteed to meet the specification against the same environment. Moreover, if the execution platform is changed for a "faster" one, with $\Delta'_P \leq \Delta_P$ and $\Delta'_L \leq \Delta_L$, then the "faster is better" result guarantees that the program is still correct.

The question we would like to ask in this paper is the following: can similar results be obtained without introducing new semantics, but using modeling instead? The question is not without interest, since, avoiding to introduce new (and admittedly complicated) semantics has a number of advantages. First, the approach becomes easier to understand. Second, the approach becomes more general: new assumptions on the program type or execution platform can be introduced simply by changing the corresponding models, in a *modular* way, without having to modify the semantics. Third, new possibilities arise, for instance, for automatic synthesis of controllers which are *implementable by construction*.

In the rest of this paper, we give a positive, albeit partial, answer to the above question. In particular, we propose an implementation methodology for timed automata which allows to transform a timed automaton into a program and to check whether the execution of this program on a given platform satisfies a desired property. This is done by modeling the program and the execution platform, respectively, as an untimed automaton and a collection of timed automata, the latter capturing the three fundamental implementation components: digital clock, program execution and IO interface. Section 3 describes the methodology.

This provides a solution to the implementation of timed automata, however, we would also like to have a property guaranteeing that, when a platform P is replaced by a "better" platform P', then a program proved correct for P is also correct for P'. We study this problem in Section 4 and show that, for a reasonable definition of "better", such a property does not generally hold. The main problems arise from the following "paradox". On one hand it seems reasonable to consider P' as being better than P if the two are identical, except that P' provides a periodic digital clock running twice as fast as the one of P. On the other hand, a program using the faster clock has a higher "sampling rate" and thus may generate more behaviors than a program using the slower clock, which may result in violation of properties. Through a set of examples, we expose such subtleties in Section 4. In Section 5 we indicate a few directions on how to pursue this issue further.

Related Work: As mentioned above, paper [21] has been the main motivation for our work.

Closely related is also the work on the tool Times [4] which allows to generate code from timed automata extended with preemptable tasks. The focus in this work is schedulability rather than semantical preservation. The generated code is multi-threaded whereas ours is mono-threaded.

Similar motivations with ours has the work reported in [13], where the model of *time-triggered automata* is proposed to capture execution on time-triggered architectures [12]. Issues like execution and IO communication times, as well as robustness of digital clocks (which cannot assumed to be perfect in other architectures than time-triggered) are not considered in this work.

Related is also the work on digitization and robustness of timed automata, e.g., see [11, 16, 15], however, the focus of most of these works is preservation of dense-time semantics by various discrete-time semantics and the use of preservation results for verification.

Finally, a large amount of work exists on code-generation from high-level models other than timed automata, for instance, hybrid automata [3], Giotto [10], Simulink/Stateflow[1] models [6, 5, 18], or synchronous languages [9, 6, 17, 19], to mention only a few.

2   Timed Automata with Inputs and Outputs

A timed automaton with inputs and outputs (TA for short) is a tuple $\mathsf{A} = (\mathsf{Q}, \mathsf{q_o}, \mathsf{X}, \mathsf{I}, \mathsf{O}, \mathsf{Tr}, \mathsf{Inv})$. Q is a finite set of *locations* and $\mathsf{q_o} \in \mathsf{Q}$ is the *initial* location. X is the finite set of *clocks*. I (resp. O) is a finite set of input (resp. output) events. Tr is a finite set of *transitions*. A transition is a tuple $\mathsf{tr} = (q, q', a, g, r)$, where $q, q' \in \mathsf{Q}$ are the source and target locations, $a \in \mathsf{I} \cup \mathsf{O} \cup \{\tau\}$ is an input or output event, or an *internal* event τ, g is the *guard* (that is, a

---

[1] Trademark of The Mathworks, Inc.

conjunction of constraints of the form $x \# c$, where $x \in X$, $\# \in \{<, \leq, =, \geq, >\}$ and c is an integer constant) and $r \subseteq X$ is the set of clocks to be *reset*. Inv is a function that defines for each location $q \in Q$ its *invariant* $\mathsf{Inv}(q)$, a constraint similar to a guard which specifies the time progress condition. We require that every guard of a transition t is contained in the invariant of the source location of t.

A TA defines an infinite transition system $\mathsf{TS} = (\mathsf{S}, s_0, \mathsf{T})$. S is the set of *states*. A state is a tuple (q, v), where $q \in Q$ and $v : X \to R$ is a *valuation* associating a non-negative real value to each clock. We require v to satisfy $\mathsf{Inv}(q)$. The valuation assigning zero to all clocks is denoted v_{zero}. The *initial state* of TS is $s_0 = (q_0, v_{\text{zero}})$. $\mathsf{T} \subseteq \mathsf{S} \times (\mathsf{I} \cup \mathsf{O} \cup \{\tau\} \cup R) \times \mathsf{S}$ is a set of *discrete or timed transitions*. A discrete transition is a tuple (s, a, s') where $a \in \mathsf{I} \cup \mathsf{O} \cup \{\tau\}$, $s = (q, v)$, $s' = (q', v')$ and there exists a discrete transition $\mathsf{tr} = (q, q', a, g, r) \in \mathsf{Tr}$ such that v satisfies g and $v' = v[r := 0]$ is obtained from v by setting all clocks in r to zero and keeping the values of the rest of the clocks the same. We also write $s \xrightarrow{\mathsf{tr}} s'$ for a discrete transition. A timed transition is a tuple $(s, \delta, s') \in \mathsf{T}$ where $\delta \in R$, $s = (q, v)$, $s' = (q, v')$ and $v' = v + \delta$ is obtained from v by increasing all clocks by δ. We require that for all $\delta' \leq \delta$, $v + \delta'$ satisfies $\mathsf{Inv}(q)$. We also write $s \xrightarrow{\delta} s'$ for a timed transition. A *discrete transition sequence* of A is a finite sequence of discrete transitions $\mathsf{tr}_0, \mathsf{tr}_1, ..., \mathsf{tr}_k$ such that $s_0 \xrightarrow{\delta_0 \ \mathsf{tr}_0} s_1 \xrightarrow{\delta_1 \ \mathsf{tr}_1} \cdots s_k$, for some $\delta_0, ..., \delta_{k-1} \in R$. The set of all discrete transition sequences of A is denoted $\mathsf{DTS}(\mathsf{A})$. We assume that A is *non-zeno*, that is, it has no reachable state s such that in all executions starting from s time converges.

3   A Methodology for the Implementation of Timed Automata

In order to obtain an implementation of a timed automaton A in a systematic way, we propose a methodology based on modeling. The main idea is to build a *global execution model*, as illustrated in Figure 1. This model captures the (real-time) execution of the program implementing A on a given execution platform and along with a given environment. In particular, the steps of our methodology are the following:

- A is transformed into an untimed (i.e., discrete) automaton $\mathsf{Prog}(\mathsf{A})$. The latter is interpreted by a generic program, and this is how A is implemented. At the same time, $\mathsf{Prog}(\mathsf{A})$ is part of the global execution model.
- The user provides models of the execution platform, in the form of timed automata communicating with $\mathsf{Prog}(\mathsf{A})$. We identify three main components permitting to model the essential features of the execution platform:
  - A timed automaton A_{DC} modeling the digital clock of the platform, that the program implementing A consults when reading the current time.
  - A timed automaton A_{EX} modeling program execution.
  - A timed automaton A_{IO} modeling the interface of the program and execution platform with the external environment.

The three models can be designed by the user, or chosen from a set of "sample" models we provide in the rest of this section. A *platform model* is the composition $P = A_{DC}||A_{EX}||A_{IO}$.

– The user provides a model of the environment in the form of a TA Env. Env can be composed with the "ideal" controller A to yield an "ideal" model of the closed-loop system, A||Env, on which various properties can be model-checked.

– Env can also be composed with the above set of models to yield the global execution model:

$$M = Prog(A)||A_{DC}||A_{EX}||A_{IO}||Env .$$

M models the execution of the program implementing A on an execution platform behaving as specified by the triple (A_{DC}, A_{IO}, A_{EX}) and interacting with an environment behaving as specified by Env. In other words, M captures the *execution semantics* in the sense of [21]. As with the ideal model A||Env, any property that the implementation must satisfy can be checked on M.

Figure 1 shows the different components of the global execution model and their interfaces. We explain these in more detail in the rest of this section.

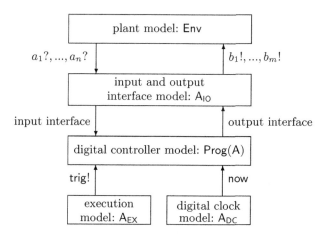

Fig. 1. The global execution model

Let $A = (Q, q_o, X, I, O, Tr, Inv)$ be a timed automaton with inputs and outputs. This notation will be used in the whole section.

3.1   The Program Implementing a Timed Automaton

The program implementing A works by *interpreting* the untimed automaton Prog(A) discussed above. Thus, we begin by explaining how to transform A into Prog(A).

Transforming A into Prog(A). Prog(A) is a finite automaton extended with a set of static variables, meaning that they do not evolve with time (as opposed to the clocks of A which are dynamic variables). Prog(A) has the same set of discrete states Q as A. For each clock x of A, Prog(A) has a static variable x_p of type "real" (initialized to zero). Prog(A) also has an externally updated variable now of type "real": now is an interface variable between Prog(A) and A_{DC}. now stores the value of the current time as given by the platform clock. The program may read this value at any time. All variables x_p are initialized to now.

Prog(A) also has an *input/output interface*, in order to communicate with the environment. For the moment, we will not be specific regarding this interface, as there as many options, depending on the program implementation, execution platform, and so on. Examples of possible interfaces are given below, along with the examples of A_{IO} models (Section 3.2).

For each transition $tr = (q, q', a, g, r)$ of A, Prog(A) has a transition $tr_p = (q, q', trig?, a_{in}, a_{out}, g_p, r_p)$, where q, q' are the source and destination discrete states and:

- trig is an input event that serves to model the triggering of the external loop of the program: the use of trig will become clear in the paragraphs that follow (Section 3.2).
- If $a \in I$ then a_{in} is an element of the input interface associated with a. As mentioned above, there are different such interfaces, so a_{in} can be of different types: if the interface is based on input variables, then a_{in} is a condition on these variables; if the interface is based on event-synchronization, then a_{in} can be an event. If $a \notin I$ then a_{in} is empty and has no effect on the semantics of tr_p.
- If $a \in O$ then a_{out} is an element of the output interface associated with a. Again, different possibilities exist, some of which are presented in the paragraph discussing how to model A_{IO} (Section 3.2). If $a \notin O$ then a_{out} is empty and has no effect on the semantics of tr_p.
- g_p is a condition obtained by replacing every occurrence of a clock x in the guard g by now $- x_p$.
- r_p is a set of assignments obtained by replacing every reset of a clock x in r by $x_p := $ now.

It should be noted that Prog(A) has no invariants: indeed, Prog(A) is an untimed automaton with no urgency associated with it. The transitions of Prog(A) are "triggered" by the input event trig, issued by A_{EX}. A_{EX} is a timed automaton that includes the urgency constraints on the execution of Prog(A).

Prog(A) will also have a set of *escape* transitions. These transitions are self-loops of the form $(q, q, trig?, g_{else})$, where g_{else} is the negation of the disjunction of all guards of all other transitions exiting q. Thus, this escape transition models the case where none of the previous transitions is enabled, thus, no transition is taken and the program does not change state. Escape transitions are simply added for modeling purposes and are not interpreted by the program interpreting Prog(A).

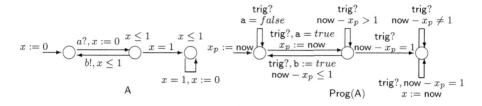

Fig. 2. Transforming A to Prog(A): the IO interface uses shared variables

In summary, Prog(A) is a discrete version of A where dynamic clocks are replaced by static variables, input and output events are replaced by conditions on input variables and assignments on output variables, respectively, and an externally updated variable now capturing global time as given by the digital clock of the platform.

Interpreting Prog(A). Perhaps the simplest control programs are the mono-thread, single-loop programs of the form "while (some external condition) do: read inputs; compute; update state; write outputs; end while". For instance, these are the types of programs typically generated by the compilers of synchronous languages [9]. This is also the type of programs we consider in this paper.

The "external condition" mentioned above can be some type of trigger, for instance, the tick of a periodic clock, or the rising of an alarm. It can also be simply "true", as in the type of programs considered in [21]. We will consider both types in this paper. We call the former type of programs *triggered* and the latter *trigger-free*.

In our case, the body of the above loop will be as shown in Figure 3. The current time is read and stored in variable now at the beginning of the loop

```
initialize;
loop forever
  await trigger;
  now  := read_platform_clock();
  in_1 := read_input_1();
  in_2 := read_input_2();
  ...
  for each outgoing transition tr of current_location do
    if (input_condition(tr) and guard(tr)) then
      perform_assignements(tr);
      current_location := destination_location(tr);
      break for loop;
    end if;
  end for;
end loop;
```

Fig. 3. The program interpreting Prog(A)

body. Then all inputs are read. Then each outgoing transition is evaluated and the first one which is enabled is taken, meaning the assignments are performed (including clock assignments r_p and output variable assignments a_{out}) and the current location is updated. Finally, the search for transitions is aborted and the program returns to the beginning of the outer loop.

Notice that the guard(t) may contain not only the clock guard g_p of a transition, but other conditions as well, for instance, a condition corresponding to an input interface element. Also note that the event trig? of a transition of Prog(A) is not interpreted: indeed it only serves the purpose of modeling the triggering of the program loop. On the other hand, if there are events corresponding to function calls (for instance, events f_1^a! of Figure 6 or f_b! of Figure 7 below), these are indeed interpreted as function calls read_input or write_output (the latter called inside perform_assignments(t)). Finally, note that escape transitions of Prog(A) are not evaluated in the "for each outgoing transition" loop. This is because these transitions correspond precisely to the case where none of the transitions of A is enabled.

3.2   Modeling the Execution Platform

Modeling the Digital Clock of the Platform. The platform clock is modeled by a timed automaton A_{DC} which updates variable now and "exports" this variable to Prog(A) (see Figure 1). Different A_{DC} models can be built: some are shown in Figure 4.

$Cl_1(\Delta)$ models a perfectly periodic digital clock with period Δ. $Cl_2(\Delta, \epsilon)$ models a clock with non-perfect period $\Delta \pm \epsilon$. In this model errors may accumulate, so that the i-th tick of the clock (i.e., update of now) may occur anywhere in the interval $[(\Delta - \epsilon)i, (\Delta + \epsilon)i]$. $Cl_3(\Delta, \epsilon)$ models a more restricted behavior where errors do not accumulate: the i-th tick occurs in the interval $[i\Delta - \epsilon, i\Delta + \epsilon]$, for all i.

Modeling the Execution of the Program. Computation is essentially change of state, and execution time is the time it takes to change state. Prog(A) is an untimed automaton, thus, does not contain this information: changes of state can happen at any time. A_{EX} is used to place restrictions on the times state changes occur. These restrictions model worst-case and best-case execution times (WCET, BCET) of the program interpreting Prog(A) on the execution platform.

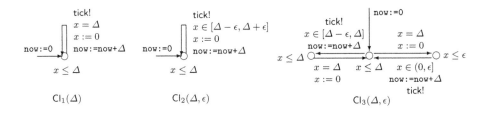

Fig. 4. Digital-clock models

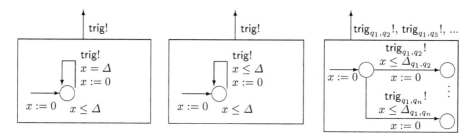

Fig. 5. Execution models

In Figure 5 we present sample A_{EX} models, corresponding to the two types of programs discussed above, namely, triggered and trigger-free programs. The model on the left is very simple: it models a periodic invocation of the loop of the program, every Δ time units. In this case, the assumption is that the WCET of the body of the loop is at most Δ. This means that the body of the loop can be completed before the next time it is invoked.

By simply replacing the guard $x = \Delta$ by $x \leq \Delta$, we obtain the automaton in the middle of Figure 5: this models a trigger-free program with WCET equal to Δ. A more detailed model is the automaton on the right of the figure (for simplicity, the automaton is incomplete: it has the same locations and discrete structure as A). This automaton models different WCETs for different changes of state: if $\mathsf{Prog}(A)$ moves from q_1 to q_2 then the WCET is equal to Δ_{q_1,q_2}, when it moves from q_1 to q_3 then the WCET is Δ_{q_1,q_3}, and so on. This automaton exports a set of triggering events instead of a single one. In this case $\mathsf{Prog}(A)$ needs to be modified accordingly, so that in a transition $(q, q', \mathsf{trig}?, ...)$, trig is replaced by $\mathsf{trig}_{q,q'}$.

Modeling the Interfaces with the Environment. The ideal controller A communicates with Env exchanging input and output messages in an instantaneous manner. Most computer programs communicate with their environment by reading and writing shared variables, or via function calls (initiated by the program).[2]

We now give some examples on how common situations of IO interfaces can be modeled. Note that these are not the only possibilities. For simplicity, let us also suppose that inputs and outputs are handled separately, so that A_{IO} is "split" in two components, one for inputs and one for outputs.

We first discuss inputs. One possible interface policy is the following. For each input event a of A, there is a boolean interface variable a which is set to "true" every time a occurs and remains "true" for a certain time bounded by $[l_a, u_a]$. This is modeled by the automaton on the left of Figure 6. Regarding the definition of $\mathsf{Prog}(A)$ given above, the input interface element a_{in}, in this case, will simply be the condition a = true.

---

[2] Interrupts are also an option. We do not consider this option in this paper, since it does not match well with the program structure of Figure 3.

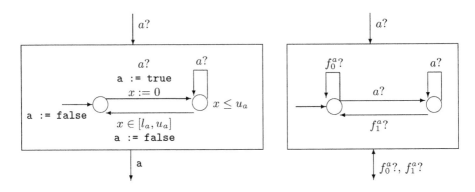

Fig. 6. Input interface models

Another possible input interface is the one modeled by the automaton on the right of Figure 6. This models the situation where the program calls a function that checks whether event a has occurred since the last time the function was called. The function call is modeled by events f_0^a and f_1^a, on which $\mathsf{Prog}(\mathsf{A})$ and the interface automaton synchronize. f_0^a corresponds to the function returning "false" (event a has not occurred) and f_1^a corresponds to the function returning "true" (a has occurred). Notice that this model is untimed. Regarding the definition of $\mathsf{Prog}(\mathsf{A})$ given above, the input interface element a_{in}, in this case, is either $f_1^a!$ or $f_0^a!$.

We now discuss outputs. One simple output interface is modeled by the automaton on the left of Figure 7. It receives a function call from the program (event f_b) and begins the process of emitting event b. This process takes some time in $[l_b, u_b]$. Regarding the definition of $\mathsf{Prog}(\mathsf{A})$ given above, the output interface element a_{out}, in this case, will simply be $f_b!$.

Another possibility is modeled by the automaton on the right of Figure 7. Here, the program sets variable b to true whenever output b is to be emitted (i.e., a_{out} is the assignment $b := \mathtt{true}$). The interface automaton "samples" this variable periodically every Δ time units. Whenever the variable is "true" output b is emitted to the environment. Also, the variable b is reset to "false", to prevent future emissions unless they are commanded by the program (which must again set b to "true").

3.3   Using the Global Execution Model for Verification and Synthesis

The global execution model M is a network of timed and untimed automata extended with discrete variables. Can M be automatically model-checked? It can, provided its discrete state-space is finite. Here, we face a potential problem, since variable now of A_{DC} can grow arbitrarily large. Similarly, variables x_p of $\mathsf{Prog}(\mathsf{A})$ are reset to now and can thus be arbitrarily large as well.

This problem can be solved in the same way it is solved in the TA case, where clocks can also grow arbitrarily. First, variable now can be removed, as

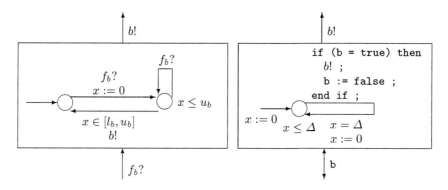

Fig. 7. Output interface models

follows. Resets $x_p := \mathsf{now}$ are replaced by $x_p := 0$ and $\mathsf{now} - x_p$ is replaced by x_p in all guards. Then, $\mathsf{A_{DC}}$ is modified so that, instead of updating now, it updates *all variables* x_p *of* $\mathsf{Prog}(A)$ *simultaneously*. For instance, in the examples of $\mathsf{A_{DC}}$ shown in Figure 4, $\mathsf{now} := \mathsf{now} + \Delta$ is replaced by a set of assignments $x_p := x_p + \Delta$, one for each x_p. It can be seen that this model is semantically equivalent to the previous one that uses now.[3]

We now have a model where x_p variables are incremented simultaneously. A reasoning similar to the one used to show finiteness of the region graph can be used: once a variable x_p has grown larger than the largest constant c_{max} appearing in a guard g_p of $\mathsf{Prog}(A)$, the exact value of x_p is irrelevant, thus can be replaced by $+\infty$ without affecting the semantics of the model. The result is a finite domain for x_p, namely, $\{0, \Delta, 2\Delta, ..., c_{max}, +\infty\}$. Using such abstraction techniques [4] and model-checking tools as Kronos or Uppaal, M can be model-checked against a given specification φ.

What if M fails to satisfy φ? Could we find *another* program Prog' such that $M' = \mathsf{Prog}' || \mathsf{A_{DC}} || \mathsf{A_{EX}} || \mathsf{A_{IO}} || \mathsf{Env}$ satisfies φ? The answer is yes, and Prog' can in fact by synthesized automatically (at least in principle). Prog' can be viewed as a controller that functions in closed-loop with a "plant" $\mathsf{A_{DC}} || \mathsf{A_{EX}} || \mathsf{A_{IO}} || \mathsf{Env}$. The problem is to synthesize Prog' so that the closed-loop system, i.e., M', satisfies φ. Notice that the controller is *untimed*, in the sense that it communicates with the "plant" via a discrete interface (discrete events and variables). The controller does observe time, but only discrete time: the tick events of $\mathsf{A_{DC}}$.

Synthesis of an untimed controller for a timed plant against a (timed or untimed) specification is possible. In fact, the problem can be reduced to a problem of untimed synthesis with partial observability. This is done by generating an ap-

---

[3] In fact we could have presented $\mathsf{Prog}(A)$ and its interface with $\mathsf{A_{DC}}$ in this way in the first place, however, we find the model with now "cleaner" because every variable has a unique writer. Instead, in the modified model x_p variables are updated by $\mathsf{A_{DC}}$ and reset to zero by $\mathsf{Prog}(A)$.

[4] In the case other $\mathsf{A_{DC}}$ models than those of Figure 4 are used, some "sanity" hypotheses need to be made. It is natural to expect now to increase monotonically by a finite number of quanta Δ_i, to diverge, and so on.

propriate finite-state abstraction of the timed plant, such as the region graph [1] or the time-abstracting bisimulation graph [20]. The controller to be synthesized for this plant is not a *state-feedback* controller, since it cannot observe the clocks of the plant (thus, neither the regions or zones of the abstract graph). The controller only observes a discrete event and variable interface, as mentioned above.

4   On Property Preservation Under Platform Refinement

There is one piece missing from our framework, namely, a result of the form:

> "given platforms P and P', such that P' is "better" than P, if $\mathsf{Prog}(\mathsf{A})\|P\|\mathsf{Env}$ satisfies φ then $\mathsf{Prog}(\mathsf{A})\|P'\|\mathsf{Env}$ also satisfies φ",

for a reasonable definition of "better".

Such a result is important for many reasons. First, it guarantees that a program that functions correctly on P will continue to function correctly when P is replaced by a "better" platform, which is a reasonable expectation. Second, it allows for abstractions to be made when modeling a platform and trying to model-check the global execution model. Such abstractions are often crucial in order to limit modeling complexity as well as state explosion. A result as above allows for such abstractions, as long as it can be ensured that the real execution platform is "better" than its model.

But what should the definition of "better" be? It seems appropriate to adopt an element-wise definition, where $P' = (\mathsf{A}'_{\mathsf{DC}}, \mathsf{A}'_{\mathsf{EX}}, \mathsf{A}'_{\mathsf{IO}})$ is better than $P = (\mathsf{A}_{\mathsf{DC}}, \mathsf{A}_{\mathsf{EX}}, \mathsf{A}_{\mathsf{IO}})$ iff $\mathsf{A}'_{\mathsf{DC}}$ is better than A_{DC}, $\mathsf{A}'_{\mathsf{EX}}$ is better than A_{EX} and $\mathsf{A}'_{\mathsf{IO}}$ is better than A_{IO}. But while a more or less standard refinement relation could be used to define "better" in the cases of A_{EX} and A_{IO},[5] we run into problems when trying to define "better" in the case of A_{DC}. We illustrate these problems in what follows. To make the discussion easier to follow, we will ignore A_{EX} and A_{IO} models (i.e., assume they are "ideal") and focus only on A_{DC}. Thus, we will assume that $\mathsf{Prog}(\mathsf{A})$ has no **trig** events and that it communicates with Env directly via input/output synchronization events, like A does.

Example 1. Consider, then, automaton A_1 on Figure 8 and let Env generate a single timed trace where $a!$ is produced at time $t_1 = 0.9$ and $b!$ is produced at time $t_2 = 1.1$. We claim that

$$\mathsf{Prog}(\mathsf{A}_1)\|\mathsf{Cl}_1(2)\|\mathsf{Env} \models \Box\neg\mathsf{bad}$$

but

$$\mathsf{Prog}(\mathsf{A}_1)\|\mathsf{Cl}_1(1)\|\mathsf{Env} \not\models \Box\neg\mathsf{bad}$$

(recall that $\mathsf{Cl}_1(\Delta)$ is the parameterized digital-clock model shown in Figure 4). Indeed, in the first case, at both times t_1 and t_2, now equals 0, which means

---

[5]   We say "more or less" because A_{IO} contain inputs and outputs, and refinement relations for such models are not that standard (e.g., see [2, 8]).

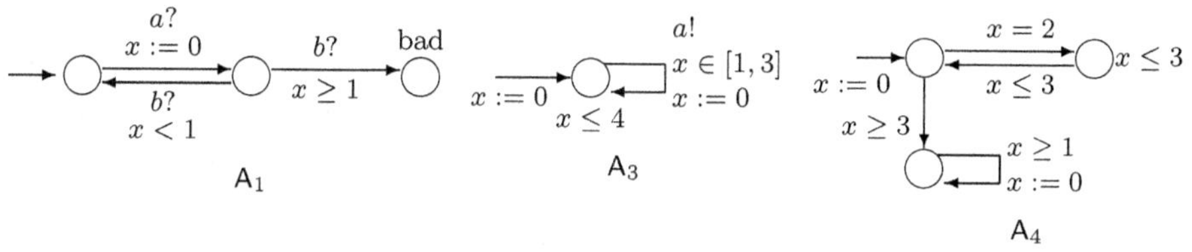

Fig. 8. Counter-examples

that the guard $\text{now} - x_p \geq 1$ is evaluated to "false". In the second case, however, at t_1, $\text{now} = 0$ while at t_2, $\text{now} = 1$, so that $\text{now} - x_p = 1 - 0 = 1$ and the guard is "true". On the other hand, it seems reasonable to expect a platform P_1 to be "better" than P_2 if the only difference between the two is that P_1 has $\text{A}_{\text{DC}} = \text{Cl}_1(1)$ whereas P_2 has $\text{A}_{\text{DC}} = \text{Cl}_1(2)$. Indeed, $\text{Cl}_1(1)$ runs twice as fast as $\text{Cl}_1(2)$, in other words, it is strictly more precise.   □

What the above example shows is that the platform-refinement property we hoped for does not hold in general. Notice that adding the assumption $\text{A}||\text{Env} \models \varphi$ does not help, since this assumption already holds in the counter-example above. Thus, we have a situation where, on one hand, the "ideal" implementation satisfies the property, on the other hand, the "slow" implementation satisfies the property, however, the "fast" implementation does not satisfy the property. In the rest of the section, we will attempt to modify our goal and examine other possibilities of property preservation.

We first examine whether the goal holds for a "chaotic" environment Chaos, that is, an environment which accepts any input and may generate any output at any time:

$$(\text{Prog}(\text{A})||P||\text{Chaos} \models \varphi) \wedge (P' \text{ better than } P) \Rightarrow (\text{Prog}(\text{A})||P'||\text{Chaos} \models \varphi) ?$$

Example 2. The above implication does not hold either. To see this, consider a modified version of automaton A_1 of Figure 8, call it A_2, where the guard $x \geq 1$ is replaced by $x = 1$ and the guard $x < 1$ by $x \neq 1$. Then the property $\square\neg\text{bad}$ is satisfied with digital clock model $\text{Cl}_1(2)$ but not with $\text{Cl}_1(1)$. The reason is that with $\text{Cl}_1(2)$, now only takes the values $0, 2, ...$, thus, the guard $\text{now} - x_p = 1$ is never satisfied. With $\text{Cl}_1(2)$, now takes the values $0, 1, 2, ...$, so the guard is satisfied.   □

The above example suggests that, for properties of the form $\square\neg\text{bad}$, a "slower" clock may be "better" than a "faster" one. This may seem like a paradox, how-ever, it is explained by the fact that a program using the faster clock has a higher "sampling rate" and thus may generate more behaviors. We formalize this observation in the lemma that follows.

Lemma 1. *Let* A *be a TA,* $\Delta \in R$ *and* $k \in \{1, 2, ...\}$. *Then*

$$\text{DTS}(\text{Prog}(\text{A})||\text{Cl}_1(k\Delta)) \subseteq \text{DTS}(\text{Prog}(\text{A})||\text{Cl}_1(\Delta)) \subseteq \text{DTS}(\text{A}) .$$

Sketch of proof: Let $\rho = \mathsf{tr}_1, \mathsf{tr}_2, ..., \mathsf{tr}_k$ be a sequence of discrete transitions of A. This sequence defines a set of constraints C on the times $t_1, t_2, ..., t_k$ where these transitions can be taken. Indeed, if a clock x is reset to zero by tr_i and tested to $x \leq 5$ by tr_j with $j > i$ (and x is not reset between i and j) then this creates the constraint $t_j - t_i \leq 5$. Then, $\rho \in \mathsf{DTS}(\mathsf{A})$ iff C is satisfiable, i.e., has a solution $t_1 \leq t_2 \leq \cdots \leq t_k$ with $t_i \in R$. When interpreted in $\mathsf{Prog}(\mathsf{A})||\mathsf{Cl}_1(\Delta)$, ρ generates a set of constraints C' which is *stronger* than C. Indeed, C' contains the additional constraint that every t_i must be a multiple of Δ. Thus, if C is unsatisfiable, so is C'. Similarly, when interpreted in $\mathsf{Prog}(\mathsf{A})||\mathsf{Cl}_1(k\Delta)$, ρ generates a set of constraints C'' which is stronger than C', since t_i must now be a multiple of $k\Delta$.   □

Notice that this lemma does not hold for timed traces, as Example 1 shows. Based on this lemma we can prove the following.

Proposition 1. *Let* A *be a TA,* $\mathsf{A_{EX}}$ *a program execution model,* $\mathsf{A_{IO}}$ *an IO interface model,* $\Delta \in R$ *and* $k \in \{1, 2, ...\}$*. Let* $\varphi \equiv \Box\neg bad$ *for some location "bad" of* A*. Then*

$$\mathsf{A}||\mathsf{Chaos} \models \varphi \Rightarrow \mathsf{Prog}(\mathsf{A})||\mathsf{Cl}_1(\Delta)||\mathsf{Chaos} \models \varphi \Rightarrow \mathsf{Prog}(\mathsf{A})||\mathsf{Cl}_1(k\Delta)||\mathsf{Chaos} \models \varphi \ .$$

One may wonder whether Proposition 1 holds for other properties except reachability of "bad" locations. A crucial property in any system is deadlock-freedom, or, in the case of timed automata, non-zenoness. Observe that, as long as the platform models $\mathsf{A_{DC}}, \mathsf{A_{EX}}, \mathsf{A_{IO}}$ are non-zeno, $\mathsf{Prog}(\mathsf{A})||\mathsf{A_{DC}}||\mathsf{A_{EX}}||\mathsf{A_{IO}}$ is also non-zeno, since $\mathsf{Prog}(\mathsf{A})$ is *receptive* to input events such as trig. We will then study another property, namely, that it is always possible for $\mathsf{Prog}(\mathsf{A})$ to take a discrete transition (possibly after letting time pass). We call such an execution model *non-blocking* and write $NB(\mathsf{Prog}(\mathsf{A})||P||\mathsf{Env})$. First note that non-blockingness does not always hold.

Example 3. Consider TA A_3 of Figure 8. If $\mathsf{Prog}(\mathsf{A}_3)$ is executed on a platform with $\mathsf{A_{DC}} = \mathsf{Cl}_1(4)$ then it is blocking, since the guard $now - x_p \in [1, 3]$ will be evaluated when $now = 0, 4, ...$, and found false at all times.   □

We next study the following property of non-blockingness preservation:

$$NB(\mathsf{Prog}(\mathsf{A})||P||\mathsf{Chaos}) \wedge (P' \text{ better than } P) \Rightarrow NB(\mathsf{Prog}(\mathsf{A})||P'||\mathsf{Chaos}) \ ?$$

Example 4. The above implication does not hold either. Consider automaton A_4 of Figure 8. $\mathsf{Prog}(\mathsf{A}_4)$ is non-blocking on a platform with $\mathsf{A_{DC}} = \mathsf{Cl}_1(4)$, simply because the guard $now - x_p = 2$ is never evaluated to true. On the other hand, this guard is evaluated to true with $\mathsf{A_{DC}} = \mathsf{Cl}_1(2)$. In this case, $\mathsf{Prog}(\mathsf{A}_4)$ is blocking, because it "gets stuck" in the right-most location with $now - x_p = 4 > 3$, thus, unable to take any transition.   □

5   Conclusions and Perspectives

In this paper we have asked a question, namely, whether timed automata can be implemented using the standard semantics and appropriate modeling, instead of introducing new semantics. We proposed a modeling framework that permits this goal to be partly achieved. In particular, we showed how to transform a timed automaton into a program and how to model the execution of this program on a given platform as a collection of (timed) automata. The models can be used to check whether the implementation satisfies a desired property. They can also be used for synthesis of another program which satisfies the property by construction. Still, subtleties arise regarding property preservation when changing the execution platform. We exposed such subtleties through a series of examples. We believe describing such failed attempts is useful, as it draws the limits of what can be done. The question is worth pursuing, and we intend to do this as part of future work. In particular, we would like to generalize Proposition 1 to more digital clock models, by introducing an appropriate notion of refinement for such models. Next would be to generalize this to entire platforms. Finally, to study the preservation of more properties, such as the non-blocking property we touched upon.

References

1. R. Alur and D. Dill. A theory of timed automata. *Theoretical Computer Science*, 126:183–235, 1994.
2. R. Alur, T. Henzinger, O. Kupferman, and M. Vardi. Alternating refinement relations. In *CONCUR'98*, volume 1466 of *LNCS*. Springer, 1998.
3. R. Alur, F. Ivancic, J. Kim, I. Lee, and O. Sokolsky. Generating embedded software from hierarchical hybrid models. In *Languages, Compilers, and Tools for Embedded Systems (LCTES'03)*. ACM, 2003.
4. T. Amnell, E. Fersman, P. Pettersson, W. Yi, and H. Sun. Code synthesis for timed automata. *Nordic J. of Computing*, 9(4):269–300, 2002.
5. P. Caspi, A. Curic, A. Maignan, C. Sofronis, and S. Tripakis. Translating discrete-time Simulink to Lustre. In *Embedded Software (EMSOFT'03)*, volume 2855 of *LNCS*. Springer, 2003.
6. P. Caspi, A. Curic, A. Maignan, C. Sofronis, S. Tripakis, and P. Niebert. From Simulink to SCADE/Lustre to TTA: a layered approach for distributed embedded applications. In *Languages, Compilers, and Tools for Embedded Systems (LCTES'03)*. ACM, 2003.
7. C. Daws, A. Olivero, S. Tripakis, and S. Yovine. The tool Kronos. In *Hybrid Systems III, Verification and Control*, volume 1066 of *LNCS*, pages 208–219. Springer-Verlag, 1996.
8. L. de Alfaro and T.A. Henzinger. Interface automata. In *Foundations of Software Engineering (FSE)*. ACM Press, 2001.
9. N. Halbwachs. *Synchronous Programming of Reactive Systems*. Kluwer, 1992.
10. T. Henzinger, B. Horowitz, and C. Kirsch. Giotto: A time-triggered language for embedded programming. In *EMSOFT'01*, volume 2211 of *LNCS*. Springer, 2001.
11. T. Henzinger, Z. Manna, and A. Pnueli. What good are digital clocks? In *ICALP'92*, LNCS 623, 1992.
12. H. Kopetz. *Real-Time Systems Design Principles for Distributed Embedded Applications*. Kluwer, 1997.
13. P. Krčál, L. Mokrushin, P.S. Thiagarajan, and W. Yi. Timed vs time triggered automata. In *CONCUR'04*, volume 3170 of *LNCS*. Springer, 2004.

14. K. Larsen, P. Petterson, and W. Yi. Uppaal in a nutshell. *Software Tools for Technology Transfer*, 1(1/2), October 1997.
15. J. Ouaknine and J. Worrell. Revisiting digitization, robustness, and decidability for timed automata. In *LICS 2003*. IEEE CS Press, 2003.
16. A. Puri. Dynamical properties of timed automata. *Discrete Event Dynamic Systems*, 10(1-2):87–113, 2000.
17. N. Scaife and P. Caspi. Integrating model-based design and preemptive scheduling in mixed time- and event-triggered systems. In *Euromicro conference on Real-Time Systems (ECRTS'04)*, 2004.
18. N. Scaife, C. Sofronis, P. Caspi, S. Tripakis, and F. Maraninchi. Defining and translating a "safe" subset of Simulink/Stateflow into Lustre. In *4th ACM International Conference on Embedded Software (EMSOFT'04)*, 2004.
19. S. Tripakis, C. Sofronis, N. Scaife, and P. Caspi. Semantics-preserving and memory-efficient implementation of inter-task communication under static-priority or EDF schedulers. In *5th ACM Intl. Conf. on Embedded Software (EMSOFT'05)*, 2005.
20. S. Tripakis and S. Yovine. Analysis of timed systems using time-abstracting bisimulations. *Formal Methods in System Design*, 18(1):25–68, January 2001.
21. M. De Wulf, L. Doyen, and J-F. Raskin. Almost ASAP semantics: From timed models to timed implementations. In *HSCC'04*, volume 2993 of *LNCS*. Springer, 2004.

Timed Abstract Non-interference

Roberto Giacobazzi[1] and Isabella Mastroeni[2]

[1] Dipartimento di Informatica - Università di Verona - Verona, Italy
`roberto.giacobazzi@univr.it`
[2] Department of Computing and Information
Sciences - Kansas State University - Manhattan, Kansas, USA
`isabellm@cis.ksu.edu`

Abstract. In this paper, we introduce a timed notion of abstract non-interference. This is obtained by considering semantics which observe time elapsed in computations. Timing channels can be modeled in this way either by letting the attacker to observe time as a public variable or reckon the time elapsed by observing the computational traces' length, corresponding to observe the program counter. In the first case abstract non-interference provides a model for abstracting the information about time, namely we can for example consider models of attackers that can observe only intervals of time, or other more abstract properties. In the second case abstract non-interference provides a model for attackers able to observe properties of trace length, e.g., the public memory during the whole computation. We investigate when adding the observation of time does not increase the attacker's power in disclosing confidential information about data. This models the absence of timing channels in language-based security.

Keywords: Abstract interpretation, security, non-interference, timing channels.

1 Introduction

The standard approach to the confidentiality problem, also called *non-interference*, is based on a characterization of attackers that does not impose any observational or complexity restriction on the attackers' power [19]. The notion of abstract non-interference (ANI) has been introduced recently in [10] as a weakening of this notion, modeling weaker attackers having a restricted observation power specified as an abstraction of the concrete domain of computation. In this paper we prove that ANI is an adequate model of non-interference, including a variety of timing channels as a special case.

The Problem. Any non-interference problem in language-based security has first to specify what an attacker can observe. Standard denotational semantics is typically not adequate for modeling covert channels such as timing channels, deadlock channels and termination channels. Consider for instance the following simple program fragment:

$$P \stackrel{\text{def}}{=} \textbf{while } h \textbf{ do } l := l; h := h - 1 \textbf{ endw}$$

In this case, the public output is unchanged, independently from the initial value of h. However, if the attacker can measure the time elapsed, then it could understand

P. Pettersson and W. Yi (Eds.): FORMATS 2005, LNCS 3829, pp. 289–303, 2005.

whether the while-loop is executed or not, disclosing some information about the initial value of h. This means that, in this case, the program is not secure. Standard non-interference does not model this behavior. Also, ANI as specified in [10] does not model this aspect of information leakage, being based on a (time insensitive) denotational semantics.

Main Contribution. In this paper we introduce a notion of abstract non-interference which captures timing channels, called *timed abstract non-interference* (TANI). This notion provides the appropriate setting for studying how properties of private data interfere during the execution of the program, with properties of the elapsed time. We will not consider in this paper the converse problem, i.e., how properties of the time elapsed during program execution interfere with properties of data. This because we do not consider here real-time system, where time is relevant to the behavior of programs [3]. We show that timing channels can be modeled as instances of ANI, simply by considering an appropriate, typically more concrete, semantics observing time. The simplest way to include time in the semantics consists in considering the maximal trace semantics of the transition system associated to programs: The trace semantics implicitly embeds the *time* elapsed during computations in the *length* of traces. Another, more explicit, way of including the information about time in the semantics consists in enriching the operational semantics of our language in order to measure the elapsed time: We consider a semantics that *stores*, in a specific variable, the time elapsed during the execution of a program. In this case we consider the time information as a public datum that can be observed by the attacker. Since, the difference between abstract non-interference in [10] and timed abstract non-interference lies only upon the semantics used, it is always possible to characterize the most concrete harmless attacker, observing timing-channels. This gives a measure of the level of security of a program under attack when the time elapsed may represent a critical information. Moreover, time, as well as data, can be abstracted. This is essential in order to model attackers that can observe properties of time elapsed, such as intervals or regular delays such as congruences. It is worth noting that, since we do not consider real-time systems, the only possible timing channels are due to a one-way interaction between data (modeled either as trace length or in the semantics) and time. We model this interaction in the framework of ANI by providing sufficient conditions that avoid timing channels in programs. Indeed, the fact that, in the most general case, an attacker may observe relational dependencies between data and time, may create problems when we want to abstract time. Hence, we provide the conditions characterizing the attackers whose capability of observing time does not increase their power in disclosing confidential information about data. In other words, we characterize in which conditions timed abstract non-interference, where attackers observe time, implies (untimed) abstract non-interference, where the same attackers cannot observe time.

2   Information Flows in Language-Based Security

Confidential data are considered *private*, labeled with H (high-level of secrecy), while all other data are public, labeled with L (low-level of secrecy) [9]. Non-interference can be naturally expressed by using semantic models of program execution. This idea goes back to Cohen's work on *strong dependency* [7], which uses denotational semantics for modeling how information can be transmitted among variables during the execution of programs. Therefore non-interference for programs essentially means that *"a variation of confidential (high or private) input does not cause a variation of public (low) output"* [19]. When this happens, we say that the program has only *secure information flows* [5, 7, 9, 16, 22]. This situation has been modeled by considering the denotational (input/output) semantics $[\![P]\!]$ of the program P. In particular we consider programs where data are typed as private (H) or public (L). Program states in Σ are functions (represented as tuples) mapping variables in the set of values $\mathbb{V}$. Finite traces on Σ are denoted Σ^{+}. If $\text{T} \in \{\text{H}, \text{L}\}$, $n = |\{x \in Var(P)|x : \text{T}\}|$, and $v \in \mathbb{V}^n$, we abuse notation by denoting $v \in \mathbb{V}^{\text{T}}$ the fact that v is a possible value for the variables with security type T. Moreover, we assume that any input s, can be seen as a pair (h, l), where $s^{\text{H}} = h$ is a value for private data and $s^{\text{L}} = l$ is a value for public data. In this case, *non-interference* can be formulated as follows.

> A program P is *secure* if $\forall$ input s, t $s^{\text{L}} = t^{\text{L}} \Rightarrow ([\![P]\!](s))^{\text{L}} = ([\![P]\!](t))^{\text{L}}$

This problem has been formulated also as a *Partial Equivalence Relation* (PER) [20, 15]. In this case we have that if the input data are equivalent under a given equivalent relation, then also the outputs have to be equivalent. The standard methods for checking non-interference are based on security-type systems and data-flow/control-flow analysis. Type-based approaches are designed in such a way that well-typed programs do not leak secrets. In a security-typed language, a type is inductively associated with program statements in such a way that any statement showing a potential flow disclosing secrets is rejected [21, 24]. Similarly, data-flow/control-flow analysis techniques are devoted to statically discover flows of secret data into public variables [6, 16, 17, 20]. All these approaches are characterized by the way they model attackers (or unauthorized users). As far as timing channels are concerned, they are avoided in the Volpano and Smith type system [23] by adding some restrictions or they can be removed by using the program transformation in [1]. Concerning timed automata, a decidable notion of non-interference has been introduced in [4]. We showed in [13] that this notion can be modeled as a generalization of abstract non-interference.

Abstract Non-Interference. The idea of ANI [10], is that an attacker can observe only some properties, modeled as abstract interpretations of program semantics, of public concrete values. The *model of an attacker*, also called *attacker*, is therefore a pair of abstractions $\langle \eta, \rho \rangle$, with $\eta, \rho \in uco(\wp(\mathbb{V}^{\text{L}}))$[1], representing what an observer can see about, respectively, the input and output of a program. The notion of *narrow (abstract) non-interference* (NNI) represents the first weakening of standard non-interference relatively to a given model of an attacker. When a program P satisfies NNI we write $[\eta]P(\rho)$, see Table 1. The problem with this notion is that it introduces *deceptive flows* [10]. Consider, for instance, $l := l * h^2$, and consider the public input property of being an even number, then we can observe a variation of the output's sign due to the existence of both negative and positive even numbers, revealing flows which does not

---

[1] $uco(\wp(\mathbb{V}^{\text{L}}))$ denotes the set of all the upper closure operators on $\wp(\mathbb{V}^{\text{L}})$.

Table 1. Narrow and Abstract Non-Interference

$$[\eta]P(\rho) \text{ if } \forall h_1, h_2 \in \mathbb{V}^{\mathrm{H}}, \forall l_1, l_2 \in \mathbb{V}^{\mathrm{L}} \;.\; \eta(l_1) = \eta(l_2) \Rightarrow \rho(\llbracket P \rrbracket (h_1, l_1)^{\mathrm{L}}) = \rho(\llbracket P \rrbracket (h_2, l_2)^{\mathrm{L}})$$

$$(\eta)P(\phi \leadsto\!\!\!| \rho) \text{ if } \forall h_1, h_2 \in \mathbb{V}^{\mathrm{H}}, \forall l \in \mathbb{V}^{\mathrm{L}} \;.\; \rho(\llbracket P \rrbracket (\phi(h_1), \eta(l))^{\mathrm{L}}) = \rho(\llbracket P \rrbracket (\phi(h_2), \eta(l))^{\mathrm{L}})$$

depend on the private data, here called deceptive. In order to avoid deceptive interference we introduce a weaker notion of non-interference, having no deceptive flows, such that, when the attacker is able to observe the property η of public input, and the property ρ of public output, then no information flow concerning the private input is observable from the public output. The idea is to compare the set of all the computations that have the same input property η, instead of the single computations. We call this notion *abstract non-interference* (ANI). When a program P satisfies abstract non-interference we write $(\eta)P(\phi \leadsto\!\!\!| \rho)$, where $\phi \in uco(\wp(\mathbb{V}^{\mathrm{H}}))$, denoting a confidential data property that we want to keep secret (see Table 1). Note that $[id]P(id)$ models exactly (standard) non-interference. Moreover, we have that abstract non-interference is a weakening of both, standard and narrow non-interference: $[id]P(id) \Rightarrow (\eta)P(\phi \leadsto\!\!\!| \rho)$ and $[\eta]P(\rho) \Rightarrow (\eta)P(\phi \leadsto\!\!\!| \rho)$, while standard non-interference is not stronger than narrow one due to deceptive interference. A proof-system has been introduced, in [11], for checking both narrow and abstract non-interference inductively on program's syntax, while in [25] the author derive a type system for enforcing abstract non-interference in a simple λ-calculus. Moreover, in [10], two methods for deriving the most concrete output observation for a program, given the input one, for both narrow and abstract non-interference are provided together with a domain transformer characterizing the most abstract property that should be declassified in order to guarantee abstract non-interference. In [12] we prove that these two construction form an adjunction in the standard framework of abstract interpretation.

Example 1. Consider the properties *Sign* and *Par*, observing, respectively, the sign and the parity of integers, and the program: $P \stackrel{\text{def}}{=} l := l * h^2$. with security typing: $h : \mathrm{H}$ and $l : \mathrm{L}$ and $\mathbb{V} = \mathbb{Z}$. Let us check if $(id)P(id \leadsto\!\!\!| Par)$. Note that $Par(\llbracket P \rrbracket (2, 1)^{\mathrm{L}}) = Par(4) = 2\mathbb{Z}$ while $Par(\llbracket P \rrbracket (3, 1)^{\mathrm{L}}) = Par(9) = 2\mathbb{Z} + 1$, which are clearly different, therefore in this case $(id)P(id \leadsto\!\!\!| Par)$ doesn't hold. Consider $(id)P(Sign \leadsto\!\!\!| Par)$. Note that $Par(\llbracket P \rrbracket (Sign(2), 1)^{\mathrm{L}}) = Par(\llbracket P \rrbracket (Sign(3), 1)^{\mathrm{L}}) = Par(0+) = \mathbb{Z}$. In this case it is simple to check that $(id)P(Sign \leadsto\!\!\!| Par)$ holds.

3   The Timed Semantics for Deterministic Languages

Consider a simple imperative language, IMP defined by the following syntax: $c ::= \mathbf{nil} \mid x := e \mid c; c \mid \mathbf{while}\ x\ \mathbf{do}\ c\ \mathbf{endw}$, with e denoting expressions evaluated in the set of values $\mathbb{V}$ with standard operations, i.e., if $\mathbb{V} = \mathbb{N}$ then e can be any arithmetical expression. $\mathbb{V}$ can be structured as a flat domain whose bottom element, $\bot$, denotes the value of undefined variables. We follow Cousot's construction [8], defining semantics, at different levels of abstractions, as the abstract interpretation of the maximal trace semantics of a transition system associated with each well-formed program. In the following,

Table 2. Operational timed semantics of IMP

$$
\begin{array}{cc}
\langle \mathbf{nil}, \langle s, t \rangle \rangle \rightarrow \langle s, t \rangle
&
\dfrac{\langle e, \langle s, t \rangle \rangle \rightarrow n \in \mathbb{V}_x}{\langle x := e, \langle s, t \rangle \rangle \rightarrow \langle s[n/x], t + t_{\mathtt{A}} \rangle}
\\[2ex]
\dfrac{\langle c_0, \langle s, t \rangle \rangle \rightarrow \langle s_0, t_0 \rangle,\ \langle c_1, \langle s_0, t_0 \rangle \rangle \rightarrow \langle s_1, t_1 \rangle}{\langle c_0; c_1, \langle s, t \rangle \rangle \rightarrow \langle s_1, t_1 \rangle}
&
\dfrac{\langle x, \langle s, t \rangle \rangle \rightarrow 0}{\langle \mathbf{while}\ x\ \mathbf{do}\ c\ \mathbf{endw}, \langle s, t \rangle \rangle \rightarrow \langle s, t + t_{\mathtt{T}} \rangle}
\\[2ex]
\multicolumn{2}{c}{\dfrac{\langle x, \langle s, t \rangle \rangle \rightarrow n \geq 1,\ \langle c, \langle s, t \rangle \rangle \rightarrow \langle s_0, t_0 \rangle,\ \langle \mathbf{while}\ x\ \mathbf{do}\ c\ \mathbf{endw}, \langle s_0, t_0 \rangle \rangle \rightarrow \langle s_1, t_1 \rangle}{\langle \mathbf{while}\ x\ \mathbf{do}\ c\ \mathbf{endw}, \langle s, t \rangle \rangle \rightarrow \langle s_1, t_1 + t_{\mathtt{T}} \rangle}}
\end{array}
$$

$\widehat{\Sigma}^+$ and $\widehat{\Sigma}^\omega \stackrel{\text{def}}{=} \mathbb{N} \longrightarrow \widehat{\Sigma}$ denote respectively the set of finite nonempty and infinite sequences of symbols in the set $\widehat{\Sigma}$. Given a sequence $\widehat{\sigma} \in \widehat{\Sigma}^\infty \stackrel{\text{def}}{=} \widehat{\Sigma}^+ \cup \widehat{\Sigma}^\omega$, its length is $|\widehat{\sigma}| \in \mathbb{N} \cup \{\omega\}$ and its i-th element is $\widehat{\sigma}_i$. A non-empty finite (infinite) *trace* $\widehat{\sigma} \in \widehat{\Sigma}^\infty$ is a finite (infinite) sequence of program states such that, for all $i < |\widehat{\sigma}|$ we have $\widehat{\sigma}_i \rightarrow \widehat{\sigma}_{i+1}$. The *maximal trace semantics* [8] of a transition system associated with a program P is $[\![P]\!]^\infty$, denoted $\langle\!| P |\!\rangle$, where if $T \subseteq \widehat{\Sigma}$ is a set of final/blocking states then $\langle\!| P |\!\rangle^{\dot{n}} = \{\widehat{\sigma} \in \widehat{\Sigma}^+ | |\widehat{\sigma}| = n, \forall i \in [1, n) \,.\, \widehat{\sigma}_{i-1} \rightarrow \widehat{\sigma}_i\}$, $\langle\!| P |\!\rangle^\omega = \{\widehat{\sigma} \in \widehat{\Sigma}^\omega | \forall i \in \mathbb{N} \,.\, \widehat{\sigma}_i \rightarrow \widehat{\sigma}_{i+1}\}$. We can define $\langle\!| P |\!\rangle^+ = \cup_{n>0} \{\widehat{\sigma} \in \langle\!| P |\!\rangle^{\dot{n}} | \widehat{\sigma}_{n-1} \in T\}$, and $\langle\!| P |\!\rangle^n = \langle\!| P |\!\rangle^{\dot{n}} \cap \langle\!| P |\!\rangle^+$. If $\widehat{\sigma} \in \langle\!| P |\!\rangle^+$, then $\widehat{\sigma}_\dashv$ and $\widehat{\sigma}_\vdash$ denote respectively the final and initial state of $\widehat{\sigma}$. The *denotational semantics* $[\![P]\!]$ associates input/output functions with programs, by modeling non-termination by $\perp$. This semantics is derived in [8] as an abstract interpretation of the maximal trace semantics: $\alpha^{\mathcal{D}}(X) \stackrel{\text{def}}{=} \lambda \widehat{s} \in \widehat{\Sigma} . \{\widehat{\sigma}_\dashv | \widehat{\sigma} \in X \cap \widehat{\Sigma}^+, \ \widehat{s} = \widehat{\sigma}_\vdash\} \cup \{\perp | \widehat{\sigma} \in X \cap \widehat{\Sigma}^\omega, \ \widehat{s} = \widehat{\sigma}_\vdash\}$. Note that, in our case, $\alpha^{\mathcal{D}}(X)(\widehat{s})$ is always a singleton. It is well known that we can associate, inductively on its syntax, with each program $P \in \text{IMP}$ a function $[\![P]\!]$ denoting its input/output relation, such that $[\![P]\!] \stackrel{\text{def}}{=} \alpha^{\mathcal{D}}(\langle\!| P |\!\rangle)$ [8]. In the following, if $|Var(P)| = n$, we consider $\Sigma \stackrel{\text{def}}{=} \mathbb{V}^n$ as the set of values for the variables, and $\langle\!| P |\!\rangle$ and $[\![P]\!]$ will denote the semantics with $\widehat{\Sigma} = \Sigma$.

Consider now a semantics containing the information about the elapsed time. In particular, consider the well-known operational semantics of IMP enhanced with time, described in Table 2, where $s \in \Sigma$, $t \in \mathbb{N}$ and $t_{\mathtt{A}}, t_{\mathtt{T}} \in \mathbb{N}^2$ are constant values denoting respectively the time spent for an assignment and for a test. In this case we suppose that the states in the concrete semantics are $\widehat{\Sigma} \stackrel{\text{def}}{=} \Sigma \times \mathbb{N}$. Namely we suppose that a state is a pair composed by a tuple of values for the variable and by a natural value representing the time elapsed from the beginning of the execution. This operational semantics naturally induces a transition relation on a set of states Σ, denoted $\rightarrow$, specifying the relation between a state and its possible successors. This transition system allows us to define the *timed maximal trace semantics* $\langle\!| P |\!\rangle^{+T}$ modeling computations by using traces of states including the information about time. By using the abstraction $\alpha^{\mathcal{D}}$ on this maximal trace semantics, we can obtain a *timed denotational semantics*, denoted by $[\![P]\!]^{+T} = \alpha^{\mathcal{D}}(\langle\!| P |\!\rangle^{+T})$.

Moreover, we can note that also the (standard) trace semantics, i.e., with $\widehat{\Sigma} = \Sigma$, can be seen as an abstraction of the timed maximal trace semantics, i.e., with $\widehat{\Sigma} = \Sigma \times \mathbb{N}$. In

---

[2] It would be the same if $t \in \mathbb{R}$.

particular, let us consider $\alpha^{st}(\langle s,t\rangle) = s$ and $\alpha_t^{st}(X) = \bigcup_{\sigma\in X}\langle\alpha^{st}(\sigma_\vdash),\ldots,\alpha^{st}(\sigma_\dashv)\rangle$, where X is a set of traces on $\widehat{\Sigma}$. Then maximal trace semantics is $\langle\!| P |\!\rangle = \alpha_t^{st}(\langle\!| P |\!\rangle^{+T})$.

Moreover, if we define the abstraction α_d^{st}, on the timed denotational semantics, as $\alpha_d^{st}(f) = \lambda s.\ \alpha^{st}\circ f(\langle s,0\rangle)$, when $f : \widehat{\Sigma} \longrightarrow \wp(\widehat{\Sigma})$, we obtain the (standard) denotational semantics $[\![P]\!] = \alpha_d^{st}([\![P]\!]^{+T})$. All the semantics, with their abstraction relations, are shown in the Figure on the left.

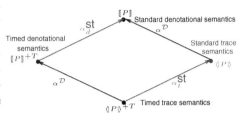

4   Defining Timed Abstract Non-interference

One of the most important features of abstract non-interference is that it is parametric on the chosen semantics. This means that we can enrich/change the checked notion of abstract non-interference for imperative languages by simply enriching/changing the considered semantics. For this reason, the idea for making abstract non-interference time sensitive, namely able to detect timing channels, corresponds to considering a more concrete semantics observing time. The first approach consists in considering the maximal trace semantics, instead of the denotational one, since the trace semantics compare the partial results at each step of computation. Indeed, the trace semantics implicitly embeds the *time* elapsed during computations in the *length* of traces since we can suppose that the time is measured as the discrete number of computational steps executed by the system. This observation suggests us that the trace semantics can be used for defining a stronger notion of non-interference that capture also timing channels. Therefore, we assume that we can have a timing channel in presence of an attacker that can count the number of execution steps, which means that the attacker observes time by looking at the program counter. On the other hand, we can also embed the reckon of time in the semantics, by considering time as a public variable observed by any attacker. In this way we can also think of modeling attackers that can only observe properties of time, e.g., intervals or regular delays as congruences.

4.1   Timed Abstract Non-interference on Traces

First of all, consider abstract non-interference, defined in [10] in terms of trace semantics. This means that at *each step* of computation we require that, what an attacker may observe does not depend on private input. This situation is possible whenever we suppose that the attacker is able to observe the public memory modified by the program. Since abstract non-interference is based on the distinction between input and output, the simplest way to extend the two notions is to consider, as output, the results of all the partial computations, and as input only the initial values (namely the initial state). With this assumption we can consider again only two closures, η for the public input, and ρ for the public output[3].

---

[3] Note that in the most general case we could consider a family of "output" observations.

Consider first narrow abstract non-interference. We can formulate the notion of non-interference by saying that starting from a state with the low property η, then all the possible observations of the states during the computation have the same low property ρ. Therefore, the new notion of narrow non-interference consists simply in abstracting each state of any computational trace. Let us introduce this notion through an example. Consider the standard semantics where states are simply tuples of values for the variables, and consider for example the concrete trace (each state is $\langle h, l \rangle$, with h : H and l : L): $\langle 3, 1 \rangle \rightarrow \langle 2, 2 \rangle \rightarrow \langle 1, 3 \rangle \rightarrow \langle 0, 4 \rangle \rightarrow \langle 0, 4 \rangle$. Now, suppose to observe the parity of public data, i.e., Par, both in input and in output, then intuitively the abstraction, i.e., observation of this trace through the property Par, is: $2\mathbb{Z} + 1 \rightarrow 2\mathbb{Z} \rightarrow 2\mathbb{Z} + 1 \rightarrow 2\mathbb{Z} \rightarrow 2\mathbb{Z}$. Formally, given $\sigma \in \langle\!| P |\!\rangle$, we define its abstraction through the observation of ρ, as follows: σ^ρ is such that $\forall i \leq |\sigma| \ . \ \sigma_i^\rho = \rho(\sigma_i^{\text{L}})$. At this point, consider only the terminating trace semantics of P, then we can define the abstract semantics: Let $\rho \in uco(\mathbb{V}^{\text{L}})$, $X \in \wp(\Sigma^+)$:

$$\langle\!| P |\!\rangle_\rho^\eta = \alpha_\rho^\eta(\langle\!| P |\!\rangle), \ \alpha_\rho^\eta(X) = \left\{ \ s^\eta \delta^\rho \mid s \in \Sigma, \ s\delta \in X \ \right\}$$

This is clearly an abstraction since it is additive by construction. Hence, we can define narrow non-interference for traces as: Let $\eta, \rho \in uco(\wp(\mathbb{V}^{\text{L}}))$ and P a program

> P is *secure* if $\forall h_1, h_2 \in \mathbb{V}^{\text{H}}, \forall l_1, l_2 \in \mathbb{V}^{\text{L}} \ . \ \langle\!| P |\!\rangle_\rho^\eta(h_1, l_1) = \langle\!| P |\!\rangle_\rho^\eta(h_2, l_2)$

In the definition above of narrow non-interference on traces, we compare abstract *observations* of concrete *computations*. This means that in order to define narrow non-interference we keep the concrete semantics and we change its observation. If, instead, we want to define abstract non-interference on traces, then we have to change also the concrete semantics by considering as initial state the set of all the states with the same public input property, namely we consider a symbolic execution of the system. In this case we have to consider a lift of the transition relation to sets: Consider the transition system $\langle \Sigma, \rightarrow \rangle$, we define the lift $\twoheadrightarrow \subseteq \wp(\Sigma) \times \wp(\Sigma)$ as follows: $\forall X \in \wp(\Sigma)$

$$X \twoheadrightarrow \left\{ \ y \in \Sigma \mid \exists x \in X. \ x \rightarrow y \ \right\}$$

Consider now the lifted transition system $\langle \wp(\Sigma), \twoheadrightarrow \rangle$, and consider the trace semantics obtained from this transition system. Let us denote also this semantics as $\langle\!| P |\!\rangle$, since it is clear from the input (depending on the fact that it is a state or a set of states) which semantics we have to consider. Let us consider the abstract trace semantics $\langle\!| P |\!\rangle_\rho^\eta$, on the lifted transition system, then we define abstract non-interference on traces: Let $\phi \in uco(\wp(\mathbb{V}^{\text{H}}))$, $\eta, \rho \in uco(\wp(\mathbb{V}^{\text{L}}))$ and P be a program.

> P is *secure* if $\forall h_1, h_2 \in \mathbb{V}^{\text{H}}, \forall l \in \mathbb{V}^{\text{L}} \ . \ \langle\!| P |\!\rangle_\rho^\eta(\phi(h_1), \eta(l))^{\text{L}} = \langle\!| P |\!\rangle_\rho^\eta(\phi(h_2), \eta(l))^{\text{L}}$

As observed above, the maximal trace semantics contains some discrete information about time, namely it distinguishes, for instance, traces that differ only for the repetition of states. For this reason we can say that it models also the timing channels due to the capability of the attacker of observing the clock of the program. In order to check this kind of non-interference, in the framework proposed in [10], we consider further abstractions of the semantics. The interesting aspect of this extension is that we can apply the transformers defined on abstract non-interference simply by considering the approximation based on *bounded iteration*. Bounded iteration, in fact, proves I/O non-interference by requiring a stronger condition, i.e., it requires that all the partial computations provide the same public output (see [10]).

4.2 Timed Abstract Non-interference on Timed Semantics

In this section we consider states which contain the information of time, i.e, we explicitly treat time in abstract non-interference. This means that we could use languages where time can interfere in the flow of computation. Suppose that the low inputs are pairs where the first component is a tuple of possible values for low variables, and the second one is the time passed, i.e., $\widehat{l} = \langle l, t \rangle$. We denote by $\widehat{l}^{\mathbb{D}} = l \in \mathbb{V}^{\mathsf{L}}$ the projection on the data component, and $\widehat{l}^{\mathsf{T}} = t \in \mathbb{N}$ the projection on the time component. In the following a state $\widehat{\sigma}$ will be the triple $\langle s^{\mathsf{H}}, s^{\mathsf{L}}, t \rangle$, and the initial states are of the kind $\widehat{\sigma} = \langle s_i, 0 \rangle$. Standard non-interference without timing channels is: Let P be a program

$$P \text{ is secure if } \forall l \in \mathbb{V}^{\mathsf{L}}, t \in \mathbb{N}, \forall h_1, h_2 \in \mathbb{V}^{\mathsf{H}} \cdot ([\![P]\!]^{+\mathsf{T}}(\langle h_1, l, 0 \rangle))^{\mathsf{L}\,\mathsf{T}} = ([\![P]\!]^{+\mathsf{T}}(\langle h_2, l, 0 \rangle))^{\mathsf{L}\,\mathsf{T}}$$

We can define the notions of narrow and abstract timed non-interference. In the following, when a program satisfies timed narrow or abstract non-interference we write respectively $[\eta]P^{+\mathsf{T}}(\rho)$ and $(\eta)P^{+\mathsf{T}}(\phi \leadsto \!\!|\rho)$, and consider $\eta, \rho \in uco(\wp(\mathbb{V}^{\mathsf{L}} \times \mathbb{N}))$ and $\phi \in uco(\wp(\mathbb{V}^{\mathsf{H}}))$.

Definition 1.

- $P \in \text{IMP}$ *is such that* $[\eta]P^{+\mathsf{T}}(\rho)$ *if* $\forall h_1, h_2 \in \mathbb{V}^{\mathsf{H}}, \forall \widehat{l}_1, \widehat{l}_2 \in \mathbb{V}^{\mathsf{L}} \times \{0\}$ *such that* $\eta(\widehat{l}_1)^{\mathsf{L}} = \eta(\widehat{l}_2)^{\mathsf{L}} \Rightarrow \rho([\![P]\!]^{+\mathsf{T}}(\langle h_1, \widehat{l}_1 \rangle)^{\mathsf{L}\,\mathsf{T}}) = \rho([\![P]\!]^{+\mathsf{T}}(\langle h_2, \widehat{l}_2 \rangle)^{\mathsf{L}\,\mathsf{T}})$.
- $P \in \text{IMP}$ *satisfies* $(\eta)P^{+\mathsf{T}}(\phi \leadsto \!\!|\rho)$ *if* $\forall h_1, h_2 \in \mathbb{V}^{\mathsf{H}}, \forall \widehat{l} \in \mathbb{V}^{\mathsf{L}} \times \{0\}$ *we have* $\rho([\![P]\!]^{+\mathsf{T}}(\langle \phi(h_1), \eta(\widehat{l})^{\mathsf{L}} \rangle)^{\mathsf{L}\,\mathsf{T}}) = \rho([\![P]\!]^{+\mathsf{T}}(\langle \phi(h_2), \eta(\widehat{l})^{\mathsf{L}} \rangle)^{\mathsf{L}\,\mathsf{T}})$.

It is clear that the only difference between these notions and the untimed ones is in the semantics, therefore we can inherit, in a straightforward way, the whole construction made in the previous sections, simply by considering the time as a further public datum. In particular this allows us to derive the most concrete property, about time, that an attacker has to observe in order to be harmless, as we can see in the following example.

Example 2. Let us consider the following example:

$$P \stackrel{\text{def}}{=} h := h \bmod 4; \textbf{ while } h \textbf{ do } l := 2l - l; h := h - 1; \textbf{ endw}$$

with security typing $t = \langle h : \mathsf{H}, l : \mathsf{L} \rangle$ and $\mathbb{V}^{\mathsf{L}} = \mathbb{N}$. Suppose that each state of the trace semantics is $\langle h, l, t \rangle$, and suppose $l \in \mathbb{V}^{\mathsf{L}}$ and $h \in \mathbb{V}^{\mathsf{H}}, h \neq 0$:

$$\langle 0, l, 0 \rangle \rightarrow \langle 0, l, t_{\mathsf{A}} \rangle \rightarrow \langle 0, l, t_{\mathsf{A}} + t_{\mathsf{T}} \rangle$$
$$\langle h, l, 0 \rangle \rightarrow \langle h \bmod 4, l, t_{\mathsf{A}} \rangle \rightarrow \langle (h \bmod 4) - 1, l, 3t_{\mathsf{A}} + t_{\mathsf{T}} \rangle$$
$$\rightarrow \langle 0, l, 2(h \bmod 4)t_{\mathsf{A}} + (h \bmod 4 + 1)t_{\mathsf{T}} \rangle$$

Therefore, if for example $h \bmod 4 = 2$ then the total time is $4t_A + 3t_T$. This means that the most concrete abstraction of the domain of time that avoids timing channels is the one that have the element $\{t_A + t_T, 2t_A + 2t_T, 4t_A + 3t_T, 6t_A + 4t_T\}$ and abstracts all the other natural numbers in themselves.

5   Timed vs Untimed Abstract Non-interference...

In this section we compare abstract non-interference defined in terms of standard denotational semantics, with timed non-interference. In particular standard abstract non-interference can be seen as an abstraction of the time component of TANI.

5.1   ...On Traces

We observed that the simple use of traces makes abstract non-interference time sensitive. We wonder how a notion of abstract non-interference on traces which is time-insensitive can be obtained as abstraction of TANI. Therefore, we want to derive a trace semantics which is not able to observe the clock, namely we have to make indistinguishable traces that differ only for the repetition of states. This is a well-known notion in literature, called *stuttering* [2]: A semantics is said to be without stuttering if it is insensitive to the repetition of states. Namely we can think of transforming the set of traces that gives semantics to the program by eliminating the stuttering and then we can check non-interference exactly as we have done before. Let X be a property on traces σ. Then X is without stuttering if $\sigma \in X.\sigma = \sigma_0\sigma_1 \ldots \sigma_n \ldots$ then $\forall i \geq 0.\sigma_0 \ldots \sigma_i\sigma_i \ldots \in X$. It is easy to show that the following abstraction, which characterizes the stuttering properties, is clearly an abstraction of sets of traces. $\langle\!\langle P \rangle\!\rangle^{\mathrm{stu}} = \alpha^{\mathrm{stu}}(\langle\!\langle P \rangle\!\rangle^{\eta}_{\rho})$ where

$$\alpha^{\mathrm{stu}}(X) = \{ \langle\sigma_0, \ldots, \sigma_n\rangle \mid \exists \delta \in X . \delta = \langle\sigma_0^{k_0} \ldots, \sigma_n^{k_n}\rangle, \forall i . k_i \neq 0, \sigma_i \neq \sigma_{i+1} \}$$

Now we can formalize the abstract non-interference in the following way, obtaining a notion of abstract non-interference on traces unable to detect timing channels.

> P is *secure* for trace-based abstract non-interference if $\forall h_1, h_2 \in \mathbb{V}^H, \forall l \in \mathbb{V}^L$.
> $\alpha^{\eta}_{\rho}(\langle\!\langle P \rangle\!\rangle^{\mathrm{stu}}(\phi(h_1), \eta(l))^L) = \alpha^{\eta}_{\rho}(\langle\!\langle P \rangle\!\rangle^{\mathrm{stu}}(\phi(h_2), \eta(l))^L)$.

Note that, in this case, as it is also shown in the following example, abstract non-interference is always an abstraction of timed abstract non-interference. Namely the timed notion always stronger than the untimed one.

Example 3. Consider the trace semantics of a program P, with states $\langle h, l\rangle$, with $n \in \mathbb{N}$ and $m \in 2\mathbb{N}+1$: $\langle\!\langle P \rangle\!\rangle = \{\langle 0, 2\rangle \to \langle 0, 3\rangle \to \langle 0, 5\rangle, \langle n, 2\rangle \to \langle 0, 2\rangle \to \langle 0, 3\rangle, \langle n, m\rangle \to \langle n, m+1\rangle\}$ Consider $\rho = Par$. We determine the abstract trace semantics relatively to Par: $\langle\!\langle P \rangle\!\rangle^{Par}_{Par} = \alpha^{Par}_{Par}(\langle\!\langle P \rangle\!\rangle) = \{2\mathbb{N} \to 2\mathbb{N}+1 \to 2\mathbb{N}+1, 2\mathbb{N} \to 2\mathbb{N} \to 2\mathbb{N}+1, 2\mathbb{N}+1 \to 2\mathbb{N}\}$ Hence, when the low input is even, we have interference. If we want to guarantee non-interference knowing that the attacker cannot observe the time elapsed, then we use the stuttering abstraction, obtaining the following semantics, which says that there's not interference, since for each abstract property we have only one possible result. $\langle\!\langle P \rangle\!\rangle^{\mathrm{stu}} = \{\alpha^{\mathrm{stu}}(\langle\!\langle P \rangle\!\rangle^{Par}_{Par}) = 2\mathbb{N} \to 2\mathbb{N}+1, 2\mathbb{N}+1 \to 2\mathbb{N}\}$

5.2   ...on the Timed Semantics

In this section, we study the relation existing between the timed notion of abstract non-interference and the untimed one, when we embed the time information in the semantics. Indeed, starting from closures $\eta, \rho \in uco(\wp(\mathbb{V}^L))$ without time, the extension to semantics with time is trivially obtained by taking the closure that is not able to observe anything about time, i.e., we interpret a generic closure $\eta \in uco(\wp(\mathbb{V}^L))$ as the closure that is not able to observe time, therefore that abstracts time to the top: $\eta^{+T} = \langle \eta, \lambda t.\mathbb{N} \rangle$. It is worth noting that $[\eta]P(\rho) \Leftrightarrow [\eta^{+T}]P^{+T}(\rho^{+T})$. In other words, since time can be treated as an additional public variable, we could see abstract non-interference as timed abstract non-interference where the time variable is abstracted to the top. Unfortunately, if we start from a semantics with time and we want to derive abstract non-interference properties without time, then the relation is not so immediate. Indeed, if time interferes with data we have that the abstraction of time is not straight. Clearly, time cannot interfere with data in the concrete semantics for the simple imperative language we are considering, but it can interfere in the abstract semantics modeling the attacker. In other words, when we consider timed abstract non-interference, the attacker model could observe *relations* between data and time, avoiding the independent abstraction of time. Namely if we abstract time we may lose something about the attacker's observation of data. Therefore, if we start from closure operators on semantics with time, namely from the closures $\eta, \rho \in uco(\wp(\mathbb{V}^L \times \mathbb{N}))$, we can obtain properties without time in two ways. We can think of erasing the observation of time only in the output, i.e., we abstract away the information about time, or we can think of collecting all the possible results for every possible time value. In this way, we are able to ignore the information about time also in the input. In the following, we characterize some necessary and sufficient conditions on the attacker model, that indeed make timed abstract non-interference stronger than abstract non-interference, and therefore the two notions comparable.

Abstracting Time in the Output. Consider the first case, namely we do not observe time in the output. Let us define the projection, of a pair $X \in \wp(\mathbb{V}^L \times \mathbb{N})$, on data or on time in the following way: $\Pi_T(X) \stackrel{\text{def}}{=} \{ \langle x, y \rangle \mid \exists y' \in \mathbb{N} . \langle x, y' \rangle \in X, y \in \mathbb{N} \}$ and $\Pi_D(X) \stackrel{\text{def}}{=} \{ \langle x, y \rangle \mid \exists x' \in \mathbb{N} . \langle x', y \rangle \in X, x \in \mathbb{V}^L \}$. In particular, given a closure $\rho \in uco(\wp(\mathbb{V}^L \times \mathbb{N}))$, we can apply these abstractions to ρ obtaining for each $X \in \{T, D\}$, $\Pi_X(\rho) \stackrel{\text{def}}{=} \{ \Pi_X(Y) \mid Y \in \rho \}$. It is immediate to show that for each $X \in \{T, D\}$, $\Pi_X \in uco(\wp(\mathbb{V}^L \times \mathbb{N}))$. It is clear that the set $\Pi_T(\rho)$ is the set of the images of the map $\Pi_T \circ \rho$. Note that, even if both Π_T (or Π_D) and ρ are closures, then their composition may not be a closure, as happens in the picture below, where we have $\langle 2, \mathbb{N} \rangle \notin \Pi_T(\rho)$. In general $\Pi_T \circ \rho$ is not an upper closure operator, so we consider $\rho^{-T} \stackrel{\text{def}}{=} \mathcal{M}(\Pi_T(\rho))$[4] and $\rho^{-D} \stackrel{\text{def}}{=} \mathcal{M}(\Pi_D(\rho))$, which are by definition of $\mathcal{M}$, closures, i.e., $\eta^{-T} \in uco(\wp(\mathbb{V}^L))$ and $\eta^{-D} \in uco(\wp(\mathbb{N}))$. The fact that in general $\rho^{-T} \neq \Pi_T(\rho)$ and $\rho^{-D} \neq \Pi_D(\rho)$ is a problem when we want to compare timed non-interference with abstract non-interference since elements that have the same image in ρ may be different in ρ^{-T},

---

[4] $\mathcal{M}(X) \stackrel{\text{def}}{=} \{ \wedge S \mid S \subseteq X \}$ is called Moore closure.

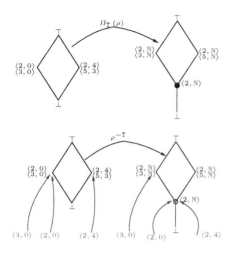

and viceversa as we can see in the picture below. So, we would like to characterize when the two notions are comparable. The picture above shows that problems arise when the Moore closure adds new points, namely when $\Pi_T(\rho)$ is not a closure. Therefore, we first want to understand when this is an upper closure operator, namely when $\Pi_T \circ \rho \in uco(\wp(\mathbb{V}^L \times \mathbb{N}))$. It is well known [18] that, given two closures $\rho, \pi \in uco(C)$, then we have $\pi \circ \rho \in uco(C)$ iff $\pi \circ \rho = \rho \circ \pi = \rho \sqcup \pi$. This means that we need a ρ such that $\Pi_T \circ \rho = \rho \circ \Pi_T$.

Theorem 1. *Let* $\rho \in uco(\wp(\mathbb{V}^L \times \mathbb{N}))$, *then* $\rho^{-T} = \Pi_T \circ \rho \in uco(\wp(\mathbb{V}^L \times \mathbb{N}))$ *iff* $\Pi_T \circ \rho \circ \Pi_T = \rho \circ \Pi_T$ *iff* $\Pi_T \circ \rho \circ \Pi_T = \Pi_T \circ \rho$. *Analogously, we have* $\rho^{-D} = \Pi_D \circ \rho \in uco(\wp(\mathbb{V}^L \times \mathbb{N}))$ *iff* $\Pi_D \circ \rho \circ \Pi_D = \rho \circ \Pi_D$ *iff* $\Pi_D \circ \rho \circ \Pi_D = \Pi_D \circ \rho$.

In [14] a method for transforming Π_T in order to make it satisfy $\Pi_T \circ \rho \circ \Pi_T = \rho \circ \Pi_T$ and $\Pi_T \circ \rho \circ \Pi_T = \Pi_T \circ \rho$ is provided. Anyway, in this context we are more interested in modifying ρ in order to guarantee completeness. In particular, let $X \in \{T, D\}$, then the following transformations of ρ satisfies forward completeness. Note that $\Pi_X^+(X) \stackrel{def}{=} \bigcup \{ Y \mid \Pi_X(Y) \subseteq X \}$ is the right adjoint of Π_X:

$$\rho_X^\uparrow(Y) \stackrel{def}{=} \begin{cases} \Pi_X \circ \rho(Y) & \text{if } Y \in \Pi_X \\ \rho(Y) & \text{otherwise} \end{cases} \qquad \rho_X^\downarrow(Y) \stackrel{def}{=} \begin{cases} \Pi_X^+ \circ \rho(Y) & \text{if } Y \in \Pi_X \\ \rho(Y) & \text{otherwise} \end{cases}$$

Then $\rho_X^\downarrow \sqsubseteq \rho \sqsubseteq \rho_X^\uparrow$. Namely we can always transform the abstractions, used for modeling the attacker, in order to guarantee that the abstraction of time is a complete upper closure operator, i.e., given a generic ρ we always have that $(\rho_X^\downarrow)^{-T}$ and $(\rho_X^\uparrow)^{-T}$ are closure operators. For the timed abstract non-interference this means that, given an attacker's model ρ, we can always find the closest model such that the observation of time does not enrich the attacker capability of observing data.

The following theorem says that the semantics for timed abstract non-interference is an abstract interpretation of the one for abstract non-interference with ρ^{-T} iff the output observation ρ commutes with Π_T

Theorem 2. *Let* $\eta, \rho \in uco(\wp(\mathbb{V}^L \times \mathbb{N}))$, *then* $([\eta]P^{+T}(\rho) \Rightarrow [\eta^{-T}]P^{+T}(\rho^{-T}))$ *if and only if we have* $(\Pi_T \circ \rho = \rho \circ \Pi_T)$.

Whenever we observe a relational property between data and time, in timed abstract non-interference we add new *deceptive flows*. Indeed, timed abstract non-interference may fail even if the program is secure and avoids timing channels, as it happens in the following example.

Example 4. Consider the program P:
$h := 2;$ **while** h **do** $l := l + 2; h :=$
$h - 1;$ **endw**. In this example, we show that
in the timed abstract non-interference we
add new deceptive flows due to the possible
relation between data and time of the abstract property. Consider a property ρ such
that $\rho(\langle 8, 5\rangle) \neq \rho(\langle 6, 5\rangle)$ (as depicted in
the picture) and $\eta = \langle Par, id\rangle$, which observes parity of data and the identity on
time. Suppose $t_T = 1$ and $t_A = 0.5$.

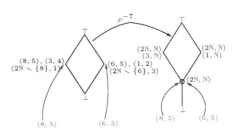

Consider the initial low values (data and time) $\langle 4, 0\rangle$ and $\langle 2, 0\rangle$, clearly we have
$\eta(\langle 4, 0\rangle) = \langle 2\mathbb{N}, 0\rangle = \eta(\langle 2, 0\rangle)$. We have now compute the semantics:

$$[\![P]\!](0, \langle 4, 0\rangle)^{L\,T} = \langle 8, 3t_T + 4t_T\rangle = \langle 8, 5\rangle \text{ and } [\![P]\!](0, \langle 2, 0\rangle)^{L\,T} = \langle 6, 5\rangle$$

At this point, since $\rho(\langle 8, 5\rangle) \neq \rho(\langle 6, 5\rangle)$, non-interference is not satisfied, while there
aren't timing information flows, namely $\rho^{-T}(\langle 8, 5\rangle) = \rho^{-T}(\langle 6, 5\rangle)$.

Note that, the presence of deceptive flows due to the observation of time arise only
when there is a relational dependency between data and time.
The following corollary provides a characterization of timing channels in terms of the
relation existing between the timed abstract non-interference and the abstract one.

Corollary 1. *If ρ commutes with Π_T, i.e., $\Pi_T \circ \rho = \rho \circ \Pi_T$, and $[\eta^{-T}]P^{+T}(\rho^{-T})$ iff
$[\eta]P^{+T}(\rho)$, then timing channels are impossible in P.*

Abstracting Time in the Input. As we said above we can think of another way of
erasing time, this is also suggested by the fact that we have two possible compositions of a closure with the projection Π_T: $\Pi_T \circ \rho$ and $\rho \circ \Pi_T$, which are the same
when they are closures. Anyway, their meaning is different, the first compute the property with time and abstract the observation, while the second abstracts time in the
input, namely compute the property on the abstracted value, without time. Let $L \subseteq$
$\mathbb{V}^L$, we can define the closure on $\wp(\mathbb{V}^L)$ as $\rho_{-T}(L) \stackrel{\text{def}}{=} \downarrow_D \circ \rho \circ \Pi_T(\langle L, \mathbb{N}\rangle)$, where
$\langle L, \mathbb{N}\rangle \stackrel{\text{def}}{=} \{\langle x, y\rangle | x \in L, y \in \mathbb{N}\}$ and the abstraction $\downarrow_D$ is the projection of the tuple
on data, i.e., $\downarrow_D(X) \stackrel{\text{def}}{=} \{x | \langle x, y\rangle \in X\}$.
    In the following, we characterize when the composition $\downarrow_D \circ \rho \circ \Pi_T$ is an upper closure operator. This is important in order to derive properties of narrow or abstract non-interference without time in programs where the semantics measures time, and therefore
for understanding the relation existing between the notions of abstract non-interference
with and without time.

Proposition 1. $\rho_{-T} \in uco(\wp(\mathbb{V}^L))$ *iff* $\downarrow_D \circ \Pi_T \circ \rho \circ \Pi_T = \downarrow_D \circ \rho \circ \Pi_T$.

The following theorem says that the semantics for timed abstract non-interference is
an abstract interpretation of the one for abstract non-interference with ρ_{-T} iff the data
projection commutes on elements closed under Π_T.

Theorem 3. *Let $\eta, \rho \in uco(\wp(\mathbb{V}^L \times \mathbb{N}))$. Let $\eta_{-T}, \rho_{-T} \in uco(\wp(\mathbb{V}^L))$, $\downarrow_D \Pi_T \circ \eta = \downarrow_D$
$\circ \eta \circ \Pi_T$, then $[\eta]P^{+T}(\rho) \Rightarrow [\eta_{-T}]P(\rho_{-T})$ if and only if $\downarrow_D \rho \circ \Pi_T = \downarrow_D \rho \circ \Pi_T \circ \rho$.*

Non Relational Attackers. A sufficient condition, in order to make the non-interference notions comparable, consists in considering only closures defined on $\wp(\mathbb{V}^L) \times \wp(\mathbb{N})$, which are particular closures of $\wp(\mathbb{V}^L \times \mathbb{N})$. Note that, if $\rho \in uco(\wp(A) \times \wp(B))$, then there always exist two closure ρ_A and ρ_B, such that $\rho(\langle X, Y \rangle) = \langle \rho_A(X), \rho_B(Y) \rangle$. Consider $\rho \in uco(\wp(\mathbb{V}^L) \times \wp(\mathbb{N})))$, we can obtain the closure $\rho^* \in uco(\wp(\mathbb{V}^L \times \mathbb{N}))$ as $\rho^* \stackrel{def}{=} \gamma \circ \rho \circ \alpha$, where $\alpha(X) \stackrel{def}{=} \langle X\downarrow_D, X\downarrow_T \rangle$ and $\gamma(\langle X, Y \rangle) \stackrel{def}{=} \{ \langle x, y \rangle \mid x \in X, \ y \in Y \}$ form a Galois insertion. Note that, in this case there are no more deceptive flows due to the observation of time, since here we cannot observe relations between data and time.

Proposition 2. *Let* $\rho \in uco(\wp(\mathbb{V}^L) \times \wp(\mathbb{N}))$, *consider* $\rho^* \in uco(\wp(\mathbb{V}^L \times \mathbb{N}))$ *defined* $\rho^* \stackrel{def}{=} \gamma \circ \rho \circ \alpha$, *then we have* $\Pi_T \circ \rho^* = \rho^* \circ \Pi_T$ *and* $\Pi_D \circ \rho^* = \rho^* \circ \Pi_D$.

Therefore, by Theorem 2 and Theorem 3, this means that in the conditions of the Proposition above, timed abstract non-interference implies abstract non-interference. This is only a sufficient condition, since there are closure operators $\rho \notin uco(\wp(\mathbb{V}^L) \times \wp(\mathbb{N})$ such that $\Pi_T \circ \rho = \rho^{-T}$ or $\Pi_D \circ \rho = \rho^{-D}$. As we can see in the picture, $\langle n, \mathbb{N} \rangle \stackrel{def}{=} \{ \langle n, m \rangle \mid m \in \mathbb{N} \}$. where In particular in the example above we can also note that $\Pi_T \circ \rho = \Pi_T \sqcup \rho$.

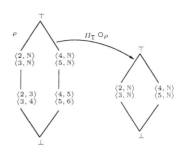

6   Conclusion

In this paper, we extend abstract non-interference in order to detect timing channels, namely those channels of informations created by the ability of the attacker to observe the time elapsed during computation, obtaining timed abstract non-interference, which embeds the time reckoning into the semantics. Afterwards, we study the relation between this new notion and abstract non-interference defined in [10]. This is an example of how, by changing the semantics, we can change the defined notion of non-interference. In the same way, we would like to define a *probabilistic* abstract non-interference, for checking probabilistic channels, considering also properties of the probabilistic distribution of values.

References

1. J. Agat. Transforming out timing leaks. In *Proc. of the 27th Annual ACM SIGPLAN-SIGACT Symposium on Principles of Programming Languages (POPL '00)*, pages 40–53. ACM-Press, NY, 2000.
2. B. Alpern, A. J. Demers, and F. B. Schneider. Safety without stuttering. *Information Processing Letters*, 23(4):177–180, 1986.
3. R. Alur and D. L. Dill. A theory of timed automata. *Theoretical Computer Science*, 126(2):183–235, 1994.

4. R. Barbuti, N. De Francesco, A. Santone, and L. Tesei. A notion of non-interference for timed automata. *Fundamenta Informaticae*, 51:1–11, 2002.
5. D. E. Bell and L. J. LaPadula. Secure computer systems: Mathematical foundations and model. Technical Report M74-244, MITRE Corp. Badford, MA, 1973.
6. D. Clark, C. Hankin, and S. Hunt. Information flow for algol-like languages. *Computer Languages*, 28(1):3–28, 2002.
7. E. S. Cohen. Information transmission in sequential programs. *Foundations of Secure Computation*, pages 297–335, 1978.
8. P. Cousot. Constructive design of a hierarchy of semantics of a transition system by abstract interpretation. *Theor. Comput. Sci.*, 277(1-2):47,103, 2002.
9. D. E. Denning and P. Denning. Certification of programs for secure information flow. *Communications of the ACM*, 20(7):504–513, 1977.
10. R. Giacobazzi and I. Mastroeni. Abstract non-interference: Parameterizing non-interference by abstract interpretation. In *Proc. of the 31st Annual ACM SIGPLAN-SIGACT Symposium on Principles of Programming Languages (POPL '04)*, pages 186–197. ACM-Press, NY, 2004.
11. R. Giacobazzi and I. Mastroeni. Proving abstract non-interference. In *Annual Conference of the European Association for Computer Science Logic (CSL'04)*, volume 3210, pages 280–294. Springer-Verlag, 2004.
12. R. Giacobazzi and I. Mastroeni. Adjoining declassification and attack models by abstract interpretation. In *Proc. of the European Symposium on Programming (ESOP'05)*, volume 3444 of *Lecture Notes in Computer Science*, pages 295–310. Springer-Verlag, 2005.
13. R. Giacobazzi and I. Mastroeni. Generalized abstract non-interference for automata. In *In The Third International Workshop "Mathematical Methods, Models and Architectures for Computer Networks Security" (MMM-ACNS'05)*, volume 3685 of *Lecture Notes in Computer Science*, pages 221–234. Springer-Verlag, 2005.
14. R. Giacobazzi, F. Ranzato, and F. Scozzari. Making abstract interpretations complete. *J. of the ACM.*, 47(2):361–416, 2000.
15. S. Hunt and I. Mastroeni. The PER model of abstract non-interference. In *Proc. of The 12th Internat. Static Analysis Symp. (SAS'05)*, volume 3672 of *Lecture Notes in Computer Science*, pages 171–185. Springer-Verlag, 2005.
16. R. Joshi and K. R. M. Leino. A semantic approach to secure information flow. *Science of Computer Programming*, 37:113–138, 2000.
17. P. Laud. Semantics and program analysis of computationally secure information flow. In *In Programming Languages and Systems, 10th European Symp. On Programming, ESOP*, volume 2028 of *Lecture Notes in Computer Science*, pages 77–91. Springer-Verlag, 2001.
18. J. Morgado. Some results on the closure operators of partially ordered sets. *Portug. Math.*, 19(2):101–139, 1960.
19. A. Sabelfeld and A.C. Myers. Language-based information-flow security. *IEEE J. on selected ares in communications*, 21(1):5–19, 2003.
20. A. Sabelfeld and D. Sands. A PER model of secure information flow in sequential programs. *Higher-Order and Symbolic Computation*, 14(1):59–91, 2001.
21. C. Skalka and S. Smith. Static enforcement of security with types. In *ICFP'00*, pages 254–267. ACM Press, New York, 2000.
22. D. Volpano. Safety versus secrecy. In *Proc. of the 6th Static Analysis Symp. (SAS'99)*, volume 1694 of *Lecture Notes in Computer Science*, pages 303–311. Springer-Verlag, 1999.
23. D. Volpano and G. Smith. Probabilistic noninterference in a concurrent language. *Journal of Computer Security*, 7(2,3):231–253, 1999.
24. D. Volpano, G. Smith, and C. Irvine. A sound type system for secure flow analysis. *Journal of Computer Security*, 4(2,3):167–187, 1996.

25. D. Zanardini. Higher-order abstract non-interference. In *Proc. of the Seventh International Conference on Typed Lambda Calculi and Applications (TLCA '05)*, Lecture Notes in Computer Science. Springer-Verlag, 2005. To appear.

26. S. Zdancewic and A. C. Myers. Robust declassification. In *Proc. of the IEEE Computer Security Foundations Workshop*, pages 15–23. IEEE Computer Society Press, 2001.

Author Index

Lecture Notes in Computer Science

For information about Vols. 1–3734

please contact your bookseller or Springer

Vol. 3785: K.-K. Lau, R. Banach (Eds.), Formal Methods and Software Engineering. XIV, 496 pages. 2005.

Vol. 3784: J. Tao, T. Tan, R.W. Picard (Eds.), Affective Computing and Intelligent Interaction. XIX, 1008 pages. 2005.

Vol. 3783: S. Qing, W. Mao, J. Lopez, G. Wang (Eds.), Information and Communications Security. XIV, 492 pages. 2005.

Vol. 3781: S.Z. Li, Z. Sun, T. Tan, S. Pankanti, G. Chollet, D. Zhang (Eds.), Advances in Biometric Person Authentication. XI, 250 pages. 2005.

Vol. 3780: K. Yi (Ed.), Programming Languages and Systems. XI, 435 pages. 2005.

Vol. 3779: H. Jin, D. Reed, W. Jiang (Eds.), Network and Parallel Computing. XV, 513 pages. 2005.

Vol. 3778: C. Atkinson, C. Bunse, H.-G. Gross, C. Peper (Eds.), Component-Based Software Development for Embedded Systems. VIII, 345 pages. 2005.

Vol. 3777: O.B. Lupanov, O.M. Kasim-Zade, A.V. Chaskin, K. Steinhöfel (Eds.), Stochastic Algorithms: Foundations and Applications. VIII, 239 pages. 2005.

Vol. 3775: J. Schönwälder, J. Serrat (Eds.), Ambient Networks. XIII, 281 pages. 2005.

Vol. 3773: A. Sanfeliu, M.L. Cortés (Eds.), Progress in Pattern Recognition, Image Analysis and Applications. XX, 1094 pages. 2005.

Vol. 3772: M. Consens, G. Navarro (Eds.), String Processing and Information Retrieval. XIV, 406 pages. 2005.

Vol. 3771: J.M.T. Romijn, G.P. Smith, J. van de Pol (Eds.), Integrated Formal Methods. XI, 407 pages. 2005.

Vol. 3770: J. Akoka, S.W. Liddle, I.-Y. Song, M. Bertolotto, I. Comyn-Wattiau, W.-J. van den Heuvel, M. Kolp, J. Trujillo, C. Kop, H.C. Mayr (Eds.), Perspectives in Conceptual Modeling. XXII, 476 pages. 2005.

Vol. 3768: Y.-S. Ho, H.J. Kim (Eds.), Advances in Multimedia Information Processing - PCM 2005, Part II. XXVIII, 1088 pages. 2005.

Vol. 3767: Y.-S. Ho, H.J. Kim (Eds.), Advances in Multimedia Information Processing - PCM 2005, Part I. XXVIII, 1022 pages. 2005.

Vol. 3766: N. Sebe, M.S. Lew, T.S. Huang (Eds.), Computer Vision in Human-Computer Interaction. X, 231 pages. 2005.

Vol. 3765: Y. Liu, T. Jiang, C. Zhang (Eds.), Computer Vision for Biomedical Image Applications. X, 563 pages. 2005.

Vol. 3764: S. Tixeuil, T. Herman (Eds.), Self-Stabilizing Systems. VIII, 229 pages. 2005.

Vol. 3762: R. Meersman, Z. Tari, P. Herrero (Eds.), On the Move to Meaningful Internet Systems 2005: OTM 2005 Workshops. XXXI, 1228 pages. 2005.

Vol. 3761: R. Meersman, Z. Tari (Eds.), On the Move to Meaningful Internet Systems 2005: CoopIS, DOA, and ODBASE, Part II. XXVII, 653 pages. 2005.

Vol. 3760: R. Meersman, Z. Tari (Eds.), On the Move to Meaningful Internet Systems 2005: CoopIS, DOA, and ODBASE, Part I. XXVII, 921 pages. 2005.

Vol. 3759: G. Chen, Y. Pan, M. Guo, J. Lu (Eds.), Parallel and Distributed Processing and Applications - ISPA 2005 Workshops. XIII, 669 pages. 2005.

Vol. 3758: Y. Pan, D.-x. Chen, M. Guo, J. Cao, J.J. Dongarra (Eds.), Parallel and Distributed Processing and Applications. XXIII, 1162 pages. 2005.

Vol. 3757: A. Rangarajan, B. Vemuri, A.L. Yuille (Eds.), Energy Minimization Methods in Computer Vision and Pattern Recognition. XII, 666 pages. 2005.

Vol. 3756: J. Cao, W. Nejdl, M. Xu (Eds.), Advanced Parallel Processing Technologies. XIV, 526 pages. 2005.

Vol. 3754: J. Dalmau Royo, G. Hasegawa (Eds.), Management of Multimedia Networks and Services. XII, 384 pages. 2005.

Vol. 3753: O.F. Olsen, L.M.J. Florack, A. Kuijper (Eds.), Deep Structure, Singularities, and Computer Vision. X, 259 pages. 2005.

Vol. 3752: N. Paragios, O. Faugeras, T. Chan, C. Schnörr (Eds.), Variational, Geometric, and Level Set Methods in Computer Vision. XI, 369 pages. 2005.

Vol. 3751: T. Magedanz, E.R. M. Madeira, P. Dini (Eds.), Operations and Management in IP-Based Networks. X, 213 pages. 2005.

Vol. 3750: J.S. Duncan, G. Gerig (Eds.), Medical Image Computing and Computer-Assisted Intervention - MICCAI 2005, Part II. XL, 1018 pages. 2005.

Vol. 3749: J.S. Duncan, G. Gerig (Eds.), Medical Image Computing and Computer-Assisted Intervention - MICCAI 2005, Part I. XXXIX, 942 pages. 2005.

Vol. 3748: A. Hartman, D. Kreische (Eds.), Model Driven Architecture - Foundations and Applications. IX, 349 pages. 2005.

Vol. 3747: C.A. Maziero, J.G. Silva, A.M.S. Andrade, F.M.d. Assis Silva (Eds.), Dependable Computing. XV, 267 pages. 2005.

Vol. 3746: P. Bozanis, E.N. Houstis (Eds.), Advances in Informatics. XIX, 879 pages. 2005.

Vol. 3745: J.L. Oliveira, V. Maojo, F. Martín-Sánchez, A.S. Pereira (Eds.), Biological and Medical Data Analysis. XII, 422 pages. 2005. (Subseries LNBI).

Vol. 3744: T. Magedanz, A. Karmouch, S. Pierre, I. Venieris (Eds.), Mobility Aware Technologies and Applications. XIV, 418 pages. 2005.

Vol. 3742: J. Akiyama, M. Kano, X. Tan (Eds.), Discrete and Computational Geometry. VIII, 213 pages. 2005.

Vol. 3740: T. Srikanthan, J. Xue, C.-H. Chang (Eds.), Advances in Computer Systems Architecture. XVII, 833 pages. 2005.

Vol. 3739: W. Fan, Z. Wu, J. Yang (Eds.), Advances in Web-Age Information Management. XXIV, 930 pages. 2005.

Vol. 3738: V.R. Syrotiuk, E. Chávez (Eds.), Ad-Hoc, Mobile, and Wireless Networks. XI, 360 pages. 2005.

Vol. 3737: C. Priami, E. Merelli, P. Gonzalez, A. Omicini (Eds.), Transactions on Computational Systems Biology III. VII, 169 pages. 2005. (Subseries LNBI).

Vol. 3735: A. Hoffmann, H. Motoda, T. Scheffer (Eds.), Discovery Science. XVI, 400 pages. 2005. (Subseries LNAI).